SOCIAL DEVELOPMENT AS PREFERENCE MANAGEMENT

This engaging book presents social development in children through the language of preference management. Conversational excerpts garnered from around the world trace how parents talk about preferences, how infants' and children's emergent language conveys their preferences, how children themselves are impacted by others' preferences, and how they, in turn, influence the preferences of adults and peers. The language of preferences is used to crack into altruism, aggression, and morality, which are ways of coming to terms with other people's preferences. Behind the scenes is a cognitive engine that uses transformational thought – conducting temporal, imaginal, and mental transformations – to figure out other people's preferences and to find more sophisticated means of outmaneuvering others by persuading them and playing with one's own mind and other people's minds when preferences are blocked. This book is a unique and sometimes amusing must-read for anyone interested in child development, language acquisition, socialization, and communication.

Rachel Karniol is Professor of Social Development in the Department of Psychology and School of Education, Tel Aviv University, Israel. She has also taught at the University of Toronto, Princeton University, Carnegie Mellon University, Tufts University, and the University of Florida. Her work has been published in several edited volumes and in many journals, including *Psychological Review, Psychological Bulletin, Journal of Personality and Social Psychology, Child Development*, and *Developmental Psychology*.

In memory of my parents
Irene Deutsch Karniol and Eugene Karniol
Holocaust survivors from Hungary and Transylvania
and their families who did not survive

SOCIAL DEVELOPMENT AS PREFERENCE MANAGEMENT

HOW INFANTS, CHILDREN, AND PARENTS GET WHAT THEY WANT FROM ONE ANOTHER

Rachel Karniol

Tel Aviv University

CAMBRIDGE
UNIVERSITY PRESS

CAMBRIDGE UNIVERSITY PRESS
Cambridge, New York, Melbourne, Madrid, Cape Town, Singapore,
São Paulo, Delhi, Dubai, Tokyo

Cambridge University Press
32 Avenue of the Americas, New York, NY 10013-2473, USA

www.cambridge.org
Information on this title: www.cambridge.org/9780521135306

First published 2010

Printed in the United States of America

A catalog record for this publication is available from the British Library.

Library of Congress Cataloging in Publication data

Karniol, Rachel, 1950–
Social development as preference management : how infants, children, and parents get what they want from one another / Rachel Karniol.
p. cm.
Includes bibliographical references and index.
ISBN 978-0-521-11950-4 (hardback)
1. Child development. 2. Preferences (Philosophy) 3. Sociolinguistics. I. Title.
HQ772.K277 2010
306.87–dc22 2009053442

ISBN 978-0-521-11950-4 Hardback
ISBN 978-0-521-13530-6 Paperback

Contents

Acknowledgments

I would like to thank Hildy Ross, Suzanne Hidi, Robert Lubov, and Caroline Bowen for their helpful comments on earlier versions of several chapters; Roberta Klatzky and John Levine for their hospitality while I was on sabbatical at Carnegie Mellon University and the University of Pittsburgh; Eric Schwartz (formerly of Cambridge University Press and now of Princeton University Press) for encouraging me to continue writing; and Simina Calin, my editor at Cambridge University Press, for bringing this book to fruition.

I also thank Karen and Orren (on whose emergent speech much of this book is based) for tolerating being followed around with a notebook during their early years as well as their comments on the introductory and final chapters and Yoram for putting up with my working hours and for sharing the pleasures of parenthood with me.

Introduction

I do not wish to arouse conviction; I wish to stimulate thought and to upset prejudices.

(Freud, 1917/1973, p. 281)

In this book, I consider children's social development from the perspective of preferences and preference management. The preferences with which I am concerned are those of adults as they interact with and attempt to socialize infants and children and the preferences of children as they acquire language and use it in the pursuit of their preferences in their interaction with adults, siblings, and peers. My goal in writing this book is to trace how infants and children come to verbally express their preferences and their emergent strategies for the management of these preferences as they interact with and experience conflict with others who also have their own preferences. Social development reflects the interplay between children's and other people's preferences as these preferences are interwoven in infants' and children's daily lives, influencing every aspect of their social world and spurring their cognitive development as they attempt to actualize their preferences in their interaction with it. Social interaction requires children to develop behavioral and cognitive strategies for navigating their own preferences in the sea of other social beings who are similarly navigating their preferences while, at the same time, parents are attempting to steer children's preferences toward normative and legal shores. Socialization is the universal meeting grounds of infants', children's, and other people's preferences. In these meeting grounds, children learn to pursue their preferences within the constraints imposed by others and society, developing necessary behavioral and cognitive strategies for the management of preferences both in oneself and in others. The need to navigate social life – to learn to express our preferences, to get others to help us actualize them, to negotiate with others about our respective preferences, and to cope with preference deferral, preference elimination, and preferential conflict – is the focus of the preference management process and this book.

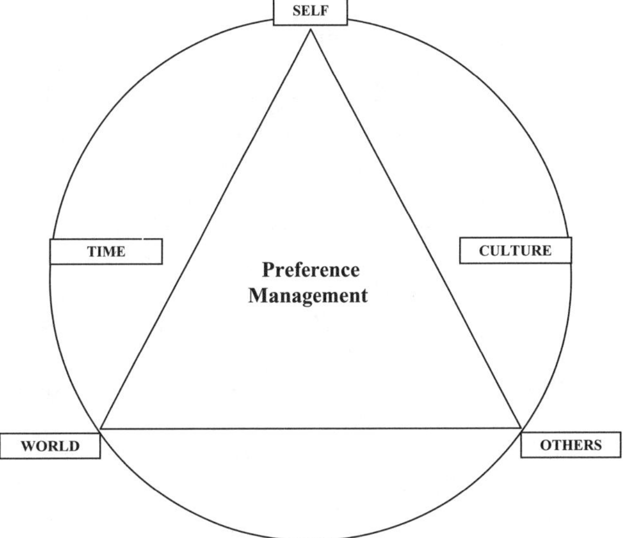

Preference Management Triangle

WHY PREFERENCES?

Why focus on preferences? In line with Bowles and Gintis (2006), I see preferences as reasons for goal-oriented behavior, as the link between ourselves, the objects and people that surround us, and the behavior that our social and physical environments afford us. Infants in all cultures are born with some preferences, and, with development, they acquire other preferences. Preferences are evident in the foods they eat, the toys and activities they select, the playmates they choose, the books they buy once they learn to read, and to some extent, the professions they enter when they grow up. As Hansson and Grüne-Yanoff (2006) argue, every choice, even a simple choice, such as choosing between two candies, "may be based on a preference for a world in which one eats candy X over a world in which one eats candy Y." This alternative world needs to be represented in order for one's preferences to be pursued in the real world, so that cognitive processes are integral to the pursuit of one's preferences. In this view, cognition evolved to serve the essential needs of an agent. Cognition, in the process of helping to satisfy needs and following motivational forces, has to take into account environments, their regularities and structures. Thus, cognition bridges the needs and motivations of an agent and its environments (be it physical or social), thereby linking all three in a 'triad.' (Sun, 2007)

Despite the triadic linkage he posits, Sun does not accord others in one's social world the importance they deserve in structuring the environment, in socializing preferences, in teaching modes of thinking, and in the intricate negotiations that they force infants and children to enter into in order to satisfy their own preferences. This intricate interplay will be of pivotal focus in this book.

Piaget (1967) noted that there are some constant functions that are common to all ages. In the realm of preferences, we can see continuity because, at all ages, individuals act in order to actualize their preferences, doing so within the constraints of their developmental stage and the social culture in which they live, using those strategies that they believe are likely to be successful in doing so. But other people and society do not always budge to accommodate our preferences so that preferences need to be managed, both to facilitate their pursuit and to cope with preference blockage. Preference management is a universal aspect of social life – infants, children, and parents in all cultures have to play the same preference management "game." The means of preference management that infants and children develop are brought to bear throughout their lives as they interact with others while pursuing their own preferences. Examining social development through the prism of preference management allows us to see how infants' social world is shaped by the preferences of those around them, how they, in turn, shape their world by expressing their preferences to others, and the way that conflicting preferences spur development by requiring preferential conflict to be resolved.

My focus on preferences does not reflect either philosophical or psychological hedonism. Rather, in line with Frankfurt's (1971, 1988) analysis, it emphasizes that although when talking of desires, we are indifferent as to which of them are actualized, preferences imply that we reflect, choose, and evaluate our desires. We have a stake in the conflict between our desires. The existence of preferences implies that one could rank the comparative desirability of one thing over another, justifying it by saying "p is better than q because . . . " (cf., Doyle, 2004). In this view, preferences are cognitive structures or mental representations that guide our choices, and our choices reflect our underlying preferences. This is evident in young children's explanations that thinking is preference centered: "You think of things you want to do" (Piaget, 1929/1975, p. 49), and that thinking of something means "you want to have it" (ibid, p. 50). In this view, preferences as mental representations can serve as anchors of comparison and guidelines in trying to align the world *as is* and the world *as preferred*.

Importantly, we tend to define ourselves with reference to our preferences. We abstract from our concrete experiences to more general statements of preference, allowing the unnamed character in *Green Eggs and Ham* (Dr. Seuss, 1960) to conclude, despite repeated protestation to the contrary, "Say, I like green eggs and ham! I do!" In fact, when children and adults are asked to tell about themselves, after listing vital statistics, they cite preferences, those psychological aspects of self that uniquely define them (e.g., "I am a Baroque music lover, Baskin Robins fan"). We can define ourselves with reference to our preferences because our preferences are remarkably stable. We repeatedly buy the same foods in the supermarket, order the same meals at our favorite restaurant, engage in the same free-time activities, and tend to live in the same house with the same furniture and significant others for many years. Preferences run our lives. We structure our lives to accommodate them, make elaborate plans that enable us to attain them, and take vacations that coddle them.

The stability of our preferences often outlives their usefulness. Many adults "love" their cars and keep investing money in their upkeep for lengthy periods of time when it is no longer financially rational to do so. My son at age 7 refused to part with his favorite shoes, bought at age 5, despite their being worn and too small to wear. I myself spent years trying to find replacements for the colorful nomad rugs that were wrecked by the cleaners when I was an adolescent, jumping for joy at accidentally finding similar rugs when my own children were adolescents. As these anecdotes illustrate, some of our preferences remain steadfast, often leading us into grief-like states when a "loved" object is broken, worn out, or is lost.

On the other hand, our preferences are not as stable as we would like to think they are. They may change spontaneously over time; as Freud (1901) noted about his own acquired taste for spinach,[1] most people do start eating spinach at some point in life. Preferences also change with exposure to the preference objects themselves. The cry "Not spaghetti again!" expresses the delicate balance between underexposure and overexposure to preference objects. The phenomenon of saying "I have nothing to wear" while looking at a full closet similarly reflects the fact that preferences are not frozen in time. Spring break provides a longed-for respite from the snow, even for those who pronounce that they love winter. Time and recurrence, then, can engender changes in our preferences. Importantly, preferences are objects of communication and negotiation with others, and they can change as a function of such negotiation, as well as through planning and deliberation (cf. Doyle, 2004). The fact that preferences can be the subject of conversation makes them ripe targets of influence for others who may want to change our preferences, both for our own benefit and for their own egoistic reasons.

[1] Freud (1901) says, "for a long time I detested spinach then eventually my taste changed and I promoted that vegetable into one of my favourite foods" (p. 639).

From my perspective, though, it is not the preferences that are important. Rather, it is the fact that not all preferences are immediately available but may need to be pursued over time, that other people can serve as agents who satisfy or thwart the pursuit of our preferences, that other people have their own preferences for what they want for themselves and what they want for and from us, and that juggling these diverse demands requires us to develop cognitive and behavioral preference management skills for dealing with ourselves and with others.

Freud's (e.g., 1933/1965) depiction of the battle between the Id and the Superego as mediated by the Ego beautifully captures the potential conflict between our own preferences and those of parents and society and underlines the need to placate both them and ourselves in our behavioral choices. In addition, from my perspective, Freud rightfully put the motivational engine prior to the cognitive cart. In contrast, Piaget (1964/1967, 1995) provided the theoretical underpinnings of an approach in which cognition drives development. Although he often reiterated the joint working of cognition and motivation, Piaget gave the motivational underpinnings of social life the short shrift in most of his theoretical work. I deliberately attempt to redress this, presenting preferences as the motivational engine that spurs the acquisition of language and communication. That is, I see the need to communicate one's preferences to others, infer others' preferences, and coordinate and align one's own preferences with those of others as the central tasks of social development.

*INTRA*PERSONAL PREFERENTIAL CONFLICT

Many of our preferences are ones we wish we did not have. I love chocolate, but whenever I eat chocolate, I regret having done so. We want not to want to eat desserts or smoke cigarettes. Philosophers (e.g., Dworkin, 1988; Frankfurt, 1988) contend that the mark of personhood is the ability to reflect on our preferences and evaluate whether or not they are preferences we should have, evaluations known as *second-order preferences*. Having second-order preferences means that there is always a potential for *intra*personal conflict with our first-order preferences. Yet children are not born with second-order preferences; they acquire them during the process of socialization. Mothers attempt to socialize children's preferences, and children gradually adopt second-order preferences about their own preferences (e.g., "I should eat spinach because it's healthy"). A wise 12-year-old reflects understanding of second-order preferences when he refers to being tempted as "you want to do something that you don't want to do" (Sonuga-Barke & Webley, 1993, p. 39).

When our second-order preferences differ from our first-order preferences – when we experience intrapersonal preferential conflict – we need to align these two types of preference. The alignment of intrapersonal preferential conflict can work in one of two possible directions. The first of these involves attempts to transform our first-order preferences to match our second-order preferences. Dieting, for instance, can be viewed as an instance of such alignment. The person says "I love to eat chocolate," while at the same time saying, "I shouldn't love to eat chocolate because it's unhealthy or fattening." In dieting, one imposes controls over one's first-order preferences as a means of aligning these two levels of preference. Activating self-control processes in the context of intrapersonal preferential conflict engages cognitive practices that work to transform our first-order preferences to align them with our second-order preferences. Of course, society plays a large part in determining the second-order preferences that individuals adopt. Cultures may foster dieting, saving money, and sexual abstinence as second-order preferences that attempt to constrain how we eat, spend money, and socialize.

However, individuals often allow their first-order preferences to override their second-order preferences and need to cope with the mismatch. Consequently, the second route we can take when our first- and second-order preferences conflict involves cognitively transforming our second-order preferences to align them with our first-order preferences. Such cognitive transformations are well exemplified in postdecisional dissonance (Festinger, 1957), which is often manifest in changes in the evaluation of preferences. As Festinger noted, however, conflict between first and second-order preferences can arise prior to decision making and can be rectified in various ways by playing with the underlying representations. Consequently, the need to resolve intrapersonal preferential conflict can activate what I call *mind play*, in which cognitive transformations are undertaken to alter our representations of reality and allow us to live more peacefully with ourselves. Socialization agents play an important role in fostering such cognitive transformations, by teaching children how to engage in such processes and specifically, by socializing the types of mind play they can adopt in attempting to cope. Viewing the emergence of such cognitive processes in developing children provides an important window to our understanding of how society shapes our motivational, cognitive, and behavioral choices and guides us into becoming the kinds of adults we become. The focus on the transformational processes employed in the resolution of conflict between our first- and second-order preferences allows us to see the parallels between behavioral and cognitive self-control, viewing them both as means of resolving *intra*personal preferential conflict.

Intrapersonal preferential conflict often involves the temporal dimension because not all preferences are available at the same time. Consequently, managing one's preferences involves the temporal dimension. As Schelling (1984) quips, "*now* I want *not* to do those things then," but as *then* becomes *now*, our preferences change. But because preferences change over time partly as a consequence of previous actions taken, they often mock us, making the socialization of the temporal dimension critical for preference management. Moreover, even in contexts that seemingly do not involve the temporal dimension, time is implicated because the likely consequences of each choice need to be forecast. March (1978) suggests that choices are guided by *guesses* – guesses about the future consequences of current actions and guesses about our future preferences for these consequences. That is, current choices are made based on what we think our preferences will be in the future; choices in the present need to be made with the future self in mind. But the way individuals relate to their future self is also a function of culture, with different cultures fostering greater or lesser concern with one's future.

*INTER*PERSONAL PREFERENTIAL CONFLICT

Preferences and choices are not made in a social vacuum; they are acquired within a social world, and this social world is not indifferent to our preferences. First, other people also have preferences, and their preferences extend into realms that impinge on us. The coexistence of preferences in oneself and in others necessarily implies that the prospect of *inter*personal preferential conflict is omnipresent in the child's life, in interaction with parents, siblings, and peers. By focusing on the preference management process, I show how social life forces us to recognize others as social beings, because they too express their preferences and demand that we take account of these preferences when we interact with them.

Within this framework, social behavior can be undertaken with or without regard to other people's preferences. In my view, there is a continuum from behavior undertaken at the expense of other people's preferences (i.e., aggressive behavior) to behavior undertaken to promote other people's preferences, rather than our own preferences (i.e., altruistic behavior). On this continuum, there are also behaviors undertaken without regard for other people's preferences (i.e., inconsiderate or egoistic behavior) and behaviors that defer to other people's preferences (i.e., considerate behavior). In this context, I see moral behavior as behavior in which the preferences of generic others guide one's behavior in settings in which one's short-term preferences would have led one to behave otherwise. The concept of generic others, with a past, a present, and a future, and preferences that need to be taken into account in guiding our behavior toward them while pursuing our preferences, is critical for this process.

Crucially, other people also have preferences as to the kinds of preferences that we *should* have. Societies, governments, educational systems, and parents all have their own ideas and preferences regarding our preferences. They all prefer that we help rather than harm other people, avoid littering in public, and generally adopt prevailing rules and norms of conduct. It is because parents have preferences regarding their children, what Harsanyi (1988) calls *external preferences*, that infants and children are first exposed to attempts to socialize their preferences. Parents know how they want their children to end up, and they try to channel, temporize, restrict, and discipline their children in their attempt to get them to mind parents' external preferences. Laws, local ordinances, and context-bound rules are passed in the attempt to impose societal preferences on us, based on the implicit assumption that our own preferences do not match them and need to be aligned via such imposition. Laws are enacted because there is an assumption that given free choice, each citizen's own preferences would lead him to behave in ways that would conflict with the preferences of others. Societal external preferences regarding the citizen's preferences differ from his first-order preferences, and the law reflects this preference gap. The Ten Commandments give voice to some of the spheres in which preference gaps are universal. Actual or assumed preference gaps result in our preferences being manipulated both by close others and distant others who also have an interest in manipulating our preferences (e.g., "Nothing comes between me and my Calvin Kleins" – from an ad for Calvin Klein jeans), not necessarily with our own best interest at heart (cf., George, 2001).

There are many occasions when we cannot attain our preferences without someone else's intervention or help. As infants and children, we rely on socialization agents, especially parents, to help us attain our preferences. As adults, we may also need others' help to do so. In such cases, we need to know how to get others' to behave in ways that will facilitate the actualization of our own preferences. We develop strategies of getting others to help us satisfy our preferences, doing so while keeping in mind that they also have preferences, and figuring out the implications of such preferences for the pursuit of our own preferences. Managing one's own preferences and managing those of others are often intertwined.

Critically, how socialization agents manage their own preferences is inexorably bound with the way they manage children's preferences. As Schelling (1984) argues, the way people cope, or try to cope, with the need to control themselves is much like the way in which they exercise command over another person. Our personalities are reflected in the strategies we adopt for interacting with the world around us (e.g., Mischel, Cantor, & Feldman, 1996), and such strategies come into play when we attempt to resolve both interpersonal and intrapersonal preferential conflict, whether with children or with adults. As I elaborate later, doing so in the context of interacting with oneself involves many of the same cognitive skills and strategies that are involved in the context of interacting with others. Adopting this perspective on social development leads to consideration of those processes that are critical to managing our preferences in ourselves and in our interaction with others: persuasion, role taking, moral judgment, and transformational thought, processes that are of interest to both academic and nonacademic audiences.

COGNITIVE PROCESSES IN PREFERENCE MANAGEMENT

Preference management requires the application of both online and offline processes (cf., Bickerton, 1995;

Gärdenfors, 2005). Whereas online processes refer to how we cognitively process and react to the world out there, offline processes refer to how we cognitively manipulate our own representations. Doing so engages transformational thought. Transformational thought (Berlyne, 1965; Karniol, 1986; 1990b) takes either external or internal stimuli and creates new internal stimuli, such as thoughts and affective reactions or a combination of both. Transformational thought involves both decontextualization and recontextualization. Decontextualization refers to psychologically removing oneself from the *here-and-now*, allowing one not to respond to the immediate features of the current context, to delay responding, and to engage in self-regulation. Bronowski (1977; but see also Gärdenfors, 2005) claims that the ability to decontextualize is the hallmark of humanity and the central factor that distinguishes us from our animal ancestors. But decontextualization is only part of the story. The other part is recontextualization, the introduction of something that has been decontextualized into a new context in which it is given a new meaning because of its new surroundings. So decontextualization necessarily goes hand in hand with recontextualization, symbolically representing current contexts in terms that transform their meaning for the individual. Transformational thought is the unique human ability that integrates both *decontextualization*, distancing ourselves from the concrete present, and *recontextualiation*, transforming the immediate environment, symbolically *re*-presenting objects and events. Piaget and Inhelder (1973) go as far as calling man "a machine engaged in transformations" (p. 8), and Piaget elaborates that

> to know is to assimilate reality into systems of transformations. To know is to transform reality.... Knowing reality means constructing systems of transformations that correspond, more or less adequately, to reality...(transformational structures) are simply possible isomorphic models among which experience can enable us to choose. (Piaget, 1970, p. 15)

Bruner (1964) further stipulates that, as part of their development, children become capable of "translating experience into a symbol system that can be operated on by rules of transformation" (p. 11), allowing for the representation of experience as well as the transformation of representations of experience that can then be used in decision making and problem solving.

It is the ability to use our thoughts to transform reality – and even our desires – that makes us uniquely human. The joint work of decontextualization and recontextualization in transformational thought enables children to cope when their preferences cannot be actualized, allowing them both to distance themselves psychologically from their preferences and to think about their preferences in the past and in the future. Transformational thought allows us to view a rose as a message of love rather than a red flower with a thorny stem, and transformational thought lets us interpret our behavior in ways that promote or undermine our control efforts (cf., Dweck, 2006). It also underlies our ability to delay gratification and keep secondary and long-term goals steadfast, deemphasizing the relevance of obstacles and temptations as they attempt to derail us from our chosen path.

Transformational thought is also critical for interacting with others. We need to heed others' preferences, to endow others with thoughts and feelings, and to use these in the attempt to impact their preferences, by negotiating, arguing, and manipulating them in the service of our own preferences. Social life requires us to get a handle on others' likely reactions to the pursuit of our preferences so we can guide our behavior in light of our reading of these psychological reactions. This guessing game – conducting mental transformations about other people's thoughts and feelings – has been of central focus in my own work (e.g., Karniol, 1986, 1990b, 2003a). It is variously discussed under the rubric of the Theory of Mind, perspective taking, role taking, and empathy – terms that in my view occlude the transformational nature of mentalizing. As I elaborate in later chapters, just as transformations are applied to ponder one's own experiences in the past and in the future, mental transformations are used for "cracking" into others' minds to link their experiences with their preferences and their likely psychological reactions.

My contention in this book is that children learn to conduct transformations along three planes of thought: (1) the temporal plane, (2) the imaginal plane, and (3) the mental plane, that they learn to do so from parents who engender transformations on these planes when they talk to their children, and that, by conducting such transformations, children become more adept at resolving both their own and other people's interpersonal and intrapersonal preferential conflicts.

THE ROLE OF LANGUAGE

Transformational thought is acquired in the context of language acquisition and social communication. Children learn not only to speak but "when to speak, when not, and as to what to talk about with whom, when, where in what manner" (Hymes, 1972, p. 277). That is, children are socialized through language, and their use of language reflects their understanding of social mores and of other individuals within the social contexts in which they find themselves. Through language, individuals become culturally intelligent beings, pursuing their preferences within a social milieu that both dictates preferences and facilitates or hinders the actualization of preferences. From this perspective, much of what we know is tacit knowledge learned through joint activities and conversations with others, others who have their own preferences and external preferences regarding our preferences, often leading to interpersonal preferential conflict with them. Because language is a symbol system, through language, children come to understand that one can refer symbolically to absent people and worlds and transform present worlds into alternative worlds that exist only in their minds.

The critical developments from the current perspective, then, are awareness of one's own preference structure, the understanding that others have preferences, the ability to figure out what preferences others have, being able to engage in transformational thought, and developing the concept of generic others. These cognitive processes yield the data that feed into the decision-making process when we decide how to pursue our preferences. They are the cognitive pillars on which social development is mounted, and which allow for interpersonal and intrapersonal preferential conflict to be resolved and for altruism and moral behavior to emerge, as I elaborate in later chapters.

PLAN OF THE BOOK

My aim in this book is to show how preference management emerges out of the infant's interaction with his mother, how it is engaged in by mothers vis à vis their infants and children, and how children become moral or immoral beings who behave in ways that manifest their concern, or lack of concern, with other people's preferences. I focus on the intricate pattern of negotiation that emerges as infants, children, and parents express their preferences to each other, cognitively manipulate each other's preferences, and behaviorally adapt and adopt ways of behaving that actualize their own and other people's preferences. It is this intertwining of our preferences, the preferences of others, and our use of behavioral and cognitive strategies in traversing the world that is the spice of social life.

First, it should be noted at the outset that this book does not offer behavioral guidelines for parents. What this book does is trace how preference management emerges in infancy, how it changes with the acquisition of language, how parents promote and foster preference management in their children, and the cognitive processes that are involved in this remarkable journey. My approach is interdisciplinary and draws on research and theorizing in psychology (e.g., developmental, social, and personality psychology), language acquisition, socialization, and communication, underlining the way these are intertwined in children's social development. I think this book would be of interest to anyone – whether lay person, parent, student, or academic – who is interested in children, in their social and language development, as well as in socialization and parent–child communication. The fact that the book is thematic rather than topical or age based, allows me to portray a coherent picture of social development that, in my view, may also make the book useful as complementary reading for courses in developmental psychology, social development, parent education, parent–child relations, communication, and language socialization.

In contrast to topical treatments of social development, then, this book is thematic, presenting preferences and preference management as the glue that integrates the different domains of social development. As such, it sheds a new and unique perspective on social development, socialization, and language socialization – a perspective that has not been adopted in any other book – placing preferential conflict at the heart of social life. I do not see this perspective as conflicting with other theoretical perspectives on social development but rather as complementing and enriching our understanding of the way language and cognitive processes serve children's development as social beings who are in pursuit of their preferences and who can help and hinder others in the pursuit of their preferences. Second, the book presents preferential conflict – both interpersonal and intrapersonal – as the force that provides continuity across social life, a continuity that is a direct outcome of the need for individuals to manage their preferences and resolve both interpersonal and intrapersonal preferential conflict throughout their lives.

This book is set up in three interlocking parts, each of which can be read independently of the others, and which together form the essence of a theory of social development. In this theory, infants first need to crack into the language system in order to facilitate their expression of preferences to those around them but also because others are incessantly telling children their preferences and want children to mind these preferences. Children need to learn to mind others' preferences because they can thereby increase the likelihood of furthering their own preferences. As part and parcel of this, children need to learn to identify their own preferences so they can develop more adaptive means of pursuing these preferences, and they need to develop means of identifying the preferences of others when others do not express their preferences directly. Children's understanding that others have preferences, both in general and about what they themselves should or should not be doing, is an important part of socialization and is conveyed to children via the strategies that parents use to get their children to adopt behaviors, delay behaviors, and terminate behaviors, often resorting to disciplinary tactics when children fail to heed. Concomitantly, parental linguistic practices allow children to disengage from the here-and-now, learning to transform on the temporal plane, the imaginal plane, and the mental plane. These transformational planes are critical for children's attempts to manage their preferences, both in interacting with others and in modulating their own attempts to cope with others as well as with the unavailability of their own preferences. Hence, language and the ability to engage in transformational thought are the keys for developing strategies of preference management and for using them when faced with either interpersonal or intrapersonal preferential conflict.

To outline the three sections of the book, the first section, Chapters 1–4, follows infants and their mothers into childhood, as they communicate about their respective preferences and infants learn to verbally express their preferences, discuss them, and get others to satisfy them, learning in the interim that others are agents with their own preferences – preferences that may lead them to opt not to satisfy infants' and children's preferences. Chapter 1 focuses on how babies and their mothers communicate with each other regarding their respective preferences. It underlines mothers' treatment of their infants as communicative and intentional beings who have preferences and can communicate these preferences to others. Chapter 2 addresses the transition to language and children's use of language to communicate their preferences to others, doing so within the context of their emergent understanding of others as social and psychological beings. I emphasize the transition from references to *here-and-now* to references to objects and events that are temporally and spatially distant. Chapter 3 traces the emergence of meta-preferences, children's understanding of both stable and unstable preferences in themselves, and their perceptions of themselves as amalgams of particular types of preferences, in contradistinction to others. Chapter 4 turns to children's understanding of other people's preferences, the emergence of the concept of generic others, and the theories that have been advanced to account for the emergence of such understanding. I consider my own theory, as well as simulation, Theory of Mind, and approaches that posit that self serves as the default for understanding others.

The second section of the book, traced in Chapters 5–9, focuses on parents and the strategies they use to influence the preferences their children have: channeling preferences, temporizing preferences, restricting preferences, and disciplining children when they don't adopt the preferences parents want them to adopt. Cross cutting these strategies are the language practices that parents adopt in dealing with their children and the transformational skills that they engender in children by virtue of how they talk of absent realities. Chapter 5 deals with parenting in general, outlining approaches that have been used to account for the relationship among parenting, language use, and social class. The following chapters address socialization strategies more explicitly. In Chapter 6, I address the means by which parents channel their children's preferences toward those objects and behaviors that they want their children to prefer. Chapter 7 focuses on temporization: how parents use the time dimension in orienting their children to objects and actions (i.e., "not now – later"; "do it right now") and how children themselves learn to use the temporal dimension in their interaction with others. Chapter 8 outlines the strategies parents use to restrict their children's behavior, to get them to avoid objects and behaviors that are dispreferred by parents. The final chapter in this section, Chapter 9, turns to the strategies parents use to discipline their children when they do not adopt parental preferences.

The third section of the book, elaborated in Chapters 10–14, focuses on the processes of preference management: the emergence of the planes of transformational thought, children's use of language to manipulate others to attain their preferences, coping with intrapersonal preferential conflict, using mind play as means of cognitively transforming our own and others' preferential worlds, and minding other people's preferences, the sine qua non of altruism and morality. Chapter 10 addresses the socialization of transformational thought on the temporal plane, the imaginal plane, and the mental plane. In particular, I consider how adults teach children to disconnect their preferences from the *here-and-now* and socialize them to imaginally enter other people's psychological worlds, often through pretend play. Chapter 11 provides a summary of the linguistic means children use to get others to do what they want them to do, how they manipulate others to become instruments of their own preferential world. Chapter 12 elaborates what children do to cope and self-regulate when they are faced with preferences they cannot have. Chapter 13 centers on *mind play*, how children and their parents apply transformational thought strategically in their daily life to change their own and other people's representations of their preferential world. I elaborate how children learn to mind play with context, with time, with pretend, and with perspective, and how they induce such mind play in others. Chapter 14 turns to altruism, aggression, and morality, elaborating how what one knows about other people's preferences is deployed to mind, or not mind, their preferences in undertaking one's actions. Finally, in Chapter 15, I tie up the threads I've woven to link this approach more explicitly with extant theoretical approaches and summarize the essence of the preference management approach.

THE DATA

The medium through which I address these issues is the language of everyday life that adults and children use in their interaction with each other. The reader may well question the reasons for this choice. First, much of children's emergent language is used to express their preferences to others. Second, language is the primary medium socialization agents use to manage infants' and children's preferences as they attempt to influence the preferences that they have and the physical and temporal dimensions along which preferences are partaken. Language is also the primary means by which others convey their own preferences and through which children learn that the social world is populated by others who are similarly pursuing their potentially conflicting preferences. It is through their conversations and verbal exchanges with parents, siblings, and peers that children construct their representations of the social world and acquire an understanding of the give-and-take of social life that preferential conflict engenders. This makes parental language critical for the representations that their children develop. Moreover, from the perspective of cognitive semantics (e.g., Langacker, 2005), language cannot be either used or understood without reference to virtual entities – fictitious objects and events that are referred to although they do not have any counterparts in reality (e.g., the sentence "your pants are getting shorter" means that the child has been growing). Yet both speakers and listeners need to engage the virtual plane in a similar manner for continued meaningful interaction between them; meaning is construed and conventionalized rather than intrinsically given. Speakers convert from the actual plane to the virtual plane as they speak and as listeners, children need to perform both transformations from the virtual to the actual plane and additional transformations that are required to interpret sentences in a manner that preserves correspondence between the virtual plane and reality as they know it. Hence, parental language plays a critical role in shaping children's construals of the world, their deployment of transformations, and their relation to others and their preferences. Garrett and Baquedano-López give voice to this view in saying,

> As a developmental process, then, language acquisition is far more than a matter of a child learning to produce well-formed referential utterances; it also entails learning how to use language in socially appropriate ways to co-construct meaningful social contexts and to engage with others in culturally relevant meaning-making activities. (Garrett & Baquedano-López, 2002, p. 342)

My book puts everyday speech in the limelight, letting us hear naturally occurring conversations in which children, parents, and peers communicate about their respective preferences, discuss preferential conflict, and attempt to manage such conflict, both interpersonally and intrapersonally. This makes the book readable, interesting – and sometimes amusing. More importantly, the book captures both the language used by children and the language used in talking to children (cf., Ochs & Schieffelin, 2001), as this language is bandied about in the process of daily living, serving as the means of children's socialization to their culture.

To capture this intricate, interactive process, I gathered samples of naturally occurring talk, relying on child language sources collected by developmental psycholinguists from the Child Language Data Exchange System (CHILDES), (MacWhinney, 2000; accessible at childes/psy.cmu.edu), both my own and other researchers' language diary studies, socialization studies, and classroom communication studies, in English and other languages – sources that have recorded naturalistic speech. This is because children "are saying amazing things all the time, if you listen carefully" (Tobin, Wu, & Davidson, 1989, p. 158). What they say serves as an index of what they know about the world, the objects and people in it, and their own role in that world. In particular, in their interactions with others, they express their preferences, both about what they want and what they want others to do, to say, and to refrain from doing or saying. In turn, others do the same to them, allowing us to see how preferential communication is used to cope with one's social world. Spontaneous speech captures the motivational platform that provides the backdrop of preference communication and preferential conflict.

In contrast to the zeitgeist of emphasizing how cultures differ, I have tried to demonstrate the cross-cultural nature of the preference phenomena that are my focus, illustrating my points with data gathered in diverse parts of the world. I provide examples from both English and non–English-speaking children and adults as they interact and communicate with each other about their preferential world. In addition to American and British children, there are samples of children's and adults' speech from Europe (e.g., Germany, France, and Italy), the Middle East (Israel), and the Far East (China and Japan). To simplify, only English is presented in the text, but the interested reader can follow the footnotes to see what was actually said in the original language in which it was said. As well, though children of different ages may differ in their cognitive abilities and the relative sophistication of their language skills, the examples of children's speech provided in each context are purposely drawn from children of varying ages to illustrate the underlying similarities of the motivational underpinnings of *what* is being expressed. Throughout the book, children's age is shown in months and days up to 36 months (e.g., 24;12 represents a child who is 12 days after his second birthday) and in years and months after that (e.g., 3;6 represents a child of 3 and a half years).

Empirical research is cited where it underlines the point being made. I have not attempted to discuss or cite all relevant research in a given domain, and I offer sincere apologies to those colleagues whose work I may have overlooked. In particular, I have explicitly avoided adopting existing classification systems of compliance gaining and persuasion because of the problems in comparing such systems and assessing the knowledge claims that can be made about their use (cf., Kellermann & Cole, 1994), an issue I will address more fully in its relevant context. Moreover, wherever possible, I have avoided using parental self-reports regarding socialization practices because of the generally low correlations between what parents believe, their self-reports, and what they actually do in interaction with their children (cf., Fivush, 1998a; Sigel, 1992). Instead, I have focused on parental socialization in terms of their strategies of channeling preferences, temporizing preferences, restricting preferences, and disciplining noncompliance as parents talk with their children and with researchers. In addition, I have discussed parental fostering of both transformational thought and mind play, cognitive strategies that are generally used by parents implicitly and that have not been incorporated into other theoretical or empirical studies of child socialization.

This book is not a compendium of research studies but, rather, it traces a developmental path from infancy to adolescence as evidenced in what infants do, children say, and parents do and say primarily to each other, but also sometimes to researchers, regarding preferences and preference management. I have taken this tack because social life reflects how we interact with others to attain our preferences in the manner in which we communicate with others, telling them our preferences, comparing our preferences with theirs, and getting them to act on our preferences. The impetus is to get what we want. However, it is the existence of others with their own preferences and their external preferences regarding ourselves that creates preferential conflict and drives the cognitive engine that finds more and more sophisticated means of outmaneuvering others, persuading them, and playing with our own minds when we do not succeed in doing so. The Preference Management Triangle shown on page 1 of this book refers to the relationship between the world – of objects and people – as they relate to self in time and within a given culture. Preferences relate to the child's physical and social world, and they involve the temporal dimension in that they concern either immediate or delayed preferences. Culture, as mediated by parents in particular, attempts to influence both children's preferences and the relationship of time and self to them, doing so within the framework legitimized in that culture. But irrespective of the particular culture in which one is enmeshed, children and parents are universally engaged in preference management. In talking to their children, parents provide us with a glimpse of this, and children, in talking to their parents and to others around them, provide us with a snapshot of how the world impinges on them and frames their means of attaining their preferences.

My own research is discussed where it has theoretical significance, but I do not see this book as a forum for summarizing my research. On the other hand, I have drawn extensively on the language diaries of my own children, Karen and Orren, diaries that were used in two previously published papers (Karniol, 1990a, 1992). Because much psycholinguistic research is dedicated to children who are just learning to speak, the book is biased in the direction of toddlers and preschool children rather than older ones. In some sense, though, this is an advantage because it serves to demonstrate how preferences drive our development from infancy onward. Concomitantly, this book provides a convenient timetable for children's emerging language skills in interacting with others at different ages and for the cognitive milestones in the realm of preferences: when children start talking about their own preferences, when they start talking of other people's preferences, when they start to attempt to influence other people's preferences, and so forth.

As will be evident throughout the book, I see preferences as providing an integrative theme that propels social and cognitive development because it compels us to face, head-on, the preferences of others who are like us in striving to actualize their preferences and who may see us as obstacles or stepping stones in the path of the attainment of their preferences, much as we may see them the same way. Although the focus on preferences may seem radical, I hope this book will demonstrate the theoretical and empirical virtue of thinking in these terms. In order to start this journey, I will start by focusing on infants' and children's first foray into the preferential world – the Baby "Preference Game," – or how infants and parents attempt to solve the preference management problem.

1 The Baby "Preference Game"

A toddler crawls into her mother's lap while the mother is drinking coffee. The mother asks, 'And what do you want, hmm? You're not having my coffee. No.' When the child looks at the observer's coffee, she says, 'You're not having her coffee either.'

(Snow, 1984, p. 81)

In this chapter, I trace the emergent way caretakers, who for the sake of convenience will be called "mothers," and infants (who for convenience will be referred to as males) communicate with each other in the context of the Baby "Preference Game," a game that can be described as "you tell me your preferences, I'll tell you my preferences, and then . . . . " First, I focus on what mothers do to infer their infants' preferences, and then I elaborate what infants do to convey their preferences to their mothers.

WHY DO I CALL THIS A GAME?

As I will try to show in this chapter, the interactive episodes that emerge between mothers and their infants are a game for all intents and purposes because both parties try to decipher the rules governing their interaction in the attempt to achieve their goals – getting more of their preferences satisfied and doing so as quickly as possible. But infant–mother interactions have many parallels with the game of charades, because one side can only use physical actions to convey meaning, and the other side needs to infer what these physical actions are supposed to imply. However, in the game of charades, players capitalize on conventionalized symbols whose meanings are socially shared, but the infant players in the Baby "Preference Game" do not know how to use conventionalized symbols. Mothers are the ones who invest time and effort in attempting to decipher their babies' behavior as signals of their babies' preferences. At first, babies do not know that their behavior is interpreted by mothers as signals of preferences. They eventually learn that mothers are attributing intentionality to their behavior and that behavior can be used to signal their preferences.

Mothers have a distinct advantage because, as adults, they already know how to play the preference game, having played it since they were infants. The game changes when their baby is born though because, as mothers, they now have a dual function: they need to satisfy their own preferences, but in order for their baby to thrive, they also need to satisfy the preferences of their baby. In contrast, babies come into this world with preferences but without knowledge of the preference game; they need to learn how to play it within the constraints of their families and their culture. For this to happen, they need to learn to communicate and interact with others whose preferences they need to take into account in satisfying their own preferences. But in contrast to many games, the Baby "Preference Game" is a non–zero sum game: if the baby wins, so does the mother; if the baby loses, its mother loses too. This is because mother and child are interdependent – a happy baby generally has a happy mother and vice versa. Tracing the emergence of this game requires us to focus on what mothers do when they communicate with their infants, what infants do when they communicate with their mothers, and what the implications of this interactive game are for the unfolding of infants' preferences.

How do mothers play the game? From the moment infants are born, mothers attempt to understand what their babies are "saying" to them. As Camaioni (1993) claims, mothers react to babies' spontaneous behavior as if it were intentional, interpreting it in terms of intentions, goals, wishes, and communicative symbols. The mother is constantly monitoring her baby, imputing meaning to his actions. When a baby spits out food, she assumes he doesn't want it; when a baby grimaces, she assumes he doesn't like it. His actions speak to her when his linguistic abilities do not yet do so. To illustrate, when an infant starts playing with his lunch, his mother interprets this as refusal to eat; she says, "No more? All right. You finish your drink then" (Snow, 1984, p. 80). In this context, Newson (1979) contends that mothers engage in a process of "adultomorphism" – attributing even to newborns the human power of social responsiveness, with wishes, intentions, and feelings that they can communicate to others. From my perspective, mothers treat their newborns as individuals with distinct preferences, and they attempt to decipher those preferences. Mothers communicate to their infants that

1. infants have preferences,
2. mothers don't know what these preferences are,
3. mothers *want* to know what these preferences are, and
4. infants can communicate their preferences to them.

How do infants play the game? They learn that

1. their world may differ from how they want it to be,
2. they can communicate their preferences to their mothers,
3. mothers will try to interpret their communication,
4. mothers can act to fulfill one's preferences,
5. mothers cannot fulfill preferences that are misinterpreted,
6. mothers may opt not fulfill some preferences, and
7. some further communication may be necessary.

As in any game, in order for it to run off smoothly, each participant needs to play his role. The infant's role – that of transmitting preference information to the mother – is one that depends on the infant's understanding that communication is necessary on his part. Communication is necessary because reality often diverges from infants' preferential state, and they need to let socialization agents know that this is the case. Infants are born with an inborn mechanism – crying – that signals their being in want. Crying is a signal that the current state of the world is dispreferred; but infants do not yet know what sort of alternative world is out there and how their current state can be improved or changed. This means that infant crying is a nonspecific cue that needs to be interpreted by a willing agent. This agent may invest time and energy in attempting to discover what aspect of the current world is dispreferred yet may not always be capable of doing so. Infants need to learn to guide their mothers. They need to acquire means of indicating *what* it is they want and to do so in ways that are both more readily interpretable and are acceptable within their culture. In Bruner's (1983) words, the infant "must travel the path from raw demand signaling to the fulfillment of felicity conditions on request" (p. 125). Traveling this thorny path is made easier by having mothers who are keen to understand and interpret the infant's signals, constantly informing him that such signals are meaningful to them and need to be emitted.

The first problem a mother may encounter in playing her role in the Baby "Preference Game" is that she may not be able to "read" the infant's communication of his preferences. As I elaborate later, mothers vary in their sensitivity in "picking up" their infant's messages; alternatively, infants vary in their competence at communicating their preferences. Infants vary in their ability to learn the rules of the game, some because they don't understand the need to communicate, others because they don't learn to communicate effectively. In either case, the game cannot be successfully played if this occurs (see Audet & Ripich, 1994). From the child's perspective, though, it makes little difference why such failure occurs because the end result is that preferences remain unfulfilled. In this light, the infant needs to learn what channels his mother attends and to refine those communicative channels that are available to him in order to maximize his mother's likelihood of interpreting his preferences. If he recognizes that she has trouble deciphering his communicative attempts, he needs to learn new means of transmitting his preferences so that reality can be aligned with his preferences and more of them can be fulfilled. As the more competent partner in playing this interactive game, mothers need to lead the way, using all the means at their disposal in the attempt to decipher their infants' preferences. In fact, as Kaye and Charney (1980) claim, "if an infant gives his mother any behavior which can be interpreted as if he has taken a turn in conversation, it will be; if he does not, she will pretend he has" (p. 227). I now turn to discussing the diverse means that mothers use to do so.

FACE READING

Mothers attempt to "read" their infants' preferences in various ways, with the primary one involving "face reading." Mothers look at their babies' faces in the attempt to try to fathom their ongoing states. Examining the interaction between mothers and their infants less than 3 months of age during feeding, Lavelli and Poli (1998) found that breastfeeding mothers looked at their infants' faces more and caressed them more than non–breastfeeding mothers. Such "face reading" enhances the prospect that the mother will catch the infant's gaze and, in fact, there were more mutual gazes in breastfed infants, with breastfeeding mothers apparently being more prepared to catch signals on the infants' part. In line with this, whereas in bottle-fed babies, interruptions in eating are primarily under maternal control, breastfed babies more often determined the interruptions of their own feeding (Wright, Fawcett, & Crow, 1980). This pattern suggests that breastfeeding mothers are more responsive to the cues emitted by the child, allowing the infant to regulate his food intake on the basis of these cues.[1]

Face reading is facilitated by the fact that there are universal, innate emotional expressions. Ekman and colleagues (e.g., Ekman et al., 1969) found a limited

[1] In some research, breastfed babies have been found to have a slight IQ advantage. Wright (1993) speculates that this reflects the fact that such infants develop greater expectations of mastery and control, possibly because their mothers are more responsive to the cues that they emit. In addition, though, breastfeeding mothers may communicate more with their infants. Still, recent research (e.g., Paxson & Schady, 2005) with more than 3,000 children in Ecuador provides little evidence for a relationship between breastfeeding and cognitive outcomes.

number of basic emotional expressions that are universally associated with the primary affects (e.g., fear, happiness, sadness). Babies' spontaneous facial expressions are apparently not random but are organized and temporally patterned (e.g., Oster & Ekman, 1978), suggesting that infants come into the world with "hardwired" instructions that drive such organization. Further evidence for hardwiring comes from the finding that anencephalic newborns (e.g., Steiner, 1973) and blind infants (Charlesworth & Kreutzer, 1973) also have patterned facial responses to certain stimuli (e.g., disgust expressions to bitter-tasting substances and smiles to sweet tastes). In this light, mothers can use their understanding of the universal features of facial expressions to attribute meaning to the facial expressions emitted by their infants.

MUTUAL ATTENTION

A critical aspect of deciphering infants' preferences is mothers' ability to get their baby to attend to them, to participate in an exchange that allows mothers to "read" the preference communication that the infant transmits. On the infant's part, establishing eye-to-eye contact with the mother represents the first milestone in this process. This interactive game, then, starts with a caregiver who observes and interprets the infant's experience, attempts to assess the infant's readiness to explore, and follows his direction of gaze to try to understand what his preferences might be. Such attentiveness on the mother's part promotes the possibility of shared attentional focus when the infant begins to explore objects. In keeping with this pattern, when their infants were 7-months-old, mothers were found to initiate interactive episodes with their infant in response to the infant's direction of gaze, and the majority of maternal utterances referred to those objects that were the infant's *current* focus of attention (Harris, 1992).

The flip side of this is that, unless the infant attends, interaction sequences initiated by the mother cannot be successful. Frequently, interaction sequences fail because the infant is inattentive; yet they can become successful if the mother implements attention-getting devices (e.g., calling the baby's name and saying "Hey, look") (Zukow, Reilly, & Greenfield, 1982). Bruner (1983) talks of *object highlighting*, either introducing objects and talking about them to direct infants' attention to them or following infants' gaze and talking about objects that are already the focus of their attention, with the latter type of highlighting often being accompanied by the placement of objects within infants' reach. Bruner found that highlighting is a fixture of the early months, dropping out almost entirely by the time the infant is about 1 year-old and linguistically more competent. Mothers also used pointing, and Butterworth (2003) suggests that infants' comprehension of pointing depends on their ability to simultaneously see the mother's pointing hand and the target to which she is pointing, using her visual gaze as an additional cue.

INFERRING PREFERENCES FROM CRYING

In addition to mothers' use of infants' facial expressions and direction of gaze to draw inferences about their preferences, mothers also use infant crying as a signal of a mismatch between the infant's preferences and current reality. Yet mothers' interpretation of infant cries depend on infants' developmental age. Up to 26 weeks of age, the cries of an infant tend to be interpreted by mothers as indicating a physical condition (e.g., hunger, pain, and discomfort) whereas after that, cries are perceived by mothers as more psychological in nature, reflecting frustration or desire for an object (Pratt, 1978). For mothers, then, a crying infant "is ordinarily seen as in want of something" (Bruner et al., 1982).

But it is unclear whether the infant uses crying as a signal and whether early crying has communicative intent. Dunn (2003) argues that although the cry of a newborn has a compelling effect on adults – babies are neither aware of this nor able to use crying intentionally. Yet Pratt (1978) suggests that infant crying itself changes in parallel to changes in mothers' interpretation of infants' cries. He found that infants were more likely to stop crying in response to physically oriented interventions when younger than 26 weeks (e.g., being picked up or comforted) and to psychological interventions when they were older (e.g., being offered an object, being talked to).

There is no disagreement, though, that during the first year of life, once children understand its powerful effects on socialization agents, crying starts to be used instrumentally, as a way of getting adult attention and help. There is research evidence that at about 8 months of age, infants' cries do actually change. They become acoustically differentiated, being marked by pauses during which the child checks the responses of the adults around him. Such behavior can be interpreted as indicating that crying has become instrumental. The fact that this transition occurs at around the age when stranger anxiety also appears suggests that it is intimately linked to cognitive changes. Specifically, this transition most likely occurs when the infant develops object and person permanence, the understanding that people and objects exist even when they are occluded or invisible. Prior to this time, the infant does not attempt to recover hidden objects, behaving as if they cease to exist when out of his perceptual field. Once object permanence develops, the infant attempts to retrieve objects out of his field of vision.

How does object permanence relate to crying? In the course of object manipulation, the infant has a variety of perceptual experiences that relate to the same object, making the infant aware that objects maintain their identity despite such variation. Objects may fall out of the infant's grip and become partially or fully occluded, yet their reappearance clarifies that they have continued existence despite being temporarily out of sight. Similarly, in the social world, when parents appear and reappear, with different clothes, hairstyles, and facial expressions,

Table 1.1.

	Age	Source
K is crying M: "Why are you crying?" K: "Mommy hold you," (i.e., wants to be held)	22 mos.	
K had been crying, I come to her room Crying stops M: "Why were you crying?" K: "It was an accident.... So Mommy hear you. Want Mommy to hold you"	22 mos.	
K is screaming and crying M: "Why are you crying?" K: "Grandma doesn't play with Karen"	23 mos.	Karniol (Diary, Karen)
Father refuses to give her the pacifier K: "Karen cries when Daddy gives Karen no moçeç" (Hebrew: pacifier)	25 mos.	
K is crying in her room M: "Why did you cry?" K: "'Cause Mummy forgot to come"	26 mos.	
K is explaining why a baby will cry K: "Because he doesn't have his diaper and his rattle and he will cry for his Mummy to do something about it"	30 mos.	

infants learn that social beings maintain their identity despite physical variation and that they exist even when they are out of sight. When infants play peek-a-boo with social partners, they similarly learn that these partners have continued existence during their temporary disappearance. Object and person permanence, then, emerge out of a comparison of the recent past in which the object or the other person is visible, to the present, when either the object or the person is not visible, and in anticipation of the near future, when they are expected to reappear. For this to occur, the infant needs to develop a representation of objects and people as separate from their perceptual image, that is, to decontextualize. Instrumental crying presumably emerges out of such development, being used by the infant to signal that the current state of affairs is dispreferred as compared to a previous one or an imagined future one in which unavailable objects and people would be available once more.

Concomitantly, though, parents start to interpret infants' cries as signals of requests, often because they are accompanied by arm extensions that involve the whole body. A 10-month-old who had been playing with the dog cries after his mother lets the dog out. The mother interprets his crying as a desire for the dog to return, says "Oh, all right,"opens the door for the dog to return, and whistles to call him back. When the dog returns, the child stops crying (Lock, 1980, p. 52). Referring to this transition, a mother says about her 1-year-old: "the minute we put him down, he begins to howl.... He wants us to keep on playing with him" (Bettelheim, 1962, p. 183). Parents become aware of the fact that infants have now started to use crying in an instrumental manner in the attempt to change their environment and the behavior of those in it.

Once crying becomes an instrumental activity, it becomes part of a routine that is initiated by parental departure or statements regarding impending departure, a routine aimed at either obviating the departure entirely or at least changing its duration. The relation between parental departure and crying as an instrumental routine is often evident in pretend play. In one example of this, when a mother and her 28-month-old daughter switched roles, the little girl, said to the pretend daughter, "I'm going. You be alone. You cry," and "I'm going to the office. You cry" (First, 1994, p. 115). This pretend interaction manifests understanding of the fact that children are "supposed to" cry when they are left alone and when mothers indicate their impending departure. Children are "supposed to" cry when they want their mothers to stay with them at bedtime, when they don't want their mothers to leave for work, and so forth. This understanding is evident in doll play, as when a child of 34 months is putting a doll in a cradle, and on being asked "what if your baby cries?" she answers, "Wants Mommy if her cry.... Her cry if her want me" (Reilly, 1986, p. 318).

Children with linguistic skills start to comment themselves on the instrumental functions of crying. Some examples, all from my diary of Karen, are shown in Table 1.1.

These comments make it explicit that she was using crying instrumentally. Children know when crying can serve an instrumental function, identifying those contexts in which they are "supposed to cry" as a means of changing some state of affairs. Karen explains this well at 31;18, when she says, "I have to cry if some things I don't like." The fact that crying can be used by children strategically is beautifully illustrated by an anecdote provided by Maccoby (1980). When the mother of a 4-year-old noticed a cut on his hand, she exclaimed, "Why, honey, you've hurt yourself! I didn't hear you crying" and her son answered "I didn't know you were home!" (p. 178). The child states explicitly that there is no purpose in crying unless someone can hear it. Crying, then, has acquired a dual function. It both serves to attract the mother's attention and to communicate the need for her to intervene in some way on the child's behalf. Mothers know that this is the case. First, they indicate that children are using crying strategically as a means of attracting their attention. When a 9-month-old cries while her mother is in conversation with a researcher, the mother comments, "She's only trying to get some attention" (Lock, 1980, p. 54). But attention isn't enough. Crying is also used to get mothers to attend to problems, as when a mother says that when the child bangs her head, the child looks up to see if there's someone around. "And if no one's around and she's in a room by herself, she just goes her own way. But if she looks first, and if someone's looking at her, she cries" (Bettelheim, 1962, p. 182).

Importantly, though, cries need to be interpreted by mothers and misinterpretations can also occur. When a 10-month-old screams because he cannot reach a toy that fell out of his playpen, his mother says, "It's no good screaming, you'll have to stay there a bit longer till I've finished" (Lock, 1980, p. 55). She interpreted his screams as reflecting his preference to get out of the playpen. Following his gaze would have told her otherwise.

TALKING AND QUESTIONING

The infants and toddlers described above were frequently responding to mothers who were attempting to infer their preferences by talking to them and questioning them, interpreting their direction of gaze and vocalizations as an index of their preferences. In interacting with their babies, mothers appear to adopt the assumption that babies' preferences are "conversationally" fathomable. As Snow, de Blauw, and van Roosmalen (1979) argue, mothers talk to babies because they think of their babies as potential conversational partners, capable of having thoughts and feelings and of communicating – perhaps not verbally – about them. The mother of a 3-month-old says to her baby, "I could play with you all day, couldn't I? You'd like that. Play all day?" The baby vocalizes, and the mother continues, "I think you prefer it to eating sometimes, don't you? Playing. It's much better" (p. 280).

As evident in this snapshot, even a 3-month-old child is thought of by the mother as having a set of preferences that are "conversationally" fathomable. The remarkable aspect of such exchanges is that mothers are apparently willing to interpret any change in the infant's behavior as indicative of intentional responsiveness to their queries. As one mother says about her 4-month-old: "she looks at you just as if she knows exactly what you're talking about, and what you're thinking about, and as if she's going to answer you any minute" (Bettelheim, 1962, p. 207). Fathers echo such perceptions, as evident in the following paternal comments: "They can't talk yet, but they know how to communicate with you. And it's like you can almost understand what they would want to say" (Palkovitz, 2002, p. 96).

In "conversations" with their prelinguistic infants, mothers do not just "talk." In many societies, mothers use "babytalk," speech that differs in its characteristics from talk addressed to adults. "Babytalk" attempts to hold the infant's attention by focusing on the "here-and-now," using many imperatives and one-word utterances, often in the context of exclamations, and engaging in partial repetitions of previous sentences. Gleason and Weintraub (1978) suggest that early maternal speech evidences features that serve two functions – the first function is to attract and hold the infant's attention, and the second function is to establish a warm bond between the infant and the mother. They argue that by the time children speak and understand language well, the functions of maternal speech change. Maternal speech is replaced by "the language of socialization," language that is filled with explicit instructions about what the child is to do, how he is to think and feel. Parents "may spell out the dangers of the physical world" (e.g., "look both ways before you cross the street"), they may disambiguate situations that are confusing for the child (e.g., when a scared child on a merry-go-round is told, "Isn't this fun?"), they instruct children in appropriate social behavior (e.g., "sit up at the table, chew with your mouth closed"), and, of course, they instruct them in the appropriate use of language (e.g., "say 'thank you' to Mrs. Jones"). As will become clear in this chapter, though, mothers use language to socialize their infants from the moment they are born; socialization, the alignment of children's preferences with that of the social world, is an ongoing process that may become more embellished as children gain facility with language, but it does not start with language acquisition.

In their "conversational" exchanges with infants, mothers also barrage their prelinguistic infants with questions regarding their preferences, interpreting their direction of gaze and vocalizations as affirmations of the questions they are asked. Leifer and Lewis (1983) found that the mothers of infants at the prelinguistic stage often attempt to decipher their infants' intentions and preferences by asking them questions despite the fact that it is clear to the mothers that their infants do not have the linguistic competence to answer. These attempts included questions, such as "What are you looking for? What would you like to do? What kind of things interest you here?" (p. 185). A very poignant example comes from Korman (CHILDES) when a British mother asks her infant: "Are you trying to tell me that you don't want ya milk you want something a little bit more substantial? Do you want ya solids? . . . or are you just tired?" In the same vein, the mother of a 3-month-old asks her: "You're telling me off, aren't you? . . . Are you bored with Mummy? . . . talk all the time" (Walkerdine & Sinha, 1981, p. 184). The mother of a 7-month-old is fixing breakfast while the child is in the highchair and says to her, "You can't wait to eat?" further explaining to the child that she is hurrying to get her food. When the child squeals, the mother asks, "You're mad at Mama. Are you mad at me?" (Lindfors, 1999, p. 45). This same mother questions whether her daughter likes the mother's dress, why she is mad today, and what she is smiling about. The direction of the child's gaze was used to infer preferences, and further questions reflected attempts to verify the mother's understanding of these preferences.

Infant crying can also be interpreted by mothers as a signal that the child wants something rather than indicating dissatisfaction with a current state of affairs, leading the mother to question the child. When a 12-month-old cries, her mother asks, "What do you want?" In response, the child gestures toward an apple and her mother gives it to her (Lock, 1980, p. 97). In the above example, it was clear to the mother what the child wanted. But sometimes extensive questioning continues because the child does not respond in a way that makes his preferences clear. When an infant of 6 months cries while on the living room floor, his mother comes in, asking, "Oh dear, what's the matter?" then she picks him up and questions whether he is thirsty, and if he wants a drink, and she offers him his bottle, which he promptly refuses, continuing to cry. She then asks him whether he is hungry, if he wants something to eat, and whether he is sleepy and wants to go to sleep, and she puts him in his pram. He continues to cry and she picks him up again. She walks around with him, stops by the window, directs his attention to a cat outside and asks, "Can you see him? Do you know what pussycats say?, Do you? They say 'miaow' don't they, yes, of course they do." The child stops crying during this episode. and the mother puts him back on the floor (Lock, 1980, p. 51). In this sequence, the mother incessantly asked the child questions, but she was unable to figure out what he wanted and finally found a means of distracting him instead.

Even when mothers think they have figured out what the child wants they often ask additional questions to get the child to affirm explicitly what he wants to be done for him. For instance, in playing with her child, a mother asks, "You want me to open it?" "You want me to shut it?" "Shall I find the car, John?" "Want me to fix it?" (Broen, 1972, p. 48). Such questioning shows that mothers want to know what their infants prefer – and suggest to infants they that have the ability to inform mothers of their preferences.

In line with this, although during the first few months mothers primarily talk about their infants' feelings and experiences (e.g., being hungry, bored, tired, and what they are looking at), when their infants are 5 to 7 months old, mothers start to talk about their infants' activities and the objects and events in the immediate environment (Snow, 1977), with between 50 percent and 96 percent of mother's speech to infants across studies concerning what the infant was looking at (Snow, 1984). In a study with infants of 11, 14, and 24 months of age, mothers were also found to talk primarily about those objects that infants were currently manipulating, and they were most likely to talk about a given toy at the point in time at which the infant started to manipulate it (Messer, 1981). The importance of this pattern is underlined by the finding (Carpenter, Nagell, & Tomasello, 1998) that the best predictor of children's speech comprehension and production at 15 months was mothers' speech to the infant regarding the focus of his attention. When mothers who respond to and talk about those objects that the baby focuses on at 9 months are differentiated from mothers who do not do so, focus-attentive mothers have babies with a larger comprehension vocabulary at 13 months (Baumwell, Tamis-LeMonda, & Bornstein, 1997).

Clearly, though, mothers cannot restrict their talk to those objects that are within the infant's current field of vision. How do objects and events that are physically removed from the current context become the joint focus of attention for mother and infant? From about 6 months of age, infants follow the head and eye movements of others in order to locate the target of their visual attention. At first, though, to establish joint attention, there has to be a salient, attention-capturing object on which the infant can fixate. Between 12 and 18 months, the infant becomes able to follow the mother's direction of gaze to locate objects outside the immediate field of vision. Butterworth (1990) identified three stages in the development of infant gaze behavior. Up to 6 months of age, infants look in the direction of the mother's gaze if her gaze is within the infant's perceptual field and not behind it, allowing what he calls, "a meeting of the minds" on the same object. At around 12 months, the infant can follow the angle of the mother's gaze as long as it is within the visual field. In the middle of the second year, the child can extrapolate to objects outside the immediate perceptual field, including those located behind the self. Butterworth contends that by following their mother's gaze, infants are learning to attend to those objects she is attending and to communicate with her about them. This intricate tale involves reciprocal attempts by the mother to follow her infant's direction of gaze and by the infant to follow his mother's direction of gaze. In fact, infants typically alternate their gaze between the object of their desire and their mother, whose attention they try to direct to the object of their desire (Bretherton, 1991).

The fact that mothers treat infants as if they were intentional beings with preferences that they can communicate to them confounds our understanding of the nature of the infant. There are two divergent views as to the nature of intentional action on the part of infants (e.g., Zeedyk, 1991). One view is that intentionality is socially acquired, because socialization agents treat infants "as if" they were intentional beings. The second view is that infants are intentional from birth, attempting to communicate desires and feelings to others directly, within the confines of the limited behavioral repertoire they have at their disposal. Trevarthen (1977), for instance, has argued that at the earliest stage, infants manifest what he calls "primary intersubjectivity," which involves the sharing of mental states with another person, mainly using eye-to-eye contact. At this stage, it's only "me and you." Gradually, secondary intersubjectivity emerges, and mother and infant start to communicate with each other about objects and situations in the external world, changing it to a triadic rather than a dyadic constellation; it becomes "me and you and the objects/people we *both* see." From Trevarthen's perspective, it is through the development of gaze alternation, the active coordination of attention both to the adult and to the object of his attention, that secondary intersubjectivity is reached. Once secondary intersubjectivity is attained, infants understand not only that they can understand the focus of another person's attention by following his gaze but also that their own gaze can be used by others to infer the focus of *their* attention. Of course, agreeing as to the sequence of this development does not clarify whether intentionality is acquired or innate, and it is unclear what kind of data could be used to resolve the controversy.

I now turn to discussing what infants do to convey their preferences to their mothers.

BODY MOVEMENTS, REACHING, AND POINTING

Although infants' body movements are most likely not used by them to convey preference messages to mothers, mothers also interpret infants' physical actions in terms of their underlying preferences. To illustrate, an infant crawls across the floor and a doll lies in his path. His mother says, "Oh you want the doll," and picks it up and gives it to him. When he tosses the doll, she comments, "Oh, you don't want it" and gives him a rattle instead. When he throws the rattle she says, "You think I'm going to play your favorite game of give and throw" (Menyuk, Liebergott, & Schultz, 1995, p. 144). As this snapshot shows, body movements can serve as means of communication because adults interpret such behavior as reflecting preferences and act to intervene so as to further such preferences.

Reaches serve the same function. An 11-month-old reaches for a toy that is beyond her reach, and her mother says, "Yes, I know you want it" (Lock, 1980, p. 110). Carter (1979a) documents an episode in which an infant sees his mother eating a cookie, reaches for it as he says "me miy" and eats the cookie after his mother gives it to him. As these examples illustrate, reaches become prevalent indicators of infants' preferences, often being accompanied by vocalizations. Reaches are replaced by verbal labeling of the desired object at around 20 months, subsequently dropping out, but being reverted to when verbal communication fails (Bruner, 1983). Here, too, though, it is important to note mothers' role in interpreting children's preferences and in accommodating their requests.

By the time they are 8 to 9 months old, children start to point, with or without accompanying sounds. But does pointing reflect communicative attempts? Butterworth (1990) denies their communicative function, suggesting that early pointing is not reliably associated with the infant's direction of gaze, and that it is only at around 15 months of age that infants check whether mothers are attending before they begin to point. The argument, then, is that pointing only becomes a truly communicative gesture *after* infants check to see if the adult is following their gaze. Butterworth suggests that the integration of three processes, (1) following mother's gaze, (2) following her pointing, and (3) producing points, represents meaningful communication on the part of the infant.

In this context, there is a controversy about the functions served by reaching versus pointing. Do they both signal wanting? Bruner (1983) interprets pointing as indicating one's preferences to others, presumably to get their help in reaching desired objects. Masataka (2003), on the other hand, does not see pointing as a request, differentiating between the functions of reaching versus pointing. In his view, reaching indicates a desire to interact with an object, expressing a *protoimperative* function that is used for getting others to act on one's preferences (e.g., "give it to me"), whereas pointing serves a different function, orienting the infant's own attention and presumably getting others to share attention, expressing what Bates (1976) calls the *protodeclarative* function (e.g., "Hey, look at that!"). Masataka supports this functional differentiation with evidence that in 8-month-old infants, reaching was used for familiar objects in the near field whereas pointing was used for unfamiliar objects and ones that are beyond the infant's reach.

An additional controversy centers on the *sequence* of emergence of these two functions (e.g., Butterworth, 2003; Halliday, 1975). Do infants point in order to signal that they want the adult to share their experience of looking at an object or do they do so to indicate that they want the object? Bates (1976) suggests that these functions co-emerge and that after their first birthday, children integrate these functions. Yet anecdotal evidence underlines the primacy of the protoimperative function of pointing. For instance, Jordan, a preverbal child of 14 months vocalizes, and his mother turns around and looks at him. He then points to an object on the counter. His mother holds up a milk container, asking "Do you want this?" He shakes his head no, vocalizes, and continues to point. His mother tries to appease him with a series of different objects that are all rejected. She finally holds up a sponge and says "This?" and the child stops pointing, relaxes in his high chair as the mother hands him the sponge (Golinkoff, 1983, p. 58). Pointing in this case was used to indicate a preference, subserving the protoimperative function, rather than to say "Hey, look at that," which would provide evidence for its protodeclarative function.

Importantly, the infant uses a variety of communicative gestures and vocalizations to indicate his preferences. He does not passively wait for his mother to interpret what he wants but rather varies the gestures he uses in his persistent attempts to get her to satisfy his preferences. The deployment of a variety of strategies was also evident in research with 12-month-olds who used combinations of gestures – for example, pointing, vocalizing, and gaze direction – to get an adult to focus on an object the infant found more interesting than the object focused on by the adult (Legerstee & Barillas, 2003). Butterworth (2003) notes that about 50 percent of acts of pointing are accompanied by vocalizations, suggesting that infants are using pointing both for expressing the protodeclarative function (i.e., to gain mother's attention and to use her as a labeler, for example, "Oh, you mean the. . . . ; no that's not for you; it's dangerous") and for expressing the protoimperative function, viewing the mother as an agent of preference fulfillment (e.g., "I'll give it to you in a minute").

The primacy of the protoimperative function is underlined further by an anecdote provided by Bates (1976). In this sequence, a 13-month-old looked at her mother and said "ha." Her mother came over to the child and as she did, the infant looked toward the kitchen, twisting her body and upper shoulders. In response, the mother, who inferred that the infant wanted something in the kitchen, carried the infant into the kitchen. But gaze direction did not suffice in this instance. The infant then pointed to the sink. The mother inferred her desire to drink, gave her a glass of water, and the infant eagerly drank it (p. 55). This anecdote shows that the infant's behavior is guided by (1) his knowledge as to the object of his preference, (2) his knowledge that this object is in a location other than where he is currently, (3) his knowledge that his mother can serve as an agent of locational change, (4) his understanding that he can use verbalization and gestures to indicate his preferences to his mother, and (5) his understanding that she will attempt to satisfy his preferences if she understands them. As before, successful termination of this sequence was contingent on the mother's repeated attempts to decipher the infant's preferences and the infant's deployment of a variety of strategies in attempting to communicate them. That is, although such sequences are initiated by the child, they progress and terminate successfully, because the mother repeatedly attempts to decipher the child's preferences.

Addressing this issue directly, Golinkoff (1986) categorized episodes into three types: (1) *successes*, which represent instances in which mothers understood and responded to children's preferences, (2) *missed attempts*, which represent instances when mothers did not understand the infant's meaning and did not actively try to comprehend, and (3) *negotiations*, with the latter two types representing contexts in which mothers attempted to further clarify the infant's intent. Only 38 percent of all episodes were immediately successful, with 49 percent requiring maternal negotiations. In fact, the average number of turns in successful negotiation episodes was 7.3. What is most remarkable perhaps is that 98 percent of all failed requests in infants 12 to 21 months of age were repaired or altered by the infant in some way, illustrating that infants display remarkable perseverance in their attempts to get their preferences satisfied (cf., Weatherby, Alexander, & Prizant, 1998).

Interestingly, Halliday (1975) suggests that in the preverbal stage, children have gestures that are differentially realized to express different types of preferences. He identified three of these in his son Nigel at 9 months of age. Nigel's grasping an object firmly was interpreted as "I want that," touching an object lightly, as "I don't want that," and touching a person or an object firmly as "Do that again." Halliday also distinguished variations in the prosody of his son's vocalizations used for indicating both "Let's do this together!" and "Look!"

In this context, Acredolo and Goodwyn (1998) differentiate two types of gestures that deaf children of hearing parents developed: (1) *indicators* (such as pointing), which were used to refer to people, places, and things in the immediate context and (2) *characterizing signs*, which were used to refer to actions and properties of objects. Children were able to combine these two types of signs to let their parents know that they wanted to eat, for instance. The interesting aspect of this development is that parents were not using the same signs in interacting with their children. Children were apparently creating these gestures and combining them idiosyncratically as communicative devices without having been exposed to such combinations, suggesting that these signs may well be precursors to language. Apparently, then, in the absence of consensual means of communicating their preferences, children develop idiosyncratic means of doing so – means that depend on the interpretational efforts of those who interact with them.

The emergence of such interactive sequences between infants and mothers also underlines both the differentiation between self and other, and the relation between self and other; it establishes a triangular representation of self, object, and other. As Hutto notes,

> the grasp of the objective world 'requires a kind of triangulation with another being who simultaneously responds to things in a largely similar way to ourselves yet in a way that admits of recognition of the possibility of friction between the different perspectives . . . it is only by locating features of a common world between two interpreting creatures that a key minimal condition for conceptual development and the formation of beliefs about an objective world is met.' (Hutto, 1999, p. 116)

Importantly, though, the sides of this triangular representation are flexible and collapsible, and each of the foci can shift in location so that the actual shape and the distance between foci are labile. This flexibility is a function of (1) preferences being communicated, (2) agents who can and are willing to satisfy these preferences, and (3) a world of inanimate objects that exists "out there" and whose mobility is engineered by these agents. This triangular representation, then, constitutes a cognitive advance that sets the stage for more complex developments. Within this triangular representation, then, flexibility emerges because both the infant and the mother are agents. The child is an agent in communicating his preferences, and the mother is an agent in choosing to or declining to satisfy those preferences that are communicated to her.

Children's object-related requests, then, constitute attempts to change the sides of the triangular representation, moving the foci either closer or further from oneself. The mother is viewed by the infant as an agent who can have an impact on the distance between two foci, either child-to-object or child-to-mother. But it is because mother and child can have different preferences as to the relationship between the child and the world that children acquire the understanding of divergences in perspectives.

One could question whether the types of anecdotes reported above capture truly communicative behavior. What kind of evidence could one garner to settle this issue? If infants and children vary their communicative attempts as a function of their audience's actual or inferred state of knowledge, this would provide strong support for the strategic function of gestures. It appears that they do so. Halliday (1975) reported that at about 18 months of age, his son differentiated in his speech between knowledge he shared with his audience and knowledge to which the audience was not privy, doing so by varying the intonational pattern of his utterances. Some languages – for example, Kwakiutl – actually require the speaker to specify whether he is talking about an entity that is or is not visible to him (Levinson, 1997), and children in such cultures apparently learn early to indicate this distinction.

Research evidence also indicates that children vary their communication by whether they think their audience knows what they are referring to. Two-year-olds were found to be sensitive to their parents' state of knowledge and changed the way they made their requests, using more gestures when they thought their parents did not know what they were referring to (O'Neill, 1996). Additional evidence for this point comes from a study (Maratsos, 1973) with older children (3 to 5 years old), who were required to describe a toy to a listener who either was, or was not, blindfolded. Pointing was the primary method used by 3-year-olds and was less prevalent in the older children. But what is important is that pointing was negligible when the listener was blindfolded. Children changed what they did when they understood that their listener could not see. Similarly, children 3 to 4 years old who had to tell a story to an adult who could not see the relevant pictures told the stories in more words and in more grammatically complex ways than those children who were telling the story to an adult who could see the pictures as they were talking (Bokus & Shugar, 1979). The fact that the adult could see was evident to the child and children even ended their stories with "You can see it all for yourself" (p. 74). Consistent with this, preschoolers seem to understand that drawings can inform others what the referent of a drawn object looks like, and they attempt to draw so as to make others "see" the referent more clearly (Cocking & Copple, 1987). In this context, children said things like, "I'm gonna draw a house – to show you how the McDonald's looked" (p. 444). They offered to draw to make a puppet called Mr. Forgetful "remember" what a car looks like, explaining, "Here, I'll show you how it looks different from a bus" (p. 445). These studies make it clear that both infants and children use gestures with the knowledge that their audience is both perceiving and interpreting such gestures in an attempt to understand what is being said.

HEAD NODDING AND SHAKING

One of the first distinctions that infants need to communicate to adults is the difference between affirmative and negative. The need to do so stems at least in part from the fact that adults are constantly asking infants and children, "Do you want ___?" and a response is expected to such queries. Counterintuitively, we know more about how infants use their heads to respond negatively than affirmatively. As well, there seems to be no evidence for head nods to indicate *yes* without concomitant verbalization. Bates, Camaioni, and Volterra (1979) noted a child indicating *yes* with a head nod at 16;2, but they do not indicate whether it was accompanied by vocalization. At 18 months, Simone, in a conversation with her mother, combines both gesture and verbalization, nodding her head and saying "mhm" when her mother asks her if she "baked a cake" when she played in the sandbox in the morning (Miller, 1979).

Negation seems to emerge much earlier. Werner and Kaplan (1963) cite the case of an 11-month-old who indicated his dislike for foods and objects by pushing them away, gradually waving *no* with his hands. Bowerman's (1986) daughter, Christy, at 16 months, tried to avoid being fed by grabbing her bottle and sticking it in her mouth, repeating this several times in the course of the feeding. It seems that infants learn early on that they can use their bodies to indicate refusal. An important aspect of the refusals noted above is that they are specific to the contexts in which they were found. Pushing one's food away and sticking bottles in one's mouth are only functional as refusals in the specific context of feeding.

Children need to learn more general means of indicating affirmation and negation. They gradually learn to use head movements as gestures of affirmation and negation. Pea (1979) found headshakes indicating rejection, at about 1 year of age, with children in the age range of 10 to 14 months, using head shakes to respond to questions such as "Do you want ___?" Eriksson and Berglund (1999) found that in mothers' reports about their children's language and gestural development, few infants were reported as shaking their heads to indicate *no* prior to 12 months and the majority was doing so by 18 months. When the mother of a 13-month-old asks, "No more egg?" her daughter shakes her head and says "no" (Carew, 1976, p. 92). Mary, at 16 months, is reaching for an iron that is plugged into to the wall. Her mother says, "Leave it, Mary. You mustn't pull it out, must you?" The child shakes her head in response (Dunn, 1988, p. 26). Bloom (1970) reports that a child of 21 months would shake her head and push an object away to indicate refusal. Although in these examples, the child only gestured, it seems that head shaking for *no* tends to be used along with some accompanying vocalization. Carter (1979a) noted headshaking with vocalization to indicate rejection and disliking between 12 months and 18 months. Greenfield and Smith (1976) report a toddler of 19;29, shaking his head, and saying "no nightnight," indicating refusal to go to sleep. Bloom's (1973) daughter Allison gestured refusal to wear a given dress or to be taken out of the bath, sometimes accompanying the gestures with verbalizations approximating *no*. Head shaking was the most frequent means of indicating negation in a child of four who was learning English as a second language; head shaking in combination with verbalized *no* emerged later (Keller-Cohen & Gracey, 1979). Iverson and Thal (1998) suggest that gesture – word combinations in which the infant shakes his head and says "*no*" at the same time emerge at around 14 to 16 months. The verbalization "ah-ah" is also used to communicate negative preferences, sometimes in conjunction with head shaking.

Very interestingly, head shaking for *no* has been documented as being used in conjunction with verbalization for negating sentences. At 20 months, Halliday's son Nigel says affirmative sentences but concomitantly shakes his head *no* to indicate that they are being negated, for example, "very old one . . . (shaking head) very good one," implying "not a very good one" (Halliday, 1975, p. 98). Similarly, Kathryn, at 22 months, says "me like coffee," shaking her head negatively but not shaking her head when she indicates that her father does like coffee and shaking it negatively again when she says that Bloom does not (Bloom, 1970, p. 153). Iverson and Thal (1998) call these "*supplementary*" gesture–word combinations in that the gesture and what is verbally expressed convey different information. They found that such combinations emerge at around 16 to 18 months, after children have started to use *complementary* gesture–word combinations in which gestures and speech convey the same information. Supplementary gesture–word combinations emerge later than complementary ones, with the former predicting the onset of two-word utterances, suggesting that they are cognitively more complex (Goldin-Meadow & Butcher, 2003). But headshaking for *no* is only useful for negating; it is not useful for affirming. Thus, when a preschool teacher asks a child whether she wants juice, milk, or a cracker, then asks her what she wants and the child shakes her head, the teacher says, "Don't just keep shaking your head. How am I supposed to know what you want if you don't tell me?" (Tobin, Wu, & Davidson, 1989, p. 134).

VOCALIZING PREFERENCES

Sometime around their first birthday, infants evidence a transition, attempting to vocalize in a more consistent manner to indicate their preferences. Painter (1989) found that at 10.5 months, her son used the sound *amamamama* in a way that was consistently interpretable as "I want that food there" (p. 27), often because it was accompanied by reaching gestures in the direction of foods (e.g., a cookie jar). In the same vein, Halliday (1975) identified several different sounds that his son Nigel used at about 12 months of age to indicate two types of affirmative answers to questions: responses to questions representing offers for visible objects (e.g., "Do you want your orange juice now?"), which the child answered affirmatively with a sound like "yi yi yi" and responses to questions that constitute offers of services or for invisible objects (e.g., "Shall I put the new record on?"), which were answered with an *a* with a high rise–fall intonation, interpreted as meaning, "Yes, you've got it, that's what I'm after." Carter (1979a, 1979b) also identified four sounds that could be reliably distinguished as meaningful communication in her son at around 12 to 18 months, conveying object requests, transfer requests, dislike and change situation requests, and object removal requests. The importance of this developmental transition is that whereas younger infants may have vocalized, they did not do so in a consistent fashion that could be associated with specific meanings. Another interesting aspect of the above pattern is that each child attempts to convey the same meanings but does so in a unique and idiosyncratic way. What determines these unique developmental patterns is not clear.

WHAT INFANTS WANT

As we saw above, infants use a variety of means to convey their preferences to others. But what is it that they want? Bruner (1983) identified three types of communication: (1) requests for objects, (2) requests as invitations to play, and (3) requests for supportive action. Requests for objects are further differentiated into requests for objects that are both close and visible, requests for objects that are visible but out of the infant's reach, and finally, requests for objects that are both out of view and out of reach. This differentiation reflects the fact that as infants develop, foci can constitute part of the triangular representation even when they are not visible and are only available as representations. Yet irrespective of whether they are physically present, they are treated by the infant as labile, and when foci collapse on one another (i.e., when the child is handed an object or when the mother is physically next to the infant), no more preference communication is needed on the infant's part. Of course, the central problem in preferential conflict is that for whatever reason, mothers need not treat foci as labile; they can view a given triangular representation as static, refusing to heed the infant's preference communication.

This is beautifully captured in the following exchange between a 9-month-old and her mother who is attempting to spoon-feed her. In between mouthfuls, the child cries and bangs the table, and her mother says, "No you can't have your spoon yet," interpreting the infant's behavior as attempts to feed herself. When the child tries to grab the spoon, the mother snaps "No!" to which the child reacts by spitting out her food and trying to grab the spoon once again. The mother now exclaims, "No! That's naughty," but when the child refuses her food, turns her head away and again attempts to grab the spoon, her mother relents, saying, "All right, you can have it; here you are" (Lock, 1980, p. 58). As we can see in this example, the mother did not originally see the foci as labile, but when she was faced with her child's intransigence and her own preference that the child eat, she relented.

Whereas requests for close and visible objects are the predominant types of request at the ages that Bruner studied (up to 24 months), such requests tend to drop off with age. This is because as the infant becomes mobile, he can induce the changes in the triangular representation himself by locomoting or reaching toward the objects that are the current foci. Concomitantly, focal objects tend to move in distance as the infant matures. Yet requests for remote visible objects and ones that are out of the child's view do not emerge until after the child's first birthday and, even then, represent less than 25 percent of all of children's requests.

By the time they are about 13 months old, children evidence a new type of gesture that appears to be more representational, for instance, extending their arms upward, indicating their desire to be picked up by someone. Bruner discusses such gestures as invitations. At times, such invitations are only geared toward being held. But at other times, such invitations are strategic, and are used as a means of satisfying some other preference. As an example of the strategic use of invitations, Jonathan, at 17 months, raises both arms and says "up"; when his mother asks him what he wants, he points to the window and says, "aere," meaning he wants to see an airplane (Bruner et al., 1982). This example shows that the infant has learned that by changing one side of the triangular representation, the one connecting self and mother, one can eventuate changes in the other side as well, by having mother serve as a means. One can use other people to achieve a goal that one cannot achieve alone. Mothers' responses to these gestures teach infants that they can produce predictable outcomes, and, as a result of maternal responsiveness, they learn to anticipate the effects that their gestures have on others. More importantly, the above underlines the fact that infants learn to use gestures to communicate their preferences prior to communicating them verbally. Their understanding of the communicative rules guiding the use of gestures and others' responses to such gestures facilitates their transition into using language to communicate. Yet even after the emergence of language, when the child's linguistic capacities are insufficient to communicate his preferences, the child reverts to using gestural communication to convey his preferences to others (cf., Bruner et al., 1982).

Infants' strategic use of invitations for parents to engage in joint activities evidences this same pattern. Infants express invitations for joint engagement in several different contexts. For instance, they can express invitations for the parent to do something during which the child is a passive experiencer, as when a parent is asked to push a child on a swing. There are invitations that are requests for joint role enactment, asking the parent to initiate routines, such as playing peek-a-boo or object exchanges, that is, routines that build on the understanding of reciprocal roles and turn taking. In addition, there are invitations for a parent to share an experience, asking the parent to look at snow falling, look at the moon, or see something that broke. Halliday (1975) contends that, to get parents to share their experiences, infants need to learn that communication also has an informative function, a function that his son Nigel did not evidence before 18 months. In line with this emergence, Bruner found that the three types of invitation he identified tend to emerge after the child's first birthday and represent about 40 percent of children's requests at age 2.

Finally, requests for supportive action, in which the infant tries to recruit an adult's skill or strength to attain a desired goal, emerge after the first birthday and represent about 25 percent of all requests at age 2. Infants attempt to signal that maternal intervention may be required in several different types of context (Bruner, 1983). *Precision help* involves actions that the infant's sensorimotor skills are not sufficiently well developed to accomplish alone, as in opening lids, tying shoe laces, and fixing uncooperative toys. In many such cases, the child brings the relevant object to the parent and gesturing may be sufficient for the mother to correctly interpret what the child wants. *Power help* involves actions that the child does not have the strength to carry out, such as moving heavy objects and opening cupboard doors. Such requests often require the child to physically arrange for the mother to come to the relevant location and depend to some extent on his linguistic skill in doing so. Finally, *translocational requests* involve actions that change the child's own location, as in going out, getting up on chairs, and so forth. Here as well, the child may not be able to convey his meaning without the use of language. In addition, the types of requests children make are clearly tied to their sensorimotor abilities and as these abilities change, as do the requests. Translocational requests tend to drop out as the child becomes more mobile. Precision and power help represented more than 40 percent of all requests made between 18 months and 24 months in the children studied by Bruner (1983).

FULFILLING PREFERENCES

Deciphering infants' preferences is one thing; satisfying those preferences is another. Even though mothers may invest time and energy in attempting to divine their infants' preferences, there is no guarantee that, once they do so, they will attempt to satisfy those preferences. Lieven (1978) found that the proportion of children's utterances to which mothers responded varied considerably between mothers, ranging from 29 percent to 76 percent. For mothers who are in the preference-deciphering business, Bruner (1983) identifies three processes that mothers need to engage in when they interpret their infant as having made a request. First, they need to find out the object of their infant's preference. Second, they need to figure out what type of request is being made by the infant. Third, they need to identify what kind of intervention is needed to fulfill the infant's preferences. But Bruner does not deal with the other side of the equation, mothers' own preferences, and consequently, he does not address the issue of when mothers will attempt to satisfy their infants' preferences. That is, mothers can be viewed as engaging in a multistep process, in which the first step is figuring out what the infant wants, the second step is figuring out what their role in satisfying that preference might be, and the third and final step is figuring out what they want to do in the context in question. Mothers try to decipher infants' preferences because they perceive their role as requiring them to help fulfill those preferences that are within their power or desire to fulfill and to obviate those preferences that their agendas dictate against fulfilling. When a child's preference is interpreted as congruent with the mother's own preferences, mothers are generally likely to fulfill the child's preferences, taking those actions that are necessary or indicating their approval of the child's undertaking such actions. For instance, when a mother interprets her child's intentions as wanting to pull apart a truck, the mother says, "if you want that that's fine" (Broen, 1972, p. 85). But infants often express preferences that mothers do not want to accommodate. In such cases, mothers may indicate that the planned action is not to be undertaken (e.g., "no, don't play with mommy's glasses").

Mothers may pose questions because they suspect that the infant's requests involve preferences that conflict with their own preferences. In such cases, mothers may ask further questions to clarify whether this is the case. For instance, at 27 months, my daughter Karen said to me, "Want Mommy to take off your sandals." My interpretation of this request was that she wanted to go barefoot, which was not a legitimate request from my perspective, and so I was going to reject her request outright. However, before doing so, I asked her why she wanted her sandals off. She answered, "Cause Karen wants to put her shoes on." Her request was instigated by the inability to take off sandals that have buckles that are difficult to undo, as opposed to shoe laces that are easy to untie. Questioning clarified that there was no preferential conflict.

REFRAINING FROM QUESTIONING INFANTS

Importantly, not all mothers ask their babies questions. There appear to be social class and cultural differences in this domain, with some cultures and classes frowning at such maternal practices. In some societies, for instance, the Kaluli of Papua, New Guinea, mothers do not treat their infants as conversational partners (Schieffelin, 1990). When children are not viewed as conversational partners, they are seldom talked to or questioned as to their preferences. In this vein, a Colombian mother says about her child, "What should I talk to him for, if he doesn't understand?" (Posada et al., 2004). Similarly, lower-class American mothers apparently believe it is silly to talk to babies who cannot yet understand (Leifer & Lewis, 1987). Hart and Risley (1995) found that in their sample of American families, about a quarter of parents' speech to their children at ages 1 to 3 years was in the form of questions. On the other hand, they found a significant correlation between social class and the number of questions addressed to children between ages 1 to 3 years, with lower-class and welfare mothers addressing significantly fewer questions to their children. Partly as a function of the higher use of questioning, children in higher socioeconomic status (SES) families consistently received three times more experience with language and interaction than children in welfare families. But, in addition, because of the paucity of language addressed to welfare children, the number of prohibitions that was directed to these children was much greater and represented a much more prominent part of these children's experience, accounting for two-thirds of their feedback experience. In fact, the children of professional parents got five times as much affirmative feedback as children of welfare parents. This is an issue that I will return to in Chapter 5.

It should be noted, though, that even mothers who do not treat their children as potential conversational partners are not unconcerned with their infants' preferences. They may not see their infants as able to intentionally convey messages. On the other hand, in many instances when mothers do not see their children as conversational partners, siblings and older children are entrusted with child care during much of the day, and these children often treat the infant as a potential conversational partner (e.g., Weisner & Gallimore, 1977; Watson-Gegeo, 2001). In fact, Morelli and Tronick (1991) found that in Zaire, both forager and farmer 1-year-olds spent more than 50 percent of their time interacting and playing with other children. Children in such communities may not be lacking conversational partners who can help guide their development, but it is unclear what the impact of conversational partners who are children rather than adults might be on children's language and social development.

Maternal agendas can also account for some mothers' apparent lack of concern with infants' preferences. For instance, if a mother is religiously devout, she may engage in practices that are religion-based and are not directly influenced by the child's needs and expressed preferences. In fact, there are parents who, because of religious beliefs, engage in behaviors that may be construed as detrimental to children's health. For instance, Jehovah's Witnesses do not allow blood transfusions to be given to children who, according to medical practitioners, need to have them. Gershoff, Miller, and Holden (1999) found that religious affiliation was a significant source of differences in beliefs about the efficacy of physical punishment and its reported use by the parents of 3-year-olds. Specifically, conservative Protestants reported using more physical punishment than parents of other religious groups, and indicated greater belief in its efficacy, expressing the belief that it prevents future transgressions.

Theories and beliefs as to the nature of child development can also impact the likelihood of questioning by mothers. Specifically, some mothers have deeply held theoretical convictions about how children need to be treated and raised. For instance, an entire generation of American children was raised with scheduled, 4-hour feedings based on Dr. Spock's (1968) advice – advice that is no longer seen as a guidepost for childraising. On the other hand, current guidelines in the Western world suggest that caring parents do not allow their infant to sleep on the stomach, a practice that for generations was deemed beneficial. I was recently privy to a battle between a 6-month-old and her mother that centered on the infant's refusal to lie on her stomach, a position that was advocated by the child's doctor as potentially strengthening her arms when she lifts up. Parents may adopt ideologies that govern their choice of schools for their children, their choice of homeschooling, and their refusal to hook up their homes to cable television or to even to have a television. Members of the Hassidic Jewish community, for instance, do not have televisions in their homes.

INFANTS AS A PROTOTYPIC CATEGORY

An additional reason why mothers may not question their infants' preferences may be that they have succumbed to a prototype-based understanding of infants and their preferences. Specifically, because mothers cannot really know what their babies' preferences are, mothers may make assumptions about these preferences, with these assumptions serving to guide their behavior. These assumptions may reflect societal or idiosyncratic beliefs about what babies like and dislike, beliefs about how preferences change with age and how new preferences are acquired. Evidence for such beliefs comes from various studies. For instance, Snow, de Blauw, and van Roosmalen (1979) found that English mothers often talk about what their young babies like to look at, and the mothers arrange visual displays in the cot and in their homes to accommodate these assumed preferences (e.g., a mother would prop a baby up in front of a window, saying that her infant likes to look out the window).

Mothers may be guided by prototype-based beliefs about babies, may then translate these beliefs into behaviors in trying to placate their own babies, and have their beliefs sustained in terms of their behavioral impact on their own infant. In line with this, Gleason and Weintraub (1978) suggest that adults have a general idea of what children are like at each age and adjust "to that ideal or canonical child" when they interact with their own children. It is as if parents have an internalized model of a "typical" or stereotypic child of a given age and this model serves as a reference point for their assumptions about what their children know, think, and feel. In fact, parents do appear to be guided by beliefs about how infants and children *generally* are rather than by perceptions of their own infant. For instance, a mother who was interviewed about her child said, "I had to learn about children and why they are the way they are. They're not adults" (Gottman et al., 1997, p. 64), using her child as an exemplar of children generally, further contrasting children from adults as a category. In saying "Children are upset by things like that" (Cook-Gumperz, 1973, p. 54), yet another mother indicates that she views her own child as an instance of the generic class of children.

In other cases, children of specific ages are viewed as a homogeneous cohort. Mothers talk of children as if they are all the same at a given age in their behavior (e.g., "They're always like that at five" and "You expect children of that age to be more careful," Cook-Gumperz, 1973, pp. 52, 247), their cognitive abilities (e.g., "You can't do much at that age. They don't really understand," Cook-Gumperz, 1973, p. 248), and their emotional reactions (e.g., "they get so upset about this sort of thing, after all they're only little really," Cook-Gumperz, 1973, p. 143). Preschool teachers are inclined to do the same, saying things like: "Don't try to reason with your child. They see it their way and that's it . . . they're five and six. They don't have the ability" (Mody, 2005, p. 66). The child-as-cohort view is well expressed in a mother who says,

> She's four and a half. Ah, their reactions are not adult reactions, they're likely to get upset about something and therefore become sad by it because of lack of understanding of the situation probably more than anything else. (Gottman et al., 1997, p. 54)

The mother is both alluding to the child's age cohort as a generic class of individuals and contrasting this cohort with another generic class, that is, adults. In these views, then, one's own child is an instance of a generic class of same-cohort children rather than a specific child with his own idiosyncratic modes of behavior, cognitions, and affective responses.

It could be, though, that parents are working with two types of theories: one that specifies how children, as a generic class, differ from adults or older children, and a second one that specifies how their own child does, or does not differ, from his own cohort. If this is the case, it is unclear whether parents infer from their own child to the generic class of children or whether they use their knowledge of children in general to develop expectations regarding their own child. In some instances, parents seem to take their child as an exemplar of their age cohort, becoming aware of having done so only when a second child arrives, saying, "now that we have Catherine we know that they're not all like that" (Backett, 1982, p. 144).

It may well be that parents are both learning what their children are really like and imposing cultural stereotypes on them. From what parents say, though, it seems that parents start off with theories about children as a generic category and then adjust these theories in light of their own child. In elaborating the principles that she and her husband were going to adhere to in raising their child, a mother clarifies this, saying, "children come along and they're PEOPLE and it just doesn't work. . . . things that you THINK are going to work with children, they don't"

(Backett, 1982, p. 14). Gleason and Weintraub echo this view when they say,

> Adults seem to have internalized stereotyped exemplars of the competencies of children at different ages and fairly limited ideas of what is appealing and interesting to children at different ages. Parents rely upon these stereotyped notions as a general guide to modify their speech to young children and then make the fine adjustments on the basis of their particularistic knowledge about their own children. (Gleason & Weintraub, 1978, pp. 213–214)

In this context, Backett (1982) draws a distinction between *abstract* versus *grounded* images of children, where abstract images emerge out of the "social stock of knowledge" and grounded images emerge out of parental interaction with their own child. She suggests that there is a mutual influence process in which abstract images change as a function of parental interaction with the child but the abstract images are used to legitimize actions in interacting with one's child and in negotiating with one's spouse as to how to socialize the child.

Viewing one's child as an exemplar of a generic class of children is advantageous, because it may help parents cope with the implications of their child's misbehavior. If all children behave this way, then one's own child is not a "bad" or misbehaving child. In the words of a Scottish mother, "If you speak to other parents of three year olds, well Joanne's at the age now, one and a half, they're all terribly irritating cos they're at . . . the negative age" (Backett, 1982, p. 156). One's own parenting skills, then, are beyond reproach. In fact, Slep and O'Leary (1998) found that mothers who were experimentally led to attribute their child's misbehavior to his own characteristics rather than to the difficulty of engaging in self-control during toddlerhood evidenced more anger at the child, engaged in more negative interaction with the child subsequently, and had children who were more likely to misbehave. Misbehavior can be more easily overlooked because the child is not responsible – his age is. In line with this, a mother says, "Well accidents happen with little children. I mean I wouldn't be terribly cross" (Cook-Gumperz, 1973, p. 146) – using his age to excuse his behavior.

Similar to age-based stereotypes, there are gender-based stereotypes. Such stereotypes are manifest when parents say, "Boys should be able to . . . ." or "Usually girls are . . . " (Cook-Gumperz, 1973, p. 52). In fact, parents often use gender-based stereotypes in attributing preferences to their children, differentiating the preferences they attribute to sons versus daughters. In a study in which parents themselves brought toys for their children to play with in a laboratory setting, sex-appropriate toys were brought for both boys and girls (Eisenberg, Wolchik, Hernandez, & Pasternack, 1985). The following interaction illustrates how such stereotypes work in action. When a boy plays with his sister's doll, his mother warns him that the sister will be upset if the doll breaks. The boy then insists that his sister would not be upset. But the mother insists that she would, explaining that it is her doll. When he counters, "My doll," she rejects this vehemently, saying, "Don't be silly! Boys don't play with dolls" (Cloran, 1989, p. 120). Similarly, when a little girl wants to play and tells her mother, "You be Mummy, I'll be Daddy," her mother says, "No, little girls should be Mummies, not Daddies. You be Mummy, I'll be Auntie . . . ," and she continues, "Let's pretend Daddy's at work, OK" (Tizard & Hughes, 1984, p. 98).

In fact, when mothers relate their children's toy preferences, they do so largely in line with gender stereotypes (e.g., Newson & Newson, 1968). In keeping with these perceived preferences, mothers tend to buy their children toys based both on their children's preferences and on gender stereotypes. The mismatch between what girls want and what they get was found to greater than the mismatch for boys, most likely because boys' actual toy preferences are more stereotyped than those of girls (Bussey & Bandura, 1992).

Parental beliefs about gender-related differences are translated into divergent socialization and interactional practices that depend on children's sex. For instance, 2-year-old girls are asked more questions by their mothers whereas 2-year-old boys receive more directives (Lewis & Cherry, 1977). Such differences in maternal practices may well underlie differences in the verbal skills of boys and girls, because questions are "conversation maintaining" and require a response whereas directives do not require a response. Yet, despite such gender-based differences in maternal behaviors, Lewis and Cherry found that these were unrelated to children's linguistic behavior and no sex differences were found in children's language performance. However, such differences do emerge later, suggesting that maternal practices have their impact over time rather than immediately, a possibility that accords with Hart and Risley's (1995) findings.

PREFERENTIAL CONFLICT

Adults do not always comply with the requests directed to them. Bruner (1983) found that adults were largely accommodating, accepting about 95 percent of children's invitations but heeding other types of requests much less often. From the infant's perspective, then, there is a need to differentiate those instances when he has failed to communicate effectively from those that arise because of preferential conflict. Preferential conflict, though, occurs between two agents with minds and preferences of their own. As Lewis (1994) states, the negativism associated with the "terrible twos" emerges out of the understanding that "me does not want to do what you want me to do" (p. 23), which Lewis sees as emerging at the same time as personal pronouns, an issue I will return to later. From the preference management perspective, though, it emerges equally out of the understanding that *others* do not want to do what one wants them to do. The child's will and that of his mother often clash head on (e.g., the mother of an

18-month-old says, "I find I can't sit down with him and make him play with the toys that I want him to play with. Like he just says, "I don't want to play with it. I'm going to play with something else") (Degotardi, Torr, & Cross, 2008, p. 267). Just as the mother recognizes that the child has conflicting preferences, coping with preferential conflict on the infant's part demands that he develop a view of the mother as an agent with a mind, free will, and preferences of her own. To quote Wolf et al. (1984), "Possibly because caregivers do not always comply or comprehend, infants gradually recognize other people as separate or independent agents" (p. 206).

How do we know that infants treat others as agents? Halliday (1975) suggests that an infant has certain fundamental goals when he communicates. He does so to "regulate the behavior of others ... to order people about, to get them to do things for him; to demand certain objects or services" (pp. 5, 11). Acquiring language is critical in getting others to fulfill one's preferences. Halliday (1975) identifies several functions that language serves. He identifies two global functions of language: *pragmatic* or those dealing with other people and impinging on the environment, and *mathetic*, related to knowing or learning. From Halliday's perspective, only the pragmatic function is of critical importance for the preference management process. Within the pragmatic function, the *instrumental* function is the "I want" function, which includes general expressions of preference and desire, expressions whose goal is to satisfy one's own needs (e.g., "I need more juice"); the *regulatory* function is closely linked to the instrumental function but differs from it in that it is directed toward a specific individual and essentially conveys the meaning, "Do as I tell you." Such directives attempt to get others to do things for oneself (e.g., "give me blanket"). They may express generalized requests for actions to be performed, for repetitions of previous actions, and for joint actions (e.g., "Let's play together"). In the mathetic function, Halliday includes *personal* descriptives, which express one's states and feelings ("I standing up; I like bunnies"), *imaginatives* (i.e., using language to create pretend environments in play or in describing pictures, e.g., "dolly tired"), *heuristics* (using language to find out things, for example, by asking why questions, repeating parental explanations – for example, "Mommy tired, Mommy go nap"), and *informatives* (using language to represent experience and to provide information from one's memory – for example, stating that something is "in Daddy's room" or telling another person of a trip to the zoo).

From the preference management perspective, though, Halliday' distinction between the pragmatic and the mathetic functions of language is only in the eye of the beholder and does not reflect the uses to which the child puts his language.[2] Language is used by the child to express preferences. These relate to (1) what the child wants to consume; (2) what the child wants to have or to manipulate; (3) whether the child wants to perform some action alone, with another person, and if the latter, who the preferred partner is; (4) what the child does or does not want to do himself; (5) whether the child wants someone else to perform an action, specifying who and how it is to be done; and (6) wanting to share perceptions/experience with another person. Adopting this perspective, all the functions identified by Halliday can be interpreted as expressions of preference, leading to the following classification scheme:

I want (something).
I want to (do something).
I want you to (do something for me).
I want you to (do something with me).
I want you to (see something).
I want you to (know something).
I want you to (do something for yourself).
I want you to (do something for a third party).

Viewing children's utterances as expressions of their preferences provides an integrative framework for viewing development. The advantage of viewing these functions in terms of preferences is that the pattern of their emergence becomes more interpretable. For instance, in this scheme, wanting something should emerge prior to wanting to do something. As well, because wanting others to do, see, or know something all represent embedded preferences they should emerge later than wanting to do something oneself. Moreover, wanting others to do, to see, and to know requires seeing them as agents, with physical motor abilities (i.e., doing) and mental abilities (i.e., seeing and knowing), and the latter should emerge later. Finally, viewing utterances as expressions of preferences underscores the role that preferential conflict plays in children's development because if others are agents with their own minds, their preferences may well differ and possibly even counter those of the child.

During the preverbal stage, though, we can only infer that these functions of language are available to the child. On what basis can we draw this inference? First, when children use verbalizations and gestures to indicate what they want, they are persistent in their efforts until those whom they are addressing as agents fulfill their preferences. Infants act as if they have expectations that their communicative acts will lead to changes in others' behavior, that is, changes that reflect the infant's preferences. Second, as long as parents attempt to decipher the agentic role being imputed to them by the child and attempt to fulfill his preferences all goes well. When parents do not, infants often express their dissatisfaction, with repeated

[2] For instance, in discussing the personal function, Halliday (1975) suggests that it expresses awareness of self in contradistinction to one's environment, referring to self as a unique configuration of interest, pleasure and withdrawal (e.g., "I'm tired"; "I like that"). But Halliday fails to consider that by expressing the personal function, the child allows those around him to take actions that reflect the specific preferences implied by such expressions (e.g., put a tired child to bed, offer more of a liked food).

gestures, flailing of their arms, and crying. This constellation strongly suggests that the parental agentic role is recognized by the infant. In this light, infants have multiple tasks in the game. First, they need to learn how to "inform" their mothers what their preferences are. As discussed earlier, as a first step in doing so, infants need to learn that getting mother's attention is a prerequisite to getting her to act on their preferences. Second, they need to develop means of getting their mothers to act on their preferences, learning to communicate these preferences in ways that will allow mothers to understand what such preferences may be. Third, infants need to learn both to cope with the delays involved in getting their preferences fulfilled and to acquire means of getting mothers to fulfill their preferences in those contexts in which mothers are apparently unwilling to do so. In essence, then, infants need to adapt current strategies and adopt new and different strategies to get recalcitrant mothers to act in line with their preferences.

Viewing preferences in this light also allows one to understand when and where mothers' external preferences may conflict with those of the child. Mothers are highly unlikely to indicate that they do not want their child to inform them of something or to show them something. They may temporize such requests, but they will not reject them outright. On the other hand, other types of preferences that the child expresses may be subject to temporization, but such preferences may also be rejected outright because of preferential conflict.

Mothers are not neutral in their reactions to preferential conflict. They vary in the extent to which they are willing to accommodate their children's preferences when these conflict with their own. The interplay between children's expressions of preferences and maternal responses to preferential conflict when it occurs may well define how children become attached to their mothers. Children's expectations as to the likelihood of their preferences being satisfied and the manner in which those around them respond to the expression of their preferences has an impact on the type of relationship that infants develop with their mothers (Riksen-Walraven, Meij, van Roozendaal, & Koks, 1996; Koos & Gergely, 2001; Gergely, 2004; Watson, 2001). To the extent that mothers act to fulfill their children's preferences and do not impose their own preferences on their children, children will form close and secure attachments to their mothers. When mothers are insistent on imposing their own preferences on the child rather than attempting to fulfill the child's apparent preferences, children's predominant attachment style will be avoidant. Finally, when children cannot build up stable expectations as to mothers' likelihood of fulfilling their preferences, they develop ambivalent attachments to their mothers. As Fonagy, Gergely, Jurist, and Target claim,

> suboptimal early experiences of care affect later development by undermining the individual's capacity to process or interpret information concerning mental states that is essential for effective functioning in a stressful social world. (Fonagy, Gergely, Jurist, & Target, 2002, p. 7)

In this light, though, we need to differentiate mothers in terms of the amount of time and energy they spend in trying to decipher their infants' preferences versus their likelihood of accommodating their children in terms of fulfilling their preferences. Whereas it may seem that logically, mothers who decipher their infants' preferences are more likely to accommodate their preferences, this may not be the case because, to the extent that infants' preferences conflict with those of the mother, she may not accommodate them, despite having invested effort in knowing what these preferences are. These are two different dimensions, although they may be related. Clearly, though, parental assumptions about children's preferences become less relevant as children become more verbal and start to make their own preferences explicit.

As infants grow, they develop preferences that are more complex in nature – they want to refer to objects that are displaced in location and in time, they want to refer to iterative actions (e.g., "again," "more") and to actions that vary on the temporal dimension ("now" or "later"), as well as to different agents who can fulfill their preferences (e.g., "me do it," and "no Mummy do it – Daddy/I do it"). Doing so requires them to refine their linguistic skills. Perhaps surprisingly, though, even as they indicate their preferences only gesturally and vocally, infants appear to have preferences that relate to both types of targets, objects, and actions, and both potential agents, self, or others. They want to have objects and want to perform actions, but they also want *others* to engage in actions and relate to objects in specific ways, persisting in their demands until their preferential world is satisfied. Infants want to convey their preferences to others so that they can intervene on their behalf and align reality with their preferences. As Tomasello argues,

> the bedrock on which the initial stages of language acquisition are built is children's understanding of the intentional actions of other persons, including their understanding of adults' social actions, such as making linguistic reference to their shared world. (Tomasello, 1995, p. 140)

But infants are limited in their ability get others to align their preferences with reality when they do not have language, and as they acquire language, they become more and more proficient at conveying their preferences. The way they acquire language is the topic of Chapter 2.

2 Children's Expression of Preferences

Eric, 22-months-old, finishes an apple and asks for more. He is told 'You ate all the apple up. There's no more apple.' He starts crying. When he is asked what's the matter, he answers, 'Want more apple.'

(Bloom, 1970, p. 122)

The focus of this chapter is children's use of their emergent speech abilities to express their preferences and the transition from their expression of preferences that are tied to the here-and-now to ones that transcend both time and space. This transition parallels a change in the way children's expressed preferences relate to those around them, with children increasingly acknowledging other social beings, both adults and children, as agents and relating these others' behavior to their own preferential world.

OBJECT PREFERENCES REFERRING TO HERE-AND-NOW

The onset of language, even before the emergence of grammar, yields a virtual onslaught of expressions of preference, initially regarding those preferences that relate to objects and events that are both close and visible. Children start using single words to express their preferences for the here-and-now, referring to objects that are physically present and visible or that have just become invisible (e.g., corn that has just been eaten – *allgone!*). The one-word stage signals that infants have learned to appreciate the correspondence between specific sounds and the objects and events to which they refer. More important, consistency in infants' and toddlers' use of words reflects their understanding that not only can a concept be evoked in another person's mind, but that by such evocation, both they and others can refer to the same object or activity (Karniol, 1990b). This incipient understanding guides their expression of preferences. The interesting aspect of this stage, which is generally reached in the second year of life, is that other people are clearly spoken to as agents who can change the environment for the child in order to align it with his preferences. The child is limited in his ability to attain his preferences without others' intervention and recognizes this in verbalizing his requests that others intervene on his behalf. Returning to the triangular relationship among child, parent, and object, the child now starts to use language rather than gesture as the preferred means of moving foci.

Why do children start to adopt verbal means of indicating their preferences? Bruner (1983) contends that children learn to indicate their preferences verbally not because their gestural requests fail, but rather, "out of some built-in preference for more economical procedures" (p. 114). This seems to wrongly impute to young children an overly sophisticated understanding of the fact that verbal requests are heeded more quickly and more consistently than gestural ones. In contrast, Halliday (1975) suggests that children start to use language because they run into trouble when they want to express multiple functions *simultaneously*. Listeners may, or may not, understand that the child is expressing several functions at the same time. For example, when a toddler recognizes animal cracker boxes and shouts, "cook cook," the multiple function of the child's utterance was acknowledged by the mother who responded, "Yes, those are cookies. Does Wendy want a cookie?" (Heath, 1986, p. 108), affirming both the declarative as correct and the request as legitimate. Yet the adult may understand the multiple functions of the child's utterance but only want to affirm one of the functions. Halliday gives the example of his son saying, "*cake*," which was interpreted by the mother as meaning both: "Oh, here is a cake" and "I want to eat some, Mummy." If the request is to be denied but the declarative is to be affirmed, the mother could answer: "Yes, this is cake, but you can't have any cake." Adult responses that make explicit the multiple functions of a given utterance and either affirm or deny one of the implied functions inform children that language can express multiple functions and that grammar can be used to disambiguate these functions.

Bates (1976) suggests yet another interpretation, contending that children know their preferences and understand the desired end state they want (e.g., getting the ball into their hands) but are less aware or less concerned with the possible means for reaching it and that this is why they express the goal without specifying the means. To elaborate, when the child utters the word "ball," he wants to have it – he is unconcerned with who gives it to him (mother, father, or sibling) and how it is given (rolled, thrown, or handed over). Bates suggests that this is why children first indicate their preferences by simply indicating the object or action of desire, for example, "water, down," evidencing little concern with the means by which reality is aligned with their preferences. As their language abilities become more sophisticated, children add more and more aspects of the desired event, "Beer... More!... to me!"[1] (Bates, 1976), still omitting the "how" of this is to be accomplished. It seems to me, though, that Bates's conclusion in this context is unwarranted. Children are concerned with both agents and means, but their lack of linguistic sophistication prevents them from specifying them. For instance, at 19;7, Gia pulls her father to the door saying "byebye," indicating she wants to go for a walk. When her father, who is not feeling well, says "Maybe you can go out later for a walk with Mommy," she answers "out Daddy," clearly indicating her preference as to who is to accompany her on the walk (Bloom, 1970, p. 87). Similarly, when Matthew is 20;10, his sister offers to cut him something, and he responds, "Mommy," indicating whom he wants to cut it (Bowerman, 1985, p. 389). Moreover, as Werner and Kaplan (1963) note, children at this stage differentiate between objects and actions and often refer differently to the same object in resting-state terms than when the object is being acted on.

Importantly, then, children at this stage need to learn that their use of a word, independently of context, does not a have one-to-one correspondence with the preferences they attempt to convey. Consequently, inferential work as to a child's implied preferences is still required on a mother's part at this stage. Just as a gesture needs to be interpreted, a single word needs to be interpreted, because it can convey several different types of preference. For instance, when a child says *ball*, he could mean: *I want the ball, Please Mommy let's play ball*, or *Catch my ball*; but the word *ball* could also indicate the existence of a shared referent as in: *I see the ball*. The fact that children at the single-word stage can use a given word to indicate more than one meaning is evident when a toddler says "shoes, shoes," first to indicate that he wants his shoes on, and a few minutes later, to show his mother that they have been put on him, lifting his foot, and pointing to the individual who had done so (Greenfield, 1980). Single words, then, may convey the topic of the child's utterance while leaving the listener in the dark as to the preference the child wants fulfilled.

This may still remain a problem when children transition into the two-word stage. To illustrate, Meike, at 19 months, whineed "more" and "auto" while holding a toy car in her hand. However, she was pointing to a kitchen cabinet at the time. It was only by combining the child's words and her pointing gesture that her mother could decipher that the child was asking to eat some more of the car-shaped chocolates she had eaten earlier (Miller, 1979, p. 113). The mother cracked into the child's meaning by using the child's utterance, her gesture, and the mother's knowledge of what had occurred earlier. She *contextualized* the child's utterance in order to infer its meaning. Contextualization is simpler when unfulfilled intentions can be inferred. For instance, when Allison, at 19;14, tries to put a horse on a chair and fails to do so, she gives it to her mother saying "horse help" (Bloom, 1973, p. 185). Similarly, when a 13-month-old child has trouble with the lid of a clothes hamper, he looks over at the adult and says "*Dada*" while trying to yank the lid (Wolf, 1982). The context can be used in such cases to disambiguate that the child wants help with the lid.

The need for listeners to contextualize is similarly evident in the following example provided by Bloom (1970). When Gia's train came apart, she said, "Train. More. More," giving it to Lois, who asked "What?" with Gia repeating, "More train," and Lois again asking "More train?" to which Gia replied, "yes." Bloom used the context, the two separated parts of the train, to infer that Gia wanted the parts connected. Of course, contextualizing can also lead to the inference that a preference is not being indicated, as is the case when Gerald, at 18 months, says, "Lorry," while looking at a book with his mother. She then repeats, "Lorry – yes. It's a lorry isn't it?" (Wells, 1985). In the context of book reading, the mother understood that the child was making a declarative statement rather than indicating a preference. Importantly, though, children's emergent language at these early stages relies on the fact that their expressions can be contextualized by others because they refer to the *here-and-now*. Attempts to contextualize and decipher children's preferences become less necessary once children start to produce more complex utterances, because there is less of a need to monitor their intentions or preferences. Kaiser and Warren (1988) view the role of parents, when their children are at these ages, as cooperators who determine the functionality of the child's communication by whether or not they respond the way in which the child intended them to respond.

The expression of preferences at the one-word and two-word stages, though, does indicate an important cognitive advance. That is, expressing a preference for a change in one's environment may indicate understanding of an immediate future in which one has objects that are not currently available, engages in activities not currently being engaged in, and discontinues activities being currently enacted. Hence, such expressions may well reflect a comparison of what was, with what is currently available, and what could potentially be and indicate a preference for the latter. This is exemplified in children's early use of words of repetition, such as *more* and *again*. Bloom's (1973) daughter Allison started using *more*, as in "more cookie" at 16;3, as she was reaching for a cookie bag. Tomasello's (1992)

[1] Italian: "Birra!.... Ancora... A me!"

daughter Travis said, "more corn" and "more that" at 17;09 and 17;16, in both cases handing her father a bowl, indicating that she wanted more of a just-eaten food. Werner and Kaplan (1963) suggest that the term *allgone!*, equivalents of which are found in all languages and that co-occur with expressions of wanting more, reflect the fact that "past and future and even present are merged or fluctuate" in children's utterances at this stage.

Reflecting their emergent understanding of the self as an experiencer of preferences, children start to use the word *want* as a pivot for an infinite set of objects, events, or desired end-states. Radford (1990) notes that young children often use *want* with demonstratives pronouns, for example, "want this," "want that," said, at 19 and 20 months, presumably because they do not have a label available for the object or activity in question. In an analysis of the language of five children from the CHILDES database (Diessel, 2004), more than 60 percent of utterances included the verb *want or wanna*, with references to *wanting something* emerging earliest, at about 2 years of age, for example, "wanna more cookie" (Bloom, Tackeff, & Lahey, 1984).

Children's use of *want* as a pivot reflects an emergent awareness that objects, activities, and the contexts in which they occur can be mentally separated. The separation between objects and their referents is evident in the fact that children can combine words differently to express various relations and combinations for the same objects (e.g., eat apple, allgone apple, allgone egg). The ability to combine, deconstruct, and recombine words in varying ways is the essence of being a generative language user who invents linguistic combinations that he may not have heard before. But the engine that drives children's language development is its instrumental function, their desire to indicate their preferences to those around them, doing so both to get others to align reality to their preferences and concomitantly voicing their own attempts to do so.

ACTION PREFERENCES

This developmental pattern is also evident when children indicate their preferences for activities, at first limiting themselves to the recurrence of actions that have just occurred. Bloom (1973) suggests that children first use *more* in the context of food requests, and only later extend it to the repetition of actions. In fact, though, children start to indicate their preferences for the recurrence of activities by using *more* and *again* at almost the same time as they use these words for objects. On the other hand, this overlap may arise because when a child says "more cookie," the intention may well be to indicate an action request, as in "I want to eat another cookie," which is grammatically more complex to express. Irrespectively, children have been documented to request action recurrence prior to age 2, as when Travis said, "again" at 17;1, indicating she wants to be tickled again, "more jump" at 18;24, and "again bubbles" at 18;23, when she wanted to blow bubbles again (Tomasello, 1992). A variant on *again* is the use of adverbs to indicate a preference for action recurrence, as when, at 17;10, Travis said, "back," indicating that she wanted a toy returned to her (Tomasello, 1992).

The second means of expressing preferences for activities is by using some version of the verb *want*. But this use of want emerges later than its use with object complements. At 22 and 24 months, Daniel says, "want again," once referring to wanting to be tickled some more and another time wanting to have a bubble container to blow more bubbles (Radford, 1990, p. 217). Children also start to use *want* with an infinitive, indicating the desire to go places (e.g., "want open door," "want go there"), see things (e.g., "want see handbag"), eat and drink (e.g., "want drink it," "want have drink") all said between 21 and 24 months (Radford, 1990, pp. 141, 162; see also Diessel, 2004). The relatively late emergence of this use of *want* may well reflect the fact that in order to ask for these actions to be performed, the child needs to have an image in his mind of the state of affairs he wants to have or to enact, indicating more explicitly that he has started to move onto the plane of the future.

As well, in the expressed preferences for recurrence above, children were alluding both to recurrences that involved their own actions and to recurrences of the actions of others, clearly indicating their understanding that others as agents can both engage in actions and repeat such actions. Importantly, children communicate their preferences, fully expecting them to be actualized by those to whom they are expressing them, reflecting the agentic role that these recipients of their communication attempts are imputed to have.

Although the children above were alluding both to actions they wanted to undertake themselves and to actions they wanted others to undertake, they did not linguistically differentiate whom they wanted to perform the action. When children do not name the subject, without reference to the specific context, it is not possible to know who is to perform the action. For example, Karen, at 17 months, says "More open that," in this particular instance, asking me to open her window wider. As children recognize that they need to indicate whom they want to perform the action, children do start to index this distinction in several ways. First, they start to use their own name as subjects, generally referring to actions that they themselves want to undertake, for example, "Paula want open box," said at 18 months and "Danny open this. This doll," said at 21 months (Radford, 1990). Then, around their second birthday, they start to use pronouns, using *I* and *me* as subjects of expressions (e.g., "Me want some juice," Ingham, 1998, p. 73; "I like more," Wootton, 1997; "I want to get in your lap," Tomasello, 1992).

Also at about 2 years of age, children start to linguistically differentiate those preferences they want to fulfill themselves from those they want others to fulfill by naming the requested agent, as shown in Table 2.1.

There are two related advances in this context. The first of these is the explicit statement of both the agent and the

Table 2.1.

	Age	Source
Asking to be taken to friend's house		
C: "Daddy take to Maria's"	20;3	Tomasello (1992)
C: "Dada get knife take skin off apple"	22 mos.	Halliday (1975, p. 100)
C: "Mommy take top off"	Toddler	Radford (1990, p. 96)
Balloon escaped and is on ceiling		
C: "Mommy stand up e chair"	Toddler	Bloom (1973)

Table 2.2.

	Age	Source
K: "Want Daddy to give Karen milk"	22;3	Karniol (Diary, Karen)
C: "You open it for me"	26 mos.	Radford (1990, p. 278)
O: "Mummy buy for Orren chicken"	27;6	Karniol (Diary, Orren)
C: "Get some more ma drink for me mummy"	29 mos.	Wootton (1997, p. 42)
C: "You hold that for me"; "You get it for me"	35 mos.	Wootton (1997, p. 142)

beneficiary of the action. Children start to indicate that they themselves are the ultimate beneficiaries, doing so in one of two ways. The first is by indicating whose preferences are involved, for example, "Want Mommy do"; "Jem want mummy take it out" (Radford, 1990, p. 96); "I want Mommy get balloon," (Bloom, Tackeff, & Lahey, 1984). The second means of doing so is by making themselves the indirect object in the sentence. For instance, Tomasello's (1992) daughter Travis, at 21 months, asks for raisins, saying, "get raisins to me."

A further advance is referring to themselves by name and then by using pronouns to refer both to themselves and to the agent being addressed, as shown in Table 2.2. Again, the importance of specifying the agent becomes clear when children reject performance of an action by one person and indicate a preference for its performance by another person. In this vein, when her father indicates that he wants to give her a bath, Sara, at 21 months, rejects his offer, saying, "I want Mummy to bathe me"[2] (Savić, 1980, p. 86).

What is also important here is that children have come to differentiate those instances in which they can act on the world and the objects in it in order to align reality with their preferences from those instances in which they need to rely on others to do so. In terms of the triangular representation discussed in Chapter 1, increased motor and verbal facility may obviate the need for parents to intervene, leaving them in the picture only as commentators who approve or disapprove of the child's own attempts to change his relation to the other foci.

SELF-SERVING VERSUS OTHER-SERVING PREFERENCES

Up to now, children's expressed preferences referred to what they wanted to have done for themselves. In this context, though, one needs to differentiate those preferences that children have with respect to what they want *for themselves* versus those preferences that they have that concern what they want others to do for beneficiaries other than themselves. To elaborate, I can say "I want you to open the door," indicating my own desire to go out (i.e., "open it for me"), but I could also indicate my desire that a friend, or the dog, be able to go out (e.g., "for Jenny," "for Spot"). Similarly, I can want my mother to buy me a specific item of clothing, but I can also want her to buy *herself* or my sister an item of clothing. The former type of expression concerns a preference that alters my preferential state directly – it provides me with something that I want; the latter type of expression only alters my preferential state indirectly, by way of its impact on those around me, for instance, by making me happy that my mother looks more attractive, or by her spending less money on her dress and thereby having more money to spend on me. *Self-serving preferences* refer to what others should do for oneself, and *other-serving preferences* refer to what others should do for themselves or for others.

Aijmer (1996) calls these *requestive* and *advisory*, respectively, with advisories being communicated to indicate that the future action is in the hearer's, and not the speaker's, own interest. Differentiating these is important for several reasons. First, *self-serving preferences*, which have as their goal directly altering one's own preferential state, should emerge earlier in development than those that do so indirectly. Second, providing justifications for self-serving preferences should be much easier and should emerge earlier because one's own preferences and wants are the reasons for expressing them. Third, self-serving preferences have the potential of creating preferential conflict with the addressee's external preferences (e.g., a mother who responds, "I don't want *you* to go out," "I don't want to buy *you* that dress"), whereas other-serving preferences may conflict with the addressee's own first-order preferences (e.g., "I don't want to buy *myself* that dress"). To the extent that children recognize the differences between these types of preferences and their likelihood of being fulfilled, they may change the way they express their preferences in light of their understanding of how the addressee will view them.

[2] Serbo-Croatian: "Oće kupa – loće mama kupa"

Table 2.3.

	Age	Source
Positive Self-Serving Preferences		
K wants to see herself in mirror K: "Want Mummy to pick Karen up to see Karen"	22;21	Karniol (Diary, Karen)
Sitting watching TV K: "Want Mommy to bring you closer to watch TV"	25;10	Karniol (Diary, Karen)
K wants the radio on K: "Mommy please put the music so Karen can hear some songs"	26;10	Karniol (Diary, Karen)
At the playground, climbing O: "Daddy guard for me my pacifier"[3]	27;13	Karniol (Diary, Orren)
C wants help with box of chalks C: "Get some chalks out there for me"	29 mos.	Wootton (1997, p. 142)
Positive Other-Serving Preferences		
K gives me one of my dresses to put on K: "Mommy's dress. Wear it"	18;18	Karniol (Diary, Karen)
Referring to my head & hat "Want Mommy to come with Karen to put on a hat"	22;4	Karniol (Diary, Karen)
Positive Third-Party–Serving Preferences		
K: "For the dolls I want water"[4]	30;18	Karniol (Diary, Karen)
K: "Mummy, buy the baby (doll) a ribbon so he'll be pretty at the party"[5]	34;28	Karniol (Diary, Karen)

Children do in fact seem to be aware of the difference between self-serving and other-serving preferences at a very young age. Children indicate what they themselves want but they also indicate what they want others to do *for them*, at first referring to others by name, and then using personal pronouns. But they also indicate what they want others to do for these others' own benefit and for the benefit of third parties, in contexts that do not appear to involve the child's own interests in any way. Examples of positive self-serving and other-serving preferences, expressed both in terms of wants and in terms of needs, are shown in Table 2.3. Of course, there are instances when it is unclear whether self-serving or other-serving preferences are involved. This is the case when Orren, at 28;13, says, "Daddy, you need to stand here by Orren,"[6] and when Karen, at 31;3, tells her father, "Daddy, you (f) need to get up – now to light Shabbat candles,"[7] because both the child's and the father's preferences may actually be implicated.

Few of the expressions above would be considered acceptable when addressed to anyone except a parent. As they mature, children learn that there are different means of telling others what they would like them to do for them and that some of these means may be more effective than others. To do so, they need to learn what choices they have in using directives. This is because directives can be expressed in various ways, including imperatives (Move!), imbedded imperatives ("Would you please . . . ," "Can you move?"), hints (e.g., "you're blocking my way," "it's warm here"), and need statements (cf., Ervin-Tripp, 1977).

Children's choice of expressions, then, reflects their understanding that the social context and the person being addressed must be taken into account in formulating the directives. One does not address a teacher the same way as a friend. Mitchell-Kernan and Kernan (1977) found that imperatives are the most common type of directive used in the speech of children 7 to 12 years old toward their peers. Younger children do the same, for example, "Put your car in there like that," "Put your brick right on top. Be careful . . . don't push it" (Tough, 1977, p. 50). In fact, though, children differentiate those directives they address to adults from those they address to peers or dolls. That is, children between 2 and 4 years old already appear to be sensitive to the age of their audience, using more imperatives toward younger children (Ervin-Tripp, 1977; Gelman & Shatz, 1977).

Diary studies, though, suggest that forms of request that do not use imperatives emerge much earlier, as shown in Table 2.4.

Children's growing awareness of others as social agents who can engage in activities and interact with objects also becomes evident when they express preferences and desires for objects and foods in the possession of others. Bruner et al. (1982) report that from 8 to 14 months, 82 percent of the objects requested were in another person's possession, being requested first only gesturally, with pauses reflecting anticipation of the object being handed over to them. Such gestures were replaced by verbal requests after this age. At first, children indicate their desire for the specific object or food that others have. In many instances, though, it is unclear whether the child

[3] Hebrew: "Abba tishmor li at hamoçeç sheli"
[4] Hebrew: "labubot ani roça mayim"
[5] Hebrew: "Ima tikni latinok seret she-yiheye yafe baxagiga"
[6] Hebrew: "Abba ata çarix laamod kan al yad Orren"
[7] Hebrew: "Abba at çrixa lakum – axshav lehadlik nerot shabbat"

Table 2.4.

	Age	Source
K: "Want the one that Evi gave you. Mommy can you get it?"	22;20	Karniol (Diary, Karen)
C: "Can you hold me?"	23 mos.	Tomasello's (1992)
C: "Daddy could lie down wiv you? Can Daddy lie down wiv you on the carpet?"	32 mos.	Peters (2000, p. 142)
O: "Daddy, can you give me all the sticks there?"[8]	34;20	Karniol (Diary, Orren)
C: "Can you shuffle them up please?"		
"Can you put the light on for me"		
"Can you move it near my seat for me"	3;1 years	Peters (2000, p. 146)

Table 2.5.

	Age	Source
Specific Objects		
Father is holding a cup		
C: "Cup hold"	18;25	Tomasello (1992)
Someone is holding an object		
C: "Use it . . . use it too"	19;26	Tomasello (1992)
Sister is holding a toy		
O: "I need this!"[9]	26;11	Karniol (Diary, Orren)
Someone is eating a lollipop		
"I want that lollipop mommy!"	34 mos.	De Houwer (1990)
Unclear Cases		
Someone is holding a popsicle		
C: "Eat-it popsicle"	19;12	Tomasello (1992)
Someone is holding a balloon		
C: "Balloon have it"	19;20	Tomasello (1992)

wants the exact item the other person has or is requesting one of the same type (see Table 2.5).

In fact, seeing objects in others' possession may induce a desire for an equivalent object, with the specific item being treated as a generic token of objects of that class. This is evident when Travis, at 20;23, asks her mother for a piece of meat like her mother has, saying, "One me too" and at 21;16, she says to her father, "Have one too myself, Daddy," when she saw her dad eating nuts (Tomasello, 1992, p. 300). Nigel, at 18 months, says, "Dada got scrambled egg . . . mummy get for you scrambled egg" (Halliday, 1975, p. 113). These requests make it clear that the child is expressing a preference for the same *type* of food that the parent is eating rather than for eating the parent's actual food. The expression of preferences for like objects extends beyond the food domain, as when bilingual Kate, at 31 months, says, "I also want a cushion"[10] (De Hower, 1990), again reflecting desires that were instigated by seeing someone else interacting with an object and indicating an understanding that the object is of a class of objects of the same kind as the desired one. A preschooler who has been asked to make Valentine's Day cards says, "I wanna have what Michael has," having no label for the requested decorations (Hall, CHILDES). Children's expressed preferences, then, reflect their developing understanding that some objects are in a class of like objects and consequently, are substitutable whereas others are not. This understanding may well underlie their willingness to accept substitute objects. Importantly, though, up to now, in the triangular representation, both mother and child could see the object that formed the third focus and this object served as a cue to identical but nonpresent objects, thus indicating that the child could allude to preference objects that were not visible. This represents a cognitive milestone to which I now turn.

EXPRESSING PREFERENCES FOR INVISIBLES

Piaget (1967) focused on the important transition from children's early sensorimotor operations on objects that are visible, physically close, and viewed statically, to the emergence of memory and practical intelligence, which allows children to generate representations of invisible objects and contexts that can be transformed to be represented both in terms of their past states and their future states. The critical aspect of thought for Piaget was "the symbolic evocation of absent realities" (Piaget, 1951, p. 67). Children's emergent ability to mentally represent what isn't there and to communicate regarding these mental representations removes the physical constraints of time and space, of the *here-and-now*. Werner and Kaplan (1963) discuss this as a fundamental transformation from objects as ego-bound things of action to objects as ego-distant objects of contemplation.

In discussing this important transition, Ochs (1979) contrasts "here and now" talk with talk about absent realities, indicating the importance of the former in early mother–child interaction. When physically present objects serve as topics, this can result in successful communication because the adult is able to link the child's utterance with

[8] Hebrew: "Abba atta yaxol latet li at kol hamakel-ot shum?"
[9] Hebrew: "Ani çarix at ze!"

[10] Dutch: "Ik wil ook een kussen"

Table 2.6.

	Age	Source
In the Same Location		
Child reaches toward the refrigerator door		
C: "Mil(k)"	15;17	Greenfield & Smith (1976, p. 145)
Referring to cereal in the cupboard		
C: "Pops get it"	17;9	Tomasello (1992)
C: "I want ice cream in the refrigerator"	34 mos.	Brown (CHILDES)
In Another Location		
Walking toward the family room		
K: "TV – watch it now"	18;29	Karniol (Diary, Karen)
Going toward the kitchen		
C: "Spoon to fetch (I) go"[11]	Toddler	Miller (1979)

something the child is attending to in the environment – and vice versa. In contrast, talk about the *not-here, not-now* may not be successful, primarily because such talk requires grammatical proficiency in referring to the past, future, or the conditional, all of which are more difficult to express and emerge somewhat later in development.

The emergence of talk about preferences for objects that are not visible and actions that are not currently being engaged in heralds this transition. Children are no longer confined to expressing preferences in the *here-and-now*, but start to glide in time and location, being able to allude to events in the past and to objects that are not in their field of vision. This transition becomes evident in two different ways. First, seeing others interact with objects can initiate a memory-based process, as when children allude to their preference for their own version of the same object. Seeing another child with a teddy bear may remind one of one's own teddy bear. For instance, when Meike, at 22 months, saw Simone with a pacifier in her mouth, she asked for one also, shouting and crying "have a pacifier"[12] (Miller, 1979). She clearly did not want Simone's pacifier but her own, being reminded of her own pacifier by the vision of Simone with her pacifier. Such expressions of preference indicate that the child has a representation of the object of desire and is reminded of that object by the sight of a similar object. But in addition, this pattern suggests that the child is comparing present reality with an alternative, future reality in which she too has a pacifier, preferring this alternative and wanting alignment processes to be initiated. The past is used as input into the future.

The second way in which children start to refer to absent reality occurs when they start expressing preferences for things that are known to be out of sight – in cupboards, hidden in boxes, or in locations out of the home. This occurs in two steps. The first of these steps is expressions of what Bruner (1983) calls *displaced requests*, requests for objects that are known to be in specific locations, for example, food in the refrigerator, vacuum cleaners in a utility cupboards, books on bookshelves. Such expressions allude to preferences for objects that have what Bruner calls "canonical locus," always being found in the same location. In Bruner's research, such requests emerged at about 14 months. A further advance is children's emergent questions regarding where invisible objects may be located, by using *where*. Note that asking *where* implies an understanding that the listener has knowledge that the child does not, evidencing a preliminary instantiation of a theory of mind. Bloom (1973) notes that Allison, at 15 months, responded to *where* questions, with *there*, both with and without pointing.

Such displaced requests are paralleled by children's statements that they are getting unobservable objects with canonical locus from their usual location. Sometimes this occurs when the child is in the same location as the object being alluded to, whereas at other times, children refer to objects with canonical locus and locomote toward them from a different location, indicating that they know where such objects are supposed to be, as evident in Table 2.6.

A more advanced step in this sequence is to indicate a preference for objects whose location is not known, using *where*. The advance inheres in the fact that to do so, the object and its location have to be disentangled. In fact, questions as to where an object or person may be located emerge later than references to invisible objects. Moreover, in posing such questions, the child has to recognize that reality is missing an element whose importation would make that reality better aligned with one's preferences. In line with this, Sachs (1983) documented her daughter's first requests for objects that were not currently in sight at 17 months; only later did her daughter acquire the construction "where + name of object," using it when she wanted something that she could not see or find. Tomasello (1992) recorded similar questions at around the same age, when, at 16;25, his daughter Travis was looking repeatedly for a spoon she had played with earlier, saying "Where spoon?" and at 18;25, when she asked "Where cake," after being told that the cake was in the

[11] German: "Loffel rausholen gehn"
[12] German: "Lala haben"

box and not finding it there (p. 286). These examples suggest that *where* is understood as referring to things that are not presently visible but that do not have a canonical locus. The fact that the child is looking for a specific object is evident when the child starts to use the definite article to describe the searched-for object (e.g., "Mommy, where is the pacifier?"[13] asked at 18 months, Savić, 1980, p. 93; and "Mommy, where me put my bus . . . ?" asked at 37 months, Brown, 1973). The latter question indicates that the child: (1) recalls having left the bus somewhere, that is, he knows that the bus has a continued presence that did not terminate when it was misplaced (e.g., "where was it the last time I saw it? . . . . I know, in the blue cabinet," Krafft & Berk, 1998, p. 646); (2) he does not recollect where this somewhere is; and (3) he thinks his mother might have knowledge that he does not have about the location of the misplaced object. A mother's knowledge of the possible location of the object in question may stem from having seen the object. But it may also be due to her having changed the location of the object, for example, a child of 31 months says, "Mum! I want it my box. Where you put it?" (Barnes, 2006, p. 141). This implies that others can know things about objects that we interact with, sometimes because they also interact with them, and we can use their knowledge in the service of our preferences. Mothers also ask children as to the location of objects, implying that children too can be privy to knowledge to which mothers themselves are not privy (e.g., when child of 28 months asks for her sandals, the mother answers, "I don't know where they are. Do you know where they are?" Barnes, 2006, p. 102).

Another means of referring to objects without canonical locus is by using infinitives of verbs relating to search (e.g., search, find, look for) and the object being searched for, as in "(I) look for the pacifier"[14] (Miller, 1979) and "awa (I want) domino find," said at 20 months (Bowerman, 1973). When children indicate that they don't know where something is, they also necessarily allude to invisible objects (e.g., "I don't know [where is] the sweater,"[15] said at 22 months (Miller, 1979). When he's asked what he was doing, Orren, at 30;23, says, "I was looking for my small car and I didn't find it."[16] Parallel to the increase in references to hidden or invisible objects, there is a drop in requests for visible objects, with this drop being partly accounted for by the fact that as children become more mobile, they can reach visible and reachable objects on their own, without parental help.

The expression of preferences that allude to invisible objects parallels the expression of preferences for activities that are not currently being engaged in. At 17;25, Travis says "eggs mouth" when she wants to eat eggs, and at 22;7, she says "Have peanut butter in it" when her parents returned from the supermarket with some bread (Tomasello, 1992). The important transition here is that the objects involved in the activities being alluded to are not within the child's sight when the child is talking about them. The child in the above examples did not see eggs or peanut butter when the expressions were uttered, implying that there is a mental representation of the object or of the related activity and that this representation is associated with the verbal label in some way. But it also indicates an understanding of how reality can be improved on, or what can be added to it to make it more palatable. This emergent ability to refer to invisible objects and related activities is not limited to food preferences. At 21 months, Kathryn pushes up her hair toward her mother and says "Mommy pigtail," clearly indicating the action she wants her mother to take and reflecting the fact that she recalls a previous "pigtail" event (Bloom, 1970, p. 48).

For such preferences to be expressed, children need to have a mental representation of their preferred state of affairs, some understanding of what conditions need to be in force for changing reality to have those preferences satisfied, and the linguistic skill to express these mental representations in some way. When children express preferences for absent objects and activities that are not currently engaged in, then, their representational skills are implicated in such expressions.

There are several different types of additional evidence for children's emergent ability to represent objects and events in the past. One type of evidence is the ability to indicate choices when they are offered in an abstract context. For instance, when a child is asked what he wants to eat when the options are not in front of him, responding with a choice necessarily implies that the child has a mental representation of the indicated preference. In this light, a 20-month-old is asked what he wants for lunch and answers, "'mato, cheese" (Painter, 1984, p. 150). Similarly, when faced with one food, specifying another food that is not currently visible and rejecting the currently available food also indicates the existence of a mental representation of the alternative food. In line with this, when a child of 35 months is offered a grilled cheese sandwich, she rejects it repeatedly, saying "I want some cheese and crackers for lunch" and refuses to be put off when her mother insists on her eating the sandwich (Gordon, 2002, p. 720). Finally, indicating a preference in the absence of any cues as to the availability of this preference also indicates the existence of a mental representation of that preference. In this vein, Painter (1984) reports that when she was out for a walk with her son, at 20 months, he spontaneously said, "drink, orange" (p. 152), indicating his desire to drink orange juice. In saying this, he had to have a representation of orange juice as a beverage that one could have, despite being temporally and locationally displaced from the home where he presumably generally has orange juice.

Finally, children start to allude to their preferential experiences in the past. At 24;10, Karen says, "Mommy gave it to you (i.e., to Karen) and you didn't want it." Justifying

[13] Serbo-Croatian: "Mama, de je cuca. Di je duda?"
[14] German: "lala suchen"
[15] German: "weiss ich nich, pullover"
[16] Hebrew: "Ani xipasti at ha-auto hakatan sheli ve-anni lo maçati otto"

Table 2.7.

	Age	Source
C pushes away worn soap, wants new bar C: "no dirty soap"	21 mos.	Bloom (1970, p. 149)
C is offered cup, rejects it C: "I want my bottle"	21 mos.	Bloom (1970, p. 149)
C: "I don't want some soup. I want some cheese sandwich"	23 mos.	Brown (1973)
C rejects spoon C: "Want nother spoon. Not that one. Want nother one"	23 mos.	Painter (1984, p. 245)
C: "No my play my puppet, play my toys"	24;2	Deprez & Pierce (1993)
C: "I want a plate-egg, not a cup-egg," i.e., a fried egg, not a boiled one	Toddler	Clark (1992)
C is asked whether she would like yogurt C: "No, I wanna drink my bottle"	26;19	Volterra & Antinucci (1979, p. 303)

why she was crying, a toddler explains, "I was crying because I didn't want to wake up, because it was dark, so dark" (Bloom, 1991). In these instances, children seem to be encoding the relationship between events and their preferences, in particular, remembering events that jarred their preferences. Importantly, though, they are referring to events for which they have a mental representation that they are alluding to in talking about the events.

COMPARATIVE OBJECT PREFERENCES

When drawing comparisons between alternatives, children often refer to mental representations rather than visible objects or settings. This is evident in two different contexts. The first of these is in the presence of the preferred alternative. The complementary context is one in which the child is in the presence of the less preferred alternative and rejects it, indicating a preference for an absent reality. In such cases, the preferred alternative only exists as a mental representation in the child's mind, reflecting the fact that such comparisons are cognitively more advanced. As examples of the latter, Greenfield and Smith (1976) recorded Nicky, at 18 months, who was asked, "Do you want some milk" and answered, "nana," meaning banana (p. 175). Perhaps more informative regarding this development, at the same age, Nicky is asked, "Do you want some orange juice," and one time he says, "chee" (cheese), and the second time he says "mee" (milk), in both instances pointing to the refrigerator. Not in the realm of foods, Painter (1984) asks her son, at 24 months, "D'you want slippers?" and the child answers, "No. Shoes" (p. 224). When Travis, at 23 months, is told to drink from a cup, she asks, "Where's my bottle?" (Tomasello, 1992, p. 287). It is clear in these cases that the child draws a comparison between an offered object and a preferred object that is not available, except as a representation in the child's memory. In an explicit example of this, a child of 19 months says, "Water, no. Drink me milk" (Clark, 1996).

As this type of comparative ability develops, the child becomes able to indicate choices between foods, objects, or activities; at times, the comparisons are implicit while at other times they are stated explicitly, as shown in Table 2.7

Note that in rejecting what is being offered, children are engaging in self-imposed delay of gratification, rejecting the currently available alternative for another alternative that is displaced in time and place, but which is nonetheless preferred by them. This may well reflect the first type of self-regulation that children evidence, an issue I will address more fully in Chapter 12.

Once comparisons emerge, references to objects need to become more differentiated because implied comparisons raise the need to specify possible distinctions among different objects of preference. Examples of such references are shown in Table 2.8.

The need to differentiate between objects also gives rise to the expression of negative preferences, which are similarly indicated in comparative form, as in "not that

Table 2.8.

	Age	Source
C: "Not wear this one, wear yellow one"	21 mos.	Church (1966, p. 273)
Child takes off bib and says "bib" M: "All right, you don't have to wear it" C: "Want that bib, want clean bib," pointing to another bib	23 mos.	Painter (1984)
C: "I want the sheets with the pink silk on top of them"	24 mos.	Tomasello (1992)
C: "I don't want it smaller cause see it has longer string. This one is better cause it has smaller string"	27;28	Feldman (1989, p. 111)
C: "No want that one. My want the little ones"	30 mos.	Budwig (1995)

Table 2.9.

	Age	Source
K: "Want to have the other one magazine what Karen read to Mommy on the carpet yesterday"	23;12	Karniol (Diary, Karen)
C found toy in bushes earlier C: "I want that toy that I found"	24 mos.	Tomasello (1992, p. 357)
K: "Want to wear the other one shoes what Mommy bought you in Toronto"	25;6	
K: "Where's the other toy they bought you, the first toy?"	26;4	Karniol (Diary, Karen)
O: "Daddy don't bring me this doll – I want Gili (another doll)"[17]	29;3	
O: "Where is the car I got from Yudi?" M shows him car; O rejects it O: "That? That I never got from Yudi, never!"[18]	30;1	Karniol (Diary, Orren)
C1: "Lisa only wants the dark brown shoes"[19]	3;6 years	
C2: "I want the short pants[20]	3;6 years	Taeschner (1983)

book" and "I don't want those shoes" (Bloom, 1970), where both of these statements imply that there are some other books and shoes that the child does want. In this context, McNeil and McNeil (1968) suggest that statements of denial often entail alternative affirmative statements, "that's not mines, that's dolly's," and that such statements require the child to hold in mind two propositions at the same time. Consequently, they posit that statements of denial would only be acquired after contrasts that involve only one proposition (e.g., denial and rejection), a possibility that has not been addressed empirically.

As the need to differentiate between different items arises, children start to use descriptive adjectives that differentiate their objects of preference and serve to guide their caretakers to identify their choices more clearly, as illustrated in Table 2.9. It is clear in the above that children want to convey the specifics of the objects being alluded to, and that in the absence of appropriate adjectives they grope for descriptions that clarify their preferences.

But children have difficulty clarifying their choices. Sachs's daughter, Naomi, at 22 months says, "I need it." On being asked what she needs, she clarifies, "I need the book." When she is asked which one, she repeats that she needs the book, getting upset when her father tries to narrow her preferences down and apparently fails to do so (1983, p. 9). When she is almost 3 years old, the same type of problem arises when she says "I need that book about dancing people.... I need dancing book. I need it," getting upset when her parents fail to understand which book she is referring to. When she is urged to "tell us more about the book so maybe we'll be able to figure out which one it is," she cries in response "I need the dancing people" (1983, p. 9). The child is referring to an absent object but is unable to describe it in ways that would allow those around her to facilitate realizing her choice. Similarly, Nigel, at 35 months, says, "Mummy, where are the ones with green in?" when she questions what he means, he repeats, "the all green ones." When his mother explains that she doesn't know what he is referring to, he answers, "The ones I had in Nairobi" (Halliday, 1975, p. 121). At this point, his mother gives up. There are two important issues here. First, children are delaying gratification, ignoring currently available but dispreferred alternatives in their search for currently unavailable, preferred alternatives. Second, in all of these cases, children assumed that their parents remember the objects being alluded to as well as the episodes in which the child interacted with these objects, again suggesting that children have an incipient understanding of parental minds.

COMPARATIVE ACTION PREFERENCES

Parallel to the development of comparative object preferences, children start to allude to comparative action and state preferences. The interesting aspect of such expressions is that the current context does not generally contain clues as to the alternative reality that is implicated in the expressed preference. Rather, children use their past experiences with activities and states, using their memory representations to guide their preference statements. They use a memory representation of an alternative reality, which in the simplest instance represents a reversal of a current state of affairs. For instance, Travis said, "open it" at 17;23 when she wanted to open the closed door so she could go out, "up here" at 17;20 when she wanted to get up on a couch, "nightgown off" at 18;27 when she did not want to have her nightgown on, and "get-out" at 17;06 when she wanted to be taken out of her playpen. Children also explicitly express the contrast between the current state of affairs and the alternative reality they prefer, as when Travis (Tomasello, 1992) says "shoes-on off" at 18;28 when she wants to take her shoes off. At 16;3, Bloom's (1973) daughter Allison said "down down up," attempting to get her mother to get off a chair and indicating her desire to get up on it (p. 89). Whereas in the previous

17 Hebrew: "Abba al tavi li at habuba haze – ani roçe at Gili"
18 Hebrew: "Eifo ha-auto shekibalti me-Yudi? Ze? At ze lo kiblati me-Yudi, af paam!"
19 German: "Lisa will nur Schuhe dunkelbraun"
20 Italian: "Voglio I pantalone corti"

examples, expressed preferences could be based on reversing the current state of affairs, cognitively more advanced expressions reflect preferences for alternative states that are not inherently linked to the current, dispreferred state of affairs. For instance, at 20;6, Travis says "watch TV pillow," wanting to lie down on a pillow rather than sit on a chair while watching TV. In doing so, she evidences understanding of the fact that people have choices, an issue I will return to later in this chapter.

As in the case of comparisons between objects, children can indicate a preference for a current context or a current activity to be continued. For instance, when he is asked if he wants to come out of the bath, Orren, at 30;7, says, "No, I want to play more," and at 35;15, when he is asked to come home from the park, he replies: "I prefer that we stay here a few minutes."[21] A child of 21 months who is being taken out of the bathtub, yells, "Stay in tub, Ruthie not ready out yet" (Church, 1966, p. 268). These children are drawing a comparison between a mental representation of the offered activity and the current setting and indicate a preference for the latter. The complementary context is one in which the child is in the presence of the less preferred context or activity and rejects it, indicating a preference for an absent reality (e.g., "I'd rather play Power Rangers," Kyratzis, Marx, & Wade, 2001, p. 402). In such cases, the preferred alternative only exists as a mental representation in the child's mind, reflecting the fact that such comparisons are cognitively more advanced.

Notice again that the children above were referring to future states they wanted to enact themselves as well as future states they wanted others to achieve for them. Children's requests underline their perception of others as agents who can change the state of the world to make it better aligned with children's preferences and also illustrate children's ability to think of alternatives to the current state of affairs. This is illustrated when Travis, at 21 months, says, "get me out there," expressing her desire to be taken out of a shopping cart and when Emily, at 22;16, says, "I want that closed," referring to shades that were currently open.

USING SCRIPTS

Above, in expressing preferences for other objects and states of affairs, children were accessing memories of specific events in which alternatives to current reality were implicated. Often, comparative preferences are expressed in contexts in which there are scripts guiding how events unfold. To elaborate, in addition to representing specific episodes, children have representations of generic or scripted events, those that happen as part of daily routines. Newson and Newson (1968) contend that because children do not have an adequate understanding of cause and sequence or the experiential base to comprehend and predict the course of everyday events, they cling to what is familiar, repetitive, and predictable. The repetitiveness of daily events provides children with a sense of security because in these recurrent patterns, they know what to expect.

In line with this, Nelson (1986, 1996) contends that scripts of routine events constitute the building blocks of children's cognitive development and that other knowledge is derived from such scripts. From Nelson's perspective, children learn about the social world by participating passively at first in routine activities and by learning the sequences of these routines and the parts played by different individuals and objects in these routines. The critical cognitive capacity that children bring to the situation is that of holding in mind a sequence of temporally ordered or causally ordered events involving oneself and others. As they start to participate more actively in routines, children learn to relate their own role to those of other participants in the same routine, and they start to contribute both by anticipating the event sequence and by incorporating relevant props. As part and parcel of such passive and active participation, children develop what Nelson (1986) calls *generalized event representations*, defined as "spatially and temporally organized schematic representations constructed from experience in real-world events that define the expected occurrence of actions, actors, and props for familiar events" (Hudson, Sosa, & Shapiro, 1997, p. 77).

Children learn that there are prerequisites to the occurrence of a given script and that sequences can fail because some precondition has not been met (e.g., when mother forgets her wallet or runs out of gas on the way to the store). They also learn that there are some open slots that can be filled by different objects and agents and they need to learn the range of possible slot fillers. Grocery shopping can be done by different agents (mothers/fathers/nannies), stores vary by what they sell (e.g., supermarkets vs. drug stores), and one can decide for or against taking a shopping cart. There are alternative actions that are allowable within the script, and with experience, the script is embellished to note these variations.

Nelson and her colleagues (e.g., Nelson & Seidman, 1984; Nelson & Hudson, 1988) contend that children experience their day as a series of scripts or routines, using these routines to understand how the world works and what the socially meaningful units are. They found evidence for the existence of such scripted representations when children report what happens in familiar settings such as day care and birthday parties. In developing such representations, children learn to distinguish those events and props that are invariable or canonical and those that are variable or unusual, doing so by using temporal words that indicate their status. This is why children can refer to the occasional nature of events by using the term *sometimes* (e.g., during the tenth week of kindergarten, children explain, "And sometimes we do some things like... and sometime we play this game" or "Sometime we play house. Sometimes I play by myself," Fivush & Slackman, 1986, p. 87). The occasional is also differentiated from the

[21] Hebrew: "Ani maadif she-nishaer kama dakot po"

Table 2.10.

	Age	Source
To doll		
K: "Dana you need to go to the supermarket, I will buy something that one needs"[22]	32;22	Karniol (Diary, Karen)
To father		
K: "Near the daycare center there is a small supermarket where you can buy things, and don't buy candy"[23]	35;17	Karniol (Diary, Karen)
Explaining supermarket shopping		
C: "We look for some onions and plums and cookies and tomato juice, onions and all that kind of stuff"	5 years	Nelson (1986, p. ix)

canonical by referring to possible actions (e.g., "we could paint," and "we could start playing," p. 88) and by indexing choice (e.g., "get dressed if you want, but you could stay in pajamas too," French & Nelson, 1985). To illustrate this more clearly, I suggest to Orren, at 34;2, that he tell his father about the "miracle" we had that day. He replies, "the miracle is that I didn't cry when Mommy washed my hair,"[24] clearly indicating his understanding that this event was extraordinary in terms of the script for having his hair shampooed.

Children's spontaneous verbalizations in language diaries provide evidence for their use of scripts to encode routine events. This is evident when Travis, at 20;20, says "Get grapes at Big Star," when she's told there are no grapes left, and when at 21;27, she says, "Go Seven-Eleven buy more Coca-Cola" when she wants more to drink and is told there is none left (Tomasello, 1992). These statements reflect her knowledge not only of what she wanted to eat and drink (grapes and Coke) but also her knowledge that these items are bought and where one ordinarily buys them, that is, a supermarket or convenience store. In the same vein, on being told that there is no more ice cream, Karen, at 20;21, says, "Have to buy ice cream for Karen. Go shopping agala" (Hebrew, *baby pram*). A child of 21 months, who had been eating chocolate and asked for more, was told, "No we've finished the chocolate now," he again says "More"; when he gets no reply, he says, "Shop . . . shop Mummy" when his mother asks him to clarify, he answers, "Some shop," and she asks "Some more from the shop?" and he says *yes* (McShane, 1980, pp. 117–118). Here, again, these children's statements reflect an understanding not only of what the child wants, but of what one does to get the item into the home. This may not be surprising in light of the finding that when they reported on the frequency of their going either grocery shopping or general shopping trips with their children in the past two weeks, 70 percent of mothers indicated that they had done so at least once and almost a third had done so twice or more (Ward, Wackman, & Wartella, 1977). Notice that in the above, the child also has to remember the valence of the events as positive in order to prefer their occurrence and to actively attempt to reinstate them. But in addition, the child has to have labeled the activity in such a way that the label would be readily accessible to be used in expressing the preference.

Children also provide evidence for their use of scripts in their pretend play of scripted activities. For instance, at 21;16, Karen says, "Bye bye" and when she was asked where she was going, she answered, "Plaza." On being asked what she was going to do there, she said, "Buy milk and eggs for you. See you later." Similarly, when a girl of 4;11 years is pretend playing going grocery shopping with her friend, she says, "I also want to buy Nutella, bread and apples because there's nothing in the refrigerator"[25] (Taeschner, 1983, p. 178).

The generic nature of such representations is underlined in the examples provided in Table 2.10. A supermarket is a place where one can buy many things and one can specify those food items that are needed on any one occasion, such as milk and eggs. These children have generalized the particular experiences that they have had in supermarkets to reflect that one can "buy things" there and that these things include "all that kind of stuff."

Additional evidence for the abstraction of scripts is that when they answer questions as to what happens in routine contexts, children employ the impersonal "you" and tenseless verbs. This contrasts with their use of the past tense and the first-person pronoun when asked about specific remembered events. As well, Nelson (1986) documents that a preschool child who cannot recall what he had for breakfast that morning is capable of answering the question when it is phrased in generic terms. When he is asked, "What do you have for breakfast?" he answers, "Usually I have Cheerios and milk, but sometimes when it's cold mommy makes oatmeal." Here, then, the child has generalized across many breakfasts, noting exceptions to what he is routinely fed. Similarly, at 34 months, a girl says, "tomorrow when we wake up from bed first me and Daddy and Mommy you eat breakfast eat breakfast like

[22] Hebrew: "Dana at çarix lalexet la-supermarket, ani nikne masheu she çarix"

[23] Hebrew: "Le-yad hamaon yesh supermarket katan she-efshar liknot dvarim – ve-al tikne sukariyot"

[24] Hebrew: "Saper eize ness haya po"; O: Ha-ness shelo baxiti ke-she ima xafefa li rosh"

[25] German: "Will ich auch kaufen, Nutella, Brot und Apfel weld a in Eisscrank ist nicts da"

we usually do . . . ." (Nelson, 1996, p. 279). Not only does the child employ tenseless verbs, but the use of "usually" clarifies that breakfast has been scripted.

It is important to recognize that script acquisition is cross-cultural. Each culture has a set of routines in which parents engage their children, primarily ones involving child care (feeding, bathing, clothing, sleeping), but also ones in which the child may only be a spectator (e.g., cooking, working, visiting). Adults socialize children as participants in these routines, using their own culture as the guideline for how this is done. In all cultures, though, children start to allude to those scripts that they know and to the preferences that specific scripts can be used to satisfy. Cultures vary in the content of their scripts. For instance, in cultures with eating utensils, children learn to eat using tools that are held and used in specific ways for eating different foods. In cultures in which utensils are not used for eating, children learn to eat the way their culture dictates (e.g., wiping up dips with a pita bread, rolling up meat in a flat bread, using chopsticks). But children in all cultures learn the scripts for eating and for obtaining food. A child growing up in rural Greece may know that one needs to go pick grapes off the vine in order to eat grapes, and a child growing up in the seventeenth century may have known that one needs to churn cream to make butter. To delineate this point, Nelson (1986) suggests that the shopping script "includes the car driving event" (p. 12) – how true of middle-class America and how untrue of so many other parts of the world! The critical issue, though, is that irrespective of one's specific culture, children develop representations of both their preferences and the culturally available means for satisfying those preferences. The culturally specific nature of scripts is evident in the high degree of overlap among different children's descriptions of those events that occur within a given script in a given culture. Such overlap accounted for between 60 percent and 82 percent of the events that were mentioned in children's scripts for dinner, lunch, and eating at McDonald's (Nelson & Gruendel, 1979).

How do scripts emerge? First, they may be based on recall of specific episodes in which the relevant behavior occurred. Children may recall an instance of going to the supermarket and buying the items specified. In fact, research indicates that children provide scripts even after a single experience in a specific context (e.g., Hudson & Nelson, 1986). This is similar to the process of "fast mapping," a strategy whereby new labels for objects are learned after a single exposure to that label and its being used in the context of an object for which the child has not had a label used previously (Carey & Bartlett, 1978). Nelson (1996) suggests that whereas the basics of the script may be established during the first encounter with it, repeated encounters with the script "overwrite" previous ones, with recurring events being absorbed by the generic memory for the event and variations being placed in episodic memory to the extent that they are deemed important or interesting.

There at least three problems with generating scripts on the basis of recall of specific episodes. First, because each trip to the supermarket is unique, it is unclear what kinds of similarities between repeated events allow for generalizations. In fact, Nelson (1996) claims that we don't know "what are the necessary similarities across events that make an event count as a repetition of a prior event rather than a novel experience" (p. 96) and that these questions remain to be investigated. Second, if specific episodes serve as the memory base, one would expect little overlap between different children's emergent scripts. Yet, as indicated above, there is a great deal of overlap in different children's reports of what happens in scripted contexts. Finally, children appear to draw inferences that are not based on specific episodes in memory. For instance, when Allison, at 20;3, wants to put a diaper on her doll and her mother says to her, "We don't have any pins," Allison answers, "Buy store" and her mother attempts to clarify, "Buy pins at store?" to which Allison answers, "Mm" (Bloom, 1973, p. 212). Similarly, Kathryn, at 22;3, looks at a picture of a mother cooking and says, "Raisins. Buy more grocery store . . . . Raisin e grocery store" (Bloom, 1970, p. 138). Both of these children had inferred that pins and raisins could be bought at the store, apparently in the absence of having such an episodic recollection.

In contrast to the above view that specific episodes form the basis of scripts, Bloom, Lightbown, and Hood (1975) claim that with repeated experiences in the same settings, children learn to mentally represent the relations between objects, the people acting on these objects and the manner in which they do, and the location of objects and how their location is changed (throwing, carrying, pushing, etc.). Because they are abstracted over repeated encounters, such representations are general and nonspecific, with the regularity being abstracted by children as they see interactions between objects and people repeated either with or without variability. It may well be, then, that children abstract scripts following repeated encounters with trips to the supermarket, for instance, learning what one does in the supermarket and an itemization of the kinds of things one can buy there. Abstraction of this kind would seem to provide a better account for the kinds of inferences that do not rely on specific episodic representations and the finding that across different children, one gets similar expectations for what one may occur in the supermarket, with only the names of the specific stores being varied.

Yet the account outlined by Bloom and her colleagues (1975) cannot account for inferences regarding objects that could not have been experienced in the context of the script specified by the child. A telling example comes from Karen at 20;25. When part of her bed broke and she was told she needs a new one, she said, "Buy it other bed grocery store." Such an inference would seem to be based on a more general understanding that all items in the home are purchased and supermarkets are replete with items – so why not beds as well? Scripts, then, would seem to provide a framework that the child uses for drawing inferences that are related to the preference-satisfying nature of scripts and as a consequence, the use of scripts can lead to errors that result from their being overgeneralized.

Irrespective of the above controversy, there is general agreement that it is by participating in routine activities that children build up scripts for how events unfold. Although this is clearly the most influential means of acquiring scripts, it is not the only one. Children may also build up scripts via questioning by adults, for instance, Shatz (1994) sees her grandson making pretend oatmeal in a pot, saying, "I cook more oatmeal." Then she tells him that he needs to stir it and asks, "What do you need to stir it with?" and the child after thought, responded with his version of the word *spoon* (p. 89). Similarly, in a study in which a mother was asked to discuss a familiar future event with her 4-year-old child, the mother queried, "Do you know what we have to do tomorrow? What do we do all the time? We have to go to the grocery store. What do we do there?" On being queried some more, the daughter answered, "We get a cart, some food, and go around," and with further prompting, she supplied, "We get cookies . . . and sometimes we get milk and eggs." The mother then answers, "Usually we do" (Hudson, 2004, p. 140). There are several important aspects of the above conversation. First, such prompted conversations are not unique to experimental settings. As I illustrate below, older children in conversation with their parents also go through similar prompted, questioning exchanges. Second, repeated conversations of this type serve to establish and solidify the tokens that the script has in it, distinguishing the canonical from the occasional aspects of the script. Third, in the above, the child appears to be basing her answers on a script rather than on a specific episode of going grocery shopping.

But when the script does not supply the answer being sought, children need to find specific episodes whose representations are likely to contain the sought answer. For instance, Bill, at 6;2 years of age (Warren, CHILDES) is talking with his father about needing to get an exercise ball for some pet gerbils. The father asks where one can get an exercise ball and the child answers that he doesn't know. The father then persists, asking, "Where do you think we can get one?" and the child answers "Uh, probably at a pet store . . . or K-Mart . . . Richway . . . that's where I got the cage." The child tries to find an answer by working through a repertoire of different types of stores, but these do not yield the sought-for information. The child finally finds the information by recalling one specific, relevant episode in which a purchase related to a pet was made. This episode was most likely recalled because the child was involved in choosing and buying the cage and because the purchase was made outside of the pet store setting where one would generally expect a cage for a pet to be bought. In fact, evidence for such expectations comes from a kindergarten girl who amusingly says "I'm going to get my gerbil a new wife." When she is asked as to where, she answers, "Pet shop where I got my gerbil" (Green & Wallat, 1979, pp. 178–179).

Children also acquire scripts in the context of being disciplined. For instance, a mother who is explaining what she would do if she found that her child has brought something home from the store without paying, says, "I'd explain to him that you had to pay for things and wait 'til someone comes to take your money and wrap up the thing you've bought" (Cook-Gumperz, 1973, p. 246). I overheard a mother at the supermarket, chastising her 3-year-old, saying, "You got to pay for it, you can't just take it. It's – it's not yours. You've got to pay for it."

Scripts can also be acquired in the context of book reading and in the context of pretend play with parents and others. A mother is looking a pictures with her son of 23;27, and says, "This is a supermarket, isn't it? Sometimes we go to the supermarket to do our shopping" (Howe, 1981, p. 127). In acting out a restaurant script, a mother says, "Do we need menus? . . . . It looks like this fork is dirty . . . I spilled some coffee on my menu" (Segal & Adcock, 1981, p. 153). When pretending to be shopping at the mall, the same mother asks her child, "Do you have money? . . . . Do you want to pack up your purchases?" (ibid, p. 154). The cited dyad also takes the elevator to the second floor, tries on different clothes, and tests different colors of lipstick. In a pretend grocery shopping episode, a mother asks her 2-year-old to buy something at the store. When the daughter says "raisins," the mother asks, "What else besides raisins" What else are we gonna get at the store?" She then tells her daughter, "You need your pocketbook," presumably to pay for the groceries (Bernstein, CHILDES).

Parents differentially emphasize different aspects of specific routines depending on their perceived importance in the script. For instance, the need to pay is underlined by parents when they engage in play with their children. Talking to her 32-month-old child in the context of hand puppets, the mother asks whether he rode the trolley, proceeding to ask him, "Did you pay any money?" (Gleason & Ely, 1997, p. 271). The need to pay then forms an integral part of children's scripts related to shopping, as illustrated in Table 2.11.

These script-based episodes underline the wide variety of script-based actions, props, and sequences that children have encoded and that they can subsequently use to guide both their expectations and their own actions in shopping contexts.

Having scripts and knowing the props and actors integral to those scripts allows children to intercede in conversations that utilize scripts and also to correct others who are deemed to have made script mistakes. Several examples of such conversations are provided in Table 2.12.

Repeated experiences of this kind allow children to play-act their own scripts, elaborating them as they go along. When a 3-year-old was pretending to have her mother for a tea party, she planned it, saying, "I want something to go with the roast. I'll make a pie – plum pie." Once the tea

Table 2.11.

	Age	Source
At play with M C: "Chocolate milk is fifty dollars.... Milk is ten dollars"	Preschool	Gleason & Ely (1997, p. 251)
Playing with girl C: "OK, I'll give you some money so you can buy some more things. Here's some more money"	5 years	Gottman (1986b, p. 190)
Pretend customer is told by pretend salesperson that the clothes are very expensive C: "That's all right. I have lots of charge cards"	5 years	Segal & Adcock (1981, p. 145)
Group playing store C1 grabs an item and runs C2: "Hey you – you're supposed to pay! Oh, you're a thief, a thief!" C2 chases C1	5 years	Kelly (2001, p. 184)
C explains going grocery shopping C: "Sometimes I get a Tootsie Roll, then I pay them, then I eat"	5;6 years	French (1986, p. 127)

party had been transformed into a dinner party, she asked, "Would you like dinner music and a candle? I'll turn the music and TV on" (Segal & Adcock, 1981, p. 47). She had learned that meat and dessert are part of dinner and that fancy dinner parties have adult props that are part of the script.

Depending on the script being enacted, some aspects of the script are invariable, even during pretend play. A 3-year-old is pretend playing being mother talking to the father and says, "Are you at the office? Come at six o'clock four o'clock. Did you cash the check?" (Paley, 1986, p. 48). Fathers go to work in the morning and come home at night. In medical settings, doctors have special concoctions and instruments they use to wield their healing powers, as shown in Table 2.13.

These children are evidencing understanding of the doctor script as involving doctors who take care of patients by performing various medical procedures, mothers who relate to doctors what the problem is, and patients who need to recuperate after being treated.

In the above, children's pretend play is assumed to reflect the scripts that children construct based on their experiences with real-world events and the routine activities that unfold in their experiences. Fein (1987) takes issue with the argument that the scripts that emerge in children's pretend play reflect veridical representations of routine, real-world experiences. She suggests that pretend scenarios do not necessarily represent events children have actually experienced and that pretend scenarios can represent fabricated events. Without denying this possibility, it is highly likely that many pretend scenarios are amalgams of different scripts, each of which is veridical within its confines but that in the context of the dominant script being played out appear to be fabricated or fantastic. For instance, Fein gives the example of a 4-year-old who is playing out a family script and says about her pretend daughter, "She picked up a knife. Was trying to kill her dad" (p. 288). Fein argues that this is unlikely to represent anything the child experienced within the family script. But children are exposed to media depictions of

Table 2.12.

	Age	Source
F: "Mummy's gone to the shop" C: "Buy chocolate"	20 mos.	Halliday (1975)
Child overhears conversation about shopping C: "Better get your cheque book"	28 mos.	Dunn (1988)
Told she'll get a hot dog at McDonalds C: "No we don't get hot dogs at McDonalds, we just get hamburgers instead"	32 mos.	Garvey (1984)
Teacher wants to buy a book in pretend library C: "You don't need to buy 'em... But this is a library. All you need is a library card"	Kindergarten	Neuman & Roskos (1991)
Friend says she bought something in a bank C: "At the bank – we get money there. They do not sell things at the bank"	4;6 years	Corsaro & Rizzo (1990)
C1: "Pretend this is in the hospital" C2: "You don't do those things in a hospital. You just do them things in the school see?"	5;1 years	McTear (1985)

Table 2.13.

	Age	Source
Pretend M to pretend Dr. M: "The baby is still sick. Give her eight vitamins".... (to another C) M: "You could be a doctor too. Give her some shots"	Preschool	Paley (1986, p. 96)
Pretend patient to pretend Dr. C: "Hurry put the medicine on me. I cut my knee. Put on the stitches, doctor. Look in my mouth. Say you see bumps. Put us in the X-Ray"	Preschool	Paley (1986, p. 103)
Pretend M telephoning Dr. M: "My baby's poorly... doctor... will you come quickly.... will you give her something special... give her a prick thing to make her better"	3 years	Tough (1977, p. 59)

family and nonfamily violence, and this may well reflect the impact of such exposure. Without knowing the particular experiences that children have had, it is difficult to know whether children are alluding to real or fabricated events. For instance, as mother, a child pretends to call up the police, finds out that the bridge is flooded, and tells her pretend child, "The river is flooded some more. We have to move our stuff upstairs" (Nourot, 1998, p. 380). It is highly unlikely that a child who has not been exposed to flooding would be able to generate this scenario. Similarly, when the first Gulf War in Iraq took place, day care in Israel was closed, homes were required to have a safe room for Scud attacks, and there were often alarms that warned of Scuds falling. Alarms were followed by quick entry into the safe room. Five days after the first Scud attack, when he is downstairs, Orren, at 33;4, says, "When there is an alarm (you) go upstairs to the safe room."[26] These events were often reflected in Orren's toy play. At 33;17, he says regarding some dolls, "In the house of these children there is an alarm – we are putting them in the safe room."[27] Being privy to his experiences, it is clear that this was a reenactment of the script of what happens when the alarm is sounded. In any case, scripts can be used to guide children's expectations for how events and behavior unfold in specific contexts.

More than that, though, scripts also become encoded as contexts within which people have generalized preferences that are typical of that script but not of other scripts. Shopping for groceries can therefore be viewed as an exercise of one's preferences to buy certain things. In this context, a child of 5;4 years explains what one does in the supermarket, saying, "Buy food, or if you wanna, you return something what you don't want" (French & Nelson, 1985), and another child of 5;6 years explains that in the supermarket you get "cheese if you want pizza." Birthday parties also entail preferences, requiring one to make choices between one's preferences. Consequently, at a birthday party, "If you feel like it, um, if you want another piece of cake, you could have another piece, then go home." Cookie baking at preschool similarly involves preferences, not only in terms of what to sprinkle on the cookies, but "you can ask if a child wants to make cookies with you – you can ask everybody else if they want to help or watch." Even restaurant scripts involve generalized preferences, as a child reports that "I like to eat whatever they have. But I like their desserts, but I don't like their meals." Ross, at 5;6 years is talking to his father and says, "I don't care if we go to Denny's or Arby's or McDonald's. I just want to go to a place that has food" (Bartsch & Wellman, 1995, p. 72). In this context, gas stations are places where "somebody wants gas," as Peter says at 33 months when he plays with a toy gas station (Bloom, 1970), and Orren, at 30;7, similarly says, "If somebody wants gas in his car, I will give him."[28] It may well be that what allows children to abstract scripts is the common preference structure of individuals within the same settings and the different preference structure of individuals in different settings. Further research is needed to validate this possibility.

CHOOSING

Alternatives imply making choices and children start alluding to the need to make choices, as evident in Table 2.14.

The most clear-cut expression of choice, though, is evident in Emily's (Nelson, 1989) presleep monologue at 33 months when she says, "Go down for breakfast see and I choose what I want cheese omelet or eggs eggs cheese omelet or yoghurt."

Making choices can be difficult.[29] To illustrate, when I walked into her room when she was 27;28 and asked Karen what she was doing, she answered, "Karen was choosing how underpants she needs to put on." Painter's son entered the room with two t-shirts, asking, "Which one d'you (i.e., referring to self) want? This one? This one?" holding up each shirt alternately. He then chooses, saying "this one"

[26] Hebrew: "Keshe-yesh azaka holxim lemala lexeder ha-atum"

[27] Hebrew: "Babait shel hayeladim haele yesh azaka – anaxnu samim otam baxeder ha-atum"

[28] Hebrew: "Im misheu roçe delek bamexonit shelo ani eten lo"

[29] The difficulty of making choices is also evident in the existence of institutions and professions dedicated to helping individuals choose among their preferences: these include guidance and occupational counselors, wedding planners, pension planners, financial advisors, etc.

Table 2.14.

	Age	Source
Sitting in high chair		
K: "Want to go out to tell Mommy what crayons you want"	24;7	Karniol (Diary, Karen)
Looking at her bookcase		
K: "Want Mommy to hold Karen to check which book Karen wants"	24;7	Karniol (Diary, Karen)
C is taking out books from bookcase		
K: "You're (i.e., Karen) taking out which books Karen wants to have"	24;13	Karniol (Diary, Karen)
Playing with puzzle with mother		
C: "Choose you (i.e., referring to self) want"	24	Thornton (2002)
M offers C a cookie from cookie jar		
C: "Can I have it down here for me to choose?"	4;7 years	Wells (CHILDES)

(Painter, 1989, p. 53). Choosing among toys does not seem easier. Given a choice of toys, a child of 35;8, sequentially picks up twelve different toys, each time saying, "Maybe this one . . . no." The exasperated mother finally said, "Why don't you get something else out?" (Manchester corpus, CHILDES). At 22 months, Nigel puts a record back on the rack and says, "what else put on . . . what else put on" as he is trying to decide on another record to play (Halliday, 1975, p. 100). An 8-year-old explains to a play therapist, "There are so many toys in here I don't know what to play with . . . I can never make up my mind" (Exline, 1947, p. 226). Even choosing what to eat can be difficult, as evident in the following exchange between a 3-year-old and his father: "I'm hungry, I'm hungry, Daddy." When the father asks what he wants to eat, the child says, "I don't know. . . . I deciding. I'm thinking. I'm thinking of something I like to eat" (Wellman, 1988, p. 82). It should be noted, though, that adults also indicate that choices can be difficult; Sproles and Kendall (1986) identify a consumer whom they call "the overwhelmed shopper" who finds it hard to choose.

As Schwartz (2004) has argued, sometimes we are overwhelmed with choices and do not know what criteria to use in selecting one alternative over another. Hence, children's difficulty of making choices may well reflect their inability to select those criteria that are relevant for making the choice.[30] This is evident in a child of 5;6 years who, using elliptical logic, says,

> Sometimes there are clean clothes that I don't like to wear so my mom wants me to wear what I have clean. But all my ones that I like are dirty and some of all the ones that I don't like are dirty, so I get to wear ones that I do like. (French & Nelson, 1985)

[30] Children's understanding of what choosing means is very interesting in this context. They appear to understand having choice as the provision of two different alternatives, not of one alternative that can be rejected. This is evident in the following exchange, when a mother asks her kindergarten child, "So you had a choice today of swimming and you chose not to?" Her child answers, "No, you didn't have a choice. If you wanted to go swimming, you could. And if you didn't, you didn't have to" (Davidson & Snow, 1996).

Further attesting to this, another child of 5;6 years, says,

> I never wear the right sneakers. Today I wanted to wear my other sneakers but I didn't wear them. And the other day I wanted to wear these sneakers and I weared my other ones. (French & Nelson, 1985)

The above may reflect the instability of the criteria used for selection but it may also reflect that fact that preferences are not stable over time. At the point of choice the children discussed above may have actually thought that they made the "right" choice, but their preferences changed over time, an issue I will return to in Chapter 3.

Another possible reason for why making choices is so difficult is that the evaluation of objects that are being compared with one another is quite different than the evaluation of the same objects independently of each other (e.g., Hsee, 1998). One can demonstrate this quite easily by asking individuals how much they would be willing to pay for a given object when it is offered to them as a sole offer versus when it is offered to them within a dichotomous choice context. Whether the comparison object is more highly evaluated or not, its presence has an impact on the valuation of the target object, making choice much more difficult. In fact, when assessed by rankings, young children's preferences are less stable than those of older children, and the process of deciding is more difficult for them (Stewart, 1958).

Despite the difficulty of making choices, children want to have choice. This is evident in several different ways. First, children make statements indicating being determined to make choices themselves. Sometimes the implementation of choice is implicit, as when Karen, at 23;21, says, "Karen will bring all the things she wants and she will read them and play with them." At other times, their determination to choose is explicit. At 28;14, Orren insists, "I want to choose. Choose for me for you."[31] At 32;25, he asks me to come and play with him and says, "Let's play together. I will choose with what (we will play) – I want these blocks."[32]

[31] Hebrew: "Ani roçe livxar. Livxarli lax"
[32] Hebrew: "Boey nesaxek beyaxad. Ani evxar bema – ani roçe at hakubiyot haele"

Second, children often object to choices that are made for them and that counter their own preferences. At 30;4, Orren rejects a shirt I put out for him, saying, "I want to choose a shirt because I don't like this shirt."[33] As well, at 26;8, Karen discusses such a conflict when she says, "These (dresses) are here because yesterday Karen didn't want to wear them and Karen cried."

Third, children differentiate *work* and *play* at preschool in terms of the former being what one *has to do* and playing as "you just do whatever your want" (Wing, 1995, p. 228). In the words of a preschooler, "You have to color, then you can play" (ibid, p. 234). Sherman (1997) found that 5-year-olds differentiated working from playing in terms of having to do the former without being given choice and being able to choose to play and to have fun.

Fourth, children may avoid contexts that do not afford them the possibility of choosing. In discussing a visit to a craft fair at Christmas time, a mother asks her preschool son why he was so mad, and he answers, "Because I just want to do whatever I want to do" (Wang, 2001, p. 713). When Sachs's (CHILDES) daughter Naomi was 4;7;28 years, her father asked her "What do you want to do in the summer?" she answers, "I don't want to go to summer camp." When she was asked why, she answered, "Because I have to do what the teachers say I have to do and I don't like to do that." The importance accorded to having choice is underlined by children when they talk of how they view their future family life. As a 10-year-old says in discussing what kind of family he would like to have when he grows up, he says, "If I have children let them choose on what they want to do" (Sixsmith & Knowles, 1996, p. 25). Similarly, a 15-year-old girl says, regarding her ideal family, "to let me do what I want, and to make my own mistakes" (Rout, Sixsmith, & Moore, 1996, p. 110).

Often, though, in the context of interacting with adults, children perceive their choices as being restricted. As one child explains, "I can't stand it when someone tells me, "No, no, you're not supposed to do it this way or that way, this way." "I want it to be from me, not anybody else" (Igoa, 1995, p. 97). As claimed by Piaget (1932/1965), peer interaction is often seen as giving children freedom to choose to do what they like, an option they do not see themselves as having at home. As a 9-year-old says about playing with friends rather than being at home, "You can do what you like. You aren't being told what to do." Another one says that with friends, "You can do what you like, go where you like" (Mayall, 2000, p. 132). When friends attempt to restrict choices, children react. A first grader refuses to write what his friends are telling him to write, complaining, "I did it the way I wanted it. And now they want me to do it how they want it. But it's my decision" (Dyson, 1993, p. 117).

Concomitantly, *wanting to* becomes a justification for doing things and *not wanting to* becomes a justification for refusing to do so. When he is asked why he is changing the places of some dolls, a child of 26 months responds, "Because I want to"[34] (Dubost, 1999) and a 5-year-old boy explains that he's not going to do anything. When he's asked why, he answers, "'Cause I don't want to" (Garvey, 1984, p. 86).

According to reactance theory (J. Brehm, 1966; S. S. Brehm, 1981), having choice eliminated in a situation in which one formerly had choice produces a motivational state called "reactance," which is aimed at restoring one's freedom to choose. As Bettelheim explains, when we pressure a child a certain direction, "It doesn't necessarily mean that the influence will be in the direction you want it to be, because... certain forces evoke counterforces" (1962, p. 145). Reactance is manifest in several ways, including lack of compliance, downward reevaluation of the alternatives, and hostility toward the freedom-eliminating agent. Often, when we feel that others are trying to impose their preferences on us, we react by sticking to our preferences even more than we would if those others hadn't tried to impose their preferences on us. Although the results are not always clear-cut, reactance has been experimentally demonstrated with children (e.g., Hammock & Brehm, 1966; Brehm, 1981) as well as with adults. Children with a choice between two candy bars who were eventually given one of these without being asked for their preference enhanced the attractiveness of the eliminated choice and evidenced some minor devaluation of the attractiveness of the one they got (Hammock & Brehm, 1966).

In line with this, children appear to react to loss of choice. As noted by the mother of a 4-year-old: "If it's *his* idea to have his bath, he does. If it's our idea, he doesn't" (Newson & Newson, 1968, p. 84). Similarly, the mother of a 7-year-old remarks: "If I get clothes for her or I choose something, *invariably*, what I like, she says, "Oh, I don't like that!" (Newson & Newson, 1976, p. 296). In such cases, it is often parents who back down rather than the child. A mother interviewed by Newson and Newson (1968) explains that in her efforts to get her child to pick up his toys, if she got down on her knees and picked up some, "then he'll start and do it willingly" (p. 83). Hence, when the child perceives the activity as one that he can choose to enact, he freely engages in it.

Research with adults has similarly shown that adults who can choose which puzzles to complete evidenced enhanced performance relative to individuals who were assigned puzzles to complete (Zuckerman, Porac, Lathin, Smith, & Deci, 1978). These findings echo deCharms's (1968) argument that

> when a man perceives his behavior as stemming from his own choice he will cherish that behavior and its results; when he perceives his behavior as stemming from the dictates of external forces, that behavior and its results... will be devalued. (deCharms, 1968, p. 273)

[33] Hebrew: "Ani roçe livxor xulça ki ani lo ohev at haxulça haze"

[34] French: "Pake envie moi"

It is not actual choice but perceptions of choice that are viewed as beneficial.

As Iyengar and Lepper (2002) have argued, though, this view of choice may be ingrained in cultures that see the self as independent and in which the expression of personal preferences is valued because choosing is a manifestation of independence. In interdependent cultures, on the other hand, choice is viewed less as a means of expressing one's personal preferences and more as a means of enhancing one's integration in the group and fulfilling one's social responsibilities. In such interdependent cultures, personal preferences may be set aside when they conflict with those of the cultural group. In fact, because it avoids the need to deal with such potential conflict, the restriction of personal choice may be beneficial to individuals in interdependent cultures. In line with these ideas, Iyengar and Lepper (1999) found that whereas performance on freely chosen anagrams did not differ between European children and Asian American children, Asian American children performed better when they were assigned the anagrams by their mothers; European American children performed worse under these circumstances. A similar pattern was evident on a computer math game when the assignment was based on presumed peer-group consensus.

However, choice can prove to be psychologically detrimental. When the range of alternatives is large and the differences between options are relatively small, choice is debilitating and individuals may refrain from choosing. Iyengar and Lepper (2000) found that potential customers who were exposed to a tasting booth with twenty-four versus six jams were more likely to approach the display with more choice but eventually bought less jam. In a similar study with chocolate, having greater choice was perceived as more enjoyable but eventuated in greater regret. The important issue here is that making choices is interpreted both by children and by others as reflecting underlying preferences that guide those choices, suggesting a stability of preferences beyond the specific time and place in which the choices are expressed, an issue that I discuss further in Chapter 3 on meta-preferences.

3 Emerging Meta-Preferences

At 35;13, Karen explains why she needs her Panda bear in her bed at night: 'Daddy you know maybe you put Panda in my bed so my pacifier won't fall – because I don't like to sleep without my pacifier.'

(Karniol, Diary)

Orren at 3;3;20 years accounts for his friendship with a boy, saying: 'I like Omri in my daycare so Omri is my best friend.'

(Karniol, Diary)

With repeated experience with offers, rejection of offers, expression of preferences, and experience with having such preferences satisfied, deferred, and rejected, children acquire an encyclopedic knowledge of their preferential world. They attempt to organize this preferential world in terms of valence: liking versus disliking, and in terms of context: cross-situational versus situation-specific. That is, they encode their preferences in terms of their stability or change across time and context. The lyrics of Cole Porter's timeless song 'I love Paris': "I love Paris in the springtime, I love Paris in the fall . . . ", capture such attempted codification of one's preferential world, the topic of this chapter.

AWARENESS OF CHANGING PREFERENCES

Some preferences are not stable. Preference instability can reflect temporary changes in hunger and interest. Food preferences may change with the degree of one's hunger; toy preferences may change in the context of playing with a toy. The instability of preferences can also reflect developmental change as children outgrow certain toys and activities. At 32:4, Orren shouts at me angrily, "Why do you give me milk in a bottle – I'm big already."[1] In the same vein, Karen, at 33;4, says to me, "Big girls don't play with such toys; I'll put those here for you 'cause I can't play with those anymore. If you want to play with those you have to move them." Both children are evidencing awareness of the appropriateness of activities relative to one's age, but, more important, they are indicating that their own preferences are changing as a consequence.

[1] Hebrew; "Lama at notenet li xalav bebakbuk – ani gadol kvar"

As I discussed in the introduction, taste also changes; we acquire taste for different foods, music, and clothes, often as a consequence of exposure to them. Building on such anticipated changes, children start to talk about their future preferences, as evident when, at 31;13, Orren says, "Tomorrow Mummy will buy me a big fat bed like Karen's, and I will sleep there without a diaper and without a pacifier. Now I need a pacifier"[2] (Karniol, 1992, p. 268). Children may, or may not, be aware of the changes in their preferences, both in the short term and in the long term. Parents need to be aware of such instability because it may entail changes in the food, objects, and activities they offer children (e.g., "Do you wann to play with David today?" Schachter, 1979, p. 195).

Children first become aware of their changing preferences in the context of food as their willingness to eat different foods at different times becomes apparent to them. When a 21-month-old asks for a cookie, her mother replies, "A biscuit. I gave you one and you didn't want it" (French & Woll, 1981, p. 165). Karen contrasts her past and present preferences at 26;10, saying, "When Izzy and Mummy and Daddy were eating Karen didn't want to eat. Now she wants to eat." In the same vein, Shatz et al. (1983) recorded a child, at 35 months, saying, "I thought I will eat my cinnamon toast first. 'Cept I decided I will eat my banana first" (as cited in Wellman, 1988, p. 81). When a child of six and a half asks for tea, her father says, "I thought you wanted some chocolate milk" (Nevat-Gal, 2002, p. 185). Such statements reflect children's realization that their food preferences are relatively unstable over short time spans.

If one knows that one's desire for food can change over short time spans, one can plan for such changes. Table 3.1 provides examples of children talking of "saving" food for later.

In the above, children are evidencing understanding of their current preferences as possibly being different than their future preferences and are planning for such changes.

[2] Hebrew: "Ima maxar yikne li mita gdola shamen kmo shel Karen veani eshan im ze bli xitul vebli moçeçi. Axhav ani çarix moçeçi"

Table 3.1.

	Age	Source
M tells K to eat her fruit now K: "I'll leave this here till I get hungry"	30;27	Karniol (Diary, Karen)
Leaving the house K: "I want some cheese"; gets cheese K: "I will eat it when I get hungry" Later, in the car, K eats cheese K: "On the way there, I got hungry"	32;15	Karniol (Diary, Karen)
C puts milk cup in fridge C: "I'm gonna save this for dinner time to drink, I'm gonna save this for dinner time for drinking"	35 mos.	Braunwald (1985, p. 524)
M picks up child from preschool, comments on sandwich not being eaten M: "he doesn't eat a thing at school" C: "I'm saving my sandwich to eat on the way home"	Preschool	Tobin (1989, p. 135)
Playing pretend C1 as mother, says she finished drinking C2 as mother C: "No, no you shouldn't drink it. You should leave it in until we get to the park"	Preschool	Cook-Gumperz (1995, p. 415)
C: "This time I'm going to save them until we go home" Sibling queries whether all the lunch C: "My dessert, that's all"	5;7 years	MacWhinney (CHILDES)

In the children's statements above, relatively short time spans were involved. Children can also plan for changes over longer time spans. At 2;7;11, after Karen comes home with a bag of candy that she got at a birthday party she says, "All this bag Karen will leave for tomorrow,"[3] recognizing that she is currently satiated in terms of sweets. When preschoolers were asked why they were packing food and drink for a picnic, they often explained that: "When I'm thirsty I will drink it" and "Because I'm gonna be hungry" (Atance & O'Neill, 2005), also evidencing incipient understanding of their future preferences.

Awareness of the instability of their food preferences allows children to hedge their statements. When she is asked what she wants for supper, Karen, at 3;0;16, says, "I will probably eat a sunny-side-up egg." Presumably, if the parent prepares the egg and it is not eaten, having hedged serves as protection against parental anger. In another instance of hedging, a 35-month-old starts eating a second egg and says, "I don't think so." When she is queried as to what she means, she says, "I don't think so need any more egg" (Braunwald, 1985, p. 518). Perner (1991) relates a humorous anecdote in which his 4-year-old daughter asks for peas and subsequently refuses them, saying, "I don't want them. I changed my mind when you didn't look" (p. 225).

As Dr. Seuss (1960) so cleverly showed in his book *Green Eggs and Ham*, awareness of the instability of preferences can emerge in retrospect, when children engage in an activity or eat a food they had resisted and discover that their preferences were different than they originally thought. As well, a child may be cajoled into eating or drinking when he thinks he is neither hungry nor thirsty and find that he was in fact hungry or thirsty. Allison, at 34 months, was told "I think you oughta drink that juice"; she whines "I don't want it," pushing her mother's hand away. Later, as she is drinking the juice, she says "I wanted it" (Bloom, 1970).

Many conflicts between children and parents arise because parents tend to assume stability in children's preferences. Consequently, they note instability of children's preferences, for example, referring to a sports team, a surprised mother asks, "Why do you not like the Ducks all of a sudden?" (Kremer-Sedlik, & Kim, 2007). In the food domain in particular, adults tend to assume that if a child ate something in the past, he or she would continue eating it in the future. This is evident when an Italian mother complains to her son, "But I can't understand Sergio. Once you liked Mozzarella any type of cheese. Now Stracchino you don't like Rubiola you don't like" (Ochs, Pontecorvo, & Fasulo, 1996, p. 31). Similarly, when her grandmother complains about Karen's refusal to eat something she used to eat, saying "You liked it always," Karen, at 28;16, answers her, "I liked it someways" – meaning sometimes. A typical interchange starts with a child saying, "Do not want the turkey." After the mother replies, "You like turkey! I made it special," the grandmother adds, "She made it just for you" (Fiese, Foley, & Spagnola, 2006, p. 72). In discussing such instability, a French Canadian mother complains, "but you ate it three weeks ago or a month ago and now you tell me that you don't like it" (Marquis & Claveau,

[3] Hebrew: "Kol haze sakit Karen tash-ir lemaxar"

Table 3.2.

	Age	Source
C1 wants to play with toy C2: "No, because we're bored with it. . . . We played with it a little while ago"	Preschool	Georgalidou (2008, p. 84)
C to parent C: "We don't want to read any more"[4]	4;4 years	Taeschner (1983)
To C2 C: "Let's put these away. I don't wanna play with them no more"	5 years	Hall (CHILDES)
To C2 C: "I'm getting bored. Let's go someplace else"	5 years	Pitcher & Schultz (1983, p. 66)

2005, p. 257). Children are often annoyed when parents assume their preferences are stable over time. When he was 10 years old, Orren was served sliced veal for dinner and shouted, "You always do this to me. Just because one time I said I liked it, doesn't mean I want to eat it all the time now!" Similarly, a child of 5;10 years complains: "Because you make spaghetti all the time I always stick out my tongue at lunchtime" (Schönenberger, 2001, p. 97).

The instability of preferences extends beyond the food domain. Having had one specific teddy bear, a panda bear, with her in her bed for several months when sleeping, Karen, at 35;9, announced vehemently, "I don't want to hold Panda at night – I'm sick of it!"[5] In a similar fashion, referring to a collection of Matchbox-type toy cars with which he played all the time, Orren, at 35;16, put aside a whole bunch of such little cars, saying, "I decided that I don't want them and that's it!"[6] Stevenson (1954) cites a 4-year-old who, referring to his blanket, announced, "I think I'm too big for Cloak and I'm not going to suck any more" (p. 206). Being sick of things is also evident when a college student explains when she goes shopping: "When I open the closet and I'm like 'Oh, I have nothing to wear.' Then I'll go to the mall and I'll buy something. So when I get sick of my old clothes, basically" (Haytko & Baker, 2004, p. 72).

Changing preferences are also integral to preschoolers' friendship choices, with the cry, "We don't like you today" and "You're not my friend today" being bandied often (e.g., Garvey, 1984; Meyer, 2003). An adult who wants to know why children are not playing with a peer asks, "Why not? You guys played with her yesterday," and a girl of 3;7 years answers, "Well, we hate her today" (Corsaro, 1985, p. 125). A preschooler asks a peer, "Why do you like her? I remember when you used to hate her" (Kyratzis & Green, 1997, p. 25). The capricious nature of such changing alliances is evident when a child of 3;5 years says to a child of 3;9 years, "We don't like you," and the disliked child exclaims, "You were my friend a minute ago" (Corsaro, 1985, pp. 131–132).

[4] German: "Jetzt woller wir nicht mehr lessen"
[5] Hebrew: "Anni lo roça lehaxzik at panda balaila – nimas li!"
[6] Hebrew: "Ani hixlateti she ani lo roçe otam vezehu!"

Temporary changes in preferences are also evident in toy play and underlie children's discontinuing activities they are currently engaged in. Although younger children do not explicitly state they are bored with a given toy or game, older ones may say so explicitly, as illustrated in Table 3.2.

Children's attention shifts with respect to toys is often a topic of parental complaint, lamenting that children request the purchase of a toy and after playing with it for a short period of time, it is forgotten. Regarding her son's habit of collecting things, a mother bemoans, "He's very full of enthusiasm for a thing to start with, but I'm afraid it sort of peters out – you know, it doesn't last very long" (Newson & Newson, 1976, p. 125). Children themselves acknowledge this pattern; an 11-year-old recounts, "My mum's friend bought it . . . . It was only fun for a couple of seconds" (Brusdal, 2007, p. 394).

In this light, parents often query children as to their ongoing preferences, as if suggesting that their current preferences may have changed. For instance, when Jeff, at 21 months, finishes playing with a puzzle, his mother asks him, "Wan(t) ta do it again? You wanna do it again?" (Warren, CHILDES), perhaps implying to the child that he may *not* want to do it again. This implication may even be stated more boldly. The mother of child of 34 months asks, "Are you going to come and play or do you want to play with something different . . . . do you want to play with something different?" (Manchester Corpus, CHILDES). Parents may even suggest to children that their preferences are supposed to change over short time spans. The mother of a child of 28 months asks her, "Wan ta play with the barn for a while . . . . Are you tired of playing with this? Let's go over there" (Warren, CHILDES). In this vein, the mother of a 25-month-old who has been playing with a boy doll asks her, "You're tired of him? All right, let's put him down," and suggests they look to see what other toys there are in the playroom (Bernstein, CHILDES). It may well be that parents are encouraging children to shift their preferences rather than responding to children's shifting preferences.

On the other hand, Hart and Risley (1995) noted a parent who, after the child started to throw cards, asked, "Are you tired of playing this? Shall we stop playing?" (p. 58). This suggests that parents recommend attentional shifts when they think the child is no longer attentive in interacting with a given toy. Alternatively, parents may suggest a shift when they themselves are no longer interested in continuing the ongoing activity. As an example of the latter, after repeatedly blowing bubbles for her daughter, Bloom (1973) does so once again, saying "Last time.... Well, that's all. We're – we're not gonna play with it anymore. We're not gonna play with it anymore" (p. 171). Similarly, a teacher asks a child what he would like to sing, and when he answers, she says, "Oh, not again. We'll sing that again tomorrow" (Willes, 1983, p. 111). When a 2-year-old asks his mother to help him build a tower, she says, "I'm tired Jack.... I wanna do something else for a while" (Menyuk, Liebergott, & Schultz, 1995, p. 116).

In some contexts, parents explicitly explain to children that their preferences may change. A mother who had gone out of the room says to her child of 34;2 months on her return, "I thought you were playing with the bricks. Have you changed your mind now?" (Wells, 1985). Similarly, on being asked whether she wants an orange or a banana, Karen, at 32;28, says "A banana, no, I don't want any fruit." I then said, "I'm having an orange, do you want to change your mind?" She asked me why and after being told "Cause you can decide to have some," Karen answers, "Changed my mind." When a child of 13;2;4 refuses to eat something, the mother says, "You have a drink first, and then think about it," also implying that one can change one's mind (Snow, 1984). In other contexts, children may also be told that they need to think about their preferences. After a preschooler puts on a scarf, the teacher says, "Do you need that this morning? You think about it" (Gardner & Cass, 1965, p. 58). Presumably, by thinking about it, the child would change her mind. Such conversations alert children to the fact that both they, and others, can change their mind about their expressed preferences, and children do start to talk of having changed their minds. After announcing to an adult that he wants to do the cleaning up, a preschooler says, "I want you to do it. I just changed my mind" (Hall, CHILDES). As said so poignantly by a child of 26 months, "I can change my mind. You can change your other mind" (Thornton, 2002, p. 231).

Parental suggestions that one's preferences may change are not limited to the domain of toy play. MacWhinney documents an instance with his sons, at 7;6 and 5;7 years of age, who are discussing marriage while in the car with their father. When the older one says he's not going to get married, the father answers, "You're going to change your mind... you're going to.... he's going to change his mind, isn't he Mark?" When Mark answers that he's not going to get married either, the father says "You're going to find when you get older that you think girls are really cute.... you just wait and see" (MacWhinney, CHILDES). Such conversations alert children to the instability of preferences and legitimize changing one's mind about one's preferences.

But changing one's mind may have a cost because some choices are not reversible. For instance, after a child of 34;2 gave his sister most of his bricks and did not leave himself enough to build a bridge he wanted to build, his mother said, "You should have thought of that before you gave her all your bricks" (Manchester corpus, CHILDES). Children need to learn when changing one's preferences is possible and when it is not. One domain in which changing one's mind is of special importance is that of becoming a consumer. In pretend play, a 4-year-old goes back to the pretend store, saying "I bought some earrings and they hurt me, so can I have my dollar?" When her request is rejected, she retorts, "Well, that' what real stores do!" (Pitcher & Schultz, 1983, p. 45). Reality can sometimes allow one to change one's mind without a cost. In fact, it is interesting in this context that the idea of a full refund policy – which is common in many stores – is the epitome of acknowledging that individuals have changing preferences. Pampered consumers are sometimes surprised when they purchase something that cannot be returned for full refund. They are so used to being able to change their mind about their purchases that they take it for granted that changing one's mind is legitimate consumer behavior.

AWARENESS OF PREFERENCE STABILITY

The other side of the coin is that children start to realize that some of their preferences *are* stable. They start to use their past and current preferences to plan for the future and to predict their future preferences. Painter (1984) found that, by 18 months, her son named his favorite foods, using a different phonological form than he used for other foods, expressing what she understood as "gleeful anticipation of his favorite food" (p. 106). If one's preferences are stable, then one can anticipate that what one wants or likes at the present time will carry over into the near future. In line with this, before going to sleep, Emily, at 29 months, tells her father her preferences for breakfast the next morning, saying "I want... yogurt... and strawberries in my cereal" (Nelson, 1996, p. 238). In the midst of eating honey, a child of 29 months is asked by her mother whether she wants to go to the shop with her father. In response, she replies "I'll leave this honey here and leave the top off.... and I will come back and eat it then" (Wootton, 1997, p. 127). She anticipates having the same preference for the same food when she returns. In the non-food domain, at 3;1:7 years, Orren says, "I want to wear this shirt tomorrow,"[7] again reflecting anticipation that at least over the implied time frame, his preferences are stable.

As attribution theory predicts, children use the stability of their preferences over time to draw inferences about their dispositional attitudes toward the objects in question. They start to refer to liking and disliking of objects or activities with which they have had repeated experiences.

[7] Hebrew: "Ani roçe lilbosh at haxulça hazot maxar"

Table 3.3.

	Age	Source
Dislike of Food/Objects		
K: "Don't like it this magazine"	19:7	Karniol (Diary, Karen)
C is eating, spits it out C: "Don't like it. Put it in rubbish"	23;27	Painter (1984, p. 246)
C: "I want breakfast" M: "Do you want some of this roll?" C: "No...... Don't like it"	27 mos.	Sachs (1983, p. 15)
C: "I don't like medsin"	28 mos.	DeVilliers (1984, p. 200)
C: "I don't like those books"	32 mos.	Toivainen (1980, p. 122)
Dislike of Actions		
C wants to stop riding C: "No ride, no like"	22 mos.	Bruner, Roy, & Ratner (1982)
C: "I don't like go in dat playground" C: "I don't like go to sleep"	28 mos.	DeVilliers (1984, p. 200)
Dislike of Others' Actions		
C: "I don't like Daddy putting my socks on" C: "I don't like Hanneke come in my house" C: "I don't like you cut my hair"	28 mos.	DeVilliers (1984, p. 200)
F accidentally gets soap in K's mouth while bathing K: "Don't do that again – 'cause I don't like it"[8]	34;9	Karniol (Diary, Karen)
Hair dryer is making noise C: "I don't like da hairdryer"	3 years	Peters (2000, p. 147)
F is coloring C: "I don't like you ta use this kinda paint"	3;10 years	Peters (2000, p. 140)

They also start to justify their choices with reference to liking and disliking. One of the interesting questions in this context is whether references to disliking precede references to liking or vice versa? This is an important issue to resolve, because, as Mandler contends, "disliking is a complex judgment, often based on the absence of a liking response" (Mandler et al., 1987, p. 647). This accords well with the finding (e.g., Herr & Page, 2004) that liking judgments are made faster than disliking judgments. The suggestion has been made that liking judgments are made spontaneously when one is instructed to evaluate disliking, and evaluation of liking seems to occur at the point of one's initial encounter with an object. Herr and Page suggest that there is a positivity bias – that is, people assume regarding most objects they encounter that they will like them. Consequently, disliking is what needs to be marked, leading one to expect that statements regarding disliking will precede those about liking.

The interesting second question is whether there a sequence in children's indicating of liking and disliking of objects versus actions? If, in fact, evaluations of objects occur as one encounters them, then one would expect children to indicate liking and disliking for objects prior to doing so for activities because engaging in activities is a process that occurs over time, is more subject to interpretation, and is likely to be context-bound (e.g., I like to take walks in the sunshine but not in the rain). The available data in naturalistic studies of child language do not allow us to draw clear-cut conclusions with respect to either of these questions.

Yet very young children do make their dislikes explicit, as shown in Table 3.3.

As evident in this table, children refer to their dislike of certain foods and objects, of certain activities, and importantly, their dislike of other people's actions both toward them and in general. But in addition, these expressions of dislike served to indicate what they didn't want to have, didn't want to do, or did not want others to do.

References to liking appear to precede or co-emerge with those to disliking, and they appear to occur primarily with regard to objects rather than actions, as evident in Table 3.4.

The issue of the sequence of references to liking and disliking as well as their application to objects versus actions is particularly interesting in bilingual children. Specifically, an important issue here is whether references to disliking precede or are concurrent with references to liking. According to prospect theory (Tversky & Kahneman, 1979), there is a psychological asymmetry between potential gains versus potential losses, with this asymmetry implying that it is more important to avoid disliked objects and activities than to attain positive ones. Explicating one's negative preferences, then, is concerned with preventing whereas explicating one's positive preferences is

[8] Hebrew: "Al taase kaxa od paam she-ani lo ohevet"

Table 3.4.

	Age	Source
Referring to food		
K: "More – I like it"	19;2	
K: "Karen like this kitty"	19;7	Karniol (Diary, Karen)
C: "Like-it bread"	19;26	
C: "Like music"	20;07	Tomasello (1992)
C: "Like that. Like that song"	22;17	Scollon (1979).
Older sib offers C1 pencil during pretend dinner		
C1: "Yum yum. I like it. I like it"	24 mos.	Dunn (1988, p. 121)

concerned with attaining, and in this light, one would expect them to emerge earlier. If the emergence of references to liking and disliking are sequential, though, one would expect the same order to emerge in both of the bilingual child's two languages. Otherwise, such references should emerge randomly. As well, if children learn to refer to likes and dislikes regarding objects prior to activities rather than vice versa or simultaneously, such a sequence should be evident in both of their languages. Although this issue has not been addressed empirically, in studies with bilingual children, references to disliking do appear to emerge prior to references to liking. A girl indicates disliking at 30 months, saying, "I don't like that one"[9]; but references to liking in this same girl do not appear until 34 months, when she says, "I really like frogs"[10] (Schlyter, 2003, pp. 25–26). Orren, who was raised bilingual in English and Hebrew, referred to his disliking, and in particular in rejecting food items, prior to referring to liking and prior to indicating liking of activities. This was the case in both of his languages. For instance, he rejects food offered to him at 23;18, in English, saying "Don't like it," and using a different sentence construction, again, rejects food at 24;9 and 24;16, saying, "Orren no like it (name of food)" and "Orren no like it this." Extending this beyond foods, at 25;22, he says, "Orren no like it the bump," after hurting his head and getting a bump on it. In Hebrew, as well, references to his dislikes emerge prior to references to his likes, and again, in the context of food preferences but not action preferences. At 24;16, he says "Orren doesn't like this"[11] incorrectly, and at 24;28, he says it correctly. His first mention of liking occurs a few days later, also in the context of food preferences, when at 24;25, he says, "Orren like it this." Within days, this construction was extended to clothes, as when he says at 24;27, "This pajama jafa (pretty), Orren like it this pajama," and at 25 months, "Orren like sweater this" and "Orren like this gufia (undershirt) clean," in each instance, liking being used as justification for wanting to wear or to buy a specified item of clothing. Expressions of liking were gradually extended beyond food and clothes, but stayed within the domains of objects rather than activities, as when, at 26;13, he says "Orren like it this playground," and at 27;4, when he says, "I like this magic markers."[12] Note that whereas the child does not say this explicitly, in both of these latter instances, liking is a justification for continued action – in the one instance, for continuing to play in the playground and in the second, for continuing a drawing activity. It may well be, though, that references to liking and disliking of objects rather than to activities are expressed because they are grammatically easier and avoid use of verbs and infinitives.

It is interesting that children extend their expressions of liking and disliking beyond objects, to indicate liking and disliking other people, often in contexts in which these others are not present. At 20;16, Karen says, "Don't like him," referring to a boy in her daycare. Orren, at 25;11, affirms his liking for an adult when he says "Orren like it this man," but at 3;3;24 years, he refers to a movie character when he says, "I no like Captain Hook.... I don't like him" (Karniol, 1992, p. 273). In contrast to contexts in which children referred to shifting dislikes of others as discussed before, children also tell others directly of their dislike for them in terms that imply stable preferences. Children unabashedly tell others of disliking them, saying things like: "I hate you Joyce," said by a kindergartner to a peer (Merritt, 1982, p. 238), "Get out of here. I don't like you," said by a 4-year-old to a peer (Pitcher & Schultz, 1983, p. 51), and "I don't like you, go away," said by a child of 7;2 years to a peer (Sluckin, 1981, p. 46). Yet even such expressions may index temporary rather than stable dislikes, as often experienced by parents in the context of disciplinary encounters. For instance, a mother tries to get child into bed, threatening and slapping her to make her obey, saying, "Karen do as you – (slaps her), put your legs down or I'm going outside right this minute without a kiss now put your legs down," the child refuses and mother continues, "Now give a kiss good night" and child answers, "I'm not"; mother asks, "You're not gonna kiss me? Why?" And the child answers, "Cause I don't like you" (Hasan & Cloran, 1990, p. 92).

[9] French: "N'aime pas celle-la"
[10] French: "J'aime bien grenouilles"
[11] Hebrew: ""Orren lo ohev ze"..... Orren lo ohev at ze"
[12] Hebrew: "Ani ohev at ze tushim"

Table 3.5.

	Age	Source
K: "Grandma has beautiful boots"	21;3	Karniol (Diary, Karen)
C to parents C: "I don't like Cynthia's drawing"[13]	32 mos.	Wijnen & Veriips (1998, p. 251)
O sees a new shirt on me O: "I really like the shirt you are wearing"[14]	34;29	Karniol (Diary, Orren)
C to peer C: "Bruce, you have a nice horse on your sweatshirt"	3 years	Pitcher & Schultz (1983, p. 64)
C to peer C: "You have a nice pin on"	4 years	Pitcher & Schultz (1983, p. 64)
C to peer C: "Your dress is pretty – so is your blouse"	4;2 years	Slama-Cazacu (1977, p. 651)
C1 discussing third child with C2 C1: "I **hate** those pants! They're **ugly**!!"	Fifth grade	Goodwin (2006, p. 207)

Children also comment about liking and disliking other people's clothes and possessions, as shown in Table 3.5.

Children's statements about their likes and dislikes may well be accepted by adults at face value – "preferences need no inferences" (Zajonc, 1984). In other instances, children may be urged to justify their liking and disliking. A child of 25 months who indicates she doesn't like the grapes she was offered is queried, "What is it about them you don't like?" (Wootton, 2007, p. 182). Asked why he is changing a doll's clothes, a child of 27;12 answers, "Because the coat isn't pretty"[15] (Dubost, 1999). When a family is being hosted at dinnertime and the guest preschool child announces he does not want mushrooms, his father says, "Michael doesn't care for mushrooms Rosa.... How can you not like mushrooms – you silly boys?" The child answers, "Cause they don't taste good to us huh?" and the host child answers, "Yeah." (Speier, 1972, p. 413). The need to justify one's preferences becomes even more pronounced with age, with constant questioning of one's preferences by others requiring more comparative work. When a child of 7;6 years is discussing his dislike of apple juice with his dad, he says "It's not like milk and water and orange juice... I just don't like the taste" (MacWhinney, CHILDES).

Children thus learn to provide justifications for their likes and dislikes. One dislikes a food because it doesn't taste good (e.g., Simone, at 25 months, says, "Doesn't taste good to me,"[16] Miller, 1979), dislikes a shirt because it doesn't suit him (e.g., Orren, at 32;11, says "This shirt doesn't suit me"[17]), and dislikes the story of Little Red Riding Hood because "He eats the grandma" (said by a child of 6;2) Applebee, 1978). One may like a shirt because it is nice looking (said by Orren at 25;14) and like a certain book "because they catch the thieves"[18] at the end of the book (said by Orren at 35;28), or because "they get the money and the gold" (said by a child of 6;2 years about Hansel and Gretel, Applebee, 1978). Children may also justify why they don't like someone, as when a 10-year-old girl says "I don't like Freddie (an 11-year-old boy) cuz Freddie say he gonna kiss me" (Goodwin, 1990, p. 154). Younger children indicate their dislike of other children, saying they are mean, bossy, or won't share.

GENERALIZED PREFERENCES

Children also start to comment on themselves as agents with generalized likes and dislikes that transcend specific situations, doing so in contexts in which the object of preference may not be present. The first such references are generalized preferences for foods, as shown in Table 3.6.

In these statements, it is evident that children have coded within the food category those items they like or dislike, and they use their liking as justifications for asking for more of those foods they like and to reject those foods they do not like, sometimes explicitly contrasting their likes and dislikes. In fact, Wesslén, Sepp, and Fjellström (2002) found that preschool children who were asked as to their dislikes often referred to both their likes and dislikes at the same time (e.g., "I don't like meatballs and macaroni, just meatballs and gravy. I like other macaronis" (p. 267)).

Such statements appear to be used to indicate generalized preferences in the context of nonfoods as well. A child of 27 months justifies using purple, saying "I do like to use purple" (Radford, 1990, p. 288). A preschool teacher suggests to a 3-year-old that she color some water and asks her to choose a color. When asked what color she is

[13] Dutch: "Ik vin Cynthia niet tekening leuk

[14] Hebrew: "Ani meod ohev at haxulça she-at loveshet"

[15] French: "pake (parce que) le manteau est pas joli"

[16] German: "mir schmeckt nicht"

[17] Hebrew: "Haxulça hazot lo matima li"

[18] Hebrew: "Ki hem tofsim at haganavim"

Table 3.6.

	Age	Source
Liking		
C refers to self		
C: "Travis love a da peanut butter sandwich"	20;08	Tomasello (1992)
K is eating cherries		
K: "Karen likes cherries very much"	20:18	Karniol (Diary, Karen)
In presleep monologue, referring to self		
C: "Emmy like cornbread and toast. I don't like (?) apples . . . Food I like and muffins too. I don't like anything . . . . 'cept for that, that bread Daddy has . . . ."	22 mos.	Nelson (1986, p. 237)
At dinnertime		
C: "Give me the fish. I love fish"	Toddler	Aukrust (2002, p. 61)
Reminiscing about Christmas at Grandpa's farm		
C: "I love chocolate"		
M: "You love chocolate? Did you have chocolate at Grandpa's house? Yes"	3;8 years	McCabe & Peterson (1991, p. 237)
At dinnertime		
C: "I think a little bit more lettuce 'cause I love the lettuce and the blue vein Mum"	Preschool	Hasan & Cloran (1990, p. 91)
At dinnertime		
C: "I'm a pasta lover"		
M: "You like pasta, huh?"	6 years	Ochs, Pontecorvo, & Fasulo (1996, p. 25)
Disliking		
M is eating celery, C refuses to eat it		
C refers to self		
C: "No like celery, Mommy. Kathryn no like celery"	22 mos.	Bloom (1970)
M offers O food, O rejects it		
O: "Orren no like it shamenet (sour cream)"		
O: "Orren no like it tuna"	24;11	Karniol (Diary, Orren)
C has tea placed in front of him		
"This is mine because I don't have no sugar in mine because I don't like sugar in it"	3 years	Hart & Risley (1999, p. 66)
Preschool visit to supermarket		
C: "I don't like that kind a food"	Preschool	Dore (1978)
O is offered cucumbers and tomatoes		
O: "I don't like cucumbers – don't buy them for me any more – only tomatoes"[19]	32;29	Karniol (Diary, Orren)
At dinnertime, C is told to eat green beans		
C refuses		
C: "I just don't like them. That's why"	6 years	Vuchinich (1990, p. 124)

choosing, she answers, "I'm going to make it red – I like red" (Tough, 1973, p. 80). Referring to miniature cars, at 35;28, Orren says to me, "Buy (me) a green car – I really like green."[20]

Contrasts between what the child likes and dislikes are evident in the context of nonfoods as well, as when Karen remarks at 31;11, "If there is rain I don't like to go to day-care – only if there isn't I like."[21] Similarly, Emily, in her presleep monologue at 25;8, refers to the tape recorder, saying, "I like it in my room when I go to bed but not for my nap" (Levy, 1989). Comparative evaluations of this sort finally engender outright comparisons, as when at 23 months, Travis says "this one I like better" (Tomasello, 1992) or when a child of 4;11 years is pretend grocery shopping and says, "Robiola is a cheese, a much gooder cheese"[22] (Taeschner, 1983, p. 178).

Liking one thing better than another implies that one can have favorites. A child of 4;10 says in reaction to

[19] Hebrew: "Ani lo ohev melafefonim – yoter al tikni li – rak agvania"
[20] Hebrew: "Tikni auto yarok – ani meod ohev yarok"
[21] Hebrew: "Im yesh geshem anni lo ohevet lalexet lamaon – rak im enn ani ohevet"

[22] German: "Robiola ist ein Kase, ein Kase viel gutter"

getting a pretend birthday present, "Oh my favorite thing. I've been wanting all year long!" (Andersen, 1990, p. 105). In the same context, a child of 6;6 years says, "Oh! Everything I wanted! I got a play helicopter. And I even got one of my favorite things! ... an ambulance that really works!" (Andersen, 1990, p. 106). In a narrative, an 8-year-old girl tells of her brother breaking a doll, saying, "He broke one of my best, my very best doll, my Raggedy Ann, she was my favorite. I got another one. I love Raggedy Ann dolls." (Peterson & McCabe, 1983, p. 234).

Although one could question whether the above statements refer to generalized preferences as opposed to specific and occurrent preferences, the contexts in which each of the above statements were said suggest that the children expressing the sentiment were making generalizations regarding their preferences. In fact, children sometimes make explicit statements, phrasing them in the grammatical forms that indicate that they have generalized preferences. For instance, Tomasello (1992) recorded Travis, at 22 months, saying "I love to play with puzzles," and at 24;28, saying, "I love to eat pretzels." A toddler exclaims, "I love chocolate frosting!" (Budwig, 1990, p. 139). There is also no doubt as to what children mean when they refer explicitly to their favorites. A 3-year-old says, "Red is my favorite color," and her teacher answers, "I do notice you paint a lot of red pictures" (Paley, 1986, p. 6). A 3-year-old is playing with a peer and suggests that they take the doll to the beauty shop and color her hair purple. When his friend asks, in surprise, "Purple?" he responds, "Purple is my favorite color" (Segal & Adcock, 1981, p. 95).

Children also spontaneously indicate their generalized likes and dislikes during storybook reading and in narratives. A child of 26 months looks at a picture book about pancakes that features eggs and says, "I love eggs" (Lanza, 1997). When a preschooler and his mother are reading a book in which wasps come into town, he offers, "I don't like wasps... because they sting me... I don't like them" (Wells, 1986, p. 153). As for narratives, a child is talking of his seventh birthday, and says of a duck with wheels "I wanted that so bad, I liked it so much. And then, Mom and Pa got me that for my birthday" (Peterson & McCabe, 1983, p. 204).

Generalized statements about preferences may emerge when script details are being filled in. When a 4-year-old is talking of grocery shopping, he says, "you can bring steak ribs. I love ribs" (Hudson, Shapiro, & Sosa, 1996, p. 996). Similar statements about generalized dislikes also emerge in the context of scripts, as when a child of 35 months says about eating lunch at preschool, "And you eat apples, and tuna fish, but tuna fish not for me," further elaborating that he doesn't like tuna fish, when queried by an adult (French and Nelson, 1985).

How do children make generalized statements about their preferences? To make such statements, children need to have abstracted a commonality of some sort between their expressed preferences in a given domain, observing how their preferences do or do not vary across time and context. This gives rise to the ability of children to make statements in terms of what they usually, or never, like. Moreover, as Byrne (1998) suggests, psychological verbs such as *like* and *hate* are used in characterizing relations; that is, they make generalization about the subject in relation to the object. They do not refer to a specific object but allude to an abstracted relationship of a given type of object in a stable relationship with the subject who expresses it. This is often stated in terms of temporal recurrence, for instance, with reference to foods (e.g., a child of 4;8 years who says, "I just like to eat cakes, so I always eat the whole thing"), to objects (e.g., a child of 50 months who says, "Well, usually I like things that have a pocket so I can carry things in the pocket"), and to activities (e.g., a 4-year-old child who says, "Or else we play Batman and Robin and that's the only thing we play 'cause we like it so much") (French & Nelson, 1985). Pointedly, a school child explains, "I don't like school. I never have and I never will" (Pollard, 1985, p. 78).

Children also become aware of their generalized preferences when they function as consumers (Ward, Wackman, & Wartella, 1977). They see objects that they like and dislike, they can compare them with one's they already have, and see patterns in their choices. Although I am not aware of such research with children, in a talk-aloud study (Haines, 1974), a female adult shopper referred to her generalized likes and dislikes (e.g., referring to a skirt, saying "drab looking but is the style I like" and "I don't like sleeveless things"), referred to her occurrent likes of specific items (e.g., "I like the print color.... I like the piping a lot"), and further implied liking and disliking by her choice of adjectives to describe both items and their attributes (e.g., too frilly looking, impractical, kind of attractive). Moreover, there were explicit comparisons to alternative items (e.g., "exact same style as the blue... very similar to the pink and blue... almost the exact same thing"), as well as comparisons to items owned (e.g., "that's just like the suit I have on, isn't it?.... I have a green dress suit at home").

The emergence of such generalized statements about preferences suggests that individuals attempt to organize their preferential world, thereby becoming aware of the fact that some of their preferences are stable across situations. Remarking on such stability, at 31;11, Karen is talking about her food preferences and says, "Some things I don't like to try. But that I would like to try." It is also clear that children organize their preferential world in terms of the valence of their preferences. This is how a child can indicate that he doesn't generally like to eat certain kinds of foods or engage in certain kinds of activities. A tomboy declares "I hate being a girl" (Blaise, 2005, p. 150), and when asked if she'd consider playing a boy in pretend, a preschooler rejected this possibility vehemently, saying, "Because I don't like boys. I don't want to be a boy" (ibid). An 8-year-old who was visiting with her parents, walked into my house and announced "Hi, I'm Sharon. I don't like avocado or ice cream." In a study on food preferences, a child explained not taking sprouts, saying, "Sprouts are green; not my favourite colour" (de Moura, 2007, p. 717). Similarly, after participating in a training session in which children were asked whether they like different fruits, a child shouted, "I do not like grapes! I do not like bananas" (Spivack & Shure, 1974, p. 33). Children can make such statements because they note the stability of their likes and dislikes over time and when one's dislikes are unique, these have to be noted.

The stability of one's preferences is taken to be an indication of one's essence, one's self. A 10-year-old boy is talking about books, saying, "I like mysteries.... I like Enid Blyton.... I like fiction most" (Wells, 1986, p. 182). Regarding school subjects, this same boy says, "I like nearly everything except Geography.... I like English.... I like the essays best of English" (ibid). A middle school girl explains about her shopping habits, saying: "I like Limited Too, and I love Bath and Body Works, and I love going to the Disney store. I just like looking at everything and all that stuff" (Haytko & Baker, 2004, p. 72). Montemayor and Eisen (1977) noted that references to liking and loving were prevalent in children's self-descriptions at all ages, with a 9-year-old including self-descriptions like "I LOVE! Sports.... I LOVE! Food.... I LOVE school" (p. 317). But dislikes can also characterize oneself, for example, a college student who says "I really don't like to shop that much," explaining that she doesn't do so unless absolute necessary (Haytko & Baker, 2004). Importantly, it is by noting the relative stability and instability of one's preferences over time that one can see oneself as an individual with generalized preferences (e.g., "We have a pizza place that we like, and we always get the same thing, every single time," Cotte, Ratneshiwar, & Mick, 2004, p. 339).

Such generalized preferences are seen as what remains constant about oneself in light of changes. A child who was asked how he knows that it's still always him, answered, "Cause I still like science, and I still like swimming. And I'd still be doing science." Queried, "So you still like the same things, so you know it's always you?" he answers, "Yeah" (Damon & Hart, 1988). Seeing consistency over time in one's preferences is critical for children's sense of self-continuity when major disruptions in their life occur – when they change countries or schools, or when parents divorce (e.g., Chandler et al., 2003). Parents may intuitively understand this. As one father says, he sees his role as

> to provide a safe environment, to provide a healthy environment, to give the child's life a sense of consistency, a sense that things are going to be here tomorrow just like they are today, that you're going to be here tomorrow just like you are today. (Palkovitz, 2002, p. 44)

To see themselves as individuals with stable preferences, children need to be able to view themselves as individuals with continuity from the past to the present, for example, a child of 35 months sees a pair of old shoes and says, "That was shoes for me when I tiny baby" (Braunwald, 1985, p. 523). Perceptions of self-continuity can be fostered by discussing past selves, in particular, when past selves are contrasted with current selves. As a 3-year-old is building a house for a toy figure, he asks, "Mommy, where's the gate I had before I was a little baby?" his mother answers, "We still have it. But you don't need it anymore because you're staying in your bed all night" (Wolf, 1990, p. 203). His behavior may have changed over time, he no longer leaves his bed at night, but he is still the same child who used to do so.

Self-continuity is also implicated when children have conversations about the likes and dislikes of their younger selves. For instance, a 4-year-old boy at preschool is talking about having soap suds in one's bath and says to a 3-year-old, "I thought of soapy when I was a baby; then I started to like it," and the 3-year-old answers, "You know what I thought when I was a baby.... I thought it was poison.... I didn't want to have any (soap) when I was a baby" (Gottman, 1986b, p. 160). Notice that, although in discussing their past selves these children are discussing how their current likes differ from their past likes (e.g., "When I was young I used to like but I don't like it now," said by a child of 7;3 years, Fletcher, CHILDES), there is perceived self-continuity from the past to the present.

On the other hand, as Karniol and Ross (1996) claim, major disruptions in one's life offer the opportunity to break with one's past (e.g., a 15-year-old says, "I'm not the angry Adrian I used to be," Frydenberg, 1997, p. 74). Immigrants are often torn between the need to preserve their old self and pursuing the new self that their cultural environment appears to demand (Timotijevic & Breakwell, 2000). In giving up addictions or debilitating habits, individuals must similarly break with their past life, often relapsing because the current context does not afford prompt or efficient preference satisfaction. To cite White (1990), breaking from addictions requires "a very major shift – something akin to a migration of identity, an act of intentionally leaving one's life behind in order to make a new life for oneself" (pp. 26–27).

DYADIC PREFERENCE TALK

Why does preference talk emerge so early? Parents are constantly attributing preferences to their children and questioning their children as to their preferences. Even prelinguistic infants are bombarded with questions about their preferences. A mother brings home a package of cookies, and as she sees her infant of 7 months looking at them she says, "Yes, they're your favorites, aren't they? (Lock, 1980, p. 57). The mother of an 11-month-old is sorting pears and says, "You like pears, don't you" (Hart & Risley, 1995, p. 79). Junefelt and Tulviste (1998) found that mothers in three cultures – Estonia, Sweden, and the United States – repeatedly probed children of all ages as to their likes and dislikes and requested ongoing evaluations of foods currently being eaten.

Such explicit questioning regarding food preferences is prevalent with older children as well. An American child of

Table 3.7.

	Age	Source
C: "Ga" M: "Yes, monkey" C: "Ga" M: "Yes, is that your favorite?"	12 mos.	Painter (1984)
C points to a picture in a book M: "That's a swing. You like swinging, don't you"	20:21	Howe (1981, p. 60)
F asks what Jeff picture shows J: "Horsey" F: "Do you like that horsey?" F again asks what picture shows J: "Monkey" F: "Do you like that monkey?"	21 mos.	Warren (CHILDES)
J plays with ball F: "Do you like that ball.... say you like that ball better don't cha?.... Say you like that ball better n anything don't you huh?"	21 mos.	Warren (CHILDES)

6;4 years was asked "How is your dinner?" a Swedish child of 5;2 years was asked, "Is it good?" and an Estonian child of 3;2 years was asked, "Is the carrot good? (Junefelt & Tulviste, 1998). When Mark was 5;7 years, his father asked, "Do you like that blueberry that you just ate Mark? .... Did you like the yogurt?" (MacWhinney, CHILDES). Nor are such questions restricted to conversations with one's parents. A grandfather asks his preschool grandchild, "You like string beans? .... You like gramma's chicken?" (Hall, CHILDES). When a preschooler announces to his teacher that he ate spinach last night, she asks, "Okay, did you like it?" (Hall, CHILDES).

As the above examples elucidate, parents may ask children as to their preferences in contexts in which having preferences may not even occur to the child. A child of 23;26 is playing with a dump truck and his mother asks, "Uhm, you like Friday mornings, don't you?" referring to the fact that garbage collection occurs on Fridays (Howe, 1981, p. 77). Similarly, the mother of a 20-month-old points to an ice cream in a picture book and asks, "You like that?" and the child answers, "I do like" (Uccelli, Hemphill, Pan, & Snow, 1999, p. 220). Reading a Sesame Street book, a mother points to Big Bird and asks her 25-month-old, "What's he eating? We ate that the other day and you loved it. Do you remember?" (Menyuk, Liebergott, & Schultz, 1995, p. 114).

Notice that the above examples occurred in the context of book reading, suggesting that parents are not just reading to the child but also engaging him by pointing out relevant likes and dislikes. Such questioning practices imply that evaluative and other criteria can be applied to a wider range of domains than the child may have thought. As well, such questioning practices may suggest to the child that one can compare different objects and activities as to the degree of liking of each activity and determine at least where the anchors of most, and least, favorite objects and activities are. Table 3.7 shows examples of parents asking their children as to their favorites, all during book reading.

In fact, in many parents' questioning practices it is clear that parents are implicitly encouraging comparisons, and when children do not spontaneously do so, parents ask for explicit comparisons. For instance, in talking to her 29-month-old about the routine involved in going to the park, the mother asks, "What do you like to do at the park?" When the child answers, "I like to play" and later clarifies, "Play on the slide...," the mother then asks, "They have a lot of slides, right? Which one's your favorite?" The question posed by the mother suggests to the child that when there is more than one type of object or activity, one should determine which one likes best. And the child answers her, "The bumpy one" (Hudson, 2004, p. 143). Similarly, a toddler is asked by her father, "What was fun about the zoo?" When the child answers that she liked the gorillas, her father asks, "What kind of gorillas did you like the best?" (Reese, Haden, & Fivush, 1996). A Japanese mother is talking of trains with her 4-year-old son, and she asks, "Then, Sho, what color train did (you) like best?"[23] and he answers, "Red" (Minami, 2002, p. 199). In the same vein, Ross at 4;3 years says, "I wish there was blue Jell-O". The father says, "That's nice. Is that your favorite color?" (Bartsch & Wellman, 1995, p. 71). There are many colors and one needs to have favorite. In fact, a kindergarten teacher suggests that one needs to use one's favorite colors for one's art work, suggesting that when making Valentines "If you do not like your color of paper.... Just let us know and we'll get you another" (Graue & Walsh, 1998, p. 171). In the context of picture book reading with her 25-month-old, a mother requests, "You show me which page you like the best," implying that children need to keep track of their preferences in such contexts as well (Bernstein, CHILDES). A Chinese mother

[23] Japanese: "Ja Sho jun wa nani iro no densha ga yokatta ka na?"

complains to her child of 3;10 years, saying, "You didn't tell Mom how fun the computer was.... you only said it was fun but you didn't say how fun it was and why you liked to play?" (Chang, 2003, p. 117). Children are similarly questioned as to what they don't like or what they like the least, as when a mother questions her 3-year-old son about the circus, asking "What part did you love the least?" (Wang & Spillane, 2003, p. 107).

In this vein, Japanese mothers have been found to ask children about their comparative likes and dislikes (e.g., "Rice balls are better (for lunch), aren't they?"[24] p. 224), often asking what object or characteristic they like the most (e.g., "What did (you) like best?"[25] Minami, 2002, p. 181, and "What color train did you like best," ibid, p. 199). After reading a book to her 4-year-old, the mother asks, "What did you find most interesting?" (Minami, 2002, p. 253). On the other hand, Wang and Spillane (2003) found that in both Korean and Chinese mothers, there is less questioning of children about their preferences in discussions of the past.

Preschool teachers and other adults who interact with children also pose questions regarding their preferences. A preschool teacher is reading a book about sweets and turns to a child, asking "What sorts of sweets do you like?" (Tizard & Hughes, 1984, p. 210). More pointedly, they also pose questions that imply the existence of favorites. In the context of discussing a picture that a child drew, a preschool teacher says, "Yeah, you really like red. Is that your favorite color?" (Applegate, 1980, p. 86). Back in a preschool class after an outing to the supermarket, the teacher asks, "What did you like best when we went to the store?" (Dore, 1978a, p. 437). After a sixth grade outing to the circus, the teacher asked the class to "think about what was your favorite act or favorite part of the circus." When in response to the above, a girl writes that she loved a certain act the best, because their act was "incredible"; because she "liked it," the teacher prompts her, saying "cause I liked them doesn't tell me why it was incredible" (Michaels, 1991, pp. 332–333). Moreover, having favorites is supposed to guide one's behavioral choices. Thus, in a kindergarten class, a teacher asks children to draw themselves, telling them that "If your favorite shorts are red, you can color red shorts" (Graue & Walsh, 1998, p. 169).

It seems, then, that not only are children expected to compare objects and activities in terms of their preferences, but they are also expected to be able to justify those preferences. Notice, though, that questions about what the child likes are often interspersed with statements about the adults' own liking or evaluation of the same object or activity. A child of 13 months is eating and her mother questions, "Love our egg? It's a good egg" (Carew, 1976, p. 92). Snow reports the following conversational exchange during book reading with a 29-month-old. The mother asks the child, "Do you like to eat cake? Do you?" and after the child answers "Eat it.... eat the cake," the mother continues, "Cakes are good to eat" (Snow, 1983, p. 53). During a meal, a Japanese mother comments, "That's good, you know" (Minami, 1997, p. 234). Yet Minami found that whereas Japanese mothers tended to ask their 4-year-olds to evaluate, American mothers tended to provide evaluations themselves, doing so significantly more than Japanese mothers.

In contrast, some parents claim that they do not need to ask their children regarding their preferences, their thoughts, or their feelings. In line with this, Newson and Newson (1976) found that mothers often report knowing what their children were thinking or feeling, for instance, "If something happened at school I can always tell (p. 263), and "I'll know what she's going to say – I can read her mind" (p. 265).

Often, then, parents do not question children as to their preferences but rather refer knowingly to their preferences, both preferences relating to food and ones referring to toys and events, as shown in Table 3.8.

Notice that the previous sentences are not phrased as questions but as a declarative statements; parents appear to have a working list of their children's preferences. This is evident when a mother who is participating in a study on multiple labels (Callanan & Sabbagh, 2004) asks her preschool child, "Do you know what kind of whale this is? It's a special kind of whale that you like" (p. 750). These examples illustrate that parents ask children as to their preferences in a manner that clearly indicates that they know their children's likes and preferences. Knowledge of such preferences extends beyond food and objects. When Mary (Warren, CHILDES) is 4;6 years, her mother asks her, "Sometimes when you get up in the morning really early and Daddy's still upstairs, what's your favorite thing to do?" The child answers, "Sneak up and scare him." Children also expect their mothers to know their preferences. Blum-Kulka (1997) recorded 4-year-old Daniel, sitting down to dinner, shouting "Me salad give me salad me salad!" When his mother asks him, "Oh you want salad Daniel?" he answers, "But with mushrooms. Yeah with mushrooms. With mushrooms. I like them! Remember?" (p. 43). In discussing his dislike of vegetables, a child of 4;5 years refers to himself, saying, "Mommy don't forget what Eric likes and what he don't like" (Gordon, 1976, p. 179).

At other times, it may well be parents who suggest to their children that they have generalized preferences. Hart and Risley (1999) cite a mother who tells her 36-month-old, "You like purple everything. Would you like your room painted purple?" (p. 101). When Mary (Warren, CHILDES) at 4;6 years is queried as to what she wants to drink, she answers that she wants apple juice. Her mother answers, "Always apple juice, right." Mary then says, "Not with pancakes, no way," to which the mother answers, "You like milk with your pancakes." The mother is the one who turns a child's simple, and perhaps context-bound, preference into a generalized one, using the term *always* and it is the child who corrects her, telling her what the exception is to her "always."

[24] Japanese: "onigiri no hoo ga ii ne?"
[25] Japanese: "nani ga ichiban suki data?'

Table 3.8.

	Age	Source
Food		
M is reading to child M: "Is that the telephone?" C: "Yeah" M: "Yeah, you like telephones"	12 mos.	Yont, Snow, & Vernon-Feagans (2003)
C asks for some soup M: "But you don't like tomato soup"	Toddler	deVilliers (1984, p. 210)
M and C looking at picture book See picture of pancakes M: "Can we have some tomorrow? . . . . I think those are your favorites" See picture of eggs M: "You don't like these kinds of eggs. You like scrambled eggs"	24 mos.	Bernstein (CHILDES)
M and C are counting strawberries on a page M: "Strawberries are your favorite" [26]	5 years	Minami (2002, p. 248)
Nonfood		
F and C are playing F: "Say we shouda got your helicopter, you like helicopters"	21 mos.	Warren (CHILDES)
M tells C of plans for day M: "You and Robby can play in the sandbox the way you love to. Yeah, and maybe we will bring your favorite truck . . . . That's going to be fun"	Toddler	Engel (1995, p. 117)
M: "I have to wash you hair in a minute. You don't like it." C fusses when hair is washed M: "I know it. You don't like to have your hair washed, do you? . . . I know you hate to have your hair washed"	22 mos.	Hart & Risley (1995, p. 88)

Yet sometimes parents have surprises in this realm and children's expressed preferences are not the ones parents assume they have. For instance, when a preschooler says, "I don't like gazpacho," his father responds, "You do like it. I know you do." The child retorts, "But I already tasted it and I hate it" (Ochs, Pontecorvo, & Fasulo, 1996, p. 35). During a fight over broccoli with cheese sauce, the child says, "I don't like cheese sauce" and his father replies harshly, "You like cheese sauce!" (Fiese, Foley, & Spagnola, 2006, p. 74). In yet another instance of this, when a child rejects turkey at dinnertime, his mother retorts, "You like turkey!" (Ochs & Shohet, 2006, p. 72).

Parents may be reluctant to accept their child's expression of preferences and evaluations, sometimes because they conflict with the parents' own, at other times because they conflict with the preferences of the canonical child, and at other times, because they are in conflict with the child's own expressed preference in the past. In addition, parents may think that by telling the child that he likes something, the child may be persuaded that his actual preferences do not match his expressed preferences. When a 3-year-old child yells to a sibling, "I hate you!," the mother responds, "You don't really do you? He's your brother!" (Dunn & Brown, 1991, p. 162).

Whereas in the above, we do not know what the child did in response, there are many documented instances of children resisting the imputation of such preferences. As an instance of the latter, at 4;6 years, Mary's mother (Warren, CHILDES) says to her, "I know your favorite book," and when the child asks what, the mother answers "Cinderella." The child says "No," and the surprised mother asks, "That's not your favorite book? What is?" When the child answers, "This one," the mother replies, "I thought Cinderella was your favorite book." Similar resistance of preference imputation is evident when a father questions his son's favorite game in a game parlor. When the son, aged 5;10 years, answers *Pacman*, the father asks, "That's not all you play. What's your favorite game?" When the son again repeats *Pacman*, the father says, "No, you know that one that you always . . . . " The child answers, "that's not my favorite game but *Pacman* is" Later, this same father says to the son, "Let's play our favorite game. Remember how to do *one potato*?" (Warren, CHILDES).

In a study on parental knowledge of their children's preferences, Miller and his colleagues (Miller, Davis, Wilde, & Brown, 1993) found that parents of fifth graders were more

[26] Japanese: "Wa kkun no suki na ichigo da"

Table 3.9.

	Age	Source
Recent Past		
M trying to get C to say *zebra* to the letter Z		
M: "It's your favorite animal. Did you see a Zebra yesterday? Did you like him"	25 mos.	Bernstein (CHILDES)
M: "Do you remember what we saw that you liked a whole lot?	Toddler	Reese, Haden & Fivush (1993, p. 423)
Distant Past		
Referring to event 2 months prior		
M: "Remember when we went to visit Daddy?.... Was that fun? Would you like to do it again?"	24 mos.	Nelson (1996, p. 166)
Discussing trip to Europe		
M: "What did you like the most about the trip to Europe?"		
C mentions castle		
M: "Why did you like that?"		
F: "What did you like the most?"	Preadolescent	Fivush, Bohanek, Robertson, & Duke (2004, p. 68)

accurate in judging their children's preferences across a wide range of categories than were the parents of second graders. They were also more accurate regarding their own child than the average child. This suggests that as children's preferences become more stable, they express their preferences more clearly and parents learn these preferences, gradually giving up their generic-based beliefs. In fact, Miller et al. suggest that knowledge of a child's preferences serves as an index of parental involvement and understanding of their children, arguing further that parental knowledge of preferences contributes to the quality of parent–child relationship and guides parental behaviors that are directly relevant to the child's cognitive development.

PREFERENCE TALK IN REMINISCING

Children may build up a picture of their preferential world in the context of reminiscing with their parents about the recent and the more distant past, as evident in Table 3.9

Children also build up views of their preferential world when they are questioned by parents and others about experiences that these others have not shared (e.g., Minami, 1997, 2002). Referring to a nonshared event while talking to her daughter of 4;8 years, a mother asks whether the child enjoyed playing in the sea and "What did (you) enjoy doing (in the pool)"[27]? (Minami, 2002, pp. 171–172). When a child of 4;6 years tells his mother that he ate cotton candy and a banana on an outing, she asks him whether the cotton candy was good and whether the banana tasted good. In a similar instance, after a boy of 4;7 years tells his mother that he bought some syrup, she asks him whether it tasted good. Minami found that Japanese mothers' requests for such evaluations of objects and activities decreased from age 4 to 5.

Preschool teachers also discuss children's experiences to which the teachers themselves are not privy, especially in discussing holidays and weekend activities. For instance, when a child explains that he was at the seaside on holidays, the teacher enters a conversation with him in which she asks "How did it feel to be home again," and when she is told *alright*, she continues, "Alright. It's nice to come home when you've been away isn't it... back to you own bedroom, eh? ... back to your own toys" (Wood, McMahon, & Cranstoun, 1980, p. 67).

In reminiscing, though, children seem to be much more aware of what they didn't like than what they did like. For instance, a 3-year-old child says, "I didn't like it in the water... it was cold and horrible and I wanted to get out and get dried" (Tough, 1977, p. 54). As this example illustrates, children seem to be attuned to those events that are emotionally charged – either because they are scary events, because they led to disciplinary encounters, or because they are simply unique in the child's stream of experience. Wang (2001) found that in reminiscing about emotional past events, parents often asked children about their personal preferences in order to set up a contrast between what the child wanted and what the parent wanted, for example, "What did Blake want to do?" and the child answers, "I wanted to take the rocks home" (Wang, 2001, p. 701), a preference that conflicted with that of the parent. In talking to her 3-year-old, a British mother is talking of preferential conflict earlier that day and asks, "Which pair of tights did you want?" and when the child indicates that she wanted the ones with a hole in them, the mother responds, "You had to have them on for about an hour before we managed to change them, didn't we?" (Dunn & Brown, 1991, p. 169). As this short excerpt demonstrates,

[27] Japanese: "don nan shite asonda?"

the mother and the child spent an hour negotiating their preferential conflict. The findings suggest that prior to age 2, children rely heavily on cues and prompts from parents to recall information and that somewhere around 30 to 36 months, they start to independently report memories of past episodes without support in the form of questions and cues (Fivush, Gray, & Fromhoff, 1987).

Rather than asking children as to their likes and dislikes during reminiscence talk, parents may remind their children of things they liked in the past. For instance, talking of an outing to an amusement park, John's father says to John, who is 5;9 years of age, "Do you remember that one? You liked that one pretty good." The child answers, "I don't remember it, but I really like it" (Warren, CHILDES). The child, who does not recall the particular ride the father is discussing, is willing to accept the father's evaluation of his own liking. But this type of conversation alerts the child not only that events in the past need to be recalled but that the valence of the specific remembered event is important.

In discussing their past preferences, children often note a contrast between their current preferences and those they had previously. For example, a child of 4 was having a conversation with her mother and said, "that block was my favorite," and when asked why, said, "I don't know. I think maybe it was my favorite color" (Nelson & Shaw, 2002, p. 50). Wellman et al. (1995) recorded a discussion between Abe, at 35 months, and his mother. After she says that grapefruit is good for you, he says, "I like it. I don't like.... I don't like it when I was.... I didn't like it... when I was a baby." His mother says, "But you like it now?" and he answers, "Uh-huh." Such discussions likely foster an understanding of shifting preferences.

Reminiscence talk can also serve to crystallize one's likes and dislikes. In being prompted to tell of a roller coaster ride the previous weekend, Eric, at 25 months, is asked whether he would like to go again. He says "I didn't go back roller coaster. No! like to. Like to. Like to," shaking his head negatively as he answers, and then adds "I no like to" (Bloom, 1970, p. 206). Similarly, when a 7-year-old is discussing a visit to an amusement park, his father asks what the child wants to do there and the child answers, "eating, popcorn, candy." The father backtracks, asking "No, I mean as far as rides?" and the child answers, "Well, I surely won't ride the M.B." (the Mind Bender). When the father persists further, asking "But what will you ride, that's what's important," the child is flustered and answers, "What important for me is not riding the Mind Bender" (Warren, CHILDES). The child remembered his negative experience with that particular ride, coding it as a ride to be avoided, rather than encoding other rides as ones to be approached.

Yet parents tend to assume that the way they have discussed and interpreted a given event prior to, during, or after it is actually experienced (e.g., fun vs. scary) is the way the child will interpret it as well. They consequently indulge in providing children with labels for past events. A father recounts a day with the child and says, "I think it was pretty nice. That was fun" (Fivush & Reese, p. 6). Similarly, in talking of a game at preschool, a mother says, "That was fun at preschool, remember?" (Ochs & Capps, 2001, p. 263), providing ways of evaluation that they assume to be the same as the child's. But this assumption may be erroneous; children have their own immediate experience which they encode as well. What enters the child's autobiographical memory is an amalgam that builds on the child's basic event knowledge, the parent's construction of the event as discussed with the child, and the child's own experience and interpretation of that experience. The fact that memories are not copies of events allows for different people to have different memories of the same event, allowing for attributional errors to arise (Ross, 1989).

Parents sometimes discover that their interpretations of events and their assumptions about the emotional experiences of their children do not match their children's interpretations or their actual experiences. For instance, when I asked Orren, at 3;2;5 years, why he turned on the light, he answered, "I didn't turn on the light – I turned off the dark."[28] From his perspective, I had misunderstood what he was trying to do, and he was telling me what his perspective was and how it differed from mine. Children can reject a given interpretation that their parents have made and provide their own interpretation of the same event or object. A father who is reminiscing with his 3-year-old about a trip to the zoo talks of the child feeding the goats and says "You were a big boy, huh? Very brave." But the child responds, "Scary" (Wolf, 1990, p. 189). That is, the child talked of his emotional experience and the father was not apparently aware of what the child experienced. Also in the context of emotions, in talking to her child, a mother says, "but you'll be glad when you go back to school, won't you?" When her child denies this, the mother asks why. Her daughter answers, "'Cause Rebecca don't go to my school anymore" (Hasan & Cloran, 1990, p. 84).

Whereas in this example, the mother did not attempt to impose her own views on the child, parents are sometimes unaccepting of the child's expressed emotion and attempt to reject it. A mother is talking with her preadolescent daughter about a friend moving out of the house, saying "You were sad this afternoon," to which the daughter answers, "No I wasn't." The mother responds "Yes you were," which the daughter again denies, saying, "I wasn't." The mother finally asks what the daughter was feeling, and when she gets the answer, happy, she is incredulous, repeating the question twice, and then finally, it dawns upon her why this may be the case and she asks, "You get more space in the house?" to which the daughter answers affirmatively (Fivush et al., 2004). Similarly, Fivush (2004) recorded a child talking with her mother about a visit to an amusement park. When the mother asks whether it was fun to go on the Ferris wheel, the child answers "No." The

[28] Hebrew: "Lo hidlakti at ha-or, xibiti at haxoshex"

mother is taken aback and says, "It wasn't fun? You said it was fun. Was it scary?" The child answers, "Yeah, I didn't like the swings," and her mother says, "I know you like to swing" (p. 92). Mothers may be reluctant to give up their version of the child's world of preferences, finding it difficult to reconcile this world with the generic child on whom they have based their beliefs.

As children develop, they become more resistant to accepting their mother's reading of their preferences and affective experiences. As a British teen explains:

> I reached a breaking point when I was about, like, 12 or 13 when –.... It just felt like she was forcing me... just have me dress the way she wanted me to dress.... I just felt like she was really trying to make me be the person she really wanted me to be... and I suppose I rebelled. (Chu, 2004, p. 95)

In fact, parents often claim that although they are aware of their young children's preferences and affective experiences (e.g., "As a child I could tell what she was thinking," Henwood & Coughlan, 1993, p. 208), this breaks down during adolescence and parents maintain that they don't "understand" their children or their preferences any longer (e.g., the mother of a 12-year-old girl explains: "Her taste and my taste are different," Palan & Wilkes, 1997). Parents consequently become less intrusive in terms of attempting to read their adolescent children's preferences and affective experiences. Doane and colleagues (e.g., 1981, 1982, 1987) found that adolescents whose parents evidenced both critical and neutral intrusiveness – defined as statements that imply knowledge of the child's thoughts, feelings states, or motives where there is no apparent basis for such knowledge – were more likely to develop schizophrenic-like disorders in young adulthood.

KNOWING OUR OWN PREFERENCES

In the previous discussion, children's allusions to their preferences, both temporary and stable, may seem to imply that they are generally aware of their own preferences. But do we always know what our preferences are? Somewhat surprisingly, it turns out that we are less aware of our preferences than we should be. When an adult suggests to a 2-year-old that he build with a construction toy, the child answers, "I don't like a construction toy." The adult answers, "But at one time you liked it." The child retorts, "No I never liked it"[29] (Antinucci & Miller, 1976, p. 179). From the adult's perspective, then, the child conveniently "forgot" his previous liking for building with construction toys. As Ross (1989) found, people do rewrite their histories in light of their current attitudes and preferences. It seems highly unlikely though that a 2-year-old is engaging in such rewriting. It is possible that the adult who had seen the child playing with construction toys in the past assumed that this reflected liking for doing so and that this was not the case. It is also possible that the child's current dislike of a given activity is so intense that it precludes the possibility of previous liking. Baars (1988) contends that whereas at the moment of choice, we may be quite conscious of alternatives, once having chosen, we enter a new context that is created by the choice and within which the original choice is not even defined. Consequently, we often cannot make previous choices conscious once we have entered the new context created by the choice points. This suggests that the child above does not in fact remember his previous liking of the toy.

In a classic study by Lepper, Greene, and Nisbett (1973), kindergarten children were given magic markers and were asked to draw pictures with them. All the children did so gladly. Two weeks later, the same children were again given the chance to draw with the markers. But this time, some of the children were told that if they would draw for the experimenter, they could get an impressive certificate, "The Good Player Award." A control group of children was not promised the award but still received it at the end of the drawing session. A week later, the magic markers were made available in the kindergarten class and experimenters unobtrusively measured how long the children drew with the markers. The group of children that had received the award contingent on drawing for the experimenter spent less time drawing with the magic markers than the group that had received the award without it being contingent on drawing, and both of these groups spent less time drawing than children who had not received an award.

How can we explain these counterintuitive results? One possibility is that children asked themselves the question, "Why did I draw with the markers? Do I like drawing with markers?" For the group that did not receive the award and for the group that received the award in a noncontingent manner the answer to this question is "Yes, I must like to draw with markers. There was no other reason why I would spend my time drawing with them." But the group that received the award contingent on drawing could provide themselves with a different answer to this question. They could answer the above question with, "I know why I drew with the markers. I only did it to get the award. I wouldn't have drawn with the markers if I didn't get the award. I obviously don't like drawing with magic markers."

Another possible route is one that focuses on the offer of the reward. Specifically, the child could question why a reward was proffered. Adults don't ordinarily give children rewards for playing with things they like. If this is the case, one possible conclusion is: "Both he and I know that I don't like drawing with magic markers and that's why he offered me the award" (cf., Karniol & Ross, 1979). In other words, in this context, children may have inferred how much they liked to draw with magic markers on the basis of their own behavior and the circumstances in which the behavior occurred. One might be tempted to jump to the conclusion that children are the only ones who exhibit such strange inference processes about their

[29] Italian: "Piace mica costruzione".... "Eppure una volta ti piaceva".... "No, mai piaciuto"

own preferences. But similar results have been found in various studies with adults (e.g., Harackiewicz, 1979). In all these studies, activity-contingent rewards led individuals to change their perceptions of their preferences for the rewarded activity.

At other times, we may have explicit preferences but we appear unable to explain why we hold these preferences. Recall the blindfold test between Pepsi and Coke? People who insisted they hated one and preferred the other were unable to tell which one they had tasted when they had blindfolds on. In a more scientific version of the blindfold test, Nisbett and Wilson (1977) found that females had clear preferences among different pairs of stockings but were unable to cite any characteristic that was consistently associated with their preferences, unaware that all the pairs were actually the same. In short, we don't always know what our preferences are, and when we do, we may know what we prefer but we may not know the reasons for such preferences.

Although it might seem from the above that we generally do not have well-established bases for our preferences, I would suggest that we don't know our preferences in those domains with which we don't deal on an ordinary basis. People know what cars they like, what clothes they like, what foods they like, what books they like, what movies they like, what kind of houses they prefer, what kind of furniture they like, and so forth. On the other hand, we can change our preferences via exposure. Popular fashion in particular changes via exposure to fashion trend setters who serve to accustom us to new styles. Going shopping can also be perceived as a means of exposure to different styles than we are accustomed to. Being put in a new context (e.g., summer camp, new high school, starting college) also exposes us to others whose preferences may differ from our own and to norms of clothing and behavior that are novel to us and that we may choose to adopt. For instance, my daughter's first adaptation to going to university was manifest in a change to the "preppy look" in clothes. She also learned to differentiate "looking cool" versus "looking serious," where the latter is the appearance needed for interviewing and job hunting. One changes one's clothes and outfits accordingly.

PREFERENCE FALSIFICATION

The children above were very explicit about their preferences, stating them clearly. Sometimes, it is unwise to let others know what our preferences are, and we engage in preference falsification (Kuran, 1995). There are many possible situations in which this can occur. For instance, a teenager is shopping with her girlfriends whose taste in clothes is more flamboyant than her own taste. Telling her friends that she likes a pale blue, button-down shirt rather than the gaudy purple one in the window may lead to her being teased and made fun of. Such expectations of social reactions are readily voiced by adolescents, as when a male adolescent says, "People might not like you if you are not fashionable" and a female adolescent poses the question in a more extreme form when she asks, "Will people hate me if I don't follow a certain trend?" (Bell & Bromnick, 2003, p. 213). When shopping with friends, then, an adolescent may prefer not to have her preferences known and may falsify them, even to the extent of buying the more gaudy shirt. Rubin (1980) provides a poignant example of this in a letter a 12-year-old girl forwarded to her teachers, asking about the likes and dislikes of the "in group," saying "I would like to know what they're interested in so in talking to them I know what they hate," explaining that "I might say something that might turn them off" (p. 100). A Japanese 17-year-old girl explains that she changes what she says in light of what she expects might be regarded negatively by other people, saying "If I say what I really feel, I could be disliked" (Shimizu, 2001, p. 209).

What does preference falsification involve? In research with 6-, 13-, and 19-year-olds, Feldman, Jenkins, and Popoola (1979) found that with increasing age, children were better able to hide their preferences. Shennum and Bugental (1982) found that 6- to 12-year-olds were able to both mask (i.e., pretend the opposite valence) and inhibit (i.e., pretend to be neutral) their preferences for disliked items and activities in terms of their expressive control of facial cues. However, they were unable to either mask or inhibit their preferences for liked items and activities. The ability to control facial expressiveness was found to be best predicted by performance on a visual perspective taking task requiring the child to predict what a scene would look like from a different physical location.

Several issues are important in this context. First, Elkind (1967) discusses the concept of *the imaginary audience*, with adolescents thinking that they are the focus of others' thoughts. He argues that adolescents can conceptualize both their own thoughts and those of others but that they do not yet differentiate between the targets of their own thoughts and those that are the focus of others' thoughts. One consequence of this is that they think they are the focus of others' thoughts and continually construct and react to an *imaginary audience*. In Elkind's words, "It is an audience because the young person believes that he or she will be the focus of attention; and it is imaginary because, in actual social situations, this is not usually the case (unless he or she contrives to make it so)" (Elkind, 1967, p. 1031). Gilovich and Savitsky (1999) similarly discuss the *spotlight* effect, the tendency to exaggerate the extent to which other people attend and notice one's presence and behavior. Both of these phenomena would be expected to lead to greater preference falsification. Importantly, though, they rely on the concept of generic others, as I discuss later.

Second, preference falsification often involves self-image manipulation. Snyder (1974; Snyder & Gangestad, 1986) has discussed an individual difference variable called *self-monitoring*, which differentiates individuals in terms of their awareness of situational demands and the likelihood of adapting their behavior to conform to such perceived situations demands. The prime example of this is Woody Allen's (1983) movie character, Zelig, the human chameleon, who changed his attitudes, his behavior, and even his appearance, to resemble those with whom he was interacting. It is the high self-monitor who would be most expected to engage in preference falsification.

Of course, not all preference falsification occurs for self-image manipulation. People often falsify their preferences to avoid hurting others. This view is expressed by a teenager who says, "If you tell a lie tryin' to keep someone from bein' hurt, it not really a lie" (FitzSimmons, 1999, p. 111). As Bok (1978) contends, people often lie as a preference management technique. In this particular context, the falsification would occur to avoid hurting another person's feelings and, as such, preference falsification is a positive rather than a negative behavior.

But at the societal level, preference falsification may lead to other, negative phenomena (Kuran, 1995). For instance, pluralistic ignorance refers to contexts in which everyone knows what their own preferences are but because no one expresses such preferences publicly, everyone thinks that others' preferences are unlike their own preferences. Noelle-Neumann (1984) has discussed this in the context of the Spiral of Silence, her explanation for the silence of dissidents in Germany during the Hitler era. Because people were afraid to voice their views, the general impression was that these views were in the minority and consequently, fewer and fewer people voiced their views in public. Preference falsification can have disastrous consequences at the societal level, even though at the individual level, it often has self-protective and beneficial functions.

The important point above is that preference falsification occurs in situations in which we make assumptions about other people's reactions to our preferences, presumably in light of their own preferences. Hence, they depend on an awareness of other people's preferences, the topic of Chapter 4.

4 Other People's Preferences

A child of 36 months is planning to put sand in a friend's watering can. She says, 'I'm going to . . . . When she comes home, she will say "There's sand in the watering can" . . . and she can't water it' When chastised by her mother for doing so, with "she doesn't like you doing that," the child responds, 'I know she doesn't!'

(Dunn, 1988, p. 146)

A 5-year-old child makes a toy lighter out of aluminum foil; his sister says, 'Well don't take that to school . . . You could get in big trouble. If I took something like that to school? And the teacher thought it was a cigarette lighter? She'd – I'd get suspended.'

(Ochs, 2004, p. 274)

In Chapters 1–3, children were expressing preferences for what they wanted to have and do and what they wanted others to do – but they did not refer to other people's preferences. In fact, Budwig (2002) found that between 18 and 36 months of age, both children and their parents used the verb *want* primarily in reference to the *child* as the experiencer of wants. Children talked of what they want and adults inquired as to children's wants, so that primarily children's preferences were alluded to over the 4 months of the study. Yet children do learn of others people's preferences in their interaction with them. In this chapter, I focus on how children learn of other people's preferences and how they indicate their awareness of such preferences. Importantly, I also discuss children's emergent awareness that others have both matching and mismatching preferences to their own preferences, thereby learning to understand both similarities and differences between people. Later in this chapter, I address the emergence of the concept of generic others and their preferences as well as the implications of this concept for children's understanding of the normativeness of their own preferences. Finally, I present extant models and my model of how we make predictions about other people preferences when others have not directly expressed such preferences to us.

BECOMING AWARE OF OTHERS' PREFERENCES

In order to consider other people's preferences, one must first become aware that others have preferences, and that these can be "known." How do children learn of other people's preferences? First, adults often express their first order preferences directly to children, indicating their likes and dislikes of objects and actions, as shown in Table 4.1.

As these examples illustrate, preferences are an integral part of adult–child conversation, with adults talking of what they like, what they don't like, and implying that they too evaluate objects and activities when they talk of their favorites. When adults talk of their preferences this way, children learn several important lessons. First, they learn that others also have preferences across a wide range of domains. Second, they learn that other people's preferences constitute relevant topics of conversation. Third, they learn the specific type of preferences that others have.

Additionally, when other people discuss their preferences, the importance of preferences in guiding others' object choices and behavioral decisions comes to light, as shown in Table 4.2.

That is, by talking of their preferences this way, others clarify that they too choose to interact with objects they like, eat foods they like, and avoid actions that counter their preferences. Children thereby learn that others share their own psychological processes, that is, the motivational underpinnings of others' behavior match their own. At the same time, though, they also learn that the actual preferences people have may well differ.

Hence, others' talk of their preferences leads children to note the basic similarities between themselves and others. Wolf, Rugh, and Altshuler (1984) suggest that the ability to understand others includes at least two basic ideas: the first is that human beings are alike in basic ways. Like ourselves, other people are both agents, the performers of overt actions that cause observable events, and experiencers, hosts to internal events such as perception, sensation, emotion and cognition. Yet despite these shared capacities, the specific preferences, intentions, thoughts, and feelings that we have do not predict the internal states that other people are likely to experience in the same situations. In this light, understanding human

Table 4.1.

	Age	Source
T: "I like those new shoes you are wearing"	Preschool	Kontos (1999)
C: "I'm making a house" T: "It's nice. I like that"	Preschool	Gearhart & Newman (1980)
T asks what flavor cake frosting they should make C: "Chocolate" T: "Good, it's my favorite"	Preschool	Hall (CHILDES)
C offers T pretend chips T: "Chips are not my favorite" T asks C as to his favorite C says he likes fish and bacon T: "I don't think I'd like fish and bacon"	Preschool	Wood, McMahon, & Cranstoun (1980, p. 135)
C asks T whether she had a cat as a child T: "Oh yes, ... but the dog was my favourite though"	Preschool	Mitchell (1982, p. 19)

Table 4.2.

	Age	Source
M: "I love meatballs, let's have some for lunch" C: "But I don't like them"	Preschool	Brigaudiot, Morgenstern, & Nicolas (1996, p. 114)
C says F ate blueberry scones at restaurant F: "Those are my favorite"	Preschool	Ochs & Capps (2001, p. 248)
In an amusement park F refuses to go on ride F: "I don't like getting wet, do you?"	4;9 years	Warren (CHILDES)

Table 4.3.

	Age	Source
M (to F): "Did you like those cranberry muffins, Stan?" F says yes C: "I wanna cranberry muffin. I like them"	29 mos.	Bartsch & Wellman (1995, p. 70)
F (to M): "I tell you, brown applesauce is cheaper. Plus I like it better"	Preschool	Gleason & Ely (1997, p. 247)
C helps T make silly putty C: "Well, I want it to be sticky" T: "You like it to be sticky?" C2: "I don't"	Preschool	Kontos (1999)
C1 hosted at family dinner by C2 and C3		
C1: "Do you like lettuce with these? Michael do you like lettuce with these?"	4;5 years	
C2 doesn't reply	3;5 years	
C3: "I do"	8 years	
Later C2: "I'm not gonna have much bread" C1: "I'm not either" C3: "I am"		Speier (1972, pp. 412–443)

Table 4.4.

	Age	Source
Getting Preferred Foods		
F doesn't want any more O: "If Daddy doesn't eat his food, I'll eat his food"[1]	33;15	Karniol (Diary, Orren)
C takes last piece of egg C: "The rest of you don't like hard boiled egg, but I do"	35 mos.	Braunwald (1985, p. 524)
M asks if C2 finished her banana C2: "I don't like it" C1: "I'll eat it then"	3;2 years	Wells (CHILDES)
Avoiding Dispreferred Food		
O: "Orren doesn't want this – Mummy eat!"[2]	24;25	Karniol (Diary, Orren)
O: "Grandma eat the chocolate – grandma eat it Orren's chocolate" M: "Why?" O: "Orren no like it"	25;8	Karniol (Diary, Orren)
K doesn't want her peas K: "Mummy, I'm to ask that you eat this"[3]	31;27	Karniol (Diary, Karen)
C doesn't like a cookie she tried C (to M): "You eat"	Toddler	Heath (1986, p. 108)
C gives F a piece of bread C: "I don't like it" F: "Why do I have to eat it? . . . What makes you think that daddy's going to like it?" C: "You are, because you like sour stuff. So eat it"	3;7 years	Bartsch & Wellman (1995, p. 86)

behavior involves an appreciation of what is common to all humans as well as sensitivity as to the limits of that commonality.

These same lessons are also acquired when children overhear conversations in which other people discuss preferences. Importantly, though, children often intercede in such overheard conversations by stating their own matching or contrastive preferences, as shown in Table 4.3.

Such conversational exchanges are a rich source of knowledge about others' preferences. But by interceding with their own preferences, children clarify that hearing others talk of their preferences invites comparisons and contrasts with their own preferences. Conversations regarding other people's preferences, then, raise the prospect of children's recognition of mismatches between their own preferences and those of others. But at the same time, they underline the similarity between people in the way preferences impact their choices and decision making.

Mealtimes in particular provide a rich forum for learning that preferences guide others' behavioral choices and children simultaneously learn to take advantage of mismatches between the specific preferences that they and others have, both to gain more of their preferred foods and to avoid dispreferred foods, as shown in Table 4.4.

As these examples illustrate, mealtimes provide abundant evidence that others too make choices on the basis of their preferences. Again, it bears recognition that other people's preferences and their comparison with the child's preferences are either implicitly or explicitly the bases for such conversations and food exchanges.

Parents also talk of other people's preferences, both in terms of their wants and in terms of their likes and dislikes, often in their absence. Turning to wants first, when a toddler wants to offer water to a visitor, she is told, "I don't think Mr. Fraser wants any water" (deVilliers, 1984). As for likes and dislikes, Mary at 4;6 years is talking with her mother about eating dessert and the mother asks her "Do you want one of our cookies?" When the child asks what kind, the mother answers, "That we made the other day that Daddy liked so much" (Warren, CHILDES). Similarly, a mother announces to her preschooler that she is going to bake cookies, explaining, "Daddy likes them," to which the child responds, "Well I don't" (Walkerdine, 1988, p. 131). During a discussion of a younger sister's dislike of sitting on a swing, the father tells his 5-year-old, "Yeah, she is not too fond of the swing, not like you were" (Fiese, Foley, & Spagnola,

[1] Hebrew: "im abba lo yoxal at haoxel shelo az ani yoxal at haoxel shelo"
[2] Hebrew: "Orren lo roçe at ze – Ima toxal"
[3] Hebrew: "Ima, ani levakeshet she-at toxli at ze"

Table 4.5.

	Age	Source
Objects		
C: "Like another one daddy?"	25 mos.	Wootton (1997, p. 148)
C (to M): "Do you want that one? . . . . Would you like a sweetie?"	26 mos.	Radford (1990, pp. 280–281)
O: "Mommy do you want your book?"[4]	27;23	Karniol (Diary, Orren)
C offers M food M: "I'm not hungry" C offers her a spoon, asking, "Want spoon?" M refuses C: "OK. You don't want a spoon. You don't want a spoon"	Toddler	Brown (1973)
C: "Want some soup mommy?"	35 mos.	De Houwer (1990)
C: "I'm going to ask mommy if she wants cakes"	3;10 years	Bassano (1996)
Activities		
To father C: "Daddy ye like do it again?	25 mos.	Wootton (1997, p. 148)
O (to sib): "Do you want to see story (book) Mommy bought me in the supermarket?)"[5]	28;23	Karniol (Diary, Orren)
O: "Daddy do you want me to make you nice-looking (i.e., comb your hair)?"[6]	29;26	Karniol (Diary, Orren)
Playing pretend mother C: "where do you want to go baby?" (addressed to C2 of 4;7)	4;3 years	McTear (1985, p. 80)
C: "You want to come over to my house one day? Ride my bike?"	Second grade	Tannen (1990, p. 182)

2006, p. 78). Such messages convey to children that other people are individuals with preferences and that such preferences need to be considered in interacting with them. Of course, as they hear of others' preferences, children may implicitly or explicitly draw comparisons with their own preferences.

Parents also interpose questions about other people's preferences when they talk of children's preferences. When a girl discusses liking Marmite, her father counters, "Yea, you do, does Eva like it?" alluding to her older sister (Forrester & Reason, 2006, p. 455). In such contexts, though, parents often talk of the preferences of generic others. When George at 4;11 years tells his father about a cupcake he ate at school, the father asks, "Did you like it?" and when George answers *yes*, his father asks, "Did everybody like it?" (Warren, CHILDES). Similarly, when a 3-year-old gets a haircut, the mother asks the child when he comes back from preschool, "So did everyone like your haircut?" (Beals, 1993, p. 503). Such questions not only imply that others have likes and dislikes but that one should be inherently attentive to such issues. This is also evident in the classroom when teachers ask as to both real and fictional others' likes and dislikes (e.g., "And did he like it? How do you know he liked it?" Torr, 2000, p. 158). As to the implication of talking of generic others in such conversations, this is an issue I will return to in later chapters.

QUESTIONING OTHERS' PREFERENCES

When others do not express their preferences, children can ask direct questions about their preferences. They can do so in terms of what others want, referring both to objects and to activities, as shown in Table 4.5.

Yet even when children pose questions that do not directly address others' preferences, they can still get responses that serve to inform them of others' preferences. This is because preferences are often used as justifications for why actions are undertaken. For instance, when a mother who is changing bed linen is questioned by her 3-year-old as to why she is doing so, she responds, "I want it all to look pretty and in the same color to look nice when Daddy comes home" (Wells, 1986, p. 57). Her response refers directly to her own preference but also implies that the father has similar preferences and that her behavior is being undertaken in service of his preferences as well.

Children also ask both parents and others, including peers and siblings, directly about their likes and dislikes, again referring to both objects and actions. Examples of such questions are shown in Table 4.6.

Of course, when children question others regarding their preferences, there is always the potential of discovering that others' preferences do not match one's own. This recognition is evident when children first announce

[4] Hebrew: "Ima at roça at hasefer shelax?"
[5] Hebrew: "At roça lirot sipur ima ikne li ba-supermarket?"
[6] Hebrew: "Abba ata roçe she-ani yaase' otxa yafe'"

Table 4.6.

	Age	Source
To Adults		
Addressing parent: C: "Do you like that one?"	26 mos.	Radford (1990, p. 279)
Addressing parent C: "Ya don't like that hah?"	29 mos.	Peters (2000, p. 147)
Hearing story of hero who gets into car C: "Mommy, do you like to ride in the front or the back?"	4 years	Lindfors (1999, p. 176)
C built house out of blocks, C: "Hey mom, you like this house?" M: "Yes, that's a wonderful house"	Preschool	Wolf (1990, p. 204)
To Children		
Addressing toddler sibling C: "Like your raisins: Like raisins? Like raisins, Jenny?"	Preschool	Howe (1991, p. 1506)
In game of pretense, referring to reality C: "'Cause you like this one don't you, don't you Lucie?"	Preschool	Cook-Gumperz (1995, p. 413)
C1 and C2 played ghosts C1: "Did you like the game? Let's play it again"	Preschool	Jordan & Cowan (1995, p. 731)

their own preferences and then query others as to their preferences,[7] or vice versa, as evident in Table 4.7.

Interestingly, children's conversations with peers are replete with discussions of their respective likes and dislikes of their own possessions and products, as shown in Table 4.8.

At times, it seems as if children only ask others about their preferences so they can tell them their own likes and dislikes. Yet whenever children make statements about their own preferences, this allows others to express their own agreement or disagreement with these preferences. Thus, when a child of 3;6 years rejects mushrooms, saying "I don't want mushrooms!!," a second child of 4;6 years concurs, "I don't either" (Speier, 1972, p. 413). Similarly, when a toddler says "I like carrots," her father responds, "I know. I do too" (Nelson, 1989). The "me too" phenomenon allows children to establish similarity across domains and to explore possible differences between themselves and others. But it is the meeting with nonshared preferences that allows for social comparisons to develop and for one's own preferences to crystallize.

PREFERENCES AND NORMATIVENESS

Discussions of preferences and of mismatching preferences in particular evoke questions regarding the normativeness of one's own preferences. When another person does not share one's preferences this may carry the implication that one's own preferences are nonnormative. Alternatively, one's own preferences may be normative and those of the other may be nonnormative. To know which of these is the case, one needs to be aware of the preferences of other people outside the dyad.

This may well engender discussion of the preferences of individuals who are not currently present or whose preferences do not directly impinge upon the child. For instance, Kate, at 3;1 years, asks her mother, "Does David like soup?" regarding an adult friend who was not present (de Houwer, 1990). Dunn (1988) noted that 2- to 4-year-old children constantly asked observers in their homes whether they like monsters, dogs, and so forth. Shatz's (1994) grandson, at 30 months, announced he was going to the grocery store to buy Coke and orange pop. After she said she likes orange pop, he asked her "You like Coke?" proceeding to ask all those present as to their preferences. Similarly, in conversations with mothers and others, children often allude to the preferences of third parties, as shown in Table 4.9.

Children's preliminary assumption seems to be that their own preferences are normative and that preferences that do not match their own need to be accounted for. For instance, a toddler asks her mother, "Do you prefer cheddar cheese?" When the mother answers no, the child asks why, and being told that the mother likes the taste of Muenster better, she asks, "Why don't like the taste of cheddar?" (Bloom, 1991). In this exchange, then, the daughter is both aware of the mother's nonshared preferences and tries to understand the basis for

[7] Telling others one's preferences can also serve as hints. For instance, Weizman (1989) gives the example of one person saying, "I love this chocolate," and the hearer responding, "So do I," When the chocolate lover retorts with, "Well, why don't you get some for us?" (p. 75), it is clear that the original statement is in fact a hint rather than a matching statement of preferences.

Table 4.7.

	Age	Source
Own Preferences Stated First		
To parents C: "I like (name of object/food). Do you?"	25 mos.	Tomasello (1992, p. 368)
Girls are drawing C: "Now which color you want. I want blue. What color you want?"	3;6 years	Bartsch & Wellman (1995, p. 78)
At preschool "I don't feel like playing, do you?"	Preschool	Beringer & Garvey (1983)
C: "Barbara, do you wonna play some more? I wonna ride the tricycle, and you?"	6;2 years	Auwarter (1986, p. 210)
To sibling C: "You want to do what I do, right? I want to go on the swings, do you?"[8]	5;7 years	Taeschner (1983, p. 217)
Questioning Others' Preferences First		
Noting Similarities		
C interacting with talking doll C: "You like string beans?" D: "Yes" C: "Uh, so do I"	Preschool	Parker (1986, p. 124)
C is interacting with talking doll C: "Don't you like going under water?" D: "No" C: "Yeah. You know what? I don't like going under water"	Preschool	Parker (1986, p. 126)
C1: "I love chocolate" C2: "Yeah"	Preschool	Gottman (1986b, p. 171)
T: "Lions are scary. I like smaller animals better" C: "Me too"	Preschool	Applegate (1980, p. 86)
Noting Differences		
Addressing parent C: "You like it?" A: "Yes" C: "But I don't like it"	34 mos.	Bartsch & Wellman (1995, p. 86)
M says she doesn't like to get wet C: "Don't like to get wet? Swim? You want you swim?" M: "No" C: "OK, I like swim"	35 mos.	Bartsch & Wellman (1995, p. 86)
C: "Do you like pancake mummy?" M: "Actually no I don't really like pancakes at all" C: "I like pancakes" M: " I know you do, yeah pancake-man"	3 years	Aukrust & Snow (1998)
C: "Do you like dinosaurs?" Gets affirmative answer C: "I don't"	4 years	Gottman (1986b, p. 166)
C1: "I **like** American Girl" C2: "I **hate** American Girl"	Fifth grade	Goodwin (2006, p. 193)

her mother's preferences. The child's implicit assumption is that the mother should like cheddar cheese. In the same vein, at 31;7, Karen asks "Karen likes a candy Mommy. Why don't you like a candy?"[9] The bases for dissimilar preferences need to be understood. More pointedly, on seeing her father eating avocado, Karen, at 29;29, says to him, "Daddy why are you eating every day things what Karen doesn't like? You should eat things what Karen likes." Here, too, the child is trying to solve the puzzle of mismatches between her own and other people's preferences.

[8] Italian: "Tu vuoi fare quello che faccio io vero? Io voglio andare in altalena, tu anche?"

[9] Hebrew: "Karen ohevet sukariya ima. Lama at lo ohevet sukariya?"

Table 4.8.

	Age	Source
Questioning Peer Preferences		
C finishes song, asks peer		
C: "Do you like it?"	31 mos.	Slama-Cazacu (1977, p. 51)
C: "Do you like my red sandals?"	36 mos.	Tough (1977, p. 81)
Discussing Positive Preferences		
C to peer		
C: "Like your brand new trouser suit jumper. That's nice. And the shirt"	Preschool	Wells (1986, p. 80)
C: "I like what you are making, Jonathan. How do you like what I'm making?"	Preschool	Corno (1989, p. 45)
C finished drawing a house		
C: "Here's my nice house. Like it?"		
C2: "Yeah, it's good"	5 years	Pitcher & Schultz (1983, p. 65)
C is drawing		
C: "You don't like mine, huh?"		
C2: "Yes I do. I always like your pictures"	First grade	Dyson (1993, p. 166)
Discussing Negative Preferences		
Drawing at preschool		
C to peer		
C: "I don't like your picture"	36 mos.	Tough (1977, p. 66)
C to peer		
C: "Do you like my drawing?"		
C2: "No"		
C: "You have to like it"		
C2: "I don't have to like it if I don't want to"		
C: "Why?"		
C2: "I don't like it, that's why"	36 mos.	Rubin (1980, p. 8)
drawing at preschool		
C to peer		
C: "I don't like your painting. Mine is pretty"	4 years	Pitcher & Schultz (1983, p. 51)
Building with construction blocks		
C to C2		
C: "Mine I like better because you didn't make a good house. I like this one, I like this one"		
C2: "I like mine the best because yours is different"	5 years	Pitcher & Schultz (1983, p. 6)

Table 4.9.

	Age	Source
M prepares C egg		
C: "Eggy? . . . Daddy like"		
M: "Daddy likes eggy"		
C: ""Doieyy (i.e., dolly) eggy" (points to doll, shaking head for no) . . . . no just baby"	19 mos.	Forrester (2001, p. 193)
C: "Nunu (person's name) no like it"	27 mos.	DeVilliers (1984)
C asks adult as to liking something		
A answers no, asks as to C's liking		
C: "I like this but Daddy doesn't"	35;8	Manchester corpus (CHILDES)
C: "I like cake. My daddy does, too, do you?"	3;6 years	Todd (1982, p. 109)
At snack time, talking of liking hot dogs		
C: "But, but but, Jill and Michael don't like hotdog"	4 years	Nelson & Gruendel (1979)

But one's own preferences are seen as normative and it is others' nonmatching preferences that are viewed as needing to be justified. To illustrate, 4 months after a visiting Dutch boy requested no cucumbers in his salad, a child of 3;5 years asks, "Why Japp doesn't like cucumbers? Cause he's Dutch?" (Snow, 1983, p. 41). The child capitalized on the one difference that was most salient to him as a possible explanation for this mismatching preference. Obviously, if Japp were American, he would like cucumbers!

Parents may well foster the assumption that children's preferences are normative when they talk of preferences as if they are shared. For instance, when a child of 3;10 years indicates that he mistakenly thought there was a snake on the ground, his father replies, "Because we like snakes, right? Do you like snakes? (Bartsch & Wellman, 1995, p. 3). The father talks of their joint preference and only afterwards questions the validity of his assumption. Of course, parents and other socialization agents can also burst the bubble of this normative assumption. After a child indicated that the food was yucky, his father said, "Don't ever call anyone else's food bad.... OK? Do you understand? Other people like their food" (MacWhinney CHILDES). Similarly, when a preschool teacher offers crackers and a child says, "We don't want any," the teacher replies, "If you don't want it someone else does" (Hall, CHILDES). Goodwin (1990) recorded an interesting exchange in which a 10-year-old "mother" chastises her "children": "Well if you don't want to go to sleep, don't go. But don't disturb your sisters. Just because you don't wanna go, maybe they wanna go to sleep." In these cases, then, children are being explicitly told that their own preferences do not match those of generic others. They can also be told that their preferences mismatch those of specific others. For example, when a preschooler tries prune juice and expresses distaste, his mother refers to his older brother and suggests, "Give it to Jimmy. Jimmy likes prune juice" (Hall, CHILDES).

Alternatively, children may discover that their preferences match those of specific others while mismatching those of generic others. Just whose preferences are normative is not very clear, then. To illustrate this point, Adam at 3;9 years is talking about eating snails, and his mother tells him that some people eat snails because they like them. He then asks his mother whether she wants to eat snails. She answers, "No I don't think I'd like to eat snails." Adam responds "I don't like to eat snails.... people eat snails" (Brown, CHILDES). That is, there may be generic others who eat and like snails but he and his mother stand in contradistinction to them in this specific domain. Similarly, a school child explains, "I don't like frogs, the French eat frogs" (De Moura, 2007, p. 718). Differences in preferences are therefore legitimized. This is well captured in the words of a first grader who explains why he disagrees with some other children, saying, "Maybe your brain and my brain think it different. People don't always agree like that" (Carlisle, 1994, p. 212).

BARRIERS TO LEARNING OF OTHERS' PREFERENCES

Children's conversational practices are not always conducive to learning of other people's preferences. Derber (1979) differentiates two types of conversational practices, reflecting alternative ways one can react to others' conversational initiatives. *Support responses* keep the conversation focused on the speaker; for instance, if the speaker says, "I just love Barbies," the listener questions, "Which is your favorite?" Such responses give the speaker license to continue speaking about his preferences. *Shift responses* change the focus of the conversation, making the listener, rather than the speaker, the subject of the conversation. For instance, continuing the above example, a shift response would be indicated if the listener replied, "I don't like Barbies," or "My mom bought me one yesterday." In using a shift response, the listener makes it difficult for the speaker to turn the subject back to focus on himself and his preferences. Adults who work with children are extremely adept at providing support responses (e.g., when a child contributes: "My uncle has a car and he took me for a ride," the teacher responds, "It must have been fun riding in your uncle's car," Krown, 1974, p. 154). Children are more likely to provide shift responses. In providing their own contrasting preferences, as illustrated above, children actually prevent conversations about other people's preferences. To illustrate this in another context, when a child of 5;9 years tells a peer that he will get a bicycle with three wheels for Christmas, his friend replies, "A tricycle. I've got one" (Piaget, 1926, p. 59). When children respond this way to what others tell them, they are shifting the focus of the conversation to themselves and disallowing others to talk of their preferences and relevant experiences.

Children use a variety of strategies to shift the focus of conversations to themselves. For instance, they often use "Guess what" or "Wanta know something?" to signal a shift in topic, usually then recounting something about self. A preschool child says to a peer, "My building is the best one in the world" and his friend answers, "I have a bigger bed than you" (Pitcher & Schultz, 1983, p. 163). The same pattern is evident in older children as well. Two 8-year-old boys are conversing and one has just been talking about his father's not caring about him. The other boy answers, "And guess what. I must study ... " (Reichman, 1990, p. 41). In another instance of this, one boy asks the other, "What games do you have on Atari?" and when he gets a list, he asks, "You wan – you wanna know what I'm getting for my birthday?" clearly wanting to inform his friend that he will get an Atari. But we should not find this surprising in light of the fact that mothers' conversational practices with their children generally allow children and their preferences to remain the focus of conversations, seldom switching to a discussion of their own preferences[10] (Budwig, 2002).

[10] Note that in adults, shift responses are often viewed (e.g., Jefferson, 1984) as a means of coping with difficult topics, being a prevalent means of making a transition out of the topic being discussed, though not always successfully. In contrast, Arminen (2004) has

PREFERENCES OF GENERIC OTHERS

In addition to learning what specific other people like and dislike, children learn about the preferences of generic others. The likes and dislikes of generic others are more important for determining the normativeness of one's preferences but we should not lose sight of the fact that concern with the preferences of specific others and of generic others go hand in hand. This is because their *joint* consideration affords a clear indication of the normativeness of one's own preferences. Reflecting this, in discussing another preschooler, a 5-year-old says, "Laura likes sour milk ... Laura likes it ... You don't know if everybody hates sour milk" (Hall, CHILDES). That is, one person's preferences cannot be used to infer those of generic others. In this vein, in a study with 6- to 9-year-olds, a child says, "I don't know if the boy or girl would want to do it ..... I think he would ... because I think he would like drawing pictures" (Reeder, 1996, p. 159). Given that others' preferences do not necessarily match one's own, one cannot be sure what generic other children will or will not like.

Moreover, as indicated before, knowing generic others' preferences also serves to reinforce the understanding that irrespective of the particular preferences involved, the motivational processes they engender are similar in everyone. Children learn that most people like sweets, don't like to take out the garbage, like to get gifts, but also that they will actively pursue their preferences and actively avoid dispreferred objects and activities. This allows children to discuss the things that kids – as a generic category – are likely to like, as when a pretend father of 5;2 years says, "I wish the kids were here with us; they'd like Alice in Wonderland" (Andersen, 1990, p. 107). That is, children's understanding of generic other children's likes and dislikes are used to draw inferences about their likely responses to different contexts. Gradually, then, children build up a picture of a generic, prototypical other who serves as an important fiction in guiding their own behavior. Damon and Hart (1988) provide a wealth of information about children's generalized assumptions about what other people like.

At the same time as they learn about the commonality of generic others' psychological processes, though, children also learn possible dimensions on which different categories of people may diverge from generic others in their preferences and behavior. First, they learn that adults' and children's preferences often differ. This understanding may emerge because parents often discuss children's preferences and contrast them with those of adults, implying that children as a social category have similar preferences. When a 24-month-old sees cheese in her mother's hand and asks for it, her mother replies, "No you won't like this this really tastes horrible." When the child cries, her mother continues, "No, no you can't have any of that Ella! .... no, I'm sorry darling you can't. It's got bad stuff in it. It's not for children." Her daughter responds, "Just daddies" (Forrester, 2001, p. 194). Similarly, when this same child, at 26 months, says she doesn't like butter, her father answers, "It's alright I'm not putting butter on," adding, "That's what all the children like" (Forrester & Reason, 2006, p. 455). Not only do adults also have preferences, but they have preferences that are contrasted with those of children.

Children can echo such understanding. To illustrate, after being told he shouldn't watch wrestling on television, Orren, at 35;15, responds, "Mommy, I really like the not nice program."[11] Similarly, when Sandra, at 6;2 years, is discussing soccer with her father, and he says, "Your mom doesn't want you to play soccer, though does she?" the child answers, "Nope – cause you get too dirty – and I like getting dirty!" (Warren, CHILDES). She knew her mother's preferences in this context and was aware that own preferences conflicted with her mother's. But do such differences between her own preferences and those of her mother reflect her being a child and her mother being an adult? Possibly, because children note that there may be developmental changes in preferences. This is evident when a child of 4;10 years who is pretending to be a nurse explaining to a pretend mother what her children should be eating while they are recuperating says, "Oh yes, like orange juice and like meat, let's see, some carrots, peas – that's my favorite. I mean when I was growing up" (Andersen, 1990, p. 119). Similarly, a child at preschool asks an adult: "Did you like baking when you was a little girl?" (Mitchell, 1982, p. 18), implying that current adult preferences and childhood preferences may not be isomorphic. The understanding of developmental changes in preferences may well emerge out of parental references to such changes. For instance, a child who refuses to eat asparagus is told, "I told you about asparagus, how weird it is," and after one of her children says, "And you hated it when you were a kid," the mother adds "I didn't like it when I was a kid" (Thomas-Lepore et al., 2004). A developmental theory of this sort can serve as a possible account for why adult preferences differ from those of children.

In this context, children also learn to differentiate the generalized preferences of boys versus girls. On being asked what's the most important thing to know about her, a girl responds, "I'm a girl." When she is asked why that's

discussed "second stories," stories told in response to an original story that has a "desired resemblance" to the prior one, focusing on a parallel experience. The parallel does not stem from factual similarity but through topic similarity and attempts to underline a point made by the prior story. In this vein, when a child tells of having been lost, his teacher says, "When I was little and got lost...." (Krown, 1974, p. 53). Second stories are often encouraged in self-help and support groups like Alcoholics Anonymous. More generally, Schank (1984) argues that this is how conversations take place, with participants being reminded by abstract features of others' stories of like examples in their own experiences that they then relate to emphasize what they see as the important aspect of the prior story.

[11] Hebrew; "Ima ani meod ohev at hatoxnit halo yafa"

the most important, she answers, "Because girls usually play with girls. And boys play with boys. So if someone wants to be my friend, they would want to know if I was a boy or girl" (Damon and Hart, 1988, p. 65). She assumes that preferences are gender-linked and that categorizing her as a boy or girl is critical to pursuing interactions with her. Parents may reinforce such gender-linked perceptions when they talk of the divergent preferences of different people. For example, when a girl announces that she does not like trucks, her mother questions her "You think most girls don't like trucks?" (Gelman, Taylor, & Nguyen, 2004, p. 97).

Stereotypes guide perceptions that certain categories of people are associated with certain types of likes and dislikes. Consequently, if "gentlemen prefer blonds," then having blond hair is good "Because boys like girls with blond hair.... If I had blond hair, maybe I could have more (boyfriends)" (Damon & Hart, 1988, p. 65). Such assumptions allow a 5-year-old girl to differentiate the likes of boys and girls, indicating that boys would like to have a Grumpy Bear because "they like bad things" like murkyish castles and Skeletors (Cloran, 1989). A 10-year-old talks of romance novels, saying, "Boys wouldn't like to read books like this. Think it's sissy to like books and romance and everything like that" (Gilbert & Taylor, 1991, p. 98). How early do girls evidence such stereotypes of boys' likes and dislikes? Karen, at 29;27, in discussing dollies, says, "Only girls have dollies." On being asked, "Can boys have dollies?" she answers, "No ... 'cause boys don't want to have dollies." Notice that behavioral differences are taken by her as evidence for differences in underlying preferences.

Boys similarly voice gender-based generalizations regarding preferences. For instance, being asked what's the most important thing to say about him, a child says "Probably that I like sports..... 'cause I don't know, that's what most of the boys like and that's what most people like to hear about boys." Another boy, on being asked what kind of person he is, answers, "I play sports." On being asked why that is important, he answers, "Because all the kids like athletes" (Damon & Hart, 1988, p. 65). Boys also allude directly to girls' divergent preferences. In their view, girls like "sissy games like ring-a ring-roses," and "long finger nails" (Delamont, 1980, p. 37), and as a third grade boy writes in an essay about disliking girls, "Do you know why I hate girls? Because they hate football. So I hate girls.... I wish girls liked football" (Dyson, 1993, p. 204). It is possible, of course, that such assumptions emerge out of exposure to girls' actual behavior in gender-linked domains (e.g., a child of 6;7 explains that girls can't play kickball, saying, "Well, girls aren't allowed to play ... Because they don't kick very good" (Andersen, 1990, p. 116). This possibility is strengthened by boys who described girls as "have to keep clean and have to help mummy in the house and are not allowed to climb trees" (Delamont, 1980, p. 37), generalizations that are likely based on behavioral indices.

Such generalized gender-linked assumptions extend to the preferences that one *ought* to have as a function of one's gender. When a 4-year-old boy wants to buy a necklace in a pretend store, the girl shopkeeper says, "No, that's for girls. Get yourself some sneakers" (Pitcher & Schultz, 1983, p. 46). When a preschool boy wants to play pink Power Ranger, he's told by his male peers, "You can't be that one ... that one's the girl" (Kyratzis, Marx, & Wade, 2001, p. 402). In line with this, Damon (1977) read children a story about George who wants to play with dolls and asked them why people told George not to do so. In response, a child of 4;8 years denied that George wants to play with dolls because "He doesn't want to be like a little baby"; but a boy of 5;11 years acknowledge this possible preference, indicating that "he should only play with things that boys play with.... he should stop playing with the girls' dolls and start playing with the G.I. Joe" (p. 255). It is evident, then, that the generalized preferences of the gender group are seen as providing guidelines for the preferences of individual members of the group. In light of this, a 3-year-old boy refuses to put on a dress during pretend play with girls, protesting, "No, no. Only girls wear these" (Pitcher & Schultz, 1983, p. 45). Being a boy, he needs to have the same preferences as other boys (Kohlberg, 1966).

It is clear, though, that what underlies the above pattern is the child's recognition that he too is a member of one gender group as opposed to the other. This recognition allows children to talk of *we*, the group of which they perceive themselves as members. Rubin (1980) documents this phenomenon when boys justified their rejection of girls by saying, "Because we like boys – we like to have boys" (p. 102). Garvey (1984) similarly found such group-based rejection of a girl at preschool when she wanted to join some boys on a swing and was rebuffed, with "We don't want you on here. We only want boys on here" (p. 163). Girls similarly reject boys as a group. This is expressed clearly in the following. When Joanie picks a girl rather than a boy to trade with, a boy says, "You always pick the girls," and she answers, "Boys pick boys and girls pick girls" (Wilkinson, Clevenger, & Dollaghan, 1981, p. 233). This type of gender-linked preference system in middle childhood is evident when a boy of 8;8 years approaches a girl on the school playground, asking, "Can I play?," the girl of 8;9 years, answers, "No, boys can't play" (Sluckin, 1981, p. 47). Preschoolers also evidence this pattern. When a preschooler is asked why his sister called him stupid, he says, "I didn't want to play with her. She's a girl" (Shure & Spivack, 1978, p. 154). Even toddlers are aware of this gender-linked preference system. Cloran (1989) recorded a toddler whose mother tells him that he can play with boys and girls at kindergarten; he denies this, saying, "I didn't play with the girls"; another toddler answers, "Oh no.... I only played with the boys" (p. 125). Note, though, that the above pattern reflects two important points: first, the understanding that specific groups of individuals can have similar preferences and second, that irrespective of which particular group they belong to and the particular preferences they hold, preferences govern everyone's choices and decisions regarding objects, contexts, and activities.

These two points are also reflected in children's talk about friendship. A child who said he doesn't want to be dumb, when asked why, answered, "Cause if you're dumb no one really wants to be your friend if you're stupid" (Damon & Hart, 1988, p. 65). In the same vein, a child discussed the importance of being smart to his friends because "My friends only like smart kids" (Damon & Hart, 1988, p. 66). Another child answered that he's friendly, indicating that this is important because "Other kids won't like you if you aren't." A seventh grader who was asked as to a pictured child being chastised at school, replied, "He'll be afraid of other kids thinking he's queer and then other kids won't want to hang around with him" (Wilson, 1974, p. 35). Finally, a child explains the importance of sharing and treating others well, saying, "It means I'll always have friends when I need them. People notice how you act to them and it counts in the long run" (Damon & Hart, 1988, p. 65). This wisdom is also apparent to a 3-year-old who says, "People don't like you if you take their things.... I don't do that" (Tough, 1977, p. 55).

PERSONALITY AS GENERALIZED PREFERENCES

Discussions of others' preferences allow children to develop perceptions of others, especially close others, as constellations of generalized preferences. In doing so, children note the cross-situational nature of others' preferences by using adverbs like *usually*, *whenever*, and *always*. In this vein, French and Nelson (1985) recorded a child of 5;4 years who said, "But you know what my sister does, she usu – whenever there's a birthday party, all she does, she wants to wear is pants." Children also use the present tense, which implies habitual constellations. In fact, Wood, McMahon, and Cranstoun (1980) noted that the majority of preschoolers' talk about family members was timeless, alluding to what mom really likes, always frowns upon, the dispositions and personal qualities of those most familiar to the child. Wellman (1988) suggests that stability of others' preferences forms the basis of children's attributions regarding enduring properties and traits in other people. In line with this, Yuill (1997) found that children as young as 4 years already have perceptions of certain traits as both enduring and changeable in others.

The importance of noting temporal stability in others' preferences is underlined by parental references to the need to remember others' preferences. In fact, just as children expect parents to remember their likes and dislikes, parents expect their children to remember parental likes and dislikes. A mother asks her children, "What's my favorite colored rose?" and when one of the children responds, "Yellow," she confirms this, saying "that's right" (Thomas-Lepore et al., 2004). Friends are also expected to remember one's likes and dislikes. A fifth grader says, "Since milk is one of my favorite drinks, and you know I like it and stuff?" and her peer responds, "You **love** milk" (Goodwin, 2006, p. 170). This is why a child can define a closest friend as "one who knows which games you like to play the best" (Selman, 1980, p. 138). If one has to remember other people's preferences, then preferences are important to them and need to be remembered in interacting with them.

In fact, children must necessarily remember others' preferences if they can allude to such preferences in their descriptions of these others. In this vein, when a preschooler talks of his 3-year-old cousin, he says, "He's a cute guy. He likes trucks" (Hall, CHILDES). In fact, older children describe their friends predominantly in terms of their likes and dislikes. A 10-year-old describes her friend, saying, "She likes to read. She likes books and she likes Harry Potter" (Engel & Li, 2004, p. 166); other children described their friends as "He likes to play video games" and "He likes to play with girls" (ibid). A girl in 5th grade tells a peer, "**You're** not a trendy person.... You like to – **you** don't like things that are trendy, or popular or anything" (Goodwin, 2006, p. 197) – and the girl agrees with her.

How do children attribute consistent preferences and characteristics to others? According to Kelley's (1971) covariation model, to do so, children examine the consistency or variation in others' behavior across objects and contexts as well as the normativeness of their behavioral choices. Perceived consistency of behavior across objects and contexts increases the likelihood of trait attributions whereas perceived normativeness decreases the likelihood of trait attributions because if many others act the same way in the same context, this makes it likely that the behavior is socially desirable rather than indicative of others' unique characteristics. This suggests that children track others' behavior over time and search for the consistencies that can lead to trait attributions. In fact, research (e.g., Gnepp & Chilamkurti, 1988) with children in kindergarten, second and fourth grade, as well as college students shows that there is an increase over this age range in the use of traits both to predict and to explain the behavior of hypothetical story characters.

This is why children can also note differences between themselves and their friends in terms of their preferences. For instance, an 11-year-old says of his best friend that he "doesn't like going to parties like I do.... and he just likes staying at home.... And he likes board games more than sporty games. I don't like board games that much" (Rout, Sixsmith, & Moore, 1996, p. 103). In an interesting example that contrasts different people's generalized preferences, Bloom (1970) recorded Kathryn, at 21 months, saying, "Me like coffee," shaking her head negatively as she says this, then continues, "Daddy like coffee. Lois e no coffee" (p. 153). Similarly, Emily in her presleep monologue at 22;22 says, "I don't like that bread. Daddy don't like. Emmy don't like."

ACCOUNTING FOR THE CONCERN WITH OTHERS' PREFERENCES

Why do children care about other people's preferences? First, similarity of preferences allows for the possibility of shared social interaction. If I want to play with dolls and you want to play with airplanes, it is highly unlikely that we will be able to engage in extended play, unless one of us is able to suggest that the dolls should go for an airplane ride (cf., Paley, 1986). Hence, questioning others' preferences facilitates the prospect of cooperation between children. As Paley (1990) notes, "If you want a certain person to like you, then you find out what makes him or her happy" (p. 122).

Second, the discovery of preference similarity is often "the occasion for jubilation, because it demonstrates that one is not alone in one's tastes and views" (Rubin, 1980, p. 70). That is, talking of one's preferences and comparing them with those of others allows one to establish whose preferences are normative. Such comparisons are built on an assumption of an inherent similarity between self and others, a similarity that presumably fosters a similarity in likes and dislikes (cf., Meltzoff, 2007a, 2007b). When Bill, at 6;2 years, refers to iguanas and says to his mother that he would hate to have one, the mother queries, "You don't want an iguana for a pet?" The child responds with his own query, "Do you?" and when the mother vehemently says *no*, the child answers, "Do you? Why should I?" and his mother responds, "Good reasoning, Bill" (Warren, CHILDES). That is, by virtue of his mother's similarity to himself, her likes and dislikes, at least in the domain in question, should translate into parallel likes and dislikes on the part of the child. It is on the basis of this assumption that the child can query why he should like an iguana for a pet if his mother would not like one. It is not surprising then preschoolers use lunchtime as a forum for discussing their comparative food preferences, talking of their respective liking of doughnuts, pizza, and tunafish (e.g., Dickinson, 1991). Of course, food preferences are not the only likes discussed in such forums. Children discuss television shows, magazines, books, and pop culture. For instance, referring to the Spice Girls, a fifth grader says, "I **never** liked **them**"; a peer then questions: "**Who** likes the Spice Girls? When one girl puts up her hand, another one says, "Emi **used** to like them" and Emi herself responds "I never liked the Spice Girls" (Goodwin, 2006, p. 197).

Third, because similarity of apparel and appearance is interpreted as evidence for an underlying similarity of preferences, it provides the grounds for establishing topics of conversation. A 5-year-old girl tells a peer, "Pretty slippers; I have some too" (Pitcher & Schultz, 1983, p. 65). A 3-year-old tells her friend, "I'm glad you're wearing pants, 'cause I am" and "Hey, we have pigtails," and her peer responds, "Yes, we have the same as mine" (Pitcher & Schultz, 1983, p. 67). Consequently, when differences are noted, they need to be justified. Piaget (1926/1959) recorded a child of 4;5 years, saying, "You've got a sweater on, I haven't. Mummy said it wasn't cold" (p. 57).

Moreover, children often use commonality of preferences to pronounce friendship, for example, "Whoever likes them (i.e. potatoes) can come to my house" (Meyer, 2003, p. 93), and a 5-year-old tells a peer: "You and me is friends, 'cause we both have red on" (Pitcher & Schultz, 1983, p. 68). In older children, similarity of preferences guides friendship choice more explicitly. For instance, a 13-year-old explains why he is friends with an age-mate, saying, "We like the same sort of things. We speak the same language" (Rubin, 1980, p. 34). A 12-year-old similarly explains that he and his friend "like the same sports." A child on a baseball team explains that he likes his friend because "We like the same stuff" (Fine, 1987, p. 80). In fact, then, friends "must become aware of one another's likes and dislikes" (Rubin, 1980, p. 37), and much time is spent talking of one's preferences (e.g., "I don't like David Potter even though they say I do") and asking others as to their preferences (e.g., "What kind of movies do you like, Heather?" asked by a preschooler, Selman, 1985, p. 227). Friends may even make a special effort to show off similarity of preferences by wearing the same clothes. As a middle school girl explains about her circle of friends: "We all try to dress the same and that," calling each other up to find out what they are each wearing and if "she'll say 'a pleated skirt' then the speaker will likewise 'put on my pleated skirt'" (Meyenn, 1980, p. 129).

In the above, there is an implicit assumption that the preferences of others who are not one's friends may well not match one's own or those of one's friends. Assumed mismatches, then, can further guide friendship choice. Heider's (1965) balance theory suggests that a triad is balanced when my friend's friend is my friend and when my friend's enemy is my enemy too. A 15-year-old girl explains, "If a new person comes in school and they hang around with somebody I don't like, I automatically don't like that person" (Rawlins, 1992, p. 82). Children are therefore concerned with whom their friends do and do not like. When first graders are talking, one asks, "Do you like Jack, Andy?" On getting a negative response, the questioning child says, "I don't either," further justifying why (Rizzo, 1989, p. 81). They also tell their friends that they must not like another child whom they themselves don't like or with whom they've had a fight. A school girl says, "My best friend didn't like her and told me not to play with her" (Goldman, 1982). In the context of a triad, a child of 3;11 is asked about what happens when his preferences and those of a good friend conflict regarding the presence of another peer during play. He says "I let 'em play.... But if he changes his mind and he don't want 'em to play – I don't want 'em to play – instead – of play, they have a fight" (Corsaro, 1985, p. 144).

ATTRIBUTING PREFERENCES TO DOLLS

Interestingly, children's preference talk is extended to dolls. First, dolls too are imputed to have preferences, much like those of babies and children. Karen, at 30;17,

Table 4.10.

	Age	Source
K playing with dolls		
K: "What color (you) want?"		
K responds as doll		Karniol
K: "Red, I'll bring you"[12]	30;17	(Diary, Karen)
Playing with stuffed mouse		
O: "Do you want Emek (type of cheese) now?		Karniol
Do you like Emek?"[13]	32 mos.	(Diary, Orren)
Boy playing with doll		
C: "Want lunch?"... "Told me she want lunch"	33 mos.	Bloom (1970)

says that one of her dolls is not eating salad. On being asked why, she answers, "Aviad doesn't like salad."[14] A child of 4;9 years explains regarding her doll in pretend "when I babysitted for her she really liked it because I tickled her so much. She likes me to tickle her" (Sachs, CHILDES). Dolls, too, react to the attainment and thwarting of their preferences. They cry when they are in want (e.g., a 29-month old explains regarding her "baby" that "she want her bottle," Fein, 1984, p. 132), are presumed to be hungry when they go unfed (e.g., a girl of 28;23 uses a stick to feed her doll, explaining: "baby hungry," Miller, 1982, p. 177), and need to be taken care of and be put to bed when they are tired. In this vein, as she is preparing her dolls for a picnic, a 35-month-old girl says, "I hope Alice can come along. And I gonna put her blanket in case her wants her blanket at night" (Hart & Risley, 1999, p. 138). In the context of doll play, Sach's daughter Naomi, at 4;9 years, explains that Dumbo is crying "'cause people are pulling his ears and he doesn't like that" (CHILDES). Pretending to wash her doll's hair, a 4-year-old asks her "Are you going to cry about it?" and as the doll, she answers, "No I won't cry when you rinse me, Kori. Kids don't cry when their big sisters rinse them." Later, she says, "Alyse, you're crying.... You don't have to cry about that. Are you crying about that?" (Segal & Adcock, 1981, p. 103).

Second, just like people, dolls are often asked what their preferences are, as shown in Table 4.10.

As well, children indicate uncertainty as to dolls' actual preferences. Reflecting this, Karen, at 30;25, says, "I'm bringing this for the dollies to draw. The dollies might not like this." Then she says to the dolls, "Do you want to draw this?"[15] again indicating uncertainty as to the doll's preferences. Third, dolls are attributed negative preferences as well. During doll play, Karen, at 24;18, says, "You (i.e., referring to self, meaning Karen) said to the baby "Want it? And the baby didn't want it." Later that day, she says, "Eat baby. You don't want it? No."

Fourth, children appear to treat dolls as if they were children, just like they are. To illustrate, Karen, at 21;27, gives her doll a bottle and says, "Like me, drinking my bottle." A child of 24;17, is feeding a toy monkey, saying, "He shall eat an apple too"[16] (Stenzel, 1994, p. 181). Dolls are put to bed, fed, dressed, taken to the potty, and sometimes spanked; dolls misbehave and need to be chastised. When Karen, at 29;13, says to me, "Karen is not happy," and she is asked why, she answers, "Because dolly is not behaving herself. She is not listening to Karen – not doing what Karen tells her." Children don't always listen to their parents and dolls are like children in this respect. Like children, dolls too can hurt and cry. A child tells her doll, "Dolly, you hold real still. I don't want to hurt you," said as she is combing the doll's hair (Segal & Adcock, 1981, p. 67). Similarly, a toddler is playing with her doll and warns her, "Okay, Dolly, we shampoo your hair. Don't worry. I get soap out of your eye" (Segal & Adcock, 1981, p. 67). When a preschool boy pokes at a girl's puppet, he is warned by her: "You could poke somebody's eye out" – and he desists (Wilkinson, Clevenger, & Dollaghan, 1981, p. 224).

Dolls are also attributed very specific wants and preferences, for instance, where they want to sit (e.g., regarding his doll, Orren, at 28;4, says to me "She wants to sit next to me"[17]), where they want to sleep (e.g., Orren, at 27;15, says, "The doll wants to sleep with me"[18]), and what and where they want to eat (e.g., at 28;18, Orren tells me: "Mommy, give to this Natali an egg to eat – she wants to eat with me at the table"[19]). Do children think that dolls are real? Apparently not, as I elaborate below.

Children know that dolls are not real people. To clarify, Orren, at 30;6, pretends that his cat puppet is talking and says, "Without a mouth he says to you, he says that to you because he's a cat."[20] Again regarding the same cat, at 31;22, he says, "Kitty, mummy will prepare for you milk in pretend and for me really. Do you know why?" and when he is asked why, he replies, "I'm a child but."[21] Similarly, while checking her dolls' heart with a stethoscope, a toddler says, "She doesn't have a real heart – the heart doesn't sound like anything," and adds, "Now the blood pressure – she really doesn't have any" (Segal & Adcock, 1981, p. 35). In yet another instance, a child says regarding a doll, "She has hair. It's only make believe," and when the mother says *Um hum*, the child continues, "People make believe. She's only a people" (Schachter, 1979, p. 141). As these statements indicate, then, there is no confusion in children's minds as to dolls' nonhuman status.

[12] Hebrew: "Ma çeva roça?" "Adom, avi lax"
[13] Hebrew: "Ata roçe axshav Emek? Ata ohev Emek?"
[14] Hebrew: "Aviad lo ohevet salat"
[15] Hebrew: "At roça et ze leçayer?"

[16] German: "auch Apfel ess"
[17] Hebrew: "He roça lashevet leyad li*"
[18] Hebrew: "Ima, titen leNatali haze le-exol beiça – he roça leexol iti leyad hashulxan"
[19] Hebrew: "Habuba roça lishon iti"
[20] Hebrew: "Bli pe' who omer at ze – who omer at ze lax ki who xatuli"
[21] Hebrew: "Xatuli, ima taxin lexa xalav be-keilu veli be-emet. Atta yodea lama?" ... "Ani yeled aval"

Rather, children's treatment of dolls appears to reflect stages in their understanding of psychological processes in others. Wolf, Rugh, and Altshuler (1984) followed nine children from ages 1 to 7, engaging in spontaneous and elicited replica play. They coded five levels of replica play with dolls. In the first of these levels, the child treats replicas as if they represent humans but does not make them act as independent agents. For instance, the child at this level may feed or dress a doll. In this context, Eric, at 20 months, feeds juice to his doll and says "juice baby" (Bloom, 1970), and Travis, at 19;26, says "Baby some too," while feeding her doll some real food (Tomasello, 1992). At the next level, the child treats replicas as independent agents but does not ascribe internal states to them. The child can make a replica doll dance, walk, sing, and so forth. To illustrate this, Travis, at 20;24, says, "Fred walking pillow" as she makes the doll walk on the pillow and, at 19;28, she says "Grover sleeping," as the puppet was in her bed (Tomasello, 1992). Next, the child ascribes sensations, perceptions, and physiological states to replicas; he may ask a doll if she is hungry or tired, whether she wants to go to sleep, see Daddy, or is in pain because of an injection that he gives her as a doctor. As the child's understanding of other people becomes more sophisticated, the child playing with replicas ascribes emotions, obligations, moral judgments, and social relations to them, with children at the highest level also ascribing to dolls cognitions like thinking, planning, and wondering. Wolf, Rugh and Altshuler (1984) coded the age of onset for each level they identified, using the second appearance of each type of behavior to index its emergence. Of the nine children studied, seven evidenced the hypothesized ordering of these levels, with two children evidencing an inversion of two adjacent orders. Children move through these levels of psychological understanding in a rather orderly sequence, but in contrast to other domains, higher levels do not supplant lower ones. All levels are represented in children's replica play, indicating the growing sophistication of children's understanding of other people as experiencers.

DEVELOPING IMPLICIT THEORIES OF OTHERS' PREFERENCES

As alluded to above, then, children appear to develop implicit theories of other people's preferences, assuming that there is a relation between people's choices, their behavior, and their underlying preferences. In such implicit theories, when an object is attractive, it provides a "pull" toward it and when it is unattractive or scary, it "pushes" away from it. People do not generally choose to interact with objects they prefer not to interact with nor do they choose to enter contexts they prefer not to be in. As they see other people behaving, then, children often comment on their actions, and they assume that these behaviors indicate choices reflecting underlying preferences. Armed with such simple theories, children can infer that infants want to play with attractive objects and that they may want to look for their mothers when they cannot see them. In this vein, a preschooler asks his toddler sister, "Maybe you want to go in there? Jennifer! Jennifer! Want to go inside?" suggesting that she climb into a play tunnel (Howe, 1991, p. 1506). Similarly, a preschooler is talking to his toddler sister and says, "Anny, if you want to go out, you can do. It's alright," reflecting his understanding that she may want to go look for her mother who's in the kitchen (Howe, 1991, p. 1506). That is, babies' behavior is interpreted by children as indicating underlying preferences, for example, "Mommy, I think she wants to go into the garden," and "I don't think she wants any more to eat" (Tizard & Hughes, 1984, p. 79).

These implicit theories also yield expectations as to both children's and adults' affective reactions to having preferences satisfied or thwarted. In these implicit theories, then, there is a relation among preferences, intentions to attain them, and psychological reactions to their attainment and nonattainment. Even 4-year-olds – close to 100 percent of them – know that people feel good when they get what they want and that people feel bad when their goals are blocked and they don't get what they want (e.g., Lagattuta, 2005). This allows children to construe others' affective reactions as indices of having their likes and dislikes satisfied or thwarted. This is why when Peter, at 33 months, hears his infant sister crying, can say, "She wants her bottle . . . think she wants her bottle" (Bloom, 1970). In this context, children know that the neighbor will be sad or angry if one takes flowers from his garden, the shopkeeper will be sad or angry if one takes something from his shop, and the teacher will be sad if the child doesn't come to school (Cook-Gumperz, 1973). A toddler asks "Are you happy that mama has bought a carriage?"[22] (Stern & Stern, 1928, as cited in Werner & Kaplan, 1963, p. 178), thereby indicating an awareness of others' affective reactions to getting preferences fulfilled.

Children develop a rich vocabulary for describing internal states in themselves and in others (e.g., Bretherton & Beeghly, 1982; Shatz & Gelman, 1973), using this vocabulary to refer to the psychological processes of babies, children, and adults. Their knowledge is first manifest in their encoding actions that are characteristic of others and gradually shift to capturing the covert psychological processes that others are assumed to experience (e.g., Eder, 1989; Yuill, 1997). Interestingly, though, children appear to encode typical and stable aspects of others behavior and only later do their representations appear to encode more specific and time-bound aspects.

Yet the tendency to see others as ensembles of stable psychological preferences and traits is not universal. Dweck and her colleagues (Chiu, Hong, & Dweck, 1997; Dweck, Chiu, & Hong, 1995) suggest that children develop implicit theories about trait stability and instability. In this view, some people are "entity theorists" who believe that others are characterized by static, fixed traits. Adoption of

[22] German: "freust du – mama Wagen ekauft hat?"

Table 4.11.

	Age	Source
K is drawing a picture K: "Karen is drawing for grandma and grandpa . . . grandma and grandpa will be terribly happy"	22;2	Karniol (Diary, Karen)
C holding a package of candy C: "Daddy like some when he come home"	26 mos.	Bowerman (1986, p. 289)
C1 to C2 C1: "Isabel likes that kind of candy. You should get her some"	4;8 years	Ervin-Tripp (1977, p. 177)
C holds shiny rocks C (to M): "I was gonna give it to Laura. . . . She'll love it, when I get it"	6;2 years	Warren (CHILDES)
Talking of making her family dinner C: "I make things that are simple, that I know they'll like. Like tuna"	14 years	Kaplan (2000, p. 489)

an entity theory leads children to use dispositions to predict and explain others' behavior. In contrast, "incremental theorists" view others as imbued with dynamic qualities that are more situationally determined and can change over time. Such children are less likely to attribute stable preferences and dispositions to others.

Nonetheless, assumptions about other people's preferences and psychological experiences then serve to guide children's behavior, and they also tell others to guide their behavior in light of such such preferences, as shown in Table 4.11.

Other people's preferences, then, are construed as needing to guide one's behavior toward them. Other people's preferences can also serve as guidelines for how one should conduct oneself in light of those preferences. A 13-year-old boy explains: "If I'm shopping for clothes, I tell that I like it and that I'd look really cool in it and the girls would like it" (Isler et al., 1987, p. 163), all being said to convince his mother to buy him the item in question.

Problematically, though, guiding one's behavior according to others' preferences makes little sense if there are temporal changes in others' preferences, and their current preferences may not necessarily predict later ones. Children do, in fact, pose questions that suggest they are uncertain as to how stable others' preferences are, for example, "Which one would you like today?" (Wells, 1985). In this vein, two girls of about 35 months are playing together and the one asks the others, "You don't want to play with these again?" (French & Pak, 1995), implying an implicit theory of short-term temporal changes in preferences. Similarly, when his father does not allow him to play with something before he goes to sleep at 32;11, Orren says, "In the morning you will allow me to play with it,"[23] indicating an understanding of the time-bound nature of his father's preferences. As a consequence, children often express uncertainty as to how current preferences may relate to later ones, for example, a toddler who says, "Maybe he'll want it later" (O'Neill & Atance, 2000). In fact, because other people's preferences may not match their own, children may indicate uncertainty as to what others' preferences might be. At 3;3;26 years, when Orren eats lunch while his sister is not home, he comments "The soup is very good. Maybe Karen no like the soup." Although other children have preferences that influence what they think about and what they do, one cannot be certain what other children will like. A college girl expresses this well, saying, "You don't know what everyone is going to like" (Haytko & Baker, 2004, p. 76).

In fact, just as parents make erroneous assumptions about their children's preferences, as discussed in Chapter 3, children can make erroneous assumptions about other people's preferences. When Siobhan, at 4;6 years, tells her friend regarding a picture she's cut out, "This is one of your favorite things to give to mummy, this is her thing right?" her friend says, "Let me see, no." Siobhan repeats, "Sure you have to give it to her . . . sure sure you have to take it home and give it to your mummy." When her friend repeatedly indicates she does not want the picture, Siobhan says "Sure it's your favorite picture," and when the friend denies this, she again repeats, "It is your favorite picture, yes it is cos that . . . . that's . . . that's sure spoons are your favorite things aren't they?" When her friend indicates they are not her favorite, Siobhan finally asks "What ones are your favorite?" (McTear, 1985, p. 96). The child made an erroneous assumption about her friend's preferences, tried to convince her that she did in fact have this preference, and when her friend rejected this attempt, she finally had to ask regarding her friend's preferences. Shure and Spivack (1978) incorporated the understanding that others have different preferences in their training program that teaches children to problem solve, with the underlying

[23] Hebrew: "Baboker atta tarshe' li lakaxat at ze"

Table 4.12.

	Age	Source
C doesn't want to throw out garbage M: "Your job is to throw out the trash. We can't always do what we want to do"	Preschool	Shure & Spivack (1978, p. 148)
C refuses to clean up at preschool T: "Cleaning up isn't my favorite thing either, but it needs to be done"	Preschool	Bergin & Bergin (1999, p. 200)
C says she doesn't want to go back to school F: "There are certain things in life that you have to do without wanting to do them, and there's a good reason to do them . . . ."	8 years	Nevat-Gal, 2002, p. 187)
C doesn't want to do homework M: "You have to do this (homework) just like I have to pay my bills or do something that I don't always enjoy"	Third grade	Xu & Corno (1998, p. 419)

assumption that in interacting with others, children need to understand how they can use this knowledge to further cooperative interactions and avoid conflicting ones.

Moreover, though, drawing inferences on the basis of others' actions can be misleading because individuals often engage in actions that counter their own preferences. For instance, Wells (CHILDES) recorded the following exchange between Ben, at 5;0;23 years, and his mother, when she says, "I don't feel like ironing." Ben says to her, "You got to do it haven't you?" and his mother answers "Yes, I have got to do it" – and she does. Similarly, when a child asks his mother not to do her housework and play with him, she answers, "I'm sorry, but I've got to" (Tizard & Hughes, 1984, p. 97). These parents are drawing a contrast between their preferences and the behavior they are engaging in, despite their preferences being otherwise. Consequently, one cannot always depend on behavioral cues that others emit.

Critically, as I discuss in later chapters, as part of socialization, children also have to engage in behavior that counters their own preferences. This may well be alluded to explicitly by parents when they tell children they have to do things that counter their preferences, as shown in Table 4.12.

OTHERS' EXTERNAL PREFERENCES

The understanding that others have preferences and that these preferences need not parallel one's own preferences is a powerful tool. It serves us well when others express their external preferences, their preferences about our own preferences and behavior. That is, others may tell us what they want or prefer that we say, do, and perhaps think. Even when they do not express their external preferences directly, we can often infer others' external preferences from what they say and do (e.g., a teen wears a skimpy outfit and a parent says, "Did they run out of fabric when they sewed that dress?"; a parent who buys a low-fat snack for an overweight child). The importance of others' external preferences is their potential of conflicting with our own first-order preferences. External preferences are especially relevant in the context of parent–child interaction because knowing parental preferences as to how one should behave, think, or feel, represents an important first step in guiding children's behavior and psychological reactions in light of such preferences. As will be discussed in subsequent chapters, parents are constantly telling children what they want *for and from* their children. Parents prefer that their children engage in those behaviors that parents want them to engage in and desist from those that they do not want them to engage in. Children's awareness of parents' external preferences about them potentiates preferential conflict when their own preferences do not accord with parental external ones.

Children, therefore, become aware of the fact that parents may tell them their preferences in order to impact their preferences. In this vein, Karniol and Ross (1979) found that kindergarten children attributed manipulative intent to adults who offered children rewards for engaging in activities that are not ordinarily undertaken for rewards. Children understood that others' behavior not only reflects intentions but that in the context of activities that are ordinarily engaged in because of intrinsic interest, the reward most likely constitutes a coercive force, meant to sway the rewarded child into performing an activity that he would not engage in otherwise. Children sometimes explicitly refer to such manipulative attempts in discussing others' behavior. When a 6-year-old girl is asked why the teacher doesn't allow children to get drinks, she replies,

> Because she wants you to get your work done . . . . Because she thinks if you go while you're doing you work, sometimes you stay there a long time and you don't want to finish your work, that's why you stay there (Mayall, 2000, p. 130).

An Italian 7-year-old, whose mother says to him, "These string beans are good aren't they?" answers her, "Only

Table 4.13.

	Age	Source
Playing pretend grocery shopping		
C: "Do you allow me to buy an ice cream cone?"[24]	27;13	Karniol (Diary, Orren)
C: "Mommy do you allow me to play with this?"[25]	27;26	Karniol (Diary Orren)
K: "Can I go on the bed with slippers? . . . Do you allow me to jump?"	33;8	Karniol (Diary, Karen)
C: "It's OK I touching this?"	39;29	Karniol (Diary, Orren)
Playing pretend mother/daughter		
C: "Mommy may we go out and play?"	8 years	Goodwin (1990)

because you want to make me eat them"[26] (Pontecorvo & Fasulo, 1997, p. 413). He understood his mother's statement as a manipulative attempt to get him to eat the food in question.

This is also evident when children interpret others' verbal utterances as an index of their implied preferences. When a mother says "It's noisy in here," referring to the television in the next room, her preschooler asks, "Do you want me to shut the door?" (Ervin-Tripp, 1977, p. 182). The child interpreted the mother's declarative statement as a statement of her preference that the child shut the door so that there be less noise. Reeder (1996) found that children acquire an understanding of indirect expressions of preference very early, construing them as statements of preference rather than as declarations as to the state of the world.

Despite the potential of interpersonal preferential conflict, awareness that parents have external preferences regarding their behavior leads children to query their parents as to what such preferences might be. Adam, at 25 months, asks his mother about getting into the car, "Do you want me get in?" (Brown, CHILDES). A 30-month-old asks his mother, "Want me to wash my face?" (Hart & Risley, 1999, p. 65). A 38-month-old asks her mother as to what both she and her sister should do: "Do you want us to wash our hands?"[27] (Taeschner, 1983). These questions indicate not only that children are aware of the fact that parents have preferences but also that children make no assumption of a similarity between their own and their parents' preferences.

Children also question their parents' external preferences when they are unsure what their parents want them to do in a given context. A preschool child asks his mother, "What's the thing what you want me to do?" (Wells, 1985). A child of 7;6 years asks his father "Where do you want me to sit?" (MacWhinney, CHILDES). The fact that a child can ask a parent as to the parent's preferences regarding the child's own behavior underlines that children are aware of potential mismatches between their own preferences and those of others. But it also indicates a willingness on the child's part to accommodate and fulfill parental external preferences.

Such willingness to accommodate parental external preferences is also evident when children ask parents what they are allowed to do, as shown in Table 4.13.

Such questions may of course yield a *no* response, pitting the child's own preferences against the parent's conflicting alternative preferences.

Finally, in this context, children comment on the contrast between their own preferences and their parents' external preferences. For instance, a child of 3;6 years who is told he must go to bed replies, "I don't want to go to bed yet. Don't let (i.e., make) me go to bed" (Bowerman, 1985, p. 389). In saying this, the child clearly recognizes his mother's external preferences as being different than his preferences and asks the mother to lay aside her preferences for the moment.

OTHERS' AFFECTIVE REACTIONS

In addition to expressing their external preferences, parents often focus on their own emotional reactions to contexts in which their external preferences were apparently in concordance or in conflict with that of the child. That is, parents are guided by an implicit assumption that if the child knows what their external preferences are in a given context, their external preferences – rather than the child's own preferences – should serve to guide the child's behavior. In fact, parents often elaborate how the child's noncompliance with their external preferences impacts them, or others, emotionally, as shown in Table 4.14.

In fact, in outlining Parent Effectiveness Training (PET), Gordon (1976) urges parents to use what he calls "I-messages" in which the parent explicates the impact of the child's actions for the parent (e.g., "When I have to talk on the phone, I get upset when there's so much noise that I can't hear," "I sure get discouraged when my clean kitchen gets dirtied up right away," p. 119).

[24] Hebrew: "Ata marshe' li liknot artik?"

[25] Hebrew: "Ima at marsha li lesaxek im ze?"

[26] Italian: "Mm che buoni 'sti fagiolini, vero"; "solo perche me li vuoi far mangiare"

[27] German: "Wollen wir Hande waschen, Mami?"

Table 4.14.

	Age	Source
M: "And you know what else made me real sad? What did you do the other night?" C says he tore up a book	29 mos.	Hart & Risley (1999, p. 103)
M doesn't want to buy C toy M: "Everytime I get you an expensive toy you or your brother break it and I get very angry"	Preschool	Shure & Spivack (1978, p. 135)
Hypothetical scenario about a child not talking to father because of a broken promise M1: "Daddy won't like it/ he'll be unhappy if you don't talk to him" M2: "You must expect mummy to be cross if you do that"	Preschool	Cook-Gumperz (1973, p. 65)
T: "I'm not happy when you don't listen"	Preschool	Mody (2005, p. 98)
T: "Put your legs down Chatinder. Don't make me cross.... Are you listening? 'Cos I shall get cross if you are going to be silly"	Preschool	Willes (1983, p. 139)
C doesn't want to draw T: "I'd be glad of some paintings for my wall. Wouldn't you do some paintings for me Ruth? For my wall?"	Preschool	Willes (1983, p. 138)

Mothers also discuss the likely affective reactions of third parties, both to having their preferences satisfied and to having their preferences thwarted. In this vein, a child who took someone's seat at preschool is told, "Sean was sitting there and now he's very disappointed" (Kantor, Elgas, & Fernie, 1989, p. 439) and a Japanese preschooler is told "If you do things that your friends don't like, your friends will cry" (Peak, 1991, p. 162). A toddler who is playing "circus" announces about the zoo animals, "They not going to do tricks today"; the mother responds, "No tricks today! Oh, the children are going to be so disappointed!" implying that children's preferences would be thwarted (Lucariello, Kyratzis, & Engel, 1986, p. 158). Chang (2003) found that Chinese mothers express affect using predicates without explicit mention of who the experiencer is, suggesting that everyone can be assumed to have the same affective experiences, a community of shared psychological experiences. In this light, preschoolers associate others' affective reactions with contexts that can give rise to such affective reactions (e.g., Gnepp, McKee, & Domanic, 1987; Karniol & Koren, 1987) and understand that cues associated with affective experiences can serve as reminders of prior events, thereby reactivating in others the related affective experience (Lagattuta, Wellman, & Flavell, 1997).

As a result, children become aware of the fact that when their behavior does or does not accord with parental external preferences, parents may have emotional reactions. A 2-year-old relates "Mama mad," and his mother replies, "That's right. I was mad. How come?" The child responds that he hit his aunt. A preschooler relates an experience relating to her sibling, saying, "I hit Joey and you got mad" (Howe & Rinaldi, 2004, p. 224). Similarly, Orren, at 27;6, says to me, "If Karen goes to throw out the balloon – mommy is angry," and at 28;9, he elaborates, "If Karen draw on this, you'll be angry."[28] Notice that the children above were alluding to maternal affective reactions in the past, as well as likely affective reactions in the future.

Children can use such emotional reactions in two ways. First, they can engage in behavior that either promotes or averts a given parental emotional reaction. They can try to make mother happy or prevent her from being sad (e.g., "I'm picking up mine because I want you to be happy," said by a child of 40 months, Kuczaj, CHILDES). But they can also use parental emotional reactions as indices of likely behavioral consequents of such emotional reactions and attempt to either promote or avert the behavioral consequents rather than the emotional reactions themselves. That is, if a child notes a consistent relation between a given emotional reaction and a specific behavioral pattern (e.g., when my mother is sad, she doesn't talk to me, when my mother is angry she yells), he may engage in actions that attempt to alter the mother's behavior rather than her emotional reaction per se.

I am suggesting, then, that there are two different processes. Children learn the contingencies between their own behavior and the emotional reactions of others. Such contingencies are in the form of "when/if I do X, mother experiences Y," referring to the impact of one's own behavior on others' affective reactions. Children learn others' reactions to their crying, to their smiling, to their requests for things, and to their own noncompliance with others' requests. They may learn that others are unresponsive, occasionally responsive, or generally responsive. For instance, a child learns that if he engages in a given behavior (e.g., hit his sister, not eat meals, wake someone up),

[28] Hebrew: "Karen holex lizrok haxuça habalon – ima koeset," "Im Karen meççayer al ze, at tixas"

Table 4.15.

	Age	Source
K: "Made kaki (i.e., had a bowel movement in her diaper). Mommy is not happy. Mommy is happy when Karen makes kaki in the potty"	24;11	Karniol (Diary, Karen)
K: "Sometimes when Karen spits out something, Mommy gets angry and then it's horrible"	25;23	Karniol (Diary, Karen)
O: "You're not happy when there's a bad boy in this house"[29]	29;20	Karniol (Diary, Orren)
F suggests he go to the bathroom O: "Making poo is a good idea – Mummy and Karen will be happy"[30]	31;28	Karniol (Diary, Orren)
K: "A mistake is like an accident. But some things are on purpose – and then Mummy is angry"	33;8	Karniol (Diary, Karen)
C: "My mom'll be cross 'cos I've got my sleeves wet"	3 years	Tough (1977, p. 56)
C asks peer for car she brought to preschool C: "Give me my car now 'cos it's nearly time for me to go home and my mum'll be cross if I don't take it home"	3 years	Tough (1977, p. 79)
C2 drew on C1's shirt C1: "Hey, don't do that. This is my nice shirt. My mommy will be mad"	4 years	Pitcher & Schultz (1983, p. 46)

others may become upset or angry; but there are other behaviors that he can engage in that may make others happy (e.g., helping with chores, being kind to old ladies). It bears recognition, though, that children also care about the normativeness of both one's own and others' affective reactions. In the words of a 12-year-old girl who explains what she does when she's angry, she says that she reads fiction because "(It helps) to know that other people have problems too and they get angry" (Brown, 1998, p. 157).

Through repeated encounters in which children hear about the likely psychological reactions of those around them to their behavior, they develop expectations for antecedent – consequent pairings in which the consequent is other people's affective reactions. When these affective reactions are positive, one presumably engages in actions to induce them; when these affective reactions are negative, one presumably engages in actions that avert them. A child who hit his aunt is further told, "But you won't do it again," and he replies, "No more" (Wolf, 1982, p. 319). Zahn-Waxler, Radke-Yarrow, and King (1979) found that six of the twenty toddlers they studied assumed that they were responsible for their mother's distress, saying, "Did I make you sad?" or, "Sorry, I be nice," apparently having learned to use apologies as a means of reparation for transgressions.

Once children become aware of their parents' external preferences and their likely emotional reactions to outcomes that relate to these preferences, they can comment on such emotional reactions and take action to either hasten or avert them. Children start alluding to others' likely affective reactions to their behavior and to their misbehavior, and by the age of four and a half years, the majority of children cite mothers as angry when children are noisy, naughty, aggressive, or cause damage and as happy when children are not noisy, are good, and do not fight (Shields & Duveen, 1986). Once they have expectations about how parents will react, children can refer to such expectations and use these expectations to guide their own behavior, as shown in Table 4.15.

This concern with mothers' likely reactions is encouraged by teachers; for example, a preschool teacher tells a child, "Put the apron on. What would Mummy say if you come home with paint on that nice new jumper?" (King, 1978, p. 52). The child is supposed to consider proactively what the likely reactions of his mother might be and guide his behavior accordingly.

Presumably then, others' emotional reactions can also be averted by not engaging in the relevant behaviors. It is important to note that these comments are not referring to parental preferences in specific contexts but rather seem to reflect a more general sort of understanding of parental likes and dislikes. This is also evident when a child of 4;8 years says, "My mom always gets angry with me if I put the wrong things out" and about baking cookies, "My sister kept eating them and so did I. So my mom didn't like us eating anymore" (French & Nelson, 1985). In this light, others' preferences are directly tied to their affective reactions and one has to be concerned with both of these in interacting with them. As a Japanese mother of a 3-year-old explains, "As long as you have to relate to other people . . . . you can't think of only your own feelings. To get along with others, you have to act based on other people's feelings too" (Peak, 1991, p. 12).

[29] Hebrew: "At lo smexa she-yesh yeled ra babait haze"
[30] Hebrew: "Kaki ze rayon tov – ima veKaren yismexu"

Note that understanding others' affective reactions needs to be differentiated from the actions that may be taken as a result of such affective reactions. It may well be that an angry mother is one who punishes and a happy mother is one who gives hugs and kisses, but the affective reaction needs to be differentiated from the likely behavioral consequents. Once we differentiate between others' affective reactions and the likely behavioral consequent, the question is whether "mother does Y" is viewed as *directly* caused by the antecedent child behavior or whether it is seen as mediated by some internal state in the other person, that is, "when I do x, mother experiences state p; when mother experiences state p, she does Y." This is important because (1) children may wish to avoid or to induce their mother's relevant experience (e.g., "I don't want you to be sad, Mommy"), (2) they may wish to induce or to avert the mother's actions while being unconcerned with her affective state ("Don't spank me"), or (3) they may attempt to unchain the contingency between the antecedent, the affective experience, and the behavioral consequent, doing so by invoking various strategies, including persuasion (e.g., "Don't' be angry Mommy") and recontextualizing (e.g., "I didn't do it – he did," "I didn't do it on purpose," "it's no big deal"). If they do not see an affective state as mediating between the antecedent and the consequent, their choice of strategies will differ and their likelihood of success will vary as well.

Another important aspect of the above is that children learn how their own affective reactions differ from those of others in the same context. That is, a mother may be angry in a given context, but the child need not be angry in the same context. Children can use their knowledge of other people's likely emotional reactions to guide their behavior, even when their own preferences do not coincide with those of others and when others' affective reactions diverge from children's own affective reactions in the same contexts (Terwogt & Rieffe, 2003). In keeping with this, Thompson et al. (2003) contend that the child can compare his direct representation of a given experience with the secondary representations of the mother, who may have shared or witnessed that same experience. As will be elaborated in Chapter 10, talking with others regarding experiences, "becomes a tutorial in divergent mental states when the child and the caregiver have different representations of the experience they shared." (Thompson et al. 2003). Awareness of divergent mental states spurs conceptual development because it confronts the child with the realization that people have different understandings of shared events and motivates efforts to understand why.

Learning parental emotional reactions to one's behavior is not enough, though, because the child must also learn the relation between others' emotional reactions and their likely behavioral responses. When mother is upset or angry, she may shout, punish, or spank; when mother is happy she may hug, compliment, or ignore. Children learn such relations by way of parental socialization strategies. Specifically, when parents channel, temporize, restrict, and discipline, children's preferences necessarily clash with those of their parents, and children need to squarely face the self–other preference gap. How do children bridge this preference gap? This is the next topic that I address.

PREDICTING OTHERS' PREFERENCES – THE SAD MODEL AND SOME ALTERNATIVES

Even though children have implicit theories about the relation between preferences and other psychological processes, they still need to be able to predict others' preferences and likely psychological reactions in specific contexts. How do they do so? In several papers (e.g., Karniol, 1986, 1990b, 2003a), I presented a model that accounts for how people make predictions about others' likely thoughts and feelings.

To elaborate, at the heart of the process are representations of *generic others* in terms of their likely thoughts, feelings, and behavior in different contexts. Predictions about others draw on generalized representations about situations or episodes (Schank & Abelson, 1977; Schank, 1982), where such generalized representations include information regarding typical characters, settings, events, temporal sequences, and causal relations, and consequently they provide a means of making sense of other people's behavior and their reactions to events. Generalized representations of situations contain knowledge about specific psychological processes like affective reactions and cognitions that people in general are likely to have in situations (e.g., Cantor, Mischel, & Schwartz, 1982; Conway & Bekerian, 1987). Memory organization proceeds by noting differences or deviations from these generalized knowledge representations (cf., Kolodner, 1984; Schank, 1982), a method of organization that reduces redundancy and maximizes economy. The implication of such a system of knowledge representation is that when no information about others is available, default values are assigned and they are assumed to think, feel, and act like a generic individual.

Who are generic others? As I discuss in Chapter 10 as well, generic others are *fictions* that are critical in our thinking, our language, and in communication. To elaborate, communication demands that we establish what Clark (1996) calls "communal common ground," a set of assumptions about others' knowledge state that emerges out of the understanding that others are members of "a cultural community" with shared expertise regarding facts, beliefs, procedures, norms, and assumptions that can be taken for granted. What defines a community is consensus, "an infinite series of reciprocating understandings between the members of the group concerning the issue. I know that you know that I know, and so on" (Scheff, 1967, p. 37). The community is an imaginary entity that is based on "a folk psychology about people in general – about human nature" (Clark, 1996, p. 106), with this folk psychology relating to generic others rather than to specific individuals with whom we have direct contact.

Yet Clark does not focus on the issue of *normalcy*. It is only by assuming that generic others have normal reactions to events and that we too are normal in our abilities, preferences, and psychological reactions that we can use language to allude to others (e.g., in using the pronoun *one*, Moltmann, 2006) and that such assumed normalcy can be used to make sense of the behavior and the psychological experiences of others. Heal (2003) makes essentially the same point when she says, "I cannot but take myself to be rational. So in order to see others as joint deliberators I need to credit them with the same capacity" (p. 6) As Jones and Nisbett (1972) emphasize, in the absence of detailed historical knowledge of others, we treat others as modal cases, drawing on our understanding of how normal people react and guiding our own behavior in light of such expectations. They elaborate that "In the absence of precise knowledge of the actor's history, the observer is compelled to deal with him as a modal case and to ignore his unique history and orientation" (p. 85). In their theory of correspondent inferences, Jones and Davis (1965) weight this aspect heavily, indicating that people are "seen as desiring the same things most persons would in a given situation" (p. 233).

When coupled with the normalcy assumption, using generic others as the default is a powerful tool for the following reasons:

1) We can assume that specific others' psychological reactions are rule-governed rather than random. That is, irrespective of who the other person is, we can assume that his psychological experiences are rule-governed (cf., Pylyshyn, 1984). In the absence of this assumption, and if others' psychological experiences are assumed to be random, we could not even attempt to predict their likely psychological experiences. As a corollary to being rule-governed, for any input stimulus or context, there has to be a transformation rule (cf., Berlyne, 1965) that can be applied to link that stimulus or context to the likely subsequent psychological reactions that others will experience. Transformation rules, then, relate targets' psychological reactions to their prior perceptions. Even though the transformation rules that account for others' psychological reactions are unknown to us, we assume that such transformation rules exist and account for the "logical" nature of others' psychological experiences.

2) Because we know a finite number of transformation rules we can assume that these rules account for other people's psychological reactions. That is, because we have no direct knowledge of others' transformation rules, we assume that the transformation rules we know ourselves account for the link between other people's perceptions and their psychological reactions. To give a mathematical analogy, if I only know of the rules of addition and subtraction and I need to predict how someone would solve a problem to which a power function may be applied (e.g., 2 (?) = 8), it is impossible for me to predict his use of the power function (or multiplication, for that matter) because this rule does not exist in my repertoire of rules. Similarly, we can only use the transformation rules *we* know for making predictions about other people's likely psychological reactions. Making predictions then requires us to select a transformation rule from the finite number of transformation rules that we ourselves know. This selection process is independent of other people's own way of relating perceptions to psychological experiences and depends only on the set of transformation rules that we ourselves know.

But why do we need transformation rules? Both the stimuli and contexts that can induce psychological experiences in others and the possible psychological reactions to these stimuli and contexts are essentially infinite. As observers and participants in interaction we need a means of reducing the potential number of possible predictions that are deemed possible in any given instance. Transformation rules serve this function; they delimit the general patterns and possible directions into which others' psychological experiences are expected to be channeled in response to stimuli and events. The selection of a given transformation rule channels the observer toward a specific line of prediction that is dictated by choice of that particular transformation rule and guides the memory search conducted to imbue predictions with content in each particular instance.

Each transformation rule represents knowledge about one possible relationship between contexts and psychological reactions to them. The actual taxonomy of rules was derived on an empirical basis (Karniol, 1986) in light of models of directed thinking (e.g., Whorf, 1956; Schank, 1982; Schank & Abelson, 1977; Schank & Wilensky, 1978) that specify the types of transformations that allow individuals to link perceptions with stored knowledge (see Karniol, 1990b). In this book, I will not reiterate this derivation and will only illustrate how the rules work in practice.

Let me take the example of a child who wants to predict how someone else is likely to react to seeing a plane taking off. If the child applies a transformation rule called "State/Characteristic of Stimulus," he may predict that the target person about whom he is making the prediction would think that the plane is relatively big or small; or this person may be expected to categorize the plane as "a 747," using a transformation rule called "Category Instantiation." If the child expects the target of his prediction to apply a transformation rule called "Stimulus-Reminded Reminiscence," he may predict that seeing the plane will remind the person of a loved one who flew overseas. As this example illustrates, selecting a given transformation rule serves to constrain the possible predictions we can make about others in specific contexts.

Given that there are several different transformation rules and more than one may be applicable for making a prediction in any given context, how do we decide which particular rule to apply? There must be a means of selecting one of the transformation rules one knows to make a prediction. Research based on my model (e.g., Karniol, 1986) implicates a heuristic that consists of a hierarchically ordered system of transformation rules that governs the selection of the specific transformation rule in each instance. This is done by accessing the entire hierarchy of transformation rules and trying each rule sequentially until the prediction generated by applying that rule seems reasonable given the context and the target in question. Transformation rules and generic knowledge representations work in concert to imbue predictions with content in specific contexts. That is, when we predict other people's likely thoughts and feelings, what we actually do is draw on transformation rules and generic knowledge about other people that we apply to the context in question. We can make predictions about others' likely thoughts and feelings because we know that others are psychological beings with thoughts and feelings that relatively predictably relate the external world to their internal, psychological world.

This heuristic also allows for great flexibility in making predictions about categories of individuals as well as specific individuals who are well known. To continue with the previous example, one's parents, for instance, are known to differ from generic others and this difference will be evident in the particular transformation rule selected for making predictions about them as opposed to about generic others. If a child knows that his parents tend to reminisce in making predictions about them, he is more likely to select a transformation rule that relates contexts to reminiscing rather than to one that relates contexts to future plans and goals. This is also the case for making predictions about old people, who are known to reminisce (Karniol & Shomroni, 1999). Similarly, if one's best friend is an expert on airplanes, one is more likely to make a prediction about him that takes this knowledge into account and to elaborate regarding the type of airplane and its technical characteristics.

From this perspective, then, there are two different processes. First, as part of socialization, children learn that there are generic others who act, think, and feel in culturally expected ways. Knowledge about generic others is used as the default in making predictions about others. Second, children learn how specific others and categories of individuals differ from generic others in their reactions and behavior (e.g., a teen explains: "Shy people don't usually like show-offs," Selman, 1980, p. 111). In this vein, Lakoff (1987) suggests that categories are necessarily defined in contrast to other categories that have opposite properties and that subcatgories are also understood as deviations from the normative case. Each category defines normal expectations for its members and serves to distinguish its members from those of other categories and from generic others (cf., Kolodner, 1984; Bond & Brockett, 1987; Bond & Sedikides, 1988)

In addition to making predictions about generic others and categories of others who deviate from generic others, we can predict how we ourselves would react psychologically to a given stimulus or context. How do we make predictions about ourselves? In the model, there are two different ways. First, just as knowledge of the psychological processes of generic others allows us to make predictions about others, we can use this same knowledge base for making predictions about ourselves in domains in which self-knowledge is not available.

Importantly, as children, we also learn how we differ from generic others. As Piaget contends,

> in order to discover oneself as a particular individual, what is needed is a continuous comparison, the outcome of opposition, of discussion, and of mutual control; and indeed *consciousness of the individual self appears later than consciousness of the more general features in our psychological make-up*.... Consciousness of self implies a perpetual comparison of the self with other people." (Piaget, 1965, p. 393, emphasis added; p. 340)

From this perspective, one's self-knowledge is comparative and only encodes one's distinctiveness from generic others in one's preferences, psychological reactions, and personal experiences. This mean that there is independent encoding of generic knowledge, specific knowledge about well-known targets and social categories, and self-knowledge, which serves to store one's own distinct or idiosyncratic points of view. For constructing a self-representation, then, children determine those domains in which they differ from others and they encode these differences within their self-representation (cf., McGuire & McGuire, 1986; 1988). This is why representations of self appear to develop later than representations of others (e.g., Eder, 1989); generic knowledge is acquired prior to knowledge about one's own uniqueness in given domains. In fact, there is evidence that children below the age of 7 seldom make psychological or dispositional generalizations about themselves or about others (e.g., Livesely & Bromley, 1973)

In the Self-as-Distinctive (SAD) model (Karniol, 1990b, 2003a, 2003b), then, there are two different ways of making predictions about oneself. First, there are many domains in which one would be expected to have the same thoughts and feelings as generic others, domains in which one's self-representation does not provide any information regarding one's possible thoughts and feelings and in which one can be assumed to be like generic others. In such contexts, one makes predictions about oneself by drawing on generic representations. This would lead to predicting that, like everyone else, on seeing an old man one would think of how sad it is to be old, on seeing a child one would think of how cute children are, and that planes are remarkable technological achievements.

Second, predictions about self can draw on a self-representation in which our own psychological uniqueness as compared with generic others is encoded. In those domains in which such self-knowledge is available, one uses this knowledge to make predictions about self's likely psychological processes in relevant contexts. In drawing on my own self-representation, I may predict that seeing an old man would remind me of my grandfather, seeing a child would stimulate my own desire for a child (cf., Boucai & Karniol, 2008), and seeing a plane taking off would remind me of my previous trip to Europe. Having a ninety-year-old grandmother who is healthy and spry may lead one to anticipate having different reactions to old people than the generic other person, who would be expected to associate old age with frailty and illness. That is, people know their own psychological quirks and make-up and differentiate their own psychological processes from those of others. I know that others are unlikely to share my thoughts and feelings in many contexts and are expected to experience thoughts and feelings that are common to most other people in such contexts. So in making predictions about others' likely thoughts and feelings, it is the store of knowledge about generic others and their psychological processes that needs to be accessed. From this perspective, then, the way we relate the external world to our own internal world need have no relation to the way we do so for others. This is because predictions about ourselves do not necessarily draw on the same knowledge source as predictions about others. On the other hand, overlaps in predictions about self and others emerge out of our use of generic knowledge for making predictions about self; overlaps that are not the outcome of the use of self knowledge for making predictions about others.

SIMULATION, SELF AS DEFAULT, AND THEORY OF MIND APPROACHES

My approach to making predictions about others' thoughts and feelings differs from three other important approaches. The first of these approaches stipulates that given the lack of access to other minds, we can only simulate, using our own psychological processes and projecting what others do on the basis of ourselves (e.g., Goldman, 1992; Gordon, 1986, 1995; Tomasello, 1999). Goldman (1992), for instance, contends that when we simulate, we use introspection to identify what mental states we would have in the same context, and then we project these states onto the target individual. In this view, then, every statement about another person's likely thoughts and feelings actually reflects our own likely thoughts and feelings in these contexts. Of course, this process is based on the assumption that others are generally like us in most respects, what Gopnik and Meltzoff (1994) have called "our deep-seated assumption that we are like other people in important ways" (p. 167). Yet, as Goldman (1992) argues, because we know that the assumption of similarity is not warranted entirely, the entire process is conducted in the pretend mode, offline so to speak, so that the results are "mental" rather than behavioral: inferences, predictions, and explanations. Nevertheless, simulation necessarily requires the assumption of similarity between self and the other to hold.[31] As Goldie argues, though, the problem with simulation is that it

> tends to retain aspects of my characterization; I might *think* I have adjusted for all relevant differences between me and the other person . . . it is not natural first to imagine hearing the news of the death of *your* loved one, and then to make adjustments. What is natural is to imagine her hearing the news. (Goldie, 2000, p. 202)

An alternative view posits that although individuals do have representations that relate to other people's psychological processes, one's self-representation "dominates" and interferes so that access to such representations is generally unlikely, unless one "suppresses" the self. In the first of these views, the *Self-Schematic Model* (Markus, 1977), the self is automatically activated in processing information about others in all domains in which one has a self-schema. Markus contends that *not* using a relevant self-schema requires concentrated attempts at suppressing the self-schema and that such efforts are likely to meet with limited success (Markus & Smith, 1981). In the second of these views (e.g., Higgins, 1982; Higgins & Bargh, 1990), simulation is developmentally primary, remaining the default heuristic in the absence of time and attentional resources in adulthood. In this view, which I (Karniol, 2003a) have labeled *Simulation as Malfunction*, there is an alternative representation that can be used for making predictions about others but the likelihood of this representation being used is quite low, given the time and effort required for self-suppression (Higgins & Bargh, 1987). The problem with both the Simulation as Malfunction view and the Self-Schematic view is that they imply that most of the time, individuals' predictions and inferences about others are in fact predictions about themselves.

The third view is one that posits the existence of a Theory of Mind. In this view, the same cognitive mechanisms are involved in attributing mental states to both self and others. These cognitive mechanisms include a body of information about human psychology, a so-called Theory of Mind (e.g., Gopnik & Wellman, 1994; Gopnik & Meltzoff, 1994; Perner, 1991). Baron-Cohen (1995) suggests that there is an innate "mindreading" module, which emerged to allow individuals to comprehend others and to make predictions about their likely behavior. In some

[31] It is not entirely clear what people do when they simulate. Currie and Ravenscroft (2003) identify three contexts in which simulation has been invoked: 1) to acquire knowledge about a situation, 2) to place oneself in imagination into a situation to determine what the implications of that situation are for what one would experience or do, and 3) to determine what the other person might experience or do in the same context. They contend that "Sometimes 'simulation' refers to the whole three-tier process, sometimes just to the bit in the middle" (Currie & Ravenscroft, 2003, p. 54), and it is unclear which of these is being invoked by which theoretician.

cases, then, the Theory of Mind is conceptualized as a special-purpose body of knowledge, akin to a mental module (e.g., Leslie 1987, 1988), but in others it is a body of knowledge, parallel to other types of theories, whether common sense or scientific (e.g., Gopnik & Wellman 1994). The distinction between these two versions is that in the former, "the child's theory of mind undergoes no alteration; what changes is only his ability to exploit what he knows" (Fodor, 1995, p. 110). That is, as the child matures and acquires new cognitive skills, he can apply his emergent cognitive skills better in using the theory of mind. What changes is only the child's computational complexity. When the theory of mind is viewed as a theory, children must first acquire this theory. Once the basic principles of the theory are set down, they are augmented and embellished as knowledge in this domain is acquired.

From the perspective of the Theory of Mind, reading one's own mind is parallel to the process of reading someone else's mind. This is because knowledge of one's own mind, like knowledge of other minds, is derived from the theory, irrespective of the target in question. As Gopnik and Meltzoff (1994) suggest, the Theory of Mind is constructed equally on the basis of information about the self and about others, and is equally applicable to both. As a result, when children's Theory of Mind is wrong, they are as inaccurate in reporting about their own mental states as they are in reporting the mental states of others. As Gopnik and Meltzoff conclude:

> even though we seem to perceive our own mental states directly, this direct perception is an illusion. In fact, our knowledge of ourselves, like our knowledge of others, is the result of a theory, and depends as much on our experience of others as on our experience of ourselves. (Gopnik & Meltzoff, 1994, p. 168)

That is, one does not have special or privileged access to one's own mental states. One relies on the same contextual information and memory processes for making inferences about oneself as about others. On the other hand, Gopnik (1993) allows for first-person psychological experiences but suggests that such experiences are both vague and unspecified, a "Cartesian buzz" (p. 11), needing to be interpreted within the confines of the same theory as others' assumed experiences.[32]

The Theory of Mind is generally tested with a task called the "false belief task" (Wimmer & Perner, 1983). Children see a puppet called Maxi put chocolate in a box and then see him leave to go out to play. Unbeknownst to Maxi, his mother moves the chocolate to the cupboard while he is out playing. The critical question is where Maxi, who did not see the chocolate being moved and cannot therefore know its new location, will look for the chocolate when he returns. Whereas 3-year-old children typically fail this task, saying that Maxi will look for the chocolate in its new location, 4-year-olds typically succeed (e.g., Perner et al. 1987; Wellman, Cross, & Watson, 2001), suggesting that there is a quantum leap in theory of mind understanding around age 4. In a parallel task (e.g., Gopnik & Astington, 1988), children are shown a candy box and surprised by its contents (e.g., pencils). Children are then asked what another child would think is in the box and what they themselves thought was in it prior to being shown the contents. Again, answers to questions about oneself were found to be significantly correlated with answers to those about others, suggesting that the younger children use self-knowledge in responding about others.[33]

Irrespective of which theory of mind one actually adopts, adults are supposed to have a full-blown version of the theory available and hence, to use the same process in making inferences and predictions about oneself and others. As a consequence, when adults make different predictions about what they would experience than what generic others would experience in the same contexts, this raises serious questions about the validity of the Theory of Mind as an explanatory tool. No definitive study in this domain has been conducted and Dunn (1988) bemoans the fact that "it is by no means evident how, if not by reference to self the child begins to understand others' feelings."

Recent research has capitalized on Hoffman's (1976) suggestion that the child's recognition that others are similar to self constitutes the first step in the process. Specifically, he suggests that children gradually learn that although others' reactions "at times may differ from his, the differences are typically out-weighed by the similarities" (p. 135). Although theoretical analyses stress the ability to take another's perspective when they *differ* from one's own, Hoffman contends that in real life, the child generally discovers that another person's perspective "is usually like his own except for minor variations" (ibid). Meltzoff (2007a, 2007b) has similarly suggested that the "like me" heuristic serves as the platform through which children

[32] Nichols and Stich (2004) draw a distinction between *detecting* and *reasoning*, the capacity to *attribute* current mental states to others vs. to *use* such attributions for making predictions about others' mental states and likely behavior (e.g., *detecting* that someone wants ice cream and *reasoning* that wanting ice cream, the person may go to places where ice cream may be found). They suggest that for oneself, but not for others, these two aspects of mindreading are subserved by different mechanisms. A separate self-monitoring mechanism allows individuals access to their own ongoing mental processes (e.g., "I was just thinking of my mother") but the same Theory of Mind used for reasoning about others' mental states is used in subsequent reasoning about one's own mental states. Developmentally, the implication is that there is a decalage during which time, knowledge of one's own preferences does not serve as input for reasoning about these preferences. The crux of the difference between Nichols and Stich's version of mindreading and that of Gopnik and Meltzoff, for instance, is that the latter claim that there would be parallel performance on the same tasks for self and other. Nevertheless, both approaches require that, in adults, there be no difference between the inferences one draws about self and about others, a pattern that contrasts with predictions based on my model.

[33] As Müller, Sokol, and Overton (1998) note, however, failing both tasks can be the result of the inability to integrate the past and the present, a notion that has not been tested empirically.

forge their way into others' thoughts and feelings. That is, he claims that the recognition of self–other equivalence in action allows children to interpret others as having similar psychological states and that the "like me" nature of others provides a means of bridging the self–other gap.

Although this is a very promising approach, it does not provide an account of self–other differentiation. Specifically, as discussed above, others are communicating agents who provide information both about how they are "like me" and how they are "unlike me." From this fluctuating onslaught, individuals need to abstract the knowledge that humans as humans share underlying psychological processes but that the contents of their psychological experiences differ. As Mithen (2007) argues, a Theory of Mind must contain two elements that are "logically separable": the ability to know that others have minds with ongoing psychological experiences and second, that these psychological experiences may well be different from one's own. The "like me" heuristic allows the derivation of the former but not the latter. It does not offer a solution for drawing inferences about specific instances of others' ongoing experiences, a solution that is offered in the SAD model. Note moreover, that in the SAD model, the direction is reverse, starting with "I am like others" rather than "others are like me."

Consistent with the above analysis, children as young as 18 months (Repacholi & Gopnik, 1997) already have a rudimentary ability to recognize differences between their own and other people's psychological experiences. In their study, Repacholi and Gopnik presented 14- and 18-month-old children with one bowl containing crackers and another bowl containing raw broccoli. All the children indicated that they preferred the crackers. An adult then tried the foods in each of the bowls, reacting with disgust to the crackers and with pleasure to the broccoli. When the children were asked to give one of the foods to the same adult, they could do so either on the basis of their own preferences or on the basis of the adult's apparent preferences. The results showed that whereas the 14-month-olds were more likely to provide the adult with the crackers that they themselves preferred, the 18-month-olds provided the adult with the broccoli that she apparently preferred, evidencing a clear differentiation between their own preferences and that of others.

This is also evident in children's spontaneous speech. Dunn and Kendrick (1982) quote a preschool boy who is watching his younger sibling as he is about to pop a balloon and says, "He going to pop in a minute. And he going to cry. And he going be frightened of me too. I like the pop" (p. 46). Similarly, a teen who is talking of her teacher, says, "She didn't' frighten… doesn't frighten me, but I think she does some people" (Delamont, 1976, p. 114), thereby contrasting her own reactions with those of other people. Bartsch and Wellman find that such contrastives emerge after age 3 in children's spontaneous speech regarding other people's thoughts and beliefs and by 25–30 months for desires. In fact, some of the children sampled were using such contrastives before their second birthday (Bartsch & Wellman, 1995).

In my own research, self–other differentiation is also prevalent. In a study (Karniol & Koren, 1987) with kindergarten children, they were asked either about their own or another child's likely affective reactions to a series of positive and negative affect-eliciting events. Children responding about how they would react made fewer negative affective inferences, offered more coping responses for transforming negative situations into more positive ones, and used different justifications for the cited affective reactions than did children responding about another child. Similarly, in research with adolescents and adults, different predictions were made about oneself than about others, both generic others and friends, across a variety of contexts like seeing a plane taking off and walking by a school (Karniol, Eylon, & Rish, 1997; Karniol & Shomroni, 1999).

Other areas of research also support self–other differentiation. For instance, one of the staples of attribution theory is that actors do not make the same causal attributions about self and about others, tending to attribute others' actions to their dispositions and their own actions to situational exigencies (Jones & Nisbett, 1972). This phenomenon, known as the actor–observer effect, occurs whether the other is a prototypic other or a friend, and importantly, is even *more* pronounced in self-relevant domains (e.g., Miller, 1975; Snyder, Stephan, & Rosenfield, 1976). The actor–observer effect can be undermined by exposing individuals to video records of their own performance (e.g., Storms, 1973) or by adopting another's perspective (e.g., Anderson & Pichert, 1978). The critical point for the current analysis is that the actor–observer effect could not occur if one's own preferences were assumed to be the same as those of generic others. As well, in research on empathy, focusing on one's own thoughts and feelings has been found to *reduce* empathy whereas focusing on distressed others' thoughts and feelings *increases* empathy (Thompson, Cowan, & Rosenhan, 1980). In a study (Barnett, King, & Howard, 1979) with children 7 to 12 years of age, children were asked to discuss happy, sad, or affectively neutral incidents that had been experienced either by themselves or by another child. They were then instructed to think further of these incidents and were given the opportunity to share their experimental earnings – thirty chips that could be traded for prizes – with children in another school who would not have the chance to earn such prize chips. Children who related unpleasant experiences involving themselves donated fewer tokens than children relating sad incidents experienced by others. Also in line with this, imagining how self versus another person would feel apparently engender different emotional constellations (Batson, Early, & Salvarani, 1997).

These findings demonstrate that there are differences between responding from one's own perspective versus from other people's perspectives. In fact, using PET measurements, Ruby and Decety (2001) found that although simulating actions from first-person and third-person perspectives produced some overlap in the regions of brain activation, certain areas of the brain were differentially associated with each of these two perspectives. In later research, Ruby and Decety (2004) again found both overlap and some differential activation of brain regions in responding about one's own feelings versus one's mother's feelings, and in responding about health-related questions from one's own perspective versus a lay person's perspective (Ruby & Decety, 2003). Ruby and Decety suggest that this differentiation is critical for the discrimination between self and others, consistent with the Cartesian view that our knowledge of our own mental states is of a radically different nature than our knowledge of the mental states of others. These independent lines of research appear to buttress the claim that self-knowledge is differentiated from generic knowledge about others and that different paths are used in making predictions about oneself and about others. I will return in Chapter 10 to discuss this issue once more in the context of transformational thought.

5 Parenting and Preference Management

'...we should listen to children, follow what they want, and take their perspectives,' Korean-American mother explaining the difficulty of raising children in the United States.

(Yang & Rettig, 2003, p. 362)

Children's preferences are guided by socialization agents, primarily mothers, who have their own preferences regarding children's preferences. The crux of the problem of socialization is that whereas infants come into this world with the apparent assumption that all of their preferences will be satisfied by aligning reality to their preferences – and on demand – mothers are not neutral with respect to their infants' preferences; they have an interest in their infants having certain preferences rather than others. They see the task of socialization as having children acquire those preferences that they want them to have. In this chapter, I discuss parenting in general, and outline approaches that have been used to account for the relationship among parenting, language use, and social class. In the following four chapters, I address the strategies of socialization themselves.

EXTERNAL PREFERENCES IN SOCIALIZATION

The philosopher Ronald Dworkin (1978) distinguishes between *personal* preferences and *external* preferences. A personal preference is a preference for a person's own enjoyment of goods or opportunities, whereas an external preference is his preference for the assignment of goods or opportunities to others. In other words, one's personal preferences are about what he himself would like to have or do, whereas his external preferences are about what other people should have or do. Viewed in this light, socialization reflects the interplay between children's personal preferences and parents' external preferences for their children. To complicate matters, though, external preferences can be *egoistic* and *prosocial* (Whiting & Edwards, 1988). Egoistic preferences are external preferences that have as their goal satisfying the socializing agent's *own* desires (e.g., "I want you to go to sleep so your father and I can have some quality time together") whereas prosocial preferences have as their goal the well-being of the target of the socialization attempt (e.g., "I want you to go to sleep so you won't be tired tomorrow").

This differentiation underlines the difficulty of understanding strategies of socialization as they occur rather than as parents report deploying them. When a mother tells a child to "go read a book," she expresses an external preference as to what the child should do – but does it reflect a prosocial preference, that the child should be literate, or an egoistic preference, that he should not disturb her because she wants some peace and quiet, or could it reflect both? Any expression of external preferences can reflect prosocial motives, egoistic motives, or both. In reporting their socialization practices, parents tend to give short shrift to their egoistic preferences and emphasize prosocial ones (e.g., a mother who explains why 7 pm is her preschool children's bedtime first says that "if they don't get their sleep, they are very cranky in the morning" but at the end admits that she does this "so I can have my evening free," Sears, Maccoby, & Levin, 1957, p. 294). Children also need to understand the motivational underpinnings of their parents' external preferences and they fare no better than researchers in this regard. They sometimes accurately recognize that parents simply want them "out of their hair" (e.g., a 5-year-old who says "I need to go to school so my Mum can have some peace and quiet," Sherman, 1997, p. 120); but they may misattribute parental motives, assuming prosocial concern when there isn't or vice versa.

This is especially problematic because of the wide range of domains in which parents have external preferences regarding their children: whom their children should play with, the objects and toys they should play with, the books they should read, the after-school activities they should engage in, the foods they should eat, and of course, how they should behave. As Ochs (1988) claims, societies even have preferences about the linguistic forms that should be used in particular contexts, with parents being the prime conduits for children's learning of such preferences.

The external preferences parents have for their children function as agendas that govern how parents satisfy their infants' and children's preferences. Baby-related agendas can center on keeping the baby safe, healthy, and relatively happy. Agendas can be related to having the baby grow up to be sociable, intelligent, moral, and a contributing member of society – a member who is not spoiled, not self-indulgent, and adopts certain religious beliefs rather than others. Maternal agendas are the bedrock that nourishes mothers' patterns of interaction with their children. Maternal beliefs about how children end up the kinds of mature beings that mothers would like them to be are translated into behaviors, rule setting, and demands that are placed on the infant and child in the present so as to yield these projected preferences and goals.

As members of a given culture, mothers have an interest in their children having preferences that relate to that cultural world. Mothers talk about this world, what happens in it, and the people and objects in it, partly to entertain the child, but primarily because this is the world in which the child will grow up and need to pursue his preferences. Mother's task is to get the child to *align his preferences* to the reality of the world she lives in rather than aligning the world to the infant's preferences. In satisfying infants' preferences, then, mothers attempt to convey knowledge to their infants, knowledge about who and what are to be avoided or approached, where danger lies, where safety can be had, and the contexts that are recurrent and ordinary versus those that are fleeting and extraordinary. She has to guide the child into becoming a functional human being within her world, as she understands it, and she does so, using those tools that she has at her disposal: her language, her love and attention, her disciplinary tactics, and those educational settings that serve as her surrogates.

However, mothers also have agendas that are not directly related to the child. These agendas can center on keeping the household running smoothly, on schedule, and without conflict, making sure that everyone in the household gets their jobs done, pursuing their own careers, and ensuring that the family is integrated within the larger social community. Another important maternal agenda is to view themselves as good mothers, however they define it. Agendas related to the child may complement, interfere, or even conflict with other, non–child-related agendas. Mothers try to coordinate their lives so these diverse agendas run off smoothly, prioritizing them as they go along. Priorities are reflected in the sequence in which activities are performed, in the activities viewed as obligatory rather than optional, and in the activities and objects viewed as forbidden versus allowed. The daily or weekly routines that need to be performed and a mother's' perception of their relative importance structure a mothers' time and dictate how and when she interacts with her baby. For instance, a mother may see herself as unable to play with an infant because she needs to work, cook, go to the beauty parlor, or socialize with friends (e.g., a mother tells her child, "Don't want to play with anything. I, I should do some cooking really.... Get the dinner ready," Walkedine & Lucey, 1989, p. 76). Mothers may even choose not to breastfeed because of the drain on their time (e.g., "I couldn't sit and breastfeed and think that the house needs dusting and hoovering," Ribbens, 1994, p. 99). Mothers' behavior may be guided by beliefs about their infant's need to sleep a given number of hours a day, eat specific types of healthy foods, or interact with other infants. The critical point here is that because mothers have agendas, their personal preferences often conflict with their external preferences for their child (e.g., "You're torn between the housework and the children, and ideally the children should always come first. But in practice, ...," Backett, 1982, p. 175), and these may further conflict with children's preferences. Preferential conflict needs to be resolved both to the mother's and to the infant's relative satisfaction. How this is done largely reflects maternal agendas because agendas have an important role in determining how mothers fulfill their infants' preferences and the likelihood of preferential conflict arising and being resolved.

One way of conceptualizing external preferences is by crossing the egoistic aspect versus the prosocial aspect with its temporal location, whether the preference relates to how the child should behave in the present or in the future. When immediate behaviors are involved, they are more likely to reflect both egoistic and prosocial preferences: one wants the child to stop screaming immediately for egoistic reasons but to stop playing with matches immediately because of prosocial ones, to avoid the child being harmed and possibly harming others. Preferences in the more distant future tend to reflect prosocial preferences. Parental concern with schoolwork, for example, generally reflects prosocial rather than egoistic external preferences. The child should study now so that he will be literate, employable, and experience economic security in the future. Parents in subsistence societies talk explicitly of egoistic preferences – that the child should not be a financial burden for the parents when he grows up and should be able to care for his parents when they are no longer able to work. But modern parents generally express more prosocial concerns. As one mother explains about her children's education, she wanted them to be educated so that

> 'they would meet people of their level or higher than them... that was one of my ambitions when I sent them to school ... that when they marry they'll marry you know, another bracket than me.' (Cohler & Grunebaum, 1981, p. 83)

Parental preferences regarding their children's immediate choices and behavior, then, reflect underlying, long-term parental preferences about what the child should resemble in adulthood: for instance, his or her sexual preferences and behavior, religious outlook, chosen profession, style of life, and so forth. As Bettelheim (1962) says, "you seem to have a certain picture of your child as a grown-up person, of what kind of a person you do or don't want her to be" (p. 70).

Socialization practices, then, reflect implicit or explicit beliefs about developmental processes – beliefs about how engaging in a certain action or behavior in the present may or may not influence the child in the long run. Bettelheim (1962) echoes this belief in developmental processes when he says, "Whatever steps you take will have consequences . . . whatever you do, you'll have done your share to make a different person" (p. 142). Sears, Maccoby, and Levin (1957) similarly say "Every moment of a child's life that he spends in contact with his parents has some effect on both his present behavior and his potentialities for future action," acknowledging that the impact of many of these moments are small but that repetition and consistency add up over the years (p. 466). This picture of children as evolving adults guides parents in socializing their children, in the way they interact with them, and in the way they channel or constrain children's behavior in the present in light of such long-term preferences. For instance, parents may constrain their children's television viewing habits (e.g., forbid their watching the Power Rangers, Bin, 1996) because they worry about the immediate impact on current aggressive behavior or because of the possible cumulative impact on perceptions of normativeness and of potential desensitization to pain cues.

Clearly, if parents believe that engaging in a certain behavior at age 6 determines what the child is like at age 18, they will be more adamant about the fulfillment of their external preferences. Few parents insist that their child play the piano at age 6 because of the immediate benefits that accrue to the child – or to the parent – at age 6. Rather, such insistence is the result of parental beliefs about the long-term benefits to the child of playing the piano, dancing ballet, or playing sports. Many parents force children to do so – despite children's resistance – because parents believe that these activities will benefit their children in the long-run. But we should not lose sight of the fact that parents may want children to have certain preferences rather than others because their own preferences may be affected by their children's preferences (e.g., "How can I hold up my head in this town if my child chooses to drop out of school?"; "If my son becomes a famous athlete we will all be rich").

In the same vein, parents often express preferences regarding the kinds of friends that their children have (Ladd, Profilet, & Hart, 1992). A Korean-American mother recounts: "Once my son made trouble, I told him not to play with a particular friend" (Yang & Rettig, 2003, p. 363). In fact, children echo this, saying, "Mom didn't like this kid so I couldn't play with her" (Goldberg, 1982). But these preferences may well be in the service of long-term preferences that the child be well-educated or morally upstanding and are guided by fears about the child being derailed from this path. As one Turinese mother says, "I shall let him choose his own friends, but I should make sure that they are suitable for him" (Pearlin, 1971, p. 42). Whereas this mother does not explicitly state her motivation for wanting those friends to be "suitable," a British mother does explain her motivation explicitly when she says, "you've got to let them choose for themselves, but at the same time, if you give them too much freedom of choice of friend, you can be running into trouble later on" (Newson and Newson, 1976, p. 218). In fact, Newson and Newson (1976) found that parents actively discourage or forbid their children from interacting with those neighborhood children whom they consider undesirable, occasionally even telling the other child to keep away from their child. Ladd, Profilet, and Hart (1992) suggest that mothers actively select, modify, and structure the environment to facilitate peer relations, managing children's social lives by arranging peer play opportunities and supervising peer play, doing so from the perspective of long-term preferences.

More important for the present purposes, it is evident from the above that parents have implicit developmental theories about critical periods of learning (e.g., "If he doesn't learn to play the piano when he's young, he never will"), about the continuous versus discontinuous nature of development (e.g., "Preschool playmates are irrelevant – it's only when they get to school that it matters who their friends are"), and about what may have an impact on their children's preferences.

Parents evidence two types of beliefs: beliefs about the continuous nature of development and beliefs about the discontinuous nature of development. As for beliefs regarding the continuity of development, such beliefs emerge in a wide variety of spheres, including appearance, neatness, and obedience. When a mother voices her fears about emphasizing appearance, Bettelheim (1962) translates her fear, saying, "you're already afraid that if you let your child talk too much about being pretty and about pretty clothes it will have certain consequences later in life" (Bettelheim, 1962, pp. 70–71). Talking of the need to train her 7-year-old regarding neatness, a mother says, "if we don't start, then he won't make a perfect job of it if you start him at eleven, will he?" (Newson & Newson, 1976, p. 250). Getting children to tidy up is "a deliberate training exercise" (Newson & Newson, 1976, p. 250) that reflects parental beliefs in the continuity of such training and is expected to pay off only in the distant future. Parents express this explicitly, as shown in Table 5.1.

The important aspect of the above comments is that they reflect parental beliefs in developmental continuity in the above domains.

Yet other parents appear to evidence beliefs about *discontinuity* rather than continuity, even in the same domains. When asked how a bad child would develop when he's grown up, mothers interviewed by Wolfenstein (1950) often stated that "You can never tell" (p. 322). Speaking of aggression and misbehavior in toddlerhood, parents generally express beliefs about discontinuity, saying "it'll only be a wee while and she'll grow out of it" (Backett, 1982, p. 158). A Japanese preschool teacher expresses the same sentiment, saying, "you have to be careful not to think that a child who hits others in the beginning of the year will always be like that . . . . . children can

Table 5.1.

	Age	Source
M: "If you don't do your own work now, when you grow up and have your own little babies you won't know how to look after them, will you? So you'll have to learn how to do those things when you're little, won't you?"	Preschool	Cloran (1989, p. 123)
M: "You start it when they're young, you tell them to do a thing . . . it grows with them through the years"	7 years	Newson & Newson (1976, p. 302)
F: "I do not see homework simply as homework . . . . I see it as a stepping stone to other things"	8 years	Xu & Corno (1998, p. 414)

change a lot" (Peak, 1991, pp. 162, 163). Talking of compliance, a father says, "you can't keep too stiff a control otherwise at the age of fourteen or fifteen they're going to rebel aren't they" (Backett, 1982, p. 23). Parental perceptions of continuity and discontinuity in different domains of behavior have an impact on the means of socialization parents adopt in those spheres. Specifically, if parents assume that in a given domain there is continuity, they may adopt different means of socialization than if they assume that there is discontinuity. A mother explains that she allows her kindergarten child to verbally aggress against her, but that "as they get a bit older, you can stop and reason with them" (Sears, Maccoby, & Levin, 1957, p. 249). Similarly, talking of leniency in giving children choice in viewing television, a parent says, "they grow up and they change and you just sort of sense it . . . you sort of know when they're mature enough" (Buckingham, 1996, p. 289).

Such parental beliefs lead parents to shape their children's environments so as to direct them into those paths that parents prefer them to take, choosing those routes they think are beneficial, setting up dead ends to other routes, and taking detours where needed. The upshot of this is that parents want to give their children choices, but they want to give them choices in some domains and not others; in these other domains, they want to limit choice. In many ways, they can be viewed as similar to the horse owner who puts blinkers on his horse to avoid his being distracted by irrelevant stimuli, ensuring that he trots forward in the direction desired by his owner. Children's problem in attempting to negotiate their own preferences in light of their parents' external preferences is that they seldom understand the preference structure that guides their parents' choices and interventions.

Parents themselves have several inherent problems in these spheres. First, their immediate preferences may sometimes conflict with their long-range preferences. For instance, parents may want their child to be obedient at age 5, but they may also want him to be autonomous at age 18, as illustrated in Table 5.2.

Alwin and Jackson (1982) found that one of the qualities American parents view as most important for preparing children for life is intellectual autonomy (i.e., thinking for oneself). They view this quality as the opposite of intellectual heteronomy (i.e., obedience to the dictates of others) and conformity to external authority. In fact, Alwin (1984) found that parents' views as to the most important things for a child to learn to prepare him for life have been changing over the years, with the view of "think for himself" as being most important gaining recent prominence, especially in higher socioeconomic groups.

As one might expect in a culture that emphasizes interdependence, in Japan, on the other hand, the most important thing to teach a child is held to be "Not to cause trouble to other people," with *people* referring to those outside the family (Peak, 2001, p. 148). American mothers, though, also claim the most important lesson to learn at preschool is how to get along with the group (Kasserow, 1999). British mothers sometimes voice similar concerns, saying, "It's important to me that they are liked and have friends, get on with people," further emphasizing that being polite

Table 5.2.

	Country	Source
M: "It's no good expecting an adult with a mind of his own if you have a wishy-washy child"	UK	Newson & Newson (1976, p. 294)
M: "I don't want to curb her completely or else she's going to be just a follower all her life. I want her to be able to lead as well"	UK	Backett (1982, p. 125)
M: "I want my children to go to college, to be somebody, to be leaders not followers, to have minds of their own"	United States	Kasserow (1999, p. 221)

will serve to make her children better and more tolerant persons in adulthood (Ribbens, 1994, p. 132). This duality is expressed in the following:

> It is your job to shape the will without breaking the spirit.... We all don't lose our individuality, but we all have to conform to an extent and this degree of conformity ... is something that has to be achieved by shaping the will. (Ribbens, 1994, p. 137)

Kohn (1969) takes a different perspective on this, contending that the need for conformity to external authority has an adaptive value for people with fewer life choices and that this is why there is a universal relationship between low SES and high valuation of compliance and conformity. In fact, middle- and working-class parents take different approaches to socializing their children for distant goals. As Kohn (1959) found, middle-class fathers and mothers differ in their perceptions of the importance of children having self-control, being considerate of others, and obeying their parents, with the latter more frequently found in the working class. Pearlin (1970) reports similar results in Italy. In line with this conceptualization, children who do not conform to external authority in school settings tend to drop out of school earlier (e.g., Delgado-Gaitan, 1988). The dilemma parents face, then, centers on ensuring compliance with others', and in particular, parental preferences in the short run, while at the same time ensuring intellectual autonomy in adulthood. Immediate goals and long-term goals may not be isomorphic.

Ensuring that parental short-term preferences are fulfilled in one domain may advance, restrict, or even prevent the fulfillment of either their short-term or long-term preferences in other domains. For instance, if a child is asked to babysit for a younger sibling, this may allow the parent to complete certain errands or to have a needed respite from daily burdens but it may also limit the older child's study time, exercise time, or peer interaction time (e.g., "Well, if I have to help my Mum sometimes, I stay in after school for the whole time," Mayall, 2002, p. 93), limitations that may not be in keeping with the parents' long-term preferences. Yet parents themselves often define good parents as ones guided by their long-term preferences. As one father says,

> I think a good father would be an individual that would look ahead in 20 years and say to himself 'What do I want my child to be 20 years from today' and then being at that moment living that goal. (Palkovitz, 2002, p. 50)

Another problem that parents have in this sphere is that they cannot assess how they are doing in terms of fulfilling their long-term, external preferences. They cannot gauge whether their success in getting children to be compliant in the *here-and-now* contributes to the attainment of their long-term external preferences. Parents have constant dilemmas in this context, wondering how their current success may relate to the fulfillment of their long-term, external preferences. For instance, a mother who is describing how she copes with her son when he has a tantrum says,

> he'll, you know, kick and holler for a while and then I'll send him to try to calm him down.... And that may be the wrong thing to do, you know, I don't know, but I really don't want him to have a bad temper. (Gottman et al., 1997, p. 67)

The issue of concern to this mother is how her current behavior and her success in the present contribute to her long-term goal in the future. Researchers (e.g., Applegate et al., 1985; Cook-Gumperz, 1975) often use a scenario of a child who brings his mother flowers picked from a neighbor's garden. What is the correct response to this situation in terms of ensuring future behavior? Is it focusing on making amends to the neighbor, refraining from future recurrence, the child's good intentions in bringing the flowers, the feelings of the victimized neighbor – all of these? The same questions arise regarding parental involvement and pressure for school success (e.g., Yang & Rettig, 2003) and insistence on performance of household chores. Does my child's refusal to take out the garbage today imply that he will not grow up to be a helpful human being? Will compelling a child to take out the garbage or clean up his room now further my external preferences more than dropping the issue? As my son argued with me at age 14, "Do you really think that punishing me for this will make me a better person in the long run?" The only honest answer to his question was "I don't know." There is no definitive feedback in current socialization contexts regarding the likelihood of long-term, external preferences being satisfied. This dilemma is captured when a mother rues, "it worries me when I smack them. You want them to behave properly, and yet you want them to be happy" (Newson & Newson, 1976, p. 320).

How, then, do parents choose what to say and do to their children? Parents do so on the basis of their *beliefs* about the relationship between their own actions and the child's long-term behavior. Parents do not socialize in the "here-and-now," but rather, are aware of their parental responsibility to inculcate moral principles that will guide their children into adulthood. To this end, they may make the rules guiding their socialization practices explicit. As one father explains, "It's up to you as a parent to know what your kids are doing, to try to teach them right from wrong" (Buckingham, 1996, p. 285). Pearlin (1970) voices this view of parental socialization when he says, "disciplinary practices are influenced by desiderata anchored in the distant future" (p. 104).

Not everyone agrees that parents' long-term goals guide their ongoing behavior. For instance, Schaffer (1991) argues that socialization does not begin with attempts to convey abstract values but begins with

> adults' efforts to induce children to comply with requests referring to the ordinary, practical, very concrete minutiae of everyday life ... constantly occurring situations where a caretaker considers it necessary for one reason or another to change the ongoing course of the child's behavior. (Schaffer, 1991, p. 168).

Hasan and Cloran (1990) similarly argue that long-term socialization goals are generally covert; it is short-term goals that are conscious and dominant in parent–child interaction, primarily in settings involving child care (i.e., providing food, giving a bath, dressing the child), cooperative action (i.e., playing, reading, cooking, cleaning up), or performance of household chores, to the performance of which the child may constitute an impediment. From this perspective, the long-term outcomes of socialization are fortuitous outcomes of socialization.

Voicing a more extreme version of the above claim, Landesman, Jaccard, and Gunderson (1991) argue that parental preferences are conveyed to children less by explicit instruction and more by *implicit* messages that children need to abstract. In particular, they suggest that children learn by observing the consequences of social interaction to both themselves and others, with these consequences including commands, suggestions, reprimands, as well as threats and punishments from adults and older children. From this feedback, children

> construct a working knowledge of the complex conditions surrounding the 'do's' and 'don'ts' of interpersonal aggression, the distribution of resources, social roles, task assignment, damage to property, etiquette, hygiene, and other matters for proper social behavior. (Landesman, Jaccard, & Gunderson, 1991, p. 253).

Research on children's social rule understanding seems to support this view of implicit learning. Bigelow, Tesson and Lewko (1996) found that children cited sixty-three social rule categories that exemplified fifteen themes (e.g., not upsetting others, reciprocating, controlling one's feelings) in managing their relationships with others. These rules are condition–action sequences that specify when and how one should conduct oneself in a specific relationship, predicated on the idea that one wants to maintain the relationship. It is most unlikely that such rules are explicitly taught by others. Rather, such rules are constructed by children as conceptual schemas by way of which they make sense of the social world and the reactions of others in that world. These schemas then govern their conduct within that world. Shweder (1982) similarly claims that social knowledge is taught informally in cultural environments that are "packed with implicit messages" (p. 56). When a preschooler is told that he needs to drink from a paper cup but sees the teacher drinking from a glass, the child draws inferences as to the preference structure that underlies the request. This view, then, places the burden more on the child's developing conceptual system rather than on the parents' socialization skills.

PARENTING AS A CULTURAL PHENOMENON

Although each parent makes choices as an individual, parents manage their children's preferences within a cultural and familial constellation with norms and rules regarding the management of one's preferences. Cultures espouse values: for example, morality, wealth, religious piety, which are formulated and symbolically elaborated in culturally distinct beliefs, norms, and ideologies. Heterogeneity is apparent across cultures in terms of how much emphasis is placed on the immediate versus delayed future, the degree to which one's own preferences are allowed to receive priority over the preferences of others, and the degree to which they view the child's preferences as malleable at various ages, if at all. For instance, whereas spanking is illegal in some Scandinavian countries, a ban on spanking was rejected by the high courts in England. A UN report (1997) estimates that about 80 percent of the world's children are subject to physical means of discipline. Yet there is no uniformity even within the United States as to what parents are allowed to do in this domain and in 2001, there were twenty-three states that allowed physical punishment to be meted out in public schools (National Coalition to Abolish Corporal Punishment in the Schools, 2001).

Cultures are relatively rigid, though, in terms of how parents are expected to socialize their children and how children are expected to behave in the process of being socialized. Many of the choices parents make in socializing their children's preferences are guided by the culture in which they are embedded and their interpretation of what the culture requires of them as parents. The force with which a culture constrains parental behavior varies depending on the nature of the embedding that parents experience. In multigenerational cultures in which grandparents reside with the family, the older generation may serve to mediate cultural expectations both to parents and to children (e.g., Cohler and Grunebaum, 1981). In cultures in which the older generation is not involved in the ongoing socialization of children, other means of disseminating cultural expectations are likely to emerge, for instance, books and magazines for parents, parent education groups, and the media can clarify norms and expectations regarding culturally appropriate means of socialization. As Grieshaber (2004) notes, parenting messages are beamed constantly from the popular media, presenting what she calls "normalized versions of parenting." Cultures, then, guide parents' adoption of long-term, external preferences, convey theories about the likely relation between short-term and long-term external preferences, and dictate how parents are to pursue both as they socialize children's preferences. As such, cultures are deeply involved in maternal agendas.

One important difference between cultures that is manifest in differences in socialization practices is temporal orientation. Every society has conceptions of past, present, and future but societies differ in their emphasis on each of these time periods. One can identify three cultural patterns of relation to time or temporal hedonic orientations (Insko & Schopler, 1972): *hedonism of the present*, *hedonism of the past*, and *hedonism of the future*. Hedonism of the present implies a lack of concern with the future, focusing on the *here-and-now*, pursuing and enjoying whatever brings pleasure *now* (e.g., A Brazilian 15-year-old explains "I'm afraid of being unemployed. I try to forget about this as much as possible and leave the problem to the future," further explaining that he devotes his thoughts and time to his girlfriend, Gibson-Cline, 1996, p. 59). The present hedonic is unconcerned with what is not currently available for contemplation, that is, the past and the future. He is unconcerned with deferring present pleasures or experiencing current pain for the sake of experiencing greater pleasure (or avoiding greater pains) in the future. Only present pleasure is valued; anticipation of future pleasure and memory of past pleasure are not valued. One reason for adopting a hedonism of the present is the lack of a sense of a temporally extended self, the sense of self-continuity over time. When this happens, one's current self is unconcerned with one's future self because there is no sense that the former evolves into the latter.

The past orientation reflects a preoccupation with the history of the family and its ancestors. Chinese ancestor worship and hungry ghost festivals reflect a past orientation. In contrast, according to Kluckhohn and Strodbeck (1961), Spanish Americans, for example, "pay little attention to what has happened in the Past and regard the Future as both vague and unpredictable. Planning for the Future or hoping that the Future will be better . . . is simply not their way of life" (p. 14). Similarly, Italians and Italian Americans "live in and for the present and seek satisfaction in the here and now. . . . Tension discharge is of greater value than the delay of immediate gratification for the sake of future accomplishment or achievement" (Cohler & Grunebaum, 1981, p. 297). This is well expressed by the statement, "there's no use worrying about the future. I try to take each day as it comes" (ibid, p. 311). In fact, there is no hope for the future since it will be as bleak as the past and dwelling on the past is useless, "the only use made of the past is to explain current difficulties" (ibid, p. 297).

Hedonism of the future is concerned with maximizing the expected value of positive future events and minimizing the expected value of negative future events. Jones (1988) argues that adoption of such an orientation is a function of: (1) the strength of the belief that if a specific act is performed in the present, the probability of some future goal state will be greater, and (2) the strength of the tendency to value such future goals. Adoption of the future orientation requires prediction, anticipation, planning, and imagining what is likely to happen. Trommsdorf and Lamm (1975) argue that because of the extensive cognitive work required – the person has to look ahead, collect information about possible decision alternatives and their likely consequences, and relate possible consequences to desired future states – the more educated the person, the more extended his or her future orientation. However, the reverse may also be the case, with individuals with a future orientation choosing to pursue higher educational goals. Csikszentmihalyi and Schneider (2000) found that in many families, parents are guided by and socialize children with primary reference to "beliefs about the immediate and long-term relevance of their actions to *future* goals" (p. 130, emphasis added). Actions are oriented toward the future and judged by their contribution to the future self rather than being concerned with their contribution to the present self. If one cares about one's future self, it makes sense to delay present gratification for the sake of future well-being. But if one doesn't care about one's future self, pursuing present gratification at the cost of future pain is a rational choice.

LeVine (1974, 1977) argues that despite cultural variation, there are universal preferences of parents vis-à-vis their children. These preferences include: (1) the physical survival and health of the child, (2) the development of the child's behavioral capacity for economic self-maintenance in maturity, and (3) the development of the child's behavioral capacities for maximizing other cultural values – for example, morality, wealth, and self-realization – as formulated and symbolically elaborated in culturally distinctive beliefs, norms, and ideologies. Kluckhohn and Strodbeck (1961) similarly assume that across cultures, there is a limited number of universal preferences and common problems for which all cultures must find solutions. Differences between cultures arise both because the specific values adopted within each culture may differ and because perceptions of how these societal preferences can be attained vary as well. Kluckhohn and Strodbeck suggest that despite the cross-cultural variability, variability is neither limitless nor random. Rather, they contend that every society has both a dominant profile and variant profiles of value orientations and that within these, there is a rank ordering of preferences. This preference structure largely determines what and how choices are enacted in each culture.

Landesman, Jaccard, and Gunderson (1991) identified six fundamental domains in which all families try to influence their children's preferences and behavior: (1) physical development and health, (2) emotional development, (3) social development, (4) cognitive development, (5) moral and spiritual development, and (6) cultural and aesthetic development. All families guide their children's preferences within these domains but the goals that families attempt to attain within each domain may differ. Some goals are universal (e.g., be healthy and strong); others may be culture-specific (e.g., be a college graduate), or family-specific (e.g., be a good Christian) goals.

The universal aspects emerge out of every culture's need to ensure that children are socialized to be contributing members of society. Every culture must guarantee that children are taken care of and learn how to behave in ways that are acceptable within that culture. Children need to be nurtured, trained, and controlled. Nurturing involves routine caregiving and giving the child help, support, and attention. It also involves responding positively to children's requests for help, comfort, support, and information. Training involves teaching children skills, social behavior, and hygiene as well as restraining them from dangerous and unsociable activities. Control involves the use of commands, reprimands, threats, and punishments to get the child to enact behaviors that are preferred by the mother but that do not necessarily represent culturally demanded behaviors.

The extent to which each of these societal functions is emphasized varies in different cultures. Based on their cross-cultural anthropological research, Whiting and Edwards (1988) argue that the "mix" of societal functions is the direct outcome of other social forces within each culture, forces that dictate the way mothers interact with their children, the amount of time they have to do so, and the presence of other children and adults who may do so in their stead. They identified three general orientations to socializing children: (1) training, (2) control, and (3) nurturing, suggesting that there is generally one dominant orientation in every culture. In sub-Saharan communities, training was found to be the dominant mode, accounting for about 40 percent of mothers' behavior toward their children. Such mothers started to train children at age 2, assigning them chores of increasing complexity. They monitored children's actions, kept them on task, and communicated their expectations about what tasks are to be completed. Children in training cultures are punished for noncompliance and for failing to complete assigned chores, but the training itself is done in a good-natured manner, for example, "Be careful in hoeing; you might hit yourself," said to 5-year-old child who is hoeing alongside his mother (Whiting & Edwards, 1988, p. 94). Whiting and Edwards suggest that this pattern of socialization emerges in cultures in which mothers are the major producers of food, there is little room for creativity in the performance of routine chores, and mothers need help with their tasks and with care of younger children.

In other cultures, including Khalapur in Northern India and Tarong in the Phillipines, the dominant mode of interaction with children is control. In this mode, children are threatened (e.g., "Otherwise I will break your face"), reprimanded. (e.g., when a 5-year-old disturbs a sleeping baby, the mother slaps her bottom slightly and says, "Do not do that"), and commanded (e.g., "Go and put that inside"), without explanation as to why that particular behavior is being controlled. Whiting and Edwards suggest that this type of socialization is prevalent where women's workloads are lighter because men do much of the work and because there are more adult women in the same household, all of whom share child care and other duties. In these cultures, children are less involved in daily chores and have more free time for undirected activities and for getting into mischief, including disturbing maternal tasks. Consequently, in such cultures, children are more likely to be reprimanded after the fact than to be warned beforehand.

In Western societies, mothers' dominant orientation is also that of control, but it takes place in the context of extensive nurturing interactions between mothers and their children. This is the case because Western mothers are residentially isolated, have fewer chores, and have more time available to spend with their children, with whom they are alone most of the day. They can play and read with children, watch television with them, take them shopping, and "play" at being helped. Hence, children in Western societies learn to play in the company of their mothers as opposed to in the company of other children. On the other hand, whereas children in such cultures do not have chores they need to complete, their mothers view this period of time as a "training period" that serves to prepare them for preschool and school. Mothers' task centers on making the child as communicative and as knowledgeable as possible to facilitate the transition into the educational settings into which he will eventually move. With this aim in mind, mothers spend much of their time talking to the child, explaining and guiding his behavior as they do chores, and verify that he is constantly occupied.

Despite these diverse cultural orientations, across cultures, several age trends were evident in Whiting and Edwards' (1988) data. First, nurturance was found to decrease as children mature. Second, training and the domain of training reflected changes in children's age. Whereas the training of younger children focused on manners, hygiene, and socially approved behaviors, older children were trained to complete chores and engage in other socially useful activities. Third, the kind of training children received tended to be related to age and gender, with girls receiving more hygiene and etiquette training than boys when they were young and more training in performing household tasks and child care than boys when they were older. This Whiting and Edwards (1988) summarized as, "girls work while boys play" (p. 125). On the other hand, the fact that boys play rather than work means that they spend less time on task and more time being rowdy and less compliant, and elicit greater intervention and control attempts than girls do.

Whiting and Edwards tie cultural variation in socialization practices to mothers' work loads in different cultures but this tie may be based on a spurious correlation. The amount of time that women allocate to interacting with their infants and children does not seem to be affected by the amount of time they have available. For instance, when girl helpers are available to take care of younger children, engage in domestic work, or economic work (e.g., basket weaving for potential sale), mothers spend no more time with their infants than when girl helpers are not available (e.g., Bove, Valeggia, & Ellison, 2002). The additional time available for mothers when girl helpers were available was found to be allocated to socializing with others in the community rather than with the child.[1]

In fact, modes of interacting with children are a product of beliefs about the psychological status of infants and children as human beings, societal values regarding children, and norms regarding parental behavior toward

[1] It may well be that in cultures in which children's survival rate past infancy is low, the investment in each child is lower and this may account for the amount of time mothers devote to their infants and children in different cultures.

them. In this context, Chao (1994) contends that cultural differences arise because of underlying philosophical differences that are reflected in child-rearing attitudes. She argues that Chinese parents, for instance, adopt the goal of "keeping the family running more smoothly and fostering family harmony" and that this goal leads to the adoption of a training orientation toward children, with training involving exposure to explicit examples of good conduct and avoidance of exposure to bad conduct. She sees such training as reflecting Confucian teaching in which relationships are structured hierarchically and subordinates are required to evidence loyalty and respect to their superiors, who in turn, are expected to guide, teach, and discipline, all of which require ongoing involvement.

Yet there is no a priori reason why the goal of fostering family harmony would result in a training orientation as opposed to any other orientation. That is, one can foster family harmony by adopting all means of childrearing. From this perspective, cultures promulgate views of infants as "minded" or not, as well as views of how children are to be treated. In addition, cultures promote value systems that families largely adopt. Yet the interpretation of that value system within each family may differ to the extent that families are insulated from one another within that culture. It is each family's value system that determines the relative emphasis in time and resources allocated to a given preferential domain. Families then devise strategies and plans that are geared toward allowing them to attain their preferences.

Gralinski and Kopp (1993) suggest that all socialization goals may be prevalent in a given society but that parental socialization goals shift as children mature. In interviewing mothers as to what they encourage and what they forbid, child safety, respect for others and their property, and temporal delay were most often demanded of children at 13 months, and a concern with safety, mealtime routines, and manners being evident at 18 months. But such changes in what parents emphasize at different ages need not index a shift in socialization goals. Rather, what changes may well be parental perceptions of how children's age, their personality, and their understanding are likely to have an impact on their adoption of parental preferences and concomitantly, changes in parental willingness to endure preferential conflict with their children. The need to avoid preferential conflict can lead parents to choose certain styles of interacting with their children, to engage in preemptive strategies that obviate the need to restrict or discipline children, and to restrict, deflect, and discipline them in ways that potentially minimize such conflict.

PROVISION OF CHOICE

Another dimension on which parents vary is the provision of choice. Csikszentmihaly and Schneider (2000) found that in families who have clear-cut rules that they are determined their children follow, children often complain about having too few choices. Parents differ in whether they see choice as important (e.g., "they should be allowed to, within reason, to do what they want," Ribbens, 1994, p. 61), at what age they view the provision of choice as necessary, and the realms in which they think choice should be provided. As one father says in defining the father role, "try to provide opportunity for your children to be exposed to things so that they can make their decision. Try to pray that they make the right decisions because you can't force them" (Palkovitz, 2002, p. 44). As to the domains of choice, although Turiel (1983) has emphasized the provision of choice in the personal domain, parents may give their children choice in domains not generally construed within the personal domain (e.g., religion), with a laissez-faire attitude being reflected in the behavioral choices provided to children, for example, "It's up to the kids if they want to go (to church), they feel free to go" (Palkovitz, 2002, p. 119). On the other hand, parents may recognize that they can dictate behavior but not beliefs, compelling their children to attend church, synagogue, or mosque while at the same time, saying, "There is room for all of us to have different views about Judaism. Our daughter does not agree with us. But she is allowed to have different opinions" (Semans & Fish, 2000, p. 133).

Yet the provision of choice may be more apparent than real. This is very evident in the domain of career choice. Despite voicing that "They've got to make their own decisions in life . . . it's got to be their choice in life" (Bennett et al., 1999, p. 38), parents work very hard at limiting children's choices in this domain. The working-class mother of a 2-year-old says,

> I guess I'd really like for her to finish school . . . by the time she gets to my age, you know, by that time she'll be old enough to make her own decisions and I really won't, you know, try to make her mind up for her. I'll just, you know, let her do what she wants. (Miller, 1992, p. 58)

Parents readily admit that they drill the importance of education into their children, as one mother says, "we have put the seed in their heads. And they may not know right now what they want to be, but the seed is there . . . to do whatever they choose to do" (Csikszentmihaly & Schneider, 2000, p. 132). Parents may pressure their children to go to college (e.g., "I really am trying to leave it up to her. Because it's her right and as long as she goes to college . . . . " Csikszentmihaly & Schneider, 2000, p. 131), emphasizing the value of a college education, both in talking to interviewers and to their children. They may also stipulate what they consider an acceptable career choice, for example, as an academic friend remarked about his children, "They can do anything they want, they can be a doctor of medicine, a doctor of engineering, a doctor of psychology . . . . " In turn, children know their parents expect them to go to college (e.g., "They want me to go to college. They expect it of me . . . . " Csikszentmihaly and Schneider, 2000, p. 131) and the kinds of professions that their parents find acceptable (e.g., "Yeah, she wants me to

Table 5.3.

	Source
M: "Children should absorb all these things at once, like ice-skating, going to see certain shows.... I think they're too young to take all this in at once... how much can children absorb at once?"	Cohler & Grunebaum (1981, p. 75)
M: "(Children) have so much freedom that they actually don't know which way they're going because it would be very confusing for them"	Ribbens (1994, p. 178)
F: "The more money they had, the more disturbed they became by the number of things that they could buy with it, and the number of things they wanted.... if (they) can't have anything, so they don't have to *tear their minds apart* wondering what they are going to spend their next 20 pence on"	Sonuga-Barke & Webley (1993, p. 62)

go to college.... She likes me (becoming a lawyer) 'cause it's a good profession," ibid, p. 137). Such expectations on the part of parents, then, are viewed as restrictions of one's options.

Why do some parents give their children choice whereas others restrict choice? First, some parents restrict their children's choices because they worry that the provision of choices will undermine their parental power and they will lose the ability to have an impact on children's preferences. Such parents often indicate that children do not have the right to make their own choices or even deny that children need to be given choices. In reminiscing about her now-grown children, a mother says, "I didn't give them a choice.... you should be able to decide what to give them and do it one way, it will be easier on you and easier on them" (Cohler & Grunebaum, 1981, p. 74).

Other parents' restriction of choice seems to index a cognitive theory, that children are overwhelmed by having too many choices (cf., Schwartz, 2004),[2] as illustrated in Table 5.3. Some parents avoid providing children with choices, fearing that such choice will be detrimental to them in the long run, as evident in Table 5.4.

The dilemma inherent in this sphere is expressed by a mother who said, "if you give them choices about too many things you never get a decision, or they find it hard to make a choice.... Perhaps in the long run it is good for them" (Ribbens, 1994, p. 182).

In fact, many parents do provide choice because they believe that the provision of choice allows children to develop their autonomy and individuality (e.g., Haswell, Hoch, & Wenar, 1982; Nucci & Smetana, 1996). This is why they provide more choice as children grow up. In fact, in a study of children in kindergarten, third grade, and sixth grade, parents were found to give older children more choice as to how they spend their money (Ward, Wackman, & Wartella, 1977). The father of a 14-year-old explains this, saying "when she was smaller, we could dress her and bring whatever we wanted to dress her in" but now she says, "Now that I'm big, I can make my own decisions" and I respect that. She's right" (Palan & Wilkes, 1997, p. 163). Similarly, in discussing his teen's spending habits, a father says that she is "more inclined to have *spending binges*, which we don't stop.... and well that's all part of the learning process, we don't stop her doing it" (Sonuga-Barke & Webley, 1993, p. 82). These parents see the provision of choice as serving an educational goal. As I elaborate below, though, the willingness to offer children choices is apparently a function of social class.

SOCIAL CLASS AND SOCIALIZATION

As discussed earlier, mothers have agendas, with some of these relating to the immediate future and some relating to the distant future. Mothers differ in terms of how their agendas are distributed in time, some because of idiosyncratic preferences, some because of preferences that are arise out of social group membership or cultural dictates. One of the most important influences on maternal agendas is social class. As Pearlin (1970) summarized years ago, "Social class position is relevant to virtually every aspect of family life" (p. 188). Social class determines agendas, socialization practices, and linguistic styles. In particular, in almost every domain, middle-class and lower-class mothers differ from each other.

In particular, social classes appear to use language differently in socializing their children. In an observational study of mothers and their preschoolers at the pediatrician's office (Greenberg & Formanek, 1974), middle-class mothers were found to talk much more to their children, using a greater mean number of words per minute than lower-class mothers, as did their children. Hart and Risley (1995) found that parents in professional families closely attended to what their children said and did and adapted their talk to challenge and guide their children, as if they were "preparing their children to participate in a culture concerned with symbols and analytic problem solving."

[2] Perhaps surprisingly, this view is also expressed by Adlerian therapists:

> parents are encouraged to offer some variety of choices within each area: What kinds of foods to eat, how much money to save, how often and what specific religious rituals to practice/observe... (but) having an unlimited amount of choice... may prove to be overstimulating to children with their limited processing characteristics. (Maniacci & Maniacchi, 1989, p. 51)

Table 5.4.

	Source
M: "I don't want a child that's aware of clothes to the extent that I've seen in some children – where they'll throw a tantrum if the ribbons don't match the dress and they have to choose their own dress"	Bettelheim (1962, p. 68, 70)
F: "When they grow up a bit then find out that they can't get all the things they want, then they'll take it much harder"	Backett (1982, p. 130)
F: (Taiwanese) "You cannot let them be too picky and wear whatever they want to.... I want to let him know that he can't always easily get whatever he wants"	Fung (1999, p. 190)

Welfare families appeared to be socializing their children to a culture concerned with established customs, in which obedience, politeness, and conformity are the keys to survival, with working-class families falling between these two extremes. In particular, social class was negatively related to the use of imperatives and imperatives were found to dampen children's development, as assessed by vocabulary and IQ at age 3. Wootton (1974) similarly found that working-class children received twice as many negative directives as middle-class children, and working-class boys were threatened twice as much as working-class girls and all middle-class children.

When the complexity of the language used in interacting with children is examined the same pattern emerges. For instance, Tizard and Hughes (1984) adopted Tough's (1977) classification of language complexity in which (1) making comparisons (e.g., "You're too big for that lorry" (p. 139)), (2) recalling events (e.g., "Last week we went to Granny's, didn't we?" (p. 139)), mentalizing (e.g., "I expect Kate is feeling very sad now"), and (3) problem solving (e.g., when a child says that they don't have enough sticks, mother says, "we'll break them in two, then," p. 140) all reflect greater complexity. They found that middle-class mothers used language for complex purposes more often than working-class mothers, and this was true for ten of the eleven categories of complex language identified. Concomitantly, middle-class children were found to use language for complex purposes more often than working-class children. The conclusion is that language is the implicit conduit for the transmission of modes of thought as well as the explicit conduit of cultural mores and values, in family dinner talk, for example, as discussed below.

Research has revealed both cultural and class differences in family talk at dinnertime. Newson and Newson (1968) found that some families perceive it rude to talk at dinnertime. A mother recalls her own experiences, saying, "When I was young I wasn't allowed to speak at table.... We could never speak unless we were spoken to" (Charles & Kerr, 1988, p. 187). In such families, parents discourage their children from talking at the table, saying, "I don't even like people talking.... I don't like kiddies talking when they're eating" (Charles & Kerr, 1988, p. 187). Children are expected to wait until adults finish talking and need to choose their input carefully; they "have to wait until it's their turn... (and) if they don't know anything about the subject, then I expect them to be quiet" (Blum-Kulka, 1997, p. 38).

Other families express the sentiment that dinnertime provides an opportunity for family members to relate their daily experiences and children are allowed to comment and intercede with no apparent limitation, save for ensuring that others are not interrupted. Such families tend to see dinners as a time for family bonding, but they also use them for socializing table manners, eating habits, and conversational politeness (Blum-Kulka, 1997). Some families even see dinnertime as a time and place to learn the value of argument. As one mother said, "she has to understand that argument is fine.... I think it's good training for adult life" (Semans & Fish, 2000, p. 135). Newson and Newson (1968) found the former attitude more prevalent in the working class and the latter more prevalent in the middle class. But such attitudes are not uniformly held in the middle class either. As Blum-Kulka (1997) found, even in some middle-class Jewish-American families, there is little apparent tolerance of child talk. Nevertheless, there is strong evidence for social class differences in language patterns.

Although there is general agreement that different social classes use language in a different manner, there is disagreement as to the basis for such differences. There are several different theoretical approaches that have been used to account for the impact of social class, and it is to a discussion of these theoretical approaches that I now turn.

A. Linguistic Codes

One dominant approach is Bernstein's (e.g., 1974) theory of sociolinguistic codes. Bernstein argues that different orientations to the organization of social relations and social knowledge are created and sustained through modes of language use and communication, which are products of the social order they sustain. In particular, different forms of speaking express underlying assumptions regarding either the uniqueness or the similarity of the psychological experiences of different individuals. Divergent assumptions concerning psychological experiences are expressed in two distinct sociolinguistic codes, which Bernstein calls *elaborated* and *restricted*, with these two codes being differentially characteristic of speech in the middle and working class. The elaborated code fosters the assumption that the motivations, intentions, and feelings of each person are to some extent unique and may differ from those shared by the group. This code is characterized as *person-centered*, fostering the elaboration of the unique qualities of individuals and contexts. In using person-centered speech, one presupposes a gap between self and others, requiring the individual to take divergent perspectives into account when communicating. As Bernstein says, the elaborated code "presupposes a sharp boundary or gap between self and others which is crossed through the creation of speech which specifically fits differentiated others" (Bernstein, 1974, p. 147). The elaborated code also requires more online planning, because it takes the situation more into account than does the restricted code.

The restricted code, in contrast, assumes that communicators share the same or similar background knowledge as oneself, allowing one to assume shared perspectives or a common denominator. It assumes that the identities of others and the meanings of their actions can be understood in terms of socially defined roles or positions (e.g., a mother, student, teacher). It is position-centered rather than person-centered, with people being viewed as interchangeable placeholders within the social system. The positional code discourages language for expressing and adapting to the unique psychological features of individual perspectives. Instead, communicators build on shared sociocultural definitions of situations, referring to the roles of participants, the authority relations between these roles, and the norms guiding behaviors between people in these roles (e.g., "Children do not answer people back when they're as young as you," Newson & Newson, 1968, p. 467). As a result, position-centered speech tends to focus on the overt behavior of self and others, judging it in terms of the relevant cultural rules that govern interaction between people in different social roles.

From this perspective, children growing up within each social class and language system acquire "sets of choices, in-built preferences for some alternatives rather than others," choices that are acquired via communication and by being encouraged to talk in specific ways. Children's social perceptions and categorizations are shaped by being addressed in person-centered versus position-centered speech and these speech codes then serve to guide them in describing, categorizing, and talking about social events and behaviors.[3] Bernstein suggests that all children learn to communicate in the restricted code but that socialization determines whether or not they also acquire the elaborated code. When communication is based on an extensive range of shared expectations and common assumptions that lead to the use of "we" rather than "I," this encourages children to use the restricted code. In such cases, rules are the same for everyone and are not individuated to specific instances, not made to fit the individual case. After a mother tells her 3-year-old child to go to bed and he refuses, she says, "Now no nonsense, time for little boys to go to bed" (Tough, 1973, p. 32). A Chinese American mother yells at her child who is running toward her with scissors, "You stop! Children don't hold scissors. It is dangerous" (Wang, Bernas, & Eberhard, 2002). The justifications in both of these instances are based on a homogeneous perception of children of a given age. The mothers are not expressing the possible adverse consequences to the child or to the individual who might get hurt.

In families with elaborated codes and a person-centered speech, children learn to differentiate their experience from that of others and learn "how to express this verbally... developing a verbally differentiated 'I,' being encouraged to focus on the experiences of others as different from his own" (Cook-Gumperz, 1973, p. 12). In such families, parents are sensitive to the unique characteristics of their children and because psychological differences are emphasized, children are better able to cope with ambiguity and ambivalence. As well, in such families, imperative controls are seen as a last resource.

Research that examined parental and child speech from Bernstein's sociolinguistic perspective has largely supported this view of differences between social classes, showing that middle-class mothers use the elaborated code for controlling their children (Cook-Gumperz, 1973; Adlam, 1977) and in turn, children whose mothers use the elaborated code tend to use it themselves (e.g., Robinson & Rackstraw, 1972a,1972b). For instance, Applegate et al. (1985) assessed mothers of first and third graders' use of person-centered communication in dealing with seven hypothetical situations, with five requiring regulatory measures (e.g., child refuses to go to bed at bedtime, takes a small item from a store) and two requiring comforting (e.g., child hasn't been invited to a classmate's party). Bernstein's distinction between position- and person-centered speech suggests that parental communication varies in the extent to which the child is recognized as an individual with a distinct psychological perspective that needs to be accommodated and adapted to. In light of this, regulative strategies were scored for the extent to which they encouraged the child to modify his behavior as a function of attention to the consequences of his inappropriate behavior for himself and others. Comforting strategies were scored for the extent to which they granted legitimacy to the child's feelings and the circumstances producing them. Additional scores reflected the extent of reflection encouraged in the child. Discouragement of reflection was scored if parents issued simple commands (e.g., "I'd tell him to take it back and ground him") or simply stated

[3] FitzSimmons (1999) suggests that lower-class children do not use the elaborated code of communication because they are "sensitive to the fact that more elaborated codes might be misconstrued as suggesting some deficit on the part of the directive's recipient..." "I won't insult you or take up your time unnecessarily by going into things you already know." Such children were found to use the elaborated code only when the hearer of the directive was reluctant to follow or asked for more information about the rationale behind the directive, but elaborated codes were never used as a matter of course (p. 144).

rules (e.g., "Taking things without asking is wrong. Now go and apologize for taking the flowers"); or if parents condemned the child's feelings (e.g., "She whines and I just put a stop to it when she does") or told the child how he should feel (e.g., "She can't expect to be invited to every party. She should just put it out of her mind. There'll be other parties"). Implicit encouragement of reflection included use of distractive strategies intended to ease the child's distress (e.g., "Take her out shopping or to a movie to get her off it," "I know you're disappointed but these things happen sometimes and we have to understand"). Explicit encouragements of reflection, including focusing on others' feelings, talking it out with people, and asking questions, were assigned the highest scores.

Applegate and his colleagues found that the effect of social class on parental communication is mediated through the interpersonal construct system of the mother. Mothers who construed others in terms of dispositions, motivations, and personality, used person-centered discipline and encouraged their children to reflect. They suggest that viewing others through a psychologically centered lens implies that in navigating the social world one needs to engage in negotiation and balancing of different perspectives. Mothers who adopt this lens teach their children that one handles social conflict by the elicitation, negotiation, and coordination of the perspectives of the parties to the conflict (cf., Bearison & Cassel, 1975). They exercise control over the child by communicating and elaborating the feelings, motives, and intentions of others, making the child aware of the domain of subjective experience. In fact, parents who focus on mental states (e.g., a victim's feelings or intentionality of actions) during disciplinary encounters have children who succeed earlier on Theory of Mind tasks (e.g., Charman, Ruffman, & Clemens, 2002).

Although conducted from a different perspective, the distinction between pragmatic versus elaborative parents in how they reminisce with their children (e.g., Haden & Fivush, 1996) fits well into Bernstein's framework. Pragmatic parents use short, directive conversations centered on specific events or questions, often inviting *yes* and *no* responses (e.g., "Did you see a giraffe at the zoo?"). In contrast, elaborative parents weave in diverse domains of experience and pose questions that require the child to do the same (e.g., "What did you think of . . . ?"). Parental styles of conversation during reminiscence talk have been found to be correlated significantly with children's own means of conversing about past events. The general conclusion in this domain is that children's "understandings of events and the psychological world are thus guided by how parents help to interpret, organize, and construct understanding though simple conversation" (Thompson, Laible, & Ontai, 2003, p. 148). This conclusion is buttressed by evidence that fifty-two core frames account for 51 percent of the utterances that are addressed to 2-year-olds (e.g., Cameron-Faulkner, Lieven, & Tomasello, 2003) and that children's own productions can be predicted on the basis of these frames. The parallel finding (e.g., Huttenlocher, Vasilyeva, Cymerman, & Levine, 2002) that both the concurrent complexity of mothers' speech and SES account for a significant amount of variation in the complexity of children's speech at age 4 also provides strong support for this conceptualization.

B. Distancing

A different approach to the impact of social class comes from the work of Sigel (1970) and his coworkers. Sigel adopted the approach of Werner and Kaplan (1963) who discuss distancing as the use of language for *transcending* the immediately given, extending thought into the realms of the nonpresent, the spatially removed, and temporally nonpresent, the past and future. Sigel and his colleagues (e.g., Sigel, 1970 Sigel, Stinson, & Flaugher, 1991; Sigel, Stinson, & Kim, 1993) suggest that parental distancing strategies play an influential role in the development of representational competence in children. They define representational competence as the ability to understand that experiences can be transformed into a symbolic model; this includes the ability to manipulate symbols mentally and conduct mental operations that influence how external experiential events are transformed and internalized into mental events. Representational competence requires an understanding that the meanings of events and objects can be re-presented in ways that are essentially abstractions of the referent. Sigel (1970) includes several types of ability as representational: anticipating outcomes, proposing alternatives, reconstructing similar prior experiences and outcomes, and interpreting transformations of objects (and events).

Sigel and his colleagues argue that representational competence is a product of social experiences within the family. Parents – as the primary socialization agents – serve as educators for their children, using socialization techniques to introduce children into the social, cultural, and physical world. Parents socialize children by communicating parental wishes, desires, goals, and notions of right and wrong. But how parents communicate with their children determines the extent of intellectual stimulation provided to the child. In communicating with their child, parents can place demands on him to think, reason, and understand. They can do so by their use of language that includes references to different temporal relations, to objects seen and unseen, and to symbols representing different objects and events. From Sigel's perspective, how the parent constructs a linguistic environment and creates discourse opportunities for the child plays a pivotal role in the child's acquisition of representational competence.

Sigel argues that children's representational competence is a function of parental use of teaching strategies that entail cognitive demands for the child to separate mentally from the ongoing reality of the *here-and-now*. This involves having the child place himself in the future (via anticipation), reconstruct the past (via hindsight), or transcend the immediate present (by engaging in hypothetical thought). From this perspective, distancing is seen as a set of parental strategies that place cognitive demands on the child, demands to create temporal, spatial, or psychological distance between himself and the ongoing present. These abilities can be fostered by parental behaviors that encourage children to anticipate possible future actions or outcomes, reconstruct past events, and employ their imagination in dealing with objects, events, and people and to attend to the transformation of phenonmena. From the perspective of Sigel and colleagues, all these behaviors serve to distance the child from the immediate environment, distancing strategies that allow the child to psychologically transform the *here-and-now* to *neither-here-nor-now*.

Distancing strategies vary in their level, from those strategies that place minimal demands on the child to separate self from the ongoing present, to those strategies that place high-level demands that require the child to engage in making inferences, proposing and evaluating alternatives, and transforming reality. Asking children what they did yesterday, what they will do tomorrow, or to evaluate their affective reactions (e.g., "Do you remember how you felt when . . . ?") requires children to use imagination. Asking children open-ended questions regarding objects and events that are not perceptually present fosters representational thinking and thereby promotes the acquisition of strategies for dealing with the *neither-here-nor-now*. One of the first critical developments in this context is the acquisition of names for locations (here and there) and temporality (now, not now, then) that signal a distance between the words that symbolize the object and the object itself. The use of such words allows language to become an instrument for communicating about abstract and remote objects and events. Distancing, which is also referred to as decontextualization, allows children to represent objects and events that are not present and the use of displaced reference broadens the possibility for information storage, problem solving, and planning, as well as hypothesizing, lying, and fantasizing.

The more experience children have with such high-level distancing strategies, the more likely they are to develop representational systems that promote competence in planning, anticipating, and recalling of experience. The more far-reaching claim that Sigel and his colleagues make is that distancing facilitates children's development "beyond these early representational systems toward transformation of competencies to academic tasks such as mathematics and reading that require representational skills in notational contexts" (p. 218). In their attempts to buttress these claims, Sigel and his colleagues examined children in various interactions with their parents. For instance, McGillicuddy-De Lisi (1985) conducted a study with 120 preschoolers who were tested on a variety of cognitive tasks and were taped in interaction with their mothers during an origami task (i.e., the children were required to make a paper plane or boat) and a storytelling task, which required imagining different things to do with an object. The interactions between parents and children were coded for use of distancing and the level of cognitive demands placed on the child, with low demand being coded when the parent required the child to observe, label, or describe verbally something in the current context, intermediate demand being coded when the parent specified sequences for the child to engage in or to reproduce something the parent had created, and high demand being coded when the parent made statements that required the child to propose alternatives, to infer cause and effect, or engage in planning. Mothers' use of distancing in interacting with the child predicted children's cognitive level across a wide variety of tasks and lower SES mothers used lower-level distancing strategies.[4]

A different line of research provides some support for the ideas proposed by Sigel and his colleagues. Specifically, young children's use of cognitive verbs like *think*, *believe*, *guess*, and *wonder* in their speech is highly correlated with their reading ability, with poor readers using fewer such words in their speech (Torrance & Olson, 1985). Torrance and Olson argue that such verbs refer to the relation between what is said and what is believed or meant, forming part of a system for decontextualizing language and thought, relating the speaker's mental state to what is being said.

C. Parental Level of Abstraction

An additional way of viewing socialization is to focus on the level of abstraction adopted by parents in conceptualizing short-term goals versus long-term goals. Landesman, Jaccard, and Gunderson suggest that the ability to engage in concrete versus abstract thinking affects parental goal setting and goal orientation. They argue that

> to reflect on long term goals or those that cannot be realized until much later requires a certain degree of abstract thought. A person who tends to think only in "here and now" terms generally will have a different goal structure (e.g., more short term goals) than will someone who thinks more futuristically. (Landesman, Jaccard, & Gunderson, 1991, p. 80)

As discussed earlier, social class also has an impact on the adoption of a time perspective, focusing on long-term versus short-term goals. There are class differences in orientation to the present versus the future, with middle-class families being more future-oriented (Daly, 1996). Newson and Newson (1976) also found that working-class families focus on more short-term goals whereas middle-class ones are more concerned with long-term goals. They suggest that the divergent focus on short-term versus long-term goals in different social classes reflects differences between wage earners and salaried workers. Specifically, wage earners get their money in tangible form and tend to use

[4] Importantly, adopting this lens was not a function of mothers' intelligence. Verbal intelligence scores were not correlated with the use of regulative or comforting strategies.

it within the week for their immediate needs. A deliberate effort needs to be made to avoid spending money in one's pocket. In contrast, when individuals have their salaries deposited in banks they are more likely to accumulate it. This is because one needs to use more abstract forms of payment for purchases (e.g., checks or credit cards), thus making money a more abstract term. One can view the proliferation of "Checks Cashed" stores in many lower-class neighborhoods, and their absence from more affluent ones, as explicit evidence for this divergent pattern.

In a theoretical approach known as Construal Level Theory (Trope & Liberman, 2003), the authors propose that individuals tend to represent psychologically distant events by their essential, abstract, and global features (high-level construals) and psychologically near events by their peripheral, concrete, and local features (low-level construals). This association between temporal distance and construal level is thought to be overgeneralized such that construals of a given event are more abstract when it is psychologically distant even if the information known about the event is equivalent. Studies have shown, for example, that increasing temporal distance from future events leads individuals to categorize objects associated with the events in fewer, broader categories (Liberman, Sagristano, & Trope, 2002). Based on construal level theory, Fujita, Trope, Liberman, and Levin-Sagi (2006) argue that self-control can be broadly conceptualized as making decisions and acting in accordance with a more global, high-level construal of the situation rather than a more local, low-level construal. From this perspective, self-control is enhanced when individuals are able to see the proverbial forest beyond the trees. In line with this, individuals' judgments, decisions, and behaviors differ as a function of construal level. When high-level construals are activated, high-level features of one's preferences and actions are focused on. When low-level construals are activated, preferences and actions are based increasingly on low-level features. A major determinant of what level of construal is activated is the psychological distance of the event or object. Imagining distant future events, for example, enhances more abstract thinking whereas imagining near events promotes more concrete and more detailed cognitive processing (Förster, Friedman, & Liberman, 2004). Fujita, Trope, Liberman, and Levin-Sagi (2006) suggest that when self-control conflicts are resolved in terms of high-level construals, one exhibits self-control. In contrast, when such conflicts are resolved in terms of low-level construals, one exhibits failures of self-control. From this perspective, any manipulation that leads to more high-level construals would engender greater self-control.

In line with this conceptualization, Fujita et al. (2006) found that changing the construal level at which individuals considered a situation had dramatic effects on their self-control. Inducing low-level construals was associated with more low-level concerns whereas inducing high-level construals was associated with greater self-control and higher-level considerations. Fujita and colleagues conclude that at the core problem of self-control is the difficulty of maintaining a focus on high-level, more abstract considerations in guiding one's behavior and making decisions. This difficulty is evident in what is known as *preference reversal* (e.g., Ainslie & Haslam, 1992; Frederick et al., 2002): as temporal distance increases, individuals make choices that are more consistent with their second-order preferences (e.g., deciding to diet versus being swayed by exposure to available foods). If, in fact, lower-class individuals have difficulty conceptualizing things in more abstract terms, this would be expected to be related to lower self-control and more short-sighted choices.

D. Child-Centeredness

Yet a different approach to socialization focuses on parental child-centeredness. Being child-centered means that the parent tries to adopt the child's perspective as she deals with the child. As one mother says, "I try to reason; I try to put myself in the child's place" (Newson & Newson, 1976, p. 445). A young mother explains: "I'm very soft, I think, I so much see it from their point of view that I overdo it.... I see everything from their point of view" (Ribbens, 1994, p. 121). A student teacher expresses the same view regarding her students, explaining "I try to put myself in their position to see.... I try to think about what they're feeling and what they're seeing" (Johnston, 1989). In keeping with attitude, Bettelheim (1962) contended that "the best way to raise children intelligently is to translate things in your own terms and ask, 'How would I feel?' (p. 105). As part of Parent Effectiveness Training (PET), Gordon (1976) urges parents to "Put yourself in the child's shoes" (p. 128). Paley (2004) urges preschool teachers that in trying to understand what the child is attempting to accomplish and what obstacles he may perceive, they themselves pretend they are children so that they can become aware of problems from the child's perspective. Ainsworth describes sensitive mothers as having the capacity to *see things from the child's point of view*, elaborating that

> A mother might be quite aware of and understand accurately the baby's behavior and the circumstances leading to her baby's distress or demands, but because she is unable to empathize with him – unable to *see things from the child's point of view* – she may tease him back in good humor, mock him, laugh at him, or just ignore him. (Ainsworth, 1969, emphasis added)

Newson and Newson (1976) assessed maternal child-centeredness, defined as being responsive to the child's demands, participating in the child's play, being willing to chat at night when the child asks, accepting the child's "I'm busy" excuse, valuing the child for himself or herself, and not making a moral issue of a child smacking the mother. Child-centered mothers were found to be from higher socioeconomic classes.

Addressing the issue of child-centeredness in a different way, Gottman, Katz, and Hooven (1997) identify three kinds of families: those that dismiss their children's emotions, those that share their children's emotions and coach them regarding their emotions, and finally, families that are accepting of their children's emotions but are low in coaching. Coaching parents value their children's emotional expressions, have a high degree of awareness of their own emotions, and assist children with their emotions, acting like an emotion coach. These parents are more comfortable in the world of emotions, and are better able to regulate their own emotions. Emotion-coaching parents (1) are aware of the child's emotion, (2) see the emotion as an opportunity for intimacy and teaching, (3) help the child verbally label his experienced emotions, and (4) empathize with and validate the child's emotion and help the child problem solve. In fact, parents often say: "What makes a good father is somebody's that really interested in what the kid thinks and feels" (Palkovitz, 2002, p. 47).

Oppenheim and Koren-Karie (2002) examined these same issues in terms of what they call *maternal insightfulness*, defined as the capacity to see things from the child's point of view, based on insight into the child's motives, a complex view of the child, and openness to new information about the child. To assess insightfulness, mothers viewed video segments of their interactions with their children and were subsequently interviewed regarding their children's and their own thoughts and feelings during the segments. The *insightful* mother is contrasted with three other types of mothers: the *one-sided* mother who tends to impose her own preconceptions of the way the child "is" onto what she sees on the tape, seeming more concerned with her own thoughts and feelings than the child's. The *disengaged* mother denies that she can understand the psychological processes in the child and tends to focus on his behavior (e.g., "How do I know what went on in his head? I have no idea"). Finally, *mixed* mothers appear to be eclectic in their attitude and are not characterized by a unique mode of interpretation. Insightful mothers were found to have more securely attached children, yet such mothers did not appear to differ from the other mothers in either vocabulary or educational level. Training mothers to be more insightful was found to reduce children's behavioral problems 6 months later.

A related framework is provided by Dix, Gershoff, Meunier, and Miller (2004) who also discuss sensitive parenting. They similarly build on Ainsworth and her colleagues' (Ainsworth et al., 1978) notion that the sensitive mother tends to "see things from her baby's point of view" instead of "almost exclusively in terms of her own states, wishes, and activities" (p. 142). Dix and colleagues suggest that sensitive parents promote their children's development in several ways: they enable them to maintain their current thought sequence and focus of attention, give them the benefit of their own skills, capitalize on children's immediate motivation to maintain their ongoing interest, and reduce the need for children to contend with the negative consequences of having their preferences thwarted. Dix and his colleagues suggest that sensitive parenting depends on child-oriented motivation – that is, on parental motivation to promote not the parents', but their children's interests and well-being. From this perspective, parents are constantly making online decisions about which specific goals, outcomes, or concerns are to be promoted at a given point in time, with sensitive parents being more likely to select ones concerned with the child (Dix, 1992, 2000; Hastings & Grusec, 1998). They further suggest that when parents are self-oriented, they are more likely to thwart the child's preferences, resulting in child defiance and mutual negative affect.

To test some of these ideas, Dix and colleagues had mothers and their toddlers interact in a laboratory setting. Initially, mothers completed questionnaires about their child while waiting for the experimenter to return with toys, allowing an assessment of how mothers cope with toddlers who have nothing to occupy their time. During a subsequent play session, children played with age-appropriate toys and their mother's task was to keep them from playing with some "forbidden" attractive toys. In a final clean-up period, mothers were asked to get their child to help clean up the playroom. After the play session was over, half the mothers viewed the tapes and reported the positivity or negativity of their emotions during the taped interaction. In addition, mothers were asked to pause the tape at points at which they experienced a change of emotion, to indicate their emotion, and why they experienced it, with each emotion coded as either child-oriented or parent-oriented. Concerns were coded as child-oriented when they indicated a focus on the child's welfare, for example, "I was pleased that he finally found something he liked," "I was worried because I thought he might fall," and "I was irritated because the study was frustrating him." Concerns were coded as parent-oriented when mothers focused on their own interests in the interaction, for example, "I was irritated because I asked him to put the toy down," "I was pleased because I didn't want to have to walk over there," or "I thought the xylophone was pretty cool." Supportive *behavior* was coded if the mothers evidenced support of the child's attempts; behavior was coded as restrictive when mothers attempted to get children to conform to rules, for instance, by using statements about keeping things clean, avoiding forbidden toys, playing gently with toys, and the like. Finally, child noncompliance was assessed by coding children's responses to all maternal requests to clean up or to avoid the forbidden toys.

The data showed that as child-oriented concerns increased, mothers displayed less behavior that was restrictive. As this view predicts, maternal behavior that supports children's intentions tended to increase as parents adopted child-oriented concerns and evidenced emotional states that promote the tendency to support children. The data suggest that mothers who display high levels of behavioral support tend to give priority to children's interests, experience relatively positive emotion, experience emotions that are more child-oriented, and are relatively free of depressive symptoms.

Table 5.5.

	Source
M: "No matter what you're doing. No matter what you think you have to do. You know that if the baby wants you, it's more important"	Raeff (2003, p. 46)
M: "It's 100% giving yourself up, you have got to put the child first although you don't want to"	Backett (1982, p. 31)
F: "You can't always be out there for yourself.... Sometimes you got to say, "I'll do it for the kids"	Palkovitz (2002, p. 247)
F: "When I'm with them I have to refocus and say what they need, what they want – .... I'd have to put what I want aside"	Palkovitz (2002, p. 71)

Finally, Ochs (1992) offers yet a different perspective on child-centeredness. She argues that despite the fact that mothering affords women both control and power, their communicative style with children and the degree to which they are accommodating and attuned to the child are a function of the social power mothers are accorded in their society. In societies where mothering is underrated, mothers engage in verbal practices that underscore their low status, doing so in their message production strategies, their interpretive strategies, and their praising strategies. Their production strategies in such societies are highly accommodating to children's perceived preferences and needs, being manifest in simplified baby talk, in mothers' "ventriloquating," that is, expressing verbally what children are presumed to be thinking, and in mothers' attunement to the child's gaze and ongoing engagement with the world around him. In their interpretive strategies, mothers in such societies attempt to take the child's perspective to infer his preferences, want the child to confirm or disconfirm these inferences, and enter into negotiations with the child to avoid preferential conflict. Finally, in their praising strategies, mothers in such societies recontextualize children's performance as successful accomplishments, undermining their own role in the performance (e.g., "You did it!"), implying to the child that his capabilities are far greater than they actually are (cf., Budwig, 1996). In contrast, in societies where mothers are accorded greater social power, they do not accommodate to children in their speech, do not engage in intensive interpretive attempts, and applaud children's accomplishments as joint products. This cultural differentiation is evident in research. Rothbaum, Morelli, Pott, & Liu-Constant (2000) found that in discussing their caretaking decisions, whereas immigrant-Chinese mothers were likely to indicate that they knew what was best for the child (indicating little need to question the child's desires and preferences), European-American mothers took their children's preferences and desires into account. In doing so, the mother has no apparent preferences – her child is given a voice whereas she is not allowed one. As Ochs (1992) summarizes, mothers are underrated in Western society because they do not socialize their children to acknowledge them; "Mother" is ignored because, through her own language behavior, "mother" has become invisible (p. 355).

PARENTING AS FOREGOING ONE'S PREFERENCES

Ochs's (1992) conceptualization fits well with the view that parenting requires one to give up one's own preferences for the potential benefit of one's children. Parents acknowledge this perpetual conflict between their own current preferences and their understanding that they cannot allow themselves to be guided by such preferences, as illustrated in Table 5.5.

In general terms, being a parent forces one to put one's own preferences on hold because one has to engage in behaviors that are demanded by one's role even when one's preferences are to do otherwise, for example, "I have to be a dad sometimes even when I don't want to be" (Palkovitz, 2002, p. 70).

Foregoing spending money on oneself is another sacrificial aspect of parenting. Discussing Christmas gift giving, a woman says regarding her husband and daughter, "I'm spending more on Bill and Kenda . . . (they) are my family. . . . That's who I need to take care of first"[5] (Lowrey, Otnes, & Ruth, 2004, p. 549). A fourth grader reflects understanding of such parental sacrifice, saying, "My mother keeps from buying stuff for her to buy for me" (Fiates, Amboni, & Teixeira, 2006, p. 160). Saving money for children's future is another aspect of this. When parents do so, they explicitly forego their own desires in the present. In discussing this, a parent says that it's important to "save money, which I'm doin' right now for him (the son) for college" (Raeff, 2003, p. 46). In justifying his investment in his family and children, a father explains,

> It's like you could be doing all that stuff . . . but why? So you can retire and go to Jamaica by yourself? . . . No, because you want to work hard so you can send your kids to school or help them buy their first house with their family. (Palkovitz, 2002, p. 254)

Moreover, giving up one's own current preferences for the benefit of one's family is not only perceived as the appropriate choice but is also seen as providing emotional satisfaction that parallels the effects of "warm-glow" altruism. In the words of one father, "I find real contentment in trying to meet to needs of my family . . . it brings me more

[5] Saving money to buy family members presents is also cited by children as a reason for saving their money; for example, an 11-year-old girl explains that she spends only part of her allowance, continuing, "I save the rest of the money for Christmas and special occasions so I can buy presents" (Webley, 2005, p. 55).

joy to do (for them) than it does to do something for me" (Palkovitz, 2002, p. 253).

MANAGING CHILDREN'S PREFERENCES

The existence of parental external preferences regarding their children's preferences necessarily implies that parents attempt to manage their children's preferences and consequently, preferential conflict is an intrinsic aspect of parent–child interaction. Far from being a simple task, managing others' preferences can include one or more of the following:

Creating new preferences and strengthening existing ones – which I am calling Channeling.

Temporizing preferences – influencing the timing and sequencing of preferences.

Weakening, changing, or limiting existing preferences – which I am calling Restricting.

Deflecting preferences – substituting alternative preferences or thoughts, which I am calling Mind Play.

Finally, one can discipline children when they fail to adopt parental preferences. All these strategies of socialization will be addressed in the next sections of the book.

Across these preference management contexts, parents can provide reasons and explanations for why preference management is being engaged in or they can use their power as parents to enforce their own preferences, without providing additional explanations. In providing reasons and explanations, they can focus on the short-term outcomes to the child (e.g., it will be fun; you'll get hurt), the long-term outcomes to the child (e.g., you'll be smarter; you'll get cancer), on material outcomes (e.g., it will break, it costs a lot), on positive or negative outcomes to other people (e.g., it will hurt Johnny, it will make me happy), or on societal outcomes (e.g., others will or won't like it, will put you in jail). To do so, parents need to teach their children to decontextualize, to distance themselves from the here-and-now, and to engage in transformational thought, to which I turn in Chapter 10.

6 Channeling Children's Preferences

In her highchair at 25 months, Amy says, 'Like get out now.' Her father asks, 'Get out now? But you haven't finished your apple.' She says, 'But like get out' and he demands, 'Finish your apple first.' She repeats 'Like get out now'; he asks, 'Can't you finish those pieces of apple first?' she replies with a prolonged *No-o-o-o!*

(Wootton, 1997, p. 82; Wootton, personal communication, June 19, 2009)

Children need to acquire new preferences as they mature: eat a wider range of foods, interact with more objects, learn to engage in new behaviors, and be able to adapt to new contexts. French mothers talk of "l'education du goût" (Suizzo, 2004), explaining that children's taste and preferences need to be educated. In this chapter, I focus on the different means parents use to channel and educate their children's preferences, as well as the multiple means of channeling preferences in the food domain.

CATEGORY TEACHING

To channel children's preferences, parents need to ensure that children know the categories to which objects and events belong – children need to learn to label and to evaluate. Parents and other socialization agents often use the fact that they have deciphered the child's preferences to comment on objects, label them, and explain what they are used for and how they are not to be used, and their potential use (e.g., when Meike, at 17;19, points to a doll's stroller and says "auto," her father responds, "No, this here is your doll's stroller,"[1] Miller, 1979, p. 283). Pens may be forbidden to the child whereas pencils and markers may be allowed; understanding the difference between pens and pencils may promote divergent behavior toward them. For instance, Peter's mother says, "That's a pencil." Peter, 29 months old, objects, saying: "No, that's not. That's not got a top on." She retorts: "Pencils don't have tops on 'em. You're talking about pens" (Bloom, 1970). Understanding the difference between windows and doors, not only in terms of how they look, but in terms of their behavioral affordances is even more important. A boy of 20;21 offers the reply "Door" when questioned about a picture in a book. His mother answers, "That's a window. Window, not a door" (Howe, 1981, p. 10). In the same vein, Painter (1989) asks her son: "Don't you want your fruit?" and he answers: "not fruit. That's apple" (p. 42) and a discussion of the category of fruit ensues. In negotiating their preferences, then, children learn generic information when mothers elaborate information about objects of focus. This is important for channeling preferences because children learn to interact with exemplars of generic categories in category-appropriate ways.

In fact, Prasada (2000) found that a single instance can be sufficient for acquiring generic knowledge. Gelman, Star, and Flukes (2002) found that generic noun phrases (e.g., birds fly) are very common in child-directed speech and that children interpret them as referring to most objects in the same category. This raises the issue of generic versus specific representations (e.g., DeLoache & Burns, 1993); that is, *dog* is a generic symbol that can be applied to any number of instances of a given species but a particular dog with a name is a specific representation. DeLoache (2002) suggests that infants and children have an early bias to treat symbols as generic representations, assuming on encountering a new symbol that it stands for a class of entities rather than a particular one and that children's initial experiences predispose them to this generic bias. In fact, virtually all pictures in infants' and children's storybooks are generic representations and stand for children and objects in general, rather than specific ones.

This generic bias may be very important in infants' developing classificatory ability. They need to learn to categorize objects as *toys* versus *nontoys*, *yours* versus *not yours*, and *dangerous* versus *safe*. Explicit labeling by mothers is not the only means of doing so. Highlighting, as discussed in Chapter 1, serves to teach infants to categorize objects in yet a different way. Mothers' means of highlighting different objects (e.g., pictures are not taken off the wall but the child is carried to look at them, lamps can be looked at but are not to be played with) informs children what objects can be manipulated and played with and what objects cannot. As a result,

[1] German: "Ne. Is doch dein Puppenwagen hier"

highlighting serves to teach children other relevant but implicit categories.

Infants need to learn to categorize events and activities as *allowed* versus *forbidden*, *optional* versus *mandatory*, and *private* versus *public*. Whereas *liking* and *disliking* and *fun* versus *scary*, are intrinsic aspects of objects and events in that they may be directly experienced by the infant, these categorizations are generally socially communicated and may be culture-specific. Although much attention has been paid to how infants learn to classify objects according to their functions (e.g., furniture, food, clothing), little research has examined how infants and children learn to distinguish these socially construed classifications. Turiel (1983) has skillfully demonstrated that by preschool, children are aware of many of these conventional classifications, using them to guide their interactions with peers and to interpret the verbal behavior of adults in those settings. The gap in our knowledge at this point is in understanding how these conventional classifications are acquired in the first place and how they combine with parental socialization strategies, such as channeling, to guide children's behavior.

FORCED EXPOSURE

Parents use forced exposure strategically to channel their children's preferences, creating situations that put the child in the presence of target object or behavior to get the child to "like" it. Teaching infants to swim, for instance, involves forced exposure, with the guiding assumption being that once the child is in the water, he will acquire the relevant preference. An 8-year-old illustrates how this works in discussing being left at his father's workplace, saying, "I don't mind, I don't mind really because the first time I minded and the second time I minded and the third time I minded, but the fourth time I got used to it, I just got used to it" (Lewis, Sixsmith, & Kagan, 1996, p. 56). In other instances of forced exposure, children are provided with dancing lessons, music lessons, and signed up for different sports, A mother who talks of her daughter's soccer playing, says, "The first year she played soccer she cried . . . second year she got around and she really liked it" (Kremer-Sadlik & Kim, 2007). That is, parents force children to get exposed to settings children may prefer not to be in (e.g., a baseball-playing child remarks, "Some people just come here because their parents make them," Fine, 1987, p. 84; an 8-year-old says, "My momma m- is going to join me up for tennis, I don't even wanna play tennis," Dorval, 1990, p. 289). Parents themselves may admit to doing so (e.g., "I have tried to pressure him into doing things like that – skateboarding and snowboarding and things like that," Brusdal, 2007, p. 395). At times, children do come to like engaging in the activity in question – but not always. Discussing her 10-year-old's violin lessons, an Italian mother says she will not sign her up for them next year because "I can't remind her everyday that she has to practice the violin and fight against her own will that she doesn't want to do it"[2] (Pontecorvo & Fasulo, 1997, p. 436).

Putting a child into any child care or educational setting also constitutes forced exposure to novel toys, activities, and ideas. When parents have choice as to the schools their children attend, they tend to choose educational and child care settings that are consistent with their own religious, educational, or other preferences. A parent who sends a child to a school run by a religious organization presumably has an interest in having the child exposed to religious teachings of that nature (e.g., Fader, 2006). In fact, children who attend educational settings run by religious organizations that put a premium on ceremonies, such as praying or lighting candles, often demand that the same ceremonies be performed at home. Further evidence as to the effect of such forced exposure is the fact that children come back from such settings asking for toys, books, and activities that are available in these settings and are unavailable in their homes.

Television and television advertising also serve as agents of forced exposure. Children are a captive audience being forcibly exposed to new products, activities, and modes of thinking that may further or curtail the preferences that parents would like their children to have. In line with this, a preschooler sees an ad on television and says, "I want that dad . . . . Daddy, I want that." The father asks "Do you know where they sell crazy straw?"; when he says he doesn't, the father says, "If I can find one, I will buy you one" (Hall, CHILDES). In a study of letters to Santa, children who watched more television were more likely to request branded items (Pine & Nash, 2002).

To the extent that parents are worried about the impact of forced exposure, they may limit children's television viewing or set controls on the programs their children are allowed to view. It is not accidental that governments, and especially nondemocratic ones, actively dictate what can be shown on television. They understand that television can be a means of inculcating values and advocating change. Restrictions on advertising in the Western world (e.g., banning cigarette advertising and forbidding exposure to drinking per se) reflect societal recognition that such exposure may contribute to the proliferation of the forbidden products and activities.

MODELING

In psychology, the notion of modeling is almost synonymous with the name of Albert Bandura (1977, 1986) who pioneered research on children's learning via observation of others. In modeling, one observes what and how another person enacts a given behavior and via such observation, acquires a preference for doing likewise. One of Bandura's seminal contributions was the distinction between observational learning and performance of the learned

[2] Italian: "no posso stare a ricordare che deve fare il violino e lottare control la sua volonta che non lo vuoloe fare eh"

behavior. Specifically, Bandura claimed that children learn new behaviors by observation, including actions portrayed on the television screen, storing images, and constructing symbolic representations of the observed actions. Children's decisions as to when and where to enact modeled actions themselves depend on their expectations as to likely outcomes. The contingencies associated with a given action – whether it is rewarded, punished, or garners no social consequences to the individual who performs it – serve as motivational guidelines for children's performance of the same action.

Modeling and televised modeling of behavior have been used to demonstrate that children learn aggressive behavior and prosocial behavior, that they can unlearn fear responses, and that they can learn new ways of thinking, categorizing, and stereotyping. Following such recognition, television programs for children have been produced that attempt to foster more positive values and behaviors, as well as new ways of thinking. Programs, such as *Sesame Street* and *Mr. Rogers' Neighborhood*, were created precisely for such reasons and children who regularly view such programs are more cooperative, more empathic, and more likely to share with others (e.g., Huston, Watkins, & Kunkel, 1989), underlining the importance of the medium for channeling.

Other people also serve as models, often telling children to model their behavior on theirs. When a 24-month-old girl is constructing a toy with felt and glue, her sitter says, "Stick it like this.... Do it like this.... Like this," showing her how to make the felt stick (Keenan, Schieffelin, & Platt, 1983, p. 120). A Japanese preschool teacher who tries to teach a child how to turn clothes inside out prior to putting them on shows him the sequence of actions repeatedly and explains, "If you don't look, you can't do it ... you can't do it because you weren't looking in the right place.... Watch carefully.... Watch, you do it like this.... Watch me one more time" (Peak, 1991, pp. 168–169). Parents do the same. They can model mundane activities (e.g., folding and putting clothes in drawers, picking up toys), or scripted activities in which children are passive (e.g., seating child in the grocery shopping cart) or active observers (e.g., "See how Mummy does the washing? First, I separate the whites from the colors, then ..."). In fact, modeling is the prime teaching method in most non-Western cultures. Children not only watch adults work in such cultures but also engage in pretend play that emulates adult work patterns (e.g., making tortillas, pretending to cut firewood, Morelli, Rogoff, & Angelillo, 2003). Kwara'ae children perform adult chores from the age of three onward, taking responsibility for younger children, for cleaning, and even for food preparation and cooking (Watson-Gegeo, 2001). Models can be used paradoxically. In this vein, a teacher tells a preschooler to put on his pants and he refuses. She counters his refusal with "I'm gonna put them on if you don't," making a show of putting them on herself. The child promptly puts them on (Kovarsky, Stephan, & Braswell, 1994).

On the other hand, children do not always follow suit. In a longitudinal study, Forman, Aksan, & Kochanska (2004) assessed children's imitation of their mother's behavior at 14 and 22 months of age. Mothers modeled simple tasks like "Clean the Table" and "Tea Party" and encouraged children to do likewise. The investigators noted children's accuracy, eagerness, and actual copying of the mother's behavior. Then at both 33 and 45 months of age, children's likelihood of obeying or cheating on games with rules in order to obtain attractive prizes were assessed. The quality of the mother–child relationship was found to be an important determinant of children's imitation of their mother's behavior and children who eagerly imitated their mothers as toddlers were more likely to follow her rules of conduct and were less likely to cheat than children who did not readily imitate at early ages.

Although parents can serve as models for specific behaviors, they are generally more concerned with serving as role models, as a father says, "it is critical that they (i.e., children) have models in terms of their future life" (Harrington, 2001, p. 365). A mother echoes this view, saying that she tries to "be a role model for the children. Children of that age are molded by the way the parents act and speak to the kids and I think it is very important to be a role model at that age" (Harrington, 2001, p. 364), contrasting this with the reduced impact of parental effects on adolescents. The burden of serving as role models may weigh heavily on parents, leading them to try to "set an example," saying, "I realize that I got to keep healthy to keep them healthy. I got to set a decent example for them because it's all imprinted in them now" (Palkovitz, 2002, p. 153).

Parents acknowledge explicitly that telling a child to engage in a behavior that they themselves do not engage in does not serve to channel preferences, explaining,

> You want them to eat better, you have to do it yourself, so. It makes you more conscious of what you're eating, you know, brushing you teeth every night, you know, every morning. So they will do it and they go by example. (Palkovitz, 2002, p. 152)

Models need not only demonstrate preferred actions, but they must refrain from engaging in dispreferred actions. As a prospective teacher explains, "If you're going to be a model for your students, you can't smoke, you can't drink ... you have to be an upright person who exercises self-control" (Bergem, 1990, p. 92). In more general terms, "you try not to do things in your everyday life that you wouldn't want your son to do ... you try to model yourself in a way that you hope your children will grow into" (Colby & Kohlberg, 1987, p. 597). In expressing these views, the above parents are guided by a belief in developmental continuity, as discussed in Chapter 5, the belief that exposure to certain behaviors during the early years allows children to acquire life-long habits. But in addition, it seems that parents want to create children in their own image, knowingly engaging in behaviors in the attempt to impact children's preferences, setting

Table 6.1.

	Age	Source
Asking Others to Serve as Models		
K: "Daddy, you want to teach Karen how to lace these shoes?"	29 mos.	Karniol (Diary, Karen)
O: "I don't know to take off the shirt so you need to teach me to do that"	33;18	Karniol (Diary, Orren)
C: "I wanta to do it like you did"	Toddler	Bloom (1970, p. 287)
C: "Show me how I'm gonna make a kite"	4;10 years	Brown (CHILDES)
Indicating that Others Served as Models		
C: "I'm 'tending like a mommy. You use knife when you eat supper. This is I use my veggies. This is I cut," showing a spoon, then a knife	24 mos.	Thornton (2002, p. 261)
Kitchen-savvy C explaining how he learned C: "(Father) started to show me how to do stuff (chop vegetables)"	Elementary/ middle school	Beach (1988)
Explaining how he learned from relations about fishing C: "I was watchin' first, then they showed me (i.e., how to fish, catch frogs etc.). After I got done watchin', they showed me how"	Teen	FitzSimmons (1999, p. 136)

themselves up as role models whose behaviors are to be emulated by the child (e.g., "the way I live is the best way to teach them . . . if you live a good life, they'll try to follow the same way," Carew, 1976, p. 122).

Whereas parents may serve as intentional models, other people may serve as incidental ones. In fact, anyone the child is exposed to can serve as an incidental model. For instance, at 25;14, Karen says, "Karen is cooking something in the pot and then Karen will be a cook like Chana," the cook at her daycare. Exposure to incidental models is taken into account in the Japanese preschool, where children are expected to engage in "learning through watching" (minararai kikan), a period of watching older children as the younger ones sit passively, a traditional feature of learning situations (Peak, 1991). Duranti and Ochs (1997) similarly document that Samoan children are exposed to prolonged periods of observation and repeated demonstrations of actions and activities during which they are not expected to take any active role.

Exposure to other children potentiates their serving as incidental models for behavior. At times, such incidental modeling is viewed as contributing to the child's emergent skills. As a mother recounts about her 2-year-old, "everything the kids do, she' gotta be a copycat and do it . . . like she used to eat with a spoon. Now that everybody else eats with a fork, she wants to eat with a fork too" (Miller, 1982, p. 57). Another mother notes her preschool daughter's new independence, saying, "she saw that her friends at school could do more for themselves and she wanted to be just like them" (Tobin, Wu, & Davidson, 1989, p. 138).

Generally, though, parents are more concerned with the negative impact of other children on their on their own child:

> if you're gonna be livin around somebody who's got kids that are real foul-mouthed and everything, I don't think it's a good atmosphere for a little one who's just learning how to talk to grow up around because they're gonna pick it up not realizing it's wrong. (Miller, 1982, pp. 56–57)

Similarly, a mother who discusses her 7-year-old's friend says, "if he goes on being very friendly with Michael, as they get bigger he will in fact pick up this (negative) attitude" (Newson & Newson, 1976, p. 209). Parents become especially concerned with possible negative influences during adolescence when children spend more time with the peer group and consequently, the potential of being derailed is much greater (e.g., a teen explains "My Dad doesn't really want me to go out with my mates," Frydenberg, 1997, p. 87). Parents may also be concerned with children's attempts to imitate real-life or media-depicted dangerous actions, as evident in the tragic case of imitators of Evel Knievel (e.g., "He tried to do Evel Knievel but it went Awful Knawful. . . . We didn't believe that he would try it," Erickson, 1990, p. 231).

Children themselves are aware of the fact that others can serve as models, both asking others to show them how to do things and indicating that they are using them as models, as shown in Table 6.1.

Amusingly, a 4-year-old who had refused to give up diapers walked into the bathroom, dropped his diapers on the floor, and asked his peeing father to give him a peeing lesson (Freeman, Epston, & Lobovits, 1997).

Children learn that they too can serve as models, telling their parents and others to do as they do. Examples are shown in Table 6.2.

As evident in the above examples, children see themselves as models for both adults and other children, telling them to emulate their behavior. Of course, the addressee may reject the modeling request. When a kindergarten child is told, "You could copy me. . . . Look what I'm doing first," he refuses, saying, "I'm not going to copy anybody except (the teacher)" (Mody, 2005, p. 62). Teachers themselves may explicitly encourage peer modeling, as when a teacher praises a preschooler, saying, "you are good, you be the teacher and teach the others" (Gardner & Cass, 1965, p. 82).

Table 6.2.

	Age	Source
K: "Karen is teaching Mommy to draw"	25 mos.	Karniol (Diary, Karen)
C: "Do it how I do it"; "I show you how to do it"; "this is the way I did it"	30 mos.	Limber (1973)
K: "Daddy please to take off shoes if to sleep; Karen also to take off shoes"[3]	31 mos.	Karniol (Diary, Karen)
As teacher, to doll K: "sit like Karen is a good girl – you're a good girl too"[4]	32 mos.	Karniol (Diary, Karen)
To peer C: "I'll show you how to get gas," shows how to pump gas into toy car	Preschool	Gelman & Shatz (1977, p. 37)
To 3-year-old C: "You must do it like that, too"	4 years	Auwarter (1986, p. 220)
Girl to female peers C: "Let me teach you a lesson about this first, you do like this. . . ."	Preschool	Kyratzis, Marx, & Wade (2001, p. 408)

Other children may also incidentally channel preferences for objects as well as behavior (e.g., "Whatever their friends have they want," Bee-Gates, 2006, p. 117). For instance, Orren, at 3;4;4 years, asks for a black watch, saying "Elad have a black watch so I want too a black watch." A preschooler asks, "Mommy for lunch will you give me a napkin tomorrow, like this? . . . 'cause Perri has these kind of napkins. I want a napkin" (Hall, CHILDES). A fourth grader explains that she wants "things that all my friends have, so I want to have it too" (Fiates, Amboni, & Teixeria, 2006, p. 159). Yet the view of children as wanting everything that their friends have is clearly overly simplistic. Only some objects in others' possession are viewed as desirable and there is no empirical research that has addressed this issue. At times, the claim "everybody has them"[5] (e.g., Axia, 1996), as voiced by a 7-year-old girl who tries to convince her mother to buy her the item, is used, suggesting that desirability may be a function of perceived prevalence. On the other hand, desirability is sometimes a function of perceived rarity, as voiced by a girl of 9;3 who tries to convince her mother to buy her some small puppets, saying, "they never sell such small ones"[6] (Axia, 1996).

DIRECT INSTRUCTION: MANNERS AND POLITENESS

There are relatively few domains in which children get direct socialization instruction. The domain of manners and politeness, including polite speech, appears cross-culturally to be one in which they do. Kaluli mothers use ELEMA (*say it like this*) to get children to use preferred linguistic forms, especially offers and requests (Schieffelin, 1990). In Tzeltal society, mothers and siblings tell children explicitly what to say, using the quotative verb "Uta" (say it), similar to the Kaluli use of ELEMA (Brown, 2002). Also in this vein, a Taiwanese grandmother instructs her grandchild, asking him what he said to his mother (i.e., "Don't hit me"), what he should have said to her (i.e., "I won't push the screen down"), and what the potential results of each expression would be (i.e., being hit versus not being hit by his mother), finally asking him, "which sentence is better for you to say to her?" (Fung, Miller, & Lin, 2004, p. 311). Demuth (1986) found that prompts for proper forms of polite language account for about 22 percent to 27 percent of adult prompts in Basotho society.

Children in the Western world are also instructed how to speak politely, being questioned *"how do you say it?" "excuse me?"* or being reprimanded for using inappropriate language. When 20-month-old Claudia says, "Give me your hand," her mother asks "How do you say?" and Claudia answers "Please you give me your little hand?"[7] (Bates, 1976). With prompting, the child changes her imperative to a more polite request. A grandfather chastises his grandson with, "Did I hear anybody say please?" (Hall, CHILDES). When a 5-year-old asks, "Can I go to the toilet," his teacher replies with *"pardon?"* The child then repeats, "Can I go to the toilet please?" (King, 1978, p. 55). He understood the teacher's question as implying that he had not asked properly.

Dinnertime is often selected as a setting in which politeness is prompted. Junefelt and Tulviste (1998) found many prompts for what children should say, for example, "What do you say after dinner then?" asked of a Swedish child of 26 months. A Japanese mother chides her toddler son, asking him "Did you say itadakimasu? (i.e., a greeting prior to eating). When he repeats the greeting, she further instructs him to put his hands together and clap when he says it (Kobayashi, 2001, p. 125). Direct instruction is also used to get children to ask to be excused from the dinner table (e.g., "What do you say when you leave the table?" Aukrust, 2002, p. 61; "I don't remember either of you asking to be excused," Aukrust, 2004,

[3] Hebrew: "Abba bevakasha lehorid naalaim im lishoned; gum Karen lehorid naalaim"

[4] Hebrew: "shvi kmo Karen yalda tova – gam at yalda tova"

[5] Italian: "ce li hanno tutti"

[6] Italian: "cosi piccolo non li vendono mai"

[7] Italian: "Dammi a mano" . . . . "Como si dice?". . . . "Poppoe, a dai a manina"?

Table 6.3.

	Age	Source
C: "I want some water, Dad" F: "Say. . . . C: "Wouldja get some water?"	35 mos.	Peters (2000, p. 145)
At dinner C: "Can I have some more orange juice?" M: "What's the magic word?" C: "Please?"	3 years	Blum-Kulka (1997, p. 203)
C: "I want more crackers" T: "That's not the way you ask" C: "Could I have more crackers. . . . please?"	Preschool	Meyer (2003, p. 70)
C: "I want a drink" M: "Pardon?" C. "Please"	5 years	Grieshaber (2004, p. 135)
Child asks for more F: "He can't have any more now. . . . He has to say please" . . . . . . "No more yogurt for Mark . . . . . . not unless he says pretty please"	5;7 years	MacWhinney (CHILDES, Mark)
At dinner C: "Mommy, bring me more fish"[8] M: "Excuse me?" C repeats the request, adds please	6 years	Blum-Kulka (1997, p. 204)

Table 6.4.

	Age	Source
At bedtime F: "When you wake up you say, 'good morning Daddy, good morning Mommy' . . . you're going to get up and you say 'good morning Daddy, good morning Mommy' "	24 mos.	Nelson (1996, p. 277)
M: "You didn't tell me 'thank you' – you gonna tell me "thank you?"	Toddler	Blake (1993, p. 487)
C tells her mother to make doll clothes M: "Can't you say, *Mommy, would you please make me some?* Don't order me on how many to make. That's not very nice"	Preschool	Becker (1994, p. 143)
C: "Mrs., tie my shoelaces' " T: "I will tie them for you. But you should say 'Please.' I don't have to tie your shoelaces' "	Preschool	Georgalidou (2008, p. 80)
M: "Thank you thank you you say thank you"	5;7 years	Junefelt & Tulviste (1998)

p. 185). When a 20-month-old asks to get down from his high chair, saying "want down now," his mother asks, "what do you say, down . . . down please" (Wilkinson, 1971, p. 69). When a 5-year-old leaves the table, her mother asks, "Did you ask if you could be excused from the table Allison?" When the child indicates that she did not, she is made to come back, sit down, and ask to leave the table prior to being given permission to do so (Grieshaber, 2004, p. 131).

Politeness related to food requests is also directly instructed, often being prompted with "Is that the way you ask?" or "what do you say?" Examples of direct instruction for requesting food, both at home and at preschool, are shown in Table 6.3.

Whereas above, children were prompted to make their requests more polite, parents also provide explicit instruction as to what children should actually say, as shown in Table 6.4.

This explicit instructional stance is especially evident at holiday times. At Halloween, for instance, parents repeatedly tell their children what to say to their hosts: "Don't forget to say *thank you*," and "Will you remember to say *Trick or Treat* and *Thank you*?" (Gleason & Weintraub, 1978). Becker (1990) found the same with respect to Christmas, as when a mother tells a preschooler, "When you give that card to your teacher, tell her Merry Christmas, OK?" (p. 17).

Direct instruction in this realm appears to take root and very young children start to thank others. For instance, Travis, at 21;10, says, "Thanks Mommy bring a chips" after her mother brought them to her (Tomasello, 1992). When I give him a goody from a birthday bag, Orren, at 23 months, says, "Toda (thank you) Mummy." They also start to comment on the need to say *thank you*. For instance, Karen at 22;14, says, "Have to say 'thank you' when saba and savta (i.e., Hebrew for grandpa and grandma) brought you the dolly." They also tell others, both adults and children, that they need to say *please* and *thank you*. Examples are provided in Table 6.5.

Children are also instructed as to table manners, being told how to sit (e.g., "mind your feet – sit properly. . . . Did you hear me – get your feet off the chair. . . . Sit on the chair properly," Tough, 1973, p. 31), and how to eat and drink. For example, April, at 35 months, is drinking a carbonated drink and belches (Higginson, CHILDES). Her mother says, "Are you gonna be a little pig and not say

[8] Hebrew: "Tavi li od"

Table 6.5.

	Age	Source
To Parents		
To mother:		
C: "Say thank you when you get it. Not please"	29 mos.	Wootton (1997)
C: "Daddy, you can also say to me "thank you very much"[9]	33;21	Karniol (Diary, Orren)
To mother		
C: "You no "gid" (i.e. say) to me thank you"	3;3 years	Karniol (1992, p. 275)
To Peers		
C: "Yesterday was Travis' birthday, and he got a lot of presents. And I had to keep reminding him to say thank you"		
Mother indicates it's important to say *thank you*		
C: "Even if you don't like what you got"	5 years	Capps & Ochs (2002, p. 53)
First grade girl to peer		
G: "Can I use your eraser, I don't have any left"		
Boy refuses		
G: "Please"		
B: "That's better" (hands her the eraser)	First grade	Maynard (1985)

Table 6.6.

	Age	Source
Mother asks what child is doing		
Child says she is wiping her chin, with her dress		
M: "How bout wiping your chin with your napkin"	22 mos.	Bloom (1973, p. 238)
M: "Don't wipe your face on your shirt please"	Toddler	Gleason, Perlmann, & Greif (1984)
M: "Francesca clean your hands with the napkin"[10]	4 years	Pontecorvo & Fasulo (1997, p. 424)
M: "Should we wipe your nose? . . . . Don't you have a Kleenex? . . . don't have a Kleenex?"	Preschool	Broen (1972, p. 88, 92)
F: "Carl, wipe the tuna off your forehead right here. That's it. Put it on your napkin"	5 years	Snow (1990, p. 230)
M: "Don't wipe on your sleeve"	10 years	De Geer (2004)

anything? Not gonna say excuse me?" The child answers "Excuse me." Later, when she is eating yogurt, her mother asks, "Why are you making those slurping noises?" When she gets no reply, she continues, "Come on, if you're going to eat like that I'm gonna take it away, OK?" Shatz (1994) answers her 18-month-old grandson's request to leave the table with, "Wait until you finish what's in your mouth. You can't walk around with food in your mouth" (p. 34). A mother tells her preschooler, "Don't talk with your mouth full. Jane, you can't tell what you're saying if your mouth is full" (Becker, 1994, p. 141). The father of a 5-year-old says, "You're talking with food in your mouth," expecting the child to understand that he is not to do so (Hall, CHILDES).

The constant reminders as to table manners appear to bear fruit. First, children comment on their own need to comply with social norms regarding eating habits. A boy of 3;4 years tells his mother, "Just a second. I can't talk now. My mouth is full, Mom" (Bartsch & Wellman, 1995, p. 118). Children also start to admonish their friends and siblings to adopt more polite ways of eating, for example, a 5-year-old says to her younger sister, "Don't talk while you're eating food" (Gleason, Hay, & Cain, 1989). A preschool girl tells her male peer, "Don't talk with your mouth full. Isn't there a rule on the wall that says 'use good table manners?'" (Meyer, 2003, p. 72). Pitcher and Schultz (1983) similarly found that 5-year-old girls often made comments of this nature to boys, saying, "You have to shut your mouth when you eat" and "Do you *have* to make those yukky noises?" (p. 37).

Personal grooming is also subject to direct instruction, as shown in Table 6.6.

Direct instruction is also provided regarding the use of utensils. When Laura, at 21 months, eats with her

[9] Hebrew: "Abba ata yaxol gum lehagid li "toda raba"

[10] Italian: "Francesca pullisciti le mani col tovagliolo"

fingers, her mother says, "You are supposed to be using your spoon" (Valsiner, 1987, p. 198). Another mother shouts at her 5-year-old daughter, "Uh Uh! Not with your fingers!" When the daughter answers, "I want to eat with my fingers," the mother responds, "Put it down! You know better than that. No! Ask for it to be cut up please." When the same incident recurs, the mother says, "You're using your fingers. What's a spoon for?" When the child answers, "Eating," and begins to eat with her spoon, the mother says, "Thank you. Yes" (Grieshaber, 2004, pp. 129, 131).[11]

In addition to attempting to foster politeness by direct instruction, parents may provide children with "words of wisdom" as to the social virtues of politeness. A German mother conveys such a message to her daughter who asked for more juice, "When one asks for (something) more nicely, one always gets something"[12] (Miller, 1979, p. 410). An American mother similarly explains to her toddler daughter, "You know, when people are polite and they ask certain things certain, in nice ways, they get it. Right?" (Snow et al., 1990, p. 302). Notice, though, that these explanations are couched in generic terms, suggesting that politeness is a universal rather than a context-specific mode of behavior.

PROMISES, REWARDS, AND BRIBES

Parents may offer inducements to get their children to engage in activities they would not otherwise engage in. Theoreticians vary in terms of how they view such inducements. For instance, Cook-Gumperz (1973) calls inducements that invoke rewards "bargaining," and categorizes them under parental concessions. Minton, Kagan and Levine (1971) call such inducements "barters" in that if the child does something the mother wants, the mother offers something in exchange. Divergence in the categorization of such strategies across studies makes it difficult to know just how prevalent their use is. Minton and colleagues found that offers of rewards were used only rarely in a home observation of 27-month-old children. This is somewhat surprising in light of the fact that promises have the same logical structure as threats, invoking "if–then" contingencies. A threat makes punishment contingent on noncompliance and a promise makes rewards contingent on compliance. The difference, of course, is that offers of rewards differ from threats in specifying beneficial rather than detrimental outcomes. Perhaps this is why many researchers (e.g., Rubin & Lewicki, 1973; Heilman & Garner, 1975) have found that promises get greater compliance than threats. On the other hand, children understand rewards as biconditionals, inferring that when a parent says, "If you do A, I'll do B," the implication is that "If you don't do A, I will not do B" (Light, Girotto, & Legrenzi, 1990). Because rewards are generally dangled when the child's preference is not to engage in the specified behavior, it may be that parents do not generally get to dispense the reward and end up responding to the nonfulfillment of the contingency.

On the other hand, diary studies provide ample examples that testify as to the prevalence of rewards and bribes in parental attempts to channel children's behavior. Parents make offers of tangible objects and of activities as inducements, both episodically and in a recurrent fashion, as shown in Table 6.7.

Recurrent associations between child behaviors and reward outcomes can be couched in more general terms, as being good, or being a good child (e.g., "He's supposed to have a shilling a week if he's good," Newson & Newson, 1976, p. 227). A mother recounts about her preschooler that "if she's been real helpful on a particular morning when I've been really busy I tend to say, 'You can have some sweeties'" (Charles & Kerr, 1988, p. 101). An adolescent girl who helps her mother with various household chores, explains, "But sometimes I get money for it, it depends on, if I've been really good the whole week"(Mayall, 2002, p. 95). In this vein, a Russian mother dangles going for a walk as a reward for her child of 19 months, saying,

> Good girls eat cutlets and carrots, yes, and they go for walks with their mummies . . . and Varja is such a good girl, who eats cutlets and carrots and goes for walks with her mummy. (Kiebzak-Mandera, 2006, p. 325)[13]

In some families, the performance of errands and household chores is consistently associated with monetary rewards, with children being paid for laying the table, helping clean up, washing dishes, and helping with their younger siblings (e.g., Newson & Newson, 1976). In a more recent study, a mother explains that her son only gets an allowance if he performs certain jobs, further relating that he "Makes his bed in the mornings, keeps his bedroom tidy, dusts it for me, brings down all the washing, puts it in the machine" (Ribbens, 1994, p. 109). In a study of 1,000 ninth graders, of those who were getting an allowance, about 80 percent indicated they had to perform household chores for the money (Mortimer, Dennehy, Lee, & Finch, 1994). In this vein, a mother asks her preschooler whether he picked up all the Tinker Toys. When he answers affirmatively, she queries, "The complete set?" and when he answers *yes*, she says, "Well I think we ought to give you a little more allowance for that . . . here we go, I'm giving you more . . . . You deserve it" (Hall, CHILDES). When

[11] However, parents may overlook children's eating with fingers when they are anxious about the amount of food being consumed, e.g., "I'm so anxious she should put it in her mouth I don't really care how she does it" (Charles & Kerr, 1988, p. 93).

[12] German: "Wenn de mer was Schones sagst, kriegste immer was"

[13] Notice that this is quite different from using "reward" objects to distract children's attention. For instance, a mother says about her 21-month-old: "you want to get him into the tub or something or to bed. So you give him a toy to distract him" (Bettelheim, 1962, p. 64). In these cases, there is no contingency between the object and the activity in question.

Table 6.7.

	Age	Source
Episodic Inducements		
M: "Will you put the top back on the washing basket please" C asks her to play M: "Well I will play if you put the top on the basket"	28 mos.	Wells (1986, p. 26)
C refuses to go to bed, asks for a sweet M: "Come on – get your things off – a sweetie when you're ready if I can find one"	3 years	Tough (1973, p. 32)
M: "You can hold the pet rat as soon as you make your bed"	Preschool	Bee-Gates (2006, p. 48)
M: "Now if you behave yourself, we'll have ice cream for tea, as a treat you see, or I'll take you to the sweet shop or you can have a lolly while you're out"	Unknown	Charles & Kerr (1988, p. 102)
Recurrent Inducements		
M: "What was my deal with you?" C explains that he was promised a Power Ranger if he used a potty and wore big boy pants instead of diapers	3 years	Wang (2004, p. 293)
M explains how she gets C to school on time M: "If you get four checks then you get cookies in your lunchbox"	Preschool	Bee-Gates (2006, p. 48)
Book shows child making bed M: "If you make your bed what do you get to do?" C: "Swim" M: "Swim – is that one of your favorite things to do?"	6;2 years	Warren (CHILDES)

the child retorts, "Everytime I deserve things," she replies, "No, not everytime, that's bargaining," clarifying that he only deserves extra money sometimes, not every time.

In fact, some parents refuse to provide children with monetary rewards for doing household chores, viewing this as bribery, saying, "We've found in the past it's been a huge mistake to try and bribe them, or you know, you can't buy them off.... They are going to do things not because they get 50p" (Songua-Barke & Webley, 1993, p. 79). In fact, there is evidence that although bribes may work in the short run, they have detrimental effects in the long run. Research (e.g., Puhl & Schwartz, 2003) indicates that adults who recall food being used for behavioral control when they were children evidence greater binge eating and greater dietary restraint.

But can rewards, even monetary ones, be dispensed in ways that are not construed as bribes? Apparently, yes, particularly if the rewards are not offered in advance. In fact, unanticipated rewards do not have the same effect as bribes, because the child cannot conduct himself in light of such expected reward (cf., Lepper, Greene, & Nisbett, 1973). A mother indicates an intuitive understanding of this difference when she explains regarding her behavior after her kindergarten son did the dishes:

> I was putting away the cookies and things, and whereas he almost never gets anything sweet in the middle of the morning, the fact that I gave him these few cookies was really quite a prize ... but it was in no way a bribe – he was already doing it. (Sears, Maccoby, & Levin, 1957, p. 320)

Moreover, rewards that are more symbolic in nature also do not have detrimental effects on subsequent behavior. In this vein, an 11-year-old explains that if he has done something good, his mother will give him a kiss, "and she takes me to shops and gets me some new clothes. My dad gives me money, about twenty pounds ... my mum, she' always proud of me" (Rout, Sixsmith, & Moore, 1996, p. 105). Children themselves may actually express a preference for symbolic rewards over material ones. At 29;20, Karen says, "Mummy don't give Karen any more chocolate 'cause it goes in Karen's teeth. When Karen makes Kaki don't give Karen chocolate. The best thing is a big hug and a kiss." The contexts that engender preferences for symbolic rewards in children have not been empirically examined. The fact that parents do use symbolic rewards is evident when the father of a third grader recounts that when the child does her homework well he gives her an imaginary medal, explaining, "We just pretend to put something around her neck, and she likes that" (Xu & Corno, 1998, p. 424).

USING IMPERATIVES

Parents can channel their children's preferences by giving them direct commands to engage in desired behaviors (e.g., "play with the puzzle"), partake of certain objects (e.g., "eat the meat"), and orient themselves in specific directions (e.g., "look at the birdie"). In this context, Whiting and Edwards (1988) found that toddlers are issued imperatives with two different goals in mind. First, they are issued prosocial imperatives whose aim is to socialize children to become acceptable members of the group, for example, "Greet your grandmother," "Give the baby part of the banana," and "Give the baby the stick";

second, children are issued imperatives whose aim is to protect them from physical danger, constituting restrictives, which will be dealt with in Chapter 8, Restricting Behavior. Using imperatives, though, may make little sense to the parent in such channeling contexts; after all, channeling is aimed at having the child develop a positive preference rather than a negative one. Consequently, parents often avoid using imperatives in channeling contexts. In fact, Becker (1994) suggests that families tend to socialize more by indirect rather than direct means.

Alternatively, imperatives can be toned down with diminutives and nicknames and mothers do so more often than fathers (Gleason, 1987). For instance, mothers tend to say things like, "Try this puzzle sweetie" (Junefelt & Tulviste, 1998), "Would you take your plate off the table sweetie" (Gleason, 1987, p. 195), and "Will you shut the door for me darling?" (Painter, 1984, p. 257). Another way of avoiding using imperatives is by prefacing them with a question that can tone down their force. For instance, the mother of a child of 4;6 years asks, "Have you finished with this Fanny love?" When Fanny says yes, her mother answers, "Well put it back then" (MacLure & French, 1981).

Another means of toning down imperatives in channeling contexts is by way of expressing utterances that have the force of directives. For instance, children attribute directive intentions to utterances such as "It's clean-up time," "It's twelve o'clock," and "Somebody's talking" (Ervin-Tripp, 1977), interpreting such statements as instructions as to what to do in the relevant context. Ervin-Tripp suggests that utterances are interpreted as directives when they break topical continuity in discourse, refer to acts that are prohibited, or give exemplars of the core arguments of social rules (e.g., "I see chewing gum," p. 169). In fact, children interpret such statements in terms of their directive force and tend to act in accordance with their intended meanings. Thus, when a preschool teacher says to a child "Jilly, I hope you're going to put that apron on if you want to paint" (Wood, McMahon, & Cranstoun, 1980), it is clear to the child being addressed that the utterance has imperative force. Similarly, when Allison is 20;21, her mother tells her to take off her coat, saying, "It's very warm.... Aren't you a little bit warm? Besides, it's not raining" (Bloom, 1973, p. 207). The message is that if it is raining, wearing a coat may be appropriate; but inside, where it is not raining, wearing a coat is inappropriate.

USING QUESTIONS

Questions can be used in many ways to channel children's preferences. When a teacher asks "Damion, have you had your milk?" and the child answers *no*, the attempt to channel the child's behavior is evident when the teacher continues, "Go and get your milk then, love" (Wood, McMahon, & Cranstoun, 1980, p. 49). Similarly, when a teacher poses the question "Do you want to run along to the loo, James?" (Wood, McMahon, & Cranstoun, 1980, p. 35), it is clear that the child is not being asked as to his preference but is rather being told to do so. Another means of using questions is to suggest the appropriate form of behavior in a given context. While working on a puzzle, when Jonathan was 3;6 years, his mother says, "Now that one goes over there, doesn't it?" (MacLure & French, 1981). She poses the question with the expectation that the child will answer affirmatively. Again, in the context of playing, a mother asks her child, "Should we put the car in there?" (Broen, 1972, p. 45), posing the question as a rhetorical device, fully intending for the child to interpret the question as a directive.

There are also questions that literally require an explanation from the child, but not literally represent a request to change the state of things. For instance, the question, "What is that Tinker Toy doing on the floor there?" (Holzman, 1972, p. 320) does not request a literal answer to the question. A child who answered literally would be considered rude (e.g., "It's not doing anything, it's resting"). Even 2-year-olds can interpret the question "Is the door shut?" as a request to shut the door (Shatz, 1974). When a mother asks, "Is that your coat on the floor again?" (Sinclair & Coulthard, 1975), she is not posing a real question but rather provides an instruction to get the child to pick up the coat, doing so in a manner that avoids giving a direct command. In posing such questions, the parent is actually making an *ought statement*, that the Tinker Toy and the coat should be removed from the floor. Teachers also pose questions in this manner, but in the following example, the "ought" nature of the statement is made explicit by what follows it: "What is your lunch bag doing here? You know you're supposed to keep your lunch bag in the cloak room. Now put it away" (Kounin, 1970, p. 94).

Questions can also be used as implicit suggestions for engaging in a given behavior. For instance, when a mother says to a child "Could you come over here please?" she does not doubt the child's ability to engage in the behavior but uses the question as a suggestion rather than using the imperative mode. Questions that constitute implicit suggestions often have the form of "Why don't you ... ?" DeVilliers (1984) provide examples of suggestions, such as "Why don't you read to me?" and "Why don't you come over here and play with the ball?" (p. 210). Similarly, when a mother asks a 9-year-old, "Aren't you having potatoes?" the child takes potatoes (De Geer et al., 2002). In these cases, the parent refrains from giving the child a direct command and the child appears to have a choice of doing otherwise.

But when parents use such questions to impose their own preferences on children, children may not cue in to this apparent imposition of parental preferences. For instance, a 4-year-old boy is told by his mother, "Evan, it's your last day of nursery school. Why don't you wear your nursery sweatshirt?" He interprets the question as offering him a choice and answers, "I don't want to wear that one." His mother makes it clear that she was not offering a choice, saying, "This is the last day of nursery school, that's why we wear it. You want to wear that one?" and he again refuses, answering, "Another one." His mother persists, "Are you going to get it, or should I?" He relents, saying, "I will" (Nucci, 2004, pp. 203–204). The child did not understand that his mother's use of a questioning mode had the force of a command rather than mere suggestion. Questions like "Would you like to . . . ?" and "Do you want to . . . ?" imply that the child's preferences are involved whereas in fact, the parent's external preferences are of issue. In this vein, a preschooler's mother asks her "Would you like to tidy up the dolls' house?" (Fletcher, 1985, p. 62). The question is not meant to clarify the child's preferences but rather to inform her that she needs to tidy up. Similarly, when a child is asked, "You wanna stop that?" (Schachter, 1979, p. 195) or "Do you want to tell Mrs. Hayes what we did?" (Hall & Cole, 1978), neither question is concerned with the child's preferences but rather directs him what to do. This is evident when the mother of a preschooler asks "Would you two like to go and wash your hands?" but then adds, "Go and wash your hands, please" (Dunn, 1988, p. 35), making it clear that the children are being told what to do.

In her research, Budwig (2002, p. 75) found that mothers of toddlers tended to use *want to*, to suggest alternative activities to their children. She summarizes by saying that the mothers' questions alluded to children's desires but in fact were disguised presentations of the caregivers' own desires. In this vein, we get "Want to turn that off? Want to turn that off now?" which the mother says to a child who has just walked out of the room without turning off the television. It is clear that such questions are interpreted by children as requests for specific types of behavior, because, in this particular instance, the child walked back and turned off the television set (Corsaro, 1979a). Garvey's (1975) study of 3.5- to 5.5-year-olds in dyadic interaction also showed that children interpret indirect requests as indicating the speaker's preferences for future action.

In fact, older children generally appear to understand the implications of such questions. In a study by Reeder (1996), 6- to 9-year-old children were asked to interpret what a teacher puppet meant by saying, "Would you like to . . . ," with different completions, such as "play on the swings, ride the bike, draw a picture." Despite the focus of the question on the individual being addressed rather than the person posing the question, the majority of children interpreted this question as a request, order, or suggestion, explaining that the speaker wants the hearer to engage in the act specified. Only 30 percent of the children interpreted it as a real question. Moreover, some children made inferences of more nefarious, manipulative intent, inferring that "The teacher probably doesn't want them bothering her so she makes them go to the play area" (p. 256), that the teacher wanted to find out if the hearer is able to perform the specified act, or that "there were too many children at the other stations" (p. 157). Children's sensitivity to the wording of utterances and the contexts in which they are uttered is evident in another study (Reeder, 1980) in which children interpreted the same question (e.g., "Would you like to play on the train?") as a directive when a puppet teacher was closer to the toy train and as an offer when the puppet child was closer to it.

USING CHOICE

Socialization agents can channel children's preferences by giving them choices between alternatives that the socialization agents themselves view as compatible with their own preferences (e.g., "Do you want to paint now, Michael, or later?" Wood, McMahon, & Cranstoun, 1980, p. 35). That is, even in offering a child a choice between doing something now or later, the implication is that the activity in question is one that needs to be engaged in by the child. In the words of one father,

> I've always thought that I would let my kids do whatever they wanted to do and I would encourage them to do whatever they wanted to do . . . as long as it's exactly whatever I want them to do. (Young, Faseluikho, & Valach, 1997, p. 41)

Similarly, as a preschool teacher says regarding preschool elections, "Let children vote on something only when the outcome doesn't matter or when you are sure before they vote what the outcome will be" (Tobin et al., 1989, p. 165). As Tobin and colleagues notes, American preschools are predicated on the idea that children are given a choice of which activities to engage in. When a preschool teacher asks, "Would you like to play at the water table or the sand table?" (Kontos, 1999), she is both providing choice and *restricting* choice by specifying those choices that are available and are considered appropriate at the moment. Preschools play with choice; in fact, when children gravitate to the same activity all the time, preschooler teachers tend to suggest that they choose other activities. But the activities provided are carefully selected to reflect the teaching agenda of the preschool.

At home as well, children are generally asked to indicate their choice between alternatives rather than asked to indicate their choice in an open-ended fashion. The mother of a 23-month-old asks, "Which book do you want to read? This one or this one? Which book"? The boy points and says, "This one" (Howe, 1981, p. 7). Similarly, children are asked in a binary fashion regarding their choice of drink (e.g., "Do you want milk or juice?" Shatz, 1994), how they want their eggs, and which cereal they want. In this spirit, Emily's father says to her, at 27 months, "you can choose what type of egg you want . . . . And you can choose what type of cereal you want, you can have either Shredded Wheat or Cheerios," and she responds, "Shredded Wheat!" (Nelson, 1989).

Children can be offered choices in an open-ended fashion, though. The father of a 5-year-old says, "You decide what you wanna play, OK?" When the child asks "*What?*" the father says, "You pick 2 or 3 things you wanna play with" (Hall, CHILDES). After Bloom's daughter Allison, at 20;21, rejects an offer to play with some toys, her mother asks, "What would you like to do?" (Bloom, 1973, p. 208). Hart and Risley (1999) found that children were often asked in an open-ended fashion, "What do you want for dinner?" (p. 32). In line with this, when a 10-year-old boy is asked as to the availability of choice, he says, "sometimes I get to choose what I want to eat" (Sixsmith & Knowles, 1996). It seems, then, that choices may be offered in an open-ended fashion in domains in which parents do not feel the need to constrain choices. On the other hand, Charles and Kerr (1987, 1988) found that at dinner, children often refuse to eat because they are not provided with choice. At other meals, children were found to be allowed to choose between various alternatives, but at the main meal of the day they had to eat what they were given and the food was in line with their father's preferences rather than their own. For breakfast and lunch, when fathers were at work, children's own food preferences often held sway. Yet American mothers provide children with more choice during mealtimes than Estonian and Swedish mothers (Junefelt & Tulviste, 1998). In fact, the provision of food choices (e.g., "Do you want any of this?") is more effective in channeling new food preferences than offering a special dessert as reward, than insisting on trying one bite, and than modeling (Hendy, 1999).

Hart and Risley (1999) found that children 1 to 2 years old were offered frequent opportunities to choose in other domains as well, being asked, "Are you ready to get dressed now?" "What do you want to read today?" "Do you want me to comb your hair?" (p. 32). Notice that some of these choices are singular and require either affirmation or negation of the offer; others are binary and require the child to specify a preference between two options; still other choices are open-ended, requiring the child to select within the domain being alluded to. But in many cases, choice is more apparent than real. A child who answered *no* would be chastised. As well, it is obviously easier for children to affirm or negate a question as to their preferred choice than to answer open-ended questions. Open-ended choices are more difficult because they do not specify possible alternatives; yet children are slower in making binary choices than in choosing an item in an array (Stewart, 1958).

Choices are often offered in what Turiel (1983) has called the "personal domain," suggesting that their provision reflects parental understanding of this domain as one in which the exercise of choice is integral. This domain includes children's hair (e.g., a mother says to her preschooler, "If you want, we can get your hair cut. It's your choice," Nucci, 2004, p. 205) and clothing choice (e.g., "You need to decide what you want to wear to school today.... Have you decided what to wear today?.... Okay, that's a good choice," Nucci, 2004, p. 205). Yet even in the personal domain, the provision of choice may be more apparent than real. When a toddler says that he needs to choose a shirt, his mother asks him "Do you know which one you have in mind?" implying by her question that he has a choice in the matter. But before he has a chance to answer, she offers him one, saying "Here, this is a new one." When he refuses it saying, "No, it's too big," she answers, "Oh, Evan, just wear one, and when you get home, you can pick whatever you want, and I won't even help you" (Nucci, 2004, pp. 203–204). Despite appearing to provide him with choice, she is stipulating what his choice must be.

The choice offered to children in the personal domain can be restricted because of gender stereotypes (e,g., when parents do not allow children to play with cross-gender toys), cultural prescriptions (e.g., being required to choose a specific other as one's future mate), or prejudice (e.g., restricting a child's choice of playmates). A 7-year-old Greek child is talking about his hair and says, "now it's straight, cause Mom had it cut ... now it's cut. Two days ago Mummy took me to the hairdresser's, and I didn't want to go and...." At this point his mother interrupts and says, "Yes, but you know... boys shouldn't have lots of curly hair, isn't it nicer like this, more masculine?" (Georgakapoulou, 2002, p. 40). We do not know how such individual differences in parental perceptions of the right to choose have an impact on their offsprings' well-being. As for the domains in which children are offered choices, Turiel and his students have generally found that those parents who offer children choice are very clear about the domains in which choice is not an option – the domain of morality and social conventions.

Yet having choice is critical for the development of responsibility and mature judgment. Morality is learned by being given choices and being able to evaluate those choices from the perspective of parental standards. As Varenne (1990) contends, parents who offer choices construct "a world of agents that may choose between alternatives" (p. 258). To quote Ginott (1965), "children who are always told what to do and who therefore have little opportunity to exercise judgment, to make choices, and to develop inner standards," are more likely to make irresponsible decisions (p. 80). Although being given the opportunity to make choices may eventuate in bad choices, children need to learn from their mistakes. It is by discussing choices that values are transmitted to children. Being deprived of that possibility is detrimental to their development. Colby and Kohlberg (1987) coded as Stage 5 a response indicating that a parent needs to "encourage an autonomy of decision, of moral choices" (p. 607).

ATTITUDE MANIPULATION

Parents can channel their children's preferences by manipulating their attitudes, doing so in a variety of ways.

Table 6.8.

	Age	Source
C takes baby's rattle M: "Hey don't do that. . . . You don't want a rattle do you? You're not a baby are you? Are you?"	3 years	Tough (1973, p. 33)
C is playing with baby rattle M: "You're a big boy – you don't want a rattle. . . ." C says he does M: "No you don' – that's for baby. Where's your car?"	3 years	Tough (1973, p. 32)
Taiwanese family M: "I've never seen any 3-year-old who behaved like you"	Preschool	Fung & Chen (2001, p. 424)
T: "You're a big boy now please . . . show me what a big boy you can be"	Preschool	Willes (1983, p. 139)
T: "Do your writing. All the other children have done some writing, and you're as clever as they are, aren't you?"	School	Willes (1983, p. 140)

ATTITUDE MANIPULATION VIA SOCIAL COMPARISON

Attitudes are often manipulated by invoking social comparisons, the provision of information as to how others behave in the context in question. Although children themselves start to use social comparisons (e.g., Ruble & Frey, 1991), before they do so, parents and other socialization agents invoke social comparisons as a way of channeling children's behavior. They draw a comparison between the child and someone else, with the child being encouraged to use others' behavior as the reference for how he himself should or should not behave. Other people's actions can be held up as models and contrasted with children's own – and inappropriate – way of engaging in actions. Sometimes these models are adults, whereas at other times, the models are other children (e.g., referring to an older cousin, a mother says, "You don't see Betty act like that" – You don't see Betty do this," Sears, Maccoby, & Levin, 1957, p. 348). Using her sister as the comparison, a mother says, "look at Shirley's plate, she has eaten her dinner up so quickly and her plate is shining; let's see if you can do it just as quickly as Shirley did" (ibid, p. 350). When toddler Eve says, "Fraser cup" as she sees the researcher drinking coffee, her mother chastises her, saying,

> Eve why don't you drink it out of the cup? See, Fraser is not drinking his coffee that way. He's not drinking his coffee with his spoon. Drink your juice out of the cup . . . . You drink it out of the cup. Fraser drinks his coffee that way. (Moerk, 1983, p. 112)

Teachers similarly encourage social comparison, for example, "Nigel, would you like to drink your milk all up like Jason's doing?" (Willes, 1983, p. 125). When a preschooler gets paint on her dress, her teacher says, "You are careless. Look how clean Margaret has kept her frock" (Gardner & Cass, 1965, p. 110). A kindergarten teacher tells the class, "I like the way Mary is sitting" (Kounin, 1970, p. 66) and another one says, "I do like the way Gillian's sitting up. Look how beautifully she's sitting up" (Kamler, 1999, p. 197). In Chinese preschools, comparisons are viewed as a means of encouraging the desire to improve. Both negative and positive comparisons are drawn to emphasize the contrast between them. In this vein, a preschool teacher says, "How about Chen Ling – is he sitting properly? Who knows what is wrong with the way he is sitting? . . . . Look at Lin Ping? Is she sitting nicely? See how straight her back is . . . . "(Tobin et al., 1989, p. 95).

Whereas above, the child's behavior was compared with that of another specific person, social comparison can refer to generic others, categories of people with whom the child is being compared, either negatively or favorably, as shown in Table 6.8.

These mothers and teachers are using negative comparisons to deter children from behaviors and positive comparisons with their age cohorts to motivate children to behave in desired ways. In doing so, they sometimes allude to "ways of doing things" that do not refer to specific others at all. This is evident in the following. A preschool teacher says, "Carry the chair properly. Not like that, dear, that's not the way to carry a chair" (Gardner & Cass, 1965, p. 64). The child is presumed to have a representation of the "proper" way of doing so and is expected to adapt his behavior to reflect this knowledge. It is unclear what *proper* means in this context; it could mean *dangerous, unmanly*, or *unladylike*. In fact, social comparison with the opposite sex often emerges in the context of socialization. In an interesting case of this, a girl who wants to take a puzzle of an airplane away from a boy is chastised by her teacher who says, "boys like aeroplanes" (Delamont, 1980, p. 31). The teacher referred explicitly to boys' preferences to imply that girls' preferences are different and that the girl should not be playing with it.

Social comparisons can also invoke parents and teachers as contrasts. A teacher says about herself "I don't talk when I'm working. No talking here," implying that her own behavior should serve as the relevant comparison (Mody,

2005, p. 61). There is also a practice of engaging in social comparisons that involve telling stories of parental youth and contrasting them with the child's current behavior. For example, a mother explains, "Look at your mummy, when she was young, just seven years old, I could fix breakfast and was very responsible" (Miller et al., 2001, p. 170). But the contrast may well include both the individual and the social group with which the individual is to be affiliated for purposes of the comparison, as when a toddler is told:

babies drink from bottles. Big people drink from cups. I drink my milk from a cup. I drink my beer from a cup too ... and Mommy drinks coffee out of a cup too. When you are big you drink out of a cup. (Moerk, 1983, p. 124)

The child's own behavior is compared with the behavior of both the parents and of adults as a generic category as a means of channeling the child's behavior to approximate that of adults and of the parent in particular. Being informed of how generic others behave may serve to channel behavior, because it provides guidelines for normative behavior in settings that are ambiguous as to what constitutes normative behavior.

UNIVERSALIZING ONE'S PREFERENCES

A. Everyone/No One Else

Parents can channel preferences by indicating the normativeness of their own behavioral preferences. They universalize their preferences, talking of how everyone else is engaging in the behaviors they want their children to engage in. Universalization needs to be differentiated from social comparisons. If my child does not want to go to camp, I can tell him that his friends are going. This constitutes a request to engage in social comparison. But this is quite different than making the child understand that the behavior in question is universally applicable and that everyone engages in the behavior. Watson (1989) illustrates universalization in the context of a child's bedtime routine, when her father says to her "everyone's asleep.... Everyone is going to sleep because you know what happens in the night-time? people go to sleep at night-time ... everybody's asleep." Similarly, a German mother tells her daughter, "Everyone is sleeping now"[14] (Miller, 1979, p. 420) and when a Hungarian child of 33 months wants to look at a sand truck outside instead of napping, his mother says, "Now let's not look at it, the sand is sleeping and we are sleeping too"[15] (MacWhinney, CHILDES). In this vein, when Karen got up in the middle of the night, we would take her to the window, show her how dark it was outside, and tell her that "Haifa is sleeping, everyone is sleeping." Universalization is advantageous from the perspective of parents because it suggests that going to sleep is not a solitary behavior; universalization makes the behavior a shared behavior, shared by absent others who are engaged in the same activity. Universalization is preferable to imposing one's wishes on a reluctant child.

Children may acknowledge the universal nature of behavior, in this case sleeping, when they themselves indicate it is time for everyone to go to sleep (Watson, 1989). In this vein, prior to going to sleep, a toddler lists all the people she knows who are sleeping, starting with herself, thereby making compliance with her father's preference not capitulation but rather conformity with a canonical action for people in general. At 29;1, Karen runs to the window before going to sleep and says, "Karen checked outside if Toronto is sleeping." Similarly, universalization is evident in Karen's presleep monologue at 3;10 years, when she says,

Karen will be a good girl. Karen will not get up nighttime and she will not get up to ask for food at nighttime. Nobody gets up at nighttime to ask for food. Karen will have supper when everybody else has supper. Even her friends don't do that, even once.

Both going to sleep and having supper at the appropriate time, then, become shared behaviors in which she needs to participate. In Hebrew, there are lullabies that universalize sleeping, telling of a doll Zehava who is sleeping, a teddy bear who is sleeping, and so forth. At 28;20, Orren says to his dad, "Daddy will sing to me 'the bear and the shadows' came to the room and everyone is going to sleep. I like this song."[16] Children start to universalize, using it as a justification, as evident when a preschooler says, "Night, night, everybody has to go to sleep now.... Doggie, time to go to sleep for you" (Schwartz, 1991). If everyone goes to sleep at night, doggie must also do so.

Universalization relies on generics. Parental use of generics in such contexts teaches children that they are individuals like everyone else and they can start to refer to themselves in a generic fashion. For instance, when Karen, at 28;18, was asked why she was crying, she answered, "Karen didn't have the time to go to sleep" (meaning, it wasn't my time to go to sleep). When asked what she means, she elaborated, "It means sometimes people don't want to go to sleep" A few days later, at 28;21, she again refers to generic others, saying, "Some people have to play at night when they're sleeping and their mothers say they can't." In other words, she wanted to play when it was time to go to sleep but she had learned that she can refer to herself and to her own preferences in generic terms as reflecting everyone's preferences. Again, at 26;26, she says, "when people go to the daycare, their Mummies take them home and they sleep." She uses the third-person narrative, referring to people in general rather than specific others or herself. Scollon and Scollon (1981) refer to "the fictionalization of self in global statements," finding evidence for it

[14] German: "Alle schalfen jetzt"

[15] Hungarian: "Most ne nezzuk meg, alszik a homok es mi is alszunk"

[16] Hebrew: "Abba yashir li "Hadooby vehazlalim laxeder bau vekulam holxim lishon"

when their daughter Rachel was 2-years old. For instance, when a girl waved to her on the street, she waved back and said, "When kids are outside all the other kids are supposed to wave their hands who are outside too" (p. 90).

When the comparison group is generic others, the implication is that children should behave like everyone else. This is sometimes said explicitly. A mother is discussing an outing during which her 3-year-old objected to putting on a jacket and she relates, "I told you 'Everybody is going to wear a jacket. Even daddy and mommy. Even K' (i.e., his sister). Then you were okay, right?" (Wolf, 1990, p. 189). Similarly, when she is asked whom she holds up as an example for her kindergarten child, a mother explains that she would emphasize to him that, "when you are with other people, you have to do pretty much what the group has to do" (Sears, Maccoby, & Levin, 1957, p. 348). In the Japanese preschool, behaving appropriately is encouraged with, "Everyone else is sitting down" and "Everyone else is sitting with their backs straight" (Peak, 1991, p. 130). The implication is that those children who are not sitting in the required manner need to change how they are sitting. Mothers can also contrast the behavior of their own child with that of everyone else. A child of 3;2 years is told, "Everybody dressed. You were the only one who took her clothes off." And the child answers, "But the dress was really hot"[17] (Figueira, 1984, p. 117). Such exchanges teach children that there are contexts in which they are to behave like everyone else; behaving uniquely is not encouraged.

B. Good/Bad Ideas

Another means of universalization is with reference to something being "a good" or "a bad" idea. Using the term implies that there is a universal applicability to the relevant idea, as opposed to parental idiosyncratic preferences. Good ideas are ones that everyone should accept and not just those who happen to live under a given rooftop. Bad ideas are ones that everyone should prefer not to engage in. These uses are illustrated in Table 6.9.

Still another means of conveying the same message is by indicating what alternative behavior is better. For instance, after a child of 20 months falls off of a big bicycle, her mother says, "You'd be better on a small one" (Howe, 1981, p. 9). Similarly, in Japanese, mothers tend refer to what shouldn't be done by using the format "that won't do" and to what should be done as "that is all right." Alternative means of doing things are indicated as "that way is better" (Clancy, 1986). Notice here again that by claiming that something is a *good*, *smart*, or *bad*, *not smart*, idea, one shrugs off responsibility for the decision to honor or refuse the child's request. A good or bad idea is a generic notion, in the public domain, rather than emanating from one's specific person and reflecting his or her idiosyncratic way of doing things. Haverkate (1984, p. 79) calls this *focalizing*, discussing it as a device for impersonalization, (e.g., "It's a good idea, it would be better . . . , the best thing is . . . , one could . . . , what about, why not. . . . "); others discuss them as "agent avoiders" (House & Kasper, 1981, p. 168) that underplay speakers' own preferences and imply that they have the listener's interest at heart. Interestingly, children learn to use such justifications to validate their own preferences, most likely without understanding their generic implications. After his request to go out to play after dinner was refused, a preschooler said, "Go out in the garden, play with the red car. That's a good idea" (Snow, 1983, p. 44).

ADJECTIVIZATION

Attitudes are also channeled by adjectivization. Parents don't just tell their children what things are, they also teach them to evaluate objects, events, and themselves, by using adjectives.

Adjectivization is used to orient children to objects and activities that they have not had a chance to evaluate themselves, to indicate the appropriate evaluation that should be attached to them. Mothers incidentally teach their children to evaluate using adjectives in describing objects and events. In this realm, it is important that infants and children use their mothers' reactions to objects and events to infer appropriate emotional reaction (Feinman, 1992). As infants develop, they begin to use emotional information as conveyed by others, especially mothers, to interpret ambiguous situations. For instance, 12-month-old infants would cross a visual cliff to reach their mother if the mother expressed positive emotion (i.e., smiling) but not if the mother expressed fear (Scorce et al., 1985).

How do mothers teach such evaluations? Adjectives such as fun, interesting, beautiful, scary, and so forth are used for evaluating objects and activities. Referring to activities first, when an observer sneezes, a 6-month-old baby looks in his direction, and mother says, "That was funny wasn't it? Sneezing" (Snow, 1984, p. 77). When 2-year-old Richard falls off a bookcase, his mother says, "Up you get. What a silly place to climb up on. . . . " (Snow, 1984, p. 76). A preschooler who climbs into the baby's stroller is told, "That's a very silly place to lie" (Walkerdine & Lucey, 1989, p. 166). A Japanese mother tells her child, "It's bad to play with matches, isn't it? . . . . Matches are not good, right?" (Clancy, 1999, p. 1414).

Referring to objects, a doll, some shoes, and a doll's brush are said to be *nice*, a puppet and dumplings are labeled as *lovely*, a monkey is *big* or *huge*, and pants are *pretty* (Howe, 1981). The mother of a toddler says about a doll, "I thought maybe you'd think she was pretty nifty" (Broen, 1972, p. 84). A preschool teacher comments, "What a pretty jumper! Is it a new one?" (Gardner & Cass, 1965, p. 77). Teachers cajole children to eat by telling them that the food in question is delicious (Peak, 1991) and urge

[17] Portugese: "Todo mundo de vestido! Voce foi a unica que tirou a roupa" . . . "Mas a roupza tava muito calor"

Table 6.9.

	Age	Source
Good Idea		
C wants to throw something in garbage M: "Dustbin, That's a good idea"	23 mos.	Bruner, Roy, & Ratner (1982, p. 122)
F is scrubbing vegetables C wants to do the same F: "Yes, that's a good idea to give it a hard rub with that"	Preschool	Wootton (1997, p. 168)
C complies with T's request T: "Ok, that's a good idea"	Preschool	Gearhart & Newman (1980)
Bad Idea		
C wants to climb into toy truck M: "Careful, don't tumble. Whoa, I don't think that's such a good idea" M helps C out of the truck	19;4	Bloom (1973, p. 190)
M offered C drink in cup C: "I don't want to drink it out cup, e want drink it out can" M: "Oh, what did I say about that? What did I say about drinking out of the can?" C: "I want drink it out can!" M: "Aw, well that's not such a good idea, honey"	28 mos.	Keenan, Schieffelin, & Platt (1983, p. 121)
T: "Everybody should be sitting in their own seats. As a general rule, we'll have no roaming around, because that's not a very good idea"	School	Torode (1976, p. 184)

them to avoid touching snails, saying, "Ug, don't touch it, it's all slimy" (Delamont, 1980, p. 31). A mother tells her 6-year-old, "Cut it a little smaller, Iris, it's too large. I think it's tastier smaller, don't you?" (Nevat-Gal, 2002, p. 184). In a more elaborate example of adjectivization, a father who is referring to a trinket that the child bought from a coin machine, says, "I can't imagine anybody paying money for that can you?" The mother then addresses the child, saying, "That's why Mommy doesn't buy you those things because they're really junky" (Gleason & Ely, 1997, p. 248). That is, adjectives that are attached to objects and events serve to classify them along evaluative dimensions that are not inherent in the characteristics of the object.

Specifying that something is interesting or fun functions the same way, as shown in Table 6.10.

In these examples, parents and teachers are adjectivizing in order to channel and motivate children to adopt behaviors that children may be unlikely to adopt otherwise.

Clearly, though, when a parent says about an activity that "it will be fun" or "it's interesting," this raises the possibility that the child may eventually reject this evaluation because he experiences the event differently, leading the child to adopt a different adjective or rejecting the one offered by the parent. When Richard, at 18 months, asks his mother to read to him, she says, "What can we find in this book? Oh, it's a boring book!" (Bruner et al., 1982). The child can dispute this claim and demand that the mother read and reread the presumably boring book. When a 4-year-old claims that orange birds are gross, his mother doesn't contradict him but offers that she thinks that red ones are pretty and he agrees with her (Lindfos, 1999).

On the other hand, when a parent says something is naughty, forbidden, and so forth, these adjectives are not directly experienced by the child as such; only those objects and events that directly impinge on the child can be evaluated as "good" or "bad." An object or event that does not directly impinge on the child cannot lead the child to experience it as "bad." The "goodness" or "badness" of such objects and events can only be inferred via others' nonverbal or verbal reactions to them. In this vein, when a child, at 25 months, doesn't answer her mother, the mother says, "What! Isn't that bad not answering" (Clancy, 1986, p. 221).[18] When an older sibling tells a younger to be quiet, the mother responds, "I don't think that it's very nice to say that" (Herot, 2002, p. 171).

Children pick up such adjectivization and start to comment on objects and activities in descriptive terms. Tomasello (1992) recorded his daughter Travis, at 24;28, as she is playing with a puzzle, saying "it's fun to play with puzzles" (p. 300). Travis used the adjective *good* in referring to foods, starting at 18;28, saying good apple, good lemon, good juice, good jello, and good bagel (Tomasello, 1992, pp. 363–364). Reilly's (1986) daughter Kate, at 28 months, climbs into her crib and says, "Climb in. Be fun." Adjectivization primes children to engage in comparisons, engenders the ability to evaluatively transform

[18] Japanese: "Okasan me tabeyo . . . Okasan mo taberuyo, issoyo ne"

Table 6.10.

	Age	Source
M wants to distract C, offers him box of socks M: "You gonna play with the socks?.... That's gonna be fun"	15 mos.	Hart & Risley (1999, p. 49)
M is talking of C being left with relatives M: "You are going to have a lot of fun"	29 mos.	Hudson (2002, p. 65)
M: "Sit right here for a minute. We'll do this game. This is gonna be interesting"	3;8 years	Sachs (1984)
Going to grandmother's house M: "You might feel less frustrated if you don't even try to watch TV at grandma's house. I'll bet it would be more fun to use her swing in the back yard"	Preschool	Denham (1998, p. 166)
In class T: "This next one is going to be fun; I know you'll enjoy it"	5–6 years	Kounin (1970, p. 130)

objects and events as needed, and allows children to learn the subjective nature of such evaluations.

FRAMING

A different approach to channeling emerges from prospect theory (Kahneman & Tversky, 1979, 1982; Tversky & Kahneman, 1986) according to which framing an outcome in terms of gains versus losses has an impact on preferences and the likelihood of choosing to pursue them. Gain-framed messages focus on the benefits of engaging in a given behavior whereas loss-framed messages focus on the losses consequent to not engaging in the behavior (e.g., brushing one's teeth as resulting in healthy teeth and gums vs. not brushing one's teeth as resulting in gingivitis). In adults, gain-framed messages appear to be more effective in some contexts (e.g., promoting use of sunscreen, Rothman & Salovey, 1997) whereas loss-framed messages are more effective in other contexts (e.g., promoting mammography examinations, Banks et al., 1995; Schneider et al., 2001). With kindergarten children, gain-framed messages focusing on the benefits of eating apples versus loss-framed messages focusing on the negative impact of not eating apples were both found to increase children's choice of apples as snacks as compared with a control condition in which apples were not mentioned (Bannon & Schwartz, 2006). However, in contrast to research with adults, there was no difference found between the effectiveness of gain-framed versus loss-framed messages. This issue requires further empirical attention as there is no parsimonious account for this difference.

CHANNELING VIA MULTIPLE METHODS

In this chapter, I have discussed different means of channeling children's preferences. It is unclear whether parents utilize all these techniques in a given domain, whether they vary their selected technique by domain, or whether they are even aware of which techniques they use and which techniques they don't use but could potentially use. Next, I will focus on one domain – channeling food preferences – in which parents appear to use a wide variety of techniques, suggesting that the importance parents attribute to a given domain may influence their likelihood of using multiple techniques. In fact, in one study (Hendy, Williams, Camise, Eckman, & Hedemann, 2009) more than seventy different strategies were identified, and these were ultimately reduced to nine dimensions that parents use in channeling children's eating behavior.

CHANNELING FOOD PREFERENCES

How do children learn to like the foods and drinks of their own culture? The initial part of the story centers on mother's milk. Flavors consumed by the mother and transmitted to her milk are detected by the infant who thereby becomes familiar with the flavors consumed by the mother (Mennella & Beauchamp, 1996). As a result, breastfed babies' first introduction to the foods of their culture occurs vicariously, and being exposed to a greater variety of flavors via their mothers' milk, they are more accepting of a greater variety of foods than infants raised on formula. In fact, the flavors of the formula provided to infants who are not breastfed have been shown to influence children's later food preferences (Mennella & Beauchamp, 2002).

As they are weaned and start to eat solid foods, children are exposed to the foods available in their culture, as reflected in the foods their family purchases, prepares, and consumes. Harper and Sanders (1975) found that 14-month-olds were more likely to try a novel food if they saw an adult taste it or if they could share the adult's food. This suggests that mealtimes are important for disseminating culturally accepted consumption habits and that experience with foods dictate preferences (Sullivan & Birch, 1990). In fact, children do not acquire preferences for foods to which they have not been exposed. Toddlers choose foods according to their frequency of exposure to them, with greater exposure leading to more choice of that food (Birch & Marlin, 1982).

Ochs, Pontecorvo, and Fasulo (1996) studied dinnertime interactions in American and Italian families and found that children's likes and dislikes of food are socialized at dinnertime and parents seem to have an intuitive understanding of this. They offer their infants and children a variety of foods, cajole them into tasting them, pose queries as to their wants and preferences, and as I discuss below, often take their children's preferences into account in planning meals. Parents tend to know what their children like to eat, predicting fairly well what choices they will make in a school cafeteria, for instance (Matta, Scheibehenne, & Todd, 2008). On the other hand, Ochs and her colleagues found that American mothers naturally assumed that children would not like the same foods that they do, often preparing different foods for children and indicating uncertainty whether children would like them.

Parents invest much time and energy in getting their children to eat. Mothers first spoon-feed their children. Later, they place food in front of children, expecting them to hand-feed themselves and to transition to using utensils. At the same time, mothers address verbal messages to their children, questioning their food preferences and desires (e.g., "Do you want milk? Do you want to drink some milk?"). Offers of food and questions regarding preferences are often intermixed, making it difficult to know whether the parent is channeling the child's preferences or restricting them. For instance, when the mother of 18-month-old Rachel says, "Just a minute, I'm gonna get you some juice, you want some juice with breakfast?" (Lucariello et al., 1986, p. 150), the mother's question makes orange juice an integral part of breakfast. Similarly, a mother asks a child whether he wants some juice before he leaves for preschool. When he declines, she asks "Do you want a piece of toast?" (Hall, CHILDES), delineating what foods are viewed as appropriate for breakfast.

Children's food preferences are channeled in other ways as well. Parents set themselves up as models for eating, telling the child to join them, see how they are eating, and so forth. As one mother explains, "I really have changed my way of eating. Like I will always take the vegetable, even though I'm not much of vegetable eater . . . so that they at least see that that sort of thing is eaten" (DeVault, 1991, p. 50). Similarly, a Japanese mother tells her reluctant preschool child, "Mom wants to eat it . . . Mom will also eat, look together (let's eat)." When asked to justify her statements, the mother said, "Because she is content if everybody eats the same thing . . . I'm teaching her we are together and we are eating the same thing. . . . If I do so, she will eat because we are (doing) the same" (Kobayashi, 2001, pp. 121–122). Mothers may even pretend to want to eat in order to get their children to eat. In an instance of this, when her child of 23 months doesn't want to eat her yogurt, the mother says, "I'll eat it all, OK?" and the child rebuts, "My eat it" (Thornton, 2002, p. 247).

In this context, then, parents see themselves as role models for appropriate eating habits. In the words of a young father,

> I mean we're more apt to eat healthier now because he's around. We don't want all the chocolate chip cookies and stuff," explaining that before, "we were, you know, get a pizza every night and a cheese steak the other night," but because of the child's presence, "we try to sit down and have a meal, a healthy meal and all that. It's not, a you know, a Burger King night and a McDonald's night the next night. (Palkovitz, 2002, p. 153)

Children do eat more of the foods that others are also eating. For instance, Travis, at 20;3, said "share me," asking her father to share his milk with her (Tomasello, 1992, p. 311), and Orren, at 32;7, sees his father eating chicken fingers and says, "I want from your chicken fingers."[19] Some mothers actually note that children only eat off other people's plates, for example, "she does nick things off his (father's) plate, even when she wouldn't eat off her own plate . . . it's one way of getting her to eat" (Charles & Kerr, 1988, p. 93). Of course, we cannot know whether the child would have eaten the food in the absence of parental modeling.

Yet research indicates that preschoolers exposed to an adult who ate the same food, but of a different color, ate less of it than when it was the same color, even though the food was introduced as a snack in both cases (Addessi et al., 2005). As well, Birch (1980) found that children who ate lunch for four consecutive days next to a peer with different vegetable preferences (e.g., peas vs. carrots) showed a shift in their vegetable preferences that persisted for several weeks. Yet Rozin and his colleagues (2004) found that the food preferences of best friends among third graders were no more similar than among those of randomly selected children of the same gender. This suggests that although modeling may work in the short run, idiosyncratic food preferences may be more important in the long run.

Food preferences are also channeled by using generic statements about what one does or does not do in the food domain. For instance, Rachel, at 17;20, pours orange juice in her cereal bowl. Her mother says, "No juice doesn't go in there sweetheart. Juice goes down your throat" (Lucariello et al., 1986. p. 149). In fact, though, there is no reason other than custom as to why a child could not have cereal with juice. In the same vein, an 8-year-old asks, "Is there any mint sauce?" His mother answers, "Don't have mint sauce with beef." He persists, asking, "Mum can I have some to try it out?" but his request is rejected outright (Sealey, 2000, p. 150). The mother makes it explicit that in her culture, mint sauce is inappropriate for a beef dish – cultural food dictates need to be accepted at face value.

Children also learn that certain foods are to be eaten at certain times of the day and not at other times. The mother of a 2-year-old asks her, "Lena, what are you going to have for lunch today?" When the daughter answers, "Cheerios," the surprised mother asks, "Cheerios? Don't you usually have a sandwich for lunch? What are you going to have, ham or bologna?" When the daughter answers with the latter, the mother says, "Bologna, Yum"

[19] Hebrew: "Ani roçe schnitzel mishelxa"

(Bernstein, CHILDES). The mother differentiates breakfast foods from lunch foods and assumes that her child has learned this differentiation. Her use of *usually* reflects the normative aspect of this differentiation. One does not eat cereal for lunch. Similarly, when a mother thinks that her 20-month-old has finished dinner yet asks for more, she answers, "you've eaten it all now and you didn't want the rest . . . want a biscuit/ want a drink?" (Wilkinson, 1971, p. 68), thereby defining what is appropriate to eat after dinner. These types of experiences allow children to develop expectations as what foods are available at each meal, as evident in children's play scenarios. For instance, a 5-year-old is playing house with a 29-month-old girl and preparing dinner is on the agenda. When the older one says she is making pudding, the younger one says she will do the same. The older one objects and tells her to make something else. When the younger one offers to make tea, she is told, "No – it's dinner time not tea-time – you'll have to do the 'tatoes." When the younger one refuses, she is told, "You'll have to. You have to have 'tatoes for dinner" (Tough, 1973, p. 54).

Cultural food norms can also be promoted by providing choice. When a child is offered dressing for one's salad, ketchup with one's fries, or beer with dinner, the offered choice implies that these are normative ways of eating and drinking. When a toddler says, "Juice, Mommy," her mother asks, "You want some juice? Apple juice or orange juice?" (Schachter, 1979, p. 184). The mother's response sets up what she considers viable juice options – she does not ask the child whether she wants prune juice. Painter (1984) asks her son, "Do you want to have an apple or a pear?" (p. 239); because both are fruits, it is clear that the current choice is between fruits rather than other food types. Similarly, questioning children as to what they want on their fries establishes the offered items as acceptable combinations. In line with this, during dinner, a mother asks her child, "You want, you want sauce on your spaghetti?" (Blum-Kulka, 1997, p. 44).

Snacking alternatives are also channeled by using choice. When Kathryn, at 21 months, asks for some more nuts, her mother answers, "You ate all the nuts. The nuts are all gone. You want some more raisins?" (Bloom, 1973, p. 45), thereby establishing raisins as acceptable snacking alternative. A 5-year-old who is offered a choice of fruit cocktail or cheese as a snack, answers, "I want my snack to be a sandwich." But sandwiches are not snacks so the father suggests making it into a meal by offering, "You want an egg?" an offer that the child refuses. The father tries again to define the offer as a snack, asking "How about cheese and jelly?" (Hall, CHILDES).

The interplay between choice and lack of choice is especially interesting in cultures in which there are food taboos. Children raised in Kosher homes, for instance, are constantly reminded of combinations that are anathema (e.g., a salami and cheese sandwich) and being offered other combinations that are defined as legitimate. But rules about combinations and sequences of foods are prevalent in all homes. When Eve asks for milk, her mother says to her, "Milk? No. You don't want milk, honey. You've just had some juice. . . . How about a drink of water? (Moerk, 1983, p. 136). Notice that the mother is not just denying the child's request; she is indicating to her that the request is an inappropriate one. This is also the case when a mother asks her preschooler, "Why do you always want white bread?" implying that she has an alternate preference and that there is something wrong with his choice (Holzman, 1972, p. 326).

Parents can channel preferences by *deflecting*, offering substitutes for the preferences expressed by children. A 7-year-old who asks for corn at dinnertime is told, "We don't have corn. We have rice and broccoli" (Ochs, Pontecorvo, & Fasulo, 1996, p. 13). When 22-month-old Francesco asks for chocolate, his father replies, "This evening you will eat the chocolate, now take the cookie"[20] (Volterra & Antinucci, 1979). In the same spirit, Bloom (1970) recorded Katherine, at 21 months, asking for raisins after having finished eating nuts. Her mother said, "You won't be able to eat dinner, Honey. I'll give you some more apple." In this context, apples, but not raisins, have been construed as appropriate to eat despite the proximity to dinner. When Richard asks his mother for a cookie, she refuses, saying, "Do you want a drink? . . . . If you want a drink you can have one . . . . Do you want a drink? Because that's all you're having . . . . " (Bruner, 1983, p. 102). Clearly, success in offering substitutes depends on both the attractiveness of the alternative being offered and the parents' willingness to stand steadfast in the face of children's resistance.

Channeling works only so far. There are innate preferences that often lead to conflicts between the food preferences parents attempt to channel and the ones children attempt to actualize. This is often evident in the realm of "eating healthy." As a mother recalls her youth, she says, "It always seemed that things you hated were good for you and the things you liked were bad for you" (Charles & Kerr, 1988, p. 127). The conflict, then, centers on parental attempts to get children to eat more of what is deemed healthy and less of what is deemed "bad for you." Parents promote consumption of foods that are considered healthy or nutritional, urging children to eat because "it's good for you" (Ochs et al., 1996), or "gives you strong muscles" (Beals, 1993). Some examples are shown in Table 6.11.

The suggestion that children eat vegetables can take on different forms, e.g., a father questions his child as to what he has eaten and when he gets a reply, he asks, "Just chicken? No potatoes . . . no salad . . . . " (Erickson, 1990, p. 230). Parents may also explicitly demand that children eat their vegetables. After a 4-year-old refuses to eat broccoli, his father says, "You always hafta have leafy greens" (Ochs, Pontecorvo, & Fasulo, 1996). A 5-year-old who announces, "I'm not having any of those," referring to peas and carrots, is told by her father, "That's your quota" and

[20] Italian: "I cioccolatini li mangi stasera, tieni il biscotto"

Table 6.11.

	Age	Source
Mother wants child to eat greens M: "Here, take a bite. Get muscles"	Toddler	Miller (1982, p. 103)
M adds peas to C's plate C: "I didn't say I wanted peas! I said I wanted sausages with potato" M: "Oh well, try the peas," puts peas on his fork, tries to feed him	5 years	Grieshaber (2004, p. 127)
M: "Jacki, I want you to eat some string beans. They're good"	School-age	Blum-Kulka (1997, p. 65)
M: "Jordan would you care for some more salad, for instance, some tomatoes?"	School-age	Blum-Kulka (1997, p. 73)
F: "I'm especially concerned about eating your vegetables, okay? They have minerals in them. . . . You eat one piece of corn and two pieces of the green . . . some broccoli . . . and take three vitamins"	Elementary school	Ochs & Shohet (2004, pp. 39–40)

Table 6.12.

	Age	Source
Scandinavian family at dinner M: "It's nice that you like porridge. It makes you strong, you know"	Preschool	Junfelt & Tulviste (1998)
M: "You need to eat different things like eggs and cabbage and rice pudding to make you grow into a big girl"	4 years	Wells (1986, p. 59)
Italian family at dinner "The meat has protein"[21]	Preschool	Ochs, Pontecorvo, & Fasulo (1996, p. 12)
Grandfather pleading A: "And its uh got ta good taste, its good. . . . I like it too. It's tasty! And I uh, he didn't want the cereal, doesn't eat. I said, "Todd it wouldn't kill ya, taste it"	Unknown	Ochs, 1983 (p. 141, citing Shimanoff, 1980)

the child was compelled to eat them (Grieshaber, 2004, p. 132). Another child was told at dinnertime that "one vegetable is compulsory" (De Geer et al., 2002). In fact, Puhl and Schwartz (2003) found that rules specifying needing to eat one's vegetables at dinner during their childhood were very frequently recalled by adults. Such parental concern may also be evident in parental offers of rewards for eating one's vegetables, as a mother explains: "we reward (son) when he eats fruits and vegetables . . . usually he gets a car or a train or something . . . . I don't think it's right to reward a child for eating vegetables, but we're so concerned about his health" (Bee-Gates, 2006, p. 47).

The health benefits of other foods are also emphasized, as shown in Table 6.12.

Such cajoling is a two-edged sword. On the one hand, children may see their parents as nagging them, for example, a 9-year-old who says "your Mum and Dad, they might nag you – take your vitamins, eat your greens or whatever" (Mayall, 2000, p. 125). In fact, being pressured to eat seems to backfire, with children eating less of what they were pressured to eat and making more negative comments regarding the food in question (e.g., Birch et al., 1993; Galloway et al., 2006). On the other hand, children learn to link certain foods with health and may see their parents' behavior as attempts to channel their food preferences in a healthier direction, for example, as a 9-year-old says, "our mum and Dad encourage us to eat things, like take vitamins and eat healthy food" (Mayall, 2000, p. 125).

Yet the repeated association with health teaches children that vegetables are healthy and they may end up eating them even when they don't like them. Eight-year-old Jordan tells his mother,

> As um Snappy Smurf would say, "I wish we didn't have to eat the vegetables." I just I just wish we could eat the little good things inside the . . . that's what Snappy Smurf said when farmer Smurf told him that there little good things in vegetables and that's why you had to eat them. (Blum-Kulka, 1997, p. 47)

The child knows that vegetables have vitamins that are good for you and that this serves as a justification for eating them even when one doesn't like them. The important aspect of the above is that children pick up on this relation between food and health. A child of 3;6 asks, "These will make me strong and healthy, will they?" (Todd, 1982, p. 110). At 30;22, Karen says to a picture of a baby, "So eat this – it's tasty; it's healthy."[22] A 3-year-old is eating pancakes and says, "They make me strong . . . . pancakes makes, makes strong" (Aukrust & Snow, 1998).

[21] Italian: "La carne ha le proteine"

[22] Hebrew: "Az toxli at ze – ze taim, ze bari"

Health-related concerns also drive parents to refuse certain food requests when they are made. A child of 18 months says to her mother, "Have it." The mother answers, "You don't want this. It's not cooked" (Brown, 1973). Some foods must be cooked before being eaten. In fact, a 10-year-old Scandinavian child says, "You can catch Charlotte (intended meaning, salmonella) if you eat raw eggs" (De Geer et al., 2002). Similarly, a child of 2;11 asks her mother to test some cake mix and the mother answers, "You can't taste it honey because it's got raw egg in it.... And that's not very safe to eat. When it is raw" (Gordon, 2002). When a 5-year-old child says he wants all the bacon, his mother answers, "No you can't have anymore it's not that good it's not even good for you really." His sister adds, "You could get sick because of bacon" (Herot, 2002, pp. 171–172). After her son asks for some chocolate, a mother responds, "This is it though. You're not having any more sugar," expressing fear of his having a sugar-high (Herot, 2002, p. 172). In fact, this concern is evident when a preschool teacher explains, "When the kids load up on sweets they can get really hyper – We notice immediate behavioral changes in children who eat high-sugar foods like candy, doughnuts, and soda" (Tobin et al., 1989, p. 161); the preschool in question explicitly prohibits such sweets and junk food. In fact, on seeing Doritos at preschool, the teacher said, "Please ask your mother not to send you to school with that kind of food, okay, Stu? Remind her about how we feel about junk food, okay?" (Tobin et al., 1989, p. 145). The teacher then relates that she specifically asks parents "not to send sweets or junk food in the lunch box" (ibid, p. 160).

In this realm, the one consistent finding is that all children like sweets and mothers are barraged by requests for sweets of all kinds (e.g., "Want sweet," "Want chocolate biscuit," "Want piece (chocolate) bar," and "Me have biscuit," Radford, 1990, p. 84, 162), all said between 22 and 24 months). Ward, Wackman, and Wartella (1977) found that more than 90 percent of children conveyed food purchase requests to their parents, asking for cereals, snack foods, candy, soft drinks, and soups. Isler, Popper and Ward (1987) asked parents to keep a diary of all the purchase requests that their children, aged 3 to 11 years, made over a period of a month. More than 50 percent were requests for snack food, candy, cereal, and drinks. The only item that changed in frequency of purchase requests with age was candy, most likely because older children have an allowance out of which they are expected to buy food snacks and this cuts into their requests (Furnham, 1999). As one adolescent says, "As a child I was able to save up.... I saved a half. The other half I bought sweets with" (Autio, 2004).[23]

Parents restrict children's intake of other foods for various health reasons as well. Wellman (1988) cites a child who says "I want some candy. I want some candy, Mommy." The mother answers "You can't have any right now. You've got diarrhea and I don't think that you should eat any more candy" (p. 82). In the same vein, Higginson (CHILDES) recorded a mother telling her child of 35 months who was drinking a carbonated drink, "Honey, don't drink so much right away otherwise you're gonna get a stomach ache, OK?" The parents of an Italian 6-year-old refer to her drinking a bottle of Coke, and say, "Gaia, look it is a lot that much of Coke," and the mother adds, "and it'll do bad to you"[24] (Pontecorvo & Fasulo, 1997, p. 432). In these instances, then, parents are restricting certain foods because of cultural beliefs about health and disease (cf., Whiting & Child, 1953).

Children learn to allude to those beliefs that are prevalent in their culture. When a preschool child pretends to cram a bunch of pretend cakes into his mouth, the pretend baker says, "You're greedy – you'll get a tummy-ache if you eat too fast" (Sylva et al., 1986, p. 261). When a girl of 3;6 years is asked what would happen if you ate three chocolate cakes, she doesn't hesitate, retorting with "You would have a tummy ache" (Reilly, 1986, p. 321). A 5-year-old child is playing doctor when the patient's pretend mother asks about special food, "How about soda and ice cream? Can I give them that?" and the pretend doctor answers, "Not unless they're better" (Andersen, 1990, p. 111). A German kindergarten child is pretending to be sick and says, "I have to, I have to drink all the soup, because I'm sick" (Auwarter, 1986, p. 214).

In preparing foods, then, mothers juggle between the health benefits of foods and children's preferences. First, as mothers become aware of their children's more chronic food preferences, they often adjust their menus accordingly, making more of their liked foods, changing recipes to incorporate more of what children like and less of what they don't like, sometimes even disguising disliked foods to ensure children eat them (DeVault, 1991; Marquis & Claveau, 2005). Mothers tell children that they have taken their preferences into account, for example, "Try the green beans, I made it the way you like it" (Orrell-Valente et al., 2007). Referring to this, a 10-year-old says, "I like spaghetti and pizza and pancakes which my mum sometimes makes me, if she feels up to it. But not very often" (Sixsmith & Knowles, 1996). Mothers also tend to ask the child as to his or her preferences. Talking of the cheeses that their son dislikes, an Italian mother asks, "Does he like the Gorgonzola?" When the child answers *yes*, she continues, "And then we'll buy that if he likes that" (Ochs et al., 1996, p. 32). As mothers learn their children's preferences, within limits, they tend to respect such preferences, as reflected in the words of the following mother:

> I decided that I would *have* to feed him on what he liked. So I make sure that in the meal there is *something* that he likes and will eat ... I have to think what he *will* eat. (Newson & Newson, 1968, p. 231, original emphasis)

[23] Mothers acknowledge that children spend much of their allowance on sweets and try to discourage them from doing so, at times noting that they give their children a monetary bonuses if they have not spent the money on sweets or ice cream, if they spent the money "wisely" (Newson & Newson, 1976).

[24] Italian: "Guarda che e tanta quella quella cosa di Coke uh"... "e ti fa male"

Similarly, Cohler and Grunebaum (1981) recorded a mother who, when reminiscing about her now-grown-up children, explains, "I tried not to fix things they didn't like . . . you can't get them to eat things they don't like . . . you try to fix things that they do like" (p. 74). A mother who is talking of her 2-year-old indicates that the child can occasionally choose what to eat, saying, "She always wants to have peanut butter and jelly," and indicates that she accommodates the child at least once a week (Wiley, 1997).

Parental concern that their children may not be eating enough is also manifest in attempts to distract children while they eat. Parents may use television as a distraction while children are eating (e.g., Cohler & Grunebaum, 1981). Other parents use story telling and other means of distraction to get children to eat. In this vein, a mother who is trying to get her 3- and-a-half-year-old to eat, tells her the story of Cinderella and when the child stops eating, she says, "But eat or I stop (telling) (Fasulo, Liberati, & Pontecorvo, 2002, p. 230). In yet another family, the older brother recites a poem and the mother says to the preschooler, "Eat Luisa and Ugo (will tell you the poem)" (ibid, p. 218).

This rosy picture, though, is somewhat illusory because not all mothers attempt to accommodate their children's food preferences. As a grandmother says, in talking about her daughter, "If the little one doesn't like what she cooked, she cooks something else. I think that's spoiling them." She then contrasts this with what she used to do, saying, "if you don't want it, look at it, don't eat it, I don't care. Mostly they ate it but if they didn't it was up to them" (Cohler & Grunebaum, 1981, p. 166). Another grandmother says, "she asks him what he wants for dinner, which I think is wrong" (Cohler & Grunebaum, 1981, p. 194). In the same vein, as one mother says about giving her 2-year-old a choice at dinnertime, "It's not a restaurant, so Rachel can't decide what's for dinner . . . . I know she won' starve to death if she misses one meal" (Wiley, 1997). Ochs, Pontecorvo, and Fasulo (1996) found that whereas in American families mothers tended to serve children different foods, assuming that their preferences are different than those of the adults in the family, mothers in Italian families did not tend to do so, rather making a variety of foods that reflected the preferences of different members of the family. Marquis and Claveau (2005) similarly found that some French Canadian mothers accommodated the preferences of different family members in a variety of ways, including offering a selection of items.

Food preferences are also channeled via exposure to food in restaurants, other people's homes (e.g., "I had them at a friend's house and thought they were really cool and tasted really nice, so I asked my mum to get me them," Wilson & Wood, 2004, p. 334), and day care. Children who are exposed to a greater variety of foods before age 4 tend to seek out a greater variety of foods in adolescence and adulthood (Nicklaus et al., 2005). As well, children exposed to a vegetable daily for 2 weeks ultimately consumed more of the vegetable in question (Wardle et al., 2003). Television can also channel children's food preferences. Research indicates that television food advertising is correlated with greater food consumption and in particular, obese children both recognize more televised food advertising and consume more of the advertised foods (Halford et al., 2004). In fact, about 40 percent of children's food purchase requests are for products advertised in the 6 months prior to the request (Donkin et al., 1993). In a study that controlled the commercials to which children were exposed, those exposed to candy commercials picked more candy as snacks; when candy commercials were eliminated, the children chose significantly more fruit as snacks (Gorn & Goldberg, 1982). As such, it is difficult to conclude whether television should be viewed as channeling or as restricting children's preferences, the topic of the next chapter.

7 Temporizing Preferences

At 34 months, Allison is playing with her mother, who says, 'So we can play now and have a snack or do anything you want now.' Allison answers, 'Not now, maybe later.' The mother answers, 'Maybe now, I'd kind of like a snack.' Allison answers her, 'No maybe later and I may eat a cookie up first.' When a few minutes later her mother offers her raisins, she refuses them, saying, 'I don't want my raisin snack.'

(Bloom, 1970)

Two children of 3;6 years are playing house. The boy says, 'Let's go to bed honey, let's go to bed.' When she answers, 'No, I'm playing with these animals .... The animals are going to bed .... '; he insists, 'Honey, it's nighttime let's go to bed.'

(Cook-Gumperz, 1986, p. 57)

Learning about the temporal dimension and how to use it relative to one's own and other people's preferences is a critical aspect of social life. Parents' external preferences often concern when their children should, or should not, engage in given behaviors. Hence, they temporize their children's preferences – pivoting them around the temporal dimension, teaching them how to allocate time by telling them when and for how long behaviors are to be engaged in and what should be done now versus later. That is, parental external preferences and children's own preferences may clash with respect to when, but not as to whether, they should be engaged in. When parents temporize, they imply that there are times at which the specified activities are acceptable and that they are not precluding the future availability of the objects or activities in question. But by temporizing, parents also convey important messages regarding the relative importance of different behaviors and domains. In the current chapter, I outline how parents temporize, how children react to parental attempts to temporize, and how children themselves start to temporize with others.

WHY PARENTS TEMPORIZE

There are many reasons why parents temporize. First, parents have agendas that dictate how they prioritize their own behavior. These agendas necessarily require them to plan and set up schedules and children's preferences may play a subsidiary role in these schedules. In the words of one father,

It's time management ... you're home putting kids to bed or giving them baths or cleaning the house, making lunches. It's time management. You don't have any time, so you ration it out to the more important things. (Palkovitz, 2002, p. 200)

In contrast to "romanticized notions that childhood is a period of unencumbered free time" (Daly, 1996, p. 87), children's time is highly structured, monitored, and controlled by schedules and priorities set up by adults. At home, life is organized in relation to mealtimes, cleanup times, sleep and nap times, and parental work schedules (e.g., before leaving for school, a mother warns, "You have three minutes before we go down," and suggests that he eat before leaving, Hall, CHILDES). At school, children's activities are also schedule-centered (e.g., a preschool teacher says, "Children, two more minutes and we shall have to clear" (i.e., for lunch), Gardner & Cass, 1965, p. 107).

Because infants and young children are generally beneficiaries of adult schedules, their expression of preferences that are external to such schedules can result in preferential conflict. When she picks up her 3-year-old from preschool, a mother is met with: "Margaret has to come to my house now." She responds, "Maybe one day soon, but she can't come today." The child cries, repeating, "Today. Today she has to" (Paley, 1986, p. 42). Children's preferences that have not been incorporated in parental schedules may derail them, as evident in the film "One Fine Day," in which a single working mother has to cope with a child who missed a school outing (cf., Hodgson, Dienhart, & Daly, 2001).

Second, family routines require synchronization of the activities of different family members. Consequently, parents temporize because of the need for synchronization, with mothers tending to take primary responsibility for such scheduling, controlling both children's and fathers' time (Daly, 2001). It is generally mothers who orchestrate family routines (e.g., when food is bought, dinner is eaten, who drops children off at school) and social forays (e.g., visiting grandma). This requires synchronizing when different individuals are ready to engage in joint action – with the potential for preferential conflict arising when children's preferences are to do otherwise and they make *others* wait. For instance, when an 11-year-old complains about her pancakes, her mother answers, "They have been warmed over several times because I thought you would be home so that we could eat an hour ago" (De Geer, 2004), clarifying the need to synchronize family members' activities.

As Benson (1997) argues, family routines contribute to the development of temporal understanding in children because they are repetitive and require children to participate and to temporize their own behavior so that the routines can continue unhindered. Moreover, Nelson (1986) claims that because routines unfold in predictable sequences, often recurring in a daily pattern, their predictability allows them to become scripted. Through repeated exposure and participation in routines, then, children develop expectations as to what will happen next, how events are sequenced in time, which events lead to particular results, and how they can participate with others in a temporal sequence of scripted actions that can further their preferences.

Parents also temporize because of social norms regarding when and for how long children should engage in activities and what objects can be had at what time. There are social norms that concern how long children should play and sleep, when meals are eaten, and what foods are eaten at what time of the day. Children need to learn the temporal norms that govern the way things are done in their culture. Dinnertime in the United States is generally at 6 pm whereas in other parts of the world dinner is later (e.g., around 10 pm in Spain). The existence of such norms and their possible conflict with children's preferences necessitate parental temporization so that these norms are not violated. This leads to parental temporization concerning the need to engage in certain actions at the present moment (e.g., "Go to sleep now!") or to delay partaking of present objects and current activities (e.g., "Stop playing and come to eat now").

Temporal family patterns and social norms also determine how the past and future impinge on our preferences. When we last ate or slept is relevant to when we eat or sleep again (e.g., "You just had one," a mother responds to a preschooler's food request, Schachter, 1979, p. 41). In addition, certain behaviors are engaged in cyclically – there are things we do daily, weekly, monthly, and annually. If we had our birthday party today, it will not recur for another year. If a child went on a sleepover last week, his request to do so again this week may be rejected. Children need to learn to relate their actions to the temporal dimension and to the norms governing the timing of events relative to each other and to the present.

Temporization is also necessary because of the need to guide one's own actions and doing so demands relating current time to past and future time. Many actions need to unfold in specific sequences in order to be successful. Doing A first often sets up the conditions for something else to be done (e.g., boxes and refrigerators need to be opened for things to be put inside or taken out). Children need to sequence their own behavior, being guided by instructions as to what needs to be done first. Underwear and socks go on before pants and shoes. Tying shoe laces is a formidable task not only because of the fine motor coordination required but also because a sequence of motor actions needs to be performed in a specific order.

Parents may also temporize because children often have multiple preferences, and these cannot be pursued at the same time. Children may need guidance in prioritizing their preferences and deciding how to sequence their activities. In this context, children need to learn that some activities may be construed as synchronous (e.g., driving and listening to music), allowing for *multitasking*. Multitasking is considered possible in some domains but not in others (e.g., Karen, at 27;15 says, "You cannot eat and play at the same time"). Again, cultures play an important role in determining the domains in which multitasking is possible. Many families do not have television sets visible from the dinner table (e.g., "We don't have the telly on and things like that, we sit and talk and have a laugh, just a bit of time with each other really," Carrigan, Szmigin, & Leek, 2006) whereas other families do, making eating and watching television a synchronous task. Recognition that multitasking is acceptable in this context is evident in a refrigerator that has a television integral to its door. Because refrigerators are kitchen staples, the implication is clear. In fact, there are claims that the vociferous response to the Vietnam War was occasioned by the fact that families were watching televised scenes of war concurrently with eating dinner (Arlen, 1969). In this light, then, children need to learn the domains in which multitasking is deemed acceptable. Teenagers often fight with parents over studying with the radio on, claiming that this facilitates rather than hinders their ability to do homework.

Of course, temporization can also be occasioned by states of the world that dictate the need for temporization: stormy weather, red traffic lights, favorite television programs, and working fathers all require children to wait. Parents talk about time in relation to these states of the world, clarifying the need to temporize. For instance, rain or cold generally delay going to the park or the beach (e.g., a child of 23 months who says "Want e go on e beach," is told, "No love, it's too cold today," Painter, 1984, p. 236; a preschooler who tells his mother it's raining is told, "If it's raining, let's not go to the park," Akatsuka, 1986, p. 341). Children need to understand these relations because they guide parental choices and often require postponement of children's preferences.

These six factors: (1) parental agendas, (2) the need to synchronize between family members, (3) the existence of temporal norms and cycles, (4) the need to guide and sequence children's own behavior, (5) the inability to pursue multiple preferences at the same time, and (6) states of the world that do not allow for current preferences to be pursued, all converge to require parents to temporize their children's preferences. Curiously, though, parents don't generally make statements about how time is valued in their culture. Instead, the importance of time is conveyed by parental statements about having or not having time, needing to be on time, and the relative temporal location and duration of different events. As well, language, clocks, and calendar systems are all used to mark the temporal location of events and their ubiquitous presence may also signify the importance of time in children's lives.

There are wide individual differences between parents, though, in how they treat the temporal dimension. Whereas some parents are lax about schedules (e.g., "he'd been fed whenever he needed feeding, I'd never try and make him wait," Ribbens, 1994, p. 119), others are regimented. This can be the case for sleep schedules (e.g., "Zoe went to sleep at the same time every day and I'd wake her up at the same time every day . . . I'm a very routine person. . . . I wasn't flexible enough," ibid, 1994, p. 100) as well as feeding schedules (e.g., "he was completely on a schedule. It didn't make any difference if he cried an hour before, he waited for the time to come," Sears, Maccoby, & Levin, 1957, p. 411). Presumably, the more often parents temporize and the more regimented they are, the more sensitized children will become to time. Empirical research has not addressed this issue but it is clear that when parents temporize, children learn to relate their own actions and those of others to the temporal dimension as well as to relate time to the current moment. This leads to the emergent differentiation between past, present, and future, as I will elaborate in Chapter 10.

TIME AND TEMPORIZATION

Parental temporization implies that children need to grasp the temporal cues prevalent in their society because these have an impact on the likelihood of their preferences being fulfilled. In most societies, the time dimension is viewed linearly and as relative to the *here-and-now*; *now* serves as the point of reference for the past (i.e., before now) and for the future (i.e., after now), so that future events are constantly approaching and past events are receding back into the past (Friedman, 2003). Developing an orientation to time means being able to determine the current time and relative time of events with respect to some temporal framework. This may well be fostered when parents reminisce with their children about what has happened (Fivush, 1993), talk to them about what is happening currently, and make plans and discuss what will happen in the future.

In addition to learning about time per se, temporal socialization involves learning what preferences can be fulfilled now versus later, which depend on the passage of time alone versus those that are contingent on human action, and whether or not one can play a role in speeding up or slowing down the occurrence of events. These types of knowledge are especially critical when current activities need to be undertaken not to satisfy some current preference but rather, to ensure that some future preference will be attained (e.g., save up money for Christmas gifts, plant in the spring to reap in the fall).

Parents' initial role in this domain is to teach children that their preferences unfold on a time scale with two points on it: *now* and *not now* (cf., Bates, 1976). This binary distinction is acquired prior to the understanding that the present moment defines both what has transpired as the past and what will transpire as the future. Learning *now* and *not now* emerges out parental temporization and children's consequent need to delay. As Couch (1984) argues, "children are commonly first introduced to symbolic sequences by being told to wait" (p. 37) – for mother to come, for the sun to rise, to grow up, and for the meal to be ready. In essence, then, acquiring the distinction between *now* and *not now* is tantamount to learning that by waiting, the *not now* may become *now* (e.g., a child of 23;23 in her crib before going to sleep, says: "not now, and now we just going to bed . . . right now it's bedtime," Dore, 1989).

These types of temporal understanding do not develop at once; with development, children also learn that *not now* can also refer to the past. Aspects of the past and the future are fleshed out with development, in part via the acquisition of words used to bridge successive activities and to indicate points on a time continuum (e.g., soon, later, etc.). Children also need to work out where events are located relative to speech time. In her presleep monologues, a toddler studied by Nelson (1989) attempted to work out the relative temporal position of events, using the words "when," "then," "yesterday," "now" and "time to. . . . " Such temporal work is important because the past as a concept that relates one's past self to one's current self is critical to self-functioning. One needs to understand a past event as something that has happened, may or may not be known to others, and may or may not leave its footprints on the present. In the words of DeLoache (2002), the hallmark of human intelligence is that "we can mentally exist in the present moment, the past, or the future, in this place or some other" (p. 75). But from the current perspective, this view needs to be embellished because not only we, but other people, the world, and the objects in it, can all transcend the physical constraints of time and space. The child and the people and objects that surround him can likewise mentally exist in other times and spaces. This makes it critical for the child to distinguish references to the *not- here, not-now* both in his own preference communication and the communication of others.

Consistent with this, the first temporal referent children use is "now!" Halliday (1975) interpreted his son's earliest vocalizations, *nananana*, as meaning "I want that

Table 7.1.

	Age	Source
C wants to be taken to his room "Now room"	18 mos.	Halliday (1975)
M talks of visit tomorrow "No! Want to visit him now!"	26 mos.	Karniol (Diary, Karen)
C: "I wanna, I wanna watch TV" P: "You can in a little while" C: "I wanna watch something now"	33 mos.	Kuczaj (CHILDES)
C: "I don't want it on later.... I want it on now"	33 mos.	Kuczaj (CHILDES)

Table 7.2.

	Age	Source
P: "I'll tickle you as soon as I put on your diapers" C: "Now!"	18 mos.	Braunwald & Brislin (1979)
C: "Mommy, you put your book down and come play ball right now!"	29 mos.	Karniol (Diary, Karen)
Mother offers child ice cube but dawdles C: "Well, get up!"	30 mos.	Garvey (1984)
C: "I want Daddy to come now!"[1]	32 mos.	Karniol (Diary, Orren)
Father dawdles in helping child with toy C: "Daddy can you help me *now*?"[2]	34 mos.	Karniol (Diary, Orren)
C1 asks C2 if he's a friend; C2 says yes C1: "Then you have to sleep in my mousie place right now this minute"	3 years	Paley (1986, p. 56)
Child asks for a sandwich, father dawdles C: "Dad, fix the sandwich" F: "OK, OK" – but doesn't C: "Now! I'm not gonna tell you again"	5 years	Hall (CHILDES)
Shopping with father, child asks for toy car F: "Come on, we will buy it for Easter" C: "No, now"[3]	7;6 years	Axia (1996)

thing now." Linguistically more mature children explicitly allude to time in their cries of "Now I want it!" Some examples of this across different ages are shown in Table 7.1.

In the above examples, children's *now* referred to themselves and to their own preferences. But they appear to understand that the temporal dimension must sweep others along if these others are to fulfill their preferences and participate with them in the specified activities, as illustrated in Table 7.2.

Children's insistence on having things done *now* often leads to preferential conflict with mothers who report that many conflicts center on their demands that children wait, telling them "not now." For instance, at dinnertime, a child of 3;6 years asks for a shake, indicating that her mother promised. The mother answers, "After supper we'll do it cause I don't have time now, okay?" The child responds, "No we have to do it now," and cries. When she continues crying her mother relents, saying, "Okay, I will make the shakes" (Gleason, CHILDES). As another mother explains about her 3-year-old:

> as soon as I stop to do housework then the trouble begins ... she cries and she lies down on the floor because I can't just drop everything. Everytime I put my hands in the water, she wants something which I'm sorry I can't do it. (Backett, 1982, p. 178)

Although at times mothers do not make it explicit that they are using "not now" to imply "later, I'm busy right now," mothers often do specify "being busy" as reasons for why children's preferences have to be put on hold, as shown in Table 7.3.

Moreover, whereas above, mothers were vague as to what *not now* or *I'm busy* actually means, at other times, mothers are explicit about what needs to transpire prior to complying with the child's request. When she is asked to play with her son, a mother explains, "I got washing to do, ironing to do, hoovering... well, it all takes time" (Tizard & Hughes, 1984, p. 97). An 18-month-old asks his mother to read to him, and the mother answers,

[1] Hebrew: "Ani roça she-aba tavo axshav!"
[2] Hebrew: "Abba atta yaxol laazor li *axshav*?"
[3] Italian: "Dai, va la, la compriamo per l'uovo de Pasqua"; "No, adesso".

Table 7.3.

	Age	Source
C asks mother for a story M: "I'm very busy. I'll read it to you later"	Preschool	Shure & Spivack (1978)
C asks to sit on mother's lap M: "Oh, but I am very busy. You can sit on my lap later"	Toddler	Moerk (1983)
C: "Daddy, Daddy" F: "Not now, honey, Can't you see I'm busy"	6 years	Blum-Kulka (1997)

"Let Mummy just iron the anorak" (Wells, 1986, p. 11). At 17 months, Nigel asks his father to draw with him and is told: "No, I'm working." When Nigel implies that his father is playing, he answers, "No, I'm not playing.... I'm writing" (Halliday, 1975, p. 90).

In such contexts, mothers clarify that household tasks that don't get done on a given day need to get done the next day, they cannot be postponed forever. The mother of a 26-month-old explains, "If I don't iron some of Daddy's shirts I shall be in a row tomorrow" (Dunn, 1988, p. 133). When a child asks why his mother needs to do the washing instead of playing with him, she answers, "Well, I didn't do none yesterday. We went out, didn't we, up to Nanny's yesterday" (Tizard & Hughes, 1984, p. 105). Specifying what the mother needs to do also serves to indicate her priorities. For example, when Anthony asks his mother to listen to records at bedtime, she replies, "Tomorrow we'll listen to records. Daddy will have his dinner now" (Weir, 1962, p. 176). When mothers temporize this way, children learn that there are priorities and listening to records is of lower priority than giving a hungry father his dinner. That is, the child needs to learn not only that housework takes priority over joint play, but also that what happened yesterday has implications for the sequence of today's activities and that what does or does not happen today also carries implications for tomorrow. In the above interactions, though, there is an implicit message that once the parent completes the specified activity, he or she will attend to the child. But note that the child is given no instructions as to how to pass the time until the parent comes.

In other contexts, parental use of *not now* refers to parents' external preferences, referring to activities the parent wants *the child* to delay enacting. The child may express a preference for doing something that the parent prefers the child *not* do at the present time. For instance, a child may want to go to sleep and a parent may prefer otherwise (e.g., Kathryn says, "e take e nap" and her mother says, "You'll take a nap after a while, Honey," Bloom, 1970). A 21-month-old who wants to have a bath and prepares soap is told, "Now it's ready for you later when you have a bath.... No we're not taking it. I said you can get in the bath later" (Dunn, 1988, p. 20). Yet the mothers above did not specify the priorities that required the child's preference to be temporarily put on hold.

There are instances in which maternal edicts of *not now* stem from maternal preferences as to alternative behaviors that the child should engage in at the specified point in time. For instance, a mother is snacking with her child and she tries both to get him to eat and to control his misbehavior at the table by saying, "How about doing it later?[4] (Kobayashi, 2001, p. 117). Trying to get her child to change toys, a mother in a playroom with a toddler says, "We'll play with the pipe a little bit later, ok? Now look at the purse, ok?.... Wanna look at the pipe a little bit later?" (Broen, 1972, p. 87, 93). Two-year-old Wendy is in the playroom when the mother says, "Do you want to do the puzzles?" When the child rejects the offer, the mother cajoles her, saying,"Yea, come on, let's do the puzzle okay? Let's do this duck puzzle, then we'll look at the book some more" (Warren, CHILDES). In all the above instances, mothers are deferring the activity the child wants to engage in and offering alternative activities that, for whatever reason, the mother prefers be prioritized in the sequence of activities. No reasons for temporizing in these contexts are provided.

In many cases, though, especially when children are required to wait in an interactive context, parents do specify what the child is to do during the wait – often to wait passively and not get into any mischief. A mother who is talking to a 6-month-old while getting him into a highchair as she goes to get his lunch, says, "You've got to sit there and be good and quiet for a bit. All right? (Snow, de Blauw, & van Roosmalen, 1979, p. 279). Similarly, in the bathroom with her 23-month-old, the mother says, "Now you wait there till I get your facecloth. Keep sitting there" (Halliday, 1975, p. 132). In the above instances, children had to wait for their mothers to enact prerequisites for a given activity (i.e., cook, run a bath, etc.). The child's waiting was an integral aspect of the activity being enacted. Importantly, even when they do not anticipate an answer, mothers add tag questions, using *okay*, as if they are waiting for infants to affirm that they are agreeable to being left alone for the duration (e.g., "You hungry? Right, I'm just going to get it ready for ya, OK? Be with you in a minute," Korman, CHILDES).

An important aspect of parental temporization in such contexts is that temporal bridges (e.g., *soon, later, in a few minutes*) are used in asking children to wait, as shown in Table 7.4.

[4] Japanese: "Ata no shitara?"

Table 7.4.

	Age	Source
M is in pantry, looking for banana C cries in kitchen M: "All right, it won't be long C cries more M: "It won't be a minute" C continues crying M: "OK, it won't be long. . . . I'll be as quick as I can"	10 mos.	Lock (1980, p. 56)
M: "Byebye. Mommy's going to give something to Roger. OK? Mommy'll be back soon"	20 mos.	Bloom (1970)
M hears bell M: "That's my timer. I have to shut off my hard-boiled eggs, Sarah. Be right back"	Toddler	Schachter (1979, p. 140)
C cries for mother F: "Mama is coming back soon"[5]	Toddler	Miller (1979)
M is cooking, C cries in other room M: "Yes, I'll be with you in a minute Kate love"	22 mos.	Foster (1986, p. 237)

Temporal bridges are emphasized as being of a short span, for example, *only a minute* or *right away*, presumably because of an implicit understanding that delays are difficult for children and this is why one has to emphasize their brevity. Again, though, the child is not instructed what to do in the meantime nor is there any indication of what will happen when the mother comes back.

Presumably, children find it easier when they are explicitly told what to do or how they should occupy themselves while waiting. For instance, when Meike, at 20;2, tries to get her mother to come with her, trying to pull her hand, her mother explains, "Mama is making sandwiches. No, it's no use, Max. You'll have to play housewife yourself"[6] (Miller, 1979, p. 126). In the same vein, when Eve, at 18 months, asks her mother to read to her, the mother answers, "No Mommy can't read. I'm busy. You read the book" (Brown, 1973). When a 24-month-old asks for a stick, her mother says, "I'll try to find it and you can play with the balloon while you're waiting" (Carew, 1976, p. 96). Another mother explains to her toddler, "You're gonna hafta play by yourself, OK, because I'm trying to make lunch and I'm gonna hafta get the baby up" (Hart & Risely, 1995, p. 58).

Such experiences teach children that delays must be endured while mothers do chores. When her mother tells her to wait just a minute, a girl of 20;9 says, "Mommy little busy now" (Church, 1966, p. 262). Similarly, when 29-month-old told her mother, "Wait cook, I cook you wait"; the mother explained to the researcher, "She knows when I'm cookin somethin for her she' gotta wait" (Miller & Garvey, 1984, p. 120). Two 4-year-olds are playing house and the pretend mother explains that she can't play: "No I have to get to work." When the pretend daughter argues with her, the pretend mother finally says, "Can't you see I'm busy?" (Katz, Kramer, & Gottman, 1992, p. 141). As mother, at 35;18, Karen chides a doll who is insisting on going "now!" saying, "We'll go visiting someone later, not now."[7]

The necessity of waiting is also alluded to when adverbs, such as *now*, *after*, and *later*, are used by children to refer to the sequence in which actions are to be undertaken by others. Table 7.5 shows some examples of such understanding in children.

As evident above, children may accept parents' need to engage in other activities as justifications for temporization. At 22 months, Painter's (1984) son goes to his mother and explains his father's refusal to play with him, saying, "Dadda busy" (Painter, 1984, p. 181). At 25;19, Orren comes into the kitchen, saying, "Orren can't bring Daddy a book." When he is asked why, he says, "Daddy doesn't have time."[8] When Kathryn, at 21 months, goes into the kitchen and sees her mother preparing lunch, she says, "Mommy busy," and her mother answers, "I'm busy. That's right" (Bloom, 1970, p. 46). Pretend play reflects such understanding as well. For instance, pretend mother and daughter are playing and daughter says "Mom, Jerry rings at the door, shall I answer it? You are busy, ha, Mom?" Later, as baby, one cries, "I want . . . " and the pretend mother whispers, "Just a minute, just a minute"(Wells, 1985).

Often, it is difficult for children to understand why their own preferences cannot take precedence. Mothers chastise children, explaining that their preferences need to take the back seat to activities that are prioritized. As a mother explains to her son, at 3;6;8 years, "I can't just drop everything for you you know" (Wells, CHILDES). Similarly, a mother who explains why she cannot read to her daughter, says, "You have to learn how to wait. You can't just have

[5] German: "Mama kommt doch gleich wieder"

[6] German: "Mama schmiert mal Brote. Nee, dann hat's keinen Zweck, Max. Dann muss du selbst Hausfrau spielen"

[7] Hebrew: "nelex levaker at misheu axar kax – lo axshav"

[8] Hebrew: "Orren lo yexola lehavi le'abba sefer"; "En le-abba zman"

Table 7.5.

	Age	Source
K: "Mommy and daddy have breakfast take you ocean"	19;28	Karniol (Diary, Karen)
K: "Mommy finish dishes read "Sad Teddy Bear""	20;7	Karniol (Diary, Karen)
K: "Grandpa has breakfast – read after"	21;10	Karniol (Diary, Karen)
C: "Want your green pen.... when Daddy finished writing with that pen and then you can have Daddy green pen"	24 mos.	Halliday (1975, p. 144)
C asks to be picked up, mother is feeding baby brother C: "Oh, Okay, first you'll feed Benjamin and then you'll pick me up so I can put this in the sky"	31 mos.	Golinkoff & Hirsh-Pasek (1999, p. 175)
Addressing grandfather C: "When you eat finish, can you play with me?"	4 years	Kwan-Terry (1990)

Table 7.6.

	Age	Source
C asks to go to the potty C: "Excuse me, Daddy, right back"	20;19	Church (1966, p. 264)
C: "I want my paper. Be right back"	27 mos.	Bloom (1970)
Mother and daughter have switched roles C: "I going to work now" M: "Don't be gone long. I'll miss you" C: "I be back soon"	27 mos.	First (1994)
Child is playing with doll C: "You want some buttercup? I'll make you some buttercup. It will take just one minute"	4 years	Segal & Adcock (1981)

everything the minute you want it" (Shure & Spivack, 1978, p. 138).

There are several important issues that relate to temporization in such contexts. First, children apparently comprehend the general meaning of temporal adverbs and phrases by about age 2.5 years (Harner, 1976, 1980; Weist, 1986). Second, children start to use temporal bridges in referring to their own actions, as Table 7.6 shows.

Third, children start to comment on themselves as explicitly "waiting." To illustrate, when she is asked what she is doing, Karen, at 28;13, answers "Karen is waiting till Grandpa wakes up." At 27;12, Orren says to me impatiently as we are about to leave for day care, "I'm waiting for you."[9] A child of 26 months tells the adult that they are waiting for his sister to come and when she arrives, he says to her, "We waited for you, Paola"[10] (Antinucci & Miller, 1976, p. 180). But children find waiting arduous, as evident when they talk to their younger siblings and to dolls as if they too find parental absence difficult and need temporal bridges to facilitate their waiting for their "parents." A preschooler tells a younger sibling "Mommy will be back soon" (Howe & Rinaldi, 2004, p. 224) and in the same vein, at 27 months, Orren refers to a father doll, telling a child doll "Very soon Daddy will come"[11] and at 28 months, he refers to a mother doll, telling a child doll "She very soon will come back."

An interesting case of temporization arises in the case of allusions to waiting for a working parent. That is, the nonavailability of the working parent is put into a context wherein the child is represented as if he is "waiting" for the parent to come back from work. A child of 19;21 who waited for her father to come back met him with: "Ruthie just waiting and waiting" (Church, 1966, p. 261). When Naomi, at 22 months, asks, "Where's Daddy?" her mother answers, "Daddy is working. Daddy will be home tonight. You'll see him tomorrow morning" (Sachs, 1983, p. 6). Knowing that his dad generally comes home at 9 o'clock, Orren, at 28 months, talks to him on the phone and asks, "Daddy, you will come at home at 9?"[12] and a few days later, at 28;6, he laments, "Daddy will come home late."[13] An 8-year-old refers to his father's working late, saying, "I don't like it when he comes home at seven or eight. I don't like it when he comes home at eight, I like seven because we've got two more hours . . . " (Lewis et al., 1996, p. 59).

Whereas parents depend on clocks in determining their departure for work, children use signals of departures for work. Picking up "his briefcase," Orren, at 31;7, says, "Bye Mummy; I'm going to work – I'm a man."[14] A girl of 28;24 takes a purse on her arm and pretends to leave, saying to her mother, "So long mommy" (Miller, 1982, p. 180). They also pick up the jargon associated with leaving for work as

[9] Hebrew: "Ani mexake' lax!"
[10] Italian: "Abbiamo aspettato Paola"
[11] Hebrew: "He od me-at taxzor; Od me-at abba yavo"
[12] Hebrew: "Aba ata yavo babaita betesha?"
[13] Hebrew: "Aba yavo habaita meuxar"
[14] Hebrew: "Shalom ima. Ani holex la'avoda – ani ish"

Table 7.7.

	Age	Source
Child to stuffed animal "child" C: "When I come back from work I'll come to take you home"[15]	33 mos.	Karniol (Diary, Orren)
Mother and daughter have switched roles M: "What time will you pick me up Mummy?" C: "I'm gonna pick you up at one o'clock. Because I'm gonna have a meeting"	35 mos.	Gordon (2002)
Two children are pretend playing house C: "Daddy's gonna come really late. He has to be working"	5 years	Andersen (1990, p. 104)
Two children are pretend playing house C: "I'm supposed to go to work now anyway.... I'm gonna have a meeting there, so I won't see you late tonight"	6;11 years	Andersen (1990, p. 101)

opposed to other types of absence. This includes references to having meetings, staying late, and specifying what time the child will be picked up, as illustrated in Table 7.7.

Fourth, despite their apparent facility in using temporal adverbs and phrases, young children do not understand the temporal implications of such words, often misunderstanding the temporal referents implied in words like *later* and *not yet*. As Shatz (1994) documents, her grandson, at 26 months, understood *later* to mean "some time in the future," saying, "Go on a school bus and a city bus. Later Ricky do that" (p. 112). Parents may inadvertently foster misunderstanding by their use of such temporal terms. To illustrate, De Houwer (1990) recorded Kate at 36 months, insisting, "I want pill!" Her mother then answered "Well that's too strong. That's for later." And Kate replied, "I want one now!!!" screaming and crying, to which her mother answered, "Well, you go in your room and cry about it because you're not gonna get one. OK?" The mother likely meant to use the word "later" as shorthand for "when you grow up," whereas the child, who is used to the word "later" being used for bridging short, temporal gaps, misunderstood and thought that crying could shorten the delay. Similarly, when a 10-year-old asks to go to the beach, his mother responds, "To the beach by yourself, not yet" (Pontecorvo, Fasulo, & Sterponi, 2001, p. 356), implying that he can do so when he's older. This is even clearer when a child who wants an electric car is told, "I'll buy you one when you're a little older" (Clancy, Akatuska, & Strauss, 1987, p. 55), a vague reference to the future.

Children also misunderstand references to absolute time, for instance, at Christmas time, at Halloween, partly because they do not have an understanding of annual recurrence or the sequence of annual events (Friedman, 2003). Playing doctor, the patient's mother asks how long the children need to stay in bed. The pretend 5-year-old doctor answers, "they'll have to stay in bed for a whole lot of years. After Christmas, then they can go back to school" (Andersen, 1990, p. 112). References to distant futures may be expressed (e.g., Karen at 28;14, says, "Next year we're going to Turtle Reef to pick up some more seashells"), but as Friedman (2003) claims, children may have little understanding of the extent of time involved. This is especially problematic when parents use birthdays and holidays as distant temporal landmarks for when desired objects may be had. In this vein, the mother of a 6-year-old explains that when he asks for toys, her response is often "Christmas is coming, maybe Santa will bring it" (Bee-Gates, 2006, p. 28).

References to past events in terms of *yesterday* fare no better. At 30;21, Kathryn refers to an event that happened 6 weeks previously, saying, "you came here last night... yes. Last yesterday. Last night" (Bloom, 1970, p. 22). Eric, at 26;3, picks up a box of puppets he has not seen for 6 weeks and says, "that the puppets from last night!" (Bloom, 1970, p. 23). Similarly, at 30;14, Orren says, "You know that yesterday Evelyn was (here)?"[16] referring to an event that took place 3.5 months earlier in Israel whereas this was said in Canada. Children understand *yesterday* as referring to events in the past, irrespective of their specific temporal location.

Talking of the immediate rather than the distant future appears to be easier for young children. Hudson (2004) found that young children were better able to relate the unfolding of future events occurring later in the same day or the next day as opposed to those in the distant future, for example, sitting in the car on the way home, Karen, at 32;13, says, "Mommy I want a cookie in the blue box. That's what I want at home, OK, Mommy?"[17] Other instances of this include, "Can I have ice cream when we get home?" and "When we get to the store, can I have a cookie?" (Golinkoff & Hirsh-Pasek, 1999, p. 184).

References to tomorrow or the next day may be problematic for two reasons. First, sleeping at night provides a landmark between the days of the week, requiring the child to bridge across the night and to contend with the

[15] Hebrew: "Ke-she-ani axzor meha-avod ani bati lakaxat otxa habaita"

[16] Hebrew: "At yodaat she-etmol haya Evelyn?"

[17] Hebrew: "Ima ani roça ugia bakufsa hakaxol. Ze ma ani roça babaita, tov ima?"

Table 7.8.

	Age	Source
Real Expectations		
K: "Play with sleeping seashells later . . . wake up go to ocean"	19;27	Karniol (Diary, Karen)
K: "Want to go to the beach. When I wake up I can go to the beach"	26;22	Karniol (Diary, Karen)
K: "When you finish your nap you can wait for Daddy to come home and then you can go on vacation"	27;23	Karniol (Diary, Karen)
C: "I gotta feel better in the morning, when we have dinner in the morning"	Toddler	Sachs (1983, p. 15)
Pretend Expectations		
C: "After the night time we're going out on a picnic"	3;6 years	Wells (CHILDES, Laura)
C: "Goodbye, Dr. Melly, we'll see you in the morning when we get up"	Preschool	Sachs (1983, p. 15)

continuity from one waking day to the next. This may be difficult because parents often discuss sleeping as an activity that has to occur before some more desirable event can take place, telling children what will happen after they go to sleep or nap. Miller (1979) explains to Simone that "Afterwards, Meike and Christiane will come, they will come afterwards,"[18] implying after her nap. When a Hungarian child of 33 months asks for a story, his mother says, "We will tell that tonight, now we'll rest, ok?" Similarly, she explains to him, "We will get up then, when we've slept," and when he insists, she repeats "We will get up, if we slept, OK?"[19] (MacWhinney, CHILDES). Similarly, Levy (1989) cites Emily's father in her presleep ritual, who after enumerating all those things that are being planned for the morrow, says "If you don't go to sleep we won't be able to do those things."

Children often repeat to themselves what will occur after they sleep, both for real and in pretend, as shown in Table 7.8.

Whereas above, children explicitly mentioned sleeping, they can talk of what will happen tomorrow without explicit mention of sleeping. Having seen a barking dog while walking home from day care, Karen, at 29;26, says, "Tomorrow when we go to daycare we'll have to tell the dog not to bark because Karen doesn't like dogs barking . . . because it's not nice when dogs bark." Similarly, before going to sleep Karen, at 32;29, says, "Mommy, you know what I'll do in the morning? I will draw a line and after that I will eat."[20] Eve, at 26 months says, "We gonna play in the swimming pool tomorrow" (Brown, 1973).

A second problem in talking of the future is that some children use time of waking as their reference point for daily activities whereas others use the present moment as their reference. Friedman (2003) argues that the flexibility afforded by use of the present as one's point of reference underlies the ability to differentiate future distances. The tendency to think about time from the perspective of the start of the day rather than from the present moment can detract from children's ability to differentiate the future distances of events.

DO IT NOW!

The picture I portrayed up to now – of parents delaying their children's preferences – represents only half of the picture. There are many contexts in which it is parents who insist on things being done now rather than later. Mealtimes are often associated with demands for *now* rather than *later*. A mother calls her child to the dinner table, saying "Come and eat your dinner while it is still warm, pet" (Wells, CHILDES). Children know that food gets cold with time; on some occasions a delay is required to let food cool down whereas at other times, a delay is unnecessary. This gives rise to the opposite pattern as well, with parents urging children to not let their food get cold. A father tells his children at dinner, "go ahead, start eating. Don't let it get cold" (Blum-Kulka, 1997, p. 72). Children themselves start to allude to these criteria. At 33;4, Karen is called to breakfast and she says, "I have to run quickly so my egg doesn't get cold."

On the other hand, mealtimes can also be associated with the opposite pattern. The mother of a 5-year-old tells him "Don't try to put it all in your mouth honey, it's hot" (Herot, 2002, p. 164). Parents tell children to wait, saying, "It's hot. Blow on it for a minute" (Hart & Risley, 1999, p. 107). At 25;13, Karen verifies the status of her food, saying, "Karen checked if the egg is not hot." On the same day, she starts eating her soup, saying, "Karen made "fu" (blew on it) and then it be not hot." It may not be surprising, then, that *hot* was the first attributive used by Travis, Tomasello's (1992) daughter, at the age of 17;14. When her mother tells Eve that the tapioca is hot, she repeats, "Eve tapioca hot," her mother responds, "By the time you have lunch it will be cool" (Moerk, 1983, p. 11). At another time, the mother explains that the tapioca is "getting cool. We'll have it in just a minute" (Holzman,

[18] German: "Nachher kommen Meike und Christiane. Die kommen nachher auch"

[19] Hungarian: "Azt majd este elmeseljuk, most pihenjunk, jo?" "Majd akkor kelunk fol, amikor mar aludtunk"; "Majd felkelunk, ha adludtunk, jo?"

[20] Hebrew: "Ima at yoddat ma any taase baboker? Ani açayer baboker kav veaxar kax ani oxal"

Table 7.9.

	Age	Source
M: "Try your toast now – it's not too hot now" C: "It is. It's too hot"	26 mos.	Painter (1984, p. 261)
M: Why aren't you eating? C: "My food is still hot." M: "No, it's not hot anymore, go ahead."	3;3 years	Karniol (Diary, Orren)
Child looks at full plate C: "Hot" M: "It's not hot anymore, Meike"[21]	Toddler	Miller (1979)
Mother tells child to eat Child responds that the food is hot M: "They'll cool off"	Preschool	Herot (2002)

1972, p. 329). Children learn to wait while food is cooling down. First (1994) cites a girl of 26 months who says "Too hot; can't eat it yet" (p. 117), indicating the need to wait as the food cools down. In a pretend play episode, a 3-year-old tells the baby, "Here's food, baby. Eat this. Too hot. Don't burn your fingers" (Paley, 1986, p. 57). A 3-year-old pretending to be a father who is feeding his family says, "Wait till these are ready because they're too hot" (Paley, 1986, p. 129). At dinnertime, a 3-year-old indicates why he is not eating his pancakes, saying, "I'm gonna eat this gets cool" (Aukrust & Snow, 1998). A grammatically innovative 3-year-old does the same thing as she plays out a birthday party scene with her mother who asks her for a cup of coffee. The child answers, "soon you get coffee – I'm colding it" (Segal & Adcock, 1981, p. 94). Judgments of how cold or hot a given food may be can give rise to conflict as to when food should actually be eaten, as shown in Table 7.9.

The implication above is that the parent knows the current state of the food in question and that the child needs to accept this parental judgment. But such conflict can take a different turn. Wootton (1981) recorded a mother–daughter episode in which the mother warns the child that her food is too hot. The daughter replies, "But I like it hot." Her mother answered, "Well just wait a few minutes and then you can taste it but it's no use burning yourself" (p. 79). In another instance, a 3-year-old refuses to eat pretend food, saying, "It's hot." His age-mate girl denies this, saying, "It's cooled down now. We can eat it any way we want" (Pitcher & Schultz, 1983, p. 44).

In this context, one day Karen was observed putting salt in her soup while waiting for it to cool down. Surprised, we asked her why and she said "I making the soup cold." Having seen the adults in her home salt their soup while she was being asked to wait for her soup to cool down, she assumed that salt cools down foods! As humorous as this example may seem, it demonstrates that children may confuse delays that are time-bound and independent of human endeavor with delays that are terminable and contingent on human action. Development also entails discriminating these two types of delay. Importantly, this anecdote also shows that children want to have control over the duration of delays and search for means of doing so.

In some contexts, parents justify their demands for *now* because of a time-bound aspect of the relevant context. For instance, when Allison asks to change her diaper, her mother answers, "I'm not going to change your diaper on television . . . we'll change it later. I think it's time for a snack now. Would you like a snack?" (Bloom, 1973, p. 213). At other times, mothers ask their children to temporize because enactment of the preference at the current time would interfere with the parent's schedule or rest plans. For example, a girl of 4;10 years asks, "Mummy have you got any of that decorated paper what's under the Christmas tree?" Her mother responds, "Not at the moment, No, I'm not moving . . . " (Langford, 1981, p. 178). Here, then, the mother's need to rest rather than her being busy was the reason for temporizing. But in some contexts, parental insistence on things occurring now rather than later is an expression of parental impatience rather than any intrinsic aspect of the situation. For instance, when a 5-year-old is asked if she wants more food and answers *not yet*, her mother gets angry and says, "I'm not waiting all day to wait on you" (Herot, 2002, pp. 174–175). Of course, as Newson and Newson (1968, 1976) found, some mothers are relatively tolerant of their children's temporization.

Parental impatience is often evident in the context of demands for autonomous behavior. A mother tells her 4-year-old daughter, "You're taking too long Lynn. You've been sitting trying to fasten that button for ten minutes" (Wooten, CHILDES). When her 7-year-old takes too long to get his pants off before going to bed, a mother urges him on, saying, "aren't you ready *yet*? . . . Come on, I'll get you ready" – it's getting late" (Newson & Newson, 1976, p. 299). Parental impatience may be especially prevalent when children are likely to derail schedules, as when a parent needs to go to work and drop a child off at preschool. Thus, a father urges a child to start eating, saying, "Come on, eat it before it gets cold . . . come on, hurry up and eat. We're running late" (Grieshaber, 2004, p. 138). After asking her child to put away his toys and being told that he wants to put them away himself, a mother replies, "Do it faster then. We have to meet your grandmother downtown" (Shure & Spivack, 1978, p. 143). As a mother bathes her child and he indicates he wants to stay in the bath to play, she says, "Come on, time to get out . . . Daddy'll be home soon. Quickly . . . come on, David" (Cloran, 1989, p. 141). In the context of toilet training, in particular, doing things quickly is generally the message

[21] German: "Das is nich mehr heiss, Meike"

and children learn to express it themselves (e.g., "I want to go quickly and make pee pee," Hamann, 1996, p. 198).

There are other situations in which parental insistence on *now* rather than later seems to be arbitrary. My own children often rightfully complained that there is no rational reason why they should "fix your room right now!" and that nothing would happen if such fixing up were delayed. Yet parents seem to have their own threshold for being able to endure a given mess. As one mother shouts, "clean up all this mess! Hurry up! Before I smack some bums really hard.... You're going to do it. Now do it!.... Hurry up!" (Grieshaber, 2004, p. 167).

Pacing can also be urged in the opposite direction, to slow down a child's actions. When a mother wants her 2-year-old to slow down eating, she asks, "What's the hurry?" (Tulviste, 2003). A mother tells her toddler "You drank too quickly"[22] (Veneziano, 2001, p. 330). Pacing is often used in the context of the performance of academic activities, to slow down or to hurry up what children are doing. A teacher says, "We're not racing. We're taking our time" (Mody, 2005, p. 98). But the opposite also occurs at school, for example, a teacher who chastises a boy regarding his drawing, saying, "That's not what I told you to do.... Hurry up or you won't be able to paint it" (Sylva, Roy, & Painter, 1986, p. 197).

In other situations, parental insistence on an action being performed now rather than later arises because of the temporal sequence in which events unfold. This is reflected in the instruction: "Let's put on your warm boots because we are going to the park later" (Engel, 1995, p. 117). As well, Eric, at 22 months says, "I ieo shoes" and his mother says "After you go to the bathroom we'll get your shoes," at which point he answers, "e need shoes." (Bloom, 1970, p. 122). The mother's insistence on this sequence makes sense within a cultural system in which shoes are removed inside the house and put on prior to going out of the house. Her demand that he go to the bathroom reflects a preemptive action taken to avoid his needing to do so after they leave the house. As evident, then, mothers are working within a cultural system that specifies the way and sequence in which time binds events normatively and children learn to accept normative sequences. When Karen, at 32;9, wanted to show me something, I said, "First you have to get dressed." She apparently accepted the need to get dressed and asked, "Can I show you something afterwards?"

Temporal delays are also an endemic aspect of scripted activities. Whereas adults tend to take such delays for granted, they are an explicit aspect of children's elaboration of script details, as evident in Table 7.10.

Delays can also arise because of unexpected violations of the routine sequence of scripted events. For instance, when Simone's mother can't find her right shoe, she tells Simone that they can't go out right now (Miller, 1979). When a 3-year-old asks her mother, "Are we going to grandma's now?" her mother answers, "In a few minutes, we need to change your sheet and get the bag ready to go" (Hart & Risley, 1999, p. 267). Not finding one's car keys is often a cause of unexpected delays as is the need to attend to infants and other children. For instance, when a child of 2;8 asks for an orange, his mother says, "Well wait a second, Mummy just change Eve's nappy ... just give Mummy a second and I'll go and cut it up." But after changing the baby, there was another delay, introduced with: "Mommy's got to go and wash her hands and then Mummy will cut that for you" (Manchester corpus, CHILDES). When a preschooler asks the teacher to draw something, she replies, "Okay, just a second, I have to do something for Kevin" (Gearhart & Newman, 1980). Such exchanges teach children that events are prioritized, often based on the "first come, first served" rule.

Going to sleep is often subject to temporization, with parents insisting on *now* and children finding means of delaying doing so. Some families are especially adamant about the time that children need to go to sleep, for example "in this house, we have a set bedtime – 7 o'clock, that's bedtime" (Cook-Gumperz, 1973, p. 240). As another mother says, "if it's bed-time that is time for bed, tears or no tears" (Cook-Gumperz, 1973, p. 143). A father who wants his son to go to sleep at 9 o'clock, says, "you have got five minutes, mate" (Grieshaber, 2004, p. 176). The mother of a 3-year-old tells him, "Time you were in bed." When he responds, "No – not got to bed," she replies, "Now no nonsense, time for little boys to go to bed" (Tough, 1973, p. 32).

Given that going to sleep is ruled by declared bedtimes, certain presleep activities have to be undertaken and many time-contingent statements are made in this context. To illustrate, during supper, a mother tells a child, "It's 8:20, you need to go and have a shower"[23] (Blum-Kulka, 1997, p. 96). When a father comes home and asks about the children, the mother says, "they are both ready (i.e. to go to sleep), they have brushed their teeth and everything" (Varenne, 1992, p. 42). Such statements reflect the fact that certain routines and activities need to temporally precede other ones, because culture dictates the steps required prior to going to sleep.

CHILDREN'S TEMPORIZATION

As evident above, children learn to allude to time in talking of their preferences. In addition, though, they start to temporize in talking to others. First, having learned that parents can make events temporally contingent on their prior behavior, children may temporize by making their own behavior contingent on parents' prior enactment of behavior that children want them to engage in. In keeping with this, Karen, at 26;4, on being asked "Are you going to eat?" says, "After you read 'Uga Uga' you will eat," requesting to be read to prior to eating.

[22] French:"t'as bu trop vite"

[23] Hebrew: "Axshav shmone ve-esrim, ata çarix lagehset velhitkaleax"

Table 7.10.

	Age	Source
Restaurants		
C: "Well, you just eat. And pay. And that's all I would say. And also wait. And that's all"	4;7 years	French & Nelson (1985)
C: "We go and wait for a little while and then the waiter comes and gives us the little stuff with dinners on it, and then we wait for a little bit. . . ."	4;10 years	French & Nelson (1985)
Cookie Baking		
C: "I put it in the freezer, then wait 'til the next day, and roll out the cookies. . . ."	5;6 years	French & Nelson (1985)
Fire Drill		
C: ". . . get outside, wait for a minute, come back in"	4;7 years	French & Nelson (1985)
C: ". . . and go outside and wait for the firemen"	5;6 years	French & Nelson (1985)
Doctor Visits		
C: "You have to wait until your turn. . . . When they say your name then you go in"	4 years	Hudson & Shapiro (1991)
Pretend doctor to child's father		
C: "So what you're gonna do is – you're gonna wait out in the – hall – in the waiting room with your wife and. . . ."	6;7 years	Andersen (1990, p. 169)
C: "Well, you go in and wait in the waiting room"	8 years	Hudson & Shapiro (1991)
Birthday Parties		
C: ". . . put on pretty socks, you wait 'til all the guests come. . ."	5;1 years	Nelson (1986, p. 27)
C: "And it's ready for the party, I wait for my friends. . . ."	5;6 years	Nelson (1986, p. 27)
C: "After you get there you usually wait for everyone else to come"	8;10 years	Nelson (1986, p. 27)
Shopping		
Asked how one pays		
C: "We wait and be quiet"		
M: "Yeah, we have to wait in line and be good"	4 years	Hudson (2004, p. 141)

Concomitantly, children start to ask others to wait for them, doing so either implicitly or explicitly. In play, a child of 34 months pretending to be mother, tells the pretend daughter, "You just sit there while I get some more tea . . . ," and "I'll be back in a minute, you stay with Granny" (Manchester corpus, CHILDES), thereby implying that the pretend child should wait. At 32;13, Karen says, "Just a minute Mommy, sit here and wait till I come."[24] A Swiss child of 5;11 years requests, "Now you have to wait here for a little while until I come back" (Schönenberger, 2001). These types of temporizing statements make it clear that children understand the notion of time as passing as one is waiting. But they also underline that time is equally applicable to themselves and to others.

Another means of temporizing is attempting to exert control over routines. Such attempts are a function of whether time is construed in an objective or a relative sense. When time is referred to in an objective sense, universal time reference is specified (e.g., at 4 pm, when the sun sets, on Sunday), with such temporal referents being both objective and unchangeable. There are no actions one can take to hasten the coming of Sunday or Christmas, one can only fill the temporal void until the relevant event occurs. On the other hand, one may be able to influence others' perceptions of when a given activity should be engaged in (e.g., go visit grandma on Sunday, not Saturday) or whether it should be engaged in at all (e.g., "Let's not got to church today"). This is not the case for scheduled events like movies, concerts, trains, and school days, all of which have preset starting times and durations. Although scheduled events are determined by social beings, they are not subject to change as a function of our individual preferences. We can either attempt to adjust to such schedules or we can fail to adapt to them with the consequent disruption of both our own and possibly others' plans.

Time can also be referred to in a relative sense. It can be relative to the present time (in 10 minutes), past time (2 years ago), relative to one's own age (e.g., "when you are older"), relative to other people's age (e.g., "when Daddy retires"), relative to specific external events (e.g., "when the bell rings"), and relative to other people's actions (e.g., "when Daddy comes home"). With respect to such relative temporal referents, there are three relevant factors: whether the past or the future is invoked, whether a given time interval is set or alterable, and whether human action can impact the time period in question. Although we tend to think of the past as irrelevant in terms of the fulfillment of one's current or future preferences, references to

[24] Hebrew: "Rak rega ima – tishvi po vetexaki ad sheani baa"

past time can be used to demand current action (e.g., "You haven't fixed your room in the past week") and to justify current inaction (e.g., "You just went to the movies last Sunday"). To deal with such claims, one can either deny their veracity (e.g., "No, I went to the movies two Sundays ago") or attack the underlying premise head-on (e.g., "Who says you can't go to the movies every week?"). In either case, it is because the current action is deemed under human control that such verbal exchanges can ensue.

With respect to the future, these same factors are involved but another relevant concern is whether the referent is positive and awaited or negative and to be avoided or averted. To the extent that some temporal referents are dependent on human action (e.g., "after I/you finish doing this," "when Daddy comes home"), they can presumably be managed, either by the child or by others. That is, human action can be used to delay, speed up, or avert the relevant event. Events that are under human control can be undertaken at times other than those specified (e.g., go to the beach at 9 am, not at 11 am), the criteria of what needs to occur beforehand can be changed (e.g., "OK, so I'll fix lunch after I take you to Melissa's house"), and the agent may be substitutable (e.g., "If you want to leave faster, you can do the dishes while I shower"). That is, one can refer to how the time dimension relates to one's own behavior (e.g., "I'll do it later") or to other people's behavior (e.g., "You'll do it later"). This may be important not only in terms of potential agent substitution, but also in terms of what can be done to change temporal contingencies.

Sequences and routines can derail (e.g., stoves can stop working) or be derailed or averted by accident (e.g., burned dinners) or on purpose (e.g., child who "accidentally" hangs up the phone when mother is on the phone with someone else). Children can try to influence parental attempts to temporize their behavior. They can try to avert the end of a routine by using strategies to delay it (e.g., bedtime), exert control over the sequence (e.g., have dessert before the meal), and attempt to speed up its occurrence (e.g., help mom clean up after a meal so she can be free to play).

Temporal justifications, such as "it's too early," "it's too late" also sensitize children to the appropriate time for engaging in certain activities. In this context, children learn the temporal justifications that regulate their behavior, using them in interaction with other children, dolls, and even pretend friends. A toddler who was refused permission to watch a movie, explained to his pretend friend, "*Bedknobs and Broomsticks* is on much too late, and you need to go to bed on time so you grow up nice and strong" (Segal & Adcock, 1981, p. 13). When a 12-year-old pretending to be mother called a 7-year-old to come, the latter replied, "We playin' cards"; the "pretend mother" shouted, "I don't care what you playing. Come on. It's time to go in. You gotta go to school tomorrow" (Goodwin, 1990, p. 128). When a child of 5;7 years who is pretending to be a doctor is asked regarding measuring the "patient's" temperature, he recommends, "put it in her mouth until the time is 4 o'clock" (Andersen, 1990, p. 112).

Importantly, temporal understanding starts to guide children's own behavior. This is evident in children's interactions with adults, when mothers indicate it's clean-up time or in kindergarten settings, when teachers announce "It's 12 o'clock" and children understand these statement as indicative of the need to clean up, wash up and so forth (e.g., when a teacher announces "John, time to go out. Put away the trains and..." and the child acquiesces, Wood, McMahon, & Cranstoun, 1980, p. 43). Similarly, when a boy wants to start playing with something new, his preschool teacher says, "Well, we must start to think about that tomorrow as it is time to clear up now" (Gardner & Cass, 1965, p. 108). Children learn to associate time with specific activities and the sequences associated with them, for example, telling of what happens at preschool, a preschooler explains that "You have to clean up and go to lunch" (Fivush & Slackman, 1986, p. 86). Similarly, a 5-year-old tells a peer, "I think it's juice and cookies time, don't you?" (Garvey, 1984, p. 159). This also allows children to deny the temporal location of events and activities. For instance, at 35 months, Nigel is asked about something at preschool and says, "No... because it was time to go home and have your pieces of meat (i.e., have lunch)" (Halliday, 1975, p. 121).

Knowing the sequence of events that occur during the day and their association with clock time allows one to recognize that the time for doing something hasn't come yet. This can result in verbal conflict regarding the appropriate time for engaging in an activity and whether the time is right for doing so. This is evident when a girl says, "It's snack time" and a peer responds, "No, its not snack time, it's crackers time... no it's floor time" (Eder, 1982, p. 228). A preschooler sees a peer taking a snack and says, "It's not time to eat snacks" (Pitcher & Schultz, 1983, p. 163). In an example with older children, two 9–10-year-olds are playing with modeling clay. Jack asks "Should we clean up?" and Jason responds with a question, "What time is it?" On being told what time it is, Jason answers, "No, we don't have to yet" (Merritt, 1998, p. 134). Clean-up occurs before lunch, and lunch is always at the same time, so that the clock determines what one does and when. When a Japanese preschool teacher sees a 5-year-old crying, she questions him and is told he's upset because he had set up his lunch but was told by his peers that it "wasn't yet time" for lunch (Kelly, 2001). The child felt bad because he had misperceived the time, engaging in a behavior too early, and was chastised for it by his peers. Children become sensitized to the sequential nature of events in different settings, viewing time in each setting as transpiring between different landmark events. Such understanding guides the sequences that children enact in their play, as evident when a child of 5;6 years who is playing house says, "Mommy, I'm all done (eating)." The pretend mother answers, "Okay, Sweetie; now it's time for your naptime" (Andersen, 1990, p. 102).

Children start to use time in attempting to guide others' behavior as well. When a preschooler starts to nap at a Japanese preschool, another child yells out, "Don't take a nap now!" (Peak, 1991, p. 139), and all the children start to giggle, clearly indicating that the timing of the nap was inappropriate. At 3;3, Orren marches into my room in the morning, asking, "It's the morning so why do not getting up?" Playing school, a girl rings a bell and says, "That means it's dinner time," requesting that others come to eat (Willes, 1983, p. 151). When a Japanese 7-year-old hears that it's clean-up time and sees boys who are still playing, she tells them, "It's time to clean up," repeating it when they do not comply (Kelly, 2001, p. 186).

Older children learn that they need to comply with a time frame allotted by parents and teachers for free-time activities. When 6-year-old Jeffrey asks to go out and play during dinner, his mother says, "No, you're not going outside. I'm sorry. This is the dinner hour" (Blum-Kulka, 1997, p. 166). In preschool, the teacher announces, "Now children it is time for assembly. Leave what you are doing and go into the Hall" (Gardner & Cass, 1965, p. 105). When no other activities are scheduled, then, one can play, as acknowledged by a girl of 4;7 who says, "it's morning time. Time to play with things" (McTear, 1985, p. 143). But one also needs to keep an eye on the clock and govern one's behavior accordingly. In pretend play, a preadolescent orders her child to "be back here at three o'clock" (Mitchell-Kernan & Kernan, 1977, p. 192). A girl who is almost 5 years old is pretending to go shopping and says to her "pretend mother," "I won't be late" (Wells, 1986, p. 5). But children find it difficult to align their preferences with parental schedules – they are late (e.g., Sixsmith & Knowles, 1996). An elementary school child explains: "you go out and play with your friends and your forget (the time) and then you go back (home) and your parents are angry" (Mayall, 2002, p. 118). A 9-year-old talks of wanting to be older because then he could make decisions about going out, "When I'm 17, I'll be able to stay out late, not too late. I'll have to come back around 9, 10. When I'm older, not now" (Mayall, 2002, p. 118).

DOMAINS OF TEMPORIZATION: FOOD AND TURN TAKING

I now turn to two domains in which parents temporize: food preferences and turn taking. Because so much research has addressed children's food preferences, this domain will be elaborated more fully.

MANAGING AND TEMPORIZING FOOD PREFERENCES

Many of the temporal contingencies that are part of children's daily life involve food. This is because parents not only have preferences regarding what foods children should eat, but they also have preferences as to when, where, and how much children should eat. Such preferences may index parental long-term preferences regarding the child's health, his maintaining reasonable weight, learning to control his food intake, and generally teaching the value of food. But what children experience is a large number of temporal contingencies that relate to their food intake. First of all, parents express their preferences that children should eat most or all of what's on their plate, and that they should do so before leaving the table. In fact, Puhl and Schwartz (2003) found that the rule concerning the need to finish everything on one's plate was one of the five most endorsed rules recalled by adults as regulating food-related behavior in childhood. For instance, at lunch, when Meike says "take off bib," her mother says, "No, first eat a little bit"[25] (Miller, 1979). Young children learn that being put in a highchair with a bib is a signal for mealtime ("Xiaociao mama wants to put the apron on you then eat OK," Quay, 2008, p. 26) and they must eat before having bibs taken off and being taken out of highchairs. When Amy wants to leave the table, asking "Shall we go upstairs? her mother says "Not at the moment." When the mother continues drinking her tea and Amy repeats that she is going upstairs, the father asks "Look well what about these vegetables here," pointing to unfinished food on her plate (Wootton, 1997, p. 162). Older children are also expected to finish their food as a precondition for being excused from the table. Jeffrey, at age 6, asks, "Excuse, can I be excused?" His mother answers, "You haven't finished your sandwich" (Blum-Kulka, 1997, p. 166) but a 9-year-old is similarly told: "Finish everything on the plate" (De Geer, 2004). Children echo these directives, as when a 5-year-old who is playing house says to an age-mate, "You gotta eat your supper first" (Pitcher & Schultz, 1983, p. 47).

Whereas above, there was no explicit statement of what would happen otherwise, children are not averse to indicating that they may be punished for not eating. A 5-year-old recounts last night's dinner experience, saying, "I started not to eat 'cause I wasn't hungry. But my mommy said I have to eat dinner. But I didn't eat dinner. So she sent me in my room" (Hudson, 1986). Food-related disciplinary tactics are often adopted in preschools to impress upon children the need to eat. A 3-year-old playing house warns the baby, "Eat up your pasta. If you don't, you'll see what happens" (Bonica, 1993, p. 63). Children who do not eat may be punished in such settings, as Karen, at 30;17, explains that one of her dolls is "in punishment" because "She is not eating."[26]

Eating or drinking become prerequisites to other activities. Allison's mother says to her at 28 months, "So hurry up and finish your snack and we can play with some toys" (Bloom, 1970). Another mother explains about her 7-year-old, "I'd tell him if he ate all his dinner I'd read him a story or we could play another game" (Cook-Gumperz, 1973, p. 61). A mother rejects her toddler's request with "No, you hafta have your lunch first" (Schachter, 1979, p. 194).

[25] German: "latzchen ab"; "Nun iss erst mal'n bisschen!"

[26] Hebrew: "beonesh"; "He lo oxelet"

Eating, then, becomes a necessary evil to be endured as a prelude to doing "fun stuff." It is not surprising then that children allude to contingencies between eating and subsequent activities, for example a preschooler tells the dolls, "You all have to eat your breakfast first, then you can play" (Segal & Adcock, 1981, p. 66). In the following sibling play conversation at 4;3 and 3;2 years, Lisa, pretending to be Daddy, says, "We want to sleep and then we'll go to the beach." Giulia answering as Mommy, says, "First eat, Daddy"[27] (Taeschner, 1983). Here, too, eating is a precondition for other activities.

Insistence on children's finishing their food may well reflect parental concern with their not remaining hungry; for example a mother who refuses a toddler's request for a snack, says, "That's your fault because you didn't eat enough breakfast" (Bruner et al, 1982, p. 109). When a child of 5;2 says he's too full to eat dinner, his mother says, "When it's bedtime and you say you're hungry, don't expect any food"; children need to eat supper at suppertime (Ely et al., 1995, p. 209) and doing so prevents them from remaining hungry. A mother tells her daughter to eat and the child asks, "Am I hungry?" Taken aback, the mother asks, "You tell me, how does your stomach feel?" and after being told that it's making noises, the mother says, "Well after you eat that you won't be hungry" (Imbens-Bailey & Snow, 1997, p. 277). The need to eat to quell one's hunger is understood by a preschooler who is playing pretend with her mother as her doll, and the doll explains that she is crying because she is hungry. The pretend mother answers, "You already had breakfast, but you didn't take your vitamin seed and your pill" (Segal & Adcock, 1981, p. 155).

A concomitant concern for parents is that children eat at mealtime rather than in between meals. This gives rise to many rejections of food requests with reference to time elapsed since eating or the period of time remaining prior to eating a "real" meal. When a 1-year-old says, "Chee," the mother says, "No, Ross, it's much too soon for cheese" (Foster, 1990, p. 3), presumably referring to the time elapsed since the infant's last meal. Mothers may also refer to the need to wait for an impending meal. After having been told that it's too early for lunch, that it's not time yet, and then having been given a single breadstick, a child of 29 months asks for another breadstick. His mother answers "Oh, no, it's almost lunch time." He repeats his request twice, and finally his mother shakes her head and says, "Honey, not now" (Bloom, CHILDES). Similarly, when Eve says, "I want have my lunch," the response is, "But it's not time for lunch yet. You wait just a little bit and we'll have lunch." When she repeats her request twice, she is told, "Not now ... not now, it's not time" (Moerk, 1983, p. 131). A girl of 33;9 says to her mother, "Bit hungry." When she is ignored, she expands, saying, "I'm a bit hungry." Her mother answers her, "Well, well, later on we'll have some tea." The child answers, "Um, I don't want tea, I'm having a . . . . " Her mother cuts her off, saying, "No, we're not having anything else at the moment" (Wells, CHILDES).

Children often voice their understanding of meal-related restrictions on their food intake. Andersen (1990) recorded a 4-year-old playing with an experimenter; the first, pretending to be a child, says, "Now I want carrot." The adult as "pretend mother" answers, "Why don't we wait 'til lunchtime for that," and the "pretend child" cries "Waah," in response (p. 149). When an 8-year-old "pretend daughter" asks for some peanuts, the 12-year-old pretend mother shouts at her, "Go to bed! You supposed – you supposed to get yours in the morningtime" (Goodwin, 1990).

Drinks can also be refused, often because mothers want to delay their children's eating and drinking until mealtimes. For instance, Melanie, aged 24 months, goes into the kitchen, saying to her mother, "Milk." The mother says, "No, not now – you go in that way and play." The child then says, "Look milk" and the mother answers, "Go and play. You can have that afterwards when you've played" (Howe, CHILDES). Similarly, when Peter, at 29 months, tells his mother he wants some milk, she says, "Well, we'll have some later, ok?" (Bloom, 1970). Wooten (CHILDES) recorded a child saying, "I want a drinkie milk. Will I get a drinkie Mummy? I'm wanting a drink." Her mother responds, "You'll get milk for your dinner." In a preschool, a child asks for a drink, the teacher smiles and says to her "You're going to have your milk in a minute," presumably with her meal (Gardner & Cass, 1965, p. 68).

Parents may also limit children's drinking in the middle of meals, fearing that it will reduce their food intake. In this vein, a mother tells her toddler, "You're not to drink any more of this until you eat some more of that egg, please" (Gleason, Perlmann, & Greif, 1984). A 9-year-old explains that his mother constrains both food and drink, " . . . not much fizzy drinks. Water, at dinnertime – we have to drink two glasses of water and then have a fizzy drink. So we're not allowed to have a fizzy drink first" (Mayall, 2002, p. 44). A related concern is how much the child has drunk prior to the current request. A child of 24 months demands a drink, saying, "Drink." His mother says, "You're only having a little more. Then that's all, All right?" (Dunn, 1988, p. 102). When Meike asks for more juice, her mother says to her "You've drank so much already today, Meike! The bottle was still this full this morning"[28] (Miller, 1979, p. 402). When a toddler asks for milk, her mother says, "You don't want milk, honey, you've just had some juice" (deVilliers, 1984, p. 210). Apparently, mothers think that children's consumption of beverages needs to be rationed in light of their prior consumption of either the same or different beverages, including milk.

Parents are especially concerned with children's consumption of sweets and temporal contingencies related to

[27] German: "Wollen wir schlaften, nachher gehen wir zur spiaggia"; "erst essen, Papi"

[28] German: "Du hast heute schon so viel gesoffen, Meike! Die Flasche was heute morgen noch ganz voll"

sweets are abundant in parent–child communication. At 14 months, a child says *ba* when he sees a cookie box. His mother interprets this as meaning "I want a cookie" and shakes her head *no*. The child reaches for the cookie box, again saying *ba, ma ma*. The mother answers *no*, removing the box from his reach and the child cries (Painter, 1984, p. 79). When Eve asks for a cookie after having had a few, her mother answers, "No more cookies, Eve. Later we'll have a cookie" (Moerk, 1983, p. 139). When Richard asks for a cookie between meals, his mother says, "Darling, it's not time." When he persists, she says, "Do you want a drink?..... If you want a drink you can have one.... Do you want a drink? Because that's all you're having...." (Bruner, Roy, & Ratner, 1982, p. 108).

Mothers appear concerned with sweets interfering with children's meals. As one mother noted, "I don't let her eat a lot between meals, but if she could, I don't think she'd ever stop" (Newson & Newson, 1968, p. 223). One consequence of the above is that in many homes, sweets are restricted before mealtimes. When a mother is questioned about having rules in the house, her preschooler answers, "Chocolate." The mother responds, "Yes, no chocolate unless they've eaten something decent beforehand" (Mayall, 2000, p. 128). When a child says, "I want a cookie," the father answers, "It's almost time for lunch" (Hart & Risley, 1999, p. 106). When a preschooler asks her mother for a cookie before dinner, the mother insists, "Absolutely not; and there's no use arguing" (Segal & Adcock, 1981, p. 82). Similarly, when Peter, at 33 months, says he wants a cookie right after finishing one, his mother says, "We're gonna eat dinner soon." When he reiterates his request, she repeats, "We'll have dinner soon," and then the child repeats "have dinner soon" (Bloom, 1970). After Kathryn, at 21 months, eats some nuts, then some raisins, and asks for more raisins, her mother says, "You won't be able to eat dinner, Honey. I'll give you some more apple" (Bloom, 1970, p. 44). A Japanese mother urges her toddler to stop eating cookies, saying "Let's make this the last one, OK?... Because you won't be able to eat your lunch." The child answered *yes* and put away the plate of cookies (Kobayashi, 2001, p. 121). When a 5-year-old girl asks for a Nutella sandwich, her mother refuses, saying "No not now"; the child then asks for bread and this request too is refused, with the mother saying, "It's tea time soon. No. You've had chips. That'll do (Grieshaber, 2004, p. 124).

Parental limitations on eating sweets before meals extend to older children who can get their own sweets. For instance, Jonathan, at 4;7;14 years asks his mother "Can I get some sweets out of the tin in the front room?" and his mother replies, "No Jonathan! I'm sorry but you're not eating sweets this early in the morning" (Wells, CHILDES). Similarly, Jason, at 5;0;19 years asks "Can I have one chip?" and his mother answers, "No. Your dinner's nearly ready. Won't be a minute." Refusing her child's request for chocolate, a mother says, "No you can't have it now. You won't eat (dinner) later" (Blum-Kulka, 2002, p. 92). A 13-year-old who indicates she's not hungry because she ate too many sandwiches is asked whether she is allowed to eat sandwiches and is told, "Yes, but that's not so smart when you're having dinner later" (De Geer, 2004). In fact, research (e.g., Birch, McPhee, Bryant, & Johnson, 1993) indicates that snacking before lunch leads to less food intake at lunch; however, this was only true for children's dispreferred foods. Their intake of preferred foods was not affected.

Further to this, many parents make dessert contingent on finishing one's meal, for example, "You can have a sweet now you have finished your dinner" (Wells, 1985). Dessert is framed in terms of what children *want to* eat and other foods, like meat and vegetables, are framed as what they *have to* eat (e.g., Ochs, Pontecorvo, & Fasulo, 1996). In this context, the mother of a 4-year-old says, "You ate all your lunch like a big boy. So I might give you a cookie now OKAY? (Beals, 1993, p. 507). The mother of a 2-year-old says,

> You did real good on your sandwich. Now see if you can eat up your carrot. Those are good for you. Can you eat your carrot up? That's the way. Let's finish your carrot because Grandma brought us some little boxes of raisins for dessert. (Hart & Risley, 1995, p. 58)

Puhl and Schwartz (2003) found that rules specifying that "you cannot have dessert until after you finish you meal" were one of the most frequently endorsed types of rules in adults' recall of food-related rules during their childhood. Orrel-Valente and colleagues (2007) found that such reward contingencies were used by about 30 percent of families with 5-year-olds and were correlated with children's eating compliance.

Children may well comply with food "bribes" even when they are phrased as threats, which are also used to induce children to finish their meals. For instance, "If you don't clear your dinner plate, you don't get any pudding" (Newson & Newson, 1968, p. 238). An American father says to his kids, "Whoever does not finish their vegetables does not get any ice cream for dessert" (Ochs, Pontecorvo, & Fasulo, 1996, p. 22). When a child of 3;8 years asks for some gum, he is told, "No, you didn't eat your sandwich" (Kuczaj, CHILDES). Orrel-Valente and colleagues (2007) found that such contingent threats were used in about 10 percent of the families with a child of about 5 years of age.

Although one might expect that children would rebel against such contingencies, as they sometimes do (e.g., a 26-month-old threw a tantrum after being denied the second half of a popsicle, shouting, "I want the nother one!," Sachs, 1983, p. 1), children generally appear to accept the food-related, temporal contingencies in force in their homes, as evident in what they say about them, as shown in Table 7.11.

Lepper, Sagotsky, Dafoe, and Greene (1982) have suggested that children learn that when something is offered contingent on having finished something else – for

Table 7.11.

	Age	Source
C: "I eat the string beans (i.e., jelly beans) after my eat my lunch"	24 mos.	Brown (1973)
C wants to eat dessert, is given fruit C: "Later cookies later"[29]	33 mos.	Taeschner (1983)
C: "First I have to eat my vegetables, don't I?"[30]	3;3 years	De Houwer (1990)
C: "When I drink finish, can I eat ice-cream?"	4 years	Kwan-Terry (1990, p. 59)
C: "Mommy, you – you 'member. If I eat a good dinner I could have a ice cream"	Preschool	Ochs & Capps (2001, p. 264)
C: "Can I have dessert if I eat two more bites?"	Preschool	Golinkoff & Hirsh-Pasek (1999, p. 184)

example, "Eat your spinach and I'll give you some peas" – the item offered as a contingency is more attractive (cf., Birch, Marlin, & Rotter, 1984). Research in which one snack was provided contingent on consuming another snack has shown that the snack constituting the means comes to be devalued as compared with the reward snack (Newman & Taylor, 1992). In essence, then, the contingency is construed as a bribe.

Children understand the use of bribes as means of getting children to eat, as reflected in their play. For example, in playing with her dolls, Karen repeats such contingencies, saying to her dolls,

afterwards if you're not a good girl, you won't get any cake"[31]; "Eat the bread and you'll get a meatball,"[32] and "drink all of it, all, so you will get a cookie,"[33] all said between 30 and 33 months of age.

In fact, mothers often acknowledge that they "bribe" their children into eating less desired foods, offering them ice cream or a fruit cocktail. (e.g., Cohler & Grunebaum, 1981)

As for absolute quantities, when Allison, at 22 months, pours out some cookies from a box, her mother says "They're too many cookies for you to eat. I think we'll put some of them back in the box.... Let's have a little more juice and we'll put the cookies way... I think you've had enough cookies" (Bloom, 1973, pp. 240–242). Sandra, at 4 years old, asks her mother whether she can have some more cookies after dinner. Her mother answers, "One more. You may have one more" (Blum-Kulka, 1997, p. 165). When a child asks for more tangerines, his mother retorts, "You've already eaten two. Your stomach is saying, 'I'm full'" (Clancy, 1986, p. 244). Similarly, a child of 23 months who saw chocolate cake on the table said, "Bibby on." The mother answers "You don't want your bibby on. You're not eating." The child replies, "Chocolate cake. Chocolate cake," to which the mother responds, "You're not having any more chocolate cake either" (Dunn, 1988, p. 21). When Simone asks for more jellybeans, her mother answers, "not now, now is enough jelly beans"[34] (Miller, 1979). Mothers seem to keep a log of children's intake of nonessential foods and to have an implicit criterion of what counts as enough. But this criterion is not absolute, it depends on its relation to meals. This is evident in the following exchange. Simon at 13 years of age comes into the kitchen as the family is about to have dinner and helps himself to a plate of potato chips he sees on the counter. His mother says "Put it away... because it fills you up" (Blum-Kulka, 1997, p. 175). Junk food is to be avoided before meals.

Additional evidence for this implicit criterion is mothers' use of previous food intake as justifications for limiting current food intake. For instance, when her mother opens up the refrigerator to get some lunch and Kathryn, at 21 months, sees cake inside, she says, "coffee cake." The mother answers, "Coffee cake! You had coffee cake this morning" (Bloom, 1970, p. 57). Similarly, when a 2-year-old child asked for candy, his mother asked "Didn't you eat a lot of candy this morning?"[35] (Clancy, 1986, p. 242). References to past consumption, then, can be used by children to justify their requests (e.g., "We haven't had any candy for a long time," Ervin-Tripp, 1977, p. 177).

In light of the temporal and absolute restrictions regarding sweets, it may not be surprising that children allude to rules relating to sweets. Ian, at 9 years old, is talking to his younger brother Jason and asks him if he wants a sweet. The younger brother answers, "We're not allowed... it's nearly dinner time." The older one nonetheless ventures into to the kitchen and asks, "Can we have a polo?" and the mother acquiesces but rations the sweets, answering, "One." Ian sees this as a concession on his mother's part and gleefully goes to tell his brother (Sealey, 2000, p. 201). A child who is out shopping with his mother expresses his desire to buy some candy; his mother replies "you'll have to wait until Saturday, then you can have candy" – and the child accepts her decision without argument (Pettersson, Olsson, & Fejllström, 2004, p. 324). Similarly, in describing what happens when she and her mother bake cookies, a child of 4;8 years explained that "Sometimes, later, she

[29] Italian/German mixed: "Dopo kuchen dopo"

[30] Dutch: "Eerst moet it imj-mijn groenten opeten he"

[31] Hebrew: "Axar kax im at lo yalda tova at lo tekabli uga"

[32] Hebrew: "Toxal at halexem ve-takebel kçiça"

[33] Hebrew: "Aval tishti hakol – hakol shetakbli ugia"

[34] German: "gummibarchen"; "Nicht jetzt ... jetzt is genug Barchen"

[35] Japanese: "Asa omochi takusan tabeta ja nai?"

doesn't let me eat them. One time I ate an ice cream cone before my dinner," reflecting her understanding that this was a memorable event that is uncommon in her social world.

Refusals to comply with requests for more food often reflect a different concern, that such requests should only be voiced *after* finishing previous servings of the item in question. Jonathan, at 18 months, chews a cookie and indicates to his mother that he wants another one. She replies, "You haven't finished that one yet, have you? You're still eating it." When he again vocalizes and reaches for another cookie, she says "You're getting a greedy little boy, aren't you?." When he repeats his request the third time, she says, "Mommy'll give you another half when you've finished that one. Mm. Have you finished that one?" (Bruner, 1983, p. 102). In this vein, when Richard holds up his cup and says, "More," his mother says, "You've got some. You can't have more" (Bruner, Roy, & Ratner, 1982, p. 109). This pattern of adult concern with finishing what one is currently eating or drinking may well give rise to Karen's statement at 20 months, when she says, "Finish that (i.e., cookie) grandpa give you another one."

Children are expected to temporize their intake of sweets in yet another way, by rationing them. When Allison, at 16;3, asks for a cookie, her mother says, "Shall we have a cookie? O.K. Let's have a snack" and gives her a cup of orange juice with a cookie. As Allison is eating the cookie, she reaches for additional cookies in the bag and her mother says, "There's more in here. We'll have it in a little while... let's save these for later" (Bloom, 1973, p. 153). Such instructions are reflected in children's own attempts to ration sweets; a child of 32 months who is offered some chocolate-covered nuts tells her friend who is holding a bag of them, "that you have to save for later" (Garvey, 1984, p. 98). As for older children, Sonuga-Barke and Webley (1993) found that many parents provide an allowance for children buy sweets (e.g., "at that age they could just about go down the local shop and buy a handful of sweets or a toy aeroplane or something"; "so they can go and buy their sweets or their birthday presents or whatever" (ibid, p. 76), with some parents expressing the view that doing so is a training exercise, for example, "to get them used to going down and asking for sweets themselves and giving the money and getting the change" (ibid, p. 76). But children are expected to ration the sweets they buy from their allowance.

Parents may also warn children of the long-term consequences of their noncompliance with food-related contingencies. A 4-year-old who didn't want to eat his vegetables was told, "You'll never grow into a big man like your Daddy – you'll never be able to drive a lorry" (Newson & Newson, 1968, p. 227). Hart and Risley (1999) found that American mothers often urged their children to eat unwanted foods by saying, "Don't you want to grow up to be big and strong?" (p. 33). Such warnings are apparently internalized by children, as evident in the following. Lisa at 3;7 years says "If I don't eat the vegetable soup I won't grow up big"[36] (Taeschner, 1983). Similarly, a 31-month-old Polish child says, "I am eating grandma, so I'll be big"[37] (Przetacznik-Gierowska, 1995). Such long-term concerns are evident in children's pretend play. Parker recorded a child interacting with a talking doll who tells the child "I'm gonna be so strong." The child answers, "... if she eats everything your mom tells you to, you will be, maybe you'll be even stronger than me" (Parker, 1986, p. 125).

Parents may also temporize food intake by warning children of getting fat. For instance, the father of a 30-month-old pats his stomach and says, "Well, you're getting fat. Maybe you eat too much candy, do you think?" (Hart & Risley, 1999, p. 48). Children echo such concern; in the midst of pretend playing, one child tells another regarding brownies, "Hey you're not getting any more. You'll get fat" (Barnes & Vangelisti, 1995). This type of comment is not limited to desserts. After Kathryn, at 21 months, asks for more meat, and her mother gives her some, but when she asks for more, her mother says, "More meat? You're gonna get fat" (Bloom, 1970, p. 43).

All these means of temporizing children's food intake results in children learning that they need to regulate their food preferences according to the time of day, closeness to meal times, and degree of "dessertiness." They also learn that different foods are eaten at different times of the day and that one does not eat the same foods twice in one day. At 3;3 years,, Francesco refuses to eat ham in the evening, saying, "I don't want it. I already ate ham this morning"[38] (Bates, 1976). This pattern is very interesting in light of research with chimps. Rumbaugh and Gill (1977) trained a chimp, Lana, to talk by using symbols. They succeeded in getting her to converse about one topic, the procurement of food and drink. All the conversations were impromptu, were initiated by Lana, and all apparently centered around things she wanted. Her expressed preferences matched what she was used to. In the morning she was used to drinking milk and in the afternoon monkey chow; she rejected food in the morning and milk in the afternoon. Importantly, not all mothers regulate their children's food preferences as a function of their temporal proximity to meals, with the mothers of picky eaters refraining from doing so for fear that their children would not consume enough food (e.g., Newson & Newson, 1968).

The extensive temporization of food preferences indicates the important role that food-related behavior is accorded. Crucially, though, parental temporization of children's food intake may backfire. Research (e.g., Fisher & Birch, 1999) has shown that for 3- to 5-year-old girls, mothers' and children's reports of restricted access to snack foods is highly correlated with girls' greater intake of these restricted snack foods when freely available, despite reports of being full after lunch. This may well reflect the

[36] Italian: "Se non mangi la minestrina non diventerai grande"
[37] Polish: "Ja jem babciu/ to bede duza"
[38] Italian: "No, non la voglio, ho mangiato gia stamattina prosciutto"

Table 7.12.

	Age	Source
C wants sister's vacuum cleaner saying he fixed it; M to the sister M: "Well, you'll have to wait your turn"	3 years	Dunn (1988, p. 57)
C pushes sister off bike, M scolds her C objects, saying it's her bike M: "Well you don't resort to violence. Wait until she's finished"	Preschool	Grieshaber (2004, p. 184)
C wants earphones T: "You have to wait 'til there's room for you"	Kindergarten	Schultz (1979, p. 291)

fact that greater external controls on children's behavior undermine their own self-control attempts, a recurrent theme in various domains discussed in this book.

TEMPORIZING TURN TAKING

Another domain in which children are taught to temporize is that of turn taking, both in conversation and in play. In fact, mothers often indicate that they expect children to learn to turn take in preschool (e.g., "I hope he'll come out . . . learning how to wait his turn and learning how not to interrupt people when they're talking," Graue & Walsh, 1998, p. 179). In the realm of conversation, children are asked to wait for their turn to speak, to wait till others finish speaking rather than interrupting them. Dinnertime is often used to teach turn taking in conversation, with some parents claiming that children "have to wait until it's their turn" (Blum-Kulka, 1997, p. 38). As one father says, "it's very important that they don't interrupt others. It's a principle here. In fact, sometimes we say to the other, 'wait, your brother is still talking'" (Blum-Kulka, 1997, p. 188). Observation of families at dinnertime reveals that parents do in fact voice these principles. When Daniel, who is 6 years old, attempts to interrupt his 4-year-old sister, his father says to him, "Daniel, can you wait until Tina finishes?" (Blum-Kulka, 1997, p. 154).

Temporizing conversational turn taking is also taught at preschool. When a preschooler calls for the teacher, she replies, "Just a minute, I'm talking to Steven. I'll talk to you in a minute, okay?" (Gearhart & Newman, 1980). When a preschooler interrupts the teacher, she says, "Sorry dear, wait until I've finished speaking" (Gardner & Cass, 1965, p. 58). Children thus learn that everyone must await their turn to speak and that they may not interrupt as others are talking.

Having been instructed in conversational turn taking, children chastise family members as to the need to turn take. When Daniel's older brother asks, "Can I say something? Is it my turn?" Daniel answers, "No! You have to wait until I finish!" (Blum-Kulka, 1997, p. 184). Parents also need to wait till others finish talking (e.g., "I'm trying to talk, mom," Aukrust, 2004, p. 185). When a mother attempts to talk about her work, her 16-year-old daughter says, "I was in the middle of the story"; the mother answers, "Sorry,"[39] thus affirming that she should have waited her turn (Blum-Kulka, 1997, p. 187). A 4-year-old makes this explicit when she tells her father, "I was talking to Mommy. You shouldn't interrupt. That's the rule, Daddy" (Becker, 1988).

This knowledge is applied outside the family as well. Children start to chastise peers as to the need to turn take in conversation. A first grader tells a classmate who is arguing with another girl, "Jameel. And don't talk when someone else is talking please" (Dyson, 1993, p. 139). A 4-year-old who is playing shopkeeper chastises a pretend customer, saying, "I'm talking to her; wait your turn" (Pitcher & Schultz, 1983, p. 45). Indicating her outrage at being interrupted, a 3-year-old chastises a peer, "Wait! I didn't finish my Halloween story . . . . Wait, it's not finished yet" (Paley, 1986, p. 38). In the middle of a discussion, a school child says to a peer, "Dennis, be quiet. Wait your turn" (Selman, Levin, & Brion-Meisels, 1982, p. 88).

The need to wait one's turn in play is similarly taught, both at home and at preschool, as shown in Table 7.12.

Having learned that these are socially acceptable ways of dealing with requests to turn take, children often deploy temporization strategies that avert the need for them to turn take. Delay strategies – such as saying *not yet, not now, in a few minutes* – are acceptable means of averting turn taking and serve to deflect from the force of outright refusals. As well, delaying may actually obviate the need to turn take if the other child gives up waiting, which may well happen when children say, "You can in a minute," "I'm not through yet," and "It's still my turn" (Garvey, 1984, p. 112). As shown in Table 7.13, children start to use such justifications to delay turn taking with both adults and peers.

Garvey (1984) found that temporizing justifications were often in terms of "now" and "not now, later" (e.g., "I'm using it now," "later you can be the Daddy"). Whether they say it explicitly or only implicitly, children use such delay tactics, indicating their understanding that social interaction requires interactants to temporally coordinate their activities.

The problem, though, is that when one is waiting for a desired object or event, time passes more slowly than

[39] Hebrew: "Hayiti be-emça ha-sipur"; "Slixa"

Table 7.13.

	Age	Source
C completed puzzle, adult asks to do it C: "No now I do e it," and redoes it	25 mos.	Bloom (1970, p. 161)
Boy is on wooden car, girl asks for turn B: "I'm doing it right now" Girl asks if she can have it when he's done B: "I'm not finished yet" A few minutes later B: "Now I'm finished" and climbs off the car	32 mos.	Garvey (1984, p. 124)
Boy asks to see girl's car G: "No, not for a couple of months ago, 'cause I wanna see it right now. I have to see it first"	33 mos.	
B: "After you're done, I see it?"	32 mos.	Garvey (1984, p. 148)
Crayoning at preschool C1: "I need . . . yellow one in a minute" C2: "I won't finish for a very long time"	4;11 years	Shields (1979, p. 264)

when one is interacting with a desired object (Miller & Karniol, 1976) so that time perceptions can differ between the one playing and the one waiting to play, resulting in conflict (e.g., "He had them for ten minutes. It's not fair," Pitcher & Schultz, 1983, p. 48). To illustrate, when a girl of 4;6 years wants the scissors she gave her friend, she complains, "She's taking very long with my scissors . . . and I want them now daddy." When her father replies "She'll give them to you in a minute," the child complains, "I want to have them now . . . cos I need them" (McTear, 1985, p. 122). The impetus for the request is the difficulty of coping with the need to wait for one's turn. This difficulty is evident to all concerned. When a teacher asks a child to go get his milk, her assistant replies, "He's only just got those cars, been waiting for ages to get them." The teacher responds, "Oh, well, play for a little while, but then you have to get your milk" (Wood, McMahon, & Cranstoun, 1980, p. 49). As we saw in this chapter, then, parents temporize across many domains of children's lives, requiring children to learn how to cope with delays. How they do so will be addressed in the chapters on Coping and Mind Play.

8 Restricting Children's Preferences

> A 10-month-old shakes a clock. Her mother takes it from her, saying, 'No let's put it back.' When the child starts crying, her mother asks, 'What's the matter? What's the matter? What do you want? What is it that you want? Is it this?'
>
> (reprinted from Lock, 1980, p. 54)

> A child of 3 shows his mother a ladybird and she see his hands are dirty. She says, 'Just look at your hands.... Go wash your hands now.' When he ignores her, she says, 'Go wash your hands now – do as I say.' When he still ignores her, she says, 'Go wash you hands and don't make a mess'; he goes to wash his hands.
>
> (Hall, CHILDES Database)

Parents' external preferences also relate to what their children should not do. Parents attempt to manage children's preferences by restricting, or attempting to restrict, behavior deemed undesirable, and they discipline children when restricted behavior is engaged in against their wishes. In this chapter, I trace how parents express restrictions to their children and the strategies they adopt in attempting to enforce compliance with their expressed restrictions. In Chapter 9, I focus on strategies of disciplining children who have failed to comply with restrictions.

THE PREVALENCE OF RULES

Children's world is full of restrictions and guidelines for interacting with objects and people. Rules, whether explicit or implicit, set limitations on behavior and set up expectations for how others will react to rule-following and rule-breaking behavior. We seldom realize the myriad of rules that guide children's behavior. Mayall (2000) questioned the mother of a kindergartener as to her house rules. She answered, "It's mainly; don't hurt each other. I do mind about that, but they do fight." Her son added, "Not break up the furniture. Not break the windows," at which point, she confirmed, "Yes I do say that. They're not allowed in my room when I'm working, and not working" (pp. 127–128). Her perception was that her rules concerned sibling conflict when in fact, she had a variety of rules concerning objects and space. Smetana, Kochanska, and Chuang (2000) found more than thirty types of rules mothers use with their infants and toddlers, with the number of rules deemed relevant by mothers increasing as children grew older. Ross and her colleagues (1994) identified 15 different rules that govern sibling interaction and Wood and Beck (1994) identified more than 200 rules that two siblings, 9 and 11 years old, cited as regulating their behavior inside their house. An 11-year-old enumerates the domains of her foster parents' decision making, saying, "whether friends can sleep over here or not.... Having a tidy bedroom.... What time you have got to come in at night.... What friends you bother with" (O'Kane, 2000, p. 142). Explaining his problems with his parents, a teen laments, "on top of that we've got that pressure as well, that you're Asian, you can't do this, and that, you can't do this, you can't drink, you can't smoke, you can't do this. You can't eat such and such things... it's like we're tied up in one circle. If we step out of it we're out of line" (Walker, 2004).

As evident above, parents set up rules to guide children's behavior in various spheres of behavior. Dunn and Brown (1991) identified five general domains of parental rules: rights (primarily regarding possessions), positive justice (primarily sharing and turn taking), harm to others (involving both kindness and aggression), destruction (of material objects), and rules of the house (concerning daily routines, politeness, tidiness, and appropriate clothing). Rules of the house proved to be the most prominent issue discussed in both England and the United States with 3-year-olds.

There are also rules for guiding conduct in public places, in schools, and so forth, with some overlap between them. Yet there are also rules uniquely associated with specific settings such as preschool or school, for example, "No fighting. No bringing toys from home to school except for show and tell... no war toys or toy guns" (Tobin, Wu & Davidson, 1989, p. 142). A kindergarten child explains that "you have to learn to walk in the hall and be quiet and don't say any jokes" (Graue & Walsh, 1998, p. 188). When they were asked regarding classroom rules, one child said, "can't come in late, no chewing, no shouting out. If everybody is doing work then you can't even talk – let them get on with the work"; another child added, "No talking, no moving about, no chewing, and just get on with your work" (Hargreaves, Hester, & Mellor, 1975, p. 36, 38). Kantor, Elgas, & Fernie (1989) found almost fifty rules that govern children's behavior at preschool circle time.

Children intuitively expect the same rules to be relevant across different settings so one of their first major tasks is to differentiate rules that are generalizable across contexts from ones that are only applicable in specific settings. Preschool teachers, who serve as the first homogenizing influence with respect to rules, are quick to point out both the similarity and differential applicability of rules at school and at home. As Pool, Shweder, and Much (1983) have so elegantly shown, children themselves pick up the rules governing behavior in preschool. Doing so enables them to note parallels or divergences from home rules, parallels and divergences that are also addressed by preschool teachers. For instance, a teacher tries to restrict a boy's behavior, asking, "Would you do that with a tea towel in your house?" (Jordan & Cowan, 1995, p. 733). She attempts to show the irrelevance of the setting for guiding his behavior. On the other hand, when a preschool teacher says to a 4-year-old, "Every time you go to the bathroom you need to stop and wash your hands," he answers her, "At home I don't." She replies, "What you do at home and what you do at school are two different things" (Meyer, 2003, p. 70). Similarly, a kindergarten teacher says, "We don't talk like that here. If you talk like that at home, that's a different story.... You can do that at home, but not here!" (Mody, 2005, p. 66). This differentiation is further underlined when a teacher instructs children before the weekend, "I want you to scream and yell and run around at home on the weekend so you can get all the energy out so you can work quietly" (ibid, p. 65). At school, one works quietly whereas at home it is legitimate to do otherwise. Similarly, when a teacher says, "In this classroom, Power Rangers are out," a preschool child says, "Power Rangers can be at home" and the teacher retorts, "If your parents say it's OK, that's fine" (Meyer, 2003, p. 83). The importance of such verbal exchanges is not only in their emphasis on the differential applicability of different rules in different contexts but also in their imbuing parents, and mothers in particular, with the power to decide about the rules and restrictions that guide children's behavior at home.

Underlining this point, when reading a book about bunnies at preschool, a child says, "We got a bunny at home.... Can I bring it to school?" the teacher nods and says, "Ask your mother if you can bring it" (Merritt, 1982, p. 257). Similarly, a teacher explains,

> If we find anything that looks like sweets, and we're not sure, we have to go and ask Mummy, don't we?... Oh but you have to ask Mummy. You mustn't eat anything without asking Mummy if it's all right, must you? (Willes, 1983, p. 130)

Mothers are imbued with the power to determine the rules and restrictions at home. In talking of the rules in his house, a 9-year-old explains that "when my mum says do something, you have to do it, not say, No, I don't want to do it" (Mayall, 2002, p. 44). Another 9-year-old further explains, "if my Mum wants to go out and I want to stay in, and we end up going out. I have to do what I'm told" (ibid, p. 118). Parents echo this, saying, "If we said something has got to be done, then it's got to be done – nothing in the world will stop it being done if we say it's going to be" (Newson & Newson, 1976, p. 302).

Concomitantly, though, mothers do not govern or police behavior outside the home – as children themselves are quick to point out. After I told Orren that he is not allowed to drink from glass cups, at age 32;25, he says to me, "We have a cup at preschool that is allowed to drink – not at home allowed to drink"[1] (cf., Pool et al. 1983). Just as mothers function as the restrictive agent at home, teachers serve the same function at school. A 6-year-old acknowledges this, saying, "you have to ask the teacher first, and if she says, No, you can't, then if she says Yes, you can" (Mayall, 2000, p. 130).[2]

Mothers themselves emphasize their power to set up the rules and restrictions applicable at home while at the same time clarifying that these rules may not have universal applicability (e.g., "They might get away with it at school, but not here," Cook-Gumperz, 1973, p. 248). The understanding that home rules do not have universal applicability allows children to capitalize on this differentiation, taking advantage of more lenient rules in different settings. Having been urged to eat with cutlery, a 30-month-old says, "When I go to Grammy's, I'll eat with my fingers" (Reilly, 1986, p. 317). The children of divorced parents often tell one parent that the other parent allows them to engage in behaviors that the more restrictive parent does not allow.

In contrast to the Western world where children intuitively expect the same rules to be applicable at home and elsewhere, in Japan, children are socialized to expect different rules outside the home. Japanese mothers teach such expectations, claiming that the most important thing to teach a child is "Not to cause trouble to other people," *people* being a term used for everyone outside of one's family (Peak, 2001, p. 148). As one mother says, "At preschool he has to follow rules... he was used to pretty much doing what he wanted to at home" (Peak, 1991, p. 148). Yet even in Japan, children's behavior is restricted by rules.

WHY RULES?

Why is children's behavior subject to so many rules? Rules are set up because of presumed preferential conflict. They are established in domains in which there is an assumption that given free reign, people would engage in precisely those behaviors that the rules are set up to control.

[1] Hebrew: "Yesh lanu kos bagan she mutar lishtot – lo babait mutar lishtot"

[2] The fact that the guidelines for behavior at home and at school or elsewhere are different may lead to the differentiation between "the school me" and "the home me." As a 13-year-old girl explains, "when I'm at home I can be myself, but at school I'm supposed to behave and stuff" (Brown, 1998, p. 151).

Unless one assumed preferential conflict, there would be no need to set up rules. Wilson (1974) refers to this in alluding to a sign in a Chinatown meat store that reads: "Do What You Are Supposed To... Not What You Want To" (p. 107). Freud (1913) expresses this pointedly, saying, "there is no need to prohibit something that no one desires to do, and a thing that is forbidden with the greatest emphasis must be a thing that is desired" (p. 69). Rules are set up in those contexts in which children's preferences and the preferences of those around them, especially parents, are likely to conflict. This is evident when a 4-year-old is told, "It's wrong to go in the bushes. You're not supposed to be there," and the child answers, "We like to go in the bushes" (Meyer, 2003, p. 69). Rules are imposed to restrict children's first-order preferences to reduce the potential of recurring conflict with others' first-order preferences and with their external preferences. This is why *ought* rules are generally less prevalent than *ought not* rules; the former do not reflect preferential conflict whereas the latter embody preferential conflict. Rules are necessary because the child's *default* assumption is that in the absence of restrictions, the object or the behavior is allowed. Rules, then, serve to restrict choice.

Parents and society have three relevant concerns here. They want the individual (1) to know what the rules are, (2) to govern his behavior according to the rules, and (3) to understand the basis for the rules, and internalize them rather than adhering to them blindly. The advantage of internalization is that it precludes the need for surveillance and continual threat of sanctions. Whereas parents have the means of verifying rule understanding, society does not have the means of doing so. For society, then, there is a trade-off between investing in methods of surveillance and sanctions versus expounding on the benefits of rule following (cf., Kelman, 1974). This is why, when new laws are passed, governments invest in elaborate advertising campaigns to inform the public as to the benefits of rule adherence (e.g., seat-belt laws). Monitoring and sanctions are in place but the investment in them is markedly lower than in attempts to alter public attitudes. This same trade-off is at play in parental enforcement of restrictions on children's behavior. Parents need to inform children of the rules and injunctions in their home and culture and of the likely outcome of their violation. Parents also need to ensure children's understanding so that they follow rules because of such understanding and subsequent internalization rather than because of fear of sanctions. In promoting such understanding, though, parents need to recognize that restrictions relating to objects and activities fall into several functional categories, as I elaborate below.

FUNCTIONAL CATEGORIES OF RULES

A. Objects

Never – objects that the child is not allowed to touch, has no exposure to parental use, but may have media exposure to (e.g., guns). For instance, talking of guns, a mother says, "I don't want you using a gun." Her child of 4;5 cries, "I wanna use it." The mother responds, "Mommy doesn't want you to play with guns or be close to one. You don't go near a gun" (Eisenberg, 1992, p. 25).

Not Yet – objects that the child is not allowed to touch but sees adults manipulate and can presumably do so himself when older (e.g., knives, plastic bags, razors). A girl of 25;15 who is watching her mother chopping vegetables, says, "Knife sharp. Let me (shaking head for no) Mummy," indicating she is not allowed to touch (Oldenburg, 1990, p. 32). A father tells his preschooler regarding a cigarette lighter, "Don't don't don't ever let me catch you with this. Okay or I'll give you a good spanking" (Clancy, Akatsuka, & Strauss, 1997, p. 36) and regarding matches, "If I see you with matches, I'll give you a spanking" (ibid).

Sometime – objects that the child is allowed to manipulate: under supervision (e.g., scissors), after being warned to be careful (e.g., "Be careful, the knife is sharp!", Wells, 1986, p. 28), after being granted permission (e.g., things that belong to others, "No, no, you can't play with Mommy's card," Carew, 1976, p. 114).

Generally – objects that the child is generally allowed to manipulate, either ones defined as belonging to him (e.g., his toys, books, replica toys) or those defined as belonging to others (e.g., mother's clothes, the preschool's toys, a sibling's or friend's belongings).

Not Here, Not Now – objects that the child is generally allowed to manipulate but are circumstantially limited to him, either because of location (e.g., "you can't take that in there," Halle & Shatz, 1992, p. 96; "Why don't you play with it in the kitchen," Carew, 1976, p. 81) or time (e.g., don't play with it at dinnertime).

B. Activities

Never – activities that the child is not ever allowed to engage in, for example, killing, stealing.

Not Yet – activities that the child sees adults engaging in and which he will presumably engage in when older (e.g., going to work, cooking, shaving, changing light bulbs). Children echo parental restrictions in such contexts, for example, at 31;12, Orren says, "We have electricity there – mummy and daddy don't allow to touch that"[3] and at 32;15, "It is forbidden to touch – only mother and father touch."[4] Children may see their parents engage in these behaviors.

Sometime – activities that the child is allowed to engage in under some circumstances: under supervision (e.g., crossing street), after being warned to be careful (e.g., climbing up on things), or after being provoked (e.g., aggressing).

[3] Hebrew: "Yesh lanu shum xashmal – aba veima lo marshim laggat beze"

[4] Hebrew: "Assur lagaat – rak ima ve-aba nogim"

Generally – activities that the child is generally allowed to and even encouraged to engage in, for example, play, watch TV, talk to people, and help others.

Not Here, Not Now – activities that the child is restricted from performing in certain locations (e.g., "Don't do that in here!" said to a 3-year-old, Dunn & Brown, 1991, p. 163) or times (e.g., "don't watch TV now"). A child of 23 months starts to hammer on the table with a block and is told, "no don't hammer on the table. It's not good for it." After further attempts by the child to hammer on the table and the father's removal of the block from the child's hand, the child asks, "Hammer floor?" and the father answers, "Yes, you can hammer on the floor," and gives him back the block (Wolf, 1982, p. 317).

Here and Now – activities that the child is encouraged to engage in but only at times and locations specified by the parent. For instance, eating, drinking, and having bowel movements are all behaviors parents want their children to restrict to specific times and places.

Only in Pretend – activities that the child is allowed to engage in during pretend play, for example, aggressing, killing, stealing, and putting out fires.

These are the functional categories the child needs to learn in terms of the restrictions in his social world. But he also needs to learn the basis for the functional categories so that when parents restrict his behavior, the child learns to assign the restricted object or activity into one of these categories. To the extent that parents differentiate their explanations for the restrictions being imposed, these categories will be well-differentiated. Otherwise, these functional categories will not be clearly defined for the child, and he will miscategorize objects and activities, leading to preferential conflict with the parent. As we will see later in this chapter, much preferential conflict arises because of miscategorization by the child and not only because of unwillingness to adopt parental preferences.

CLASS ACTION – USING GENERIC *ONE, YOU, WE*

Although one generally thinks of rules as being stated in terms of activities being forbidden (e.g., "No bouncing, no standing, no jumping, no fooling around on the furniture, understand?" Piotrowski, 1997), rules do not have to be stated formally to serve as restrictions. Rather, when rules are expressed they tend to have three characteristics. The first characteristic of rules is that they are generally stated in the simple present tense, which is used to convey common or habitual actions. By expressing rules this way, one implies that the restriction has force beyond the present moment, with roots in the past and continuing into the future. For instance, at 32;22, Karen says, "In the room it's not allowed to draw" and at 3;7 years, Orren says, "It's not allowed to play on the road, it's dangerous, a car can come and hit you in the leg."[5] Use of the present tense conveys their understanding that the restriction is not time-bound; this is always the case. Notice that irrespective of whether household rules or societal rules are expressed, the words *not allowed* convey the force of the restriction.

The second important aspect of such restrictions is that the agent who stands behind the rule is amorphous. The actions are forbidden but the rule is independent of the agent who originally expressed it. This is evident when Karen, at 20;23, says, "Hairbrush not go in the garbage – just paper go in the garbage," conveying her understanding of both the timeless nature of the edict and the irrelevance of whose rule it is.

The impersonal nature of rules leads to their often being expressed with generic pronouns that indicate class action or class inaction. Mulhausler and Harré (1990) discuss four different ways of expressing generic reference to people: using the indefinite pronoun *one* or the personal pronouns, *you*, *we*, or *they*. Using generics extends the realm of individuals who fall under the rule beyond the scope of the persons present and "helps speakers to conceal the subjectivity of their arguments" (ibid, 1990, p. 196). This aspect of generics is useful to parents in conveying the transsituational aspects of those rules they try to get their children to adopt. Importantly, generic pronouns refer to hypothetical others who, like the individual being addressed, need to be concerned with rule following.

Many languages use the third-person singular or plural to indicate the generic nature of rules. Budwig (2002) found that in German, mothers repeatedly use generic agency in instructing their children how things should or should not be done, using the term *Man*, roughly translating as "One." In French as well, *one* is used to express generic agency in stating rules (e.g., "One doesn't throw balloons in the house,"[6] Veneziano, 2001, p. 330). In using the term *one*, although the mother is the one telling the child how and what to do, she phrases her actions in terms of how *one* does things this way rather than in other ways, making it seem that there is a normative basis for her demands. French children appear to understand this use of *one* very early, as evident in the following directives, for example, "(If) one is drinking now, one says 'To your health,'"[7] "one doesn't speak now. One first eats,"[8] the first of these directives being said by a child of 33 months and the second by one of 3;2 years (Schlyter, 2005, pp. 45, 47).

In English, the use of *you* is a more common means of restricting and parents use this means of restricting their children's behavior in many domains. They use *you* to indicate their expectations for how children should behave inside the house, to restrict how children play, eat, and interact with others, with examples of generic *you* shown in Table 8.1.

[5] Hebrew: "Assur lesaxek bakvish – ze mesukan – auto efshar lavo velaten maka baregel*"
[6] French: "On lance pas les ballons dans la maison"
[7] French: "On boit maintenant. On dit 'sante!'"
[8] French: "On parle pas maintenant. On mange d'abord"

Table 8.1.

	Age	Source
C drew on doorway M: "Nicky, y'know you must only draw on paper, only on paper, not on the doorway"	24 mos.	Wootton (1986, p. 151)
C coloring an elephant M: "You don't do elephants red" C says it's blue M: "You don't do elephants blue either" C says it's purple M: "You don't do elephants purple"	30 mos.	MacLure & French (1981, p. 215)
C scribbling in coloring book M: "You colour in the pictures.... Samantha, they're not for drawing on, they for colouring in"	Preschool	Tizard & Hughes (1984, p. 142)
Dinner in a Dutch home M: "You don't eat bread with a spoon. You eat it with a fork, don't you?"	Preschool	Elbers & van Loon-Verwoorn (1998a)
Dinner in an American-Israeli home M: "You don't touch lettuce with your fingers"	12 years	Blum-Kulka (1997, p. 147)
At dinnertime, C says egg is disgusting C2 (older sib): "You don't say disgusting about food"[9]	6 years	Blum-Kulka (1997, p. 205)

What is common to all the above examples is that the mothers are not using *you* to refer to the child being addressed; they are using *you* in a generic fashion, as a "*second*-person exophoric," a pronoun that has no explicit reference within the communicative context (Cook-Gumperz, 1973). The generalized nature of their claim is also evident when mothers combine the use of the generic *you* with the use of generic pronouns that refer to other people, generalizing the applicability of the rule beyond the preferences of the individual imposing the restriction. Examples are shown in Table 8.2, with the generic pronouns italicized.

The parents and teachers above do two things. First, they use the pronoun *you* exophorically, fully expecting the child to understand that it applies to expectations that are applicable to everyone's behavior. Second, they generalize beyond their own preferences, referring to *somebody* and *people* and their preferences, conveying that the restriction does not emanate from their own idiosyncratic preferences. These three characteristics of rules, (1) their phrasing in the present tense, (2) their use of exophoric pronouns, and (3) their allusion to the preferences of generalized others, serve to establish them as desiderata that do not emanate from the person but from society. Notice that rules may also refer to inappropriate ways of enacting a given behavior but they need not necessarily specify the "correct" way of enacting it. It is implicitly assumed that knowing that the current way is inappropriate will guide the child to do it normatively.

English also allows the use of *we* as a generic. The pronoun *we* can be used in several different ways. It can be used to indicate the speaker's unit relationship with one person while serving as an exclusionary tactic toward the person addressed as "you." It can also be used to refer jointly to the person speaking and to the person being addressed in which case it is an *inclusive we*. For instance, referring to a fight, the teacher says to the class, "yesterday we had a little problem between two boys... because all of us have this problem at one time or other" (Mishler, 1972, pp. 286–287). The fight, which was restricted to two boys, has been reinterpreted as a class problem. The exclusionary versus inclusive nature of *you* and *we* is well illustrated in the words of an elementary school teacher who commends her class for the orderly way they walked back from the cafeteria, saying "You people have been doing a very good job," but then adds, "We're still not good about coming back into the room (Mehan, 1979, p. 39).

As well, the *inclusive we* can be used to allude to joint action both in directives ("let's do ...) and in permissives "Can we ... "). Ervin-Tripp (1977) discusses its use in directives as indicating that the addressee is subordinate whereas its use in permissives indicates that the addressee is higher in status. Aronsson and Thorell (2002) found that both preschool and school children used the *inclusive we* in playing doctor more than in playing a parent, suggesting that they understand the status differences involved.

There is also a *royal we* in which the speaker speaks for himself but uses the plural pronoun in doing so. Budwig (2002) found that American mothers tend to use the *royal we* in talking to their infants (cf., Ochs, 1992, as discussed in the chapter on Parenting). For instance, a child is playing with a truck and the mother says, "did it come apart, let's see if we can fix it; there, we fixed it" (Broen, 1972, p. 77). It is the mother who does the seeing and the fixing. She uses the *royal we* to make her child feel included, as if she is referring to joint action and the *inclusive we*. Similarly, a mother talks to her 2-year-old, referring to a newborn, saying, "Shall we give him something to eat first, okay?

[9] Hebrew: "Bixlal lo omrim al oxel mag-eel"

Table 8.2.

	Age	Source
C tickles mother's head M: "That's not where *you* tickle *somebody*" "*You* tickle somebody under the arm"	29 mos.	Bloom (1970)
M: "When *somebody* sneezes *you* say *Bless you*"	Preschool	Becker (1994, p. 141)
C ignores F's question F: "When *people* talk to you they want you to answer them. They don't want *you* to just be quiet. That's not right"	Preschool	Becker (1994, p. 141)
C wants to interrupt book reading T: "Wendy, stop that, you be quiet when *someone* is reading to you"	Preschool	Heath (1986, p. 108)
C trying to dislodge another C from seat T: "You can't pull *people* off their seats. Ask them if they'll move"	Preschool	Paley (1990, p. 81)
C1 was running at preschool, C2 got hurt T: "Someone has been hurt because someone didn't remember the classroom rules"	Preschool	Jordan & Cowan, 1995, p. 739)

Yes – I think so," and she then starts nursing the baby (Schutze, Kreppner, & Paulsen, 1986, pp. 137), clearly not intending for the older child to participate. In the case of restrictions, the use of the *royal we* is more interesting, as when the mother of a 13-month-old who climbs up on a chair says to her, "Laura, no! I thought we made a rule about those chairs" (Carew, 1976, p. 93). The mother does not imply that the child had a voice in determining the rule.

We can also serve what Rastall (2003) calls a "paternalistic" or "condescending" function, being used instead of the second person pronoun *you* in statements or questions that are couched as suggestions for joint action when they in fact serve as restrictives meant to alter the child's behavior, as exemplified in Table 8.3.

In the above, it is children whose behavior is to be restricted but the use of *we* sidesteps the imperative "don't scream" or "stop screaming." The restrictive nature of this use of *we* is evident in the following example. The father of a 23-month-old asks, "Should we go in the bath?" and when his request is rejected, he says "Yes." When the child repeats *no* four times vehemently, the father replies, "Yes, you must go in your bath" (Reeder, 1985 p. 692). The father's original *we* was an attempt to avoid the imperative, but when the child resisted, the father made the attempt to compel the child clear. This is also evident in the following example. A Japanese school teacher tries to get a child to put on his shoes, saying, "Let's put our shoes on, okay?" but when the child does not do so, she rephrases, saying, "Hey, hey. Put *your* shoes on" (Peak, 1991, p. 176, emphasis added).

The more important use of *we* for restrictive purposes is when it is used generically to indicate *people* in general, as shown in Table 8.4.

None of these mothers or teachers means that she and the child are the reference for *we*. As in the case of the generic *you*, the pronouns *everyone*, *no one*, and the noun *people* could all appropriately replace *we* in these contexts since *we* actually could refer to all of humanity in these contexts (cf., Kamio, 2001). This meaning is also conveyed by Japanese mothers' reference to *no one* as a generic group, for example, a child who is pretending to eat a plate, is asked, "no one eat plates, do they?"[10] implying that such behavior is nonnormative (Clancy, 1986). Universalization in the negative sense allows children to refer to what "no one does" or what *people* should not do, for example, "the teacher has to go home . . . nobody sleeps in a school," said by a 3-year-old girl at play (Nelson & Gruendel, 1979). Interestingly, Hebrew allows the pronoun to be dropped entirely, conveying the force of rules generically by using the third-person plural form of the verb; for example, when something he eats falls, Orren, at 32;7, says, "Don't eat off the floor – only take and throw in the garbage."[11]

One can also use *you* in a generic fashion in order to affirm restrictive rules. For instance, a preschool teacher asked her class, "Do you wipe hands on your clothes?" (Meyer, 2003, p. 69), waiting for the children to affirm that one does not do so. Similarly, a first grade teacher in a Hasidic girls' school asks, "Can you say "no" to a teacher?" fully expecting and getting a unified "No" in response (Fader, 2006). Notice that again, this type of question builds on the understanding of *you* as a generic form of stating behavioral expectations that are applicable to everyone.

The problem with rules is that they are often conveyed the same way across domains and irrespective of whether they are context-bound and have no force beyond the immediate confines of the context to which they refer. Consequently, children need to weed out those rules that have trans-situational force from those that do not, those that entail societal responses from those that do not. At times, this is quite easy and children recognize that rules

[10] Japanese: "Osara tabeturu hit inai deshoo?"
[11] Hebrew: "Lo oxlim me-hariçpa – rak lokxim vezorkim lapax"

Table 8.3.

	Age	Source
C is screaming M: "Let's not scream while I'm on the phone"	2;11	Gordon (2002, p. 685)
C refuses to go to bed M: "We wouldn't like to be tired in the morning, would we, so off you go to bed"	Preschool	Cook-Gumperz (1973, p. 142)
C gets up from the table at preschool T: "Yukari, let's stay sitting down, okay?"	Preschool	Peak (1991, p. 134)
C wants to continue drawing T: "We're not doing any more pictures today. You'll do another one tomorrow. All right?"	Preschool	Willes (1983, p. 110)
T: "What must we do when we've finished painting?" Children answer: "Wash our hands"	Preschool	King (1978, p. 55)

are being cited when *you* or *we* is used in a generic fashion. For instance, April's mother (Higginson, CHILDES) says to her "When you're naughty in the car you have to stay home, don't you?" April, who is 35 months, repeats, "Have to stay home." Carol, at 30 months, is playing house with her mother. The mother says, "You have to have sheets on your bed, don't you?" When her child answers "I'm gonna have sheet on baby," the mother says, "That's right, baby has to sleep on sheets" (Warren, CHILDES). The mother's use of "has to" carries imperative force and the implication that some adverse outcome may result otherwise. The mother also uses *you* in a generic fashion, applying the rule not to a particular doll or baby, but to dolls and babies in general.

In the above examples, mothers' use of *you* was generic and it could well be replaced by the pronouns *everyone* and *everybody*. Whereas this use of *you* was quite clear above, this is not always the case. A British mother tells her 4-year-old regarding drawing on a jigsaw puzzle, "You aren't supposed to draw on them, Clare. You should know better. You only draw on pieces of paper. You don't draw on puzzles" (Dunn, 1988, p. 60). Note that the mother's uses of *you* are not coreferential. She uses the pronoun *you* both in a generic fashion, referring to everyone, and as a personal pronoun referring to her child, requiring the child to differentiate between these two divergent uses. Children aren't always able to do so. For instance, a 30-month-old is told by his older brother, "You're not allowed to put knives in your face." The child asks, "Just you?" After seeking further clarification, the older sibling says, "No. Not anybody" (Dunn, 1988, p. 135). Using *you* in a generic fashion serves to contextualize actions in terms of normative or general procedures for doing them rather than as reflecting the idiosyncratic preferences of the speaker. A sophisticated understanding of this is evident as a child of 4;10 years is playing with trucks and trees; he puts a tree on a truck, then puts it next to a house, saying, "He put it on his lorry and planted it in his garden." But then "the traffic lights said. You shouldn't take things from other people's gardens . . . so he said alright . . . and he went and bought one from a shop" (Shields, 1979, p. 261).

As above, it is sometimes difficult in the case of *we* to know whether it is being used as an inclusive pronoun or as a generic one, as evident in the examples shown in Table 8.5.

It is not possible to conclude whether these parents and teachers are referring only to those present or to people generically. Although they may mean the pronoun *we* inclusively, to indicate the immediate family around the table, it is more likely that they are referring to a *generic we*, human beings in general, and intend the rule to have has cross-situational force (cf., Rastall, 2003).

Table 8.4.

	Age	Source
C touches microphone M: "No. That's a wire, right. We don't play with wires, do we?"	16 mos.	Bloom (1973, p. 151)
C puts toy penguin in mouth M: "No. We don't eat penguins, do we?"	Toddler	Howe (1981, p. 78)
C tore up book, M says she's sad M: "We don't tear up books, do we?"	29 mos.	Hart & Risley (1999, p. 104)
C screams at preschool T: "We don't say "Eeee!" do we?"	Preschool	Peak (1991, p. 137)

Table 8.5.

	Age	Source
At dinnertime		
M: "No Per, we don't sit and make a mess with our soup like you"	3;2 years	Aukrust (2002, p. 72)
In preschool		
T: "We don't want to put any more mud on the floor"	Preschool	Gleason & Weintraub (1978, p. 187)
C is singing at dinnertime		
F: "Daniel, we don't usually sing at the table"	School-age	Blum-Kulka (1997, p. 153)
M: "Lena when we eat we sit still in the chair"	5;6 years	Junefelt & Tulviste (1998)

This gets even more confusing because parents not only use *you* and *we* as both personal and generic pronouns in the same sentence, but they also can move back and forth with great agility from using the second-person exophoric to the third-person exophoric. Bloom tries to get her daughter to take her coat off, saying,

> No, we don't eat with a coat on, do we? You have to take your coat off... you know we don't eat with your coat on... you have to take your coat off. "We don't have a snack with our coat on." When her daughter still refuses to take off the coat, she says, "No... let's take the coat off first. That's the rule." That's the rule." (Bloom, 1973, pp. 213–216)

Alluding to a rule makes it clear that generics are involved. What is interesting here, then, is that in the same context, children can be exposed to pronouns referring to them uniquely (e.g., "you spilled it"), to others uniquely (e.g., "Mommy'll get a tissue"), to *you* referring to generic others, and to either an inclusive *we* (e.g., "we'll have some a little later," Bloom, 1973), a *royal we*, or a generic *we*. Children need to figure out whether in using the pronoun *you* or *we*, the person speaking is referring only to those present or to people in general. As Mehan (1979) notes, the same confusion is prevalent in classrooms and "to be competent in the classroom, students must differentiate between these different uses of the same pronoun" (p. 166).

Despite this apparent difficulty, children do in fact acquire the concept of generic others. Oldenburg (1990) cites a child of 27;27, who, after seeing two clowns in a play knocking a hole in the wall, says "People... people... people not allowed knock down walls. People should (shaking head for negative) knock down walls" (p. 32). At 29;22, Orren says, "I behave like that people told me I'm not a good boy"[12] – roughly translating as "if I do that, people will say I'm not a good boy." Similarly, asked about telling the truth, a 7-year-old boy says, "because if you always tell the truth people will come to trust you" (Robinson & Strawson, 1972b, p. 317). When a peer refuses to share, a preschooler says "Miser. Later on people won't give you things either" (Kyratzis & Guo, 2001, p. 58). The generic concept of a society that is made up of people who react to one's behavior is evident in these statements. As well, in making such statements children acknowledge the force that generic others' preferences have in guiding and restricting both their own and others' actions.

[12] Hebrew: "Ani etnaheg kaxa anashim amru li ani lo yeled tov"

USING IMPERATIVES

Imperatives, rather than statements specifying rules, tend to be used when rules are violated and parents want to stop children's behavior in midstream. For instance, the mother of a toddler who's putting a finger in a cup, yells, "Do not put your finger in it" (Tulviste, 2003) and a child who is shouting is told, "Don't make so much noise" (Whiting & Edwards, 1988). Although imperatives are generally stated as *don't*, imperatives stated in the affirmative can still convey restrictions. For instance, while on a bus with her son, a mother wants to read a magazine. When he asks her questions, she says, "be quiet now and play with your cars"; when he keeps talking to her, she says, "Sit down and let me read, there's a good boy" (Tough, 1976, p. 27). In both cases, the mother avoids telling him what not to do, that is, not ask her questions or talk to her, and instead tells him what he should do. Similarly, in a preschool, when a teacher says, "Tory, go over to the sand table" (Kontos, 1999), she is restricting his choice to do something else.

Imperatives have been differentiated (e.g., Harsanyi, 1976) into *advices* and *demands*: demands are imperatives conducive to the speaker's own ends (e.g., "don't disturb me") whereas advices are imperatives conducive to the ends of the addressee (e.g., "don't run in the street"). Yet a third type of imperative refers to the outcome to others, what Whiting and Edwards (1988) found prevalent in many societies and called prosocial demands: "Don't play on your brother's bed," "Don't pull the dog's tail," where neither the addressee nor the speaker is the direct beneficiaries of the action in question. Yet another type of prosocial demand has the general public as its beneficiary (e.g., "Don't let the dog out without a leash"). These different types of imperatives have not been differentiated in terms of children's understanding of them. One might expect that children's compliance may well reflect their understanding of who the beneficiary of the restricted action is. They may well choose to comply with restrictions with themselves as beneficiaries prior to ones that have the speaker as beneficiary, with the latter being complied with prior to ones in which either a third party or the general public is the beneficiary. Nonetheless, children's ability to cite the many rules that guide their behavior in various contexts undergrid the prevalence of imperatives of all these types in children' lives.

On the other hand, parents are often reluctant to issue imperatives. Imperatives are mitigated, especially in the contexts in which there is no apparent urgency to stop the child's behavior. One way of mitigating is by using *please* (e.g., a mother who wants her child to stop watching television, says, "Sandy, turn the TV off please," Wilson, Cameron, & Whipple, 1997). Using the child's name either before or after issuing the imperative similarly serves to mitigate the force of the imperative (e.g., a preschool teacher who says, "Elise, use your walking feet," or "Put the caps back on the markers, Jana," Kontos, 1999). A related means of mitigating imperatives is by using diminutives and nicknames in addressing the child. A mother whose son refuses to eat warns him that she will hit him unless he sits down. When he objects to being hit, she replies, "sit down, you have to eat.... you have to eat Jorgito,"[13] using the diminutive of his name, Jorge (Cicourel, 1978, p. 278). Combining both the diminutive of the child's name and *please* softens the impact of imperatives even further. For instance, an Israeli father asks his child to leave the bicycle alone, using the diminutive "Ranilé," rather than "Rani," saying, "Ranilé, please leave the bike"[14] (Blum-Kulka, 1997, p. 147). A Swedish mother combines all of these and says, "Listen sweet little darling, would you please finish your food Rebecca" (De Geer, Tulviste, Mizera, & Tryggvason, 2002). Blum-Kulka found that about 45 percent of direct requests addressed to children by their parents at dinnertime were mitigated.

Using justifications for why the imperative is being issued also serves to mitigate. For instance, Bloom says to her daughter as she is crushing a paper cup, "Oh, don't break up the cup, we won't be able to have more juice" (Bloom, 1973, p. 196). Rather than simply telling her daughter to stop, she provides a justification for doing so, a justification that carries implications for the daughter's preferences to drink more juice. As I discussed in Chapter 5, not all mothers provide such justifications. When a child of 20 months says, "I wanna turn the TV on," her mother replies, "No, you can't turn on the TV" (Hart & Risley, 1999, p. 105), offering no rationale as to why. In contrast, when a 24-month-old whines that she wants to go out like her brother, her mother offers to put on a record for her, explaining "You see, your nose is dripping and you have a little cold, so you'll be staying in" (Carew, 1976, p. 95).

[13] Spanish: "Sienta te, debes comer ... debes comer Jorgito"
[14] Hebrew: "ta'azov et haofnayim"

USING QUESTIONS AND DECLARATIVES TO RESTRICT BEHAVIOR

Rather than issuing imperatives, questions can be used as restrictives, serving to mitigate the force of imperatives. This can be done by simply adding a tag question to an imperative, for example, a mother who asks her 4-year-old "Sweetie, stop that please, OK?" (Blum-Kulka, 1997). Weizman (1989) argues that parents use hints, often in the form of questions, rather than directives in attempting to restrict children's behavior. In this vein we get mothers' questions of the following sort: "How come you get everything so dirty?" and "When are you going to learn to put your shoes on yourself?" (Holzman, 1972, p. 320). Despite being phrased as questions, the above are statements of the mother's preferences, that the child keep clean, that he put on his shoes by himself, and so forth. Similarly, instead of telling a child to be quiet, a kindergarten teacher asks, "Cory, who is talking now?" and when the child answers *You*, she continues, "then listen please" (Graue & Walsh, 1998, p. 171). Schieffelin and Eisenberg (1984) found that the Kaluli often use questions to control children's behavior, calling attention to actions or utterances that the mother considers inappropriate, for example, "who gave it to you?" literally means "it's not yours to take."

Do children understand such questions as implying parental preferences? Apparently yes. Weizman (1989) gives an example of a mother who says to her child who is watching a movie on TV, "Haven't you seen it at least twice?" This question could be interpreted as demanding a real answer (e.g., "Yes, I have"). But in fact, it is viewed as a directive meant to restrict behavior, with the child answering, "O.K., I'm going to do my homework" (p. 78). He understood the question as a means of getting him to stop doing what he was doing and engage in an alternative behavior.

But such questions are not always understood as directives. Gumperz (1982) cites a mother talking to her 11-year-old who wants to go out in the rain and asks him, "Where are your boots?" Her son interprets this as a literal question rather than as a directive and answers, "In the closet." The mother, who had assumed the child would interpret the question as a directive, replied, "I want you to put them on right now" (p. 135), clarifying that she was using the question as a means of getting the child to put on boots.

Declaratives can also be used to specify restrictions. This can be done either directly or indirectly. A preschool teacher says to a child, "That is not a paper cup," implying that children are not to handle glass. This implication is borne out when she takes the glass away from the child, saying, "No, that's just for snack time when the teacher is at the table." But it is clear that the child interpreted the teacher's declarative statement as a restriction even before it was elaborated because in response, the child whimpered, "I want to put it down" (Shweder & Much,

Table 8.6.

	Age	Source
Getting ready for preschool M: "it's time for you to get your shoes on baby" C ignores her M: "Will you please go get your shoes on please" C ignores her M: "Would you please go and get your shoes and socks on?" C does	3 years	Hall (CHILDES)
Family at dinner C comes down without a shirt F: "Mark could you wear a shirt. . . ." C ignores him, sits down F: "Mark could you wear a shirt please" C ignores him F: "Could you wear a shirt please?" C: ignores him F: "Could you go up and put a shirt on?" C leaves the table and goes upstairs F: "Thank you"	5;7 years	MacWhinney (CHILDES)

1987). Hence, the statement had the force of a command, "Put that glass down!" Similarly, when a teacher says "My rug doesn't like (children's snacks)" the implication is that children should not be eating there (Mody, 2005, p. 58). As an example of an implied restriction, after her child throws papers on floor, the mother says, "You know I happen to be cleaning up. I'm cleaning up, Felicia" (Schachter, 1979, p. 137); despite the fact that the mother is making a statement as to what she is doing, the implied meaning is that the child should not engage in her current behavior. Similarly, in the context of being badgered by an 11-year-old whose request to watch television she refused, the mother finally says, "this I have heard already four times" (De Geer et al., 2002), meaning that the child should stop badgering her. Finally, in this context, a kindergarten teacher says, "Math table, less talking and more working!" (Mody, 2005, p. 62), avoiding the imperative, both for restricting talking and for channeling continued work.

RULE REPETITION

Parental reluctance to deploy their power is also evident in a strategy I call *rule repetition*, simply repeating restrictions and instructions until they are followed. Several examples are shown in Table 8.6.

In the above examples, the parents' message is expressed with minor variations until the child indicates his compliance in some way. Importantly, these parents are evidencing remarkable patience with their children's noncompliant behavior. The child in each of these cases does not reject the parent's request but ignores it, as if the parent had not expressed his preference to the child. Under such circumstances, repetition is a way of making the child "hear" what is being requested. Once the child "heard" the request, he took steps to comply.

Repetition does not always suffice or succeed in getting children to comply. Children can refuse to heed parental requests, insisting on their own preferences being fulfilled instead. Whereas parents' power position within the family enables them to have their way, parents often defer to the child's preferences, choosing to avert head-on conflict with their children when they are unsuccessful in getting the child to do what they want. Parents admit that they are not good at standing their own ground (e.g., Newson & Newson, 1968) and language diary studies show that this is often the case. Mark, at 27 months, was trying to get up to see out the window. His mother said, "No, leave the curtain." Mark answered, "Oh up please." The mother repeated, "Leave the curtain please." Mark answered "No," at which point the mother repeated, "Leave the curtain Mark!" He again answered "No," and went on to explain why he wanted to look out. The mother then relinquished her request for him to leave the curtain (Wells, 1985).

In parent–child research, the common finding is that the majority of cases of preferential conflict are not resolved but come to a stand-off and are dropped, with parents relinquishing their requests (e.g., Eisenberg, 1992). Yet even when parents do not succeed in getting their children to heed repeated requests, children may still learn the restrictions that parents wish to impose. At 26:21, on being told to get off the sofa, Orren says, "I don't want to get down." When the request is repeated, he says, "I don't have to get down." At this point, the issue was dropped. However, he had learned that the sofa was "off limits" because, at 28;9, he says, "Daddy doesn't allow me to get on the sofa."[15] Nevertheless, this knowledge did not translate into avoidant behavior. Using the sofa as a play space the same day, he got hurt by falling off the sofa. When he

[15] Hebrew: "Ani lo roçe laredet" . . . "Ani lo xayav laredet"; "Abba lo marshe' li laalot al hasapa"

was asked how it happened, he said, "I played wildly on the sofa."[16] The point being made here is that even though parents may not follow through with their own restrictions, stating the restrictions repeatedly does seem to work in terms of children's being able to verbalize the restrictions, if not follow them.

PARENTAL COMPROMISE

There are occasions when parents realize that the current preferential conflict is one that cannot be resolved in the direction of their preferences being fulfilled. As one mother explains, "nine times out of ten I end up doing it because it's just not worth the hassle of arguing" (Ribbens, 1994, p. 111). In fact, language diary studies show that this is often the case. During a bath a child, at 15;9, waves his arms and says "darg," to which his mother replies, "not now." He repeats the word, waving his arms and making it impossible for his mother to continue bathing him. She says, "Oh, all right then!" She goes out and returns with a toy dog, gives it to the child, and the bath continues peacefully to its end (Lock, 1980, p. 19). Similarly, a mother explains that when her preschooler asks for sweets, she sometimes gives in, "if I know that a sweet will keep her quiet" (Charles & Kerr, 1988, p. 100). With older children, parents may choose to offer a compromise solution that averts the need to escalate the conflict and partially fulfills the preferences of both parties (e.g., Eisenberg, 1992). As an instance of parental compromise, a father says to his kindergarten-age child, "Can I ask you a favor Margaret? Can you take the fork instead of your fingers?" The child repeats twice, "I hate the fork." Her father relents, saying, "Why don't you finish that piece with your fingers and then use your fork from now on" (Davidson & Snow, 1996, p. 230). The father compromises his preferences. Notice as well that he does not express his preference as an imperative; taking the fork is presented as a favor to the father, making noncompliance an act of "not being nice to dad" rather than an act of defiance. Wootton (1997) similarly describes a situation in which his 29-month-old daughter Amy tries to persuade him to play with toy animals, and he says, "it's – no it's too late to start playing – now it's – it's – time to be thinking of bed now" (p. 154). When she repeats, "play with them," he compromises, saying, "Well we'll have one game . . . one quick game with them. Right?" (p. 154).

Yet parents may resist compromises because they fear that children will take advantage of their "softness," saying things like: "You give in to them once you'll have it everyday you know what I mean?" and "If you give them an inch they'll take a mile" (Cook-Gumperz, 1973, pp. 147, 142). Parental unwillingness to compromise is a function of how parents view their role and the importance they assign to the domain and the issue of conflict.

Compromises can be negotiated in an anticipatory manner in order to avoid conflict. For instance, a father is speaking with his 7-year-old about an amusement park, saying, "We're going to pick a weekend to go," and then asks, "Remember the deal with made about Six Flags?" and the child answers, "That I would only have to ride one of the things with you that I wanted to" (Warren, CHILDES). Compromises are often negotiated with older children, with parents offering their children "deals" and compromises (e.g., Palan & Wilkes, 1997), such as "you pay half and I'll pay half."

RESTRICTING BY INVOKING PREFERENCES

Restrictions are often expressed in terms of the restricting agent's own preferences. When a 13-month-old is playing near the fireplace, his mother picks him up, saying, "Come on, I don't want you playing there" (Lock, 1980, p. 97). Referring to a toy pipe, a mother says to her toddler, "but I don't want you to put it in your mouth." When the child persists, she says, "but honey I don't want you to put it in your mouth," and still later the mother says, "honey, mommy doesn't want you to put that in your mouth though" (Broen, 1972, p. 82). The parent engages in repetition and invokes her preferences as the reason for why the child should comply. In a more extreme case, the mother both commands the child and states what she doesn't want, saying, "Now shut up, I don't want to hear another word" (Newson & Newson, 1976, p. 298).

Teachers also tend to cite their own preferences, both positive and negative, as ways of restricting children's behavior. Some examples are provided in Table 8.7.

Notice that in some of these cases, the teachers indicated what they wanted children to do – doing so while referring to themselves in the third person (e.g., Staton, 1993). Even in attempting to mediate between children, contexts wherein the adult's preference is not an issue, adults may attempt to restrict children's behavior by expressing their own preferences. After a child annoyed a peer, the teacher said, "leave John alone . . . I don't want you bothering him . . . . Would you please leave him alone?" (Genishi & Di Paolo, 1982). Whereas the context is one that could be used for moral teaching, it is misconstrued by the teacher and her own preferences are invoked.

Mothers similarly invoke their own preferences in such contexts. A mother who is attempting to get older siblings to play with a younger one, says, "I don't want you to be mean to her" (Shure & Spivack, 1978, p. 112). A child who grabs a doll from a peer is told, "Mommy doesn't want you to act like that when you have company" (Shure & Spivack, 1978, p. 125). Sports coaches likewise refer to their own preferences. In this spirit, a baseball coach says to his team, "I don't want any monkeying around out there, I want no talking to them . . . " (Fine, 1987, p. 70).

Parents and teachers can also attempt to restrict children's behavior by indicating what the parents do, or do not, like or prefer. This can be done either subtly or explicitly, as shown in Table 8.8.

Presumably, such statements of adult preference should serve to guide and restrict children's future behavior.

[16] Hebrew; "ani lishtolel al hasapa"

Table 8.7.

	Age	Source
Positive Preferences		
T: "Now then I want you to. . . ."	Preschool	Sinclair & Coulthard (1975)
T: "Ms. Lane wants you to get your crayons and close your box"	Preschool	Staton (1993, p. 159)
T: "Martin, raise you hand to give other people a chance to think. That's why I want you to raise your hand to give other people a chance to think"	Grades 1–3	Mehan (1979, p. 101)
Negative Preferences		
T: "You cannot come in here with mud on your shoes. I don't want mud in here. This is a clean classroom and it's going to stay clean"	Kindergarten	Mody (2005, p. 58)
T: "I don't want to see anybody off their seats"	School	Torode (1976, p. 185)
T: "I don't want any rubbish on the floor"	Preschool	King (1978, p. 109)
T: "Now this is a lovely new book and I don't want to see it left on the floor for people to walk all over"	Preschool	King (1978, p. 109)

Rather than using themselves as the restricting agent, third parties can be invoked as the restricting agent who does or does not want or like children to do certain things, what King (1978) calls *reference control*. In this vein, the mother of a 20-month-old tells him, "I don't think Jane wants you to climb up on her desk, Kate" (Ninio & Snow, 1996, p. 164). Absent fathers are often invoked this way; it isn't Mommy, but absent Daddy, who restricts the child's behavior. This allows mothers – or fathers – to portray themselves as the good guys who are simply voicing the more restrictive and potentially punishing parent's preferences, for example, "I'm going to tell your father on you when he comes!" (Widdowson, 1979, p. 71) and "Don't say no to me. Your dad'll see to you" (Tough, 1973, p. 32). A mother who does not want to deal with a child's infractions says, "sometimes I fall back on the old dodge of telling him when his father gets home he will deal with him" (Sears, Maccoby, & Levin, 1957, p. 379). Grandparents can also be invoked this way. When a boy chews on a blind cord, his mother says, "I don't think Nana wants her blind cord chewed" (Cloran, 1989, p. 135). In line with this, Clancy (1986) found that Japanese mothers use third parties, especially grandparents, as authority figures, thereby "distancing themselves from actual imperative" (p. 234). The mother anticipates that the respect the child feels for the grandparent and the imagined anger of the grandparents will make the child comply. Teachers may invoke the school principal in the same fashion, for example, "Now, nice and quietly down the corridor. You know Mrs. Brown does not like noisy children" (King, 1978, p. 52).

Interestingly, children themselves also invoke third parties this way. For instance, an older sibling complains to her mother about what her younger sibling is doing to the dog, saying, "If Daddy was here, he wouldn't do that" (Wells, 1986, p. 75). Similarly, a child tries to stop a peer's behavior, saying, "if the counselor were here *you* would be plenty scared" (Selman, Levin, & Brion-Meisels, 1982, p. 85). This seems a fruitful issue to pursue empirically.

IF–THEN CONTINGENCIES

If–then statements specify contingencies between antecedents and consequences. In some cases, the contingency referred to describes how the world is structured, reflecting the usual state of affairs that follows when a given antecedent occurs, with this antecedent not being a human action (though it may be mediated by humans). For instance, pulling a light cord turns the light on or off, opening the screen door allows mosquitoes to come into the house, and leaving ice cream out makes it melt. I call such contingencies *externally mediated* ones and they can be described as: "If you/I do x, y inevitably happens." The consequent is a physical regularity. Its occurrence is more or less stable and predictable, barring unforeseen circumstances – the light may not work, there may be no mosquitoes around. When a 3-year-old says, "And the ice cream was all soft 'cos we forgot to put it in the fridge" (Tough, 1977, p. 55), the statement recognizes the contingency between putting things in the refrigerator and the inevitable outcome of leaving ice cream out – unless one is living in Arctic conditions. Similarly, in discussing groceries in the refrigerator, a 30-month-old says, "If you don't put them in for very long they won't get staled" (Bowerman, 1986, p. 393). Going outside when it is raining results in getting wet, not going out prevents this consequent. This is understood by Bowerman's daughter, at 25 months, as reflected in her statement, "I don't want go outside 'cause I get wet in my diapers and in my shirt" (Bowerman, 1986, p. 291). She understood the contingent nature of the consequent, getting wet and indicated her preference to avert it by preventing the antecedent from occurring. In this vein, when two preschoolers are playing house, the pretend child yells at the pretend mother, "Nobody send children out when it's raining . . . you don't know how to be a mother at all" (Tulviste & Koor, 2005).

When the consequent is intrinsic and there is one-to-one correspondence between the antecedent and the consequent, the child does not need for others to be prophets

Table 8.8.

	Age	Source
C asks M to open up powder box M: "Oh Mickchen! You know how I hate for the powder to be open"[17]	18 mos.	Miller (1979)
C pretends to be firing a gun M: "Guns again. Why Maachan? Mama already doesn't like guns", i.e., is tired of them[18]	28 mos.	Clancy (1986, p. 244)
M: "I'd rather you made less noise darling"	Preschool	Bernstein (1971)
T: "I could do with a bit of silence . . . I don't like this chattering away . . . . Look, I'd prefer it if you belted up"	School	Stubbs (1976, p. 160)

of the apocalypse who forewarn of the consequent. If the same outcome occurs each time the antecedent occurs (e.g., if every time I turn the tap, water comes out), experience exposes the intimate tie between the antecedent and the consequent. Infant toys are generally manufactured in ways that ensure such one-to-one correspondence between the infant's own actions and the consequent (e.g., noise). Children's first experience with intrinsic "if–then" contingencies occurs in the context of toy play (cf., Karniol, 1989). The infant learns that if he pulls the string of a toy, it starts to move and make music. Subsequent pulls on the string are aimed at making the toy respond. More generally, children learn that pulling strings, pushing buttons, and shaking objects can make things happen. Children evidence much joy at this discovery and engage in repetitive actions that savor it. When they are old enough to comment about the contingency, they do so. A child of 24 months explains: "hold e handle, puppy dog go wuff-wuff" (Bowerman, 1986, p. 295). When the antecedent–consequent relationship is discontinued for some reason, as when a toy breaks, children often become distraught, providing evidence for their understanding of intrinsic contingency. When Allison, at 22 months, squeezes a rubber pig to make it say "oink," she turns it over, saying "no oink," and her mother says, "It didn't make a noise when you squeezed it, did it? Well, it doesn't sweetie. That pig doesn't say oink oink" (Bloom, 1973, p. 245).

The second type of contingency, *self-induced outcomes*, is one that can be described as "if I do x, y could happen to me." The consequents again can be either positive or negative and it is the negative ones that are especially problematic. For instance, if I run, I could fall; if I go into the street, I could get hit by a car; the consequents are not guaranteed but they do have some probability associated with them and they are aversive; the likelihood of their happening could be averted by not engaging in the antecedent behavior. A mother warns her child who is trying to cope with shoe laces that are too long, "Don't pull your laces. You might break them. All you need to do is tie them and then they won't be so long" (Hart & Risley, 1999, pp. 161–162). The consequent is only probabilistic but the conditional specifies what can be done to avert this consequent. To the extent that parents are aware of the fact that a given consequent only has a probabilistic relation with the antecedent, they need to specify the antecedent and the consequent as well as to indicate the steps that can be taken to either promote or avert the consequent. Parents may engage in only the first of these steps, only the second of these steps, both of these steps, or neither. When children indicate how to avert consequents that are probabilistically associated with antecedents, they have clearly been instructed in both steps.

Yet contingencies are often conveyed to children as guaranteed rather than in probabilistic terms. This is especially the case with respect to the prudential domain (Nucci, 2004) in which behaviors need to be avoided because they could be harmful to the child. In the prudential domain, parents may want their children to avoid these consequents, making it seem that these consequents are inevitable or nearly inevitable. When Allison indicates she wants to make a tower fall over, her mother says, "If you knock this tower over, honey, you'll spill the juice and that's not a good idea" (Bloom, 1973, p. 254). The mother states the consequent as an inevitable one – she does not indicate its probabilistic nature – there is some probability that the juice will not spill; moreover, she does not take preemptive measures (e.g., moving the juice) to avoid this possibility.

One interesting domain in which probabilistic outcomes are converted by parents into guaranteed ones is the domain of weather-appropriate clothing. The consequence of wearing inappropriate clothing is not phrased probabilistically; getting colds and being sunburned are presented as inevitable consequents, both by parents and by children, as shown in Table 8.9.

Both adults and children, then, present these preemptive measures as having one-to-one correspondence with the consequent so that if the antecedent occurs, the consequent is eliminated.

When the consequents do occur, parents appear to be omniscient prophets – "I told you that's what would happen!" Teachers are also prophetic in this context. A child

[17] German: "Ach Mickchen! Das weisst du doch, dass ich das hasse, wenn der Puder offen ist"

[18] Japanese: "Mata tep. Nani de Maachan? Teppo wwa moo mama iya da ne. Iati ne"

Table 8.9.

	Age	Source
M: "I wish you'd put your overalls on. I'm afraid your legs are gonna get cold"	32 mos.	Hart & Risley (1990, p. 161)
O: "I won't be sick because I put on shoes"[19]	33;4 mos.	Karniol (Diary, Orren)
C1 pretend playing doctor, patient C2 opens window C1 closes it C1: "You can't.... Else you'll get a worser cold...'cos it's windy today"	4;2 years	Shields (1979, p. 256)
M: "Do you need your coat?.... You going in the garden?.... Well, if you go in the garden come and get your coat okay...'cos I don't want you ill as well"	10 years	Sealey (2000, p. 147)

of 3;5 years comes to tell the teacher that another child is crying. The teacher says, "I know he's crying. He fell down because we told him not to run and he wasn't listening and he fell down" (Aukrust, 2001a, p. 71). Post hoc specification of possible antecedents of adverse outcomes may seem as prophetic to children. When a 3-year-old complains that she got hurt, her mother explains, "That's because you weren't watching what you were doing!" (Dunn & Brown, 1991, p. 163). A baseball coach on whose team a child's head got seriously hurt by a bat explained that it was the child's own fault for not wearing a helmet (Fine, 1987).

But parents and teachers do sometimes convey the probabilistic nature of consequents. For instance, when her son of 4;9 years wants to use a grater, the mother warns, "You can tear your finger if you're not careful"; when he questions her, she explains, "you can catch it on the sharp part and scrape the skin off" (Wells, 1986, p. 54). Warren (CHILDES) recorded George, at 4;11 years, talking with his father about a creek close to their house, with the father saying,

> There might be some water moccasins around here. That's one reason Mommy doesn't want you to go down around the creek. She's afraid there might be some snakes back there. And she doesn't want you get bit, by a snake.

Similarly, when a Polish child of 3;7 years is playing with a electric plug, his mother admonishes him, "You mustn't do that Jasiu!" When he is undeterred and asks why, he is told that it could give him an electric shock. When he again asks why, he is told, "Electricity is very powerful. It could even kill" (Przetacznik-Gierowska & Ligeza, 1990). The consequent is stated as probabilistic rather than as inevitable.

Yet because the aversive consequents involved in prudential behaviors are not inevitable, it is difficult for children to abstract the relation between the antecedent and the consequent. Parents need to spell out the possible consequents. After Allison, at 22 months, hurts herself on a truck, her mother says, "It's sharp. So you have to be careful" (Bloom, 1973, p. 252). Being hurt by the toy is not an inevitable consequent but one that can be averted by taking appropriate measures. A child of 21 months is standing on a table to look out the window, and his mother says, "Mind you don't fall" (French & Woll, 1981, p. 176). If one stands up on things, one can fall so one needs to be careful. Crying because she fell off a chair, a child is told, "An' when you stand up on things Angela you must be very careful where your feet are" (Wootton, 1986, p. 150). Potential danger is everywhere and one needs to be careful so as to avoid self-harm.

It is precisely in these domains that children are given no freedom to choose. Parents convert the probability of danger into guaranteed danger, offering children no choice about injuring themselves (e.g., Hart & Risley, 1999). Nucci and Smetana (1996) found that mothers indicated that they give their children choice over personal issues such as play activities, playmates, food, and clothes but set limits on choice when actions counter social conventions or pose risks to the child or to others. When a child of 4;7 years asks to play with the tape recorder, her father answers, "Not when you're in the tub. That's dangerous" (Sachs, CHILDES). A Russian mother tells her child of 27 months "If the mother says you can eat those berries, it means you can pick them up and eat them, and if she says you cannot, it means you can die" (Kiebzak-Mandera, 2006, p. 324). The nature of the danger is spelled out and parents justify such restrictions by specifying the safety concerns that guide them.

In some homes, safety concerns are predominant and serve as justifications for why certain antecedents are to be avoided. As a grown woman says about her own childhood, "I couldn't have roller skates because you might fall and get hurt, you couldn't have a bike for the same reason, you couldn't go out on the streetcar because some bad man might molest you" (Cohler & Grunebaum, 1981, p. 81). A woman suffering from chronic schizophrenia said that her father always warned her that she must not go out because someone will kidnap her, "the big bad wolf will come after me – the world is full of big bad wolves" (Laing & Esterson, 1990, p. 62). Her father believed that the neighborhood was "infested by gangs of marauding youths" and that it was unsafe for a young woman to go any distance alone.

[19] Hebrew: "Ani lo eheye xole ki ani naalti naalaim"

Table 8.10.

	Age	Source
C is asked if he wants to climb up C: "I too big to climb on my plate. I *might* fall and cry"	25 mos.	Bowerman (1986, p. 291)
C on top of a jungle gym C: "Sit here. Fall down"	28 mos.	Reilly (1986, p. 317)
Prior to crossing street with mother C: "If Christy don't be careful, she *might* get runned over by a car"	32 mos.	Bowerman (1986, p. 299)
O gets into car O: "If I not sitting with a belt, I *can* bump the head in the window"	3;3 years	Karniol (Diary, Orren)
C: "I'm holding on very tight, because I *might* fall off if I don't hold tight. If you fall off the ambulance comes to take you to the hospital because you're hurt"	Preschool	Tough (1976, p. 87)

Children's language reflects their understanding of the probabilistic nature of the consequents in many contingencies as well as their awareness of how they can avert the consequent. Some examples are shown in Table 8.10.

These statements reflect children's understanding of the consequent as probabilistic and their knowledge of alternative actions that can avert this probabilistic adverse outcome.

Other-mediated contingencies are ones in which the antecedent is the child's behavior and the consequent is a response undertaken by another person, usually the one who specifies the contingency. Parentally mediated *if–then* contingencies have been described as being of two types: *Desirable leading to Desirable* and *Undesirable leading to Undesirable* (e.g., Clancy, Akatsuka, & Strauss, 1997). In the first instance, parents specify a consequent that is desired by the child in response to desirable behavior exhibited by the child; in the second instance, parents specify a consequent undesired by the child in response to an undesirable behavior by the child (e.g., "If he's doing something and I want him to stop I would probably say "Well you don't get any sweets tomorrow," Charles & Kerr, 1988, p. 101). Yet in both cases, the contingency is set up because of the assumption that children have preferences that are different from those of their parents in the specified domain and that only by specifying a contingency between the antecedent behavior and subsequent parental action could such preferences be impacted. To the extent that the consequent is one the child prefers to obtain, the antecedent is likely to be undertaken. To the extent that the consequent is one the child prefers to avoid, he has an interest in averting its occurrence (e.g., "Come on eat your breakfast now, or I will get mad. *I will get mad Peter*," Grieshaber, 2004, p. 139). Higgins (1998) has discussed individuals as being promotion-focused versus avoidance-focused, suggesting that parental socialization strategies tend to emphasize one of these poles at the expense of the other. What is important from the current perspective is that *if–then* contingencies pit parental preferences against children's preferences and are used by parents to restrict their children's behavior.

Socialization agents may specify only partial contingencies, telling the child the "if" but leaving the "then" unspecified. This may happen because the parent thinks the child knows the contingency and does not want to repeat it. At other times, this is the case because the parent does not really intend to make any contingent response when the antecedent condition does not get fulfilled. For instance, a mother tells two siblings of 32 months and 4 years, "Guys, I'm gonna say three and then you better be out from under the bed. One. Two" (Hart & Risley, 1995, p. 83). She doesn't specify what will happen if they do not emerge from under the bed, perhaps assuming that they know. Similarly, a mother tells her son, "I said if you wanted to stay in the kitchen you had to remain quiet" (Beals, 1993, p. 507); here again, the mother does not specify what will happen otherwise. A father tells a child of 23 months who is using a block to hammer on the table, "You can use it if you don't hammer with it" (Wolf, 1982, p. 317). Harris and Núñez (1996) found that preschoolers understand that contravening such contingencies implies naughtiness.

Contingencies need not be stated in *if–then* terms, as illustrated in Table 8.11.

These mothers are not specifying the possible consequents of continuing the specified activity. In fact, though, mothers often cite children's awareness of what is likely to happen when contingencies are underspecified; as one mother says, her child "knew that if I counted to three before he responded I would spank" (Prusank, 1993, p. 141). Allusions to such knowledge are not restricted to toddlers. Yet parents report that with some children, counting, even in the absence of contingency specification, works (e.g., Backett, 1982).

Similar underspecification of contingencies often occurs in the context of school settings. A teacher warns her students, saying "Dean and Neil, I shan't tell you again to turn round and sit up please, Come on, sit up please" (Willes, 1983, p. 111). Similarly, a teacher at preschool said to the children, "I'm going to count to three, and by then I want you at the door," and "I'm going to count to two, and you'd better be back over here" (Meyer, 2003, pp. 78, 82). The children presumably know what the consequents are

Table 8.11.

	Age	Source
M: "Don't shout or I won't give it to you" M: "No, banging won't produce it"	14 mos.	Bruner (1983, p. 97)
C is crying M: "Sandy, the crying doesn't work so stop it"	Preschool	Wilson, Cameron, & Whipple (1997)

likely to be. In their play, children also underspecify contingencies (e.g., a preschooler who yells at a doll, "Eat up your pasta! If you don't, you'll see what happens" (Bonica, 1993, p. 63). It may well be that when contingencies are underspecified, children symbolically complete the contingency, specifying it as, "If I don't stand by the door/eat my pasta, something awful will be done to me." They may comply in order to avoid this unspecified but dispreferred outcome. In line with this, a mother tells her son of 34;7 months after he knocks over a toy train station, "Naughty boys get into trouble for knocking the station, don't they?" (Wells, CHILDES). In other cases, the consequent may be specified and the child may refrain from engaging in the behavior because he knows what consequent to anticipate. A high-school teacher tells his class, "Somebody's talking. You know what will happen. No five minute break" (Torode, 1976, p. 183).

At times, the consequents regarding which children are alerted are removed in time from the point at which the antecedent is to take place. Such long-term contingencies may be expressed in the affirmative (e.g., if you eat your vegetables you will grow up healthy, if you smoke you will get cancer) but they can also be expressed in the negative (e.g., if you don't do your homework, you won't succeed at school, if you're not nice to your friends, you won't have friends). Parents can combine contingencies, expressing both the immediate consequent and possible long-term consequents; the expressed contingencies can refer to short-term outcomes for the child, or long-term ones, for example, "If you don't go to school . . . you won't do any painting, you won't be able to have a job like daddy" (Cook-Gumperz, 1973, p. 66). As well, the consequent specified may be reasonably linked to the relevant behavior or it may be incidental. The mother of a child of 4;7 years who was acting silly at home told him that "they don't let little boys go to school if they don't behave" (Wells, CHILDES). A mother who tried to prevent her 4-year-old from sleeping in her parents' bed told the child that little girls don't grow if they sleep with their parents (Newson & Newson, 1968). A 13-year-old relates what happens in school, saying, "they tell you that when you are grown up you won't have a job and your family will go hungry . . . . My Dad says it too. He says that we'll only have raw onions to eat if we don't work (at school)" (Knowles & Sixsmith, 1996, p. 124). To the extent that children think the undesirable consequent is a likely outcome, they may be less likely to undertake the relevant antecedent action.

A related means of getting children to understand restrictions is by voicing antecedents and asking as to possible consequents, asking, "What if?" That is, the parent refers to the child's behavior and asks as to its logical consequences. For instance, when a child of 3;10 years is asked to pick up some papers, he says, "Somebody please help me." His mother retorts, "Now . . . What would happen if every time mummy did something, she didn't want to tidy up an' she 'ad to shout 'Will somebody please come and help me?'" (Wootton, 1986, p. 154). Similarly, when a child asks his mother to buy him a puzzle, the mother asks, "What would happen to my pocketbook if I bought you toys that cost a lot of money every time you want something?" (Shure & Spivack, 1978, p. 137). The child is presumed to understand that the logical consequent is a negative one and to desist from similar behavior in the future. Notice that by doing so, the mother avoids refusing the child's request outright.

USING POWER TO ENFORCE RESTRICTIONS

Greenhalgh and Chapman (1995) suggest that there are several alternatives when one has conflicting preferences with others. First, one can use one's power – defined as the ability to impose a solution to resolve the conflict. Second, one can reconceptualize the conflict in less divisive terms, cognitively restructuring it in ways that actually diminish the perceived incompatibility of preferences of the parties to the conflict. Finally, one can negotiate, compromising one's own preferences and accepting outcomes that only partly reflect each party's preferences. In a sense, then, negotiation serves to reconcile the preference structures of two individuals, each of whom has a preference structure that is based on his or her own unique interests. Negotiation and cognitive restructuring tend to arise when conflict occurs within the context of an ongoing relationship and preservation of the relationship is one of the primary objectives of the interactants. There are several problems with using power, especially the fact that using power results in external compliance rather than internal commitment. Using power also tends to alienate the party that the solution is imposed on and can be detrimental to the relationship. Many parents opt not to use their power because they are more concerned with the relationship than with the behavior they want to restrict (Pearlin, 1970).

On the other hand, power holders can ultimately wield their power if the need arises. The difficulty in classifying parental strategies of socialization is that parents can employ different levels of prompts when children resist their requests. They may avoid using their power at first but may end up wielding it when other expressions of restrictions fail to yield compliance. Hart and Risley (1995) suggest that at the first level, parents may prompt with a statement of a social or family rule, for example, "It's cold. You need to put on a coat before you go outside." At the second level, when the child has not complied, the parent may question, "Can you get your coat?" If the child still does not comply, the parent may move to the third level of prompting, with a demand, "Go get your coat," perhaps adding, "now" (p. 104). Further noncompliance may elicit more stringent attempts to get the child to comply, including threats, bribes, and so forth. The important point here is that parents engage in successive strategies when the issue in question is one they deem important (e.g., Wilson, Cameron, & Whipple, 1997).

INVOKING IDLE THREATS

Parents often invoke idle threats, specifying consequents that they have no plans of carrying out (e.g., "With me it is just a threat. I very rarely carry it through," Sears, Maccoby, & Levin, 1957, p. 356). Newson and Newson (1976) found that parents often threatened that they will not take a child to some upcoming event, like the circus, a fair, or holidays at grandparents' homes, knowing full well that they are unlikely to implement the consequent. In this vein, a mother who tries to get her child into bed warns her, "put your legs down or I'm going outside right this minute without a kiss." But then she promptly says, "now give a kiss good night," despite the fact that the child had not done what she was asked to do (Hasan & Cloran, 1990, p. 92). Another mother warned her 4-year-old that she would make him sleep on the floor if he wet his bed again (Newson & Newson, 1968). These types of consequents – and the fact that they are not carried out – teach children that there are various types of idle threats.

Yet it may be difficult to know whether a threat is an idle one. For instance, a child who dawdles at picking up strewn toys is warned, "If these toys are not in your room in five minutes, you will not watch TV tomorrow!" The child responds by crying, suggesting that the threat was not construed as idle. But the mother then went and picked up the toys herself, obviating the need to carry out the threat (Shure & Spivack, 1978, p. 142). Again, a mother warns her child, "If you don't move faster, I'm going to leave without you"; but the child takes the threat seriously, saying "No, Mommy," precluding the possibility of knowing whether the threat was an idle one (ibid, p. 143). When a teacher warns a preschooler "I'll get a piece of Sellotape and put it over your mouth if you spit" (King, 1978, p. 99), does the child know whether the threat is idle or not? He doesn't dare take a chance that it might not be an idle threat.

Anthropologists have found that in some societies, idle threats are a prevalent form of social control. In Tzeltal society, for instance, parents use what Brown (2002) calls *lying threats*, which the person who makes them has no intention of carrying out.[20] They threaten the child with outcomes that are used symbolically. Brown claims that because overt threats are seldom carried out, by age 3, children learn that speech does not necessarily convey true propositions and they develop a sensitivity to the intentions of utterances. For instance, a mother might warn her child, "I'll pour water on you if you don't pipe down" (Brown, 2002, p. 244). But this sensitivity seems to be necessary given that lies are a prevalent means of controlling child behavior.

Referring to the use of such apparently idle threats, Milburn and Watman (1981) suggest that parents use idle threats to inculcate norms of behavior, knowing full well that their children understand the fiction involved. Parents hope that the child will understand the parent's goal as attempting to control a class of behaviors rather than as construing the threat literally. When a father warns his preschooler "I'll break your head if you go there" (Gleason, 1987), presumably both father and child understand the fiction involved and the child does not fear as to the welfare of his head. Parents do not actually want to carry out their threats; it's as if they are saying that they are issuing the threat precisely because they do not want to follow through with the threatened action.

Examining the prevalence of idle threats in socialization is difficult because researchers have included such threats under different categories of parental behavior. For instance, Sears, Rau, and Alpert (1965) did not include threats in their study of socialization. Hoffman and Saltzstein (1967) included threats of punishment and withdrawal of privileges under the category "power assertion," which also includes the actual use of physical punishment. Oldershaw, Walters, and Hall (1986) similarly classified the use of threats as power assertive control, labeling them "negative contingencies" (e.g., "If you don't clean up, you won't get dinner tonight"). They did not address the issue of whether such negative contingencies constitute real or idle threats. Cook-Gumperz (1973) included threat of punishment under the label "indirect punishment" but did not focus on whether they were idle.

Even more problematic is the fact that in many studies of socialization, promises of rewards were not included as categories of parental behavior (e.g., Sears, Rau, & Alpert, 1965). Cook-Gumperz (1973) included promises of reward – which she labels as bargaining – under *concessions* and classified them as positively oriented control strategies (e.g., "if you clean up the toys, I'll give you candy"). Crockenberg and Litman (1990), though, included bribes, rewards contingent on compliance, as control strategies, including them with prohibitions. Yet

[20] Mothers may also use lying in channeling contexts. A Japanese mother whose son refused to go to preschool explained that "the only way I could get him into his uniform in the morning was to lie to him, saying we were going to the supermarket" (Peak, 1991, p. 148).

the conceptualization of promises as positive inducements and threats as negative ones is wrong for several reasons. First, both promises and threats can be used to restrict children's behavior. Second, as Giddens (1968) notes, because inducements and promises offer rewards in exchange for compliance, inducements always have the potential of being transformed into negative sanctions. Wolfenstein (1950) found that mothers often promised their children special outcomes and when children misbehaved, they were threatened with their potential loss. For instance, after an argument with her 3-year-old, the mother asks, "How about I won't make you a nice birthday cake for your birthday party?" (Dunn, 1988, p. 98). Similarly, the mother of a preschooler says, "you drink all your juice and I won't put (on) the vacuum cleaner," whose noise the child objected to (Clancy, Akatsuka, & Strauss, 1997, p. 37). Finally, threats and promises may co-occur in a given parent–child encounter.

INVOKING IMMANENT JUSTICE

In coining the term *immanent justice*, Piaget (1932/1965) referred to the tendency to believe that punishments emanate from things and events themselves. The collapse of a bridge that occurs after a child has stolen is construed as punishment for the theft and a child who falls after lying is viewed as being punished for lying. Building on their understanding of if–then contingencies, young children, especially those below age 7, infer a causal relationship between misbehavior and adverse outcomes that they construe as consequents of the antecedent misdeed. Children can offer other types of explanations for the contiguity between misdeeds and adverse outcomes, doing so more readily when the adversity is self-producible (e.g., falling, cutting oneself) than when it is naturalistic (e.g., being hit by lightning) (Karniol, 1980). Yet parents and teachers explicitly *encourage* beliefs in immanent justice even for self-producible outcomes. When a child at preschool says he got hurt and the teacher asks how, he indicates that he was running. She says, "You weren't supposed to run in the classroom, that's why... you're not supposed to be running in the classroom." She makes it seem that getting hurt is a "natural" consequence of violating the rule.

Parents invoke immanent justice in more fearsome ways. In Tzeltal society, a mother might attempt to get her child to engage in a given behavior or to refrain from a given behavior by invoking a scary insect, saying, "It might squat on your back in a moment if you don't play" (Brown, 2002, p. 247). Widdowson (1979) found that parents warned children of horrible outcomes like, "Next time you stick out your tongue, a big knife will drop down from the sky and cut it right off" (p. 304), "If you don't take your thumb out of your mouth a big worm is going to come out of it and bite your tongue off" (p. 57), and "If you touch that, your hand will drop off" (p. 59). Similarly, Cook-Gumperz (1973) reported that a mother who didn't want her 5-year-old to continue watching television indicated she would say to him "he'll get square eyes if he goes on watching" (p. 248). The mother of a 4-year-old who wanted to prevent thumb-sucking warned her child that her thumb wouldn't grow and a 4-year-old who played with himself was told that his penis would drop off and he would have to be hospitalized (Newson & Newson, 1968).

Notice that the severity of antecedent behaviors does not have any logical relation to the horrible consequences with which children are warned. Whereas invoking immanent justice may be helpful in restricting young children's behavior, who may comply out of fear, older children may treat such threatened outcomes as idle threats. Then, as children discover that there is no one-to-one correspondence between the antecedents and immanent consequences, their ability to serve as restrictors of children's behavior is diminished (Karniol, 1982).

THREATENING WITH POWER FIGURES

Parents can invoke power figures, either real or imaginary, in the attempt to restrict their children's behavior. Widdowson (1979) found that children are warned with power figures for several reasons: (1) to express family or societal disapproval of behavior regarded as unacceptable or inadvisable, because the use of threats is simpler then explanations that the child may not understand; (2) to protect children from danger and maintain their physical health and well-being; and (3) to alleviate adult anger and frustration, with the verbalizing of the threat serving "as a release mechanism through which the person concerned can give vent to his feelings... he is less likely to seek a release for his anger in some kind of aggressive physical action" (p. 68). From Widdowson's perspective, adults use power figures to threaten instead of threatening with their own power because invoking oneself as a direct threat undermines the parent's role as the child's protector and presumably undermines the child's feelings of security. Furthermore, Widdowson identified twenty-eight contexts in which threats invoking power figures are used to control children's behavior, where each of these categories includes a wide range of behaviors, for example, breaking things, tearing things, marking walls, throwing stones, and hurting animals.

One of the power figures that parents used in Widdowson's study was the policeman. As the symbol of civic authority, the guardian whom society appoints over its own behavior, the policeman would seem to be the person children should turn to for help and support. But parents engage in deliberate misrepresentation of policemen, using them as a threatening figure who could jail a misbehaving child or take him away (cf., Newson & Newson, 1968). In this context, though, one needs to differentiate invoking policemen as enforcers of the law versus their use as individuals with punishment potential. As an instance of the former, a mother is explaining what she would do to cope with her child's taking something from a supermarket, and says, "I'd tell him if he did it again the policeman might catch him" (Cook-Gumperz, 1973,

Table 8.12.

	Age	Source
M1: "Go to sleep or I'll phone the doctor to give you a needle"	Adult reporting childhood experiences	Widdowson (1979, p. 261)
M2: "The doctor will give you a needle if you are bad"	Adult reporting childhood experiences	Widdowson (1979, p. 59)
M3: "You better eat those beans, Sharon, or the doctor will come for you"	Adult reporting childhood experiences	Widdowson (1979, p. 264)
M tells C1 (2;3) that injection-giver will come if she cries		
C3: (6-year old) "Pipe down. You'll get injected soon if you keep crying. If you cry"	3;9 years	Brown (2002, p. 258)

Table 8.13.

	Age	Source
A: "Santa Claus was checking to see if we were being good all year, and if he saw us being bad, we would get nothing for Christmas.... Santa was watching our every move"	Adult reporting on childhood	Widdowson (1979, p. 210)
M: "Santa Claus is watching; if you don't be good, he won't give you anything for Christmas"	Adult reporting on childhood	Widdowson (1979, p. 55)
M: "You have to be a good girl. If you're not a good girl Santa Clause doesn't bring you anything"	Preschool	Clancy, Akatskua, & Strauss (1997, p. 26)
Preschooler Tommy refuses to stop shouting M threatens him that Father Christmas would bring him no toys this year C "Father Christmas don't get Tommy any toys, Mummy"	3 years	Dunn (1988, p. 65)
C complains to mother C: "Sister said no presents"[21] (that is, he would get no Christmas presents for misbehaving)	27 mos.	Antinucci & Miller (1976, p. 180)

p. 248). Children in Newfoundland were told, "Quit slinging rocks; the policeman's coming" (Widdowson, 1979, p. 55). This sort of invocation presents policemen as law enforcement agents. The more common use of policemen, though, is as potential punishers when the child misbehaves at home and when he doesn't listen to his mother. Newson and Newson (1968, 1976) found that policemen were invoked across a wide variety of settings, with both 4- and 7-year-olds, generally in the attempt to get them to stop behaving in an undesirable fashion. Both Widdowson (1979) and Wells (1985) found that some mothers threatened that they would call a policeman to have the child taken away. The deliberate misrepresentation of policemen as potential punishers is evident in the words of a 3-year-old who is playing house and says, "Get that little girl and put her in jail. She's waking up the baby" (Paley, 1986, p. 37).

Doctors are similarly invoked, sometimes in realms relevant to their medical backgrounds (e.g., "if you don't take your cough syrup I'll call the doctor," Widdowson, 1979, p. 262) – but sometimes not, as illustrated in Table 8.12.

The use of doctors as power figures is evident in the pretend play of a 5-year-old who attributes doctors with the power to send a recalcitrant child to bed, explaining that the mother is supposed to say, "You better get in that bed or I'll send you to the doctor" (Andersen, 1990, p. 118).

Supernatural power figures are also invoked by parents. Kenyan grandmothers allude to witches (e.g., "Stop crying or I will send you to the dark to be eaten by hyenas or taken away by witches," Oburu & Palmérus, 2003, p. 508). In the Western world, Santa Claus serves as an effective figure because he holds the promise of potential rewards if the child behaves (e.g., "If I'm good Santa will bring toys," Bretherton, 1991, p. 65). But Santa is more commonly used as a potential withholder of potential rewards, as shown in Table 8.13. More unfortunate children were even warned that their bad behavior would prevent Santa from coming at all at Christmas time, for example, "If you aren't good Santa won't come" (Widdowson, 1979, p. 59).

[21] Italian: "Suora ditto niente regalo"

Irrespectively, in these threats, Santa was a supernatural, godlike presence who was to be feared.

It should be noted, though, that it is difficult to know whether both parents and children interpreted these as idle threats. On the other hand, children who know of supernatural beings from storybooks invoke them in threatening contexts. A child of 30 months says about her sister that she "is naughty, she doesn't eat, the witch will get her" (Przetacznik-Gierowska, 1995). Similarly, an Italian preschooler of 3;8 years, warns a peer during pretend play "But if you're bad no, okay?".... If you're not good.... However, now if you are good, we won't use the wolf"[22] (Bates, 1976). Fantasy "bad guys" from the media can also be invoked to threaten children.

Parents can also invoke God, doing so as a deliberate means of socialization. Here again one needs to differentiate two different ways in which parents can invoke God in disciplinary contexts. Parents can invoke God in the religious context, as the determiner of who goes to heaven and hell. But this is quite different from invoking God as a disciplinarian who punishes children for misbehavior in the immediate future. As an instance of this, a mother threatened her child that God will do something to her hand if she smacks her mother (Newson & Newson, 1968). A mother explains regarding her kindergarten child: "We've always told her that any little girl who tells a lie, God always does something terrible to them," further explaining that when a neighboring child was hit by a car, the child assumed that God was punishing him for some wrongdoing and the parents did not disabuse her of this notion (Sears, Maccoby, & Levin, 1957, p. 380). In my research (e.g., Karniol, 1981), children often invoked God when they were unable to explain the relation between a cause and effect for adverse outcomes. For instance, God was invoked to account for a child being hurt by lightning after committing a theft. Similarly, Widdowson (1979) found God being invoked for thunder, for example, "someone's done something very wrong, and the thunder is God's anger, and if you are not a good child, it will come and hurt you. Be a good child and it won't hurt you" (p. 57). God knows when a child is misbehaving and has the means of punishing that child for his misbehavior. In research (Karniol & Jabaly, unpublished) with Moslem children in the fourth and sixth grades who were required to explain the contingency between misdeeds and adverse outcomes, God was invoked both as a punisher and as responsible for one's fate, with children explaining that the misdeed may have been irrelevant but that "God wanted it to happen this way," and "God determined his fate." These two views of God have not been identified in prior research and hold promise that there is both a sophisticated and a more primitive conceptualization of the relation between beliefs in God and morality.

[22] Italian: "Se non state buoni.... " "Ma se siete cattivi no, eh?....." "Pero adesso se state buoni, non l'adopriamo il lupo"

Because adults invoke supernatural figures who are omnipresent and cite immanent justice, which similarly occurs without visible means of human intervention, it may not be surprising that children learn that punishment can be immanent. For instance, a child who needs to answer questions regarding a story target who faces the dilemma between summoning the parents of a fallen child and consequently missing a birthday party, says, "If he didn't help, someone would find out and punish him" (Eisenberg & Miller, 1992, p. 32). Who the someone is remains unspecified. It is clear, though, that parents do want to scare their children into behaving. As one parent says,

> ...tell about things, what happened when you don't follow such certain rules and regulations about society.... I guess it scares them at first until they get older.... But then maybe they'll think about some of the things you told them in the past, and it might help them out. (Palkovitz, 2002, p. 137)

Parents use such strategies because they believe that such scare tactics have long-term benefits.

PREEMPTING

One way for parents to avoid preferential conflict regarding the restrictions they impose is to take preemptive steps that prevent its eventual occurrence. Preemption can be in the form of teaching and preaching, being taught the "do's" and "don'ts" of social life. Another means of preemption can take the forms of steps that prevent outcomes that may otherwise be expected to occur (e.g., a mother who tells her 18-month-old, "Come, run this way, Sonja, there's (broken) glass there," Carew, 1976, p. 95). Preemptive action can take many forms and different mothers can take different preemptive actions with the same goal in mind. For instance, a parent who expects that a child may spill things may attempt to preempt it, as the following mothers explain, "I put paper down when he paints or he does it in the bathroom so he can make as much mess as he likes" (Cook-Gumperz, 1973, p. 58) and "I only fill their cups half-way up – so there's less to spill – it used to happen a lot" (p. 241). This type of contextual preemption is quite different from the following: "We put Marley tiles on the kitchen as soon as we started a family so that spills wouldn't matter" (p. 58). Yet another mother explains "I put off buying bedspreads for two or three years, because they would get on the beds with their shoes" (Sears, Maccoby, & Levin, 1957, p. 280). As these examples illustrate, preemptive actions vary in terms of the temporal perspective adopted. Contextual preemption is much more difficult because it requires constant monitoring, for example, "It's difficult with children to keep things out of their reach all the time" (Cook-Gumperz, 1973, p. 143). Many parents do engage in contextual preemption with breakables being removed from children's reach, for instance. Similarly, a mother who is questioned as to her likely response to minor shoplifting responds,

"I've always kept an eye on him in supermarkets to make sure that doesn't happen" (Cook-Gumperz, 1973, p. 247). Preschool teachers (e.g., Gardner & Cass, 1965) often take preemptive steps, covering tables with newspapers before children begin painting, providing aprons before they play with water, suggesting to other children that they go to play areas that are less crowded, and so forth (e.g., "only two at a time on the bench," Sylva, Roy, & Painter, 1986, p. 27). In a Chinese preschool, the teachers see their role as a preemptive one, saying, "We control them by stopping them from misbehaving before they even know they are about to misbehave" (Tobin, Wu, & Davidson, 1989, p. 94), doing so by active monitoring of children's behavior and attending to signs of impending transgressions.

There are alternatives to preemption. Some parents merely advise their children to be careful around breakables. Many parents avoid giving their children adult-size scissors to avoid their being cut. Yet other mothers think that children should learn to deal with adult-size scissors and to be careful in doing so. In this vein, a preschool teacher warns children, "Mind, Katie, mind John! You might cut yourself on that spade" (Gardner & Cass, 1965, p. 69) – but she does not forbid their touching it. This latter attitude is evident when a 4-year-old who is pretend-playing mother, says to her child, "Be sure you don't cut yourself" (Pitcher & Schultz, 1983, p. 71).

Holden (1983) suggests that preemption is a more general strategy involving attempts to deal with anticipated problems before they occur. For instance, in a naturalistic study of mothers' behavior with their toddlers in the supermarket, children of mothers who took steps to preempt misbehavior by engaging the child before preferential conflict arose instead of reacting to it after it happened evidenced less misbehavior. To examine this issue empirically, Holden and West (1989) provided 2- and 3-year-olds with dull toys with which to play and exciting toys that were "forbidden." Mothers were asked to adopt each of three attitudes in interacting with their child when the exciting toys were restricted. They were first asked to interact with the child as they normally would at home. Then they were asked to adopt a preemptive stance in which the child gets to play with the unattractive toys and to refrain from playing with the restricted ones. Last, mothers were asked to adopt a reactive stance in which they rebuke the child for playing with the restricted toys and respond as they normally would if they violate the "rule." During adoption of the proactive stance, mothers were more involved with the child, made more suggestions, and participated more in play with the child than during adoption of the reactive stance. In turn, children spent less time looking at and touching the forbidden toys and more time engaged with the available toys during the preemptive trials than the reactive ones, with a developmental trend such that older children were better able to resist playing with the forbidden toys.

But what were mothers doing while being preemptive versus reactive? Both when uninstructed as if playing at home and when preemptive, mothers were distracting their children in two different ways. First, they were offering children alternative activities that would engage them and keep them away from the "forbidden" toys. Second, they were actively engaging the children in play with those objects that were available. The reactive role is a different one, requiring mothers to monitor the child's behavior, "catch" the child in the act, and respond to his transgression, much like a policeman. From an attributional perspective (e.g., Lepper, 1981), the reactive role is one that undermines children's emergent ability to cope. Specifically, children need to justify to themselves why they are complying with injunctions and why they are not playing with forbidden toys. When they are engaged in exciting, pretend play with their mother, the attributional problem is circumvented. Who needs to play with those toys when one is having so much fun playing here with these toys? But if the mother does not engage them in exciting play with the available toys, these toys become even less attractive because the only justification for playing with them is that the other more attractive toys are forbidden. But because no explicit contingency is specified as to what will happen if the child violates the rule and plays with the forbidden toys, the child "runs the red light" in the hope that nothing serious will happen. Once he does so, though, the mother intervenes, emphasizing her "policing" role. The child, then, learns to comply because of her adoption of the policing function.

Japanese mothers seem to understand that they need to make the child feel that he is spontaneously restricting his own behavior and that "anything that makes the child do a task reluctantly should be avoided." Japanese mothers use hints "providing the child with chances to perform an expected task as if it were his/her own decision" (Kobayashi, 2001, p. 131). As well, the child is expected to mind-read what others expect him to do and maternal hints help the child know what is expected.

Gardner, Sonuga-Barke, and Sayal (1999) conducted a study in which the mothers of 3-year-olds, with or without behavior problems, were taped as they played at home with their children and then engaged them in a toy clean-up task. Mothers were advised in advance that toy play would be terminated after 10 minutes and that their task was to get the child to tidy up the toys, using the strategies they normally use in that setting. The strategies the mothers used were categorized as positive versus negative, with positive strategies including: *Reasoning*, in which a plausible explanation or justification for the behavior is provided (e.g., "we'll have to clear these up because it's time to go out soon"); *Bargaining* in which a positive incentive to comply is offered *conditional* on the child's compliance (e.g., "if you tidy up the man will give you a new toy," or "tidy it up. We'll play something else"); *Compromising*, which was coded if the parent explicitly offered to help the child or reduce scope of task (e.g., "I'll help you put the jigsaws in the box," or "you can just do the tracks"); and *Imaginative strategies*, which were coded if the mother used humor or pretend (e.g., "Racoon will help you to tidy up. He wants to see how fast you can pick everything up"). As well, the strategies were coded as being either *preemptive* or *reactive*. Strategies were coded as preemptive if the mother used any of the above strategies to persuade the child to carry out her instructions. Preemption had to occur *before* the child evidenced any noncompliance. Strategies were coded as reactive if any of the above strategies were used *after* the child has evidenced noncompliance or resistance. Mothers who used any preemption were coded as preemptive even if they subsequently used reactive strategies during the clean-up. Whereas there were no differences between the two groups in mothers' use of positive strategies, the mothers of children with behavior problems were less likely to use preemptive, and more likely to use reactive, strategies. As well, the frequency of noncompliance was lower in children of preemptive mothers as compared with the reactive mothers. A 2-year follow-up of some of the children found that mothers' use of reactive strategies at age 3 predicted children's behavior problems at age 5, even after controlling for behavior problems at age 3.

USING CHOICE TO RESTRICT

Another means of restricting preferences is to set up choices between two dispreferred alternatives. For instance, before Emily, at 22;16, goes to sleep her father states,

> Okay, you have two choices. You can either just lie like that and Daddy'll leave, or you can like down, the other way, and Daddy's put a blanket on you . . . you remember you have two choices . . . Would you like . . . for Daddy to just go out, or do you want to put your head down here so Daddy can put the blanket on you? (Watson, 1989, pp. 268, 270)

He offers her two negative choices, assuming that one of these will be preferable to her. But she is not offered a choice as to his staying in her room or her coming out of bed. Ten days later, she herself reiterates the choices, saying, "Either Emmy go to sleep or put blanket at either side." When her father asks what she prefers, she rejects both options, answering, "Nothing!" But recognizing that her father's preference will prevail, she chooses the lesser of two evils, the one in which she goes to sleep with her blanket. The father starts off with the premise that the child must go to sleep and the only question is how this will occur. Similarly, a father whose starting assumption is that the child must eat broccoli says, "Two pieces of broccoli any two you want" (Ochs, Pontecorvo, & Fasulo, 1996, p. 16). The issue thereby becomes which pieces of broccoli will be eaten rather than whether broccoli is to be eaten at all. In a preschool, when a child ignored her request to leave another child alone, the teacher says, ". . . Either leave John alone or move over here" (Genishi & Di Paolo, 1982, p. 65).

Parents can also give their children choices in the context of threatening them with punishment, asking them whether they want to be punished. Dunn (1988) reports an instance of a child crying and being unable to calm down. His mother says, "Do you want me to smack you?"; when he answers no, the mother answers, "Then just stop it, please" (p. 94). In fact, then, the mother gives the child a choice between being physically punished or to stop crying, neither of which the child wants to do. Knowing full well that the child is unlikely to prefer to be physically punished, the mother assumes that giving the child a choice of this kind will facilitate his attempts to stop crying. In a similar context, when a child has been crying nonstop after being told she cannot watch TV, her mother says, "You have a choice, You can either quit your crying or you can go upstairs in your bedroom . . . you got a choice." Later, the mother explains, "Well honey you had a choice. You could've either stopped crying and stayed downstairs or you could a kept on crying and went to bed . . . that's why you're in bed now" (Wilson, Cameron, & Whipple, 1997).

Parents may present such choices as if they were indifferent to which choice is selected but it is clear that they are not indifferent. They have implicit external preferences and when children do not pick up on this, parents may withdraw the offer of choice. Jeffrey, at age 6, asks his mother if he can invite his friend Adam over to do an experiment with an ice cube. His mother suggests that he can either do that or have another friend come to watch TV with him. She says to him, "You have the choice of two things." When it becomes clear that he prefers the option she doesn't want him to choose, she eventually says, "There are so many things you want to do, you can't decide" (Blum-Kulka, 1997, p. 170). Here, then, despite the fact that he was presented with a choice, the child had no choice. In fact, mothers admit this to be the case, saying, "what I usually do is try to talk him into my choice" (Nucci & Smetana, 1996). This use of "choice" is evident in a baseball coach's attempt to deal with children's apparent lack of motivation. He says: "If you want to swing, go ahead and swing; if you don't want to swing, don't swing. If you want to catch the ball, go ahead; if you don't want to catch the ball, that's OK too . . . . Like I said you can go out and do anything you want" (Fine, 1987, p. 66). Both he and his players know that he is not offering them a choice.

In this chapter, I have intentionally avoided discussing children's reactions to their behavior being restricted, with such reactions being discussed in the chapters on manipulating others, coping, and transforming. What still remains to be discussed, though, is parents' reactions to children's noncompliance with their restrictions, the way parents do or do not discipline their recalcitrant children, the topic of Chapter 9.

9 Disciplining Noncompliance

A mother refers to her problems with getting her 4-year-old to eat, saying, 'We used everything in turn. He was forbidden ice-cream and sweets; we did have a spell when we smacked him, but we gave up, because we don't believe in smacking children if it has no results; and I think we did have a time when he was sent to bed. But we also gave that up pretty quickly, because obviously it had not effect.'

(Newson & Newson, 1968, p. 231)

Preferential conflict between parents and their children does not necessarily dissipate when parents temporize or restrict children's preferences. What happens next depends on children's reactions to their preferences being temporized or restricted and on parental responses to children's reactions. In this chapter, I focus on how parents discipline their children and what they do when their children are recalcitrant. In particular, I see disciplinary contexts as ones that entail choice on both the child's and the parent's part as to how to behave. Children can make what parents perceive as wrong choices in continuing to be defiant or avoiding to take responsibility for their misbehaviors. Parents can choose how to respond to their child's behavior; they can prevent or promote the escalation of conflict depending on the strategies they themselves adopt during disciplinary encounters, as discussed below.

ESCALATION OF PREFERENTIAL CONFLICT

When children go along with the imposed restrictions on their preferences, interaction with their parents can generally proceed smoothly. That is, children may acknowledge the conflict but behave in ways that reflect their parents' preferences rather than their own. A 5-year-old child is talking about not liking school and says, "My Mummy woke me up and got me up. And I didn't wanna go to school. So she said, you have to. So I had breakfast and then I got to school" (Mayall, 2000, p. 126). A teenager similarly explains with regard to such conflict, "I'd rather be home, lyin' 'round, watchin' TV, but my mama won't let me. She say I gotta come to school" – and the child comes to school (FitzSimmons, 1999, p. 182). But preferential conflict may escalate if children resist parental restrictions or violate parental expectations.

Whether or not preferential conflict escalates depends on at least three factors. First, it depends on the importance parents assign to those domains in which they impose restrictions. The more important they view a given domain, the more likely is conflict to escalate. On the other hand, to the extent that parents have not crystallized their values, the way they view the domain can be amorphous and labile, often changing in the midst of a disciplinary encounter. The occurrence of such online changes in importance can lead parents to drop the issue, or it can lead them to stand on their hind feet and battle their children head-on.

Second, the escalation of conflict depends on how parents view the context of the disciplinary encounter. Prusank (1993) argues that behaviors that were subject to past discussions and warnings are treated differently than first-time offenses. References to previous discussions abound in disciplinary encounters, as evident in Table 9.1.

When behaviors have been the subject of past discussion or discipline, parents may see the behavior as more problematic, they may perceive their previous strategies as ineffective, and they may perceive the child as intentionally violating explicit rules. In interviews with parents regarding disciplinary encounters, they often relate current disciplinary encounters to previous ones. For instance, a father tells of a child who had returned to the living room after being sent back to bed once, and was told "in no uncertain terms to go back to bed and not to get up again or he would be spanked hard" (Prusank, 1993, p. 139). As well, a child who took off his sister's diaper was grabbed, spanked on his bottom, and put in his room because the mother said "I have repeatedly told him not to do that" (Prusank, 1993, p. 146).

The need to repeatedly discipline a child in a given domain can be viewed as a failure on the parent's part to convey his external preferences to the child. In such cases, the child may be viewed as defying the parent, leading

Table 9.1.

	Age	Source
M: "What did I say about those wax crayons Abbie?"	Preschool	Halle & Shatz (1994, p. 91)
M: "I told you yesterday you can't go in there"	Preschool	Clancy, Akatskuka, & Strauss (1997, p. 54)
Baseball coach to player A: "How many times have I talked you about clowning around. I can't count the number of times"	Preadolescent	Fine (1987, p. 55)

the parent to engage in disciplinary tactics geared toward eliminating defiance (e.g., a child who had previously been told not to close a door and shuts it, is warned "Sally, open that door now! Close that door again and I'll give you a smack," Walkerdine & Lucey, 1989, p. 24). This is generally the view of discipline expressed in English, with the dictionary defining discipline as "punishment or bringing under control." Viewing discipline in this manner entails strategies that suppress defiance rather than ones that attempt to align preferential conflict. In other cultures, the child's nonadoption of parental restrictions is viewed as a failure on the child's part – he has not come to understand the need to impose restrictions on his preferences or the need to adopt the external preferences of his parents. In Japanese, for instance, to discipline is to teach the child how to tell what is good and what is bad (Kobayashi, 2001). Discipline is viewed as an educational tool whose goal is preference alignment, making the child realize the importance of adopting parental preferences in the interest of harmony – at home and in society (e.g., Chao, 1994).

In this vein, then, one of the reasons that parents react differently to offenses that have been discussed in the past is that such offenses are in domains in which the child is assumed to know the difference between good and bad (cf., Prusank, 1993). When the child is assumed to have knowledge in a given domain and "should have known better," parents are much more likely to discipline the child. In fact, then, disciplinary encounters are conducted in light of what the parent believes the child "knows." Parents believe that disciplinary encounters lead children to share their views of the world and of the rules in that world; they can therefore refer to what the child should have known when they discipline. In recounting disciplinary encounters, parents often allude to children's state of knowledge, elaborating the mismatch between it and the behavior undertaken. For instance, a mother explains regarding a disciplinary encounter, that "she knew paint on the floor was unacceptable" (Prusank, 1993, p. 141) or "She knows that we have a family rule for that" (Cook-Gumperz, 1973, p. 64). The child's state of knowledge is assumed to be the relevant criterion for guiding children's behavior. As one mother says, "Children of that age know quite well how to behave to their parents. I'd make him get down from the table 'til he could pay attention" (ibid, 1973, p. 241).

Teachers similarly refer to children's state of knowledge in chastising and disciplining them, In referring to the need to clean up, a preschool teacher says, "Come on, Kerry, you know you are responsible for cleaning up toys you take out" (Tobin, Wu, & Davidson, 1989, p. 132). A preschool teacher chastises a misbehaving group of children, saying, "Don't do that please boys. You know better than that" (Kamler, 1999, p. 207). In explaining why a child was disciplined at school, the teacher explains, "she was eating a sweet and she's not supposed to eat sweets in school and she knows as well as I do" (Hargreaves, Hester, & Mellor, 1975, p. 41).

From this perspective, not only do parents and teachers make assumptions about what the child knows about appropriate behavior in different domains, but they also assume that this knowledge is to be used as a behavioral guide. In fact, then, disciplinary action is undertaken not to remedy the inappropriate behavior but to align it with the knowledge state relevant to it. It is as if the parent is saying, "I'm disciplining you because your behavior did not reflect your knowledge state." Voicing this view, a child who is describing being punished in a Vietnamese school explains, "I knew why I got hit. They don't tell you why. You're supposed to know yourself" (Igoa, 1995, p. 95). Given that children's state of knowledge about those behaviors that are considered good and bad changes with age, parental discipline should be age-appropriate. Taking something from a store without paying is the same illegitimate behavior but the underlying state of knowledge is quite different when done by a 4-year-old versus a 14-year-old and should be handled differently.

Third, the likelihood of conflict escalation depends on the relative importance parents assign to their immediate versus long-term goals and whether they see the fulfillment of their current external preference as impacting the child's adoption of their preferences farther down the road. In each disciplinary encounter, parents are not only concerned with the current context, but they are worried about how their treatment of the current context will impact the child's future adoption of their preferences. When a parent compromises and says, "only this once," this reflects his worry that his future preferences will not be adopted by the child. Because parents have both immediate and long-term goals in disciplining their children, they continually face dilemmas; whereas one goal may be approximated by adopting a certain disciplinary tactic, another goal may be thwarted. For instance, if the current issue looms larger in the parent's mind than the child's happiness or the nature of the relationship with the child and the possible impact that current actions may have on it, parents will be differentially likely to let the conflict escalate. Consequently, disciplining children requires parents to walk a tightrope, maneuvering between their current and future goals, with little certainty as to what they will find when they get to the end of the walk.

Parental goals in disciplinary encounters have been discussed in various ways. Dix (1992) suggested that parental goals in disciplining children can be divided into three categories: (1) parent-centered goals (such as obedience and short-term compliance) and two kinds of child-centered goals: teaching values or lessons (i.e., socialization goals) and satisfying a child's emotional needs to promote positive feelings (what Dix calls empathy goals). Grusec and Goodnow (1994) proposed yet another goal – fostering a close and harmonious bond between family members (i.e., relationship goals). Hastings and Grusec (1998) suggest that each of these goal orientations can focus on the long term or on the short term. In a study in which parents were interviewed over the phone as to recent problem interactions with their child who is in the 5- to 7-year age range, Hastings and Grusec found that short-term, parent-centered goals were the most frequently cited as the focus of disciplinary encounters. On the other hand, parents could be differentiated by whether they were pursuing primarily parent-centered or child-centered goals, with parents espousing parent-centered goals using more power assertion and those espousing child-centered goals using more reasoning. It is evident, then, that parental goals relate to the way parents behave during disciplinary encounters.

On the other hand, it would be highly surprising if parental goals did not relate to the disciplinary strategies adopted by them. But because all parents have both short-term and long-term goals, the more relevant question is to what extent parents can *coordinate* between their short-term goal, of having their child adopt their preferences – which is the immediate goal in restricting and deflecting children's behavior – and their long-term goals of having the child become a well-functioning adult within their society. In this context, individual differences between mothers become relevant.

INDIVIDUAL DIFFERENCES IN MOTHERS

Mothers differ in terms of: (1) how many preferences they have, (2) how these are distributed in time, (3) the level at which these are represented, (4) how they think long-term preferences are related to short-term events and behaviors, (5) how tolerant they are of noncompliance, and, finally, (6) how long they will wait before disciplining. For instance, of the two mothers observed by Bruner, Roy, and Ratner (1982), one mother generally handed over requested objects to her child as soon as the child had made the request. The other mother withheld the object for a while, teased her child, interposed comments, and only then handed over the object. This of course resulted in more fretting and vocalization by the second mother's child. Her goal, though, most likely was not to enhance fretting but rather, to socialize the child into being better able to cope with delays. Whiting and Edwards (1988) suggest that both mothers and cultures vary in norms regarding how quickly one should respond to children's demands for comfort, care, and attention. In some cultures, to avoid "spoiling the child," it is normative to respond only after delays and persistent crying, for example, a Parisian mother who explains about her 16-month-old: "So I don't want to come running right away, I think that she needs to learn to be patient or to figure out how to calm herself" (Suizzo, 2004, p. 309).

Mothers and cultures also differ in their beliefs about how children's preferences can be influenced or changed. They may think that the best means of doing so is via discussion and via participation (e.g., take a child to church, to the opera), explicit commands, use of threats, bribes, or rewards). Mothers also differ in terms of their reactions to a child's nonenactment of their external preferences, their tolerance for discrepancy between what they prefer the child to do and what the child does, and their ability to tolerate delays that are related to their external preferences, that is, how long they will wait for a child to enact a behavior that the mother prefers. For instance, a mother explains, "I myself expect her to obey the moment I speak to her" (Sears, Maccoby, & Levin, 1957, p. 301). This demand for immediacy is evident in parental self-reports as well as parent–child interactions, as evident in Table 9.2.

Mothers sometimes recognize that it is their own impatience that is the critical issue and not the child's misbehavior, pondering, "What if the mother just isn't patient enough to constantly distract the child or think up ways to get out of it? Maybe it would be better for her to train the child fast and not take any chances?" (Bettelheim, 1962, p. 164).

An additional problem in this context is the range of behaviors that mothers have in their repertoire of socialization strategies. Clifford (1959) found that parents ranged from using only one strategy to using as many as seven strategies within a given disciplinary encounter. Zahn-Waxler, Radke-Yarrow, and King (1979) found that in responding to incidents in which their children caused another person distress, some mothers used as many as nine strategies, some as few as one strategy, across a 9-month period. However, within any given incident, most mothers tended to report the use of a single strategy (59% of the incidents), with more than two strategies being reported in only 17 percent of the incidents. Consequently, many mothers do not apparently have a variety of strategies in their repertoire and use physical punishment as a default (e.g., as a mother questions: "Well, what I want to know is, what's the alternative to slapping?" Bettelheim, 1962, p. 167). The problem, then, is two-pronged: mothers may think that children need to comply immediately and

Table 9.2.

	Age	Source
Parent–Child Interaction		
M wants children to clean up		
M: "Clean up all this mess! Hurry up! Before I smack some bums really hard"	Preschool	Grieshaber (2004, p. 167)
M: "Ryan, if you don't go and get your shoes in five seconds, I'm going to smack your bum. Go!"	Preschool	Grieshaber (2004, p. 183)
Parental Self-Reports		
M: "She knows if I get to three then it's a spank on the bum"	24 mos.	Wiley (1997)
M: "I used to count to five . . . and I thought, no, five's too long, so I said I'd count to three, and I never get to three, I mean I very rarely have to smack them"	Preschool	Ribbens (1994, p. 175)

they may have only a limited range of responses in their behavioral repertoire. Research has not addressed how such individual differences in mothers may be related to how they discipline their children or how they are reflected in their children's behavior (cf., Marfo, 1992).

In this context, though, Baumrind's (1967, 1971, 1989) research is noteworthy. She examined the relation between parental childrearing styles and social competence in children of preschool and school age. Data on nursery school children were obtained from observations in a school setting and in laboratory test situations when the children were in preschool. Data on the parents were obtained via home observations and interviews with both parents. Baumrind identified four parenting styles: *authoritarian*, *permissive*, *rejecting*, and *authoritative*, which differ on two major parenting dimensions: the amount of nurturance and the degree of control over the child.

Authoritarian parents tend to be low in nurturance and high in parental control. They set absolute standards that are not to be questioned by the child, they do not see their restrictions as open to negotiation, and they expect children to comply without questioning their authority; they enforce compliance, often using forceful discipline and demanding prompt obedience, providing little affection, praise, or rewards when children are compliant. In contrast, permissive parents tend to be higher in nurturance, but very low in parental control. Permissive parents place relatively few demands on their children, are less likely to monitor their children's behavior, and tend to be inconsistent disciplinarians. Permissive mothers avoid using their authority and are averse to using control or to setting limits; they are viewed as tending to spoil their child. Rejecting mothers tend to be unconcerned with their children, beyond meeting their immediate needs. Finally, authoritative parents tend to be high in nurturance and moderate in parental control in dealing with their children. They are flexible in that they stand their ground when needed, but they also listen to their children. In Baumrind's research, authoritative parenting appeared to be the most facilitative to the development of children's social competence.

However, there is an assumption in such research that children are exposed to a uniform style of childrearing, an assumption that is highly tenuous. For instance, Gleason (1987) found that fathers use more imperatives than mothers in talking to their children, that fathers' speech to sons contains more imperatives than speech addressed to daughters, and finally, that fathers use more threats (e.g., "I'll break your head if you go there") in talking to their sons than to their daughters. Parents also differ in their socialization practices and disciplinary tactics for sons and daughters (e.g., Fivush, 1998b). Bentley and Fox (1991) found little difference between mothers and fathers of children 1 to 4 years old in terms of their parenting expectations, use of discipline, or nurturance. However, in interviews, mothers and fathers themselves say they differ from each other in terms of their childrearing attitudes. In some families, it is the father who is deemed the disciplinarian and the mother who is the lenient one (e.g., "we have two different philosophies in raising the children . . . . My wife is pretty permissive with them. I have to clean up the consequences of her permissiveness," Palkovitz, 2002, p. 172). But in some families the opposite is the case. It is the father who is the "pushover" and the mother the more stringent one (e.g., "My wife's the disciplinarian and I'm the pushover. And that's probably out biggest area of disagreement," Backett, 1982, p. 173).

As a consequence, the disciplinary encounters and relationships children have with their mothers versus their father are quite different. A mother refers to this, saying, "it's a different relationship altogether," indicating that the father is the "softie," and that her child "knows how to get round her Daddy" (Newson & Newson, 1976, p. 268). Children themselves also refer to the differentiation between their two parents, saying, for instance, "my dad tells me t'do one thing and my mom tell me tuh do the other" (Hutchby, 2005, p. 315). Some children indicate that their father is the more strict parent, for example, "Mum thinks about it more . . . . Dad gets into a rage . . . says whatever comes into his head, and kind of roars . . . . It's much worse when it's Mum" (Kagan & Lewis, 1996, p. 46). Reflecting the opposite pattern, an adolescent reminisces, saying, "When I was 4–5 years old . . . I got anything I wanted with no more than a pleading look at my father" (Autio, 2004). Parents sometimes acknowledge that this is the case, lamenting that their children react differently to disciplinary encounters that are undertaken by mothers versus fathers. As one mother bemoans, her husband does not need to smack the child whereas she does, and "one word from Daddy and that's it" (Newson & Newson, 1976, p. 278). Yet another mother complains, "what he says is law. For me, they just couldn't care less" (ibid). Expressing the same lament, another mother says, "if I'm cross with her it's just 'oh', you know, mummy again, but if he says anything she's heartbroken" (Backett, 1982, p. 171).

In addition to differences between mothers and fathers in their strategies of socialization, across domains, individual parents differ in their strategies of channeling behavior, temporizing behavior, restricting children's behavior, and finally in how they discipline children when they fail to adopt their preferences. In their longitudinal study of forty-two American families, Hart and Risley (1995) found that "the amount of freedom parents could give their children was directly related to the number and diversity of the strategies they could call on for anticipating, distracting, redirecting, and persuading their children" (p. 56).

As discussed in Chapter 5, differences between mothers and fathers in their behavior during disciplinary encounters may also reflect underlying beliefs about how the current context may relate to future ones. For instance, if I want my child to be religious, have a given profession, or be kind, what do I believe I have to encourage/forbid today? How will allowing a child to sleep while the rest of the family goes to church impact the child's long-term religiosity? Implicit theories of discontinuous versus continuous developmental trajectories in the domain in question are often the bases for the means of discipline that parents adopt. I now turn to discussing the various strategies of discipline that parents use when children fail to adopt parental external preferences in guiding their own behavior.

TIME-OUT

Children are often disciplined by being removed from the presence of those around them, sometimes by being sent to their room (e.g., Hart & Risley, 1995; Wells, 1985), a period generally referred to as *time-out* (e.g., a child who made a mess on the kitchen floor was told, "Now go up to your room," Shure & Spivack, 1978, p. 149). In this vein, a mother explains that her child is given a series of warnings "and when you get to 3 it's an automatic take a break, time-out" (Bee-Gates, 2006, p. 48). Shatz (1994) notes that her toddler grandson was often punished with a time-out during which he was sent to his room, with the child apparently accepting this form of discipline, as evident when he says, "Oday (okay), time out" (p. 80). Some parents claim that this is the only successful means of disciplining at least one of their children (e.g., Backett, 1982) and children's reactions to this disciplinary strategy suggests that children do find it aversive. Gordon (2002) recorded an episode in which the mother was on the phone and her daughter of 2;11 was screaming. The mother said, "If you scream while I'm on the phone, you will have time-out," and the child responds, "No time-out," apparently objecting on the basis of prior experience with this disciplinary strategy. DeVilliers's (1984) son, at 28 months, says, "You no put me up in my room," similarly objecting to a time-out. In fact, the mother of a kindergarten child relates: "I just put him in his room, which has a terrible effect on him" (Sears, Maccoby, & Levin, 1957, p. 379), with some mothers admitting that this is their main strategy of disciplining the child precisely "because he is a child who doesn't like it" (ibid, p. 250). In being questioned as to why a child should not be punished, a 4-year-old explains, "She doesn't like it when he sends her to her room .... It makes her cry" (Selman & Damon, 1975, p. 65).

Older children are also subject to time-out. An 8-year-old boy is discussing arguments with his parents, indicating that his father says, "Get into your bedroom Thomas," imposing a time-out on him. He further states that when he's naughty, "my mum and dad send me to my room and I just play... and then come back and say, 'I'm sorry' (Lewis et al, 1996, p. 62). The mother of a 7-year-old relates that after being in time-out, "half an hour later a rueful Hilary will reappear and say she's sorry" (Newson & Newson, 1976, p. 303).

In child care settings, time-outs are often used as a disciplinary strategy, especially when children disturb the rest of the group or after they engage in aggressive behavior. As an example of this, a preschool teacher puts two children in the corner and tells a child, "Now you and (Child 2) be good for 3 minutes and you can come back and sing" (Applegate, 1980, p. 79). A kindergarten child explains what happens at school, saying, "like if one of the teachers says to go pick up that stuff and you don't do it and she says it again and then you don't do it and then if she says it again and you don't do it. And then she says, 'You're on time out!'" (Graue & Walsh, 1998, p. 188). At the age of 32;7, Orren relates an event at preschool, saying, "Yesterday I was going wild with Omri and Tehila put me in her room."[1]

In these contexts, the time-out was ended by the child returning to the presence of the parents and pronouncing an apology. Time-outs can also be ended by imposing a prior time limit on them, by the parent deciding to question the child as to his being repentive, or by both sides ignoring the incident and continuing as if nothing has transpired. Time-outs, then, provide an opportunity for the child to reconsider his actions and for the parent to reassess the importance of the misbehavior in question and decide whether any further discussion of the issue is warranted. As a mother explains, "send them up to their bedrooms and give them time to calm down, and then perhaps we can talk about it...." (Ribbens, 1994, p. 131). When I told Karen, at 31;9, "You go to your room and

[1] Hebrew: "Etmol ani hishtolalti im Omri ve-Tehial sama oti baxeder shela"

Table 9.3.

	Age	Source
In pretend play with dolls K: "You are a big menace – sit here, I don't want to see you, sit in the corner"[2]	32;10	Karniol (Diary, Karen)
Pretend play, doll pooped C: "And now you, you poop in panties. You get in time-out. . . . Time-out for you miss, right here. Sit in time-out"	35 mos.	Hart & Risley (1999, p. 137)
Pretend play, doll pooped K: "You will be here 10 minutes – you made in your diaper"[3] . . . . (to father) "Daddy be careful when you go to the bathroom, Dana is sitting there for 10 minutes, until she is 3 years old."[4]	35;26	Karniol (Diary, Karen)
Pretend play, C is preschool teacher C: "You guys are going to sit in time out. . . . all of you go sit in time out. You're gonna be in time out the whole time"	Preschool	Barnes & Vangelisti (1995)
Pretend play, dolls climbed to the roof, C as pretend M C: "See I told you guys that you would get hurt if you climbed up here. Now get in your rooms and have a time-out!"	5 years	Engel (1995, p. 52)

think about being a good girl," she answered, "After I finish thinking I will come back here and I will be a good girl."

Children's experience with time-out is manifest in their doll play, as illustrated in Table 9.3.

A time-out, then, is used by children to punish pretend dangerous behavior, toileting accidents, and general misbehavior by dolls and peers. The variety of settings in which children threaten their dolls and peers with time-out suggests that it may be quite a prevalent disciplinary strategy on the part of parents. How frequently is a time-out used? Straus and Mouradian (1998) found that 18 percent of mothers admitted to using it more than twenty times in the past 6 months, primarily with their younger children.

LOSS OF PRIVILEGES

Parents often use loss of privileges to discipline their children. Parents seem to gear the privilege to be withdrawn to the age of the child being disciplined. For instance, when asked how she would deal with a child who refused to leave a television program and go to bed, a mother says "I'd stop her watching the TV tomorrow" or warn the child, "if you stay up now, you'll not be able to have a story" (Cook-Gumperz, 1973, pp. 60, 107). Similarly, a mother who explains what she would do if her child didn't talk to his father, says, "if he went on being silly I'd get cross with him and make him go to bed without a story that night" (Cook-Gumperz, 1973, p. 243). After a toddler threw a crying tantrum, her father warned that if she didn't "straighten up," he would not read her a book (Prusank, 1993, p. 144). A Korean preschooler who was excited and hit her father was told, "If you keep doing this, I won't take you to the movies" (Clancy, Akatsuka, & Strauss, 1997, p. 30).

Older children are more likely to be disciplined with a different type of loss of privileges, such as being grounded (e.g., "I have kept him home even from a school party," Sears, Maccoby, & Levin, 1957, p. 337). For instance, a 10-year-old boy explains that "whenever I'm late home playing out, and not like keeping the house tidy. They would probably ground me for the rest of the week" (Sixsmith & Knowles, 1996). As a 15-year-old girl relates:

> my mum had a go at me, shouting, then she calmed down. . . . I explained to her what happened. She talked to me, she told me why, what was wrong and why I shouldn't have done it. . . . I was banned from TV and going out for a bit. (Rout, Sixsmith, & Moore, 1996, p. 109)

A related loss of privilege is being prevented from staying up late. When a teacher asked a first grader, "What kind of punishment don't you like?" she got the response, "Go to bed." The teacher then elaborated, "To be sent to bed early," and the child agreed (Mishler, 1972, p. 287). It is clear that the child viewed being sent to bed as a means of discipline. As evident in the above reports, though, children seem to take such loss of privileges in their stride, at least in retrospecting about them. Interestingly, when children discuss how a problem should be solved, they themselves may suggest loss of privileges as a solution, for example, a 4.5-year-old who says, "I could go to my room and not play with the kids a couple of days" (Gordon, 1976, p. 178).

In children's play, threat of loss of privileges is often used as a means of controlling their dolls and their friends. A pretend mother of four chastises her children saying, "If you're not good, you can't stir" (Pitcher & Schultz, 1983, p. 45), with helping mother cook being construed as a privilege that could be withdrawn. Similarly Karen, at 31;10, tells a male doll, "You're not behaving nicely – you won't

[2] Hebrew: "Atta shovav gadol – teshev kan, anni lo roca lirot otxa, taamod bapina"

[3] Hebrew: "At tiheyi po esser dakot – at assit baxitul"

[4] Hebrew: "Abba tizaeher sheata holex lasherutim – Dana yoshevet shum 10 dakot – ad she he tiheye bat 3"

dance today."[5] Dolls who do not adopt "adult" preferences are warned that they will have positive incentives removed, disciplinary tactics that are used frequently at day care. In fact, children are often warned of loss of privileges in day care and preschool. Staton (1993) found that teachers often threatened, and carried out, such disciplinary tactics, for example, "You will not get to see the movie with the rest of the class if you continue to talk" (p. 159). When a teen refuses to throw out her ice cream in class, her teacher grabs her hat off her head and says, "When you have put your sweet in the bin as I asked you can have your hat back" (Furlong, 1976, p. 37). By doing so, the teacher essentially announced that wearing a hat in class was a privilege that could be lost by misbehaving. In this context, it is interesting that choice is sometimes treated as a privilege that can be withdrawn. Willes (1983) found that in preschools and elementary school where choice among activities is the norm, choice is viewed by teachers as a privilege that can be forfeited if children do not behave appropriately, for example, "Choice time is no longer choice time if you haven't gotten your work done" (Graue & Walsh, 1998, p. 171).

LOSS OF REWARD

Rather than losing privileges, children may be disciplined by loss of rewards, losing out on a promised sweet or gift (e.g., Wells, 1985; Newson & Newson, 1968, 1976). In this vein, when 4-year-old Raymond drops his coat in the living room, his mother repeatedly asks him to pick up the coat and take it upstairs. After he consistently ignores her request, she warns him: "Well you'll get no threepence at lunchtime" (i.e., to buy sweets) (Newson & Newson, 1968, p. 499). It seems that children do take such threats seriously, largely because parents do in fact carry them out. Thus, in discussing her daughter's willingness to make up her bed, a mother explains, "the only reason she does that (i.e., making her bed) is because she'll lost two bucks off her pocket money, otherwise she wouldn't do it" (Bennett et al., 1999, p. 40). On the other hand, when threats refer to larger, promised items, the loss of reward is more likely to be interpreted – both by the parent and the child – as an idle threat. Threats like "I won't buy you that bike for Christmas" (Newson & Newson, 1968, p. 420) are likely to be either conveniently forgotten or *camouflaged* (Newson & Newson, 1976), with parents finding evidence of "improvement" in children's behavior that obviates the need for the threat to be carried out.

Children's task in this context, then, is to sort out those potential lost rewards that are likely to be withheld from those that can potentially be gained, a task they seem to accomplish quite readily. This is evident in two different ways. First, children explicitly tell parents what kinds of rewards they are willing to lose, for example, a 7-year-old boy who refuses to put on his pajamas tells his father, "Oh no, Daddy, I'd rather go without my sweets for the weekend" (Newson & Newson, 1976, p. 335). Second, children threaten their dolls with loss of rewards in interacting with them during pretend play. Pretending to be the preschool teacher, Karen, at 32;16, chides her doll saying, "Orr won't get a surprise today; Orr is not nice today; Orr is doing something that I don't allow him."[6] Again, a few days later, she chides her doll, saying, "Afterwards if you're not a good girl you won't get cake."[7] In another instance of threat of loss of reward Karen, at 31;10, is playing with her dolls and she reports that "All day dolly doesn't sit nicely," and when she was asked why, she answered, "I think because she doesn't want a surprise,"[8] an implicit threat that those who do not sit nicely at day care do not get surprises.

There is some evidence that parents sometimes treat supper as if it were a reward and send their children to bed without giving them supper, using this as a disciplinary strategy (e.g., Grieshaber, 2004). On the other hand, parents do not report using such a strategy but in doll play, children give voice to the prevalence of such a strategy, as shown in Table 9.4.

Although we cannot be sure that the above children are reflecting parental practices that invoke loss of reward, it seems highly unlikely that all of these children invented the contingency between being good and getting fed at night without ever having been exposed to such a contingency.

THREATENING WITH PHYSICAL PUNISHMENT

In home observations and in parental interviews some parents indicate that they threaten their children with physical punishment, with several examples shown in Table 9.5.

Some mothers indicated that they threatened their children with straps, belts, canes, and yardsticks (e.g., when a 5-year-old annoys the dog, his mother warns, "I'll get that stick in a minute," Wells, 1986, p. 75) but often denied actually using them when interviewed (e.g., Newson & Newson, 1968, 1976).

There are two important questions that can be raised in this context. First, do mothers who threaten with physical punishment eventually administer it? Second, do mothers actually use various instruments to punish their children? Home observations indicate that in some cases, the answer to both questions is yes. Carew (1976) relates a situation where a 15-month-old pulls the blanket off a visiting baby. After being told to get out, she runs into the bathroom. Her mother yells, "Get out of that bath! I'll beat your ass too! Out! Out!"; catching the child, she slaps the child's bottom and says, "Get in there (living room) or I'll get the strap" (p. 131). Cook-Gumperz (1973) found that whereas mother's use of threats and punishments did not correlate

[5] Hebrew: "At lo mittnaheg yafe – at lo lirkod hayom*"

[6] Hebrew: "Orr lo tekabel haftaot hayom; Orr lo xamud hayom; Orr osse masheu she ani lo marsha lo. . . . . ."

[7] Hebrew: "Axar kach im at lo yalda tova at lo tekabli uga"

[8] Hebrew: "Kol hayom buba lo yeshevet yafe" "Ani chosehevet he lo rotza haftaa"

Table 9.4.

	Age	Source
C1 says he's C2 Is warned not to make this claim C: "Because his mommy will be angry at you. She'll put you to bed without your supper"	3 years	Paley (1986, p. 58)
During pretend play F: "I won't give you any food if you're not good" Pretend baby protests that he's good F; "No, you're not. You're crying. Only good babies get food"	3 years	Paley (1986, p. 129)
Playing a feeding mother C: "Because I'm not giving you any more if you're not good"	3;2 years	Slama-Cazacu (1977, p. 94)
Playing mother C: "Well, then, I'll send you to bed and you'll never have a sweet – your dinner, all right?"	Preschool	Sheldon (1990)

Table 9.5.

	Age	Source
Child is throwing something M: "If you throw it once more, I'm gonna smack your bottom. M: "What's going happen when you throw it again?" C: "You going hit my bottom"	26 mos.	Brown (1973, Eve)
C repeatedly touches table M: "No, you are not playing with the table. If you do it again, I'm gonna spank"	Toddler	Hart & Risley (1999, p. 107)
C laughs about spilling milk on M M: "You do it again and I'll whack you"	Unknown	Cloran (1989, p. 134)
M: "Now what's going to happen?" C: "I guess I have to be spanked" M: "That's right"	Kindergarten	Sears, Maccoby, & Levin (1957, p. 379)
M explaining handling refusal to go to bed M: "I'd tell her that if she didn't go to bed now she'd get a hiding"	7 years	Cook-Gumperz (1973, p. 60)

with children's reports of mothers' use of threats, mothers' use of threats and children's reports of actual punishment did correlate. It seems that mothers who threaten to physically punish their children tend to do so – at least as reported by their children.[9] It may well be, though, that mothers who threaten do not need to carry out their threats because children suspect that the threat may be implemented and change their behavior accordingly. As one mother explains, "I do smack them, but I don't very often have to smack them because if I tell them not to do something they know I mean it" (Ribbens, 1994, p. 174).

[9] We should be wary of drawing any conclusions about this pattern though for several reasons. Children's reports of their mothers' actions rely on children's memory of disciplinary encounters. Children may be generalizing over several disciplinary encounters as opposed to recalling any specific instance, and they may recall actual punishments better than the threats that preceded them. As well, since actual punishments may elicit affective reactions in the child, it is possible that affective reactions are used as recall cues in guiding the memory search conducted by the child in responding to questions about disciplinary encounters.

Interestingly, threats of physical punishment are apparently differentially used by different social classes, with greater use in the working class than in the middle class (e.g., Cook-Gumperz, 1973).

PHYSICAL PUNISHMENT AS PARENTAL LOSS OF SELF-CONTROL

Straus (1994) defines corporal punishment as "the use of physical force with the intention of causing a child to experience pain but not injury for the purposes of correction or control of the child's behavior" (p. 4). It is the goal of the infliction of pain rather than the production of injury that defines physical punishment as punishment rather than as abuse. But Straus sees this goal as being in the service of another goal, the goal of correcting child behavior and bringing it in line with social norms and parental expectations for behavior. It is this latter goal, of correcting and controlling the child's behavior, that is at the center of a controversy over the use of physical means of disciplining versus punishing (e.g., Gershoff, 2002; Holden, 2002), where the former implies instruction and guidance and the latter implies response suppression. As I argue below, even parents who do not accompany their physical behavior with verbal induction often perceive their physical behavior as conveying disciplinary messages. In fact, in an interview study, parents were found to use multiple justifications in accounting for their use of physical punishment (Gough & Reavey, 1997).

As Gershoff (2002) claims, though, it is often difficult to differentiate physical means of punishment from physical abuse, to delineate the point at which one changes into the other. The problem is compounded in studies in which parents self-report; parents may underreport harsh and abusive means of physical punishment, for fear of being reported to the authorities, for shame of being considered an abusive parent by the interviewer, and so forth. In studies that track parental behavior in interaction with their children, parents may even alter their disciplinary techniques because of such observation.

The major problem with the above definition of physical punishment is that not all instances of punishment, in particular physical punishment, reflect parental goals. Parents don't always behave the way they would like to behave. As one mother poignantly lamented, "you very often don't come anywhere near the picture of what you'd like to be" (Newson & Newson, 1968, p. 539). All parents want to be calm and reasonable during disciplinary encounters, but they often fail. The apparent reason for their failure is that mothers interpret the child's actions or inactions as having willfully defied their external preferences.

Yet the proximal cause of parental failure to maintain composure during disciplinary encounters may have less to do with the child's prior behavior than with parental inability to self-control; as Bettelheim (1962; but see also Gordon, 1976) says, "you slap your child because you're out of your wits" (p. 160). Very few mothers start off by shouting or hitting their children. Whereas parents may use a variety of methods of control within a given incident of socialization (e.g., Clifford, 1959), using a variety of methods is distinct from an *escalating* series of methods. Many parents report that their methods of discipline escalate, becoming progressively harsher as the child continues to resist (e.g., Backett, 1982). The mother of several children explains,

> I don't hit them to start with . . . I try and tell them straight that I don't agree, and then if they still continue then I threaten a smack, and then if they don't, I do do it. I do hit them, and I don't think it does them any harm once in a while. (Ribbens, 1994, p. 131)

The sequence referred to by these mothers indicates that parents add more extreme means as the child continues to resist (e.g., Ritchie, 1999). As one mother relates,

> We try explaining, you know, saying 'no, you must'nt, no you mustn't, two or three times. Try explaining, and if that doesn't do any good then I just smack her, or smack her and put her out of the room. (Backett, 1982, p. 183)

In fact, in a Swedish study (Palmérus & Jutengren, 2004), the parents of children 3 to 6 years old were asked to respond to hypothetical dilemmas in which their child supposedly continued to evidence misconduct. Parents changed verbal strategies to more coercive ones, including physical punishment, when misdeeds continued.

In this context, it is clear that parents are polarized into two groups; those who expect to smack or threaten with smacking; and those who explicitly refrain from using or threatening their children with physical punishment. It is important to note that even those who expect to physically punish their children generally start off in a reasonable fashion – but things escalate when the child does not comply and the parent loses self-control. How do we know that parents lose control? Straus and Stewart (1999) found that more parents reported administering physical punishment of some sort to their children between the ages of 2 and 8 years than indicated that they threatened to do so. This suggests that some parents were not intending to administer physical punishment although they ended up administering it.

Losing self-control, though, is not a unitary phenomenon. There seem to be several kinds of parental loss of control. One kind of loss of control reflects parents' inability to cope with their own anger, for example, "I'm angry, I want to punish them" (Gough & Reavey, 1997, p. 424). Describing a context in which her daughter defied her, a mother says, "I was about ready to murder her. . . . So she got walloped" (Newson & Newson, 1976, p. 80). Some parents who react to their own anger with physical punishment see this as an inevitable cycle that resolves, rather than creates, problems. Physical punishment inflicted on the child is seen as cathartic for the punisher in such cases – "I don't use it as a punishment. I use it as a relief for me" (Sears, Maccoby, & Levin, 1957, p. 329). This is also expressed by a mother who elaborated: "It's necessary for *me* – it's like a thunderbolt – crash, bang, wallop, and then it's over and you're happy again!" (Newson & Newson, 1968, p. 436). Other parents readily admit to having a problem with controlling their tempers, acknowledging that they tend to "fly off the handle." Understanding the problem as reflecting their own troublesome temper, rather than the child's misbehavior, though, does not help these parents find a solution. They seem unable to divert their anger into nonphysical means of dealing with their children. In the words of one mother, "I sometimes spank him. Putting him to bed works better, but sometimes I've spanked him before I think of that. Spanking is partly to let off steam" (Hess & Handel, 1959, p. 43). Her words reflect her inability to use alternative strategies despite her understanding that physical punishment is not conducive to her own long-term goals.

Another kind of loss of control is evident in parents who attribute their "losing it" to temporary bad moods, induced by having a bad day, the time of day, or being tired. As a mother explains what she would do when her child spills wine on a tablecloth, she says, "Well sometimes I mean I think it all depends on what kind of mood you are in, when I'm in a pretty you know good sort of mood then I'd probably not scold him and tell him to be more careful" (Cook-Gumperz, 1973, p. 146). But when a parent is "in a bad mood," parental loss of control may follow. One mother who exemplifies this type of loss of control, said, "I believe in smacking . . . you can't help yourself if you've had a bad day" (Ribbens, 1994, p. 176), explicitly attributing her loss of control to "having a bad day."

Long, tiring days are another source of loss of parental self-control. In this vein, a mother explains: "after a rotten day at work, and he's being a real mongrel . . . . I do lose my cool," further explaining that she apologizes afterwards (Grieshaber, 2004, p. 110). In fact, "going nuts" at the end of the day is evident in a mother who says, "I've only swatted my kid twice, but it was hard, and it was at five thirty, just the way everybody else does . . . at the end of the day" (Bettelheim, 1962, p. 166). Notice that the above mother justifies her behavior by seeing herself as instantiating a general phenomenon of parental loss of control. Expressing this sentiment as well in a different way, a mother says, "everybody gets to that pitch sometimes when they've just got to smack them" (Newson & Newson, 1968, p. 447). These mothers, then, see themselves as being similar to everyone else in finding it difficult to cope – everyone has bad days, everyone gets tired at the end of the day – wrongly assuming that this difficulty is generally translated into physical means of dealing with one's children. In fact, though, young children are spanked more often in the evening than at other times of the day (Holden, Coleman, & Schmidt, 1995).

Yet parents often blame their children for their own loss of self-control. They see the child as "getting on their nerves," and think that the child is the one who should be able to stop getting on their nerves rather than the parent who should maintain self-control. The mother of a preschooler who repeatedly asks for a book to be read, is warned "You're getting on my nerves" (Shure & Spivack, 1978, p. 138). As the mother of a 4-year-old says, "she gets on my nerves that much, I just put my things down and smack her one" (Newson & Newson, 1968, p. 94). In these cases, then, it is the child who is deemed responsible for the adult's loss of control. Straus and Mouradian (1998) found that of mothers who admitted spanking their child in the past 6 months, only 11 percent took responsibility and admitted doing so because they "lost it."

PARENTAL REACTIONS TO LOSS OF CONTROL

Parental reactions to loss of control in administering physical punishment to their children range widely. Some parents merely acknowledge that such behavior is inappropriate and label it negatively. As one father explains, "When I feel like spanking them on the spur of the moment just because I'm mad, I shouldn't do that" (Hess & Handel, 1959, p. 45). A mother who is asked whether she ever loses her temper answers that she gets aggravated and when she is asked how she handles it, she responds, "I just paddle them, which isn't good" (Hess & Handel, 1959, p. 242). Explaining about her 18-month-old who wailed repeatedly at night, a mother says, "I ended up spanking him, but I felt that was not the right way" (Gordon, 1976, p. 215). A similar sentiment is expressed by the mother of a preschooler:

> If I've had like a bad morning or something, usually I'll give him a whack or something, send him to his room, that's really not the right way to deal with it, I don't think, I should try to talk to him . . . when he calms down we can talk it out. (Gottman et al., 1997, p. 68)

Other parents speak more explicitly of their own inability to maintain self-control and refer to their administration of physical punishment in terms of their own loss of self-control. In this vein, a mother bemoans: "I'm the adult, I should be able to cope with this situation . . . I get annoyed with myself that I've got to the state where I've had to smack her" (Newson & Newson, 1976, p. 317). Similarly, a mother is explaining what happens when her child "throws a fit," saying "It makes me so mad, it gets me so nervous. Then I hit her and then I feel bad about it" (Miller, 1982, p. 65).

In more general terms, some parents do evidence awareness of their own loss of control and feel bad about their own inability to maintain it.

Whereas some of the above parents expressed contrition about having engaged in physical punishment, it is unclear when they actually experience being contrite. In some cases, regret and the attendant guilt feelings are experienced immediately after engaging in the behavior, as shown in Table 9.6.

In many cases, though, regret appears to emerge only when parents have calmed down and have had time to think about the preceding events. As the mother of a 7-year-old says, "I regret it afterwards; and when it's all over, I sit and say to myself "I'll never do it again" (Newson & Newson, 1976, p. 311). In fact, when parents have had time to think about it, they may explicitly question their own behavior, wondering whether their child was actually at fault or whether their anger got the better of them.

Not all parents are contrite after they use physical punishment. First, some parents only experience guilt when they see the child's negative reaction to being physically punished. As one mother says about herself, "I feel bad (i.e., about hitting her) and I pick her up and start huggin her" (Miller, 1982, p. 65). After a mother slaps her son for touching a kettle and he cries, she says, "No don't cry – there – don't cry – Oh come on you baby – you're not hurt now. Come on – give us a cuddle and a kiss" (Tough, 1973, p. 31). Yet another mother relates, "I'd bawl him out and then give him a bun to stop him crying" (Cook-Gumperz, 1973, p. 247). In these instances, then, the parents' own behavior does not elicit regret or guilt; the child's

Table 9.6.

	Age	Source
M: "I will land one at him, I feel sorry straight away; I always regret it afterwards"	4 years	Newson & Newson (1968, p. 447)
M: "I smack purely to relieve my own feelings... but I never fail to feel guilty and I always feel myself to be the loser"	4 years	Newson & Newson (1968, p. 447)
M. "(When I) shout at him, or get angry with him... I'm immediately overwhelmed with guilt feelings"	Toddler	Bettelheim (1962, p. 48)

reaction to the disciplinary encounter elicits contrition in the parent.

Second, some parents see physical punishment as a legitimate last resort – to be used when all else fails or when the mother acknowledges that she doesn't know how to get her child to adopt her preferences. In the theoretical controversy over the use of physical punishment, Larzelere (2000) has taken the stand that restrained physical punishment should be used as a back-up for when other strategies do not work with children. Acknowledging this attitude, mothers report: "I don't like to spank, but I do resort to it at times" (Prusank, 1993, p. 148), and "As a last resort I will smack him" (Newson & Newson, 1968, p. 441). Of course, here parents vary in terms of what it means that "all else has failed." Some parents may try one tactic and when that fails they may see this as a situation in which "all else has failed." They may eventually realize that had they taken the time to clarify the situation prior to deciding that "all else had failed," other solutions may have been likely. The father of a 7-year-old says, "I ought to have tried a good telling-off, a really good one, and it might have saved my smacking, I don't know" (Newson & Newson, 1976, p. 318). Straus (1994) suggests that spanking as a last resort is worse than spanking per se, because by that time parents are usually angry and act impulsively, suggesting to the child that when one is extremely angry, hitting others is justified.

Some parents do not express regret about using physical punishment but rather regret the *extent of force* with which the physical punishment was applied, as shown in Table 9.7.

For such parents, children's complaints about being physically punished are translated into complaints about the *force* of the punishment rather than about the punishment per se (e.g., when a child of 19 months complains about being slapped, the mother responds, "I didn't hit you that hard," Carew, 1976, p. 133).

The important question here is, why are parents unable to parlay their feelings of regret into guidelines as to how to behave toward their children in the future? One explanation provided by Straus (1994) is that parents tend to forget incidents in which spanking did not work because such incidents contradict the almost-universal American belief that spanking is something that works when all else fails; in contrast, they tend to remember when nonspanking methods did not work.

VIEWING PHYSICAL PUNISHMENT AS AN EDUCATIONAL TOOL

Many parents who resort to using physical punishment believe that this serves either short-term or long-term socialization goals. In Wells's (1985) study, the majority of British mothers of preschoolers sampled indicated that they would discipline a child for various infractions, but irrespective of the type of infraction, the mothers' preferred strategies for dealing with these transgressions were to explain (e.g., why the behavior was naughty, why it makes the mother angry, or telling the child that he or she is naughty) and to smack. Smacking the child was viewed as an efficient means of getting the child to understand the severity of his infraction. Expressing this view, a mother says, "I don't smack to relieve my own feelings, but for something he really must understand was very wrong" (Newson & Newson, 1968, p. 411). The perception is that if the child is physically punished, he would understand "the right and wrong of things" (Newson & Newson, 1976, p. 310); children have to "learn what's right" (Gough & Reavey, 1997, p. 422). Expressing this explicitly, a mother interviewed by Ribbens (1994) indicated that if one uses physical discipline "it's got to hurt.... So if I smack mine they get a good smack, they know they've done something very wrong" (Ribbens, 1994, p. 101).

Whereas some mothers claim that physical punishment is used by them to teach "moral" lessons to their child, other mothers indicate that they use physical punishment as educational tools for emphasizing dangers to be avoided. Safety concerns can lead parents to use physical means of prevention, as evident in the words of the mother of a kindergarten child who says,

> I would be the one that would be sorry if you were hurt. I would never forgive myself, because I slipped up in not teaching you the danger. It's a sorrowful thing for me to have to teach you through pain. (Sears, Maccoby, & Levin, 1957, p. 379)

Reflecting this educational approach, when a 3-year-old plays with an electric kettle, his mother slaps him, pulls the kettle away and asks, "Haven't I told you not to touch the kettle? You do as I say or you'll get hurt" (Tough, 1973, p. 31). As well, a preschooler tells a visitor, "Remember the time I put a little ball marble in my nose?... I'm not going to do that no more... If I do it again, I'm a get I might get spanked," and the father affirms the contingency (Hall,

Table 9.7.

	Age	Source
M: "If I lose my temper, I perhaps smack him harder than I mean to"	4 years	Newson & Newson (1968, p. 538)
F: "When I do spank Jim I'm too hard on him"	Preschool	Hess & Handel (1959, p. 49)
F: "this smack the last time, I've wondered whether I smacked her too hard, and thought, "you big bully"	7 years	Newson & Newson (1976, p. 318)

CHILDES). Tough (1976) recorded a mother with her 3.5-year-old at a launderette. When he starts crawling away, she slaps him, carries him back, and says, "Now sit still and be good" (p. 22). In another such instance, a working-class mother who is worried about traffic in her street, says, "I told my neighbors if I'm working and Mon doing cleanin or something, if they see her out there and she even so much as starts to put her foot on the street, to paddle her ass," which the neighbor promptly did when the occasion arose (Miller, 1982, p. 59). In a similar fashion, another mother explains that "when he was $1\frac{1}{2}$ and was first walking, I always cold-bloodedly slapped him for crossing (the street) and now he's just fine.... And what harm has it done?... I'd stop doing it if I could see something wrong with it" (Bettelheim, 1962, p. 163).Whereas above, parents were using physical punishment to curtail ongoing behavior, parents may see the purpose of physical punishment in a more extended temporal context. In this vein, the mother of a 7-year-old explains "If I can knock good manners and common sense into them now, by the time they get to 9 and 10 they should be all right" (Newson & Newson, 1976, p. 454). That is, physical punishment is viewed as a means of inculcating rules and norms in the long run. Physical punishment is used as an "insurance policy"; although it did not provide immediate results, it is expected to prove beneficial over the years.

Some parents who see physical punishment as an educational tool think that as children grow older, spanking is no longer an educational tool. In fact, parents report that they use less physical punishment with older children than with younger ones (Straus & Mouradian, 1998). In the words of one father, "They are too old to be taken over the knee. They are of an age where reasoning is of more value" (Hess & Handel, 1959, p. 196). Also referring to children's age, a mother says, "My daughter is too old to spank" (Hess & Handel, 1959, p. 43). Such parents change their "educational tactics" when they perceive that their children's cognitive abilities have changed.

There are many cultures in which beating children – with the hand, with sticks, or with belts – is entrenched as a pedagogical strategy, accepted by parents, teachers, and even children themselves as a means of punishing misbehavior of various sorts, including lying, stealing, impoliteness, and even not eating one's food (e.g., Smith & Mosby, 2003). In such cultures, parents express expectations that children should be physically punished following transgressions. In this context, a British father born in the West Indies says,

> But over here it's different. For instance, if one of these kids did something terrible, and I decided to give him a few straps, and then he ended up with marks on him, he went to school and the social worker sees the marks on him, then I'll be in trouble.... In the West Indies you'd get a good hiding, you get marks, then the teacher knows you got the marks because you did something you shouldn't do and you know you got disciplined for it. Even the teachers in the school they used to discipline children, with strap in school. (Mayall, 2002, p. 57)

The major problem in such cultures is that parents who do not physically punish their children are seen as being derelict in fulfilling their parental role. Such attitudes are unlikely to change without legal changes that restrict or outlaw the use of physical means of punishment.

In cultures in which physical punishment is viewed as an educational tool, parents may use reminiscence as a means of clarifying to the child why he has gotten punished in the past. In this vein, a Chinese mother asks her son why he cried last night and he answers, "You and Grandma didn't let me watch TV.... I insisted on watching it." His mother replies, "So you got spanked, right?" (Wang, 2001, p. 713). From this perspective, spanking is viewed as a justified, contingent outcome of transgressing and is discussed as a means of enforcing both such socialization practices and the values that guide them.

DIFFERENTIATING DISCIPLINE BY CONTEXT

Parents may view different types of discipline as appropriate in different locations. For instance, one mother explains that whereas she is relatively tolerant of misbehavior on the child's part when this happens in the home, she is not tolerant when the same thing happens outside the home. She explains, "if they show me up inside, then I would talk to them and explain to them... but if they showed me up outside, then I would smack them most definitely" (Newson & Newson, 1968, p. 59). This is because in such a context the parent perceives it as having lost face. If the same behavior had been undertaken by the child in the house it is highly unlikely that the parent would have engaged in physical punishment. A mother admits this, saying, "I told them off at times because I felt the pressure of people watching" (Ribbens, 1994, p. 103). In a recent study (Karniol & Assor, unpublished), Kibbutz mothers were found to differentiate their disciplinary tactics less than urban Israel mothers by whether the child misbehaved at home or in public.

DIFFERENTIATED PHYSICAL PUNISHMENT

Some parents use physical punishment only with a specific child, being convinced that for that particular child, physical punishment is warranted. That is, the use of physical punishment may arise after parental experience with one particular child as opposed to other children. Parents may be sensitive to individual differences between their children and select the means of regulating their behavior that seems to work for that particular child (e.g., "I would have maybe smacked Edward, whereas I wouldn't smack Robert," Ribbens, 1994, p. 119). In the words of one mother,

> spanking doesn't work good for R., never did. You know, we tried it.... Ah, like my younger son, J., spanking works... you don't have to spank him hard or anything else, just the physical, you know, I did spank you, that is enough. You had to be more logical with R. You know, 'Time out because you did this wrong'.... You just put him in his room, let him calm down, give him five minutes, and he's ready for try something else again. (Gottman, 1997, p. 69)

Newson and Newson (1968) similarly recorded a mother who indicated that her children differ in their temperaments; with her son, "you've just got to give him a tap and he shuts up. But if I smack Michelle, she just screams all the more" (p. 497). Yet another mother explains regarding her two children, "Mark was the other way around – he'd rather take the spanking" (Gordon, 1976, p. 189). In line with this, Deater-Deckerd (1996) found that parents respond in child-specific ways to child misbehavior scenarios. They adjust the way they interact and discipline the child, depending on the particular child being disciplined. This indicates that parents are interpreting the child's personality and adjusting their own behavioral tactics in light of their understanding of the child's personality. In reminiscing about her grown-up children, a mother says, "Some I could be more stern with and some of them I had to go a little easier or they would rebel" (Cohler & Grunebaum, 1981, p. 75).

Whether such differentiated disciplinary tactics are in fact warranted and successful in dealing with different children is difficult to examine empirically. However, research in this domain indicates that parents' perceptions of their children as different and warranting different treatment may be wrong. Specifically, Saudino, Wertz, Gagne, and Chawla (2004) used both parent ratings and objective measures to assess the activity levels and shyness of ninety-five pairs of same- and mixed-gender siblings between 3 and 8 years of age. The objective measures were obtained in the laboratory and assessed children's level of shyness, for example, if they took a toy offered to them or clung to their parent instead. As well, motion recorders were attached to the children's dominant leg and arm for 48 hours. To assess parents' perceptions, parents completed questionnaires about their children's temperaments. The researchers found that the objective measures, as measured by children's actual behavior and via motion recorders, correlated little with parents' reports. How parents viewed their children differs substantially from children's actual temperaments. Moreover, parents reported negative correlations between their children's temperament dimensions. Parents didn't just say that their children were dissimilar, but said that their children were opposites – if one was shy, the other was outgoing. Why would parents see differences between their children if such differences do not actually exist? First, defining one child through contrast with another child may be a simple way to better understand and interact with each child. Second, seeing each child as different may justify differentiated behavior toward each child.

WHAT CHILDREN LEARN FROM PUNISHMENT

What constitutes successful punishment? One could argue for several different criteria. One of these criteria would be the extent to which the child is a "repeat offender." As discussed previously, parents are more likely to "lose it" in the contexts of behaviors that have been subject to discipline in the past. On the other hand, we do not know the extent to which children engage in repeated offenses after being disciplined (Gershoff, 2002). Research in this context does indicate that when aversive outcomes are anticipated, children are less likely to engage in those behaviors that lead to such aversive outcomes (Bandura, Ross, & Ross, 1961). Either direct or vicariously experienced aversive outcomes are critical to abstention.

A different approach to gauging whether a given disciplinary encounter is successful or not is one based on Kelman's (1974) tripartite division of the processes of attitude change: compliance, identification, and internalization. *Compliance* refers to an apparent change that is undertaken when the primary concern is the social consequence of agreeing or disagreeing with powerful others who can distribute rewards and punishments. *Identification* refers to an apparent change that is undertaken to either establish or maintain a relationship with another person, who may be perceived as hinging the relationship on the change. It is based on perceptions of self and other as in a unit relationship. Finally, *internalization* occurs when the individual adopts a given position because the position itself appears to be logical, reasonable, or especially compelling. Internalization is the presumed outcome of the message being advocated having been carefully scrutinized and considered. Consequently, the message itself is relevant for internalization but not for either compliance or identification. Concomitantly, in internalization, attitude change would outlast the particular relationship between the person delivering the message and the one receiving it. From this perspective, then,

Table 9.8.

	Age	Source
Playing house F tries to get pretend baby to sleep B refuses to put her down head F: "Okay, I will spank you. Bad boy," spanks	2;9	Garvey (1977, p. 84)
In doll play as pretend teacher K: "Itamar, you will not do that again – you will be punished"[11]	33;16	Karniol (Diary, Karen)
C: "I'm sorry, Dolly. I have to spank you for running in the street. It won't hurt you"	Toddler	Segal & Adcock (1981, p. 67)
Pretend mother to pretend daughter M: "Well, Linda Faye, you just come up these stairs before I whup your behind"	Preadolescent	Mitchell-Kernan & Kernan (1977, p. 202)
Pretend father to pretend son F: "You just turn yourself over here. You gon' get a spankin' for today"	Preadolescent	Mitchell-Kernan & Kernan (1977, p. 203)

disciplinary actions that do not result in internalization are not successful because they do not engender a long-lasting attitude change that is independent of the relationship between the persuader and the target.

Another manifestation of internalization is posttransgressive atonement. That is, if the individual has internalized the values in question, then violating them represents violating one's own standards of behavior. Such violation requires atonement. As a mother explains, "I always say to him if he *knows* he's in the wrong, then he should admit it and say that he's sorry.... But children don't do that, not very often, do they?" (Cook-Gumperz, 1973, p. 201). In a recent study of children's apologies, there was a developmental trend found, with older children expressing more apologies than younger ones across all kinds of contexts, not just in the context of violations (Ely & Gleason, 2006).

Although I am not advocating physical punishment, children learn many things from being physically punished. They may learn what kinds of behaviors lead to what kinds of consequences. As the mother of a 4-year-old explains, after she smacks him, he cries, sits and thinks, and then conjures up alternative behaviors and asks about each one whether his mother would physically punish him for engaging in them (Newson & Newson, 1968). The child was apparently trying to figure out the relevant contingencies for getting physically punished. Children do abstract such contingencies. After a child relates to his mother what he did, she asks "Now what's going to happen?" and he replied "I guess I have to be spanked" (Sears, Maccoby, & Levin, 1957, p. 379). In fact, children often express their understanding of the kinds of consequences that are associated with restricted behaviors. A 17-month-old asks, "If not you'll spank me?"[10] (Bates, 1976). A 5-year-old child repeatedly asked his father, "You going to spank me now?" (Hall, CHILDES). Such questions imply both that the child knows that the behavior in question is subject to restrictions and that the child is aware of the fact that violating such restrictions may have negative consequences. They reflect an awareness of an "if–then" contingency in which one's own behavior constitutes the antecedent and parental reactions constitute the possible consequents. This understanding is also evident in children's pretend play, with children giving expression to their expectations regarding the kinds of misbehaviors that are followed by physical punishment, such as warning dolls that they will be punished, specifying how and why this will happen, as shown in Table 9.8.

The elaborate explanations these children provide as they enact their pretence suggest that they have intimate knowledge of such physical punishment.

In addition, children often state outright the means by which their parents punish them. A 3-year-old who pushed another child off his chair, explaining that she did it because he pushed yet another child, says, "Daddy spanks me to push Leslie," her younger brother (Paley, 1986, p. 27). A 32-month-old child says that her mother wants to hit her, explaining that "Because I wet my pants in the morning"[12] (Eisenberg, 1985, p. 199). In the same vein, two girls, 4 and 5 years old, are discussing being bosses when they grow up and the one says, "maybe we won't know how to punish." The second says, "I will.... I'll put hand up and spank 'em. That's what my mom does" (Corsaro, 1985, p. 96).

Children also indicate that parents use various instruments to administer physical punishment, as evident in the following. A school boy is discussing what happens when his mother is angry, saying, "It's always the same. Me mam, she yells at me... So she yells some more.... In the end I'll probably get a belt or not watch telly" (Kagan & Lewis, 1996, p. 45). In a more extreme fashion, an adolescent girl is talking of parental punishment and says, "in

[10] Italian: "Se no mi dai le botte?"

[11] Hebrew: "Itamar atta lo taase' at ze od paam – atta tekabel onesh"
[12] Spanish: "porque yo me orine' en la mañana"

my family, my dad used to do the wooden spoon thing" (Mason & Falloon, 2001, p. 108), using a euphemism rather than stating explicitly that her father used to beat her with a wooden spoon. When a mother warns her son that unless he gets his shoes she will smack his bum, her daughter adds, "Yep. Smack it hard with a belt" (Grieshaber, 2004, p. 183) and the investigator notes that the mother did, in fact, use a belt on a regular basis to discipline her children. In these instances, then, children incidentally provide portrayals of the means of punishment that are used in their homes.

In fact, many parents interviewed by Newson and Newson (1968, 1976) reported using various objects (e.g., wooden spoons or canes) to administer physical punishment and Wolfenstein (1950) found cross-cultural evidence for the use of wooden spoons and hair brushes as punishing instruments. In a 1995 Gallup poll phone interview of more than nine hundred parents (as cited by Straus & Stewart, 1999), close to 30 percent of the parents of children 2 to 8 years old reported using an object to physically punish their children, suggesting that the use of objects in disciplinary encounters is not an uncommon phenomenon. This is a remarkably high number of what is considered physically abusive parenting and has not been verified in other research.

Irrespective of how physical punishment is administered, children expect that once a child is spanked, he will not repeat the same behavior. Although it is less surprising to hear such expectations from adolescents (e.g., a 15-year-old explains the purpose of punishment as "think over what you did wrong, next time maybe you will make a better decision," Selman, 1980, p. 125), even preschoolers voice the same expectation. As a preschooler who is playing teacher with her dolls says, "Clown, you're not listening. You need to be punished. You need to be good or I'll hit you." After she hits him, she adds, "Now you got to go home and tomorrow you better listen" (Segal & Adcock, 1981, p. 68). Moreover, children may think that they should be physically punished so they will learn to conduct themselves better. When I shouted at Karen, at 31;16, she said to me, "Don't shout at me all the time when I don't behave nicely." When I then asked what I should do, she surprisingly answered, "Just hit me."

Children may also learn to differentiate those circumstances under which their parents do, and do not, manage to maintain self-control. They may learn, for instance, that sometimes their parents "lose it" whereas at other times, they don't. As one child says, "she's always shouting and in a temper. Sometimes she just goes crazy" (Kagan & Lewis, 1996, p. 46). Another 12-year-old says, "you get on your mother's nerves when you do something wrong" (Mayall, 2002, p. 115). In other cases, children may recognize the impact of alcohol on their parents' behavior. As a 5-year-old says regarding his father's drinking, "I don't want him to drink beer. He get real mad, grr, grr, grr, like that" (Singer, 1993, p. 43). Two preschoolers are playing and pretending to be mothers and when one insists on being a "beer drinking mommy," the other refuses, and finally, they agree that the mothers will drink beer, but "it's the kind of beer that doesn't make you mad" so they won't be mad at their babies (Trawick-Smith, 2001, p. 343). Also in this vein, a 7-year-old discusses his father saying,

> our Dad don't drink beer.... My Dad used to.... I know what it does too. It makes you get mad at your friends.... Also, makes you kill people. Makes you get mad to hunt for a gun and you'll find it, then shoot people down. (Peterson & McCabe, 1983, p. 188)

As a consequence, children may attempt to avoid their parents in those circumstances in which they suspect that the parent will lose self-control, a possibility that has not been researched.

As for the processes by which children learn from physical punishment, Holden (2002) suggests that physical punishment activates a two-stage process, in which there is an immediate physiological and emotional reaction to the punishment, with these being followed by secondary cognitive appraisal. It is these secondary cognitive appraisals that determine whether the child complies or defies the parent. Gershoff (2002) suggests that there is a third stage of long-term, cognitive processing that makes possible the long-term child outcomes that have been found to be associated with physical punishment (i.e., increased aggression, etc.). These long-term effects include learning that compliance after physical punishment generally reduces the chances of further physical punishment or that that the use of physical means of coercing others are acceptable means of getting them to enact your preferences. From this perspective, a child who is disciplined without attendant explanations has greater difficulty generalizing across situations because the common factor among them may not be self-evident. As well, without being provided an explanation, the child may well "manufacture" his own incorrect explanation for why a given behavior is inappropriate. More importantly, as discussed in the context of Lepper's (1981) research, when children comply after physical punishment, they may attribute their compliance to the punishment itself, thereby undermining the potential for internalization processes to be initiated. A 13-year-old child crystallizes this view, saying,

> he would think I really shouldn't have done it, because he didn't get punished. But if he gets a punishment, he will think, "that is all that is going to happen, I just worry if I'm going to get a punishment." (Selman, 1980, p. 127)

As for parents, their problem may be that when they spank, the salience of their action is much greater than that of the attendant verbalization and they may attribute the child's compliance to the spanking, rather than to any possible internalization of the message.

The above suggests that there is a causal link between parental self-control and children's self-control. In line with this, one of the basic tenets of Gottfredson and Hirschi's (1990) self-control theory is of a link between parents' self-control and children's self-control by way of the ineffective childrearing practices of parents who are themselves low in self-control. From the perspective of self-control theory, "people who lack self-control will tend to be impulsive, insensitive, physical, risk-seeking, short-sighted, and nonverbal" (p. 90). Gottfredson and Hirschi argue that raising a child high in self-control requires consistent efforts to monitor the child's behavior, recognize deviance when it occurs, and exert effort to correct such deviant behavior when it does. Doing so requires parents to lay aside their own current preferences and address the needs of their children. In particular, they need to ignore their own reactions to the child's deviant behavior and exert self-control in dealing with the child. From this perspective, parents who are low in self-control themselves would be expected to fail to adequately supervise, recognize, and correct deviance in their children. In line with this, parents with a criminal record have been found to use discipline that "tends to be easy, short-term, and insensitive – that is, yelling and screaming, slapping and hitting" (p. 101). On the other hand, parental supervision and monitoring of children's behaviors as well as consistent discipline have been found to increase children self-control (e.g., Hay 2001; Polakowski 1994; Pratt, Turner, & Piquero 2004; Unnever, Cullen, & Pratt 2003), and children's self-control increases with consistent discipline (Gibbs, Giever, & Martin 1998; Unnever, Cullen, & Pratt 2003). In a recent study, Nofziger (2008) found that parental socialization practices serve as the link between the self-control of the mother and her child. In a study of maternal self-reports of self-control-related behaviors (e.g., smoking, excessive drinking, frequent change of partners and jobs) and maternal assessments of child behavior (e.g., the tendency to seek immediate and easy gratification, engage in high-risk behaviors, or indicate the subjects' level of temper, impulsivity, and self-centeredness), maternal means of dealing with children's anger and swearing, discussion of television programs, and consistent expectations as to household responsibilities were the socialization practices examined. There was a significant correlation between maternal and child self-control, which was partly mediated by maternal socialization practices. For instance, children who were spanked when they were 6 or 7 years old had lower self-control when they were 10 and 11 years old.

ESCHEWING PHYSICAL PUNISHMENT

Those parents who intentionally refrain from physically disciplining their children seem to espouse different views as to the virtue of physical punishment. First, some parents do not believe in the adequacy of physical punishment, saying things like:

> I've tried everything. I've tried bribing her, I've tried being nice to her... I've tried hitting her... there's not one thing that makes any difference whatsoever. She just sort of comes round in her own time. (Backett, 1982, p. 184)

Second, some parents believe that parental disciplinary tactics must eventuate in children's acquisition of self-control. This philosophy is evident in a parent who says,

> all discipline is finding your own discipline, isn't it... if children haven't got their own discipline, it doesn't matter what external disciplines are imposed on them.... But if they've got a sort of reasoning in them that this is just a sensible thing to do and I've got other people to think of not just myself, well... (Backett, 1982, p. 164)

Third, some parents refrain from administering physical punishment because they think that physical punishment serves to drive misbehavior underground, only stopping it from happening in front of parents. In this view, children learn to be experts at avoiding being caught, heeding their parents' warning of "Don't let me catch you doing that again!" (Wyckoff & Unell, 1984, p. 4). Research does in fact support the notion that children behave differently when they expect to be caught than when they think no one will know of their misdeeds (e.g., Dienstbier et al., 1975). It is unclear how prevalent each of these views are.

Interestingly, Holden and his colleagues (1997) found that two-thirds of the mothers interviewed reported having changed their beliefs about corporal punishment once they actually became parents. A majority of those mothers who became less in favor of physical punishment indicated that this was partly because of their own, or their child's, negative reaction to such punishment, demonstrating that parents' experiences as socializers can induce changes in their beliefs and disciplinary tactics.

KEEPING IT – AVOIDING LOSS OF CONTROL

Parental loss of control is not inevitable; parents can try to maintain self-control, even when it is difficult to do so. Sometimes, they attempt to do so because they think there are long-term benefits to doing so. For instance, a wife is explaining that her husband "gets provoked, but he doesn't lose his temper at any time. He has a world of patience. He doesn't see the sense of losing his temper – you can't gain" (Hess & Handel, 1959, p. 241). Other parents expressed the sentiment that words have a greater long-term impact, for example, "when they've been smacked the smack is gone, and they are more likely to forget what it's even for; whereas things you say are likely to come back in their minds a little bit" (Newson & Newson, 1976, p. 315). In fact, Gibbons and colleagues (1986) found that actions are recalled better than utterances by young children, most likely because of their salience.

Given the importance of what is said, one way of controlling the situation is by avoiding saying things that are pejorative. As one mother said when interviewed by Gottman and his colleagues, "if I get angry at them, I really try to bite my tongue and to be careful not to say something that I wish I hadn't" (p. 64). This parent realizes that she could do or say something that she would later regret and maintains her cool in order to avoid this anticipated regret.

In line with this, in advising parents, Bettelheim (1962) suggested that one needs to "Be careful. Use forethought" (p. 167). A father expresses such forethought in saying: "At that point where I'm not in control I start to get angry, and with anger you either repress it or you lash out, so you can't lash out at three kids. So I have to control myself there" (Palkovitz, 2002, p. 104).

One common means of controlling oneself involves imposing a temporal distance between oneself and the problematic event. Doing so can merely acknowledge the benefit of the passage of time on the dissipation of anger. As one mother says in describing this, "If I'm angry with the kids, I'll set myself down and say, you know, "You can't yell at them, or you can't, you know, I'll set myself down and cool off before I talk with them" (Newson & Newson, 1976, p. 311). Another means of doing so is by imposing both temporal and physical distance between the mother and the target of her anger. With reference to physical distance, though, there are two different options, with one option involving the mother removing *herself* from the anger-arousing setting. For instance, a mother says to her toddler, "When you hurt me, I don't want to be near you. I am going away from you" (Zahn-Waxler, Radke-Yarrow, & King, 1979). A 14-year-old similarly acknowledges the usefulness of this strategy in peer conflict, saying, "you got to get away for a while. Calm down a bit so you won't be so angry" (Selman, 1980, p. 11). The other option in such cases involves removal of the child from the mother's presence, usually by suggesting that the child leave the current setting until the mother calms down. For example, a mother explains that to avoid administering physical punishment she sends her child upstairs, saying "You must go to bed until *I've* calmed down a bit" (Newson & Newson, 1968, p. 447, emphasis added). In Israel, this strategy is quite common, as manifest in the command, "fly away from my eyes"[13] (literally, get out of my sight), being used by parents and teachers to cope with intransigent children. Note that this is quite different from the situation in which the child is sent to his room to calm *himself* down.

Another related strategy is to warn the child that the parent is reaching tolerance level and is about to lose control. When parents recognize that they are approaching their tolerance level, they can warn their children, either expecting them to change their ways of behaving in the current context, or moving out of harm's way. This is evident when a mother tells her 2-year-old, "You getting on my nerves start talking smart" (Hart & Risley, 1999, p. 122). Preschool teachers often warn children of their rising anger, as evident in Orren's speech to his dolls at 32;25, "Why do you annoy me – I love you but today you are annoying me and I can't play with you . . . today you're not a great kid."[14]

[13] Hebrew: "Oof li me-ha-einayim."

[14] Hebrew: "Lama at margiza otti – ani ohev otax aval hayom at margiza oti vegum ani lo yaxol lesaxek itax . . . . hayom at lo yalda nehederet."

Engaging in self-talk is another means of self-regulating and preventing oneself from "losing it." Gottman et al. cite a father who is trying to control his anger and says,

> the intelligent half of my head talks to it, It says, "All right asshole, don't screw up . . . . You're gonna go out, and you're gonna do something dumb, you're gonna get in all kinds of trouble, embarrass your family, and slow down and stop. (Gottman et al., 1997, p. 72).

In fact, in attempting to teach criminals in a corrections program to control their physical aggression, self-talk is encouraged, with facilitators specifying that the major aim of the program is "to teach you not to be violent by developing an awareness of how you're thinking about things so you can catch yourself" (Fox, 1999). Children recognize the value of self-talk, as when a middle-school child explains that coping with anger is to "have a conversation with yourself or with like God or something" (Brown, 1998, p. 100)

Other strategies of "keeping cool" involve self-distraction and self-calming. For instance, as some mothers note, taking the dog out for a walk allows them to calm down, "I can think and go over things that are bothering me and the time. It is calming for me" (Harrington, 2001, p. 371). Similarly, engaging in gardening can serve to calm oneself down, "I can turn everything off . . . and turn off to the kids. It's relaxing" (ibid, p. 371). Finally, parents can use their spouses when they are going to lose it. For instance,

> we use certain buzz words if one thinks the other's overdoing it . . . . So in the heat of anger, if you are really angered and the kids really get you mad or something like that and you hear this word and it's like, oh, yea, yea, I must be going over the edge . . . and we both look after each other to make sure we don't overdo it. (Palkovtiz, 2002, p. 173)

AUGMENTING, SHAMING, AND INDUCING GUILT

There is a series of techniques that all reflect the induction of posttransgressive reactions. They constitute attempts to alter the way the individual relates psychologically to a behavior that was interpreted as a transgression by the socialization agent. In general, such attempts are aimed at inducing aversive affective reactions in the individual perceived as a transgressor. In *augmenting* (sometimes called "catastrophizing") the outcome of the transgression is made to seem more serious than it really is. For instance, after her son's team loses a baseball game, a mother tells her son that it was his fault that they lost and didn't make it to a tournament (Fine, 1987). In shaming, the hypothetical reactions of others, whether specific or generic, are brought to bear on the outcomes of the transgression. Finally, guilt induction is a means of making the individual who has committed the transgression dispositionally linked to the transgression. An individual who engages in such bad behavior is a bad person and should suffer psychologically and eventually atone for his transgression.

Table 9.9.

	Age	Source
Non-Western Culture		
Kaluli C of 39 mos. took cousin's gourd A1: "Is it yours to take?! Elema" A2: "Aren't you ashamed of yourself? Elema" C2: "Be ashamed! Elema"	24 mos.	Schieffelin (1979)
Basotho C does not address elder properly M: "What kind of person are you who doesn't respect elders?" C does not thank her mother. Sibling of 5;3 responds C: "Thank you mother." "Don't you know how to say "Thank you, mother" yet?"	28 mos.	Demuth (1986. p. 63)
Basotho C grabs a share of cut apple M: "Hey – that greedy person" C doesn't say *thank you* M: "If a man the size of you still doesn't know how to thank. Really!"	5;3 years	Demuth (1986, pp. 62–63)
Western Culture		
C threw toys all over the floor M: "I'm disappointed in you. It hurts my feelings when you do that"	Preschool	Shure & Spivack (1978, p. 143)
T: "Oh, Wendy, I'm ashamed of you. It's packing up time. How can Peter clear up properly when you are doing that?"	Preschool	Gardner & Cass (1965, p. 107)
C runs around instead of sitting down T: "You should be ashamed of yourself" T sits C down, facing wall C sits with his head down during shaming period	Preschool	Grieshaber (2004, p. 4)

Posttransgressive socialization is prevalent across various cultures, as shown in Table 9.9.

Fung and Chen (2001) also found that Taiwanese mothers used shaming explicitly and repeatedly with their preschoolers, alluding to both family members and generic others while doing so.

Although mothers themselves seldom report using shaming, children often provide evidence for its use. A child of 4;11 years explains, "My mom would say 'Abe Duncan! You should be ashamed of yourself'" (Kuczaj, CHILDES). In a play context, when a child refuses to go to bed, a pretend mother says, "Oh, why do you want to stay up all night," and a 5-year-old child corrects the "pretend mother," saying, "No," the mother has to say: "Ashamed of you, Andrew" (Andersen, 1990, p. 118). Older children provide more direct evidence for the induction of guilt and shame. For instance, an adolescent boy says about his mother, "she's very calm and shows us how disappointed she is in us. She makes us feel terrible, really small" (Kagan & Lewis, 1996, p. 46). A 10-year-old child contrasts his experience of being disciplined by his mother and his grandmother, saying, "With me gran it's different. She can make me feel bad . . . and good" (Kagan & Lewis, 1996, p. 45). In line with this, a teen explains why he doesn't talk to his parents about his grades, saying, "they give you the whole 'I'm very disappointed' routine." And I just get sick of that" (Rawlins, 1992, p. 96).

In line with strategies that attempt to engender shame and guilt, children actually do express such affective reactions. Another ten-year-old says, "like, er, in the playground, if I hit someone or something, I feel sorry inside me" (Wells 1986, p. 210). In the same vein, a sixth grader tells of a fight with her dad, saying, "so me and my dad got into a big fight and everything yknow? And um, oh god, and I bit him. I couldn't believe it. Oh god . . . . I went in my room. I locked the door" (Tannen, 1990, p. 186). Similarly, a teenager is explaining why he's trying to stay out of trouble, because "when I do get caught I hate it. I don't like it at all . . . it's just I don't like the feeling of guilt as well." When he is asked whether he only feels guilt when he gets caught, he explains "I feel guilty when I get caught, or I know I'm about to get caught" (Walker, 2004, p. 41).

Does inducing shame and guilt work? Children in a school where shaming was used actually indicated that they avoided behaviors that could lead to such an outcome, saying, "So I don't get my name on the board" (Staton, 1993, p. 158). A teacher explains to a Japanese preschool child who ran outside after hitting a peer, "You were ashamed, so you ran outside to hide, didn't you?" (Peak, 1991, p. 160). There is also empirical research evidence with both children and adults that the induction of shame and guilt does work. For instance, Dienstbier et al. (1975) had preschoolers "guard" a toy train from getting off the tracks, in the presence of a distracting clown. Once the child was distracted, the train derailed. Children were assigned to three groups: a no-emotion group, a shame group that was told that they feel bad because both they and the experimenter knew that they had done something bad, and a guilt group that was told that they feel bad because they knew they had done something bad and would have this experience even if the experimenter did not know of it. Their subsequent behavior in a temptation situation was observed. Children who had been in the guilt-induction group resisted temptation subsequently more than did children in the other two groups. This suggests that the anticipation of experiencing guilt and shame works as a deterrent to misbehavior (cf., Karniol, 1982).

In fact, parents can specify a priori the kinds of affective reactions that children would be expected to experience if they were to engage in a given behavior. For instance, a child could be told how great he would feel if he were to win a tennis game, get an A on his report card, or help an old lady across the street. Parents can also do the opposite, telling a child how awful he would feel if he were to lose a game, fail a subject, or harm another person. In doing so, parents may alter the expectations children have about their own likely affective reactions and this may serve as a motivational resource in determining behavioral choices. The role of anticipatory affective reactions in guiding behavior has not been well-researched and deserves further empirical attention.

Importantly, children's reactions to being disciplined depends on their ability to decontextualize, to transform the *here-and-now*, to manipulate others, and to cope with preferential conflict and preference deferral, issues I address in the next several chapters.

10 Planes of Transformational Thought: Temporal, Imaginal, and Mental

> Doll falls out of bed. 22-month-old girl says, 'Oh-oh, need bandaid,' adding: 'J (own name) fall down... hurt here (shows eyebrow)... ouch... Mommy ice... Poor J... J cry... Dada car... J. car... Go hospital.... All better,' referring to an incident several weeks earlier.
>
> (Wolf, 1982, p. 320)

> Playing house, a 3-year-old girl tells a boy 'You're the baby.' He counters, 'No I'm not; I'm the Superman getting away from you, witch.'
>
> (Pitcher & Schultz, 1983, p. 45)

Thinking need not remain tied to the here-and-now. As Bickerton (1995) contends, although much of our thinking is online, devoted to the immediate environment, we also engage in extensive offline thinking, performing computations, and transforming our internal representations. Gärdenfors (2005) differentiates *cued* versus *detached* representations, with the former referring to representations that are cued by something in the current external situation and the latter being independent of the current context. Our minds can create imaginary objects, situations, and people that are independent of any apparent changes in the external environment but despite their imaginary status may nonetheless be as powerful as external cues in terms of their motivational force. In this chapter, I focus on the emergence of transformational thought and how parents foster it in three planes of representation: (1) the *temporal* plane, as evident in talking of the past and future, (2) the *imaginal* plane, as manifest in pretend play, and (3) the *mental* plane of transformation, as evident in talk of covert, psychological experiences.

TRANSFORMATIONAL THOUGHT AND SYMBOL USE

Transformational thought invokes both decontextualization and recontextualization. The former refers to the ability to dissociate oneself from the observable present; the latter refers to the re-presentation of what has been decontextualized. For instance, in acting out a play, one recontextualizes the words of the playwright (Silverstein, 1976). But one also transforms reality, imbuing the stage with a life that previously existed only in a verbal format. In recontextualizing, one engages in transformational thought, which builds on the capacity to *symbolize*, "the process by means of which human beings can arbitrarily make certain things stand for other things" (Hayakawa, 1972, p. 21). That is, symbols are representations that serve to signify something other than what they are.

Symbols, then, have two important characteristics: independence from the objects they signify, and arbitrariness. The independence of symbols implies that they can be removed in time and place from their referents, they are decontextualized. This independence means that symbols and what they stand for need to be mapped onto each other. But since anything can become a symbol, the specific mapping is arbitrary and idiosyncratic. Reality-to-symbol mapping is an *intra*personal process. Others are not necessarily privy to our use of symbols. Children who are just learning to talk invent words as symbols whose referents are not always clear to parents. Karen used the words "sidamatop" and "popolo" without a clear-cut indication of what they referred to. The former remained a mystery and disappeared from her lexicon; it gradually became clear though that "popolo" was her word for computer. This arbitrariness of words and what they stand for is reflected in Shakespeare's claim: "That which we call a rose, by any other name would smell as sweet." Words, then, are symbols that have arbitrary connections to the objects and ideas they represent.

Given this arbitrary nature of symbols, if one wants to publicly refer to symbols, others need to be informed of the specific mapping and to acknowledge it. For instance, a flag is a symbol of a country; but flags are arbitrary creations that are conventionally determined; the Unites States could hypothetically swap the "Stars and Stripes" for Canada's "Maple Leaf." When countries merge, they adopt the same flag to represent their new merged identity and many wars have been fought to resist the imposition of such new symbols on a given territory. Moreover, if I use a red light as a symbol for "stop" and you use it for "go," the outcome could be disastrous. This underlines the need for people to align their use of symbols. Symbols are conventionalized by having people agree or make rules about the mapping function that governs their use.

In addition, though, in mapping objects onto their mental representation, one needs to distinguish different objects and different mental representations from one another (e.g., "that's not a dog, that's a cat"). As Saussure (1983) claimed, concepts are not defined positively, but negatively, in terms of their contrast; they are defined by what they are not. Contrast is particularly important in the use of both deictic and personal pronouns. *Here – there, today – yesterday, next week* and *last week*, are both contrastive and decontextualized, relative to the time and place at which they are spoken and relative to each other.

The argument has been made that consciousness of self is also experienced in contrast. In this view, "I use *I* only when I am speaking to someone who will be a *you* in my address . . . reciprocally *I* becomes *you* in the address of the one who in his turn designates himself as *I*" (Benveniste, 1971, pp. 224–225). Communication is possible because *I* is a mobile sign that refers to the speaker at speech time; yet each person becomes *you* when addressed and *he* who was absent yesterday, can become *you* when present today.

Young children do not intuitively understand the mobility and arbitrariness of pronouns as symbols. First, they often refer to themselves in the second and third person (Budwig, 1995; Peters, 2000) and have difficulty with first-person self-reference. To illustrate this difficulty, a child of 35;15 asks, "Want me to help . . . want you to help . . . want to help me color?" (Church, 1966, p. 686). Similarly, when her mother says, "Say I, Nelly is I," Nelly, at 2;6 answers, "No. Nelly is not I. Nelly is you!" (Broeder, 1991, p. 121). Children need to learn that *I* refers to the speaker, being relative both to the individual who is speaking and to the moment of speaking. The use of pronouns requires their detachment from persons, an understanding of their mobile and symbolic nature. Our ability to transform, contrast, and reverse speaker and listener in referring to self and others is at the heart of pronoun use and social communication. The mobility and arbitrariness of symbols is the structural foundation of pronoun use and pronoun comprehension.

Our ability to use symbols, then, relies on the use of comparison and transformation, the two fundamental processes that according to Piaget and his colleagues (1992) epitomize our ability to signify. These two functions, in turn, combine in different ways in cognitively transforming the *here-and-now*, making it *neither-here, nor-now*, as evident in all three planes of transformation, to which I now turn.

PLANES OF TRANSFORMATIONAL THOUGHT

The temporal domain has been uniquely identified as critical for transformational thought. In particular, the temporal domain has been discussed as critical for preference deferral, as discussed in Chapter 7. In this vein, Bischof-Kohler and Bischof (2007) argue that

> humans are able to conceive of a temporal axis analogous to space that provides a buffer on which competing desires, including future ones, may be shifted, postponed, adjourned, delayed, or anticipated, according to their expected consummatory value and success, thus overriding the imperative of instant gratification. (Bischof-Kohler & Bischof, 2007 p. 317)

Discussing the temporal axis in a different manner, Suddendorf and Corballis (1997) talk of *mental time travel*, linking it more directly to self, suggesting that mental time travel builds on the ability to meta-represent one's knowledge about the past and to attribute past mental states and experiences to one's earlier self. The *I* who had fun at the circus or was afraid during a scary movie is not the same *I* who is currently speaking of these earlier experiences. In mental time travel, one ideationally removes oneself from the current context, moving into the past or moving into the future. Suddendorf and Corballis further suggest that future time travel builds on representations of the past that enable projection of self into the future.

But as Merker (2007) aptly notes, thoughts about the future are not limited to anticipations and projections that replicate the past. The future also includes "prospective fantasy," the possibility of transforming the present on the imaginal plane as well as the temporal one, allowing us to transform the world we inherited from our ancestors into a world without kings or slaves, with skyscrapers, flying machines, and cell phones. Hassabis and Maguire (2007) found neuropsychological evidence for the distinction between episodic future thinking, which relates to the plausible future versus what they call "imagining fictitious experiences" that are not based on past experiences. In his discussion of the life space, Lewin (1951) differentiated these two planes of transformation: the temporal plane and the plane of the imaginal. He suggested that young children's psychological environment is restricted to the present and the real, gradually expanding backward and forward on the time dimension and differentiating reality from irreality. Similarly, Piaget (1969) suggested that "we gradually build up within ourselves a plane of reality, a plane of possibility, a plane of fiction, and so on" (p. 245). To envision a future *unlike* the past, then, requires the plane of the imaginal which yields the irreal, of the world and the self as they could potentially be. It is only by transforming reality both on the temporal plane and on the imaginal plane that the future as distinct from anything that has happened in the past can be conceptualized. Moreover, pretend play often invokes the *imaginary past* (Blum-Kulka, Huck-Taglicht, & Avni, 2004), a linguistic device in which the past tense is used for descriptions of the pretend world, underlining the linkage between the temporal and imaginal planes of transformation.

There are several important corollaries to this. First, mental time travel is a joint enterprise, sweeping along other passengers who also traverse this temporal plane with the child; it is in talking to others about the past and the future that mental time travel is legitimized as a human endeavor (cf., Desalles, 2007). Second, transformational thought in which time and reality are spun allows for the construction of an alternative world in which absent realities can be represented and can serve to guide current behavior. Hazlitt (1969) suggested that imagination underlies the concern both with one's future self and with other people's future, paving the way for altruistic and moral behavior. Transformations on the imaginal plane also allow for fantasy and fiction to come alive in our minds. This makes reality monitoring critical; one must always be aware of the world as is and the world as transformed in our minds, whether in realistic or fantastic terms. Only by doing so can we develop plans for pursuing our preferences in ways that will support their being actualized. In fact, people normally appear to be able to cordon off the past in dealing with the present (e.g., Melara & Nairne, 1991), suggesting that they have some control over the temporal and imaginal transformations that they engage in.

The above picture, though, is still far from complete. Interacting with others requires alignment of our preferences with their preferences and such alignment cannot take place without yet another plane of transformational thought, *mental* transformations, endowing others with thoughts and feelings and using such transformations in attempting to negotiate with them, to change their preferences, argue with them, and manipulate them in the attempt to actualize our own preferences. The plane of mental transformations allows us to venture into other people's minds and attempt to capture their covert experiences. In *mentalizing*, one transforms the here-and-now into imaginary lines of thought and affective experiences in the minds of other people. Importantly, then, mental transformations also involve the imagination. This view of mental transformations accords with Corballis's (2007) definition of Theory of Mind as the "ability to imagine what might be going on in the mind of another individual." Just as temporal transformations serve to ponder one's own experiences in the past and the future, mental transformations are used for "cracking" into others' minds, to link their experiences with their preferences and their likely psychological reactions to having their preferences fulfilled or thwarted. This is critical for our ability to understand and mind other people's preferences and engage in altruistic and moral behavior.

From my vantage point, then, transformational thought takes place on three planes, as illustrated in Figure 10.1.

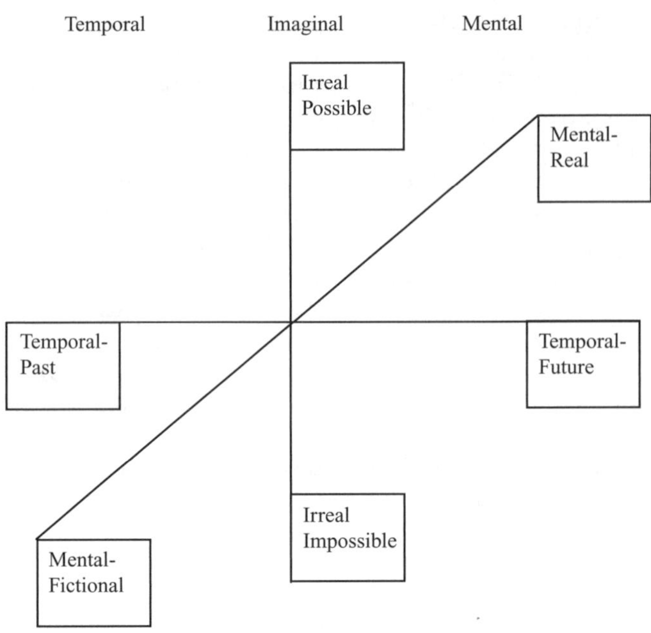

Figure 10.1

To elaborate, the temporal plane allows for mental time travel into the past and into the future and affords us the possibility of using the past as the basis for planning for the future. But the temporal plane offers little potential for pondering unknown futures that are disconnected from the past. This requires the plane of the irreal, which allows us to imagine both possible and impossible worlds and engenders the prospect of turning the imagined and impossible into the imagined and possible.[1] This is the plane of transformation that allowed man to adapt nature to his needs and preferences, venturing to the moon and discovering cures for disease and genetic malfunctions. The plane of the mental, though presented last, may be even more critical for our social life. It is the plane that affords us the magical ability of interacting with others, both real and fictional, to comprehend and anticipate their actions and reactions, using this knowledge both for our own benefit as well as theirs. In this light, transformational thought is necessary for managing both *inter*personal and *intra*personal conflict and forms the basic cognitive building block on which social life is predicated.

Critically, when the three planes of transformation are applied at the same time, one can think of others' past experiences, their likely future experiences, and venture into the realms of fictional characters and their psychological experiences. It is not by simulating other people, but rather by contemplating possible worlds and the possible psychological reactions of people in such possible worlds that we can appreciate fiction, have affective reactions to it, and still maintain our awareness that we are immersed in a fictional world that has no bearing on the world outside the written page or the theatre (cf., Meskin & Weinberg, 2003). In fact, recent neuroimaging research suggests that transformations on the temporal plane, the imaginal plane, and the plane of the mental are supported by the same core brain network (e.g., Botzung, Denkova, &

[1] Although it has been suggested (e.g., Swan, 1995) that only tense is necessary and that the subjunctive is a special tense used for imaginary situations, including counterfactuals, there are alternative proposals (e.g., Mezhevich, 2008) in which tense and mood are independent dimensions, as I argue here. This view is more consistent with the finding that in some languages, counterfactual worlds are indicated by clitics (e.g., Kockelman, 2004).

Table 10.1.

	Age	Source
C touches Pinocchio doll C: "Screwdriver . . . mend Pinocchio foot", what F did a few days earlier	22 mos.	Halliday (1975, p. 100)
C holds train C: "It got bent . . . it not bent now . . . it was broken yesterday but Daddy had to mend it with a screwdriver"	24 mos.	Halliday (1975, p. 144)
C points to arm C: "One time I had a (siydow = mosquito) bite . . . when I go to my Gramma's house"	32 mos.	Reilly (1986, p. 319)

Manning, 2008; Buckner & Carroll, 2007; Hassabis & Maguire, 2007). It is man's ability to engage in these different types of transformational thought *simultaneously*[2] that allows him to bridge the self–other preference gap, to use transformational thought to manipulate others, to cope, and to traverse the bridge into altruistic and moral behavior, as I elaborate in later chapters. I now turn to elaborating how cognitive transformations on each of the planes of transformation are fostered in parent–child conversation and emerge in young children.

TEMPORAL TRANSFORMATIONS INTO THE PAST

Verbal references to the past implicitly involve a comparison of the time of the speech event with a prior time referred to in the speech event (Silverstein, 1976).[3] Engaging in such comparison may first require concrete manifestations of the past in the present. In fact, Antinucci and Miller (1976) claim that children's early references to the past occur *only* when past events leave a visible trace. In line with this claim, at 17 months, Painter's (1984) son says *badboy*, referring to being chastised earlier that day for intentionally spilling a drink on a coffee table. At 18 months, he said *Dadda* while touching a fence where his father nailed up some loose planks two days earlier (p. 112). In both instances, the relevant objects – the coffee table and the fence – were visible at the point of speech, serving as reminders of the past events. In more verbal children, the association between present objects and the episodes in which they featured is more explicit, as evident in Table 10.1. Something in the current context reminds these children of the event being alluded to and they clarify that the past is being talked about (cf., Gärdenfors, 2005).

[2] Mithen (1996, 2007) makes a similar point in discussing what he calls "cognitive fluidity," which allows for sharing of knowledge across domains. He argues that this is precisely how the mind of modern man differs from its predecessors, in its ability to integrate knowledge from domain-specific knowledge modules. But modularity need not be assumed for the present purposes.

[3] I do not address this here but temporal transformations are also critical for sentence production because the sequence of words in sentences does not mirror the temporal sequence of the world events that sentences attempt to capture (cf., Müller, Sokol & Overton, 1998).

Yet children also refer to near and distant past events for which there are no apparent cues in the present, as Table 10.2 shows.

Yet events to which children refer in the distant past and for which there are no cues in the present are often ones with strong affective components, as shown in Table 10.3.

Although events may be recalled because of their emotional significance, long-term recollections may well be mediated by repeated prior discussions, as suggested by the following example. A girl of 22;2 talks of being turned over by a wave at the beach the previous day, saying, "Laura turn over. Laura get scared." Then 1 month and 9 days later, while being diapered at home, she relates, "water tip me over. Wave tip me over. I didn't like it" (Braunwald, 1995, p. 86). Although in this instance, the mother's input was not recorded, mothers do reminisce with children about affect-laden events. Because such conversations overlay the child's own experience, it is difficult to disentangle children's representation of their personal experiences from their re-presentations of such experiences following mutual discussion. One may well ask "whose memory is it?" because if mothers' interpretations are more coherent than the child's, they may overlay the child's own recollections. On the other hand, involuntary memories – spontaneous personal memories without retrieval attempts – are also cued by others who shared the experience (Berntsen, 1996) and by virtue of their omnipresence in children's lives, parents may serve as retrieval cues for past episodic representations.

Another means of temporal transformation is by invoking comparisons of the *here-and-now* with what is *neither-here-nor-now*. Comparisons are drawn by finding correspondences (Piaget, Henriques & Ascher, 1992), features of entities that are similar on some criterion and establishing correspondences using that criterion. But not all comparisons involve temporal transformations. Correspondences can be grounded in the *here-and-now* when both objects are visible (e.g., when a 31-month-old notes: "Hey, this is red," her mother responds, "Yes, it's red. Your shirt's red too. The ball and your shirt are the same color." Carew, 1976, p. 65). Temporal transformations are involved when the comparison object

Table 10.2.

	Age	Source
Near Past		
Events the previous day		
C: "Saw swans yesterday"	19 mos.	Karniol (Diary, Karen)
C: "Go for walk grandma see seagulls yesterday"	20 mos.	Karniol (Diary, Karen)
Event earlier that day		
C: "Children rain. Walk rain"		
M: "We saw the children walking in the rain, didn't we?"	20 mos.	Bloom (1973, p. 207)
Event earlier that day		
C turns over an imaginary cup		
C: "Juice on a floor"	24 mos.	Shatz (1994)
Distant Past		
Ten days after Thanksgiving		
K: "Pumpkin pie – Amy's house"	19 mos.	Karniol (Diary, Karen)
Event 2 months earlier, in Canada, K in Israel		
K: "Karen 'membered with Grandpa"		
M: "What do you remember with Grandpa?"		
K: "Snow"	22 mos.	Karniol (Diary, Karen)
Event 1 month earlier		
C: "Remember we went to Rhode Island?"		
M: "Goodness yes. That's a month ago"	24 mos.	Brown (1973)

is a mental representation in one's mind, an absent entity or context, for example, a toddler who sees the moon, runs into the house, says *moon*, points to moons in two books and says, "Moon, moon" (Painter, 1989, p. 43). Halliday's son Nigel, at 23 months, finds a toothbrush and referring to two absent toothbrushes, says, "have daddy green toothbrush"; when his father assents, he continues, "but you can't have Daddy new toothbrush" (Halliday, 1979, pp. 84–85), referring to yet another toothbrush. As I discussed in Chapter 2, temporal transformation is also involved when seeing someone with an object similar to children's own equivalent but absent object engenders demands for their version of the object (e.g., crying for one's teddy when one sees another child with a teddy).

Slightly older children express comparisons that reflect temporal transformations more explicitly, as shown in Table 10.4. Notice first, that children are generally drawing comparisons within the same category, ignoring the fact that the present object is a child-sized replica and not its real-world sized equivalent. Second, it is unclear what specific features serve to remind the child of the absent object or context. Shape seems to play an important role, though, as evident when a child of 24 months responds to his mother's statement "that's a wolf," with "Wolf. Like a big dog" (Painter, 1984, p. 246).

Instead of focusing on correspondences, children can focus on lack of correspondences, what McCabe (1997) calls *disparity* comparisons, as evident in Table 10.5,

Table 10.3.

	Age	Source
T talks of lonely old people		
C: "One day when were uh when uh we just been in the bookshop we went to find a toilet and on the way we saw a man lying on the floor..... and the – uh outside the – shop and an ambulance came to take and we put a jacket over him"	Preschool	Cuff & Hustler (1981, p. 117)
T reads a story about a bike		
C: "My sister's bike got run over by the car and smooshed"	Preschool	Lehr (1988, p. 42)
Referring to birthday party		
C: "Someone cried and she ruined my whole party"	5;3 years	Hudson (1986, p. 114)
C: "And when we went to Holland, my brother spilled two glasses of soda on this person next to him"	7 years	Hudson (1986, p. 114)

Table 10.4.

	Age	Source
C: "That's like my one"; "That one's like yours"	26 mos.	Radford (1990, pp. 278, 279)
C is playing with toy cars C: "This one's like my grandad's isn't it? It's got bumpers on"	4 years	Tough (1976, p. 27)
C: "That's the same table as our one isn't it daddy?"	4;6 years	McTear (1985, p. 123)
C: "This slide's the same like the slide when I go to Grannie's"	Preschool	Donaldson & Wales (1970, p. 251)
C1 and C2 are building a fire engine C1: "I saw a big wheel like that. We saw big tractors at the farm, at my granddad's farm, and they had big wheels" C2 : "I've got a tractor at my house. I can ride on it outside"	Preschool	Sylva, Roy, & Painter (1986, pp. 58–59)

which also shows combined similarity and disparity comparisons. In the above instances, current objects or contexts engender transformations mapping them onto other objects or contexts which though similar in some respects, also differ in ways that children find important to note.

A developmental advance is conducting temporal transformations based on correspondences between present objects and absent but *unrelated* objects that share common features. For instance, Nigel, at about 18 months, says something interpreted by his father as "uncle . . . pipe . . . smoke . . . train" (Halliday, 1975, p. 68), apparently drawing an analogy between the smoke of trains and pipes. Similarly, a child of 21 months spills milk on the carpet and says, "Look. Look. Moon. There moon" (Dunn, 1988, p. 19). A child of 32 months surprises his mother when he looks at a tent and says, "That look like a sausage"; she agrees that it does (Ingham, 1998). When Karen at 31;28 walks by a window at night, she notes, "Mommy, this is like a mirror." Asked why, she responds, "'cause I can see myself." A school child indicates that he dislikes cauliflower, saying, "It looks a bit like sheep" (De Moura, 2007, p. 717).

Parents may foster the emergence of such transformations by pointing out similarities and disparities between present and absent objects. For instance, at dinnertime, looking at an apple, a mother asks her toddler, ". . . is this a different color than we usually have?" When the

Table 10.5.

	Age	Source
Disparity Comparisons		
Looking at object C: "I used to have one with seats"	26 mos.	Radford (1990, p. 286)
Looking at picture of a beach C: "I've been to a different one, not the same as that"	Preschool	Tough (1977, p. 53?)
Looking at toy tractor C: "I've got one of those . . . but it's not like that one . . . ."	3 years	Tough (1977, p. 53)
Similarity and Disparity Comparisons		
M: "Nadav and Gil are like you" K: "Nadav and Gil are not the same, they're similar" M: "Why?" K: "Like Karen has no diaper and they have a diaper"	33;1 mos.	Karniol (Diary, Karen)
K: "My dollies know English and Hebrew like me and they know French what I don't know"	3;3 years	Karniol (Diary, Karen)
C: "Hey Dad . . . that man has the same umbrella I got." F: "Yeah, he sure does" C: "It doesn't have plastic on it . . . it does have the same color as me"	5 years	Hall (CHILDES)
Looking at picture of girl C: "Oh, she has a headband like mine . . . but hers is white, mine is pink . . . hers is wider . . . mine has a design on it, hers doesn't"	First grade	Chittenden, Salinger, & Bussis (2001, p. 108)

Table 10.6.

	Age	Source
Similarity Comparisons		
Looking at picture book M: "That's a bear you like you have"	12 mos.	Yont et al. (2003)
Looking at picture book M: "See the doggie, Keith? . . . . He looks like the dog that Mr. Owen has, doesn't he?"	13 mos.	Golinkoff & Hirsh-Pasek (2000, p. 100)
Looking at picture book C: "Tree there" M: "Uhm, where's the tree in our garden?"	20 mos.	Howe (1981, p. 12)
During unstructured free play M: "That truck's just like Eve's truck, huh?" M: "that's like a van . . . . that's like daddy's car" M: "it's like mommy's purse"	Toddler	Broen (1972)
Disparity comparisons		
During unstructured free play M: "Is that a mouse? It doesn't look like a mouse, it's so big, it looks like a beaver"	Toddler	Broen (1972)
During free play in toy room M: "Is this a shirt? It's like a dress. It's so big"	Preschool	Callanan & Sabbagh (2004, p. 750)
Looking at egg in storybook M: "Who eats eggs in our house? . . . . I don't think I've ever seen you eat an egg cooked like this. Daddy eats them like that though"	32 mos.	Imbens-Bailey & Snow (1997, p. 269)
C is building a fence M: "Oh my that's a big fence Angus. It's more like a snake, isn't it eh? . . . . I think it's more like the Loch Ness monster, mmmm?"	4 years	Wootton (1974, p. 281)

child responds with *green*, the mother says, "And what color apples do we usually have?"; getting the response *red*, she says, "So these are a little different" (Gleason & Ely, 1997, p. 238). Apples of different colors retain their "applehood." The child is thereby taught about the category of apples and the relevant dimensions for inclusion in the category. Again, though, making the comparison requires the child to draw on her memory representation of apples in general, thereby solidifying such prototypic representations. Similarly, looking at a toy pipe in a playroom, a mother asks, "Is that a pipe? . . . Does daddy smoke a pipe? . . . sometimes, doesn't he?" (Broen, 1972, p. 87). The mother refers to child's own past experiences and relates them to the current context. Trying to get a 24-month-old to search for a scarf, a mother suggests, "Granny's got a scarf. D'you remember? In her shopping bag. You see if you can find one like Granny's scarf" (Bridges et al., 1981, p. 127). The specific features of the scarf are rendered irrelevant while the intrinsic quality of "scarfness" is rendered critical.

Whereas above, similarities were noted, parents draw both similarity and disparity comparisons between current and past events *strategically* in diverse contexts, as evident in Table 10.6. These mothers are encouraging children to transform a currently available object into a mental representation of another, absent object (i.e., a dress, a snake, or the Loch Ness monster) in order to compare the two along some dimension which mothers find relevant. In doing so, children are "invited" to do the same, either by acknowledging the similarity, noting a different correspondence, or noting a disparity. In book reading with preschoolers, parents have been found to devote about 10–15 percent of their talk to objects and events unavailable in the immediate environment (e.g., De Temple & Beals, 1991). Doing so both engages the child in making the connection between book illustrations, replicas, and their real-life counterparts and induces him to conduct temporal transformations, drawing on his past experience as a framework for looking at the world; whether the child can do so depends on his ability to access the representation being alluded to by the parent.

Such comparisons also serve to underline the irrelevance of the dimensions of divergence and clarify what are deemed relevant criteria for comparison. As a mother attempts to put shoes on her 18-month-old, she looks at a Mothercare catalogue and says, "Find the shoes in the book" (Wells, 1986, p. 11). Pictorial representations of shoes and real shoes are all categorized as shoes and disparities are waived. Children's ability to do likewise is underlined when a child of 25;21 draws a comparison between her falling off a chair and the fall of a book character, saying, "fell down wall like Tom Kitten" (Oldenburg,

Table 10.7.

	Age	Source
Looking a picture book M: "I cut your hair with scissors like that"	24 mos.	McGlaughlin et al. (1981)
Looking at picture of jelly beans M: "You had jelly beans at your birthday party"	24 mos.	Bernstein (CHILDES)
Showing C new book about ducks, drawn in yellow M: "Remember the duck on College Lake?" (refers to grey duck)	Toddler	Heath (1986)

1990, p. 31). Similarly, when her mother gets down on her hands and knees to wipe up a spill, a child of 24;3 comments, "Just like poor Cinderella" (Church, 1966, p. 286).

As these last two examples illustrate, temporal transformations often involve past episodes rather than objects, as shown on Table 10.7. These mothers conduct temporal transformations in which current objects and events are compared with ones that feature as an experience in the child's past. The comparisons require the child to ignore the fact that the pictured items are not real, not of the same size, color, or texture as their real life counterparts and differ from other exemplars in the child's past and the mental representation being alluded to.

The interesting aspect of such temporal transformations is that adults do not randomly refer to a memory representation of ducks, jelly beans, or dogs. They *strategically* select memories shared with the child and which they assume to be available in their child's memory system. But it is the parent who is reminded of the relevant object or event being referred to. Hence, there are two processes involved: the first is of parents themselves experiencing what Schank (1982) calls "analogical reminding," usually category-based, and the second is using such reminding *strategically*, to guide their children's interpretation and understanding of objects, contexts, and experiences.

This two-step process is also evident in parents' strategies for teaching children names for new objects and categories. For instance, in a study in which mothers had to provide names for two instances of the same category, they referred to items in their preschooler's past experience (e.g., "that's a blue birdie and that's a turkey like you saw at the turkey farm"; "this is a cactus like we have in the house," Whitehurst, Kedesdy, & White, 1982, p. 417). Similarly, in introducing her daughter to bubble liquid at 16;3, the mother says, "I have something you've never seen before . . . would you like to have some bubbles? Remember bubbles in the bath?" (Bloom, 1973, p. 166).

The same strategy is also evident in parental reminiscence talk, examples of which are shown in Table 10.8.

Again, parents attempt to guide children to conduct temporal transformations, to access the same memory representation that they themselves have accessed. Imbens-Bailey and Snow (1997) suggest that the transition from the *here-and-now* to experiences removed in time and space from the present depends on two processes: (1) discussion of topics related to the present (e.g., asking about Spot when a dog is featured in a book) and (2) shared experiences in the recent past (e.g., how the child tripped and fell earlier that day). They claim that such discussions widen the child's knowledge base about the properties of things, their use, and the normative affective reactions to them, relating this knowledge to the child's immediate environment. In particular, Imbens-Bailey and Snow (1997) argue that because the emphasis is often on generic functions and characteristics, such talk also serves to clarify norms of behavior or generalities (e.g., the father of a 32-month-old asks, "when somebody rings the doorbell, does Steamer bark?" ibid, p. 268). This allows children

Table 10.8.

	Age	Source
Looking through magazine F: "This reminds me of a building we made a few months ago, remember that big building we made with blocks? Remember? We had towers like that too"	3 years	Engel (1995, p. 192)
Looking at picture of bone on doghouse M: "That's kind of like the bones we had last night, isn't it? Those big spareribs?"	Toddler	Olsen-Fulero (1982, p. 557)
Looking at car M: "Look, this car is much the same as the one we saw the other day in the car park"	Toddler	Stella-Prorok (1983, p. 207)

Table 10.9.

	Age	Source
M looks at a can of Bumble Bee tuna, refers to child going to hospital after bee sting C: "No. I remember the bee bite me in the belly, though, but don't remember I don't had to go to the doctor's"	$4^1/_2$ years	Snow (1990, p. 242)
Talking of sweater M: "That's the one Kelly gave you for Christmas" C: "No for my birthday . . . at the party"	Preschool	Dunn & Munn (1987, p. 793)
C: "Where's the pen what Papa um gave me? Mummy?" M explains it was left somewhere C: "No. I want it. I want it please, Mummy. Mark – Mark brings it home, think so"	Preschool	Wells (1986, p. 29)

to differentiate the canonical from the deviant or unexpected, serving as a proxy for culture when violation of expectations, norms, or morality is discussed.

Talk about the past, then, can also serve to inculcate values and norms. In talking of events that happened, parents also teach children to evaluate others' behavior in light of such values and norms. This is a critical aspect of moral socialization and the development of the ability to judge events and actions from a moral perspective (e.g., Morton, 2003). Mother–child conversations about the past that focus on behavioral standards and adherence or deviance from them also influence emergent conscience and moral understanding (Dunn, Brown, & Maguire, 1995; Kochanska, 1995).

In addition, the use of comparison and analogy by parents feeds into the systematization of children's knowledge, what Gentner and Medina (1998) discuss as the gradual replacement of the idiosyncratic perceptions of childhood by the relatively uniform representations of the adult world. In fact, both Schank (1982, 1999) and Hofstadter (1995) argue that all memory processes work by analogical reminding. In this view, the mind works so that interpretation of the present context is driven by automatic reminding processes that activate similar contexts in memory (e.g., a child of 3;7 comments after another child tripped and hurt her knee, "She'll be all right. She just needs a band-aid . . . . I bumped my knee once and it just hurt for a minute," Corsaro, 1985, p. 178). In this vein, a child explains that he likes a story because "it reminds me that I might be having another baby . . . my mom is really fat" (Lehr, 1990, p. 41).

In this view, people are constantly interpreting new situations in terms of old ones and "analogy making is going on constantly in the background of the mind, helping to shape our perceptions of everyday situations" (Hofstadter, 1995, p. 187). Decision making is also viewed (e.g., Klein, 1993) as driven by recognition of current contexts as instances of a given type, guiding retrieval of appropriate responses based on similarity with stored memory patterns. Sun (1995) has explicitly incorporated similarity-based reasoning in his Artificial Intelligence (AI) model of how people draw inferences and answer questions based on what they already know.

Parents' use of comparisons and analogies may unwittingly foster such processes. Somewhat surprisingly, though, parental use of comparisons and analogy-making appear to *depress* the conversational input of 2-year-olds (Stella-Prorok, 1983). This may occur because children lack the relevant memory representation, may not understand the comparison or analogy being drawn, or may disagree regarding the similarity invoked and lack the verbal skill to refute the claim of similarity. The latter may well occur, as evident in Table 10.9. All these children are disputing their mothers' representations of the past and claiming that their representations are the right ones. Since both mother and child are conducting transformations, though, there is no objective means within a dyadic context for determining whose version is correct.

Looking at family picture albums may also serve to crystallize differences between mothers' and children's memories of shared episodes (cf., Aschermann, Dannenberg, & Schulz, 1998). Yet such occasions serve both to cement the continuity of portrayed objects and individuals from the past into the present and to relate the child's present self to his former self, fostering the development of children's own early autobiographical reference (Hudson, 1990; Miller, Fung, & Mintz, 1996). They also facilitate the extraction of events of personal significance from the stream of events and clarify the framework within which they should be contextualized. For instance, as a 3-year-old is looking at photographs, he tells of an outing during which he objected to wearing a jacket, saying "I was mad, Mommy . . . I cried?" (Wolf, 1990, p. 189). The following exchange between a 21-month-old and his mother is illustrative. When the toddler alludes to an argument at breakfast, saying "Eat my Weetabix. Eat my Weetabix. Crying," his mother elaborates, "Crying, weren't you? We had quite a battle. "One more mouthful Michael." And what did you do? You spat it out!" (Dunn, 1988, p. 32).

We should not lose track of the fact that children themselves also spontaneously experience temporal transformations and attempt to strategically guide parents to access relevant episodic representations. For instance, a preschooler explains, "like those you know those things like Target... the tub things that you can put outside"; the mother asks, "like at Target... the little swimming pools?" (Imbens-Bailey & Snow, 1997, p. 287). The child assumes that his mother can map his description onto the relevant episode. Similarly, a preschooler points to a drawing of a flower on a pot and says, "This is like Anne's flower. Like at her house...." Further questioning clarified that his playmate has similar flowers on her underwear (Garvey, 1984. p. 69). In such conversations, then, mothers serve to create bridges from the present to the past, helping to embellish children's own event representations (Nelson, 1989, 1996).

Parents may engender temporal transformations by asking about children's affective reactions to events. This is often the case when children are questioned as to how they felt after being victimized. When a 4-year-old complains that a peer hit him, the mother asks, "How did that make you feel?" (Shure, 1985, p. 201). Similarly, a preschool teacher questions a child: "Stu, when Mike took the block from you, how did you feel? Did you tell him that made you angry?" (Tobin, Wu, & Davidson, 1989, p. 131). Both of these adults transformed the *here-and-now* along the temporal plane to get the child to relate past experiences of victimization to his past psychological reactions to these experiences. Of course, as we saw above, children may spontaneously talk of their own affective reactions to past events.

Children also strategically attempt to guide peers to perform temporal transformations and discuss shared event representations. When his friend talks of something funny at the circus, a child of 5;11 years asks him, "Do you remember when the gymnastic man but who couldn't do gymnastics, fell down...?" (Piaget, 1959, p. 62). An 8-year-old tells a peer, "Johnny, remember when I got cut right here?... Wanna see my stitches? Look, they're right under here.... I got six took out" (Reichman, 1990). Of course, peers may be less successful than parents in finding the event representation being alluded to and may invest less effort into attempting to do so. But such conversations also serve to link children's mutual past to their current selves. This is evident when a girl of 4;9 years tells her friend "we don't have to fight," her friend of 5;1 years answers, "I know because big girls like us don't fight, but we used to fight didn't we?" (McTear, 1985, p. 146).

Talking of events that are not shared with others changes the nature of talk about the past. Imbens-Bailey and Snow (1997) contend that the prototypical problem of communicating is that of getting another person to understand a nonshared experience. They suggest that the basis for doing so is in a gradual shift in parent–child conversation from talking about the present, to talking of recent past events, to talking of the shared nonpresent, and finally, to discussions of nonshared events. Imbens-Bailey and Snow found that at 14 months, only 29 percent of parents discussed the nonpresent with their child, increasing to 57 percent by the time children were 32 months old. This is generally the pattern in other research as well (see, for example, Moerk, 1975; Sachs, 1983).

Conversations about non-shared events often emerge when children are asked about their experiences at preschool. Sachs's daughter Naomi started to talk about her preschool experiences in the routine of being picked up and asked "What did you do today?" Sachs (1983) suggests that such conversations form a bridge between reference to events in the current context and reference to past events in general. Eisenberg (1985) found that more than 50 percent of past talk by young children was elicited by parental urging to "Tell Daddy what we did today." Dinner time is often the context in which children are asked to relate nonshared events (Blum-Kulka, 1997).

Parents pose questions regarding nonshared events, requesting elaborations, serving to solidify children's representations as well as to clarify to them that others' lack of knowledge regarding the event needs to be taken into account. For instance, a 4-year-old child tells his grandparents of a train trip and is asked, "did the man come around and get your ticket?... he just come around and took the money?" (Imbens-Bailey & Snow, 1997, p. 274). Adults in a given culture know the scripted aspects of train rides and can ask about them. Children can then use their own knowledge of these scripted aspects to play out the same scripts (e.g., a preschooler climbs into a "train" and says, "I bought a ticket. Let's go to the seaside," Sylva, Roy, & Painter, 1986, p. 57).

Children's introduction of nonshared experiences into their conversations alert us to their recognition that information to which they are privy is not shared by their conversational partner. That is, when children recount nonshared events, they implicitly indicate their understanding that their listeners do not have the same knowledge they do. This is quite clear in the examples shown in Table 10.10. These children are describing events in their past of which their addressee can have no possible knowledge. But in doing so, they are indicating their awareness that their temporal transformations cannot be known by others who have not shared their experiences. As we will see in discussing pretend play, this is of critical importance in performing transformations on the imaginal plane as well.

TEMPORAL TRANSFORMATIONS IN TALKING OF THE FUTURE

As children start to conceptualize future time, they can start to talk of what has not yet been experienced, allowing

Table 10.10.

	Age	Source
K: "Mommy, the car did Boom Boom Boom and Daddy stopped. . . ." M: "I don't understand" K: "Daddy will come and Daddy will tell what Karen is saying about the car making "Boom Boom Boom""	25;7	Karniol (Diary, Karen)
C playing with boats, to C2 C: "You know, my granddad fell off a boat – he told me. And he fell in the water and grandma threw a rope, to pull him"	3 years	Tough (1976, p. 77)
C to T C: "The other day, the other day my Mom and me and my Dad and, we went to the Big Island the other day"	Preschool	Tobin, Wu, & Davidson (1989, p. 151)
C to C2 C: "I used to live at Salève. I lived in a little house and you had to take the funicular to go and buy things"	5;11 years	Piaget (1926, p. 58)

them to reach points in time that are both close and far removed from the current moment. As Vygotsky and Luria (1994) contend,

when, thanks to the planning assistance of speech, a view of the future is included as an active agent, the child's whole operational psychological field changes radically and its behavior is fundamentally restructured. (Vygotsky & Luria, 1994, p. 122)

As discussed earlier, this restructuring is a function of the ability to generate transformations and integrate them across the temporal plane and the plane of the imaginal. As we saw in Chapter 2, young children start to talk of the near future, referring to "when we get home" while sitting in the car and to "tomorrow" when they go to sleep. Likewise, a girl of 35 months is preparing her dolls for a picnic and says, "Not ready to go yet . . . Oh no, not ready yet" (Hart & Risley, 1999, p. 138). Perhaps the most interesting aspect of references to the future is that children do not only refer to their own future but also to others' future. For instance, Orren, at 31;5, says, "When Daddy comes home I want to show him the scratch I got from there,"[4] referring to the edge of the table. Time travel occurs in a spaceship with room for others who are travelling into the same future point in time.

Although the future has specific points that can be referred to, such as *Tomorrow, on Tuesday*, it also extends into unknown realms and children use temporal words to indicate their understanding of this. Karen, at 27;8, says, "Mommy I want to go to the beach sometime with a slide and you'll go on it." Her use of the term *sometime* conveys indefiniteness, a future beyond today and tomorrow. In a similar fashion, Nigel, at 18 months, says, "one day might go on fast chuffa (train)" and when the father says, "Yes, we might," Nigel continues, "one day go on blue chuffa . . . . next chuffa coming . . . go on that one" (Halliday, 1975, p. 113). Such indefiniteness is also evident in children's talk of the distant future. In discussing her 2-year-old, a mother says,

she's talking about when she gets bigger how she'll be able to go to school and walk across the street by herself and go to the store for me. That's all she's talking about when she gets bigger. (Miller, 1982, p. 57)

Such indefiniteness may be fostered by parental talk of the distant future. As a mother explains regarding her third grader, "I'm trying to get him to see that he will grow up and he'll have a job, and his boss will say you have to do X, Y, and Z" (Xu & Corno, 1998, p. 431).

Talking of the future often requires some consideration of the past as well because "past experience serves as the foundation on which alternative perceptions and conceived futures are built" (Buckner & Carroll, 2007). The need to consider the past in talking of the future is often evident in comparisons of these two time periods. When an almost 2-year-old questions what they will eat in the morning, her father answers, "*tomorrow morning*, you're going to have yogurt, and bananas and wheat germ, like mommy *gave you this morning*, remember that?" (Nelson, 1996, p. 237, emphasis added). Similarly, at 29 months, in discussing breakfast, the same father says, "*Today* you had strawberries, *tomorrow* I think you'll have raspberries" (Nelson, 1996, p. 238). Such comparative talk allows the child to bridge the past which only exists as a memory trace, and the future, an image of which has to be created on the basis of the comparison, generating expectations of what will happen on the basis of what has already happened. This is also evident in the following example. Speaking of baking cookies, a mother asks her daughter,

Do you remember the ones you made when Nanny came down? . . . Could make some of them for Daddy tonight . . . . And you put them in the tray, like you did before. They were nice . . . . Like you were making when Granddad come down that night. (Tizard & Hughes, 1984, p. 174)

[4] Hebrew: "K'sheaba yavo habaita ani roçe lirot lo at hasrita shekibalti mishum."

The past is used as input for planning a future based on similarity with the past. Again, though, both the past and the future referred to pertain to the child and those in his social universe, all of whom are time-travelling together.

Yet children may have difficulty forging the connection between the past and the future. When a mother tells her preschool child that Father Christmas comes around at Christmas time, she suggests to the child, "you could ask him for a ballerina outfit for your little doll." When the child indicates uncertainty how to do so, the mother explains, "We'll do what you did last year, and you can write a letter to him. Remember?" (Tizard and Hughes, 1984, pp. 115–116). In such conversations, parents attempt to use children's memories of past events as input to guide their future behavior, forging a connection between children's past, present, and future.

Children themselves allude to the past in forming expectations of the future, again referring to those in their social universe who are travelling with them from the past into the future., Emily, at 34 months, says, "tomorrow when we wake up from bed first me and Daddy and Mommy you eat breakfast eat breakfast like we usually do...." But she then goes on to contrast this with "but today I'm going to nursery school in the morning" (Nelson, 1996, p. 279). Time sweeps everyone along, producing threads of continuity that allow projection from the past to the future.

Children expect their parents to understand that they are using the past as input into expectations regarding the future, as evident when a preschooler tells his father: "Daddy, I wish we could go back to that store where Marky and me ride that white horse" (Bartsch & Wellman, 1995, p. 71), providing his father with clues to facilitate his accessing the relevant episodic representation. This is clear when a girl of 3;8 years says, "I wish I was on the other boat" when driving past the docks. Her father replies, "Yes, do you remember when we went in a boat? We'll have to go in a boat again some time" (McTear, 1985, p. 67). Having shared the episode with her, the father evidenced understanding that memories can provide fodder for wishes regarding one's future. To cite Freud: "past, present, and future are strung together... on the thread of the wish that runs through them" (Freud, 1908, p. 148).

How the threads of continuity are spun to allow us to distance ourselves from the present is a question of theoretical importance, with different theoreticians focusing on different aspects of the future. Markus and her colleagues (Cantor et al., 1986; Markus & Nurius, 1986; Markus & Ruvolo, 1989) focus on the distant future, suggesting that individuals develop images of possible selves, representations of how they might act, look, or feel in the future. In this view, social forces serve to shape and delimit the possible selves one constructs, leading one to obliterate ones that are inconsistent with social norms and moral principles. There are positive possible selves to be approached (e.g., "I like that class 'cause I know it is going to help me achieve my goals and help out a lot in the future," Csikszentmihalyi & Schneider, 2000, p. 156) and negative or feared possible selves to be avoided (e.g., "when I get older, I don't wanna be on welfare. I wanna have my own job so I can pay my own bills and' get my kids things.... An' feed my kids without no welfare helping' me" (FitzSimmons, 1999, p. 69). If individuals can construct representations of self that are displaced into the future, they can envisage themselves approaching their desired possible self or avoiding their feared possible self. In this conceptualization, then, individuals move from the present to the future by building a bridge of self-representations between their current states and their desired futures. In fact, instructing individuals to develop more distal and varied possible selves has an impact on the objectives they set for themselves (Day, Borkowski, Punzo, & Howsepian, 1994) and the inability to envisage one's future is associated with feelings of despair and adolescent suicide (Chandler, 1994; Chandler et al., 2003) and delinquent behavior (Nagin & Pogarsky, 2004).

Different views of how the present is transformed into the future are provided by theoreticians who focus on the near future. There are two major views, *forward chaining* and *backward chaining*. In forward chaining, we image a desired outcome and plan a sequence of steps by which we successively approximate that image (e.g., Beach, 1990). The steps toward the future are specified prior to the endpoint. In contrast, proponents of backward chaining suggest that individuals work backward from the future to the present (e.g., Allen & Perrault, 1980; Melges, 1982), constructing plans that chain end points to points closer to the present, providing a blueprint for reaching the end point. For instance, filling the tank with gas is a prerequisite for driving out of town, possibly requiring prior actions like verifying the presence of a credit card and withdrawing cash from an ATM. White (1976) humorously captures the essence of backward chaining in an illustration of a child and his father standing before the lion's cage, with the child asking, "Dad, if the lion got loose and ate you up, what bus would I take home?" (p. 267).

Yet neither forward planning nor backward planning capture the piecemeal nature of young children's planning, with steps being apparently selected haphazardly. For instance, when a toddler says, "Paper find. Paper write. Daddy suitcase go get it" (Brown, Cazden & Bellugi, 1968), finding paper is expressed prior to the goal of writing and the goal is expressed prior to the necessary antecedents. Is the problem in sentence production or in action planning? Bruner (1983) argues that children find it difficult to assemble in advance both the required plan of action and the relevant linguistic descriptor. To illustrate, Richard, at 22 months, approaches and says *Mummy*. When asked "Mummy do what?" he answers, "Mummy get up," and when he is questioned again what he wants her to do, he gestures and says, "up cupboard," wanting to be raised to open the cupboard door (Bruner, Roy, & Ratner, 1982, p. 121). In this light, the child needs to integrate his emergent knowledge of means–end relations in the physical world with his knowledge of how to communicate in the social world.

Piecemeal planning may result because other goals become salient and distract children in the midst of goal pursuit, making them "forget" the original goal. To illustrate, a girl of 22 months set out to the garage to get her "baby," saying "Bring my baby. Baby's blanket. Carry my baby in the box. Come out baby" (Nelson & Bonvillian, 1978), p. 526). In getting the doll, the goal of finding a blanket and something to carry the doll became salient. Segal and Adcock (1981) note that children's planning of their pretend play may be so elaborate that they forget to enact the planned scene. For instance, a child who was taking her dolls to the beach, brought along beach towels, a hair dryer, sunscreen, and dry clothes. Then she said, "They need more supplies at the beach – they need a carousel" (p. 52). At the end, she was so distracted by the preparations that she did not take her dolls to the beach. Hudson, Sosa, and Shapiro (1997) found that 3- to 4-year-olds had difficulty remembering their shopping goals and being reminded of their goals boosted their performance. Five-year-olds were able to keep their shopping goals in mind, even when given simultaneous goals and when faced with multiple distractions.

Yet children do evidence forward chaining in guiding their own behavior. Karen, at 22;17, organizes everything needed for going to the beach (e.g., a towel, a pail, and a bathing suit), and says, "Karen is putting everything in the kitchen. When it's nice weather can go to the beach with you." Similarly, a 2-year-old trained her dolls on the potty chair, and saying "That baby poop. Go get a Pamper," she left the room and returned with a fresh diaper (Miller, 1982, p. 53). A girl of 34 months is getting ready to cook, and says, "I want to have everything I need for cooking"[5] (Stenzel, 1994, p. 184), setting out the appropriate play things needed for cooking. In line with the above, Segal and Adcock (1981) found that children spent much time organizing the props needed to enact a given play theme, creating offices, spaceships and doctor's offices, using replica toys when available and substitute objects otherwise.

Yet instances of backward chaining in children are also evident. A 3-year-old is looking for a blanket for a doll, saying "Where's a cover? I'll have to find a cover . . . in the box". She turns over the box, looks through the contents and says, "that'll do for a cover, there . . . put it round . . . make you warm . . . . There . . . that's nice and warm baby" (Tough, 1977, pp. 48–49). She appears to move backward, asking herself where she might find something to serve as a blanket, locating the box as a possible solution. But children's comments during a drawing activity (Cocking & Copple, 1987) also reveal the emergence of backward chaining (e.g., "I'll need blue to make the sky," p. 449), and a combination of both forward and backward chaining (e.g., "I'm making the body first so I'll have room for it all," ibid, p. 453), suggesting that backward chaining may represent a more sophisticated strategy. In the above study, children's comments as to how their creation differed from their planned drawing also reflect the interaction of the two types of chaining in guiding their activity. Children commented how their creations differed from what they desired (e.g., "I made the arms too long" and "I just did a mistake," p. 453), and on their inability to undertake the necessary steps (e.g., "I don't remember how her tail is [a duck]" and "I don't know how to make a duck," p. 453).

Self-talk may facilitate children's focus on their goals. Feigenbaum (1992) found that 4- to 8-year-olds who had to help a toy bus full of children get to an amusement park by constructing roads increasingly used self-talk to guide their actions. Successful planners engaged in self-talk in formulating, executing, and monitoring their plans. In both Feigenbaum's and others' research (e.g., Krafft & Berk, 1998), children interrogated themselves to "figure out" what to do (e.g., "How do I . . . ?"), interrupted their actions (e.g., "Wait a second . . . "), and guided their actions (e.g., "where was it the last time I saw it? . . . I know, in the blue cabinet," Krafft & Berk, 1998, p. 646) by talking to themselves. In addition, they often reminded themselves of their goal (e.g., "I want to cut this out," ibid, p. 646).

As for self-talk, Vygotsky (1936/1962) argued that private speech has its origins in social speech and whereas social speech continues to be used for communicating with others, private speech becomes used for communicating with self, providing self-regulation and self-direction. According to Vygotsky, when speech becomes internalized, this "signals a universal moment of human development when language and thought interact, transforming the course of intellectual development" (Diaz, 1992, p. 57). Bruner echoes this view when he says,

> Thought and imagination begin in the form of dialogue with a partner . . . the development of thought may be in large measure determined by the opportunity for dialogue, with the dialogue becoming internal and capable of running off inside one's head on its own. (Bruner, 1986b, p. 82)

In this view, private speech is a precursor to inner verbal thought, becoming internalized and transformed into a silent dialogue which because it is self-directed, can be abbreviated for directing and controlling one's own behavior. Sfard (2008) also adopts this view in defining thinking as "an individualized version of (interpersonal) communicating" (p. 81).

In line with this, very young children accompany their motor actions with speech, especially when a physically challenging activity is involved. For instance, Tomasello's daughter Travis said, "lock it" at 18;25 as she was trying to lock something, and "out . . . . tape out," said at 18.25, as she is trying to take some tape out of a box. A 30-month-old engaged in block building says, "Take a blue! Now take a red! Now take a white! . . . Now take all the blues . . . now take a red" (Carew, 1976, p. 97).

[5] German: "ich will alles zu kochen haben."

In order to explore the self-regulatory function of private speech in somewhat older children, Vygotsky (1934/1962) presented them with obstacles to their planned activity. Those children whose actions were interrupted increased their private speech. For instance, a child would say to himself, "Where's the pencil? I need a blue pencil. Never mind. I'll draw with the red one and wet it with water, it will become dark and look like blue" (p. 16). Older children paused and redirected their behavior without speaking aloud; but when asked, they described thoughts similar to those voiced by the younger children, suggesting that their private speech has been transformed into inner speech. As Ericsson and Simon (1984) argue, people can externalize their private speech, reflecting the way they use it to guide their own actions.

Private speech is generally defined as speech addressed to self for the purpose of self-regulation. But it is difficult to distinguish descriptive speech that accompanies behavior (e.g., "(I'm putting) marbles in the box") from speech that has a self-guiding function (e.g., "(I have to put) marbles in the box") (Berk, 1992, p. 35). For instance, a 24-month-old child says "Go put crayon in my pocket. I trying put crayon in my pocket. There. I put crayon in my pocket' (Brown, 1973). Is this descriptive or self-guiding? Perhaps both. Yet Diaz (1992) found that children who were told they could talk while performing semantic and perceptual tasks doubled the amount of private speech, underlining the usefulness of such speech in self-guidance. But the issue is far from resolved because children's private speech is more prevalent when there is a receptive audience than when they are alone. Speech used only for self-guidance should not vary by audience presence.

In the tasks undertaken above, children used the current context as a guide for how obstacles should be overcome. But when obstacles arise and when events do not transpire as planned, one often needs to draw on the past. Hammond (1990) and Schank (1982) proposed that a crucial part of planning is being able to learn from past mistakes and to use knowledge of past failures to predict when failures are likely to occur again. In Schank's model, strategies for solving problems encountered in familiar events are represented to include information about how to replay and modify event sequences when plans fail. In Hammond's model, memories of successful episodes can be retrieved to generate viable plans for future events and memories of failed plans are used to anticipate and avoid problems in the future so that individuals can guide their actions in trying to transform the present into the future.

Envisaging the future may prove counterproductive when desired outcomes do not materialize. An 8-year-old who was told that the family was going out for breakfast, imagined the particular restaurant, saw herself smelling and eating blueberry pancakes with maple syrup, and saw herself playing on the swings in the park afterwards. When none of what she imagined materialized, she had a temper tantrum (Freeman et al., 1997). This shows that imagining desired outcomes is an important motivational resource, impacting the perceived likelihood of the imagined events, intentions to engage in related activities, and the actual undertaking of relevant behavior (e.g., Sherman et al. 1981; Anderson, 1983). O'Hanlon & Weiner-Davis (1989) deploy this motivational resource therapeutically. For instance, they ask a person with a weight problem, "When you lose 15 pounds, which will be your favorite store to buy new clothes? Will you need dresses or slack? What color . . . (p. 110). They attempt to motivate the individual to engage in behaviors that would enable imagined outcomes to become a future reality. In this context, the act of choosing objects that can participate in pretend play would seem to use knowledge of the past in transforming the present into an imagined future, the topic of the next section.

IMAGINAL TRANSFORMATIONS

One can leave the plane of reality and move to the world of the irreal, engage in *imaginal* transformations that either take what is available and transform it into what is not available, conjuring up figments of the imagination, or contemplating what could have been in the past or could possibly happen in the future. In fact, as Lewin (1951) noted, *hope*, *regret*, and *guilt* are all affective experiences on the plane of irreality, varying in whether they involve temporal transformations that take us forward or backward in time. Imaginal transformations create fictional worlds, which like sorcery and magic, can lead us to contemplate imaginary numbers, people, objects and events. As a projective technique, Corsini (1966) tells patients that "on the table there is an invisible book, an invisible candle, and an invisible pencil" to be dealt with. Patients read the pretend book, tore out its pretend pages, used it as proof in a pretend argument, and even burned its pretend pages with the pretend candle.

Although above, it was the therapist who called imaginary objects into being, children conduct imaginal transformations in the context of pretend play, voluntarily transforming *This and That*, *Here and Now*, and *You and Me* (Garvey, 1977). In pretend play, present reality is imaginally transformed into something other than it is, with objects, people and spaces being transformed into other objects, other people, and other spaces, and time being turned backward, forward, or standing still. According to Vygotsky (1966), pretend play imbues contexts with meanings created in the child's imagination and reflects the separation of contexts from the transformed meanings attributed to them. Before such separation occurs, though, the 2-year-old is unable to repeat sentences that do not capture reality (e.g., repeat "Tanya is standing up," when she is sitting down). Words are taken as descriptive of reality and in the absence of the ability to decontextualize and conduct imaginal transformations, to separate meaning from reality and transform reality into something other than what it is, the child cannot engage in pretend play.

I differentiate three types of pretend play: (1) *similarity-induced* pretense, (2) *similarity-creating* pretense, and (3) *imaginal* pretense.

SIMILARITY-INDUCED PRETENSE

In both *similarity-induced* and *similarity-creating* pretense, a present object, the signifier, is used to represent an absent, signified object. In *similarity-induced* pretense, the pretense is triggered by the physical characteristics of the present object, as when a ball is "eaten" as an apple. The shape of the ball is reminiscent of the shape of apples and this allows it to serve as a stand-in. The pretense is engendered by both comparison and transformation in which the child notes features of a present object and symbolically transforms it into an absent object with shared features. The shared, relevant features of the signifier determine its applicability in serving as the signified object. Children's ability to spontaneously draw comparisons and to find correspondences and lack of correspondences stands them well in engaging in similarity-induced pretense.

The second part of similarity-induced pretense is using the signifier in a *storyline*. The *storyline* is the real-world context or script in which the signified object plays a part. Adopting a given storyline reflects children's understanding of the physical and social world and the people and objects in them. But it is a storyline, a recontextualization of something that has been captured symbolically and is being "staged" within the pretense. To elaborate, let me turn to Tomasello's (1992) daughter, Travis, when at 19;22, she says, "Make dinner, make soup," while playing with a bowl and water. She uses a bowl which has the curvature of the pots used in real cooking. She also indicates her understanding of dinner foods, of food preparation, and of people as agents who decide what to do and for what purpose. Similarly, in the sandbox, at 19;29, she says, "Make birthday cake," shaping the grains of sand to look like a round cake. The similarity of flour and sand is evident; mothers may bake in rectangular cake pans but the prototypic cake is round, as are pretend cakes. The child is guided by a representation of the absent, signified cake and uses some characteristics of what is currently available in a reactive manner. But it is the real world, the objects and the people in it that serve to guide her storyline. The pretense is in her playing at being a mother who is cooking and baking, using currently available and similar-looking stand-ins for the absent objects needed. Play is behavior in the simulative mode (Bruner, Jolly, & Sylva, 1976); it mimics the behavior that would be displayed if the goals and intentions of the players were actually being pursued.

Although similarity-induced pretend play occurs in very young children, engaging in it is far from simple. First, the representation of the signified objects has to be sufficiently embellished to allow the transformation to take place (e.g., Volterra et al., 1979). In pretending that a banana is a telephone, for instance, the functions the telephone serves, the way it does, and how telephone conversations are conducted all have to be mentally represented for the pretense to take place. If a child were to pretend a banana is a telephone without having a mental representation of telephones as means of communication, he would not talk into it, pretend to listen, or "hang up." Although at first, children only have cursory knowledge of the functions of objects and contexts, they gradually acquire such knowledge, adding more aspects that can be included in the storyline. As well, the child has to be able to disentangle the present signifier and the object signified in terms of the way they are treated. When a banana is a telephone, it is not smelled, peeled, eaten, or treated as a member of the fruit category.

Similarity-induced pretense also requires the child to pretend to carry out activities outside of their usual context, to decontextualize. Decontextualization is evident when a child pretends to go to sleep in his cot, signaling the pretense by laughing, for instance (e.g., Piaget, 1936/1952). It is also evident when a child lies down on the living room floor at a time not associated with sleeping or napping. But when he covers himself with a newspaper, laughs and says, "I sleeping," the child has transformed reality on both the temporal and imaginal planes and created an alternative world in which newspapers can be transformed into blankets, floors into beds, and so forth.

Similarity-induced pretense is facilitated by the availability of replica toys that capture some of the relevant features of the real-world objects they represent. In using replicas, one sets up correspondences (Piaget, Henriques & Ascher, 1992) by finding features that are similar according to some relevant criterion and establishing correspondences to a mental representation of an absent, signified entity using that criterion. For instance, the shape of a toy phone allows the establishment of correspondences to a real telephone whereas other features, such as size or color, may prevent correspondences from being established. Children adapt by ignoring those features of replica toys that differ from their real counterparts.

Replica toy play becomes possible once the functional correspondence between the replica and its real world equivalent is established and the child understands that noncorrespondence of the size dimension or other dimensions is irrelevant (i.e., toy toilets do not generally flush and toy stoves do not cook foods). Replica toys make similarity-induced pretense easier because of the correspondence between them and the real objects they signify. In line with this, replica toys are children's preferred objects of play, representing 100 percent of children's pretend play at 12 months and about 70 percent of their play at 48 months (Haight & Miller, 1993).

Why then don't children recognize the relation between realistic scale models of rooms and the actual room they represent? To elaborate, DeLoache and her colleagues (e.g., 1997) have examined how children deal with scalar replicas of real rooms. Some of the children in DeLoache's research were led to believe there were two rooms, whereas for others the room was "magically" shrunk by a shrinking machine. Toddlers 29 to 33 months old observed the experimenter hide a large troll in the room and were told that the equivalent small troll would be hidden in the same place in the scalar model of the room, or vice versa, with the small troll being hidden and the large one needing to be found. Those children who thought there were two different rooms performed very poorly, with six of the fifteen children not succeeding in finding the troll even once. Those children exposed to the shrinking machine which magically created the "shrunken" troll and the "shrunken" room were more successful, with twelve of seventeen children retrieving the troll repeatedly, and seven doing so without error. DeLoache and her colleagues suggest that the magic task only requires children to recall where the troll was in the original room whereas children exposed to scalar models need to engage in dual representation, mentally representing the two rooms in order to find the correspondences between them.

What do these elegant studies tell us? First, they clearly show that toddlers have trouble maintaining two representations active at the same time, making it unlikely that they will be able to find the correspondences between them, something that is necessary for success at this task. Second, they underline the fact that toddlers' experience with replicas has taught them that size is not a relevant variable in functionally interacting with objects. This is also evident in toddlers' attempts to behave with toy replicas as if they were full scale models, trying to slide down toy slides and putting their feet through toy car doors (e.g., DeLoache et al. 2004).

Problematically, though, parents, actively encourage children to draw correspondences between replicas and their real world equivalents. The mother of a toddler looks at a play kitchen and says, "Look at this, I know it doesn't look like the room in our house, but what do you think this room might be?" and after several tries, the child says it looks like a kitchen (Olson-Fulero, 1982, p. 559). Parents tend to encourage what Gentner and Loewenstein (2002) have called re–representations – altering one or both representations so as to increase the number of correspondences between them. They found that providing size labels (Daddy, Mommy, and Baby) facilitated children's relational mapping of physical objects varying in size. Parents themselves may foster this when they engage in relational mapping. As a girl of 26 months is reading with her mother, and her mother says, "Kittens are baby cats . . . the mommy is the cat; the babies are kittens" (Teale & Sulzby, 1987). Yet children also engage spontaneously in relational mapping, with a 3½-year-old labeling objects that varied in size and color saturation: *Daddy*, *Mommy*, and *Baby* (Smith, 1987) and a 24-month-old spontaneously calling a partially inflated balloon *baby* and a fully inflated one, *Mummy* (McShane, 1980). The size discrepancies between the balloons led the child to draw two parallel correspondences, one based on size, and one based on categorical similarity (cf., Piaget, Henriques & Ascher, 1992). Hence, ignoring differences between representations is also the hallmark of similarity-induced pretense.

SIMILARITY-CREATING PRETENSE

In *similarity-creating* pretense, instead of being triggered by characteristics of a present signifier, storylines guide the search for present objects that can be transformed to represent something other than what they are, something needed for the current play context. In similarity-creating pretense, a currently available object is transformed, "moved" into the current context, and recontextualized as a temporary place-holder for the absent object being signified. When first graders are arguing about a piece of Lego being used as a muffler, one child says, "You can make it what it is" (Chittenden, Salinger, & Bussis, 2001, p. 103), expressing the fact that any object can take on whatever qualities one imagines or attributes to it. Necessity, then, becomes the mother of invention. An 18-month-old put a small teddy bear in a drawer, saying "night, night" (Painter, 1984, p. 114), pretending the drawer was a bed for the bear to sleep in. Children search for signifiers that can serve as placeholders in the storyline, making comparisons and compromises as they search for objects that have more shared features with the object to be signified so that correspondences can be established.

Although at first, only objects physically similar to the signified object are used in similarity-creating imaginal transformations, with development, children start to pretend in the absence of physical correspondences. They latch onto some feature that makes a correspondence reasonable and imaginally transform the currently available object by stating what it is in pretend, saying "this is a . . . "and "pretend this is a . . . " A 3-year-old takes an upturned box and says, "That's a hospital now" (Tough, 1977, p. 75). A preschooler takes a hat and says, "This is not a hat, this is a ship" (Ariel, 1984). Although children about 4 years old are able to engage in pretense with objects that bear no similarity to the signified object (e.g., a child holds up some blades of grass and suggests, "pretend these stems are our candy," Kyratzis & Guo, 2001), ones similar to the referent are still preferred by them (Forys & McCune-Nicolich, 1984; McCune-Nicolich & Fenson, 1983). Yet in the majority of non-Western cultures, children do not own toys and cannot rely on replicas (Watson-Gegeo, 2001; Whiting & Edwards, 1988), requiring them to be more innovative in the variety of objects they use in their similarity-creating pretense.

In fact, children appear to devote much time and thought into choosing signifiers that can be imaginally transformed into the objects needed for a given storyline. They set up correspondences between present and absent but needed objects, note lack of correspondence, and find compromises that facilitate imaginal transformation of the signifier into the storyline. Cocking and Copple (1987) found that preschoolers have standards about what constitutes an appropriate object to be transformed and devote much thought to choosing them. Children commented as to the suitability of a given object as a choice (e.g., "This is a shoe because it's got string," p. 434) and as to the shortcomings of a rejected object as a possible choice (e.g., "Not this one. This can't be good . . . ," "This one doesn't have a handle. Needs to have a handle," Cocking & Copple, 1987, p. 434). Fascinatingly, children created imaginary correspondences. They commented how they *could* imaginally transform an object to make it correspond despite its deficiencies (e.g., "This would be better with a handle" and "I'm pretending something's right here" [i.e., a scoop], Cocking & Copple, 1987, p. 434). Children appeared to consider how the object could be transformed to imbue it with the required identity, for example, "that's not a spoon but it could be a spoon" or "I know how to make one of these into a telephone," holding the object to his ear as he says this (Cocking & Copple, 1987, p. 434). Children also transformed objects by adding pretend elements (e.g., "there's no elevator there, but I want to make one" (Cocking & Copple, 1987, p. 456).[6]

The verbalization of pretend elements above served to facilitate the imaginal transformation necessary to bridge the gap between the object as it really is and as required for the pretense. In similarity-creating pretense, then, there is an interplay between the storyline, the need for specific slot-fillers, and the actual or imaginal correspondences that can transform present physical objects. When two 5-year-olds construct a "spook house" from cardboard boxes, they stand back to look at it, decide it doesn't look spooky enough, and say "We'll need more scary parts, like a dark place here" (Trawick-Smith, 1998, p. 448).

In most discussions of children's play, the distinction between *similarity-induced* and *similarity-creating* pretense has not been drawn (e.g., Fein, 1987; Sperry & Sperry, 2000)[7] Yet this distinction is important for several reasons. First, to the extent that pretense is reactive, with the correspondences induced by similarity of physically available objects to the absent objects they signify, it restricts and limits the child's ability to enact coherent episodes of play. Second, to the extent that similarity-creating pretense is undertaken to allow for a storyline to unfold, signifiers need to be created to fit in as needed. A child who cannot set up correspondences, either real or imaginal, and creatively transform available objects to fit the storyline will be limited in the ability to follow the storyline to its denouement.

An issue that has been the subject of theoretical controversy concerns the status of the physically present objects used in pretense. Does the banana temporarily cease to exist psychologically when it is used as a telephone? Is reality suspended? Leslie (1987, 1988) argues that by "decoupling" present signifiers from the absent things they represent, reality is "quarantined" and suspended with respect to the actual properties of present signifiers. Veneziano (2002) argues the opposite, claiming that the representational aspect of pretense implies children's ability to consider one object as *simultaneously* having the properties it has in "real" life and those acquired "by virtue of the meaning transformation it has undergone in pretend" (p. 59). According to Veneziano, the hallmark of pretense is the ability to maintain both representations simultaneously. From her perspective, children can shift in and out of similarity-induced pretense depending on their momentary needs. A hungry child may eat the "banana-telephone"; a child who has announced that a roll of toilet paper is "a policeman coming . . . coming to see the fire," can still use the toilet paper to wipe her runny nose.

Although to the best of my knowledge there is no research addressing how children's momentary needs impact their pretense, Veneziano's portrayal seems to be more accurate since it implies a seamless transition in and out of pretense. Several types of evidence seem to support seamless transitions. First, children are able to snap-in and out of pretend frameworks to go to the bathroom, answer the telephone, and heed maternal requests. To illustrate, in the midst of a pretend birthday party with his dolls, Orren at 33;0 declares, "I decided something Mummy – I will first pee and then I will come back to the birthday party"[8]. More pointedly, a 3-year-old refuses his mother's call, saying, "I can't talk, I'm dead" (Becker, 1988). In making this assertion, the child's one foot is in reality and his other foot is immersed in an imaginal world.

Second, children's ability to direct metacommunication to their peers during pretend play, telling them how a given object should be treated during the pretense (e.g., "No, no, not there! You don't press there, you press here!," Musatti & Mayer, 1993, p. 35) similarly underlines the fact that reality and pretense coexist harmoniously in the interim. Related to this is the fact that children comment to others what they need to do in pretend versus in reality, also implying that this duality is maintained during pretend play. In line with this, a preschooler admonishes, "don't really pull it out, just pretend to pull it out" (Garvey, 1993, p. 255) and Orren at 28;12, yells at me, "Don't open the door – only pretend to open."[9] Similarly, Sachs's daughter at 4;9 years asks her mother for bandaids while playing doctor. When her mother answers alright, she

[6] Interestingly, in studies on cognitive cuing and emotional change, 39 percent of 4- and 5-year-olds transformed cues similar to those responsible for prior negative emotions in others into the actual cues that were originally associated with the negative emotion, e.g., "she's sad because maybe that's the same clown . . . and he dyed his shoes red and his hat red" (Lagattuta, Wellman & Flavell, 1997, p. 1096).

[7] Fein has discussed both types of pretense as *material transformations*, since they incorporate a physically present object into the scene being played out as substitutes for another, unavailable object. Sperry and Sperry referred to *fictional displacements*, suggesting that the unique feature of such transformations is their being enacted in the present through transformation of immediately present objects, persons, or locations.

[8] Hebrew: "Ani hixlateti masheu ima – ani kodem aase' pipi veaz ani axzor la yom-huledet."

[9] Hebrew: "Lo liftoax hadelet – rak ke-ilu liftoax."

Table 10.11.

	Age	Source
Playing firefighter, C takes a long stuffed snake C: "This is a hose – I'll take care of the fire, 'kay?"	Preschool	Eisenberg & Garvey (1981)
C wants to make hamburgers, takes a wastebasket C: "This is gonna be a grill"	4 years	Fein (1987, p. 285)
Child shows younger sib toy comb C: "This is my cheese cracker," "eats" it	5 years	Haight & Miller (1993, p. 87)

responds, "real ones," requiring that her mother go to get them (CHILDES).

Third, children's comments during pretend play regarding the relation of pretend objects to their real-life counterparts (e.g., a preschooler who plays with plastic tools and says, "My Mom has these tools, but they're too sharp," Trawick-Smith, 1998, p. 438) and their ability to continue treating these objects in their pretend versions also underlines the ability to maintain both representations at the same time. In this view, when a pretend race car driver says, "My dad drives real fast like this" or declares during a pretend shopping spree: "I go to the mall with my grandpa," the child is moving back and forth between the two planes. These three phenomena all indicate that the transition in and out of pretense is virtually seamless.[10]

SOCIAL PRETEND PLAY

There is no limitation on the kinds of correspondences between real world objects and absent realities a child can incorporate in pretend play alone. But children engage in pretend play in social contexts and similarity-creating pretense is not necessarily self-evident. The fewer the correspondences between the signifier and the object or context being signified, the more necessary it is to communicate relevant transformations to others to get them to align their use of the signified object. In social play, similarity-creating pretense can only work if correspondences are mutually agreed upon by others who are party to the same storyline. This social aspect of similarity-creating pretense is evident in children's public statements as to what signifier corresponds to what signified object or setting,[11] as shown in Table 10.11.

Another index of the social nature of similarity-creating pretense is that children suggest to others what these others should pretend, or what they should *jointly* pretend. As an instance of the former, a girl of 3;1 years says, "now you pretend this is Spencer's Mommy" (Diessel, 2004). Of course, such directives need not explicitly specify that pretense is required, for example, in saying to another child "These can be your wings" (Engel, 2005, p. 519), the speaker also establishes the domain of imaginal pretense. As for jointly pretending, a child of 3;10;25 years, says, "let's say that this is a tree"[12] (Müller, 1994, p. 251). At 33;9, Orren says to his sister, "Karen, I decided that this will be our house. It's important that we have a house."[13] Because in similarity-creating pretense children may use objects that do not have apparent correspondences to the object being signified, they need to publicly announce their transformations to verify their mutual acceptability, for example, "Let's pretend we're going to cross the bridge" (Williamson & Silvern, 1991, p. 84). The use of such announcements, in the form of "make believe that," "pretend that" and "let's pretend," increases dramatically over the ages of 2;10 to 5;7 (Garvey & Kramer, 1989).

In addition to declaring their similarity-creating transformations, children also often ascertain agreement prior to continuing to play (Giffin, 1984). This is because they need to coordinate their imaginal transformations with others and to guide their behavior in this light. Consequently, they often make suggestions using tag questions, for example, "Let's pretend . . . okay?" The need for others to express their acknowledgement is also evident in children's suggestions as to what they should jointly imagine, and their delaying doing so until their peer indicates acknowledgement of the proposed transformation.

When others agree to a specific imaginal transformation this restricts how that object can be treated during the play episode. If the playground swings are a boat, one cannot just step off them; one needs to jump to avoid drowning in the surrounding water (Musatti & Mayer, 1993). If the teacher pretend plays that she is in jail, then one needs to

[10] One possible crack in this picture comes from research on bilingual children. Bilingual preschool children differentiate between metacommunication about play and pretend play in terms of the language used, with bilingual 3-year-olds speaking English when in their pretend roles but Spanish when informing and directing their peers what to do during play (Orellana, 1994). One could argue that such language shifts reflect the independence of the pretend representations from reality. This particular issue is far from settled, though, and the balance of the findings seem to support the seamless transition view.

[11] Children may publicly announce imaginal transformations when others who are not interacting with them are present. At 30:14, Orren comes into the kitchen where I am and says, seemingly to himself: "my whistle is called birdie and she flies in the sky in pretend" (Hebrew: "la çafçefa sheli korim çiporet vehee afa bashamaim be-keilu").

[12] German: "sagen wir mal das is ein baum."

[13] Hebrew: "Karen hixlateti she ze yiheye habait shelanu. Xashuv sheyiheye lanu bait."

Table 10.12.

	Age	Source
Child plays at giving doll a bath, uses an imaginary bar of soap, scrubs doll's head C: "Scrub, scrub"	19 mos.	Bloom (1973, p. 49)
Child puts doll on toy potty, waits, peers into pot C: "See poop. I see it. See it. Ah, I see it", screws up face in distaste, laughs, dumps out "poop" C: "Baby done"	24 mos.	Miller (1982, p. 53)
C walks around with coasters, offers adults pretend foods	24 mos.	Shatz (1994)

find means of getting into the jail to free her (e.g., "Don't worry. We'll rescue you. We have super power" (Elgas, Klein, Kantor, & Fernie, 1988, p. 146).

Children as young as 24 months can adopt the imaginal transformations of others but they may modify or refuse them. For example, a child of 3;1 years demands of her peer, "Get out of the road, all right?" When she asked what road, she answers, "the one I'm driving in." But her playmate of 29 months, protests, "No this is . . . no, this is a rug" (Garvey, 1984, p. 138). One child attempted to imaginally transform the rug and the other resisted, possibly, because she was unable to do so. But often rejections of proposed imaginal transformations appear to arise when proposals conflict with the peer's preferences.

This is evident when children counter with their own proposals, claiming that the specified object not be transformed or proposing an alternative transformation. As an example of the former, at 33;4, Orren cries, explaining that "Karen doesn't want a cat in her room."[14] He was pretending to be a cat and his sister objected to this pretense. Similarly, a child objects to another child's saying his name and the teacher explains, "Simon doesn't want you to pretend he's in your airport" (Paley, 1990, p. 63). Refusing to enact a proposed transformation of a shawl into a poncho, the rejecting 3;5 year-old peer says, "No, I wan' to. No I don' wanna. I wanna be it, a shawl" (Iwamura, 1980, p. 44), rejecting the proposed transformation outright.

Children can offer alternative transformations. On being told that something will stand in for rice, a child counters, "No, this is meat, not rice" (Schwartzman, 1978, p. 239). When a preschooler suggests to a peer, "This could be your home," the peer counters, "but it could be a shopping place too" (Gallagher & Craig, 1987, p. 31). Since the issue of mutual acceptance of others' imaginal transformations recurs in the context of imaginal pretense, I now turn to discuss it.

IMAGINAL PRETENSE

Imaginal pretense differs significantly from other types of pretense in that correspondences are not established. Rather, imaginal pretense is uniquely indicated by behavior that mimics absent objects, contexts, and people. It is "as if" these absent objects, contexts, and people are physically in the child's milieu and in his behavior, he takes their presence and their implied impact on both self and others into account. We already saw a preliminary version of such imaginative work in children's creation of imaginal correspondences to facilitate the transformation of available objects into a storyline. Children imaginally "added" missing features to real objects to allow them to correspond better to signified objects. The advance here inheres in the imaginal creation of the signified object or context. As children evidence decreasing reliance on the physical properties of the signifier for setting up correspondences, they get to a point at which they no longer need to set up such correspondences. They are able to perform imaginal transformations that do not require the presence of a signifier. In Vygotsky's (1966) words, they no longer need a pivot for their pretense.

Imaginal pretense has been called *invention* (Fenson, 1984) and *ideational transformations* (Galda & Pellegrini, 1991; Göncü & Kessel, 1988) but irrespective of the label used, gestures and speech are used to indicate that a pretend element has been added to the current context. Taking a drink from a nonexistent cup represents imaginal pretense whereas drinking imaginary water from a replica cup does not. Imaginal pretense, then, represents an important developmental advance. Although he does not use my terms, Fenson (1984) found that whereas both similarity-induced and similarity-creating pretense were evident in the play of children at 20 months and older, imaginal pretense was hardly evident at these ages. In this context, Furrow (1992) examined the speech of Bermudan children aged 2 to 2;6, and 18 months later, in toy play with replica toys. Among the aspects of speech coded were verbal transformations of objects or events, whether present or not. Such transformational utterances accounted for about 5 percent of utterances when the children were younger and about 15 percent of their utterances in children's speech when they were older.

On the other hand, imaginal pretense is readily apparent much earlier in many studies of child and language development, as shown in Table 10.12. There are two

[14] Hebrew: "Karen lo roça xatul baxeder shela."

Table 10.13.

	Age	Source
Girl baking B: "Can I have some muffins?" G: "Don't touch then, 'cause they're very hot." (boy sprinkles pretend sugar on pretend muffins) B: "I'm gonna put a little sugar on your muffins, all right?"	32–33 mos.	Garvey (1984, p. 112)
Two children are preparing a meal One points to two locations on an empty plate C: "Now this is cheesecake and this is ice cream"	Preschool	Garvey (1984, p. 87)
Children at daycare, C1 says he saw a wolf outside C2 says he's scared of the wolf C2: "He's got a saw in his hand"[15]	4 years	Camaioni (1979, p. 331)
C1: "The monster is coming! He's almost here" C2: "Get the magic belt! When you put it on, he gets froze"	Preschool	Paley (1990, p. 80)
C1 pretends cardboard box is a cave C2: "Alright, it'll be a spooky, dark cave"	Preschool	Trawick-Smith (1998, p. 439)
Child announces it's winter C2: "Okay, so it' s, like, windy and stormy"	Preschool	Trawick-Smith (1998, p. 439)

defining features of such imaginal pretense. First, the elements added to the physical context are critical aspects of the storyline, which often represents scripts of real life events and sequences. In such scripts, dolls cannot be washed without soap, people cannot be fed without food, and going to the potty is necessarily associated with certain physical products. Second, it is the child's use of *physical* mimicry (e.g., pretending to wash the doll) and accompanying verbal expressions (e.g., "scrub, scrub") that constitute the imaginal pretense. Yet in some of the above examples, there were physical elements (i.e., real objects or replica toys), that supported the creation of these imaginal elements.

Often, in imaginal pretense, the child is guided by a mental representation of the imagined object or context and there is nothing in the physical environment to support these mental activities. This can occur both in solitary play and in social play. For example, when a child announces to a peer, "Now is tomorrow" (Ariel, 1984, p. 222), there is clearly nothing in the current context to support this transformation of the here-and-now. A preschooler announces that it is now after dinner and the teacher acknowledges, "Yes, I see, darling, so it is afternoon now" (Gardner & Cass, 1965, p. 77). A girl instructs a peer: "pretend it was afternoon . . . and it was wintertime but you weren't wearing a winter coat" (Garvey, 1993, p. 259). These children's statements serve to transform the time frame rather than anything concrete that can be referred to in the current context. In this vein, a toddler who referred to someone knocking on the door, refuted her mother's statement that "Nobody is here," saying, "Humble and Gerch are here. Come in Humble and Gerch. You want some crackers and cheese? You want some water without chlorine in it?" (Segal & Adcock, 1981, p. 14).

Playmates can agree to adopt the offered line of imaginal pretense, as illustrated in Table 10.13. In their play, one child acts like a magician, inventing objects, and the other is a willing participant in the magic, collaboratively creating an imaginary world that has no trace in the physical world.

Here as well, children tell both mothers and peers what they should imaginatively pretend. When I told Karen at 30;17 that there's no water in her cup, she answered, "You can just pretend there's water in here". A girl of 35 months gives her mother a pretend cup of coffee, saying, "You drink it for pretend" (Menyuk, Liebergott, & Schultz, 1995, p. 30). A girl of 3;10 years says to a peer, "just pretend you have a hurt" (Diessel, 2004). Playing doctor, a preschooler says to a peer, "Now play like you . . . on the bed . . . You have . . . you go . . . play like you went ahead and laid down on the bed" (Genishi & Di Paolo, 1982, p. 62). Yet another preschooler asks a peer to "pretend there's something wrong with my leg . . . somebody has to operate on it" (Ervin-Tripp & Kuntay, 1997).

But the magic being advocated by one child may not appeal to the other child. A first grader imaginally transforms a sand table into a graveyard, saying, "Watch it! A lady is buried in the sand there!" But his friend objects, saying "I don't see no lady," and interprets his transformation as a means of keeping her out of the play area, purposely digging where the lady was buried (Chittenden, Salinger, & Bussis, 2001, p. 149). When a 3-year-old wants to pretend to color the doll's hair purple and his peer does not, the refuser insists that the doll has soap in her eyes, and the colorist first denies this, saying "There's no soap in her eyes," and finally relents, saying, "Okay, I'll wash it"

[15] Italian: "Ha visto fuori il lupo"; "ci has la sega in mano."

(Segal & Adcock, 1981, p. 95). Similarly, 3-year-olds are playing house, and the pretend mother says, "but we need to have cookies"; her pretend child answers, "They are on the table. Don't you see them in the brown plate?" and the pretend mother answers, "Oh yes, but I like big fat cookies." Her pretend daughter retorts: "Well then, they are big fat cookies" (Weininger, 1988, p. 142). One child imaginally transforms thin air into cookies and then imaginally retransforms them into big fat cookies to align them with the pretend mother's preferences.

This is quite different from the following example in which a preschool child has cut out dough circles and baked them in a toy oven. He offers them to his friends, saying, "Now you have to be careful 'cause these cakes are very hot... they've just come out of the oven so watch you don't burn your tongue." His playmates proceed to pretend to eat the cakes (Sylva, Roy, & Painter, 1986, p. 261). In making dough circles that represent cakes baked in a replica oven, the child has engaged in a similarity-creating transformation. A given play episode can, of course, provide evidence for both similarity-creating and imaginal pretense. Sluckin (1981) gives an instance in which a 4-year-old insisted that "if that's the sea you mustn't walk on it"; a playmate accepted the transformation of the outlined area as the sea but announced that his magical powers let him walk on the sea (p. 100).

In some of the above examples, only one of the children engaged in imaginal pretense. There are also instances when both players do so, trying to impose their respective imaginal worlds on each other. In the play of siblings, when the pretend baby says "I want chocolate cookies," the "pretend mother" answers, "You are allergic to chocolate cookies, and you must not eat any." She further explains that "chocolate cookies are no good to eat, he gets sick." When the pretend baby then says, "I want to eat chocolate and I'm not sick," the "pretend mother" reiterates, "We will pretend you are sick." He rejects this, saying "I don't want to be sick" and when she says "Well, you have to," he responds "I won't play with you then" (Weininger, 1988, pp. 142–143). In this example, both children were imaginatively transforming reality, but they were not interested in sharing the same pretend world and did not accept each other's imaginal transformations.

Veneziano (2002) suggests that children's verbalizations are meant to get others to make "the same meaning transformation as the child has imagined," implying that the child understands the need to change other people's representations of signifiers or to adopt the transformation being proposed. In her view, children have an intuitive understanding that (1) representations about pretense differ from representations about reality, (2) another person may not have access to others imaginal transformations, and (3) language is a good means of letting others know about these imaginal transformations. Veneziano suggests that such understanding is evident in the way children announce their pretense to observers – even ones who are not participating in the pretense (e.g., by looking at and approaching the interaction partner). In fact, toddlers have been found to look at adults longer immediately after performing symbolic actions, as if they are verifying shared construals with them (Striano, Tomasello, & Rochat, 2001).

Veneziano further contends that if verbalizations regarding imaginal pretense are more common than other types of talk, this reflects the child's understanding that his transformations are not patently obvious to others. To examine this issue, she categorized the verbalizations of four children between 18 and 23 months who participated in a longitudinal study with their mothers while playing at home. More than 50 percent of children's verbalizations reflected *meaning* transformations which transformed reality by verbalizing the imaginal transformation (e.g., "the doll is sleeping" or "she's hungry now.") Veneziano concludes on this basis that children have an intuitive understanding about imaginal transformations, the fact that they are performed idiosyncratically, and understand the consequent need to voice them to share them with others. A 10-year-old with a language disorder expresses this well in referring to fantasy pet monkeys, saying, "Monkeys in ours head. Nobody knows us got monkeys in our head" (Chiat, 2000, p. 247). The developmental pattern observed indicates that even very young children understand the need to announce their transformations to each other because they know that these cannot be known by others.

Notice that in the examples of imaginal pretense above children were creating objects and contexts out of thin air, but they were also sometimes pretending to be someone else (e.g., "Pretend I'm your mom, okay?"; "I'm the auntie, so I'm getting married," Blaise, 2005, p. 168). Fein (1987) calls these *person transformations* and Volterra and her colleagues (1979) call them *decontextualization through role reversal*, but both suggest that these represent a cognitively advanced activity. Yet their emergence at such young ages seems to belie their apparent sophistication. How do we reconcile this? First, many of the contexts in which children engage in person transformations are ones in which they simply adopt the reverse role, usually that of the parent. At 31 months, Orren says to me, "Let's say that you're a kid and you will sit here and I will take you to Tehila's kindergarten."[16] A girl of 35 months often reenacted with her mother disciplinary encounters by reversing the disciplinarian and the one being disciplined, with the pretend play version being an almost word-for-word replay of the disciplinary encounter experienced by the child (Gordon, 2002).

Children's ability to adopt other roles emerges within scripted, well known routines in which the role of the individual being played out is fairly circumscribed. Siblings pretending to be trains used a children's story as their basis, adopting the storybook train names to label themselves, to pretend being squirted by an elephant, and

[16] Hebrew: "Bo nagid she at yeled ve-at yishev po ve ani yikax ottax lagan shel Tehila."

to brush their teeth (Dunn, 1988). In fact, Chaillé (1978) found that when they were asked how they pretend to be someone else (e.g., a mother, a doctor), references to in-role behavior was the primary response of 7- to 11-year-olds; 5-year-olds indicated a need for both props and resemblance props (i.e., appropriate costumes like Batman capes, make up). To play doctor, a child only needs to know medical props and their means of use (e.g., a stethoscope to check a doll and something wrapable to administer a band-aid, Andersen, 1990). Pretend doctors take patients' blood pressure and write out prescriptions, just like real doctors ("that's what doctors do," Lederer, 2002, p. 251). In this vein, a preschool "doctor" tells the patient, "You make sure you take 100 of these every hour until you're better. Keep warm and go to bed" (Morrow & Rand, 1991, p. 153). When a plastic figure falls out of the "elevator," a preschooler says, "I'll take him to the clinic. I will bandage the man in my car. I have a first-aid kit" (Krown, 1974, p. 92). There are also things doctors do not do. When a "doctor" laughs, his playmate says, "No, don't laugh because doctors do not laugh" (Genishi & DiPaolo, 1982, p. 62); when a "doctor" who is changing a baby's diaper says, "Look at all the poo poo," her playmate objects: "I'm gonna tell. Doctors don't say poo poo" (Galda & Pellegrini, 1988, p. 94). Out of script behavior is unacceptable so when a boy wants to cook dinner, he is admonished, "Daddies don't cook" (Garvey, 1977, p. 91). In this vein, a preschooler tells a peer, "You're the daddy and you'll have to go to work 'cos daddies do" (Tough, 1976, p, 85).

Role transformations, then, actually involve a series of limited and recurrent actions, structured activities undertaken by those in the roles with a limited number of role-related props. Because they are highly scripted, others who are similarly aware of the role and relevant props can join the child in play. They can do so by adopting a complementary role, helping the child's own role, or suggesting additional roles and props. For instance, a preschool child says, "I'll fix supper for the kid and you get the groceries" (Garvey, 1984, p. 167), assigning the mother and father roles with their associated tasks. In another instance of this, a "pretend mother" tells the pretend baby: "I'll make tuna fish for supper. But you have to eat baby food" (Segal & Adcock, 1981, p. 66). Similarly, a pretend executive mom tells the stay-at-home pretend dad, "I'm going to work. I need you to vacuum this floor" (Denham, 1998, p. 173). As El'Konin (1971) showed, role transformations in play emerge when children understand the functions different individuals play in the relevant scenario. When children were taken to the zoo but were not informed of the roles of the zoo staff in the daily running of the zoo, pretend play did not emerge, even when toy animals were available.[17]

[17] Importantly, in their fantasy play, girls adopt the *possible* pole of the imaginal plane whereas boys appear adopt the *impossible* pole. Girls' fantasy play focuses on realistic themes of home and relations (even when princes were involved) and boys' play focuses on heroic fantasy themes, often including superheroes (cf., Maccoby, 1998).

Importantly, though, role transformations provide children with the opportunity of adopting the goals and motivations of the individual whose role they adopt, thereby glimpsing what alternative perspectives on the same context imply, an issue that will be addressed more fully later.

The fact that different children have similar experiences and develop similar representations of the activities within scripts allows them to play out diverse roles and to determine when they need to adopt or terminate a specific role. In the play of 3½-year-olds, one says, "Now you be Dracula." The newly anointed Dracula, delays, saying, "Wait.... I gotta put my cowboy hat on first"; once the hat is on his head, the game can proceed (Fein, 1984, p. 136). Another preschooler yells, "We need a Batman!" Turning to a peer, he asks, "you want to be Batman?" (Paley, 1986, p. 75). Children know the powers imbued by Batman's cape; so one needs to get a cape to become Batman (e.g., denied access to a Batman house, a preschooler says, "I need a cape to get in their Batman house," Elgas et al., 1988, p. 151). As well, a 3-year-old who draws a figure, says he is drawing capes, adding "I am making Superman," on another occasion explaining that "to be Batman you have to put on his shirt with this... and his boots and capes" (Wolf, 1990, p. 201).

But children need to verify that others acknowledge the transformed role being enacted. An interesting case of this occurs when a pretend cat says, "I'm not – I'm not a kitty anymore," and the other child asks, "You're a husband?" and when the reply is *yes*, says, "Good. We need two husbands" (Corsaro, 1985, p. 103). But proposed role transformations can be rejected by others. When her offer to play mother is rejected, a preschooler says, "I can be the grandmother," and when this possibility is also rejected with "No, we don't need a grandmother," the rejected mother/grandmother addresses a third girl and says, "You and me can be a sister, you and me can be sisters, and Lee's the mother, OK?" (Genishi & Di Paolo, 1982, p. 60). Similarly, when a girl asks whether she can join other girls at play, she is told, "Yeah, you can be the dog." She resists, saying, "I wanna be the sister," and is rejected with, "No, we already have enough sisters" (Pitcher & Schultz, 1983, p. 8).

Role transformations in play eventually need to be terminated and reality has to be re-instated. DiLalla and Watson (1988) found that over the ages of 2 to 6 years, there was a developmental trend such that older children were better able to continue their play after experimenter-initiated interruptions in superhero pretend games. Yet children are quite concerned with role termination, often announcing that they are no longer playing pretend roles (e.g., "Please don't push me 'cause I'm not the dragon anymore," Garvey, 1977, p. 83, and "I'm not the sister anymore," Schwartzman, 1978). Labeled *back transformations* (Garvey & Berndt, 1977) or *disconnection statements* (Schwartzman, 1978), their importance is underlined in the following. A child who after roaring with anger agreed that he was a lion, got upset when his mother suggested

Table 10.14.

	Age	Source
C: "The hunter doesn't know I'm hiding here, alright James?"	Preschool	Trawick-Smith (1998)
Playing with dolls C1: "let's pretend that she didn't know that this girl put on one of her ballet slippers, ok?" C2: "And she was angry with her"	Preschool	Shuy & Griffin (1981, p. 281)
C: "Pretend I had a winter coat on and you couldn't believe me was walking across the street with a winter coat, all right?"	5 years	Garvey (1993, p. 259)
Pretending to be baby C: "Now, make believe I'm scared of the dark . . . . Now Mama could I sleep with you in your room?"	First grade	Chittenden, Salinger, & Bussis (2001, p. 151)

he roar some more, saying, "No. I not a lion. I not a lion. I John" (Dunn, 1988, p. 164). As well, a 5-year-old in therapy says to the therapist "No more pretend," adding, "You made me frustrated when you kept pretending" (Downey, 1987, p. 114).

But how does one stop being someone else? A 3-year-old discusses being Batman and asks his father, "Then do you take the shirt and the boots off? And the cape? And then are you a man? Or Batman still?" (Wolf, 1990, p. 201). He is not entirely sure. The same problem arises when a preschooler wants to give his teacher a jam sausage roll and the teacher says "Oh, well I think I've eaten quite enough. I shall be getting fat now, won't I?" The child counters with "It's pretend!," requiring the teacher to explain, "Well, I'm pretending I'll get fat, aren't I?" (Wood, McMahon, & Cranstoun, 1980, p. 151).

The important aspect of role termination statements is that they indicate the child's ability to terminate role play at will. This is critical because in many clinical settings, the individual is unable to do so. In fact, in the film "Don Juan de Marco," the decision as to whether to institutionalize Don Juan rested on his stating that he willfully adopted the role of Don Juan and that he could, at will, disengage from the role. A child who pretends he is a helicopter is told by a peer who wants him to play puppy, "You're really a helicopter really but you're pretending a baby, okay, Jason, okay" (Paley, 1990, p. 135). The child acknowledges the peer's pretense, asks him to stop this pretense to play at being a puppy, and he does. In line with this, a child who refuses to stop pretending she is a cat, is told by a peer, "You can't be Boots for the rest of your life, Amy. You pretend you turn back into a kid, okay?" (Barnes & Vangelisti, 1995).

In this context, Harris (2000) found that role playing, and in particular, statements regarding roles adopted during pretend play, are associated with higher false belief understanding. He suggests that the adoption of different roles during pretend play facilitates the emergence of understanding of other minds and, concomitantly, false belief understanding. He accords pretend play a *causal* role. Following Veneziano, I would argue to the contrary, that children announce adoption of different roles during role play precisely because of their *prior* understanding that others do not share their own mental states and cannot be aware of their imaginal transformations. This analysis accords well with the view of Volterra and her colleagues (1979) that the advance that inheres in the development of social pretend play is that it requires the child to coordinate his actions with that of others by stating how reality is to be transformed for the duration of play.

There are several patterns of findings that support Veneziano's and Volterra's view. First, children often phrase their suggestions for joint imaginal transformations in the conditional mode, indicating what transformations *could* be undertaken, presumably if the other child were willing. For instance, a preschooler tells his peer, "You could play with this. This *could* be a snake" (Genishi & DiPaolo, 1982, p. 52, emphasis added). Similarly, when a child of 5;11 years suggests playing hot air balloons, and is queried how, he answers, "You see, we *could* pretend we're in the sky" (Piaget, 1926/1959, p. 62, emphasis added).

Second, children attempt to get others to adopt the mental states that they want them to adopt for the duration of play, telling them the psychological states they should adopt (e.g., "Pretend you hated baby fish," Garvey, 1977, p. 87; "pretend I'm angry because . . . ," Paley, 1990, p. 89). They also specify the mental states of the pretend characters that are incorporated in their play, as shown in Table 10.14. Mental states are related to both one's own and others' behavior. If both players adopt certain mental states there are behavioral implications for how their joint play needs to proceed (e.g., a 4-year-old Cinderella tells her peer, "You need to yell at me to clean . . . cause you're the mean stepsister," Davidson, 1998, p. 175). But moreover, children recognize that by saying "pretend," both they and their peers are entering a fictional world that has its own rules and regulations, ones that differ from the real world. This is clarified by a preschooler, who explains, "If we just tell them and don't say "pretend," they'll think it's real life" (Curran, 1999).

Third, children's ability to reconstrue events retroactively also indicates that they understand that others do not share their mental states. For instance, a boy who sits with a dragon puppet growls at a peer who walks by. She says, "S (boy's name), I'm telling." He replies, "I'm the baby dragon." She answers "Oh," and continues on her way (Curran, 1999). She understood that although his behavior was unacceptable as a child, it was acceptable as a pretend dragon. More importantly, he understood that he needed to disabuse her of her belief that he was growling at her as a real child.

Clark (1996) analyzes social pretend play as layered actions. In layer 1, the pretense of being someone else takes place, and consists of *serious* actions that are seriously undertaken. In layer 2, the roles and actions that are part of the pretense are taking place but they are *nonserious* because they are not really occurring, "they are created out of a whole cloth as a joint pretense" (p. 354). Clark describes this metaphorically as the foundation on top of which is a theatrical stage which requires players to coordinate or imagine themselves together on the same stage. Establishing the ground rules for the pretense takes place in layer 1 and the actions that occur within the pretense take place in both domains but are simply different construals of the same behavior in the two domains (e.g., a pebble taken out of the sand is a gold nugget found by a gold miner during the Gold Rush). Hence, there is a correspondence function that maps elements of level 2 onto level 1. Access to the levels is asymmetrical so that participants in level 2 have no access to elements of level 1 and the pretend people created in level 2 cannot interact with the real people in level 1. But statements made by the pretend people in layer 2 can be used by the people in layer 1 to "help them simulate imaginary experiences" (e.g., "look, I found a gold nugget," p. 359). Clark summarizes this by suggesting that the primary participants (i.e., the real individuals in level 1) are intended to imagine what is happening in the higher layers (the pretend layers) and to appreciate the purposes and techniques used to create the higher, pretend layers. The primary participants jointly develop a correspondence function that maps entities of domain 2 into entities of domain 1, allowing entities in domain 2 to be caused by occurrences in the corresponding entities in domain 1 (but not vice versa). In this context, then, metacommunication serves to coordinate children's understanding of the transformations that allow the two levels to relate to each other and acknowledges the centrality of shared construals for the unfolding of the pretense.

Trawick-Smith (1998) developed a typology of preschool children's metacommunication, which from Clark's perspective represents the means of coordination of the two layers. He identified thirty-eight different types of metacommunication that increased significantly between the ages of 2 to 5 years. Five-year-olds engaged in twenty-three times as much metacommunication as 2-year-olds. Children announced their imaginal transformations that related to objects (e.g., "This will be the broom, alright?"), contexts (e.g., "Let's say a hunter's coming" or "Let's say I'm baking these pies"), roles (e.g., "I'm Cinderella the princess, alright?"), and the mental states of different characters (e.g., "Let's say the mother is really angry, okay?"; "You're the mother who doesn't know her baby ran away, so you just make the dinner, alright?"). Regarding the spook house alluded to earlier, one of the children says, "Little kids are coming and let's say they will be sad when they go in, right?" When a child says, "Let's pretend the queen doesn't know about the hunter," (Trawick-Smith, 1998, p. 434), the act of pretending involves both a pretend role and a pretend mental state.

Concomitantly, though, one needs to ascertain understanding of how one's peers set up the correspondences between layers. Trawick-Smith (1998) found that children asked their peers as to their imaginal transformations of objects (e.g., "Is this going to be your telephone, Hanna?"), settings (e.g., "You're just sweeping and sweeping the kitchen to clean up the baby's mess, right Sara?" "Is the carnival starting today, James?" p. 437), joint actions (e.g., pretending to shoot a gun, a child says "We're shooting them, aren't we, Seth?" "Are we nailing this, James?") and roles (e.g., "Am I going to be the older sister?"). They also told others what to pretend in their actions (e.g., "Pretend you to go in the cave now, Jeremy"), who to pretend to be (e.g., "You'll be one of the good guys, alright Marcie?" and "Will you be a hunter?"), sometimes using props to do so (e.g., placing a plastic firefighter's hat on a peer's head). Finally, children also told others what to pretend to see and think (e.g., "Pretend you don't see me and I'm in my squirrel hole and then you see me but first you don't," Paley, 1990, p. 35). Such talk reflects children's awareness of others as possessing internal psychological processes that need to be taken into account in setting up their transformations, perhaps consolidating their understanding of such psychological processes but contrary to Harris's (2000) claim, certainly not being causal in producing them.

In line with this, Fonagy and his colleagues (2002) maintain that, "Pretending requires a mental stance involving the symbolic transformation of reality in the presence of, and with a view to, the mind of the other" (p. 48). This may account for why engaging in group pretend play enhances children's ability to choose sex- and age-appropriate toys for others (Burns & Brainerd, 1979), choices that require one to engage in mentalization. As Paley (2004) notes, children work hard at "deciding who to be and who the others must be and what the environment is to look like," with perhaps their greatest difficulty being "getting others to listen to *you* and accept *your* point of view while keeping the integrity of the make-believe" (p. 2). It is by doing so that they come to a full-blown understanding of others as psychological beings. They learn that others have preferences, that others' preferences may not match their own, that their plans can clash with those of others, and they need to integrate their preferences with those of these others in order to stay within the play context. But there are additional virtues to play. As Rubin (2007) argues, "fantasy, play, and imagination function as a developmental time machine . . . transporting its occupants between past, present, and future" (p. 16), thereby solidifying the ability to decontextualize as well.

FOSTERING ADOPTION OF THE *PRETEND* FRAMEWORK

Do parents play a role in fostering children's pretend play? In the Western world they do. As Lancy (2007) reviews this domain, mother–child play and especially, pretend play, is a relatively new cultural phenomenon that is rare in many societies and is prevalent in societies that expect children to "eventually, function at the top of the information economy" (p. 274), being conceptually linked to literacy development. In their hallmark American study, Haight and Miller (1993) found that pretend play develops as a social activity with another person, usually the mother, starting at about 12 months. About 70 percent of pretend play was found to be social, with mothers being the primary partners in their children's pretend play. But mothers' participation was found to decrease as children acquire playmates and enter settings in which more peers are available. When playmates were available prior to 24 months, children took little advantage of opportunities to pretend with them. It was mothers who initiated pretend play at 12 months, prompting the child to pretend but getting little sustaining responses from him. Kavanaugh and colleagues (1983) similarly found that mothers both initiated and directed most of the pretend play of children between 12 and 27 months. By 24 months, children in Haight and Miller's (1993) study were equally likely to initiate pretend play, but mothers' sustaining responses are critical, with those episodes in which mothers participate and sustain play, lasting significantly longer. Pretend play with mothers is also more elaborate and more complex than pretend play alone (Howes et al., 1992). In fact, Slade (1987) found that mothers' availability as verbal commentators or as active participants in children's play increased both the level and the duration of play episodes in children of 20–28 months.

But what role do mothers play in children's adoption of the *pretend* framework? Mothers both legitimize and provide guidelines and instructions how the *pretend* framework is to be adopted. This becomes evident in looking at what mothers actually do to foster pretend play. Kavanaugh and colleagues (1983) found that by the time children were 2-years-old, mothers were recontextualizing, talking of nonexistent imaginary objects and encouraging their children to add imaginary elements in their play. When an 18-month-old inspects a purse, takes out some coins, puts them back, and repeats the procedure once more, his mother asks, "Going shopping?" (Dunn & Wooding, 1977, p. 52). As her son of 23;24 is pushing some cars, the mother asks, "Who are you going to see?" The child answers, "Going, going to gramma" (Howe, 1981, p. 10). The physical act of moving a toy car back and forth on the floor has been transformed with the mother's help into an imaginary scenario that has a goal, visiting the grandmother, and into which additional imaginary elements can be added at will. One could bring grandma flowers, play with other grandchildren, and eat grandma's famous roast turkey. A mother hands her child an empty cup, saying, "Here is some juice. You can give it to the doll to drink" (Veneziano, 2001, p. 331).[18] In this context, in participating in pretend play with her toddler, a mother transformed dolls into movie stars and hospital patients, coffee tables into stoves, and nesting bowls into pots and hats (Miller, 1982). When 3-year-old Nancy is bored, her mother suggests she drive her car, tells her to "Buckle up for safety!" and asks, "Where are you going? Are you taking a trip?" becoming a passenger going with her daughter to Havana (Haight & Miller, 1993, p. 1). Wells (1986) recorded James at 3;9 years as he is playing trains with his mother, sitting on the sofa as the driver. When the "train" starts, the mother suggests he wave goodbye to his friends, says her breakfast is rumbling in her tummy, and that he should slow down the train. Then she says, "Look at the cows in the field, James" and when he mutters, *Mm*, she continues, "and there's a farmer, look. The farmer's waving to you" (p. 64). It is the mother who is teaching the child that imaginary transformations are legitimate, that one can invent objects and settings at will (e.g., "Pretend you're at the ball . . . and I'll be the Prince," said by a mother to her 24-month-old, Haight & Miller, 1993, p. 105), and that there are no boundaries on doing so. People and objects can be invented, scenarios can be created and tossed, and physical and psychological reactions can be tried on and turned off. Morelock, Brown, and Morrissey (2003) found that during play, mothers were engaging in transformations of present objects and contexts earlier than were their toddler children, providing a scaffold for their children's eventual use of similar transformations and analogies. In line with this, Striano, Tomasello, and Rochat (2001) found that children's early symbolic acts are mostly in imitation of adults rather than truly symbolic so that when no replica toys were available and no symbolic acts were demonstrated by adults, 2-year-old children were unable to use objects symbolically.

Teachers also foster adoption of the *pretend* framework by elaborating the scenarios created by children and encouraging children to do so themselves. Faced by a "bank teller," a preschool teacher asked to open an account, provided her address, asked "Can I deposit ten dollars in my savings account?" telling the "teller" he needs to sign a form indicating she deposited the money (Schrader, 1991, p. 206). In other preschools, teachers served as shopkeepers, bank tellers, and customers (e.g., Gardner & Cass, 1965). Preschool teachers actively participated in children's pretense and even excluded children

[18] French: "Ici il y a du jus. Tu peus donner à boire à la poupée."

from playing because of the requirements of the pretense. For instance, when several preschoolers were playing nurse, the teacher prevented another child from joining the game, telling her she would have to wait "because I don't think there's another nurse's outfit" (Wood, McMahon, & Cranstoun, 1980, p. 183).

Parents even encourage adoption of the *pretend* framework when children appear unwilling to do so. When a Japaneses mother urges her bathing preschooler who is blowing bubbles to pretend to be riding a soap bubble to Osaka and the child expresses fear, the mother says, "If you fall, I'll save you" (Clancy et al. 1997, p. 29). It is the mother who both initiates and fosters the pretense and not the reluctant child. Similarly, when Bloom (1973) suggests to her daughter Allison at 19;14 that her doll is dirty and needs a bath, Allison says "home," which is where baths are taken and given. But her mother answers, "Home. When we get home? Well, let's pretend we'll give her a bath now. O.K. Shall we give her a bath? . . . Let's pretend there's water in the cup" (p. 201). The mother transforms the cup into a bathtub and conjures up imaginary water to bathe the doll. In other contexts, mothers may encourage adoption of the pretend framework when reality counters their own preferences. When a child wants to put sunscreen on her mother, the mother refuses to open the bottle, saying "You can pretend (to put) it on . . . . I don't want you opening that . . . now you can pretend to just go like that and put it on me." When the child hollers *no*, the mother answers, "Well I don't want it opened . . . just pretend" (Gordon, 2002, p. 712).

Mothers also adopt the pretend framework during book reading. Reading with her 1-year-old who points to a picture in the book, a mother says, "Guitar. Can you pretend to play a guitar?" and the mother strums an imaginary guitar and sings (Carew, 1976, p. 65). In a similar book-reading incident, a mother warns her child "Don't put your finger in there. The lion will eat it up." When the child does, the mother roars loudly, scaring the child into withdrawing her finger (Segal & Adcock, 1981, p. 144). During book-reading as well, children can resist the pretense being suggested by the mother. While reading a Dr. Seuss book with her preschooler, a mother pretends to pick a green egg off the page and tries to feed it to her daughter, asking, "Do you like green eggs and ham"? When the daughter shakes her head vigorously, the mother says, "Oh, come on, just try one little bite" (Segal & Adcock, 1981, p. 144), with the child vehemently rejecting the offer.

Of course, children can also initiate the pretense. At 31;24, Orren says to me, "Mommy prepare for my mouse milk in pretend."[19] In the same vein, the mother of a child who had an imaginary cat was told, "Mind my cat! Don't tread on him, will you?" (Newson and Newson, 1968, p. 174). As one incredulous mother said about her daughter, "she'll get the table out and set it out for different people, and she'll talk to them, but there's nobody there . . . she's talk to them as if they're all sitting down and having a good conversation with her" (ibid, p. 174).

Parents can do one of several things when their children initiate pretense. First, they can ignore children's pretense, allowing children to maintain the pretense but taking no action to either encourage or discourage it. Second, parents can acknowledge it. When a girl of 30 months says to her father, "Don't wake teddy up will you Daddy?" he answers, "No I won't" (Wells, 1986, p. 63); the father does not deny the possibility of waking up an inanimate object. Similarly, a mother interviewed by Newson and Newson said about her 4-year-old daughter,

> At one time she used to pick things up and give them to us – pick them off the table. There was nothing there; and my husband used to say to her "You've dropped it! And she'd bend down to pick it up. (Newson & Newson, 1968, p. 174)

In both these instances, the parents adopted the same *pretend* stance in seeing imaginary objects but did not actively participate in the child's activity. Yet by going along with children's pretense they legitimized children's imaginal transformations.

Third, parents can become active participants in the pretense. When a 4-year-old "terrorized" his mother by becoming ghosts and robots who popped out behind doors or leapt from boxes, his mother had to be "appreciative, frightened, surprised and amazed at the appropriate moment" (Segal & Adcock, 1981, pp. 104–105). One mother indicated that when her son plays Robin Hood, she is the Sheriff of Nottingham and another mother explained that she and her son go on a rocket – "he puts all the chairs out and touches the knobs . . . . " 'Hold on Mummy, we're off,' so we hold on" (Newson & Newson, 1968, pp. 176–177). When a 24-month-old pointed a straw at her mother, waved it, and said *magic*, her mother replied, "Oh, You turned me into a frog," becoming a participant in the child's pretense (Haight, 1998, p. 259).

Moreover, mothers willingly participate in pretending that dolls and stuffed animals are real, needing to be fed and taken care of. At lunch, Kathryn, at 21 months, asks her mother for some more meat for herself and then pointing to a toy cat, asks for more meat for the cat. The mother fed the cat (Bloom, 1970, p. 43), later evidencing the same behavior toward a toy bear. A mother who said that her son asked her to smack his imaginary cat because it had scratched him indicated that she pretended to smack the cat (Newson & Newson, 1968). Mothers even acknowledge the presence of imaginary people. A child with a pretend friend Susan asked "Can Susan come for tea?" and the mother says "All right" and explains, "and we sit there and we pretend" to be having tea (Newson & Newson, 1968, p. 191). A mother whose 4-year-old had an imaginary baby lamented, "I have to carry it about in my arms – I'm as daft as her!" (ibid, p. 198).

How common is mothers' acceptance and participation of their children's pretense? It appears to be quite common. Newson and Newson (1968) asked mothers whether

[19] Hebrew: "Ima taxin la-axbar sheli xalav be-keilu."

Table 10.15.

	Age	Source
M asks about doll M: "Do you think she'd like to go for a ride in the truck now that she's all clean?"	19;14	Bloom (1973, p. 204)
Mother and child are playing; mother picks up doll M: "Wanna rock Nancy to sleep?"	22 mos.	Zukow et al. (1982, p. 77)
Child feeds doll C: "Dolly have a dinner" M: "Uhhuh, she likes it, doesn't she"?	24 mos.	Howe (CHILDES)
Child plays with doll C: "Crying" M: "You'll have to give her a cuddle and make her better"	Toddler	Howe (CHILDES)

they ever act as participants in children's pretend play. Of the seven hundred mothers sampled, two-thirds said they did. On the other hand, there is a limit to how far parents are willing to go along with pretense. Limits may be imposed because children refuse a given transformation proposed by the parent. When a mother gets tired of "walking on the moon" and suggests they take a streetcar, her son snaps: "There are no streetcars on the moon" (Segal & Adcock, 1981, p. 33). Parents may also limit pretense because they are displeased with the storyline, as when a child wants to pretend to be someone else, indicating that he himself has gone away (e.g., Segal & Adcock, 1981). Parents can also discourage pretense because they fear the child will lose his grip on reality, for example, "I tried to stop it, because I didn't want him to go from an imaginary story to a downright lie – because there's not much difference between the two" (Newson & Newson, 1968, p. 199). Parents' implicit understanding of the virtues of pretend play guides them in dealing with their children's adoption of the pretend framework.

MENTALIZING AND SOCIALIZING MENTAL TRANSFORMATIONS

M*ental* transformations provide us with access to other people's psychological experiences, using our knowledge of human preference systems to draw maps of others' likely thoughts and feelings and to use such maps in guiding our expectations and in guiding our own behavior in interacting with others. My concern below is with how parents foster children's mental transformations.

SOCIALIZING MENTAL TRANSFORMATIONS

Mothers take an active role in fostering mental transformations, doing so first in the context of doll play. In this context, mothers actively encourage children to anthropomorphize dolls. Mothers are often the voice of the doll, telling children what they like and don't like, telling children that they need to go the potty, are cold, hungry, sick and in need of other things. When a 2-year-old tells her mother that she can't find her teddy bear, her mother asks, "where could he have gone?" and the child retorts, "run away" and the mother accepts this (Schutze, Kreppner, & Paulsen, 1986, p. 140). As well, in talking for the doll, mothers ask children questions that mimic real questions that another person would pose. For instance, the mother of an 18-month-old child asks her child in a doll's voice, "hello, how do you like my blue jeans?" (Bernstein, CHILDES).

Mothers also suggest explicitly that dolls have needs and preferences. Some examples of this are provided in Table 10.15. More generally, Sachs (1984) found that in doll play with children, mothers were the ones who described the ongoing activity in terms of the motivations and covert psychological processes of the dolls. For instance, when a child put a blanket on a doll, the child was likely to say "blanket on," but the adult was likely to say "the baby's tired" (p. 124). In this vein, a 24-month-old who covered her teddy with a blanket was told, "Not over his face. He won't be able to see" (Wells, 1986, p. 8). A toddler who asks for her doll is told that the doll is sleeping and that the child has to be quiet so as to not wake her (Clancy, Akatsuka, & Strauss, 1997). In research with children 12 to 27 months old, Kavanaugh and colleagues (1983) found that mothers made attributions about the feelings, actions, and functions of animate and inanimate objects, with virtually no responses from the younger children.

Mothers also draw parallels between dolls and babies, instructing children how to take care of the "baby." A working class mother tells her toddler daughter to comfort the doll because she is crying (e.g., "Say 'don't cry'," p. 110), tells her to "Burp it. Burp the baby.... Put her on your shoulder and burp her...." (Miller, 1982, p. 105). The child was encouraged to change the doll, comb its hair, take her for rides, and show her toys and pictures (e.g., "Show the baby the picture. Go over there and show the baby the picture. Tell her about the picture" (p. 108). She was also encouraged to feed her, telling her to say "take a bite...chew it up" (p. 106). Even by calling the doll "a baby," the mother creates an equivalence between the doll and human children.

Table 10.16.

	Age	Source
Referring to doll M: "Want her hat on too? Just like you put it on yourself?"	Toddler	Broen (1972, p. 94)
Referring to doll's diaper M: "I guess maybe she's a wetting doll. It's just like mom puts it on you"	Toddler	Broen (1972, p. 84)
Referring to doll's clothes M: "I'll bet one time these booties belonged to a real baby . . . the booties are the size of some that you and Jeffrey had when you were little . . . she's about the size of a real baby isn't she?"	Preschool	Broen (1972, p. 76)
Child put teddy to sleep, saying "night night" M; "Have you read him a story?" C: "No, he doesn't want a story" M: "He doesn't want a story? Ooh, you have a story when you go to bed. Why don't you get your caterpillar book and read him that?"	3 years	Dunn (1984)

Moreover, mothers also make explicit comparisons between humans and dolls (e.g., as a teacher looks at a doll that a child brought to preschool, she says, "She really looks like a school girl, really," Kamler, 1999, p. 201) and between dolls and their children, as shown in Table 10.16. As evident above, mothers legitimize children's treatment of their dolls as children by engaging in all of the above activities. Children appear to be accepting and following their mothers' anthropomorphizing rather than spontaneously treating their dolls as if they were human.

This is also evident in the anthropomorphization of animals in children's stories. For instance, when a preschool teacher tells a story about a lonely donkey, she draws a parallel between the donkey and human children, asking, "When did you feel lonely Colin? . . . What about you Richard have you ever been lost or felt lonely?" (Cuff & Hustler, 1981, pp. 113–114). In a study conducted with my students (Karniol, Foor-Eisenberg, & Caspari, unpublished), preschool children listened to a children's storybook about an animal character who was bullied, with reading being terminated at three different points in the story, or at the end. After their understanding of how the animal character felt was assessed, children were asked to draw and the strength of pressure on the page, as assessed by attached carbon copies, served as the index of arousal. Then they responded how another child or they themselves would feel in response to three short, aversive vignettes. As compared to their control level of arousal, all children hearing the storybook evidenced increased arousal, irrespective of the point of story termination, but this increase was only evident in those children who evidenced empathic understanding of the affective reactions of the animal character in the storybook. Hence, animals, like dolls and children, have psychological reactions to their experiences and children are taught to respond to such experiences as if they were being experienced by humans.

Why do mothers and teachers do so? First, they may want children to learn about the covert psychological processes of other people. Second, in anthropomorphizing dolls and pointing out the similarities between them and the child, they may want to underline to the child the similarity between different individuals in terms of their psychological processes. That is, dolls, and the child hurt, cry, smile, and laugh, just like everyone else, as shown in Table 10.17. By doing so, mothers are putting dolls, pictures of people, the child, and other people into a generic category of everyone, and everyone has similar psychological processes. As we saw in Chapter 4 on other people's

Table 10.17.

	Age	Source
M sees picture of pointing baby in book M: "Look the baby's pointing. Just like you do"	12 mos.	Yont, Snow, & Vernon-Feagans (2003)
Korean C throws doll M: "If you throw her, she'll go 'ouch' "	Toddler	Clancy, Akatsuka, & Strauss (1997, p. 55)
Japanese C breaks doll's hand M: "Well then, if we don't take him to the doctor, it's no good"	Toddler	Clancy, Akatsuka, & Strauss (1997, p. 56)
C playing with a doll M: "Can you hear her heart? Is it beating?"	Preschool	Perlmutter & Pellegrini (1987, p. 272)

preferences, children do in fact mentalize about other people's psychological experiences and do so for both specific and generic others. This is critical for altruism and moral behavior, as I discuss in Chapter 14.

TRANSFORMATIONAL THOUGHT: TIME, REALITY, AND THE MENTAL

As we have seen in this chapter, children learn to both decontextualize (i.e., distance themselves from the current context) and to recontextualize (i.e., transform the present on the temporal plane, the imaginal plane, and the plane of the mental) with parents playing an important and guiding role in such development. The imaginary present created in pretend play provides the child with a forum for replaying past situations, both with and without changing the way they actually unfolded, and for venturing into the possible and impossible future in a setting that does not pose any danger. It also provides the stage for children to venture into other people's minds, making predictions about their likely preferences, thoughts, and feelings. Pretend play, then, allows children to integrate the world of *what is* with the world of *what if* (Engel, 2005) and to investigate the boundaries, limitations, and possible overlaps between them. It is the stage on which transformations of time, reality, and the mental are rehearsed. But inexplicably, pretend play disappears in middle childhood. Why? My contention is that pretend play is the dress rehearsal for the real work of transformational thought. The ability to transform the *here-and-now* on the temporal, the imaginal, and the mental planes allows us to deploy transformations *strategically*, to change how we and others think and feel about contexts, objects, and even ourselves. Pretend play disappears after middle childhood because the planes of transformational thought are ready to be used for the work of real life, as I discuss in Chapter 13.

It is critical to note, however, that the imaginary present children create is not random. As Vygotsky (1966) argues, pretend play follows rules of behavior; the child playing mother obeys the rules of maternal behavior, the child playing doctor behaves like a real doctor, and so forth. Only limited leeway is accorded for engaging in rule-violating behavior. Children use the rules they have abstracted regarding the context being played out and use them to guide pretend play, telling themselves – and others– what is or is not allowed within the context of the pretense. Yet abiding by such rules implies that one cannot be guided by current preferences. According to Vygotsky,

> by subordinating themselves to rules, children renounce what they want, since subjection to rule and renunciation of spontaneous impulsive action constitute the path to maximum pleasure in play. (Vygotsky, 1966, p. 14)

From this point of view, pretend play teaches children new preferences, the preferences they have as a fictitious "I," as mother, father, or doctor. But it also teaches children to subjugate their current desires in the interest of playing out the game. This subjugation is reflected in coping, self-regulation, and mind play, which will be addressed in subsequent chapters.

11 Manipulating Others

A 3-year-old shouts at a preschool peer, 'Just shut up, Erik! Don't talk to me. Just be quiet. Don't crawl all over me neither. Don't do anything to me.'

(Paley, 1986, p. 114)

In several earlier chapters, I discussed infants' and children's expression of their preferences. Telling others one's preferences is an effective strategy when others are willing accomplices who *want* to satisfy these preferences. But this is not always the case. Others may have conflicting preferences or may simply be unwilling to accommodate children's preferences. Concomitantly, others may express their external preferences as to what children should, or should not, be doing and these may conflict with children's own preferences. In this chapter, I discuss two types of interpersonal preferential conflict: (1) ones in which others represent obstacles that need to be overcome and what children do in their attempts to overcome them, and (2) ones in which children pose obstacles to others' attainment of their preferences and children's strategies of resisting others' imposition of their external preferences on them.

COPING WITH INTRANSIGENT OTHERS

Other people who are unwilling to resolve interpersonal preferential conflict with us represent either obstacles that need to be overcome or insurmountable barriers that need to be coped with psychologically. This distinction parallels that drawn between *problem-focused and emotion-focused* coping (Folkman & Lazarus, 1985), with the former geared toward changing external conditions so as to alter the situation, and the latter geared toward altering one's own *experience* of the situation rather than modifying the relevant external circumstances. Weisz and colleagues (see, for example, Band & Weisz, 1988; Rothbaum, Weisz, & Snyder, 1982) have similarly differentiated *primary* and *secondary* control, where primary control refers to attempts to influence objective conditions or events and secondary control refers to attempts to maximize one's goodness of fit with conditions *as they are*. I am more comfortable with the parallel distinction Selman (1985) has drawn between an *other-transforming orientation* in which the individual attempts to change the thoughts, feelings, and actions of others and a *self-transforming orientation* in which one attempts to change one's own thoughts, feelings and actions. The commonality across these conceptualizations is the distinction between what one does toward having the world and others accommodate to one's own preferences and what one does to accommodate one's preferences to an intransigent world, altering one's own psychological state in coping and self-regulating, and in *mind play*. The focus of this chapter is the former – what children do in their attempts to get others to yield or to avoid yielding themselves. Coping and mind play, in which children deal with others as insurmountable barriers, will be the focus of Chapters 12 and 13. Note that in addressing these issues, I have explicitly refrained from using extant classification systems of coping; Skinner et al. (2003) identified four hundred ways of coping, with each theoretician cutting up the pie in a way that best fits his or her theoretical orientation.

RECOGNIZING PREFERENCE GAPS

The realization that others need not heed one's own preferences requires children to squarely face the self–other preference gap and invoke strategies that attempt to bridge this gap. As O'Keefe and Benoit (1982) note, even preschool children recognize each other as primary obstacles and primary means of achieving preference satisfaction. That is, they perceive each other as serving to impede satisfaction of one's preferences but also of being able to satisfy those preferences *when they want to* do so.

To the extent that children deploy manipulative strategies to resolve interpersonal preferential conflict, they contradict Piaget's contention that young children assume other people's interpretations of events to be identical to their own and to be widely shared. Piaget argued that given such shared perceptions,

> the child thinks for himself without troubling to make himself understood nor to place himself at the other person's point of view. . . . The child feels no need to socialize his thought so he is so little concerned with others. (Piaget, 1926, p. 9)

Preschoolers' apparent use of egocentric speech, their solitary and parallel play patterns with their peers, and their apparent inability to adapt their speech to their listeners in communicating (e.g., Glucksberg & Krauss, 1967; Flavell, 1974) have all been viewed as supporting the conclusion that children view others as sharing their perspective. This view is also echoed by Fonagy and colleagues, who argue,

> Perhaps one reason that toddlers are so prone to outbursts of rage and frustration is that as the world and individual minds are not yet clearly demarcated, they expect other people to know what they are thinking and feeling, and to see situations in the same way they do. Thus, frustration of their wishes seems malign or wilfully obtuse, rather than the result of a different point of view, alternative priorities, etc. (Fonagy, Gergely, Jurist, & Target, 2002, p.)

Yet this view of children as locked in an egocentric bubble that disallows perspective taking flies in the face of reality. In Bruner's (1986a) words, "the prevailing view of initial (and slowly waning) egocentrism is, in certain respects, so grossly, almost incongruously wrong and yet so durable, that it deserves to be looked at with care" (p. 61).

To elaborate, if one takes the linguistic approach seriously, "the human capacity for taking multiple perspectives must be present in some workable form in order for the child to master language" (Bruner, 1986a, p. 109, emphasis added). MacWhinney (2005a, 2005b) undergrids this argument, claiming that perspective taking is critical for language acquisition. In addition to the fact that many linguistic syntactic devices require perspective shifts, MacWhinney argues that grammar emerges as a method for supporting accurate tracking and switching of speakers' and listeners' perspectives and that sentences link perspectives across the cognitive domains of space, time, perception, action, belief, and social roles. The use and understanding of language requires an understanding of perspective – if someone *came* in, the speaker is inside; but if someone *went* in, the speaker is outside (cf., Levinson, 1997). Without perspective taking, children would be unable to use personal pronouns, differentiate *come* versus *go*, or *give* versus *take*, all of which are dependent on one's perspective. Tomasello (1999) voices a similar argument, saying, "the back-and-forth of discourse involves the child in a constant shifting of perspectives from her own to those of others and back again."

Moreover, even very young children are apparently aware of when interpersonal preferential conflict exists and engage in attempts to resolve such conflict with children, siblings, and adults. As shown in several previous chapters, in their everyday speech, children appear to be aware of the two prerequisites for resolving interpersonal preferential conflict: recognizing that others do not share one's preferences, and recognizing that one has possible means of influencing others' preferences. What then is their problem? As I see it, they need to acquire strategies of resolving interpersonal preferential conflict and to learn which of these strategies are more successful and in what contexts. Many child treatment interventions are geared precisely to this end (e.g., Selman, 1979, 1985; Shure & Spivack, 1978; Spivack & Shure, 1974).

EMERGENT STRATEGIES FOR MANIPULATING OTHERS

In fact, children have a myriad of strategies they deploy when others pose obstacles to the attainment of their preferences. Social development involves learning which of these are more effective in resolving interpersonal preferential conflict. Troop-Gordon and Asher (2005) identified more than 3,000 strategies in the proposed solutions offered by 9- to 12-year-old children to six hypothetical vignettes depicting others as obstacles. Yet Troop-Gordon and Asher found that instead of resolving the hypothetical conflict, children often changed their goals in the relevant context. My concern here is with what happens when children maintain their goals and attempt to "remove" the obstacles posed by others.

Children evidence two broad types of strategies. The first of these are aimed at changing others' *behavior* and evidence little concern with the psychological state that may have led others to pose obstacles to preference attainment. The second types of strategies are aimed at changing others' psychological states or construals that are assumed to pose impediments. Younger children adopt the first type of strategy, trying to change others' behavior; and with age, they recognize the need to change others' *construals*, being implicitly guided by the understanding that changing others' construals may lead to changes in their behavior. Children's early focus on behavior rather than on construals may index two different problems. The first may well be that young children do not yet have a model of other minds in which what one says and does is intimately linked to what one thinks and prefers. That is, they do not understand that changing others' construals may promote a change in their willingness to heed one's own preferences. A second possibility is that children recognize the importance of others' construals but do not know how such changes in construal can be implemented. Once they do, they can attempt to change others' construals in various ways, including changing these others' construal of one's own preferences, changing others' construal of their own preferences, or by changing others' construals of the situation at hand. Whether they focus on others' behavior or on their construals, children actively communicate with others who represent hurdles to the fulfilment of one's preferences and, as will be shown in this chapter, their communication in such contexts gradually indexes their awareness of others as agents who serve to mediate between them and their preferences. I now turn to the strategies children deploy in such contexts.

DIRECTIVES – TELLING OTHERS WHAT TO DO

Searle (1975) defined *directives* as "attempts by the speaker to get the hearer to do something" (p. 355). They are expressions that require an action from the person being addressed and much of children's early speech reflects their use of directives. Wells (1985) equipped children with tape recorders to be worn at home and found that at 15 months, attempts at controlling others' behavior accounted for about 12 percent of children's utterances, increasing to about 18 percent at 19 months and to almost 32 percent at 3 years. A decrease in children's use of directives at age 5 most likely reflects the fact that older children can act on the environment themselves, without the need for others' help. But directives can be issued in two different contexts: when others are viewed as likely to perform the specified action and when others are viewed as unlikely to do so. Very young children apparently differentiate these contexts (e.g., Marshall & Levy, 1998), recognizing when preferential conflict is likely to be involved and they invoke different strategies when they view others as likely to be accommodating versus resistant.

Before they become fully verbal, children often attempt to cope *physically* with preferential conflict. When Gia, at 19 months, was told, "Maybe you can go out later for a walk with Mommy," she pulled her mother toward her stroller, indicated wanting to go outside and said, "Go byebye" (Bloom, 1970). Meike, at 20 months, cried and tried to hold onto her mother's hand to prevent her from leaving, saying "Mama with (i.e., come)"[1] (Miller, 1979). These physical means of dealing with preferential conflict need to be differentiated from cases in which gestures, including physical ones, are used to convey one's preferences, for example, when Karen, at 21;9, takes my hand and pulls me to her room, saying, "have to show Mummy animals." The distinction between these examples lies in the assumption of the first two children that the parent is unwilling to accommodate their preferences. In the latter example, and in similar ones discussed in Chapter 2, physical gestures are used as expressions of preferences, but there is no assumption on the child's part that the parent may be an unwilling partner.

Physical attempts to get others to comply give way to verbal directives that express one's preferences, with children indicating what they want others to do primarily by using imperatives. In this vein, Travis, at 16 months, says, "move," when her father impedes her way when getting a toy (Tomasello, 1992), and a 20-month-old who wants her father out of her way commands, "Father go away, sit down"[2] (Mikeš, Dezső, & Vlahović, 1972, p. 169). In talking to her dolls in Hebrew, Karen, at 19;20, echoes the words of her day care teachers, telling her dolls to "get up, sit down, come draw a triangle, go to your seat, sit nicely and don't move."[3] In children's early imperatives, though, it is not always clear whether they recognize that others may have alternative preferences that need to be taken into account. For instance, in issuing two-word imperatives, such as "fix this," "catch ball," and "see this" (Tomasello, 1992), all said between 18 and 20 months, there is no indication of the child's awareness of possible preferential conflict.

The repetition of imperatives may well signal the child's emergent anticipation of preferential conflict. For instance, when Travis says, "read this ... book ... read this," asking to have a book read to her (Tomasello, 1992), such repetition may index her assumption that the addressee may not want to do so. Similarly, at 22 months, Nigel feels a bandage on his forehead and tells his father, "tell Mummy take it off," then runs to his mother and demands, "take it off, take it off!" (Halliday, 1975, p. 73). His insistent repetition may well index awareness that his mother may have conflicting preferences.

Children's first use of *please* in mitigating their imperatives may also reflect their understanding that others' preferences conflict with their own and that they are unlikely to accede. For instance, well after her bedtime, Karen, at 20;3, pleads, "Take me out bed please" and when I attempt to take off her shoes at 21;15, she requests, "Mommy please don't take off your ... Karen's shoes." Wootton (2007) notes that this type of *please* often occurs when adults do not immediately respond, and that there is often a temporal gap prior to the addition of "please" (e.g., "Do it all, Mummy (0.7 temporal gap) please" (p. 173). In fact, the use of *please* for anticipated refusal appears to precede its emergence as a form of politeness by several months, for example, Orren, at 24;2, says, "Please Daddy read that," and Karen, at 26;20, says, "Daddy please help me to open Karen's drawer." In both these cases, the father's preferences were not assumed to be in conflict with the child's. Bates (1976) also found that at around two and a half years of age, children tend to soften their imperatives by using *please* but she did not address the possible role of anticipated preferential conflict in its emergent use.

Children also use directives as *protests* (e.g., Dore, Gearhart, & Newman, 1978) to get others not to do, or to stop doing, what they are doing, apparently starting to do so at around 18 months (Greenfield & Smith, 1976). Table 11.1 shows the types of protests children voice at these ages, relating to actions taken toward the child himself, to actions taken toward objects, and relating to locations.

These protests all reflect conflict between what parents are doing and what children want them to be doing, clearly marking children's ability to contrast between self and others and between their own preferences and the preferences of others. This is also evident in protests that are voiced in the affirmative. For instance, when Travis, at

[1] German: "mama mit."

[2] Hungarian: "apu menj innen csucsuj le."

[3] Hebrew: "Kumi, shvi po, boee leçayer meshulash, lex makom shelxa, shev yafe' velo lazuz!"

Table 11.1.

	Age	Source
Self-focused Protests		
Wants to stop swinging C: "Stop push me"	19;27	Tomasello (1992, p. 303)
To father who is changing his diaper C: "Don't touch Orren's stomach"[4]	23;26	Karniol (Diary, Orren)
To mother O: "Don't shout (pl.) at Orren[5]	24;18	Karniol (Diary, Orren)
To father who is dressing her K: "Daddy don't put Karen's dress the wrong way" (i.e., backward)	25;11	Karniol (Diary, Karen)
C: "You cannot do that to me!"[6]	29 mos.	Guasti (1993, p. 14)
Object-focused Protests		
K: "Don't want Mummy to play with Karen's toys"	21;27	Karniol (Diary, Karen)
O: "Karen don't touch Orren's red car"[7]	23;22	Karniol, (Diary, Orren)
C playing with 1-year-old cousin C: "Leave it alone .....don't touch it"	3 years	Cohler & Grunebaum (1981, p. 143)
Location-Focused Protests		
To M O: "No be here"	22;25	Karniol (Diary, Orren)
F is reading newspaper at table Orren is drawing at the same table O: "Not do that kan" (Hebrew, *here*)	23;15	Karniol (Diary, Orren)

Table 11.2.

	Age	Source
Other-Serving Positive Directives		
Pulling me toward my bed K: "Mommy please go to sleep in bed"	22;10	Karniol (Diary, Karen)
Father snoozing on sofa K: "Daddy, maybe you should go to sleep in bed"	25;15	Karniol (Diary, Karen)
K: "Daddy you go to sleep in your bed – I don't allow people to sleep in places like that"	33;4	Karniol (Diary, Karen)
Other-Serving Negative Directives		
F snoozing on sofa C: "No sleeping here!"	24;2	Karniol (Diary, Orren)
I lay down on K's bed, O wants me in my bed O: "No sleeping Karen room – hamita (i.e., bed) Shel (of) Daddy"	24;27	Karniol (Diary, Orren)
M is calling for Grandpa C: "Mummy no shout for Grandpa"	26 mos.	Karniol (Diary, Orren)
Orren is watching M get dressed O: "Don't want this (dress) on you!"	30;29	Karniol (Diary, Orren)
F is brushing teeth C: "Daddy don't talk if your teeth are with soap"[8]	31;17	Karniol (Diary, Orren)

19;15, says, "stay here rug," she objects to its being taken out of the room, and when at 20;1, she says, "Watch this TV program," she voices her refusal to having the television channel changed (Tomasello, 1992). This affirmative manner of expressing protests may well be a function of the complexity of expressing equivalent protests negatively (e.g., "don't take out the rug," "don't want you to . . . .).

Protests can be *other-serving* rather than self-serving, being voiced to change others' behavior in contexts that do not impede the child's own preferences in any way, as shown in Table 11.2, with all examples from Karen and Orren.

As evident above, other-serving directives appear to reflect understanding of preferential conflict between others' preferences and the child's *external* preferences, being issued because the child assumes the addressee's preferences are not the same as his own. Yet the child adopts the role of a socialization agent vis-à-vis parents in these examples, attempting to alter parents' behavior because their behavior conflicted with the child's preferences as to what *they* should be doing. Yet children would not benefit directly from the adult's compliance since children's *external* preferences are involved. Gordon and Ervin-Tripp (1984) found that 2- to 3-year-olds often issued what they call *corrections*, when they perceived that some rule or norm was violated and the child wanted to change what was going on, not for direct personal gain but on normative grounds. Rakoczy and his colleagues (cf., Rakoczy, Warneken, & Tomasello, 2008) similarly

[4] Hebrew: "Al tiga beten shel Orren."
[5] Hebrew: "Al tiçaku al Orren."
[6] Italian: "Non poi fammi quetto!"
[7] Hebrew: "Al tiga Karen auto adom shel Orren."
[8] Hebrew: "Abba al tedaber im hashinaim shelxa im sabon."

Table 11.3.

	Age	Source
Using *We*		
To father who told her a story K: "We don't read without a book!"	26;13	Karniol (Diary, Karen)
To peer C: "We don't put books on our head. That's not nice!"	26;17	Karniol (Diary, Karen)
To father who is whistling "Daddy we don't sing this way, we sing properly Daddy"	32;22	Karniol (Diary, Karen)
Playing with toddler sister C: "No Peggy, we don't do that.... that's not the way I want to play"	4 years	Bettelheim (1962, p. 49)
2- and 5-year-olds after mutual name-calling C: "We don't talk like that"	5 years	Golinkoff & Hirsh-Pasek (1999, p. 204)
Using *You*		
To father C: "Don't lick that knife daddy. 'pposed to cut it up"	27 mos.	Wootton (1997, p. 73)
To peer of 33 mos. C: "You hafta go poop in the bathroom. Big boys go in the potty"	35 mos.	Garvey (1984, p. 178)
Pretend mother to pretend baby M: "You have to take naps, honey"	Preschool	Schwartz (1991)
To peer C: "You are 'posed to cut those things... you are 'posed to – do you know that?"	4;10 years	McTear (1985, p. 92)
Justifying refusal to make younger brother hot chocolate C: "I can't make a drinking chocolate I'm not old enough. You shouldn't play with matches so I can't make you one"	9 years	Sealey (2000, p. 155)

identified *normative protests* that children 2 and 3 years old voice when others' behavior violates norms of transformed object use during pretend games (e.g., using Lego as food vs. as soap).

Normative protests are often expressed by using generic pronouns like *one*, *you*, and *we*. This is evident when Claudia, at 26 months, says, "One doesn't touch it," differentiating this from the negative imperative, "Don't touch it."[9] (Bates, 1976) Orren, starting at 24 months, repeatedly says to his sister and dolls, "One doesn't put that here,"[10] and "one doesn't do that/like that,"[11] and he, at 24;22, yells at a doll, "one doesn't poo here – in the potty!"[12] Karen, at 32;10, yells at her doll: "How are you sitting? One doesn't sit like that!"[13] The use of generics in these expressions reflects children's understanding that normative rules have trans-situational force, as evident in their ability to specify what the rules are; for example, Claudia at age 2, says to an adult who is sitting on the floor, "It is forbidden to sit down on the floor"[14] (Volterra and Antinucci, 1979, p. 292).

[9] Italian: "Non si tocca" vs. "Non la toccare!"
[10] Hebrew: "Ze lo samim kan"
[11] Hebrew: "Lo ossim kaxa"
[12] Hebrew: "Lo ossim kaki kan – basir"
[13] Hebrew: "Ex ata yoshev – kaxa lo yoshvim!"
[14] Italian: "No si sta per terra"

As discussed in Chapter 6,, generics can also be expressed by using *we* and *you*. Children's use of both *we* and *you* to express normative protests is shown in Table 11.3.

As evident in the above table, these children have all learned the concept of class action as a category of social behavior that can be used to attempt to alter others' behavior. Notice as well that in pronouncing why she is unable to make the hot chocolate, the girl in the last example above was using *you* both generically and to refer specifically to her brother.

Of course, at times, children's directives and protests are self-serving rather than other-serving. This can be expressed implicitly, when the child's own preference as to what the other person should be doing is not stated, or explicitly, when the child indicates what his preference is in the specified context, as evident in Table 11.4.

In the above instances, the child prefers that the adult do otherwise; it is the child who would be the beneficiary of the adult's action or inaction and his own interests rather than the adult's interests that would be served by the adult's action or inaction.

Do children themselves recognize the distinction between self-serving and other-serving directives? Apparently yes. The most clear-cut indication of awareness

Table 11.4.

	Age	Source
Implicit Cases		
C wants M to stay with her C: "Don't have a shower"[15]	19 mos.	Deuchar & Quay (2000)
M is drawing C: "No! Not like that!"	21;8	Tomasello (1992)
M wants to feed baby C: "No Mommy giving baby Sarah milk"	21 mos.	DeVilliers & DeVilliers (1979)
K wants me to stay with her K: "Mommy don't go in the kitchen. I don't allow it"	23;0	Karniol (Diary, Karen)
Grandma is singing, C doesn't like her voice C: "Grandma no should sing "Horsey"!"	23;15	Karniol (Diary, Orren)
C doesn't want M to watch TV C: "You're can't watch"	23 mos.	Thornton (2002)
O: "What are you writing? I don't want you to write"[16]	33;21	Karniol (Diary, Orren)
Explicit Cases		
C doesn't want her mother to have a shower C: "You can't take a shower! You can play toys. You're can play toys"	23 mos	Thornton (2002)
K: "Mommy, you don't go out to the kitchen – I want to show you some drawings"	28;29	Karniol (Diary, Karen)
O: "I'm requesting that you don't go to the office just work at home"[17]	33;17	Karniol (Diary, Orren)
O: "I don't want Daddy to work, only you stay at home lots and lots and later only you will work"[18]	32;13	Karniol (Diary, Orren)
M tells son she can't play, has to do housework C: "I don't want you to do hoovering and washing"	Toddler	Tizard & Hughes (1984, p. 97)

of the distinction between self-serving and other-serving directives is that children appear to be able to transform self-serving directives into other-serving ones, most likely when they anticipate that self-serving ones may not be successful. To give an example, a child of 19;21 whose request for candy was refused, even when phrased as "Just a tiny bit?" went to her room, brought out a doll, and said, "Please candy for Peter, Peter cry" (Church, 1966, p. 260). In yet another example, the same child at 23;5 asks her father if he wants candy. When the father assents, the child goes to the mother, tells her "My Daddy needs candy," takes two pieces, gives them to the father, and says, "Daddy has two pieces – one for Ruthie, please" (Church, 1966, p. 281). White (1976) captures this idea beautifully in an illustration of a child reaching into a cookie jar, with mother and dog looking on; the caption reads: "Oh, The cookie isn't for ME, Mom, FLUFFY asked me to get him one!" (p. 43).

Referring to the need to share is another means of transforming self-serving directives into seemingly other-serving directives. At age 20;1, Travis asks her dad to "share this pen" when she actually wants him to give it to her. When three-year old Ricky has had his quota of ice cream for the day and heard his mother say she was getting ice cream for herself, he asked, "Can we share? You take a lick and I'll take a lick, and that's how we can share" (Shatz, 1994, p. 175). He understood that making a direct request would not work but that alluding to sharing may be a way of getting around it. Referring to himself as *you*, at 30 months, Halliday's son similarly tells his father, "you want to have half of Daddy's biscuit and Daddy have the other half." His father assents, thereby affirming the value of references to sharing. These type of requests exhibit sophisticated understanding of preferential conflict and show how the anticipation of preferential conflict guides children to choose diverse means that can circumvent the conflict, amusingly perhaps in that they assume that adults are more likely to comply with a preference expressed by someone else – even a doll – than by themselves. This is poignantly illustrated when a toddler who wants to go to sleep says, "My bed is crying because I'm not in it" (White, 1976, p. 41); presumably, parents do not want the bed to cry and would put the child in bed to terminate the bed's crying. Importantly, though, by not making the self the beneficiary of the request, self-serving

[15] Spanish: "no ducha"
[16] Hebrew: "Ma ata kotev? Ani lo roçe sheata tixtov"
[17] Hebrew: "Ani levakesh al tilex lamisrad rak taavod babait"
[18] Hebrew: "Lo roçe she-aba yaavod rak tisha-er babait harbe' harbe' ve-axar kax taavod"

directives were transformed by these young children into other-serving ones, most likely because they recognized that others' preferences did not match their own.

PLEADING AND BADGERING

In the face of refusals to comply with their preferences, children may simply plead, both with parents and with other children. A child explains how he gets what he wants in the supermarket, relating, "sometimes you just keep saying please mum, please mum, please mum, and then she gets it" (Wilson & Wood, 2004, p. 334). When a child of 4;2 years tells his peer of 3;4 years, "I'm not playing space trees any more," his peer responds, "Oh . . . please," and the older child concedes, saying "All right" (Shields, 1978, p. 325). A Rumanian child of 4;2 years, who is ignored by her friend, pleads, "Come, I beg you nicely, Ilenuca" (Slama-Cazacu, 1977). Read and Cherry (1978) found that whereas saying *please* and *pretty please* was very common in the speech of $2^1/_2$ year-olds trying to persuade a puppet who did not want to share, by the age of $4^1/_2$, they changed to using imperative and embedded imperatives. On the other hand, Finley and Humphreys (1974) found that older school children also invoked pleading as one of their strategies when facing recalcitrant mothers and best friends (e.g., "Oh come on, please try it. Oh, please please," p. 77). Pleading was also found to be frequent in the appeals of preschool boys to preschool girls but not in their play with male peers (e.g., "I'll do anything you say, please? Please Jenny? Please?" Kyratzis & Guo, 2001, p. 66).

Another related strategy is badgering, persistent repetition of one's preferences. In the context of playing, a girl of 4;9 tells her 5-year-old friend, "'tend you heard your telephone ring ding ring ding dong," but her friend responds, "pretend I wasn't there." But the younger one continues, "pretend you got it, pretend you got it," yet her friend refuses, saying, "No pretend I wasn't home." Again, the younger one reiterates, "Pretend you were," and her friend relents, saying okay, and picking up the phone (Sheldon, 1992). To illustrate badgering at home, a mother repeatedly rejects louder and louder requests by her 2-year-old for her pacifier, "Want Ninny!"; the mother repeats, "I said NO" but when the child rocks violently back and forth in a recliner, the mother gives in and lets the child have the pacifier (Miller, 1982, p. 61). In an instance of badgering with preschool siblings, when the ice cream truck's chimes were heard, they asked their mother for ice cream and she refused, saying, "No, not on a wet day like this." Their second request was rejected with: "No, you can't, you've already had all that Skeggy rock (candy)." Their third request was rejected with: "I said NO, you heard me!" But they persisted and she finally gave them money to buy it (Newson and Newson, 1968, p. 540).

Children learn from such experiences that if they are persistent enough in voicing their preferences, adults may give in. This is explicitly expressed by an adolescent who says, "If I really want something bad, I just keep asking her (i.e., the mother) over and over again, except if she's in a bad mood . . . if I keep asking, she caves in and I get what I want" (Bigelow, Tesson, & Lewko, 1996, p. 211). As another adolescent put it, "sometimes I have to do that (reiterate requests) over a long period of time" (Isler, Popper, & Ward, 1987), with another child indicating that she's "been at it for 4 months now," with success seemingly around the corner. That is, children gauge their parents' state of mind in terms of their likelihood of "giving in" to badgering attempts.

In discussing this issue, parents often admit that they give in to their children's requests, even when they don't see these as particularly justified. For instance, when asked to stay up to watch television, one mother said, "I'd sometimes give in on that and say just five minutes more" (Cook-Gumperz, 1973, p. 61). It is difficult to know whether such acquiescence occurs when parents are less convinced regarding the virtue of their preferences, when they are persuaded by the child's insistence, or because the child's persistence wears them down. Perhaps all of these play a role.

TELLING OTHERS WHAT TO SAY

Another strategy that deals with others as obstacles to preference attainment focuses on telling them what to say, for example, "Say yes, Mommy!" or "Oh, please don't say no" (Clark & Delia, 1976, p. 1010). A child of 20 months, whose mother refused her request for fruit, replied, "Fruta si!" (Deuchar & Quay, 2000). Selman's son at 29 months appealed to his father to allow him to go down a hill by insisting: "Say *yes*, daddy!, don't say no!" (Selman & Damon, 1975, p, 64). In doing so, the child seems to be unaware that saying *no* is based on a different state of mind than saying *yes* and that the other's state of mind needs to change. This is also evident when on being told that I was angry at him, at 27;25, Orren says, "Don't be angry to Orren."[19] The same problem underlies children's use of the *"say yes"* strategy with their peers. When Stephanie, at 4;6 years wants to play with Suzie, she asks her "like some eggs?" When Suzie answers "no," Stephanie says, "No, you say "yes." She then repeats, "Would you like some eggs? You say "Yes." Suzie finally says "Yes," and Stephanie answers, "O.K. Two?" (Schwartz, 1991). A 3-year-old in preschool asks her friends in a sequence if they are her friends, and when she gets negative replies, she says, "Now say yes. Now we all have to say yes, okay?" (Paley, 1986, p. 41). Cook-Gumperz (1981) recorded an interaction between two playmates, one of whom wanted to get rid of part of an apple. She says to her friend, "no, I don't want it you can have it. D'you want it? Say yes and I'll give it to you." When the peer says no, the child says, "no say yes. What did I say, yes, yes say yes," her friend replies, "If I don't want to say yes I don't want to, 'cause

[19] Hebrew: "Al tiheyi koesset le Orren."

my sister says if you want to say yes, you don't want to, my sister . . . ." The target child then says, "you do want to say yes, you don't don't say you don't want to" (p. 43).

Although the use of *say yes* may seem to implicate children's lack of understanding of other minds, such an interpretation is unwarranted. Specifically, parents also plead with their infants to *say yes*, doing so primarily within instructional contexts (Zukow, Reilly, & Greenfield, 1982). For instance, when Sarah refuses to change shirts, her mother says, "You can practice, "Yes, mommy, yes, mommy, yes, yes, yes" (Garvey, 1984, p. 126). After a toddler asks for some water in a bottle, her mother says, "You can't have it if you're gonna spill it. You gonna spill it?" When the child answers *yes*, the mother says, "You're supposed to say 'no . . . I'm not gonna spill it this time" (Miller, 1982, p. 101). Parents, then, appear to use *say yes* as an instructional technique, akin to the use of ELEMA (i.e., *say it like this*) in Kaluli society, as discussed in Chapter 6. This may well serve parents as an alternative to telling their children what they should think. In an extreme instance of this, when a child of 2;10 says "I'm a-scared of it." The father answers, "no, don't be scared so much, ok?" And then when the child repeats that he is scared, the father says, "say ok, Dad, I won't be scared." The child repeats, "ok, Dad, I won't be a-scared" (Peters, 2000, p. 144). Also in this vein, when a child of 13 months complained that he has no toy cars, his mother responds, "Don't say that kind of thing. Will you say, "It's all right if there are no cars?"[20] (Clancy, 1986, p. 242), again, telling the child what to say rather than what to think.

The use of *say yes* in children, though, would appear to stem from an inability to use alternative justifications that do not allude to their own preferences. That is, children do not appear to have an understanding of the kinds of information they could provide another person in order to change the other's preferences or underlying state of mind. Reiterating one's own preferences, then, is the predominant means they have for engaging in such attempts (e.g., "But I want it Mummy!"). This is quite clear in their interactions with other children. Not knowing how to justify their requests, when a request to be given a toy is refused with a *no*, two girls of 4;0 years and 3;8 years, get into an impasse in which the requester said *yes*, and the refuser said *no* six times before changing the nature of the request (McTear, 1985, p. 119). When a 3-year-old asks "Do you like my monkey" and the response is "that's not your monkey," each side in sequence, repeats, "it's my monkey," "my monkey," twice, and no resolution to the impasse is found (Phinney, 1986, p. 57). When a girl of 31 months announces that she's getting down, her friend objects, saying "don't get down," and each repeats her statement three times, when finally the first says, "Oh yes" and her friend answers, "Oh no!" (Slama-Cazacu, 1977, p. 117). Given their difficulty with providing justifications that allude to something other than their own needs and desires, children often simply repeat their preferences. Garvey (1984) found that whereas repetition, with or without greater insistence, was the common response among young children, by third grade, this strategy accounted for less than 10 percent of dealing with others' unwillingness to accommodate to one's preferences.

[20] Japanese: "Sonna koto iwanai de. Bubu najute mo ii tte?"

TURNING TO AUTHORITY FIGURES

Another strategy for dealing with others as obstacles is turning to authority figures, a strategy often used with other children, including siblings. For instance, Dunn (1988) found that in 66 percent of incidents in which siblings behaved aggressively toward them, children turned to their mothers for help. It is unclear whether children engage in this strategy because they assume that direct appeals to the other child will be rejected or because they assume that others who have power over the peer or sibling may both gain compliance and reprimand the other child. Alternatively, they may simply worry about the possibility of conflict leading to aggressive altercations (e.g., a 5-year-old "pretend mother" says to one of her "pretend daughters," "take turns, don't fight," Pitcher & Schultz, 1983, p. 8).

The earliest instances of turning to authority tend to occur with siblings because these are the children who are most readily available as playmates and they tend to occur in several contexts: when the sibling does not allow children to engage in some behavior that they want to engage in and when the sibling does not yield to their object requests. In some cases, the child's own preferences are implicit whereas in others they are explicit. Examples are shown in Table 11.5.

Similar complains are voiced about peers, both at home and at preschool. In a series of home interactions at age 3;8 and 4;9 years, a child complains about her playmate: "she's not making it go forward daddy, she's not putting the bus forward daddy"; "Heather won't take this thing that you be the queen (i.e., a shawl) for away from the bed"; "Heather won't let me be the baby daddy" (McTear, 1985, pp. 89, 82). At preschool, children tell teachers of conflicts with other children: "He made sand go in my eyes" and "Jason's trying to take my stuff" (Ervin-Tripp, 1977). Children appeal to those in authority in settings in which parents are not present and in which preferential conflicts with other children arise.

Whereas all the above statements could be viewed as statements of fact, they are not declaratives but are attempts to get parents and teachers to relieve the aversive conditions being experienced by the child. They are complaints geared to get adult intervention. How do we know this? First, children "whine" when making these statements. Second, they often persist in their complaint until adult intervention occurs. The fact that adult intervention often does occur in response implies that adults too interpret these complaints as requests for intervention on their part. Third, children may state

Table 11.5.

	Age	Source
Behavioral Conflicts		
To mother		
C: "I want to go there, brother won't le me"[21]	26 mos.	Savić (1980, p. 168)
To father		
O: "Daddy, Karen won't let me sleep there"[22]	27;13	Karniol (Diary, Orren)
To mother		
O: "I don't want that Karen should play here"[23]	34;9	Karniol (Diary, Orren)
C wants to shell maize with sibling		
C: "Mama, she won't let me do it"	4 years	Whiting & Edwards (1988, p. 218)
To mother		
C: "Mommy, I don't want this that Giulia writes with my colored pencils"[24]	5;7 years	Taeschner (1983, p. 216)
Object Conflicts		
To mother		
C: "She won't let me have the bicycle!"[25]	27 mos.	Savić (1980, p. 114)
Sister refuses to give her a bag		
C: "Mommy, this is my bag, why"[26]	31 mos.	Miller (1979, page)
Sib is playing with desired object		
To father		
C: "I don't want him to play with it"	3;6 years	Peters (2000, p. 148)
Siblings eating marshmallow topping out of a jar		
2-year-old won't let 4-year-old eat		
CO: "He won't let me have some."		
M to CO: "You're getting your share"		
M to CY: "Now give her some"	4 years	Whiting & Edwards (1988, p. 216)
Younger sib (3-year-old) is taking more than his share of salt (a prized commodity)		
C: "Abi keeps eating salt"	9 years	Whiting & Edwards (1988, p. 216)

Table 11.6.

	Age	Source
Peer of 36 mos. took her toy "Want Mommy to ask Yochai to give it to Karen"	23;21	Karniol (Diary, Karen)
A 5-year-old sib tries to lift her shirt		
C runs into the family room shouting		
C: "Mum, Mum, please tell him to stop!"	School age	Grieshaber (2004, p. 185)
A 4-year-old sib interrupting play		
C: (To mother) "Make Andy leave us alone"	8 years	Whiting & Edwards (1988, p. 217)
Sib took something from C		
C: (To mother) "Make Steven give them back to me"	Unknown	Gordon (1976, p. 239)

explicitly what they want the adult to do, as evident in Table 11.6.

As well, even when the complaints are not stated explicitly, questioning by adults often reveals the true nature of such complaints. For instance, when Orren, at 3;4 years, told me that he saw Karen touching the window, I asked him, "What should I do? His answer was, "You should tell her not to do that." In another instance, a child tells a teacher, "Please, Miss. Dawn is eating." When the teacher asks, "What's that got to do with me?" the child replies, "Miss, you are the teacher, you are supposed to stop her" (Delamont, 1980, p. 79). A 6-year-old explicitly explains the goal of turning to authority, saying, "I go and tell the teacher, so she'll punish him" (Piaget, 1932, p. 303), referring to a child who had hit him.

[21] Serbo-Croatian: "Mama, ja tamo, bate!"
[22] Hebrew: "Abba, Karen lo noten li lishon shum."
[23] Hebrew: "Ani lo roçe she-Karen tesaxek po."
[24] German: "Mami, ich will das nicht dass Giulia mit meine Buntstifte schreibt."
[25] Serbo-Croatian: "Ona mi ne da bicikli!"
[26] German: "Mami, dies ist meine Tasche, warum!"

Table 11.7.

	Age	Source
Mother as Threat		
C: "If you throw that iron at me I'm gonna tell"	3;8 years	
C: "I'm telling, when I get home to my mummy, I'm gonna tell"	3;8 years	Garvey (1977b, p. 93, 94)
C thinks girl tripped him C: "I'm going to get my mum"	7;6 years	Sluckin (1981, p. 42)
Peer punching C2 C1: "Leave him alone, his mum's coming in a minute"	8;8 years	Sluckin (1981, p. 65)
Teacher as Threat		
C: "Better give that purple back! I'm telling on you Alison!"	Preschool	Kyratzis & Green (1997, p. 25)
C: "If you spoil my castle I'll have to tell the teacher"	3 years	Tough (1977, p. 67)
C: "You better stop that Fredrick! I'm telling the teacher"	Preschool	Paley (1986, p. 76)
Two girls are annoying boy C: "If you won't be quiet, I'll get the teacher and then she'll be really angry"	Preschool	(Danby, 1998, p. 183)

Rather than turning to authority to settle interpersonal conflicts, children can merely threaten to do so. A child of 3;7 years, asks a younger sibling, "you want that Mummy takes it away right?"[27] (Müller, 1994, p. 251). Whereas the child does not say this explicitly, the implication is that he would approach the mother and she would take action against the younger sibling. Nonsiblings can also be warned with the authority of mothers and teachers, as shown in Table 11.7.

It is unclear whether such threats are interpreted as idle threats or whether peers actually worry about impending parental or teacher intervention. Importantly, though, in issuing such threats children are implying that parental and teacher preferences are aligned with their own preferences and counter those of the child who is being threatened with such intervention.

Yet as parents often explain to children, using authority figures is a problematic strategy; it does not offer solutions when authority figures are absent. As one mother tells her preschooler, "How will that help you when I'm not here?" (Shure & Spivack, 1978, p. 147). Knowing that this is the case, children can attempt to invoke their own authority to get others to comply with their preferences. In preschool, a bossy child yells at a more docile one, "Move! When I tell you to do something, you're to do it!" (Meyer, 2003, p. 98). The child's own power is invoked to manipulate the other child. In such instances, though, the invocation of authority is often ignored, unless accompanied by threats.

[27] German: "du wi dass nimm das weg ne?"

USING THREATS AND CONTINGENCIES

Another set of strategies that underlines children's inability to deal with others' construals is their use of contingencies and threats of negative sanctions in their interaction with adults, peers, and siblings. Such strategies use *if–then* conditionals in which the antecedent is the action or inaction they want the other to take or avoid taking and the consequent is their own reaction to the antecedent they specify. But the threats and contingencies children specify are varied. In one set of such contingencies, the "threatened" consequent is the child's anger reaction. For instance, a child can threaten that he will get angry or shout if someone does something that contravenes his preferences. When I ask Orren, at 31;20, to remove a row of miniature cars he had placed on the stairs because someone might fall on them, he refuses; when I tell him that I will move them, he replies, "You take it apart I will shout at you."[28] Similarly, in talking of his dolls, at 28;19, he says, "I will be angry at them, I don't allow them the magic markers."[29] Children can also "threaten" others with "self-removal," as when a child of 29 months who is angry at his mother, yells, "don't want to talk to you! I go to my room. I slam the door! Good-bye" (Chapman & Zahn-Waxler, 1982). Children who were given the task of persuading parents to buy them things like pets often invoked threats of this kind, saying, "If you don't let me have a pony, I'll run away from home" (Clark & Delia, 1976, p. 1009). The understanding of such contingencies

[28] Hebrew: "At tefarek li anni eçak alax."

[29] Hebrew: "ani tixas lahem – anni lo marshe' lahem at hatushim."

Table 11.8.

	Age	Source
Threats of Reward-Withdrawal		
K is pressured to stop wearing diapers K: (in English) "If they don't say "no more diapers" I will let them come to my birthday" . . . . . (In Hebrew) "Only if grandpa and grandma don't say "there's no diaper" I allow them to come to the party"[30]	32;33	Karniol (Diary, Karen)
Peer refuses to share C: "You have to. Or I won't . . . . give you a piece of gum when my daddy buys some"	Preschool	Paley (1990, p. 11)
C: "If you're not my friend, you can't come to my house to see my Batman"	4 years	Meyer (2003, p. 39)
Peer refuses to turn take C: "You know what? I won't invite you to my birthday party if you don't let me have a go . . . you'll miss out on my party"	Preschool	Alloway (1999, p. 161)
C asks peer for hairbrush, is refused C: "I won't let you sleep with my bear tonight"	6.5 years	Geva (cited in Olson, 1980, p. 96)
Affiliative Threats		
Peer refuses to play with C C: "If you don't build ships with me, I won't be your friend anymore"	4 years	Meyer (2003, p. 35)
Child asks C2 to cover up eyes in game C refuses C: "Stop it or I won't be your friend"	Preschool	Pitcher & Schultz (1983, p. 45)
Child wants her turn, peer refuses C: "If you don't give me a turn I won't be your friend"	Preschool	Alloway (1999, p. 161)

is evident in a 4-year-old who is playing out a school scene in which she is both mother, as Big Bird, and child, as Grover. When the mother says "I have to go home and make lunch," the child says, "No, you got to be a parent helper. If you don't be a parent helper, I'm going to run out of school and never come back" (Segal & Adcock, 1981, p. 104). Threatening parents with not talking to them serves the same function. In this vein, Orren, at 33;3, yells at me, "I'm not talking to you because you are not buying me what I want."[31] He did not know how to get me to buy what he wanted and assumed that this threatened consequent was sufficiently aversive for me to comply.

Such threats often invoke the withdrawal of rewards and of friendship, with the latter generally referred to as *affiliative threats*. Examples of both types of threats are shown in Table 11.8.

In this context, a colleague reported an experience in which a 3-year-old, who didn't let the other child on a car to play, was told by the peer, "one day the ocean will come all the way to my house and I won't let you go swimming." In a more sophisticated version of an affiliative threat, a preschooler says to a peer, "You have to go out of the family if you don't cooperate with this family" and suggests that the other child leave the country (Sheldon, 1990).[32] Notice that such threats necessarily build on the assumption that the contingency is one that is dispreferred by the target of one's threat. In using such threats, then, children are implicitly alluding to others' underlying preferences and are assuming that because the consequent is one that the threatened individuals do not want to happen, they will comply with the child's request. Threats also necessarily invoke the future plane and reflect children's understanding of others as travelling into the threatened future with them.

This aspect of threats is much more explicit when children threaten others, both siblings and peers, with the use of physical force, as shown in Table 11.9.

Garvey (1984) found that threats of physical force were generally unsuccessful in terminating conflicts between peers, possibly because they focus on the other child's preference to avoid being physically hurt rather than on the interpersonal preferential conflict that instigated the need to threaten. It is also possible that such threats do not work because children understand the irreal element of

[30] Hebrew: "Rak im sava versavta lo omrim "ein xitul" anni marsha lavo laxagiga."

[31] Hebrew: "Ani lo medaber itax biglal she at lo kona li at ma she ani roçe."

[32] Parents also use affiliative threats. For instance, a mother tells her preschooler, "You have to learn to share the chores if you're going to be part of this family!" (Shure & Spivack, 1978, p. 148).

Table 11.9.

	Age	Source
Threatening Siblings		
Older sibling to younger C: "Don't do it again. If you do, I'll smack your bottom for you"	School/preschool	Wells (1986, p. 30)
Older sibling to younger C: "Hey Zoe, if you play with my rubber bands any more I'll kill you"	School/preschool	Hall (CHILDES)
Younger sibling plays with hood of her jacket C: "Don't put that down. Put that back up. It's supposed to be that way." Younger sibling protests C: "You always showin' off. You always actin' smart. I'm a spank you. . . . That's what you get for bein' so fresh" (spanks her)	School	Goodwin (1990, p. 155)
Threatening Peers		
C1 is bothering C2 C2: "Stop that Kevin or I'll shoot you dead"	Preschool	Newman (1978, p. 246)
C1 is bothering C2 C2: "If you do not go away, I'll crack this here (a piece of a spaceship) on your head"[33]	Preschool	Corsaro (1990, p. 49)
C1: I'll punch you if you touch it"	Preschool	Tulviste & Koor (2005)
C1 asks C2 to play, is refused C1: "I'll beat you up"	9;9 years	Sluckin (1981, p. 49)

many of these threats and consequently interpret them as idle threats that do not need to be taken into account.

REQUESTS, INDIRECT COMMANDS, AND MITIGATION

Directives can be issued in ways that reflect children's emergent understanding that others' do not respond well to imperatives and threats. As their pragmatic skill increases, at around ages 3 to 4 years, children start to use indirect commands (Bates, 1976). There are various ways in which indirect commands can be stated; Levin and Rubin (1983) found that children's indirect requests were more likely to be stated as declaratives (e.g., "You have to give me the crayon") rather than as interrogatives (e.g., "Can you give me the crayon?"). Gerhardt (1991) found that preschool children often used *hafta* and *needta* (e.g., "You hafta do/give . . . "). Yet children in dyadic play at ages 3 to 6 and 5 to 7 years apparently produce many more direct requests than indirect requests, with indirect requests increasing with age (Bellinger, 1979; Garvey, 1975) and being addressed more frequently to older children and adults than to younger children (Ervin-Tripp, 1977; Gelman & Shatz, 1977). Children also use declaratives as indirect imperatives, saying things like: "Okay everybody, the airplane's starting," to get peers to take their place and play (Gordon & Ervin-Tripp, 1984) and "that cookie sure looks good" (Read & Cherry, 1978), in attempting to get one. Interestingly, Garvey (1975) found that more indirect requests than direct requests were complied with in preschool peer interaction.

Children can also mitigate the force of imperatives by creating the semblance of collaboration. Instead of telling others what their preferences are, in such expressions, children may indicate what they themselves are planning and suggest how others are to collaborate, by adopting the same plan for instance (e.g., a preschooler who says, "I'm going to put a big pile here . . . you bring yours . . . you build the wall," Tough, 1977, p. 51). Children also use the inclusive *we* to indicate the possibility of joint action. To illustrate, a preschooler says to her friend, "Let's do it like this, you'll be the mother and I'll be the child" (Tulviste & Koor, 2005). Karen, at 30;17, asks me to play with her, saying, "let's play with this"[34] and at 30;25, she says, "Come to my room and let's play with a spinning top."[35] Orren, at 24;27, similarly calls to his sister, asking, "Karen come draw (with me) Karen."[36] Such "suggestions," as Dore, Gearhart, and Newman (1978) call them, and "proposals," as Aijmer (1996) calls them, generally reflect the preferences of the speaker. Yet they make it appear that preferences are shared and only subsequent compliance by the addressee can provide evidence as to whether they are actually shared.

[33] Italian: "se te non te vai, ti spacco questo qui sulla testa."

[34] Hebrew: "Boey nesaxek at ze."

[35] Hebrew: "Boey baxeder sheli ve-nesaxek be-sevivon."

[36] Hebrew: "Karen bo leçayer Karen."

This becomes clear in several different contexts, the first being a context in which children ask others outright as to whether they agree to their joint proposal (e.g., Orren, at 28;4, asks, "Karen do you agree that I clean you?"[37]). The second context is when children reject joint proposals outright by expressing their lack of agreement with them (e.g., Orren, at 33;13, says, "I don't agree to that, that you put this car here"[38]). The third is a context in which children reject proposals by using terms like "let's not," evidencing their understanding that a given proposal does not reflect their own preferences (e.g., a Finnish girl of 27 months says, "Let's not read that" and a boy of 25 months says, "Let's not go over there," Toivainen, 1980, p. 57). When Peter, at 29 months, is playing with the experimenter, she says to him "Let's put it back in the box, all right?" She wants him to engage in the action, possibly with her help. But he answers her "No, let's not." Clearly, he interpreted her suggestion as reflecting a preference he did not share and this led him to reject it.

Another means of mitigating requests is by posing them as questions, using words like *maybe*, *perhaps*, and so forth. or adding tag questions. In this vein, Orren, at 35;8, wants to stop playing dress up and asks Karen, "Maybe we will take off the tights?"[39] His question makes it clear what his preference is but he phrases it in a way that gives her choice, possibly because he knows that he cannot compel her to do so. Tag questions (e.g.,"okay?"), which are especially prevalent in interaction with peers, both mitigate requests and convey the implication that others' preferences may not match those of the speaker. In this vein, a child of 32 months says to her peer, "Tom, don't you touch my things, all right?" (Garvey, 1984, p. 110). This use of tag questions is also evident when Kate, at 3;3 years, warns a peer, "You can't touch, okay?" and when playing a hiding game, she says, "If you want to look, then then you will, then I will tell you, okay?" (De Houwer, 1990). The use of *okay* is not only rhetorical because children do know that others can reject their request.

In this context, Olson and Hildyard (1981) differentiate *rights* versus *favors*. A right involves a request that is viewed as legitimate, for example, for the return of one's property, whereas a favor involves a request that has no inherent legitimacy and is only legitimate in the context of a relationship (e.g., one gives things to one's friends) or a role (e.g., teacher asks child to clean blackboard). They found that children varied the type of request by whether they were asking for rights versus favors and by who the request was addressed to. In fact, children often ask others for favors, recognizing that they are favors and not rights. When kindergartner Sejal requests of another child, "Could you go check the color of the kite?" he is told, "After I'm done with this." A few minutes later, he addresses the same child, asking, "Could you do me a favor Ashok? Could you go check if her shirt is orange or green?"; the request is viewed as legitimate because of the friendship between the two children and is granted, with the child acknowledging the service with *thank you* (Mody, 2005, pp. 62–63). Favors are treated differently.

Here again, it is important to note that children change the nature of the directives they use in play when they pretend to be a parent giving directives to a child versus when they pretend to be a child giving directives to an adult (Andersen, 1990). Also in this context, Marcos (1991) found that when their requests for objects were ignored, 18-month-old children often reformulated their requests rather than abandoning them. Wootton (1981) similarly found that after a nonresponse, children tended to modify their requests to mothers, often adding "Mummy." The fact that children know that some forms are more polite is evident in the finding that when their requests do not succeed, children change the way they verbalize them. Claudia, at 20 months, says to the experimenter whom she wants to play a telephone game with her, "Let's do "Hi grandma!" When the experimenter does not comply she softens her voice and says, "Paola, we do "Hi Grandma?"[40] (Bates, 1976). She interpreted the experimenter's noncompliance as an indication that the request needs to be mitigated in some fashion. In a study on communication failures, a toddler who said *ball* and was told "I don't know what you mean," responded with *please*, interpreting the statement as implying that the request was not sufficiently polite (Fagan, 2008, p. 65). When others ignore children's requests, children also revert to more polite forms. A child of 22 months says to his grandmother, "Want peaches." When the grandmother waits and does nothing, the child repeats, "Please peaches"[41] (Savić, 1980, p. 94). Similarly, a child of 3;5 years at dinner first says, "Somebody give me some milk." He then repeats the request in a more polite manner, saying, "Please can I have some milk?" (Speier, 1972, p. 412). Bates (1976) found that Italian children at these ages know that directives differ in politeness and vary them to express different levels of politeness under different communicative constraints.

In fact, children's choice of which directives to use appears to depend on their expectations that their audience will comply with their request. In line with this, Gordon and Ervin-Tripp (1984) found that the 4-year-old they studied used different forms of directives when she assumed that the listener was unlikely to comply with her request. As well, Levin and Rubin (1983) found that younger children were more likely to reiterate their requests verbatim or with minor modifications whereas older children were more flexible, for instance, changing a direct request to an indirect one. In a study in which elementary school children were asked to write letters appealing to adults to adopt puppies, even second grade children were found to change their appeals in light of their

[37] Hebrew: "Karen at maskim she-anni naki otax?"
[38] Hebrew: "ani lo maskim at ze she-at sama at hamexonit haze kan."
[39] Hebrew: "Ulay norid at hagarbiyonim?"
[40] Italian: "Ciamo potto nonna!"; "Paola, ciamo potto nonna?"
[41] Serbo-Croatian: "Oce beske'. Molim beske."

Table 11.10.

	Age	Source
C asks for hammer C2: "you can have the pliers," C: "No, I'll give you the flashlight if you give me the hammer"	Preschool	Garvey (1977, p. 13)
C wants airplanes others are holding C: "Could I please play with that" C2: "I'll trade you," indicating a car in C's hand	Preschool	Meyer (2003, p. 91)
C wants friend's truck C: "Yael let's trade trucks. I guess you take my baby dinosaurs and let me have that truck"	Preschool	Sheldon (1992, p. 111)
C: "Will you please give me the scissors and then I can have the stool and you have this?"	4;6 years	McTear (1985, p. 107)
C wants male doll, C2 refuses C: "I'll trade you the boy for that"	School-age	Miller, Danaher, & Forbes (1986, p. 545)

audience, but older children evidenced greater change than younger ones (Cameron, Hunt, & Linton, 1996).

OFFERING TRADES, EXCHANGES, AND BRIBES

A strategy that indicates emergent understanding of the need to align preferences includes offering trades, exchanges, and bribes. As Clark and Delia (1976) found, children appear to learn very early that offering parents something in exchange for what they want can hasten attainment of their preferences. To illustrate, a child of 4;2 years asks, "if I be real good at the community center will you get me a prize?" (Kuczaj, CHILDES). But this strategy is also prevalent in children's interactions with peers; Table 11.10 provides some illustrations of such sequences.

Garvey (1984) found that other children generally accept such offers, with more than 50 percent of object-centered conflicts being settled this way. In a study of conflict resolution in pretend scenarios with peers, parents, and teachers, sixth graders were found to provide more suggestions for a compromise and solutions to the conflict with peers than with parents or with teachers, with such responses accounting for about 40 percent of their responses (Borbely et al., 2005).

Notice that offering others exchanges builds on several implicit assumptions. First, in offering exchanges, children tacitly acknowledge the right of the individual who has the to-be-exchanged item to the item in question and that the items are not shareable or subject to turn-taking. When a mother intervenes in a conflict between her child and a peer, asking him what he can do to get back a racing car from the peer, the child replies, "I could let him have my match-box cars" (Shure & Spivack, 1978, p. 37). He thereby acknowledged the legitimacy of the other child's right to the racing car. The second assumption is that the offered item is desirable to the person to whom it is being offered. Desirability can enhance the likelihood of trading. In one preschool, bringing sweets to school is prohibited because "it drives other kids nuts . . . the kids make trades, like they trade their whole sandwich for three Cheetos" (Tobin, Wu & Davidson, 1989, p. 161). An offer to exchange can fail when this assumption is erroneous and the other person does not want what is being offered. Third, there is an assumption of an equivalence of sorts between the to-be-exchanged items. But assumed equivalence is problematic because when an item being offered is not perceived as sufficiently valuable, the offer can be rejected.

Exchanges need to be differentiated from bribes; in the former, there is an implication that the items can be returned if one of the parties regrets the exchange, but this is not the case with bribes. A preschooler offers "If I can play, I'll show you what's in my pocket" (Schwartzman, 1978, p. 238). Similarly, a boy of 7;11 years asks to borrow a friend's football boots, saying, "I'll give you two little sweets and two big ones" (Sluckin, 1981, p. 62). The first child only wants to play in return for the gesture and the second child expects to get the football boots back and for the sweets to be consumed by the lender. Bribes of this sort turn out to be quite common in interactions between children. Weiss and Sachs (1991) had preschoolers play a puppet game in which they engaged in two hypothetical persuasion tasks. The first of these involved convincing a playmate to let them play with a toy; if they succeeded they would get a prize. For the second task, they needed to convince their mother to buy something while shopping when the mother refused to do so. The data showed that offers and bargains were the most common strategy and increased with age. In a real life context, Sluckin (1981) found that school children who were rejected from a playgroup on the playground often offered sweets as bribes for being allowed to play. Such expectations regarding offers and bribes are often voiced explicitly, "You've got to give her some crisps if you want to play," said by 6-year-old girl to an age mate (Sluckin, 1981, p. 48).

In any exchange or attempted bribery, the objects being offered need to be assessed for their value. Such

Table 11.11.

	Age	Source
C: "Can I help color? I'll be your best friend"	3 years	Pitcher & Schultz (1983, p. 67)
C1 wants tricycle C2 is using C1: "Can I have a go of that please? Please? I'll be Your best friend"	Preschool	Mitchell (1982, p. 20)
C: "Say yes"; peer refuses C repeats "say yes" several times C: "I'll be your best friend if you say yes"	4;6 years	McTear (1985, p. 117)
C: "Who gives me the brown (marker) is my friend"[42]	Preschool	Corsaro & Rizzo (1990, p. 44)
C: "Can I have the gun? I'll be your friend"	8;2 years	Sluckin (1981, p. 63)

assessment can lead to their value being contested and rejection of offers may well ensue. For instance, a boy of 9;2 years offers his friend a sweet in return for playing with him. The child being offered the sweet asks to see it, and upon inspection, rejects the offer with *no* (Sluckin, 1981, p. 49). Exchanges require that both individuals have preference scales, that objects be evaluated as to their relative worth, and that each party recognize that there needs to be a mismatch between their relative assessments for the trade to be implemented (Mishler, 1979). A child interested in trading needs to indicate his interest in the object he does not have, while making the one in his possession seem desirable to the child being offered the trade (e.g., "I got something interesting," Mishler, 1979, p. 235). Generally this is done while devaluing the desired object – how much smaller, less attractive it is relative to the offered one. Mishler found that in first graders, it is the person being asked to trade that makes an initial statement "directed to diminishing the strength of the first speaker's position before the explicit bargaining begins," belittling the offered trade (p. 277). This ability forms the basis for food exchanges and opens the door for exchanging toys, sports cards, and so forth. In fact, then, exchanges and bribery depend on children's ability to foster evaluative transformations in which they make the relative value of the items diverge in the eyes of others. Piaget (1995) discusses the problem of equilibrium in exchanges between individuals, saying that it depends on "whether one underestimates or over-estimates the services rendered, whether one forgets them or exaggerates their importance in memory, whether one distorts memory into a greater or lesser estimate of the partner, etc." (p. 58).

Children appear to understand the need to glorify the object being offered, whether in an exchange or as a bribe. For instance, a 4-year-old child suggests to her friend that they trade lunch boxes. When her friend refuses, she says "you'll have a bigger one so you will" (McTear, 1985, p. 109). When her friend refuses to trade toy animals, the above girl, at 4;9 years, says, "change over, there, the elephant is much more nicer" (McTear, 1985, p. 119). The child understood that in order to make the trade, the relative value of the objects needed to diverge in the eyes of her friend, and she did so by making the one in her possession seem more attractive. Of course, this is counterintuitive because if the elephant were in fact nicer, the one making the suggestion to trade should not be making it. Children "up" the value of the object in their possession and "down" the value of the object they actually prefer. Mishler talks of this as "structured downgrading." In a study in which 10-year-olds had to persuade others to taste a cracker, children enhanced the value of the cracker, saying "it's good for you" and "it tastes good" (Bragg, Ostrowski, & Finley, 1973).

But what does one do when there are no tangibles to offer? One can offer intangibles. This is underlined when a preschooler whose friend ignored her request to zip up her "fairy dress," changes her request, saying, "If you zip my fairy dress up, I'll make you a pie" (Smith, 1977b, p. 145); the offered pie may be imaginal but it serves to legitimize the request by construing it as an exchange of goods and services.

OFFERING FRIENDSHIP

As we saw above, children often use affiliative threats with other children. The flip side of this are offers of friendship, as evident in Table 11.11.

The importance of offers of friendship is that they reflect children's perception that friendship is a valuable commodity to offer other children. Why else would they offer them?

PERSUASION

Persuasion is a means of getting others to change their *construals*. Persuasion builds on the recognition that (1) others do not share one's preferences, (2) others' construals can be changed, and (3) if others' construals can be changed in specific ways, they may be more likely to adopt preferences they do not currently hold and that one can thereby facilitate pursuit of one's own preferences. Attempts to persuade, then, both contradict views of the

[42] Italian: "Chi me da il marrone e il mio amico."

Table 11.12.

	Age	Source
Spontaneous Reference to Needs and Wants		
K: "Daddy please come here – I want to talk to you"	23;22	Karniol (Diary, Karen)
K: "Daddy come for a minute, I want to talk to you"[43]	32;3	Karniol (Diary, Karen)
O: "Karen, I need for you to help me find it"	3;4 years	Karniol (Diary, Orren)
Needs and Wants as Justifications		
C asks F to fill squirt gun, F asks why		
C: "Because I want to play with it"	33 mos.	(Kuczaj, CHILDES)
C: "Open it"		
C: (In response to *why*) "Because I want you to open it"	28;1	Hood & Bloom (1979)
Two preschoolers are playing		
C1 wants to be fireman		
C2: "I'm the fireman 'cause I want to be the fireman"	Preschool	Eisenberg & Garvey (1981)

child as egocentric and provide evidence for children's developing theories of other minds. That is, developmental changes in children's strategies of persuasion index their emergent knowledge that construals can be changed but, more important, their knowledge of the specific ways in which construals can be changed to further the pursuit of one's own preferences. As discussed below, all three of these prerequisites emerge with age.

A. Using Justifications

Children's use of justifications provides a glimpse of their emergent understanding that preference alignment needs to be implemented by changing others' construals. Providing, justifications that can serve to persuade others requires an understanding of the possible reasons why these others may choose not to satisfy our preferences. That is, persuasion builds on the understanding that others have preferences, that they have external preferences regarding ourselves, that their preferences and ours may not be the same, and that justifications can serve as a means of preference alignment. For instance, children learn that justifications that allude to needs are more likely to succeed than ones that allude to desires (e.g., Karen, at 27;22, says, "Mommy can you come – I have a serious problem"; Orren, at 35;8, says, "Mummy I need soap"[44]; and Thornton's (2002) toddler daughter says, "Mummy, I need you're help me," p. 260). Moreover, they learn that justifications that refer to others' needs are more successful than ones that only allude to one's own needs. In light of such understanding, children start to justify their requests and directives, especially when they assume that others are unlikely to comply. But the basis for engaging strategies of persuasion is the understanding that others' preferences may conflict with one's own and that preference alignment is required. Preference alignment, though, can be attempted in different ways. It can focus on why our preferences are primary (e.g., as a 12-year-old says, "You try to get him to see why you want [it]," Selman, 1980, p. 110). It can focus on why others' preferences are not primary. A more sophisticated alignment strategy is to make our preference appear to be a preference that the other should also adopt for his own benefit (e.g., "If I were you and I lived alone, I'd like a good watchdog like this," Clark & Delia, 1976, p. 1010).

A child's first strategy is to state his own current preference as the reason why others should comply or act on their behalf. Dunn (1988) found that in conflicts with both their mothers and their siblings, 3-year-old children generally referred to their own needs, wants, and feelings in justifying why their own preferences should prevail. This can occur both spontaneously and when children are asked to justify, as shown in Table 11.12.

These types of justifications are reminiscent of research on mindlessness (Langer, 1989; Langer, Chanowitz, & Blank, 1978). Langer and her colleagues found that requests were honored more often when justifications for the requests were provided. However, the actual nature of the justification did not impact compliance with the request; as many people agreed to let someone use a Xerox machine when the request was justified with "I have to make some copies" as when the request was justified with "I'm in a rush." It is the appearance of a reason that triggers compliance with requests, rather than the reason itself.

Children appear to understand this and provide justifications that appear to serve as reasons. For instance, a girl of 3;2 requests, "pour me some water. I don't have any" (Slama-Cazacu, 1977, p. 83). Obviously, if she had water she would not be asking for it to be poured. This is also the case with a preschooler who requests, "Can I use your eraser for a minute Sandy? I made a boo-boo"

[43] Hebrew: "Abba bo rega – anni roça ledaber lexa."
[44] Hebrew: "Ima ani çarix sabon."

Table 11.13.

	Age	Source
C: "That string's stuck . . . come help me"	21;2	Tomasello (1992, p. 296)
C has trouble lifting lid C: "I wanna drink it my juice. Help me my cup"	22 mos.	Thornton (2002, p. 231)
C gives mother doll C: "Mother redress the doll – I can't"[45]	26;14	Dubost (1999, p. 69)
Toy has come apart, C hands it to adult C: "I can't fix it"	27;1	Bloom (1970)
C: "Could you read this to me cause I don't know how"	35;2	Hood & Bloom (1979)
C: "Do it for me. I can't reach up"	4 years	McTear (1985, p. 109)
C gets ready to water-paint C: "Mommy, I want you to open all of them the paint, so I won't have to trouble"	5 years	Ervin-Tripp & Gordon (1986, p. 83)

(Wilkinson & Calculator, 1982, p. 97) and "Oops. Hey, can I borrow your eraser again? I made a mistake" (Wilkinson, Clevenger, & Dollaghan, 1981, p. 224). Here, as well, it is clear that erasers are needed to erase something that was done wrong – they have no other use. In line with research on mindlessness, Garvey found that justified refusals were much more likely to be accepted by peers than simple refusals without reasons.

Ervin-Tripp and Gordon (1986) suggest that children under third grade tend to assume compliance in addressing requests to others whereas older children acknowledge the possibility that the listener might not comply with the request and take the viewpoint of the addressee more into account. In this light, they suggest that children's strategies differ by whether they expect the justification to be accepted or rejected. In the first case, children only need to supply the listener with a just cause for carrying out the desired action so that their role is basically that of supplying information. In the second case, the child anticipates an obstacle to the listener's cooperation and attempts to neutralize it. Their role in this case is to serve as persuaders.

What do good persuaders do? First, they attempt to legitimize their requests. For instance, in asking others to do things for us when we might be expected to do these things by ourselves, we need to justify why the imposition on others' time is deemed necessary. Socialization agents anticipate that as children grow older, they will become more autonomous and will do things by themselves. When they are unable to do so, children may be expected to justify asking others to intervene, citing some limitation on doing something by themselves. Very young children start to indicate why they are requesting others' intervention. A child of 1;7 whose mother ignores a request for help after he says *Maman*, looks at her, pushes a box in her direction and says, "e' pa" (presumably, *peux pas*, *I can't*) (Gauthier, 1999, p. 51). Gauthier documents that in this child, justifications for requests tended to follow failed attempts to solve a problem, for example, dressing a doll, with 91 percent of justifications in the context of *trying* referring to what the child was trying to accomplish and could not do so alone. In more verbal children, the justifications seem to be clearer but the context also seems to be the same, as shown in Table 11.13.

In this context, a sophisticated boy of 33 months explains to his parents, "If you help me I can do it better. If you don't help me I can't do it better" (Clark, 2003, p. 267). As children mature, they start to employ justifications that evidence greater understanding of the needs and preferences of the individual being addressed. Clark and Delia (1976) found that children used a greater variety of strategies of persuasion that were more sophisticated with age and their use of strategies indicated they were taking the perspective of the target of persuasion into account.

B. Universalization

Another means of persuasion is by universalizing one's preferences, implying that they are generic rather than idiosyncratic. A child who wants to play doctor says, "Hey, I've got a, I've got an idea. We can play doctors. This is a great idea. Great idea" (Hatch, 1992, p. 112). Whereas in the above example, the power of the words "good idea" is not evident, in the following example, it is clear that the child uses it strategically. When Molly, at 4;6 years, does not want to accept another girl's suggestion regarding building a house, she says "No, I want . . . I have a good idea. Let's make a bridge" (Sheldon, 1992, p. 109). She phrases her suggestion in a generic fashion rather than as a personal preference. A preschool boy similarly tries to convince his friends, saying, "Hey, I have a good idea that reminds me we can make haunted house" (Kyratzis, Marx, & Wade, 2001, p. 394). When two girls are arguing about who will be mother, one says, "I got a better idea.

[45] French: "Maman resabille' lui – peux pas moi."

Table 11.14.

	Age	Source
C wants bracelets adult refuses to give her C: "You give me the bracelets a minute please, Virginia, you give 'em to me?"[46]	30 mos.	Bates (1976)
C1 asks to borrow a green marker from male C2 Request is refused C1 bats her eye lashes, smiles C!; "Please, just for a second?"	Preschool	Blaise (2005, p. 169)
O to father O: "Daddy can you give me one minute the big bag with presents? Just for one minute I want the bag."	3;5 years	Karniol (Diary, Orren)
C: "Will you give me the scissors for a wee minute? I won't be very long with them"	4;6 years	McTear (1985, p. 123)
C1: "Joan, you want to trade puppets?" Request is refused C1: "Just for a while"	First grade	Wilkinson, Clevenger, & Dollaghan (1981, p. 225)

We'll both be moms" (Chafel, 1987, p. 35). As discussed with reference to parental use of universalization, good ideas are in the public domain and serve to remove the burden of having to justify one's preferences to others. As well, universalization transforms the context from one in which the two individuals have conflicting preferences to one in which they need to resolve whether the idea is or is not good.

C. Adjectivization

Children also adjectivize in attempting to persuade others. A preschooler who is trying to convince a friend to play ghost with him, says, "It's fun... it really fun, Bob" (Kyratzis, Marx, & Wade, 2001, p. 404; Finley & Humphreys, 1974). Axia (1996) found that children adjectivized in trying to persuade adults to buy them toys; they would "advertise" the qualities of the toy, for example, a boy of 7;6 years says to his father about toy cars, "look Dad, aren't these lovely,"[47] and a girl of 6;4 years tells her mother "look mummy, what a beautiful Barbie. I want it."[48] Similarly, a toddler who wants a balloon says, "That balloon is so pretty. It would make me so happy if I could have that balloon" (Spivack & Shure, 1974, p. 116). Of course, the reason for using adjectives as means of persuading others regarding one's preferences may well be that others' are reluctant to accept "I want it" as a justification. In the words of the father of a 13-year-old: "We really just want to know why she wants to buy something and basically she has to give us some reasons. It just can't be "because I want them" (Isler, Popper, & Ward, 1987, p. 166).

D. Request Minimization

Another strategy that children use constitutes a variant of the strategy of persuasion known as the "door in the face" (Cialdini et al., 1975). Often, when volunteers approach individuals to donate money to charity, only relatively large amounts of donation are mentioned. Once the individual declines to donate the large amount, surprise! – it turns out that smaller amounts can be donated as well (e.g., \$20 vs. \$2). What is the basis of this technique? First, it works on the basis of contrast; donating \$2 seems significantly less when it is contrasted with \$20 than with zero. Second, once the individual refuses the first request, the refusal seems to induce a change in one's self-perception. This is because refusing to donate makes one a "cruel and heartless individual." Since most people are unwilling to adopt this new self-perception, they tend to comply with the second, smaller request. In this technique, then, the initial request is deemed unreasonable and is rejected outright. When it is followed by a more reasonable request whose rejection would make the individual seem unreasonable, the second request is more likely to be accepted than when an equivalent request is made without prior rejection of a larger request.

Children appear to intuitively understand the power of this technique, as evident in Table 11.14.

Children appear to be aware of the fact that if one minimizes the size of the request, there is a greater chance of the request being responded to favorably, especially after it has already been rejected by a noncompliant partner.

[46] Italian: "Mi dai I bracciale un momento per favore, Virginia, me li dai?"
[47] Italian: "Guarda babbo che belle queste!"
[48] Italian: "guarda mamma che belle la Barbie. Lo voglio."

REFUSING TO ACCOMMODATE OTHERS

As indicated in the beginning of this chapter, the other aspect of manipulating others is refusing to accommodate others when they indicate their preferences. Children are often faced with requests to do things they prefer not to do. Once they develop verbal facility, they start to express rejection of such requests in a variety of ways, gradually learning to deploy strategies that serve as justifications for their own refusals to accommodate others. Yet in contrast to their use of wide variety of strategies to manipulate others into furthering their own preferences, they appear to be less innovative in rejecting others' preferences. First, as we saw in previous chapters, they often ignore others' requests and appeals, as if they hadn't heard them. Second, they can avoid listening to the request. For instance, a 9-year-old who is arguing with siblings over rights to the top bunk in a bunk bed, yells, "Leave me alone! You're gonna try and talk me out of it and I don't want to be talked out of it" (Allen, 1995, p. 353). Third, they can reject the underlying premise. For instance, they can suggest that they are not the ones who should enact a requested action (e.g., when I say, "Can you go get your slippers?" Orren, at 31;13, responds, "You bring it to me"; when I tell Karen, at 30;8, to crawl under her bed to get a ball, she says, "Mummy can go"). Wilkinson, Clevenger, & Dollaghan (1981) found that children often rejected others' requests by attacking the underlying premise, saying things like, "Ya gotta get your own crayons" in rejecting a request to give a peer crayons, or refusing to answer a peer's request for help by saying, "You gotta read the directions yourself" (p. 226). Children can also reject the underlying premise that the action requested needs to be undertaken (e.g., when I ask about some toys, "Can I take them back to your room?" Karen, at 26;17, responds, "No you can leave them here"). Similarly, in refusing to turn take, children can reject the underlying premise that the object is subject to turn taking, claiming, "It's mine" or they can reject the categorization of the requested object (e.g., being asked for the car, responding "it's not a car, it's a truck") as a means of side-stepping the request (Garvey, 1984).

As for rejecting others' requests, Wilkinson, Clevenger, and Dollaghan (1981) identify three types of refusals: outright refusals, temporizing refusals, and accounts of why the refusal is being made.

A. Outright Refusals

Outright refusals constitute statements of one's lack of willingness to comply. The word *"No!"* standing alone emerges very early in such contexts. Greenfield and Smith (1976) document that Matthew, at 11;28, protested his mother's putting on his undershirt with "no! no!" Most researchers document the emergence of *no* somewhat later, ranging from 14 months (e.g., Deuchar & Quay, 2000), to almost 17 months (e.g., Tomasello, 1992), to 18 to 19 months (Bloom, 1970; Halliday, 1975; Painter, 1984), in many cases emerging first in the context of rejection of foods and later expanding to other objects and activities. Pea (1980) found that the use of negation to reject parental offers emerged between 13 and 15 months in four of the six children he studied, with two of the children not yet evidencing verbal negation at 18 months when the study was terminated. Negation is very interesting in this context because it suggests that these infants compare reality with the alternative reality that is being offered to them and they prefer the former to the latter.

Rejection can be expressed by combining *no* with the object or activity in question (e.g., a child of 19;21, who refuses to go to bed, saying "not bed," and rejects a cucumber with "no cucumber,"[49] Deuchar and Quay, 2000). In more verbal children, rejection may be expressed in terms of one's negative preferences, with examples shown in Table 11.15.

Notice that above, in addition to rejecting the specific objects, foods, and activities currently being offered, a concomitant development is the child's emerging ability to indicate rejection by using the terms *nothing*, *anything*, and so forth.

Rejecting requests by citing one's preferences can also be expressed positively, without saying *no*, indicating actions the child refuses to undertake. For instance, Travis, at 19;08, refuses to get out of the bath and the pool, saying, "more bath," "more swimming" (Tomasello, 1992, p. 291) and, at 19;17, she rejects her father's request to come, saying, "stay here" (ibid). These rejections differ from protests in that they are responses to action requests by adults. That is, they are responses to others' expression of their external preferences as to what the child should or should not be doing. The children above rejected parental requests because they envisaged alternatives to the state of affairs they were offered and rejected them, indicating an alternative that was preferable to them.

Interestingly, children also start to indicate who should not serve as an agent of action, rejecting parental offers to do things for them, often because they want to do the activity themselves or because they have a preferred agent. Painter (1984) reports that by 18 months, when her son said "light" he would indicate dissatisfaction if someone turned the light on or off; he expected to be lifted up to perform the action himself. When a mother tells her 20 month old child that she is going to pack his suitcase, he answers "Guillaume," meaning that he wants to pack it himself. Similarly, when his mother starts to read him a story, he protests, "non Guillaume," explaining that he wants to read it himself (Brigaudiot, Morgenstern, & Nicolas, 1996). In this context it is interesting to note that the Kaluli of Papua New Guinea have a pronoun *nisa*, which translates roughly as "I, not you" (Schieffelin, 1981), indicating the importance of establishing this

[49] Italian: "no cama"; Italian: "no pepino."

Table 11.15.

	Age	Source
Rejecting Objects		
C is asked: "Do you want cornflakes?" C: "Alexia doesn't want cornflakes"[50]	13 mos.	Tsimpli (1996)
C is offered a book C: "Book don't want it"	19 mos.	Wilkinson (1971, p. 66)
K is offered food K "Want nothing"	20;25	Karniol (Diary, Karen)
M: "Do you want to drink some milk?" K: "No" M: "Do you want some water?" K: "No, don't want to drink nothing."	24;13	Karniol (Diary, Karen)
C is asked if she wants meat C: "Want no meat"	26 mos.	Miller (1982)
C is offered fish C: "I don't want any fish"[51]	33 mos.	Stenzel (1994)
Rejecting Activities		
C is offered to play on the slide wants to play alone in play pen C: "No, Kathryn playing self"	22 mos.	Bloom (1970, p. 161)
M suggests she bake a cake C: "Want not bake cake"[52]	22;3	Miller (1979)
M asks K to come K: "I don't want to come here"[53]	27;28	Karniol (Diary, Karen)
C doesn't want to get into car seat C: "No wanta sit there.... No, I don't want to sit seat"	30 mos.	Brown (1973)

Table 11.16.

	Age	Source
M wants to help C: "No Mommy, wipe my butt off myself"	20 mos.	Tomasello (1992)
Being offered help by parent C: "Alone do"[54]	22 mos.	Miller (1979)
Being offered help to get off chair C: "I want get down self.... No, I wan myself"	22 mos.	Thornton (2002)
Adult wants to close a door C: "No no, I close"[55]	24 mos.	Volterra & Antinucci (1979)
Adult offers to read a book C: "No Mop Top".... "I wanta read new Mop Top... I wanta read e my book"	Toddler	Bloom (1970)
M tries to feed K K: "You don't feed Karen. Karen is eating alone"	27;26	Karniol (Diary, Karen)

contrast. Some further illustrative examples are shown in Table 11.16.

Outright refusals can also be expressed in terms of alternative activities that the child prefers to engage in, as when Karen, at 29;22, responds to her father's statement "you're going to sleep," with "No – you're going to play."[56] That is, children's alternative wants and preferences are cited in refusing others' requests so that when others state their external preferences as to what children should do,

50 Greek: "Ohi seli confe Atsia."
51 German: "ich will ni keinen fisch haben."
52 German: "mag nich kuche backe."
53 Hebrew: "Lo roça lavo lekan."
54 German: "Leine mache."
55 Italian: "No, no chiudo io."

56 Hebrew: "At holexet lishon"; "No – at holexet le-playing."

Table 11.17.

	Age	Source
Adult offers to read a book with C C: "No... because I want to play records"	34;2	Bloom (1970)
Adult suggests C wants TV program C: "I don't wanna watch TV. No. Because I just wanna watch news"	4 years	French & Nelson (1985)
C2 makes offer to trade C1: "No let's change over puppets please cos cos I want the dog"	4;9 years	McTear (1985, p. 109)

children counter with their own preferences. Further examples are shown in Table 11.17.

In all the above examples, the child is expressing a preference for an alternative action or state of affairs, using his own contrasting preferences as the justification for noncompliance. This is also the case when children make counterproposals that cite their own preferences when engaging in pretend play with peers (e.g., "I want to be the mother," "You be the baby," Garvey, 1984). Yet citing one's own preferences is not terribly useful when confronted with others' preferences and neither party has a good reason for why his preferences should take precedence. For example, when a preschooler rejects an offered pretend role with, "I want. I would rather be the patient now" (McTear, 1985, p. 197), the interaction is stalled until one of the two preferences is compromised.

Rather than rejecting adult requests outright, children can specify the conditions under which they are willing to comply with the request. For instance, they can specify *if–then* contingencies, offering "good behavior" on their part if someone else satisfies one of their preferences, for example, a child of 3;5 years offers that he and his brother will behave, saying "We'll be good if you give us chocolate." When he is further queried, "You won't be good without it?" the child responds, "Because we will be good if you give us that" (McWhinney, CHILDES). Similarly, a child who had been warned not to put a bottle of cleaner in her mouth says to her mother, "I will if you, if you don't get a, a, a, saucer for my dolly" (Walkerdine & Lucey, 1989, p. 113). Orren, at 35;28, doesn't want to go have a bath and finally says to me: "if you give me the red car from there then I will come with you to have a bath."[57]

Whereas in their interaction with parents, children learn early that simple rejections are inappropriate means of rejecting requests, in their interactions with other children, they apparently continue to do so. For instance, a preschool child refuses to trade with another child, saying, "I don't wanna trade with you" (Wilkinson, Clevenger, & Dollaghan, 1981, p. 226). In a variant on the above, a preschooler who is 3; 10 years of age approaches a 3;8-year-old in the playroom, speaking to her like a puppet that she holds in her hand. The girl being addressed says, "I not playing puppet games now." When she is asked why, she answers, "I don't feel like it" (Garvey, 1984, p. 58). Although other children may accept rejections that merely cite preferences in this manner, adults may be less accepting of such rejections, implying that having contrastive preferences and needs does not constitute appropriate justifications for rejecting others' requests.

In addition, though, in their interaction with other children, children mitigate their refusals in several ways. First, they often use "yes, but" (e.g., "You're the doctor, but I havta lie on the couch," Kyratzis & Guo, 2001, p. 67), affirming what others have said but adding their reservations or amendments. For instance, when one preschooler says of two figures "They're twins," her peer answers, "Ya, um, but they're boyfriend and girlfriend too" (Kyratzis & Ervin-Tripp, 1999, p. 1334). Second, they mitigate by offering substitutes. For instance, when a preschooler asks a peer for a puppet, his friend refuses, but does not do so explicitly. Instead, he offers a substitute, "I'll let ya read the book" (Wilkinson, Clevenger, & Dollaghan, 1981, p. 227). Similarly, when her request for cards is rejected, a 5;5 year old protests, "I'll have no cards," and in turn, is told, "I'll give you a whole puzzle" (McTear, 1985, p. 117). These attempts at reaching "deals" indicate that children recognize that even in interaction with peers, outright rejection is inappropriate. They try to placate others whose requests they reject, offering them substitutes to "soften" the rejection and make themselves out to be still friends despite the rejection.

B. Temporizing Refusals

An important means of rejecting requests is by temporizing them. In some instances, it is clear that children anticipate having to comply eventually, after they finish temporizing, while in other cases, children use this as an avoidance tactic and do not anticipate having to accommodate the other's preferences at all. One cannot always tell from children's statements whether temporization is being used as an avoidance tactic (e.g., "I'm busy now" said by a 21-month-old to her mother, Bloom, 1970). This is often

[57] Hebrew: "im at titni li mi-shum at ha-auto haadom az ani eese itax ambatia."

Table 11.18.

	Age	Source
Activities		
M asks K to stop playing to go shopping		
K: "Not yet go shopping"	19;6	Karniol (Diary, Karen)
M asks child to put doll in stroller		
C: "Wait a minute"	28;07	Miller (1982, p. 180)
M asks K to come		
K: "I need to finish this and I need to go pee"[58]	30;21	Karniol (Diary, Karen)
C is asked to come		
C: "Now I don't want"[59]	3;2 years	Taeschner (1983).
Routines		
M asks O to come have a bath/shower		
O: "I'm not ready to have a bath"[60]	28;19	Karniol (Diary, Orren)
M asks K to come eat, need to go sleep		
K: "I'm just finishing the book. That's it. . . . I finished"[61]	30;29	Karniol (Diary, Karen)
K: "I to pick up all this and to eat supper and then I to sleep, OK?"[62]	31;15	Karniol (Diary, Karen)
M asks O to come eat		
O: "I'll just arrange my big cars"[63]	32;2	Karniol (Diary, Orren)
O: "First I will finish the house I said"[64]	32;3	Karniol (Diary, Orren)
O: "A few minutes I will play with Karen with this, she will buy this for me pretend, and then I will have a shower"[65]	32;29	Karniol (Diary, Orren)

the case when children reject others' preferences, especially peers' preferences, by claiming that they are busy. When a preschooler asks a peer "You wanna be my husband," he replies, "No, because I'm busy" (Paley, 1990, p. 118). Similarly, a 4-year-old boy rejects his friend's request to join him in play, saying, "No, I'm too busy with my work" (Pitcher & Schultz, 1983, p. 46). In their interaction with parents, temporizing by claiming busyness more likely reflects children's understanding that eventual compliance will be required. In this vein, First (1994) recorded a girl of 27 months saying, "I'm busy. I'm working," when she didn't want to be "found" by her parents. She clearly knew that eventually she would be found be her parents.

When children explicitly refer to time in temporizing, the issue is clearer. Specifically, children often use *not now* and *now yet* as means of rejecting requests, as shown in Table 11.18 for both simple activities and routines.

These children are justifying temporizing using the same temporal terms that parents use to delay complying with their requests (e.g., "I'll just," "I only have to," "very soon," "first"). Garvey (1975) calls these *temporizing acknowledgements*, indicating awareness that requests need to be complied with at the earliest opportunity or be rejected outright.

Such temporizing rejections are also evident in children's interactions with non-parents. When in the context of playing house a preschooler tells her friend, "well go and get some nappies," her friend, at 4;7 years, responds, "I'll do it in a minute now" (McTear, 1985, p. 110). When an age-mate says to a 3-year-old, "Now you do it to me, Mollie,," she answers, "After this game, okay? Because I'm playing this lotto game" (Paley, 1986, p. 50). In this latter statement, the responding child makes it clear that the supplicant and his request are less important than the child's current undertaking. Note, though, that the unique aspect of temporizing rejections is that compliance with the request is being delayed rather than being rejected outright. That is, children also acknowledge that they are not refusing to engage in the specified activity, they are only temporizing it, thereby also legitimizing the request addressed to them. On the other hand, they may temporize in the hope that the other child will give up and the request will not be renewed. This is clearly the case when children reject requests with reference to not having had enough time to engage in the activity. A preschooler

[58] Hebrew: "Bo-ee hena." K: "Ani çrixa gamarti z eve-ani çrixa laasot pipi."

[59] Italian: "Allora non voglio."

[60] Hebrew: "ani lo muxan laasot ambatia."

[61] Hebrew: "kodem ani yigmor at habait. . . . gamarti." "Ani rak gomeret at hasefer. . . . Zehu gamarti."

[62] Hebrew: "Rak ani yesader at hamexoniot hagdolot sheli."

[63] Hebrew: "kodem ani yigmor at habait amarti."

[64] Hebrew: "Kama dakot ani asaxek im Karen beze, he tikne li at ze bekeilu veaz ani esse tush."

[65] Hebrew: "Ani leesof at kol ze veani leexol supper veaz ani lishon, OK?"

explains, "I just got it off Claire... I don't want to give it up yet" (Mitchell, 1982, p. 20). When a 10-year-old says, "Let me hold your yoyo," an 11-year-old answers him, "I just got it" (Goodwin, 1990. p. 168), thereby implying that the other child should defer.

Of course, others need not necessarily accept children's attempts to temporize. When a teacher tells a 3-year-old that a peer wants to tell him something, he says, "I'm busy waiting for John." She answers, "You can still wait for John. But let Christopher speak to you" (Paley, 1986, p. 114). When her friend Heather repeatedly calls her, Siobhan, at 4;6 years, protests, "I'm too busy to talk." Heather answers her, "you are not, you aren't," and Siobhan, says, "Yes I am" (McTear, 1985, pp. 42–43). Importantly, though, children learn that claims of being busy are considered valid justifications and are acceptable means of delaying compliance with others' requests.

PROVIDING ACCOUNTS

Children also learn to provide accounts that justify their rejection of others' requests. Simple accounts serve to reject the presumed premise underlying the parental request. For instance, when a parent wants a 3-year-old to go to sleep, she responds, "I don't want to sleep because I'm not tired"[66] (Taeschner, 1983). When her grandfather offers to take Karen, at 28 months, to her room to sleep, she refuses, saying, "Grandpa I explained to you before, Karen will take Karen to bed."

Wilkinson, Clevenger, & Dollaghan (1981) found that children also rejected others' requests by citing alternative norms that presumably clash with the need to comply with the request. In this vein, Nigel, at 22 months, objects to being put to bed saying, "didn't clean your teeth" (i.e., I haven't brushed them yet) (Halliday, 1975, p. 101), referring to the norm of brushing one's teeth before bedtime as the reason why he cannot go to bed. Similarly, Orren refuses to go to sleep at 3;4 years, saying "now it's not the time to go to sleep. I see the clock. It's not the time for sleep."

Rejections can also cite one's own clashing needs. A preschooler asks for a syringe and the peer refuses, saying, "I'm gonna need to use the shot in a couple of minutes." She replies, "But I – I need this though," and her request is granted (Sheldon, 1997, p. 234). Referring to needs in rejecting a request, a 3-year-old says, "Don't take all my bricks 'cos I need some more to finish my castle" (Tough, 1977, p. 65). The child's needs and desires are viewed as valid justifications for refusing the request.

USING PRETEND TO REJECT REQUESTS

Accounts may also invoke the pretend framework, as shown in Table 11.19.

[66] Italian: "Io non voglio dormire perche' io non sono stanca."

Children's pretend play often gives voice to this type of manipulative rejection, as when a preschooler who doesn't want to eat his dinner in pretend says, "I gotta go to the office now" (Garvey, 1993, p. 256). In general terms, though, the means children use to reject requests, both those of adults and of peers, as well as their reasons for choosing a given rejection strategy, have not been adequately empirically addressed.

INDIVIDUAL DIFFERENCES IN CHILDREN

There are wide individual differences in children's ability to convince others that they need to compromise their own preferences. Trawick-Smith (1992) found that more persuasive preschool and kindergarten children varied the way they framed their requests when they met with refusal the first time, even resorting to deception. In addition, persuasive children appear to have sophisticated compromising and mediational skills. A preschooler whose friend rejects her request to be the queen in pretend play says "I know – we'll both be queens, because we both want to," and then specifies how this will occur, saying, "you'll have the crown first, then it'll be my turn" (Dunn, 1996, p. 192). In getting preschoolers to vote on a new nickname for their group, when the boys wanted "Ghostbusters" and the girls wanted "Golden Girls," one child suggested "Goldbusters," and this name won (Tobin, Wu & Davidson, 1989, p. 165). Similarly, when a 4-year-old wants to pretend to drive to New York City, and a peer announces that it's too crowded there and they should go to McDonald's instead, the first child offered a compromise solution: "We'll go to McDonald's. Then we'll got to New York for the show" (Trawick-Smith, 1998, p. 241). When several preschool girls were in conflict over a doll, one approached her sister and "borrowed" her doll to resolve the conflict, giving it to the girl whose request for a doll had been rejected (Hayes, 2005).

Children who serve as mediators in such contexts evidence several characteristics. Mody (2005) found that there were six distinct roles in boys' block corner play, with that of mediator (which she calls "negotiator") being fulfilled by a child who could articulate feelings and negotiate friendship rules. When a child yells at him, the mediator says, "That doesn't mean you scream at me. Are you my friend?" and when the child shakes his head *no*, he continues, "Even if you're mad at me, you have to be my friend" (p. 104). Mody (2005) found that the mediator used his skills for his own advantage as well, gaining access to the toys and roles he preferred in play. In a recent study with adolescents (Karniol & Ziskind, unpublished), three types of mediation were examined: (1) self-serving mediation, in which the mediator's own interests are the reason for mediating, (2) victim-serving mediation, in which the potential victim of a noncompromising choice is the reason for mediating, and (3) group-serving mediation, in which the group's interests are the reason for mediating. Across these different types of mediation,

Table 11.19.

	Age	Source
C doesn't want to wear pajamas selected by mother C: "But I can't wear pajamas to bed. The mouse and the kitty (i.e., on the pajamas) run all over and tickle me all night long"	Preschool	Segal & Adcock (1981, p. 81)
C doesn't want to attend playgroup takes all his clothes off C: "I'm in Africa. You can't come in, it's against the rule"	Preschool	Newson & Newson (1968, p. 444)
C: "I don't want to play any more"; peer asks why C: "Because the fox bit me, that's why I don't want any more"	3;9 years	Auwarter (1986)
C: "I don't like PE so I usually pretend to lose my pumps. . . . we pretended I'd lost an earring so we went round all the classes looking for it"	School	Pollard (1985, p. 71)

more empathic individuals (as assessed by the Interperson Reactivity Index [IRI], Davis, 1980) and ones who were higher in self-monitoring, were more likely to engage in mediation.

LEADERSHIP

Leaders are individuals who are adept at getting others to do what they prefer them to do rather than having others do what they themselves would prefer to do. Good leaders can manage to do so without alienating others and without making others feel they were compelled, giving them the illusion of choice. How do leaders manage to impact others this way? According to Fiedler (1967), there are two types of leaders: (1) *task-oriented leaders*, individuals who are single-minded in their efforts at getting the job done, irrespective of how others feel, and (2) *relations-oriented leaders*, whose major concern is with group members and their interpersonal relations, possibly at the expense of task accomplishment. In highly structured contexts, having a task-oriented leader may be more conducive to group success whereas in highly ambiguous tasks that require much direction and coordination, a relations-oriented leader may be more successful.

In research with children's groups, Sachs (1987) found that boys tend to intuitively adopt a task-oriented leadership approach whereas girls tend to adopt a more relations-oriented approach; these diverse approaches are evident in boys' greater use of imperatives and girls' greater use of mitigated imperatives and greater use of tag questions like *okay? right?* Goodwin (1990) similarly found that in playing with their friends, black boys use directives (e.g., "Gimme the thing") as commands for actions that should be taken immediately whereas girls are more likely to talk of *we*, as in "We need to . . . " and "let's do . . . ," indicating greater awareness of the need to maintain relationships with their peers. FitzSimmons (1999) reported that seventh grade girls commanded their friends with imperatives using the inclusive *we*, for example, "We gotta go!" These findings emphasize that girls are sensitive to the need to psychologically create an "egalitarian" relationship between themselves and those being addressed whereas boys' directives stress position and hierarchy, reflecting an adversarial style of interaction in boys and an affiliative style of interaction in girls (cf., Miller, Danaher, & Forbes, 1986; Sheldon, 1990).

Barner-Barry (1988), who studied leadership in children's groups, identified several different types of directive behaviors that leaders engage in, all of which involve attempts to regulate others' behavior:

Regulation of ongoing activities – telling others what to do;

Inclusion or exclusion – determining who can or cannot join a group;

Conflict resolution – settling conflicts with others;

Distribution of resources – determining what to give each member of the group;

Rule articulation – stating rules and having others' conform to these rules;

Rule interpretation – interpreting rules and having others accept his interpretation; and

Rule enforcement – eliciting compliance with no challenge of his right to do so.

In addition, Barner-Barry identified several behaviors that did not reflect attempts to regulate others, but rather were prosocial behaviors that were also exhibited by the leaders: giving aid, giving information, protection, retaliation on behalf of another, giving attention, and showing affection. In research conducted with preschoolers aged 2;6 to 4;6 years old in a nursery school, and children aged

3;6 and 6;6 years old attending a summer playground program, Barner-Barry found that six children in each group could be characterized as leaders by virtue of the number of leadership behaviors they exhibited. These six children accounted for 48 percent of the directive behaviors in the two groups (i.e., as calculated from Tables 11.1 and 11.2), and 52 percent of the prosocial behaviors.

Critically, the other children apparently *accepted* these children as leaders, acknowledging their leadership role by engaging in the following behaviors: expression of proximity desires, solicitation of their attention, imitation, attempts at appeasement, permission seeking (e.g., "Can I play too?"), and deference (e.g., yielding their place in line). In fact, the children identified as leaders received 33 percent of the leadership-acknowledging behaviors that were displaying in the groups. Leaders are the ones who decide how to allocate roles, apportion rewards (e.g., "I decided John gets two," Kyratzis & Guo, 2001), and decide who can or cannot play. It is the perceived leaders who are approached during play, with their veto on one's joining their play sufficing to exclude the rejected child. When a girl asks "Can I play?" she is told "Yeah, you can be the dog." When she counters with, "I want to be the sister," she is told, "No, we already have enough sisters" (Pitcher & Schultz, 1983, p. 8) – and the edict is accepted. Similarly, in a boys' group, the boy who served as gatekeeper barred the entry of others, marked his own terrain, and aggressively demanded entry into extant groups, with little resistance on the part of the other boys (Mody, 2005). When a high-status girl returns to a play area where only four children are allowed at a time, she tells the girl who replaced her, "Lisa, you have to go out," and the child leaves tearfully, but without resistance (Mody, 2005, p. 107).

Garvey's research suggests that leaders and nonleaders also differ in their ways of dealing with others' noncompliance. First, they revise the content of their requests, making them appear less costly, as elaborated earlier. Second, they make their request more polite, by adding *please*, softening their voice, and so forth. Third, they may add a threat or a warning as to what the consequences of noncompliance may be. As evident in Barner-Barry's research, because leaders can threaten others with being outcast from the group and may have the power to enforce this threat, this gives them additional power that other children do not have.

Leaders also look out for their constituents' interests. A first grader protests, "Vera was working here, Daisy. She's coming back . . . Vera is working here. So shoo, turkey, shoo" (Dyson, 1993, p. 97). The girl being shooed away accepts this and moves away. A kindergarten boy comes to the defense of a new girl in class, saying, "Don't tease her, you guys!" (Dyson, 1993, p. 88) and they stop doing so. When a boy of 9;9 threatens that he will beat up an age mate who doesn't want to play with him, a third agemate interferes, saying, "You leave him alone," and the threatener heeds the request (Sluckin, 1981, p. 49). Leaders assume that they can interfere on others' behalf and protect them.

Even leaders, though, do not always succeed in getting others to do their bidding. Consequently, both leaders and nonleaders need to develop means of coping in those contexts in which they have not succeeded in getting their preferences, which is the topic of Chapter 12.

12 Coping and Self-Regulating

A 12 year old explains, 'If you are really upset about something you don't really forget about it that easy . . . you are thinking about that thing most of the time. So it is real hard to forget about it.'

(Selman, 1979, p. 82)

In many contexts, other people, primarily parents and teachers, impose their external preferences on children and prevent them from pursuing their preferences. In other contexts, others may be unwilling to yield to children's expressed preferences. Except for voicing their own preferences or attempting to alter parental injunctions – strategies that were addressed in previous chapters – children need to learn how to cope with contexts in which others have set up preference blockage. In addition, children eventually develop second-order preferences that lead them to impose barriers on their own preferences and preference-seeking behavior, engaging in self-regulation to do so. In this chapter, I discuss children's strategies for coping with preference blockage, contexts in which others prevent children from either temporarily or permanently pursuing their preferences, as well as the psychological processes involved in self-regulation in which children put the brakes on their own preferences for the benefit of their own second-order preferences.

EXTERNALLY VERSUS SELF-IMPOSED DEMANDS FOR SELF-CONTROL

The strategies children use to cope with preference blockage are generally discussed under the umbrella term *self-control*. But this umbrella covers two different contexts in which self-control is required: coping with externally imposed demands and self-regulation. When others thwart preference attainment and impose demands for self-control, coping is required. Parents may impose their external preferences on the child, forbid his interaction with desirable objects (e.g., "don't touch Daddy's pipe"), demand that the child refrain from engaging in specific actions (e.g., "don't jump on the sofa"), or demand that he temporize his preferences (e.g., "you can't play with it until I pay for it"). In such contexts of *interpersonal* conflict, the child's preferences and the parents' external preferences as to what the child should do are in conflict; but parents' power to impose constraints and to discipline accords them a power advantage so that children need to cope with the restrictions rather than continue the pursuit of their own preferences unless they want to risk possible sanctions. The aversiveness of such contexts, then, stems both from needing to delay or forgo one's preferences and from their pitting one's own preferences against those of more powerful others who have the potential of imposing negative sanctions. Wrong (1979) contends that the power of the parent over the child precedes the child's internalization of parental rules and thus, submission to power is the earliest and most formative experience in human life. In Piaget's (1932) theory as well, submission to parental power is seen as the critical factor in the formation of children's heteronomous (i.e., externally imposed) morality,

In contrast, in self-imposed demands for self-control, one chooses to deprive oneself of something positive or to expose oneself to something negative, usually for anticipated long-term benefits (e.g., resisting eating chocolate because of concerns with one's weight or future health). These settings involve what economists have called conflicts between one's own *first-order* and *second-order* preferences. Specifically, first-order preferences are preferences for immediate gratification whereas second-order preferences are for more distant and perhaps abstract outcomes. Economists have discussed this as a conflict between two selves (e.g., Elster, 1979), a self that knows what one should do in light of one's future preferences and a self that knows what one actually prefers to do in the present. It is the *intrapersonal* conflict between these two selves that epitomizes self-imposed self-control contexts, requiring individuals to self-regulate. Intrapersonal conflicts are often evident in self-talk in which one speaks to oneself as a *you*, which Bredel (2002) calls the *self-positioning you*, suggesting that it emerges to allow one to address oneself from the perspective of others. In intrapersonal conflict, one conducts an inner dialogue between self as *I* and self as *you*, splitting one's perspective from that of the actor who wants to engage in the behavior in question to that of the restricting observer of the planned action.

Contexts characterized by *inter*personal conflict and ones characterized by *intra*personal conflict evidence some similarities. First, both may involve the same subjective problem (i.e., the need to deal with current preferences that cannot be satisfied); they may even invoke the same strategies (e.g., self-distraction). Nonetheless, subjectively, these are different psychological contexts. Young children do not generally have second-order preferences that require them to self-impose demands for self-control or to self-regulate and they do not generally choose to endure something aversive or to give up something positive of their own free will[1]. But children do have such demands imposed on them by others. Consequently, children often need to cope with contexts in which due to the intervention of others, their own preferences need to be put on hold or dropped altogether. Of course, once children are socialized to value long-term outcomes, they develop second-order preferences and may start to engage in self-regulation of their own accord.

Importantly, whereas in a given home, a specific behavior may be viewed as requiring coping, being regulated by parents, in other homes, it may be viewed as requiring self-regulation. To illustrate, in some homes, giving up pacifiers and transitional objects (e.g., blankets) is perceived as requiring self-regulation. Children may be pressured to give up such objects of their own accord, but essentially children are viewed as having to self-regulate in this domain. In other homes, children are forced to cope with the removal of such objects by parents who deem the child old enough to do without (e.g., a 3-year-old who is told, "Now, when you're four, you've got to throw your dummy away," Newson & Newson, 1968, p. 330). Parents may use a wide range of strategies to prevent their continued use (e.g., put pepper on the pacifier, a band-aid on fingers that are sucked, Newson & Newson, 1968). For instance, a mother says to her toddler, "Stop sucking your finger," but then says, "Buy you some red stuff" (i.e., bad tasting fluid to prevent thumb sucking) (Schachter, 1979, p. 134).

Another domain in which this contrast is evident is television viewing. Many studies (e.g., Gehring, Wentzel, Feldman, & Munson, 1990; Laursen & Koplas, 1995) have found that both adolescents and parents report frequent conflicts concerning the regulation of their activities, including watching television, with parents imposing restrictions on children's viewing habits. In contrast, in China (Bin, 1996) and Japan (Peak, 1991), parents believe that children should voluntarily regulate their own behavior, including television viewing. Peak (1991) generalizes this point, claiming that Japanese society

> expects a high degree of self-control and suppression of personal desires and feelings.... But the wish to assume this control must be initiated and sustained by the child himself, or else, it is believed, the long-term effectiveness of the child's social adjustment will be impaired (Peak, 1991, p. 85).

Specifically, the Japanese believe that less salient external controls result in greater internalization of culturally appropriate behavior by the child. In line with this, Lepper (1981, 1983) contends that salient external controls are detrimental to the internalization process because they provide children with salient, external causal attributions for their compliance. The child who complies in the presence of strong controls can attribute his compliance to the presence of such controls rather than to his own preference to comply. In fact, strong controls function to make forbidden fruit sweeter. To illustrate this, Lepper (1973) had preschool children comply with a request to refrain from touching attractive toys under a mild or a strong threat. Children subject to a mild threat subsequently refrained from touching the toys when the threat was no longer in force whereas those subject to a strong threat did not evidence similar restraint. Why? Lepper claims that the former children had to account to themselves why they refrained from playing with the attractive toys, surmising that the toys were actually not so attractive. This devaluation of the toys carried over into the later period when there were no threats. In contrast, those children who were strongly threatened could use the strong threat to account for their not playing with the toys. But the toys remained as psychologically attractive as they had been, so that when the threat was no longer in force, they played with the still attractive toys. Mild threats, then, led children to see themselves as having *chosen* to refrain from playing with the attractive toys whereas strong threats led children to see themselves as being compelled to do so. This precisely captures the distinction between *coping* with externally imposed restrictions versus *self-regulating* under self-imposed contexts.

COPING WITH EXTERNALLY IMPOSED RESTRICTIONS

As discussed above, children need to learn to cope with restrictions unless they want to face the possible sanctions consequent to contravening them. This means that they need to learn to defer or suppress their own preferences and abide by the preferences that others, especially parents, express. In the words of the mother of a preschooler when her child's request to engage in an activity is rejected, "he stops – he's that sort of child" (Newson & Newson, 1968, p. 93).

In submitting to adult power, though, children still need to cope with preference blockage. As discussed in

[1] As discussed in Chapter 2, though, in the food and toy domains, children do sometimes opt to reject a less desirable alternative and hold out for something that is preferable to them.

Table 12.1.

	Age	Source
C: "Leave Stu's beer alone"	20;27	Tomasello (1992)
C gestures toward parrot on shelf Shakes her head C: "Can't take it down"	23 mos.	Wootton (1997, p. 72)
Presleep monologues C: Don't touch Mommy Daddy's desk.... Don't go on the desk; Don't take Daddy's glasses; Don't take it off. Don't take the glasses.... leave it"	28–30 mos.	Weir (1962, p. 121)

Chapter 11, Manipulating Others, of the two kinds of coping identified by Folkman and Lazarus (1985), in *problem-focused* coping the child attempts to change external conditions; in *emotion-focused* coping, the child attempts to alter the *experience* of the situation. Problem-focused coping invokes strategies that attempt to deal head-on with the problem of interpersonal preferential conflict and as discussed in Chapter 11, children attempt to deal with the problem – the recalcitrant parent or peer – using a wide variety of strategies. But others do not always accede to children's demands. As one father describes what happens after the child's request for a dollar is refused, "he'll just carry on and on hoping that I will give in and *I don't*" (Harrington, 2001, p. 367, emphasis added). What do children do to cope with parental intransigence? There are two different paths. One of these paths involves complying with parental demands. The second path involves what I call mind play, using cognitive transformations to deal with the problem, as will be discussed in Chapter 13. I now turn to the first of these paths.

The march toward internalization of parental restrictions appears to start with self-prohibitions that echo parental ones. Children issue themselves self-directed restrictives, both before and after engaging in prohibited activities. Pea (1979) found infants who engaged in headshakes for self-prohibition at around 12 months, with the expression of such self-prohibitions emerging between 14 and 21 months in four of the six children he studied. For instance, a child of 14 months, after being told by his father not to touch the radiator, lifted his hand toward it, saying "Oh-oh, sooooo hot. Noooooo," looking at his father as he said this (Wolf, 1982, p. 313). Tomasello's (1992) daughter Travis, at 16;23, said "no" to herself as she reached for a forbidden pen, and, at 16;25, she said "no" to herself as she was playing with a light cord with which she had been warned not to play. Similarly, a child of 20 months says "no 'chine," while pointing to the tape recorder after he'd been told he could not play with it (Bloom, 1970, p. 152).

Whereas the children above voiced the restrictions without specifying the relevant verb (i.e., play, touch, move), more verbal children do say the rules aloud while specifying the forbidden activity, as shown in Table 12.1. These types of self-directed restrictives are notably different from self-regulative speech in which children attempt to physically guide their own actions. For instance, at 23;18, a toddler who is carrying nesting bowls says to herself, "don't drop this over here" (Miller, 1982, p. 175), and a child of 28 months repeats to himself, "don't step on Daddy's feet!" (Peters, 2000, p. 147). Although these latter statements are phrased in the negative and have the same surface structure as the previous self-directed restrictives, they differ in their goals. The former statements constitute restrictives that attempt to manage and divert children's preferences. But the latter children are not desirous of dropping the bowls nor of stepping on the father's feet, and hence their statements do not represent attempts to cope with preferential conflict. But the former children do want to engage in the actions they are telling themselves not to engage in and their statements represent restrictives aimed at coping with preferential conflict. In line with this, Kochanska, Coy and Murray (2001) used children's self-directed restrictives (e.g., "No – no toys"; "no – touch") as indices of committed compliance in mothers' presence and as indices of internalization in maternal absence.

Whereas any given instance of self-directed restrictive could be viewed as originating within the child, on questioning parents, one discovers that children are essentially echoing injunctions and rules they have repeatedly heard expressed to them (cf., Aukrust, 2001b). This is evident in the fact that children may first repeat restrictions immediately after hearing them. For instance, when his mother says to a toddler, "Don't do that!" he answers, "Okay don't do that" (Wagner-Gough, 1975, cited in Hatch et al., 1979). When toddler Simone plays with the tape recorder, her mother admonishes her: "Simone, no, that you need not (do)" and her daughter repeats, "this – this – not,"[2] walking away from the tape recorder (Miller, 1979, p. 382). Sears, Maccoby, and Levin (1957) relate an anecdote about a visiting 17-month-old who twice was told "Now, Martha, *don't touch*!" regarding a lamp and then deliberately approached it and chastised herself: *"Don't touch"* (p. 365), but then laughed excitedly, clearly reflecting her echoing of her father's restriction.

Importantly, though, the same pattern emerges in parental absence, as when a toddler tells himself, "Be quiet, grow up!"(Becker, 1988). The echoing of parental injunctions is evident in a 4-year-old child, who as a nighttime ritual, said to himself "Don't get out of bed and don't open the curtains." His mother remarked that she used to

[2] German: "Simone! Nein, das darfst du nicht"; "da – da – nich."

say it, elaborating, and "I don't say it any more, he just says it now!" (Newson & Newson, 1968, p. 307), reflecting that "it's just this constant voice coming at them 'don't' do this, don't do that'. It just rubs off" (Backett, 1982, p. 167). Behaviors that were verbally prohibited by adults become subject to self-restriction, with the child repeating to himself the same admonitions he has heard from adults.

Of course, the child may reiterate the prohibition but engage in the behavior nonetheless. As deVilliers (1984) notes, the child's utterance is not always effective in stopping the act, regardless of whether the speaker is the parent or the child himself. In line with this, a girl of 28 months put a piece of Lego in her mouth while saying to herself, "We don't eat it" (Garvey, 1984, p. 131). My daughter Karen, at 20;23 comments outloud as she engages in forbidden behavior, "This is not nice (what) Karen is doing." Even more telling, a boy, at 22 months, yells "don't open e fridge!" – as he slams the fridge shut after opening it (Painter, 1984, p. 170).

Children's understanding that the actions being engaged in are forbidden is evident in a different way as well. They may engage in self-evaluation while undertaking behavior that is subject to restrictions. A child of 15 months says "Babo" (meaning *Bad boy*) as he presses the forbidden television switch (Painter, 1984). He subsequently came to report to his parents about misdeeds, using some version of *Bad boy* to do so. In one such instance, when at 19;1, he is scolded by his mother for pulling the cat's tail, he relates this event to his father, saying, "tail, pussy, bad boy" (Painter, 1989, p. 52). When he rips up a flower, he says, "broken, flower, naughty" (ibid, p. 45). But occasionally, he wants to verify whether his actions are viewed as bad. When he pours salt on the table, he looks at his mother and questions, "Naughty?" (ibid, p. 40). Such evaluations are clearly learned, as evident when Halliday's son, Nigel, at 30 months, says about himself, "The train picture you tore up that was very bad," using the pronoun *you* to refer to himself.

In general, in contexts in which they have contravened parental injunctions and were disciplined, children apparently internalize both the negative evaluation of the behavior that is subject to restrictions and the expectation of some parental reaction that reflects this evaluation. This is evident when a 3-year-old is heard saying, "Don't do that Jenny . . . ," then whispering to herself, "I'm sorry" (Becker, 1988). Such internalization is poignantly illustrated by Bloom (1973). After Allison, at 16;3 tries to touch the microphone and is stopped both with "no" and with "I'm sorry. Can't play with the microphone," Allison spanks her own hands, saying "no no no" (p. 91). A girl of 19;6, when she was spanked or scolded said, "Ruthie tired – in crib, please" (Church, 1966, p. 258). Shatz (1994) describes an event in which after being chastised, her grandson, at 30 months, gave himself a "time out," first standing in a corner, facing a wall, then lying down in another room. The children above were restricting their own behavior verbally, and echoing both the restrictions imposed by parents and the disciplinary encounters that followed when they failed to abide by parental preferences.

COPING WITH TEMPORIZATION

Many restrictions constitute demands for temporization, to be coped with for a period of time as determined by the socialization agent. For young infants, all delays are externally imposed ones that are initiated by parental temporization and in which termination of the delay is not under the infants' control. Infants are dependent on adults who decide when and on what terms, a given delay will be terminated.

In this context, there are two different types of delay: people-initiated delays and event-induced delays. People-initiated delays involve waiting for other people, often because they need to complete activities. Mothers need to finish cooking, get up from their nap, and get off the phone. Experimenters need to come back and provide temporarily forbidden toys and foods. Event-induced delays require "the right time" to arise. The weather has to be good for picnics, the sun has to shine for going to the beach, December has to roll around for Santa to bring his gifts, and nighttime has to give way to morning for children to get up and go to preschool.

This distinction is important for children to learn. First, event-induced delays are ones in which the child's actions are limited in that they cannot generally be hurried up. Christmas and birthdays roll around at their own pace. One has to await the conditions or times specified for the event's occurrence. For instance, when a child asks for drinks to be bought, her mother explains that she doesn't have enough money, saying, "when Daddy gets paid I'll get some more money and then I'll go and get the rest [i.e., of the list]" (Tizard & Hughes, 1984, p. 75). Except for persuading his mother to do otherwise, the child's range of potential actions in this context is relatively limited.

Event-induced delays are especially difficult to cope with because children (and adults) are poor judges of time elapsed. Time appears to pass quickly or slowly depending on the nature of the activities undertaken in the interim. This is evident in children's experiences at school; being bored makes the time period appear endless. A 10-year-old girl talks of school and says, "it just gets real boring . . . . Sometimes, when it's boring it just feels as though the day's never gonna end" (Christensen & James, 2001, p. 70). In contrast, when individuals are busy or engaged in interesting activities, time is experienced as passing quickly and vice versa (Fraisse, 1981). Elaborating this distinction, an adolescent says, "If we've got real good lessons it goes real quick and when we've got really boring lessons it goes slow" (Christensen & James, 2001, p. 82). A 6-year-old ponders this puzzle, asking, "How can an hour be long sometimes and so short another time?" (Reilly, cited in Greenfield, 1980, p. 274).

Are there strategies that can be used to manage event-induced delays? As stated by the school children above, one strategy is to fill the time till the relevant event arrives. For instance, children can be taught to mark the calendar for the number of days left till Christmas, look for signs of the rain abating, and be given clocks to watch for the appointed hour to arrive (e.g., Miller & Karniol, 1976b). The mother of a 30-month-old explains to him, "We'll go out at 11:30 when we take Ricky to school, alright?" (Carew, 1976, p. 84). A Japanese mother explains that to deal with her son's difficulty in waiting to go to preschool in the morning, she "taught him to watch the clock . . . he watches the clock every morning and calls, "It's almost time Mama, let's go" (Peak, 1991, p. 146). Yet obviously these strategies do not actually change the length of the required delay. They may, however, change the subjective duration of the delay and the difficulty of coping with it. In talking of a good teacher, a teen expresses this, saying, "you don't keep looking at your watch for the end of the lesson . . . you don't have time" (Delamont, 1976, p. 114). In this vein, a boy explains why he hates sitting where he does at school: "I hate looking this way 'cos you're like looking this way and your eyes are always pointing to the clock and then your belly starts grumbling. Like at twelve or quarter to twelve, got to eat" (Christensen & James, 2001, p. 84); for him, then, clock watching made the delay more, rather than, less difficult.

In many places in the world, children's difficulty with event-induced delays is acknowledged – in restaurants, medical offices, and supermarkets – which have created solutions for waiting children. Many family-style restaurants provide children with coloring tasks that can make the wait for food more enjoyable, supermarkets often offer supervised children's play areas where parents can leave children while they shop, and medical and dental offices are often replete with toys and books to entertain children as they wait. Denham (1998) gives an example of a father who thinks the wait in the doctor's office may be difficult and suggests his son look at a waiting-room-provided book to distract himself. Such practices indicate a societal sensitivity to children's difficulty with waiting and index acknowledgment of the need to help parents in this endeavor. The provision of such "child-entertaining" services is an expression of the underlying belief that delays require children to use coping strategies they may not yet be adept at using. As well, such provision indicates that society does not entirely trust parents to be skillful in guiding their children in such contexts and to some extent, undermines the important parental role of teaching children to cope with delays, an issue I will return to later. On the other hand, adults too are offered entertainment, with televisions and magazines being standard fare in waiting contexts, reflecting the societal view of waiting as a difficult endeavor.

In general, then, there seems to be an intuitive understanding that offering children various forms of "entertainment" while they wait is conducive to their coping with event-induced delays. When a mother at a laundromat has trouble controlling her son, the manager offers the child a book to read to pass the time until the machine finishes its cycle (Tough, 1976). A 5-year-old child tells of a hospital stay for having his tonsils removed, saying, "I hadda wait a few hours but, but while I was there they had brought stor – library stories along" (p. 229). Children indicate their understanding of the beneficial effects of such "entertainment," as evident when a 4-year-old child says, "I have to take some toys with me because I was bored once before" (Schönenberger, 2001, p. 253).

In contrast, people-induced delays may be controllable, both by the individual who sets up the delay and the one who has to cope with it. The one who sets up the delay can make up lists of what needs to be done, estimate the time required to complete different tasks, prioritize tasks, make schedules to organize his time, and attempt to use the time allotted for different tasks more efficiently. One can devise daily routines that reduce cognitive load and choice, strategies that allow one to experience a sense of control over time, and to manage time by making it appear to be more concrete and more structured. In fact, mothers apparently deal with delays that they control by specifying extended plans. Friedman and Sherman (1985) videotaped mothers' interaction with their 2- to 4-year-old children in a homelike environment. Mothers' statements of their own plans were recorded (e.g., "When we leave here, we will stop at the market first, then we will pick up your sister, and then we will all go to visit Grandma"). Mothers made many statements that related to such plans, with about 80 percent of them involving the child in planning. Doing so may make it easier for children to wait.

Alternatively, children who need to cope with people-induced delays can attempt to control them, implementing several possible strategies. First, they can avoid disturbing the prerequisite events from unfolding. When mother says she is busy with something, for instance, they can permit her to carry on without interruption so prerequisite activities can be completed. To illustrate, when a child wants his mother to set up an easel for drawing and she indicates she's busy, she explains that she will do it when she's finished, adding, "But I can't finish as long as you bother me" (Shure & Spivack, 1978, p. 138). Children need to occupy themselves when mothers are busy. Some mothers acknowledge children's difficulty in doing so, saying, they "can't amuse themselves, and there's ironing to be done and washing to be done" (Backett, 1982, p. 176). But the need to find things to do while mothers are otherwise occupied is impressed upon children and mothers explain: "They've got used to that routine of knowing that they've to play on their own till after dinner" (Newson & Newson, 1968, p. 91) and "When I'm busy in the mornings I expect him to (amuse himself)" (ibid, p. 91). Children learn that parental busyness requires them to occupy themselves until the parent is no longer busy.

Second, as they get older, children can facilitate the termination of the prerequisite activity. For instance, if mother says she needs to put laundry in the washing machine prior to going on a joint outing, the child can offer to perform the required activity so as to shorten the delay, eliminating mother's need to engage in the activity herself. As one mother says to her 5-year-old, "you help and tea gets on the table faster. If you don't want to help the tea's longer" (Grieshaber, 2004, p. 127). An appreciative mother tells her child, "I was sure happy to have your help tonight, because without it dinner would have been late" (Gordon, 1976, p. 166).

Third, children can attempt to change mothers' *perceptions* of the necessity of completing the prerequisite activity. For instance, a mother may indicate her need to iron before taking the child to the playground and the child may try to convince her that ironing can wait. For the child, delaying the mother's actions seems as logical as being asked to delay his own. In this vein, when Abe's mother tells him at 34 months that she has to do the dishes first, he retorts, "No, no dishes first. Why you have to do dishes?" (Kuczaj, CHILDES). When a mother tells a preschooler that she has no time to play with her, child asks, "Why? Why do you have to do your washing?" (Tizard & Hughes, 1984, p. 105).

As we saw in Chapter 10, because the ability to persuade others is slow in its emergence, children often resort to actions that prevent mothers from completing the planned sequence that led to temporization. Children can cry to get their mothers to stop doing what they are doing; in some studies, they can summon the experimenter (e.g., Mischel & Moore, 1973). Nagging and badgering their mothers can also result in her changing the sequence of activities, thus shortening the delay the child needs to endure. To the extent that such badgering is successful, children learn to shorten delays this way rather than by using alternative means.

The difficulty of coping both with people-induced delays and event-induced delays stems primarily from the immediacy of children's desire to satisfy their preferences "here and now." Children often comment on their difficulty of coping, referring to their inability to wait. A 3-year-old tells the preschool teacher, "Can I tell mine (story) right now teacher? I can't wait a minute!" When the teacher answers that he's not next on the list, he replies, "I have to! I can't wait!" (Paley, 1986, pp. 51–52). Indicating his frustration after calling me repeatedly to come and being told that I'm busy, Orren, at 2;10;23, says to me, "All the time you're not coming and I will already be angry at you."[3]

The implementation of strategies to cope with delays depends on the understanding that a delay period has been initiated and that strategies can be useful to cope with it. Yet young infants may not be aware that a delay period has actually been initiated, possibly because they do not yet comprehend the language used to explain delays to them. Even if they were to understand that a delay period has been initiated, they may not know what strategies could potentially enable them to cope better with delays. However, infants and toddlers do have a wide variety of behaviors in their repertoire and they engage in them *indiscriminately* when they need to cope. Bridges, Grolnick and Connell (1997) exposed 12- to 14-month-old infants to an externally imposed delay situation in which they were to temporarily refrain from touching an attractive visible toy. Alternative toys were available and the parent was either "busy," or free to interact with the infant during the delay. Similarly, Grolnick et al. (1998) used an externally-imposed food and gift delay of 3 minutes and 6 minutes, respectively, with mothers being sequentially active or passive during the delay period. When mothers were allowed to interact with their child during the delay, they were found to engage their child actively with objects that were not forbidden to the child, attempting to redirect his attention and to distract him from the forbidden toy. The average number of strategies used by mothers was four; mothers were sensitive to their children's fretting and used a variety of strategies to help children cope with delays.

What did infants do during the delay? Their strategies included: playing with alternative toys, physical self-soothing, focusing on the forbidden toy, and focusing on the parent, with all of these increasing when the parent was "busy." The fact that all these behaviors increased during the more difficult delay period when the mother was unavailable indicates that children were using their behavioral repertoire indiscriminately. In similar research, Braungart and Stifter (1991) differentiated three kinds of strategies used by young infants in coping with such delays: people-oriented strategies, which include looking at mother and trying to communicate with her, object-oriented strategies, which include looking at toys and attempting to interact with them, and self-comforting, which includes attempts to physically soothe oneself. They found that 12-month-old infants engaged in all of these strategies, but there were individual differences in terms of the amount of time different infants engaged in each. This indiscriminate pattern of coping suggests that infants need to learn which of the behaviors in their repertoire facilitate their delay better.

In fact, such learning does appear to take place and in research with 2-year-olds (Grolnick, Bridges, & Connell, 1996), active engagement with substitute objects was the most prevalent form of coping with delays. Relative to 24- and 32-month-olds, 12- to 18-month-olds are less likely to actively engage in play with substitute objects during both delay and mother separation (Bridges & Grolnick, 1995). Cournoyer and Trudel (1991) found that although, at 33 months, the most frequent behavior while waiting for a delayed reward was fidgeting, including physical self-soothing, those toddlers who exhibited longer delays were better able to shift their attention from the delayed rewards. It is likely, then, that these older children have learned that strategies that constitute self-distraction facilitate coping with delays.

[3] Hebrew: "Kol hazman at lo baa vekvar exas alaix."

Table 12.2.

	Age	Source
C is throwing cards instead of playing M: "Do you wanna play with your chalk or do you wanna get your pegs out?"	24 mos.	Hart & Risley (1995, p. 58)
C1 wants toy in C2's possession C1 asks mother to intervene M asks C2 to comply, C2 refuses M looks for another toy, puts it next to C1 M leaves the room, C1 plays with toy	33 mos.	Garvey (1984, pp. 108–110)
M is on phone C wants help with derailed train M: "Why don't you look at your storybook now?"	Preschool	Shure & Spivack (1978, p. 139)
C complains sister won't play with him M: "Why don't you play with your new spinning top for a while. Maybe Carrie will play with you later"	Preschool	Shure & Spivack (1978, p. 111)
C wants to use earphones, needs to wait his turn T: "How about if you go and play with the plasticene. Make me something – a snake"	Preschool	Shultz (1979, p. 291)
C can't find a book M: "Whyn'tcha play with your babies for a while?"	Preschool	Clancy, Akatskua, & Strauss (1997)
C is mad at peer who wouldn't sit next to him T: "Think of something that makes you feel good and do it"	Preschool	Paley (1990, p. 115)

The ability to activate successful coping strategies appears to be a function of the infant's level of distress. Grolnick and her colleagues (1998) found that more distressed infants played less with alternative toys. Similarly, in a study with 18-month-olds who were exposed to a series of frustrating delays, two involving plastic barriers that the child could attempt to remove and two involving passive, externally imposed delays for a toy or food, Calkins and Johnson (1998) found that those infants who were more distressed – as indexed by crying or fretting – reacted with aggression and venting and were less likely to attend to their mothers, to distract themselves with other objects or to engage in constructive behaviors to overcome the barriers. In turn, maternal positive guidance (i.e., positive verbal expressions, physical expressiveness, and verbal suggestions) was significantly related to the infant's use of distraction and constructive coping.

USING DISTRACTION TO FACILITATE COPING

As children become older, parents can suggest to children what they can do while they are waiting; they can send them to watch television, listen to music, and to play, as shown in Table 12.2.

These examples all implicate alternative activities that constitute distractions. Note that the parent is suggesting that the child engage in the alternative activity to pass the time until a preferred activity can be engaged in. Hence, distraction in these contexts was undertaken as a time filler. It essentially engaged the child with an activity that was less preferred than the unavailable activity.

Attempts to distract are also prevalent in restrictive contexts where they serve a different function, as shown in Table 12.3. In the above instances, distraction was used to stop the child from engaging in an activity that the child preferred but that the adult did not want the child to engage in. It was suggested in contexts in which adult external preferences conflicted with children's own preferences. This is more explicit in the following. A mother wants to prevent her preschool child from eating a candy given to her by the experimenter; she suggests, "Let's play a game of hide and seek with the candy" (Stansbury & Sigman, 2000, p. 191). In line with this, teachers indicate that they use distraction about 10 percent of the time to intervene in children's misbehavior (King, 1978). Miller (1982) found that a working-class mother used instructional routines (e.g., naming, reciting rhymes) as a way of distracting her toddler from engaging in activities that were considered undesirable by the mother. As Miller says,

> even though the sequence originated with the mother, it was an effective distraction because it captured and sustained the child's interest, bringing about a realignment of the purposes of the child and the caregiver. (Miller, 1982, p. 127).

In this vein, Holden and West (1989) found that in contexts in which they were asked to prevent their children from playing with attractive but forbidden toys, mothers sang songs, rehearsed letters and numbers with the child, and carried out naming exercises. Mothers spent their time distracting children in two different ways. First,

Table 12.3.

	Age	Source
C opens drawer despite being told not to M: "No, we'll get you something else to play with" (takes C to playroom)	19 mos.	Carew (1976, p. 11)
C discovers a forbidden box of toys M: "Go and play with the other box"	20;19	Howe (1981, p. 129)
C repeatedly hit M with toy hammer M: "Would you like to draw me a picture . . . or would you like to play the cello"?	35;9	Howe (1981, p. 34)
C is misbehaving T: "Vanessa, will you put these crayons away for me?"	Kindergarten	King (1978, p. 53)
Two boys fighting T: "Paul will you come and do this puzzle for me please?"	Kindergarten	King (1978, p. 99)

they offered children alternative activities that distracted them and kept them away from the "forbidden" toys. Second, they actively engaged the child in play with those objects that were available, an issue I will return to later. Importantly, maternal use of distraction strategies during toddlerhood has been found to be significantly correlated with children's ability to delay gratification at age 5 (Lecuyer & Houck, 2006).

Distraction is also used when children have nothing to do during an interval and could potentially interfere with parental caretaking functions. Hart and Risley (1999) found that when changing baby's diapers, parents often gave the baby a toy to explore so that the baby would lie still, often saying things like "Just lie still. I'll be through in a minute" (p. 76). This use of distraction is also prevalent during meals. A mother who is discussing how she deals with her $2^1/_2$-year-old daughter says, "she's got to be holding something while she eats . . . if there was something to keep her amused, she'd eat all her breakfast, her fruit or cereal" (Cohler & Grunebaum, 1981, p. 139).

On the other hand, eating itself can constitute an instrumental distraction. In this vein, when a girl of 19;1 indicates that she wants to go into another room but her mother does not want her to, she tries to distract the child by asking her if she wants a biscuit (Lieven, 1978, pp. 229–230). In another instance of this, when a child chews a blind cord, his mother attempts to distract him by offering, "Would you like some mandarin to put in your tummy instead" (Cloran, 1989, p. 135).

As evident above, then, mothers use strategies in which they concomitantly keep the child's attention on currently available alternatives and off currently unavailable ones. Interestingly, parents also offer children food to distract them and get them out of their way (e.g., "if I give them a biscuit or a dish of smarties or something it keeps them out of my way while I get on," Charles & Kerr, 1988, p. 100). Mothers who indicated that they used distraction with their children to get their minds off Hurricane Andrew were found to have children who were more likely to use both positive coping and self-distraction themselves (Prinstein, LaGreca, Vernberg, & Silverman, 1996).

Pretend play can also be initiated as a means of distracting children. Haight, Masiello, Dickson, Huckeby, and Black (1994) found that mothers often initiated pretend play instrumentally to redirect their children's behavior and to distract them from dangerous, annoying, or forbidden activities. To illustrate how this works, when a Japanese 2-year-old wants a toy held by his friend, his mother distracts him with a toy cat, and speaking as the cat says to him, "Click, click, hello, Yotchan, hello" (Clancy, 1999, p. 1408); pretend play served as a distraction from a currently unavailable preference. Holden and West (1989) found that in contexts in which they were asked to prevent their children from playing with attractive but forbidden toys, mothers "transformed" mundane objects and situations that were currently available into exciting forms of entertainment. Cylinders became crowns, rugs became acrobat's mats, and pretend meals were prepared and eaten.

SELF-REGULATION

In the above discussion, the need to cope was engendered by being in contexts in which the delay was imposed by others. But there are many instances in which one imposes second-order preferences on oneself, contexts that require one to delay a given preference and to self-regulate in the interim. Self-regulation emerges when (1) one knows what one's preferences are, and (2) one has second-order preferences about those preferences. For instance, I may love to gamble, smoke, and eat ice cream, but I know shouldn't want to do any of these things because they are bad for me. On the other hand, I do not like to exercise and yet I know I should like to exercise because it's good for me. Self-regulation processes are engaged when one wants one's preferences to be different than they are (Frankfurt, 1988). That is, the possibility of self-control emerges because we can reflect upon, evaluate, and identify our first-order preferences and reach conclusions about whether or not we should have these preferences. Once we do so, we can engage in strategies that help us align our first-order preferences with our second-order preferences.

The classic example of self-regulation is in the context of noncotemporal choice. For instance, one needs to refrain from eating a potentially fattening food in order to maintain one's long-term dietary or health goals or avoid buying on impulse because of a desire to save. In this context, then, self-imposed delay is manifest in resisting temptation. In such resistance to temptation, both the immediately available alternative and the delayed alternative (e.g., being thin or healthy) are positive. However, it is the immediately available alternative that tends to sway the choices made; the delayed alternative seems to be a dim flicker on the far-away horizon, presenting only a minor annoyance at the point of choice (cf., Trope and Liberman, 2003). As discussed by addicted adult shoppers, the temptation is all but impossible to ignore because "the candy bar was staring there at me," "the pants were shrieking 'buy me," and "the sweater was following me" (Rook, 1987). The alternative, of saving one's money or keeping one's figure, cannot withstand such temptation. The problem of course is that as the future becomes the present, the dim flicker becomes a blazing light, often leading to regret about having chosen the immediately available alternative.

Other instances in which one imposes self-regulatory processes on oneself include contexts in which one has immediate preferences that are in conflict with other preferences that are not currently available. For instance, a child may be taken to a toy store to buy a desired toy only to find out that the desired object is out of stock and will not arrive for another week (cf., Yates, Yates, & Beasley, 1987). In such contexts, parents are quick to point out the possibility of choosing another toy that is currently available. On the other hand, choosing the currently available toy generally eliminates the possibility of receiving the more preferred toy when it arrives (i.e., "If I buy you Sporty Barbie now, you can't have Bride Barbie later"). The question here is whether the child will choose to wait for the preferred toy to arrive or whether he will he opt for the currently available but less desirable alternative. In such contexts, children often opt to reject the currently available alternative, deferring to their original choice.

In another type of self-imposed self-control, both the preferred and the less preferred alternatives are available but the preferred one is metaphorically under temporary lock and key whereas the less preferred one is not. Will the child choose to wait until the preferred alternative is no longer under lock and key or will he opt for the freely available option and thereby lose the preferred one? Harriet Mischel (1984) suggests that in such contexts, two different psychological processes are involved. The first of these represents making the choice to delay for the preferred alternative that is not currently available. The choice to delay is determined by the subjective value of the delayed alternative relative to the immediately available one, as well as the child's belief that the preferred alternative will be available after the delay (e.g., is the shipment from China really going to arrive next week?). If the child does not trust the social environment to guarantee that the delayed alternative will in fact be available at the specified time as promised, he has no reason to undertake the delay in the first place because delays are inherently aversive.

As Harriet Mischel elaborates, committing to defer gratification in order to attain more preferred alternatives is but the first step in self-imposed delay. Maintenance of the delay in the face of ongoing temptation to terminate it as the delay continues is the crux of the problem. The second ability involved in delaying, then, is the deployment of strategies that facilitate keeping on track toward obtaining the delayed but preferred alternative, avoiding being derailed as time passes. The research program of Walter Mischel and his colleagues (e.g., Mischel & Moore, 1973; Mischel & Baker, 1975) focused on delay maintenance within such self-imposed delay contexts. In Mischel's delay paradigm, preschool children are asked to agree to wait for a preferred reward contingent on passive waiting. The child's task is to resist pressing a buzzer that can be used to summon the experimenter, thereby forfeiting the preferred reward and getting a less preferred reward. The unique aspect of this delay paradigm is that as long as the experimenter is out of the room, the child has continually available the option of escaping the situation by pressing the buzzer. So there are really two questions one can ask about this context. Why do some children choose to terminate the delay and what facilitates children's coping with the delay? Mischel's findings indicate that children who choose to terminate the delay do so because they do not know how to cope with the aversiveness of the delay. They do not appear to have readily available strategies that enable them to delay. Although we saw in Chapter 7, Temporizing Preferences, that children learn very early that they need to wait for certain outcomes, children vary in terms of what they do to cope with delays.

What specific strategies would one expect to facilitate children's delay ability in such contexts? Mischel capitalized on Freud's (1911) notion of primary process thinking in attempting to answer this question. Specifically, primary process thinking refers to generating a mental image of the desired object in one's mind, representing a process analogous to hallucinatory wish fulfilment. Freud suggested that infants cope with delays by forming such mental images of the delayed, but absent object (e.g., the mother's breast or a feeding bottle), and such mental images facilitate their coping with the mother's absence. Translating this into the current context, delay of gratification in the self-imposed delay paradigm should be facilitated by generating mental images of the delayed but preferred reward. This would suggest that children who have the rewards available and visible would be better able to continue waiting than children who do not have the rewards visible during the delay. Yet Mischel found the opposite to be the case. Having the rewards visible during the delay significantly hindered delay maintenance and those preschoolers who did not have the rewards visible were able to maintain the delay longer. Mischel and Moore (1973) found that children varied in terms of what they did during the delay. Some children sang, others attended the electric outlets in the walls, talked to themselves, and one child apparently even had a short nap. These activities were interpreted as reflecting strategies of self-distraction and so it seems that engaging in self-distraction is beneficial for children in coping with delays. This suggests that children need to learn strategies for distracting themselves without forgetting the relevant outcome for which the delay was undertaken.

In further studies using the same delay paradigm, Mischel and his colleagues attempted to experimentally manipulate children's cognitions during the delay. Some children were instructed to think about the reward objects, how good, chewy, and crunchy they would taste. Other children were given instructions to think of fun things like finding frogs. Children who were instructed to think of the reward objects in consummatory terms were less able to maintain the delay than those children who were given no instructions or than those children who were given instructions to ideate about fun things. Mischel concluded that successful delay requires children to occupy themselves with thoughts and activities that interfere with focusing on delayed rewards. In further studies, children were instructed to think of the reward objects in transformational terms. When children were instructed to cognitively transform the reward objects, for instance, thinking of marshmallows as little clouds floating in the sky or pretzels as logs floating down the river to the saw mill, their ability to maintain the delay was significantly increased. Similarly, children who were asked to transform the rewards into pictures in their heads or were actually exposed to pictures rather than to the rewards themselves were also better able to maintain the delay period (Moore, Mischel & Zeiss, 1976).

Importantly, children who waited longer in a self-imposed delay with rewards visible and without experimenter-provided delay strategies during preschool had higher SAT scores 15 years later, with correlations of 0.42 with SAT verbal scores and 0.57 with SAT quantitative scores (Mischel, Shoda, & Rodriguez, 1989). From Mischel's perspective, those preschool children who can effectively self-regulate during delays have a distinct advantage because they acquire strategies to reduce frustration in situations in which self-imposed delay is required to attain desired goals. By using these strategies to make self-regulation less frustrating, these children can more easily persist in their efforts, becoming increasingly more competent as they develop. Note, though, that this account does not provide an explanation for the higher correlation of preschool delay times with the quantitative SAT score than with the verbal SAT score, an issue I will return to in Chapter 13.

Yet many preschool children do not appear to be aware of the strategies that are conducive to maintaining delay (H. Mischel & Mischel, 1983). When queried as to the strategies they think would facilitate their ability to maintain delay, only older children specify strategies that are in fact helpful to delay maintenance. These older children cited cognitive strategies, including redirecting attention, transforming the goal object into something that is temporarily less desirable, and engaging in self-monitoring. For instance, a sophisticated 5-year-old said "if it's covered, I could wait all the time"; (if it's covered) because that will sort of get my mind on something else." Similarly, older children seemed to know that thinking about the rewards abstractly is better because "it would make me not think of eating them. Also, it would make my mind drift to the thought of something different than the marshmallows" (H. Mischel, 1984, p. 127).

In their research, Mischel and Mischel (1983) found that by the ages of 5 to 10 years, children not only discover delay strategies, but they also shift from reliance on physical ploys such as covering up tempting objects, to mental strategies, such as thinking about something else (e.g., "You can take your mind off it and think of Christmas or something like that but the point it to think about something else," said by a child of 11;3, p. 618). At about age 10, children begin to understand that there is a difference between planning to deploy a strategy and actually carrying it out and their knowledge of delay strategies begins to be correlated with their ability to maintain a delay.

Related to this, Altshuler and Ruble (1989) asked 5- to 11-year-old children how they would control their reactions to two positive and two negative delay situations: waiting for candy or a birthday party and waiting for a dental filling or a medical injection. They were asked explicitly what they could do to change the situation, change their cognitions, or change their feelings. Older children generated more strategies, with younger children generating more situation-avoidant strategies and older ones generating more behavioral distractions (e.g., do something else or something fun, play, read, watch TV) and cognitive distractions (e.g., think of something else or something fun). Altshuler and Ruble suggest that young children have not yet learned that their thoughts and feelings can be strategically manipulated and deployed to cope with delay contexts. This is generally the same conclusion reached by Cole, Bruschi, and Tamang (2002), who found that the understanding that emotions can be strategically manipulated by how one thinks about a situation was only evident in older children. That is, younger children generally attempt to change the restrictions placed on their behavior rather than employing strategies that facilitate their coping and self-regulation.

COMPARING COPING VERSUS SELF-REGULATION

Whereas Mischel's data have been interpreted as disproving Freud's contention regarding the value of focusing on the reward objects during the delay, Dale Miller and I (Miller & Karniol, 1976a, 1976b; Karniol & Miller, 1981b, 1983) claimed that Mischel's paradigm does not address Freud's contention. Specifically, Freud was discussing the infant who must bridge the delay until his mother appears, having no recourse to terminate the delay, whose termination is solely in his mother's hands. Mischel's paradigm, on the other hand, provides the child with the choice of terminating the delay, using a buzzer that summons the experimenter, making the delay self-imposed, rather than externally imposed as is the case in Freud's context. Consequently, Freud's context involves coping while Mischel's paradigm involves self-regulating. Capitalizing on Freud's notion of primary process thinking as repeatedly imaging the delayed reward during the delay, we argued that whereas in self-imposed delay, thinking about the delayed reward may be debilitating to delay, repeatedly imaging the delayed reward during externally imposed delay would facilitate children's ability to delay.

In keeping with this conceptualization, in our research, we found that waiting during an externally imposed delay in which the child has no recourse but to wait until the experimenter returns and gives the child the preferred reward is *facilitated* by having the reward objects present and hindered by having them absent. When one has no choice but to wait until a preferred outcome occurs, thinking of this outcome facilitates one's ability to sustain the delay. When one has a choice during the delay period, as is the case in Mischel's research, thinking of the outcome hinders one's ability to delay. Why would this be the case?

We (Karniol & Miller, 1981, 1983) argued that this occurs because having choice initiates a process of reward reevaluation, which goes on during the delay period. The two reward objects start off being evaluated somewhat differently and this slight difference between them allows for one to be selected as preferred. As the child starts to wait, because the delay itself is aversive, the delay "chips" away at the value of the preferred reward, making it more similar in value to the less preferred reward. Once the two rewards are perceived as more similar in value, continuing to wait for the preferred reward no longer makes sense, leading the child to terminate the delay by pressing the buzzer. For those children who press the buzzer, then, this occurs because the two rewards have seemingly converged in value. In contrast, those children who do not press the buzzer are able to maintain the divergent evaluations of the two rewards, either by engaging in self-distraction or by consciously attempting to make them diverge in value from each other.

This suggests that first, for those children who can self-distract, such convergence would not occur and second, that one could prevent convergence from occurring by selecting reward alternatives that differ from each other greatly in their original evaluation. In one study (Karniol & Miller, 1983) that manipulated the relative similarity of the two reward alternatives, our findings indicated precisely that. We found that those children who were waiting for two rewards that were relatively discrepant in their original evaluation were able to maintain the delay for much longer than children for whom the rewards were originally of nearly equal value.

This pattern of findings suggests that transformational instructions are successful because they prevent convergence from occurring and may even be conducive to the occurrence of divergence, making the reward objects seem even more discrepant from each other than they originally were. Some preliminary evidence for this possibility comes from two sources. First, Mischel and Mischel (1983) found that some of the children in their studies suggested a strategy of devaluing the delayed rewards, saying things like "the marshmallows are filled with an evil spell," "I hate marshmallows. I can't stand them" and "I don't want to eat the marshmallows. They are yukky" (p. 609). Second, in a study (Yates, Yates, & Beasley, 1987) in which children 4, 6, and 8 years old were asked to indicate how either they or another child would be able to opt to wait for an iced cake that needed to be baked versus a plain one that was readily available, older children evidenced reward-oriented thoughts, thoughts that appeared to index a divergence strategy. Children embellished the waited-for cakes, saying that they thought things like "those lovely yummy cakes," "the icing looks nice and really good to eat."

In a study (Karniol, unpublished) conducted to explicitly test this, children in second to the fourth grade were asked to select their preference between three M&M's and a piece of Bazooka gum. All the children preferred the gum. Children in the control condition were asked to "help" write an ad for the Bazooka gum immediately after making their selection. Children in the experimental conditions were asked to wait for the experimenter to return prior to receiving the gum. To assess the possibility that convergence and divergence are a function of the length of the delay period, in one condition, the experimenter stayed out of the room for 5 minutes and in the other condition, the experimenter stayed out of the room for 10 minutes. Upon the experimenter's return, children in both of the experimental groups were asked to "help" write the same ad as the children in the control group. Whereas boys and girls did not differ in the ads they wrote in the control condition and in the 5-minute delay condition, boys in the 10-minute delay condition were more likely to indicate that they liked *both* the gum and the M&M's the same or to provide only descriptive adjectives for the gum. Girls in the same 10-minute delay condition were more likely to make an explicit comparison between the gum and the M&M's and to indicate that gum was their favorite. These data suggest that one can prevent convergence from occurring via devaluation of the immediately available alternative or by bolstering of the deferred alternative. In the above study, such bolstering was engaged in via explicit comparison of the two items, making the preferred item seem much better than the other, dwelling on how much one likes it, and so forth. In contrast, one can facilitate convergence by bolstering the immediately available alternative or by devaluing the deferred alternative. In this study, the boys allowed the two items to converge in value, often indicating how good both the gum and the M&M's taste. The finding that boys and girls differed from each other in their means of coping is interesting and consistent with the general pattern of boys of these ages evidencing less self-control than girls (e.g., Silverman, 2003).

From this perspective, then, coping with delays largely involves engaging in convergence and divergence. Convergence involves a cognitive process by which choices are made to seem more similar to each other whereas divergence represents the opposite cognitive process by which choices are made less similar to each others. Both convergence and divergence can be used to convince oneself that an immediate choice is better than a later one, and to convince oneself that a delayed choice is better than an immediate one. Notice that both convergence and divergence processes were engaged in by children when trading objects with other children, as discussed in Chapter 11. It may well be, then, that trading objects and learning to make objects seem evaluatively different from each other is a critical precursor to the deployment of convergence and divergence in self-imposed delay contexts.

COPING WITH COTEMPORAL CHOICE

Above, convergence and divergence were discussed as critical to the ability to self-regulate in contexts that require one to await delayed rewards. These processes also play an important role in resolving intrapersonal preferential conflict in cotemporal choice. Such conflict arises in three different contexts: approach–approach conflict is when available choices are both positive, avoid–avoid conflict occurs when available choices are both negative, and approach–avoid conflict occurs when a single available choice has both positive and negative valence (Lewin, 1935). The critical factor in all these conflicts is that choices are between mutually exclusive options and consequently, there is psychological pressure on the individual to resolve the conflict as I elaborate below.

Approach–approach conflict arises when two different alternatives are equally attractive and the options are mutually exclusive, such that choosing one implies not choosing or rejecting the other. Imagine the proverbial donkey standing midway between two equally sized piles of straw. How does he move in the direction of one pile versus another pile? In the classic version of this dilemma, the donkey dies of hunger, because there is no way to resolve the conflict. The problem with this type of conflict is that the closer the two options are in valence to each other, the less important it is to make the best choice but the more difficult the choice itself. Minsky (1986) discusses this as Fredkin's paradox, "the more equally attractive two alternatives seem, the harder it can be to choose between them," irrespective of the importance of the actual choice.

In the human version of this conflict, something has to happen to make the individual psychologically closer to one of the two piles. This can occur if he hears laudatory comments about one pile of straw or derogatory comments about the other pile; it can also occur if he determines that one pile is fresher than the other. The individual can also come psychologically closer to one of the alternatives by engaging in evaluative changes, making one pile seem superior. This can be done by making the one pile better, making the other pile worse, or doing both simultaneously. Once the person has successfully made the two piles seem to diverge in their value to him, the conflict is resolved. Approach–approach conflicts, then, are resolved by engaging in divergence processes.

Avoid–avoid conflict is similar to approach–approach conflict in that two different alternatives are available, with both of them having negative valence. In colloquial terms, such a conflict is "out of the frying pan, into the fire." Obviously, no one ever wants to either step into the fire or to jump into the frying pan. For such conflict to be relevant, some outside force must restrain the person from leaving the situation in question (Lewin, 1935). Socialization agents often act as such restraining forces, compelling a child to do one of two things, both of which are anathema to him (e.g., take out the garbage or do the dishes). Clearly the child would prefer to do neither. But as long as socialization agents act as constraining forces, having such choice requires a resolution of the conflict. Similar to the situation that arose with approach–approach conflict, here as well the person needs to psychologically make the two alternatives diverge. This can be done by making one alternative better (e.g., taking out the garbage is better because it takes less time), making the other alternative worse (e.g., I should do the dishes – the garbage smells so bad!), or doing both. Unless the socialization agent changes the situation to eliminate choice, the child himself must engage in divergence processes in order to resolve the conflict.

In some cases of avoid–avoid conflict, the restraining factor is unchanging reality. For instance, an individual who is dentist – phobic but is suffering from excruciating dental pain is faced with an avoid–avoid conflict. The problem in such cases is that as one comes closer to the dental office, the fear of the dentist looms larger and the pain seems less excruciating, often resulting in ambivalent behavior (e.g., turning the car around to go back home, etc.). When the pain starts throbbing again, going to the dentist seems less scary than living with the pain and the conflict is reinstated. Unless the person is compelled by others, the only real solution is engaging in divergence processes that make one of the aversive alternatives so much more aversive than the other that the choice becomes crystal clear and the conflict is resolved.

The final type of conflict is approach–avoid conflict in which a single alternative has both positive and negative features that are more or less balanced. Such a conflict is evident when a child at an amusement park is both excited and terrified of getting on a specific ride. The critical feature of such conflict is that the avoidance gradient is generally greater than the approach gradient. This means that as we get closer to the alternative, the negative features seem to outweigh the positive ones, making us vacillate. Again, the way out of this conflict is by engaging in divergence processes that make the positive features outweigh the negative ones, or vice versa. In the amusement park example, the child could decide that the ride is too terrifying or that the potential enjoyment of riding it is sufficiently compelling to ride it nonetheless. In either case, unless the two valences are made to diverge, no decision will be made and the child will remain on the ground.

POSTDECISIONAL DISSONANCE

Postdecisional dissonance often emerges in resolving approach–approach conflicts. Specifically, every decision can be viewed as involving choices between alternatives that have both positive and negative aspects. In choosing what car to buy or college to attend, one car has more leg room, the other gets better mileage; one university is smaller, the other is in a better location. Dissonance theory does not address the issue of how one makes decisions between alternatives. In fact, Festinger claimed that there are no systematic changes in the evaluation of alternatives in the predecisional stage. But after making a choice between alternatives, the negative aspects of the chosen alternative and the positive aspects of the unchosen alternative loom larger, making us question the wisdom of our choice. Facing the future with our wisdom assailed and a lemon for a vehicle, for instance, is debilitating and undermines our belief in our own wisdom. To avoid this debilitating situation, we engage in divergence processes that serve to justify the choice we made. We do so by making the two choices diverge in their values, cognitively spreading them apart so as to make it seem that we had made the wiser choice. This can be done by devaluing the unchosen alternative, by bolstering the apparent value of the chosen alternative, or by doing both. In fact, in postdecisional dissonance research, individuals have been found to primarily *devalue* the unchosen alternative. Why would this be the case? They do so because they have less of a chance of having their decision proven wrong. Those aspects of the decision that are firmly grounded in reality (e.g., the car that doesn't start twice a week) are unlikely to be changed. As Festinger (1957) claimed, though, there are other means of reducing dissonance. One can add more consonant cognitions, change the importance of the decision, change one's perception of having had choice at the time, and so forth. Irrespective of which mode of dissonance reduction one selects, all the modes involve evaluative changes, changing one's cognitions as to the value of the alternatives as a means of coping.

Whereas Festinger discussed divergences that follow decision making, other theoreticians have argued that whenever a decision is made the decision maker always "seeks a greater divergence in attribute scores of alternatives because a small divergence renders decision making more difficult" (Zeleny, 1982). From this perspective, decision making requires that the alternatives be made to differ from each other. In line with this, both Montgomery (1983, 1994) and Svenson (1992; Salo & Svenson, 2001) contend that all decision making necessitates the use of convergence and divergence processes in which the subjective values of alternatives are cognitively transformed *prior* to decisions being made.

WORKING DURING DELAYS

Up to this point, the delays discussed all required passive waiting. But delays can involve a work requirement, fulfilment of which is prerequisite to the attainment of rewards. How do work-contingent rewards impact delay behavior? In one study that addressed this question, preschoolers were required to feed a toy Baby Bird with marbles until an experimenter returned. Children worked harder when the contingent reward was visible during the work period than when it was not visible (Patterson and Carter, 1979). In a similar study (Peake, Hebl, & Mischel, 2002) in which the same task (i.e., feeding the toy Baby Bird with marbles) was presented as a requirement for getting the preferred reward versus something fun that the child could engage in while waiting, the impact of reward visibility was opposite, with visible rewards leading to longer task engagement when the reward was contingent on "working" and leading to shorter task engagement when the fun activity was independent of the delay contingency. In a study (Karniol, Feldman, & Cohen, unpublished) in which the same card sorting task was presented either as *work* or as *play*, children younger than 6 years old all engaged in the activity for less time when rewards were visible than when they were absent; but children older than 6 years old, engaged in the task for less time when rewards were visible and the task was presented to them as *work*. These results indicate that children's ability to conceptualize the contingency and the "work" task may well play an important role.

An important issue that has not been examined is what happens when the contingency is self-imposed versus externally imposed and when it involves a work-contingency versus a temporal contingency. Specifically, as shown in Table 12.4, contingencies can be set up by others and they can involve a work-contingency versus a temporal contingency. The fact that not all aspects of these delay contexts have been examined in previous research limits our understanding of the dynamics of coping versus self-regulation.

Table 12.4.

	Externally-Imposed	Self-Imposed
Work Contingency	"Read one chapter before watching TV"	"I'll read one chapter before watching TV"
Temporal Contingency	"Read till the show comes on at 8 pm"	"I'll read till the show comes on at 8 pm"

APPLYING SELF-REGULATION: SAVING AND SPENDING

An important domain of self-regulation is that of spending and saving money. Research indicates that the majority of school children get money from their parents, often in the form of an allowance[4] (e.g., Webley, 2005), but also in birthday and holiday gifts (Fiates, Amboni, & Teixeira, 2006). Some children indicate that they work for at least part of their money, engaging in babysitting, lawn mowing, and other assorted summer jobs (e.g., Belk, Rice, & Harvey, 1985). In many cases, providing children with an allowance is viewed by parents as a training exercise for getting children to defer immediate purchases and to save their money over time. This attitude is expressed by the parents cited in Table 12.5. That is, parents are encouraging their children to see saving as something that they can control over time, with some parents explicitly stating their desire to inculcate long-term saving by providing an allowance (e.g., Barnet-Versat & Wolff, 2002; Furnham, 1999). Children come to understand this, as when a third grader refuses an offered penny in an ultimatum game, saying, "You can't buy anything with a penny. It's not going to do you a lot of good, unless you save up your pennies, which could take a very long time, because it takes 25 to equal a quarter" (Murnighan & Pillutla, 1995, p. 264).

In some instances, parents explicitly pit the possibility of spending money right away versus saving it for later (e.g., "if you spend the money right away, you may miss what you really want by not waiting. I'm trying to teach him to make his own choices," Bee-Gates, 2006, p. 29). Yet other parents do so with the hope that over time, children will forget the specific object wanted in the present and use the money more wisely in the future (e.g., the mother of a 7-year-old says, "I make him save purposely to make him wait, in the hopes that the thing he wants he'll go off before he's got his money," Newson & Newson, 1976, p. 241).

When parents are aware that large items are beyond the scope of children's savings, they may offer solutions that reflect this awareness, often proposing solutions that indicate parental willingness to chip in additional money (e.g., Newson & Newson, 1976; Ward et al, 1977). As one father explains,

> they see something in the shop they like, which costs a lot and well... we either buy it for them, for their birthday or Christmas or something,... (or) we will say, 'look, you save half of it and we'll put the other half towards it. (Sonuga-Barke and Webley, 1993, p. 77)

What do children actually do with their money? First, although children do spend part of their allowance, they also save part of it. A mother discusses her 7-year-old who hides his weekly allowance, indicating that when he is asked why he doesn't spend it, he responds, "I can't spend that. I'm saving that" (Newson & Newson, 1976, p. 239). Similarly, a school child explains "if I get 5 pounds for my birthday that's the money I put in the bank" (Sonuga-Barke & Webley, 1993, p. 56).

In fact, seventh graders indicated that they saved about 30 percent of their money (Belk, Rice, & Harvey, 1985). Fiates, Amboni, and Teixeira (2006) similarly found that about 30 percent of their Brazilian sample of 7- to 10-year-olds could be classified as savers, with many of those who were classified as savers indicating that they were doing so in order to purchase a larger item. On the other hand, Belk and his colleagues found that children who worked for their money saved more than those who received their money from gifts or from their allowance.

The trade-off between spending one's money versus saving it is evident in the words of an adolescent who says, "every time I decide to buy something, something in my head tells me that I might need the money later for something more important" (Autio, 2004). Similarly, a 12-year-old explains, "I get 5 pounds a month from my mum cos if I got say a bit each week, I'd just spend it all" (Sonuga-Barke & Webley, 1993, p. 58).

Saving money both in banks and piggybanks is an explicit strategy of self-regulation that parents encourage. In fact, there are apparently two different views of this strategy. One of these views putting money in the bank as serving to avoid constant temptation. A 9-year-old explains "I won't take it out of the bank as I don't want to be tempted" (Webley, 2005, p. 58). In the words of a 12-year-old, it's good to put money in the bank "so I don't spend it as well... if it was left over I wouldn't have any cos I would always be at the pictures of swimming or something" (p. 58). In fact, Brazilian children were often found to discuss bank accounts as preventing them from having ready access to spending money (Fiates, Amboni,

[4] There is a correlation between getting an allowance and parental SES, irrespective of the size of the allowance (e.g., Mortimer et al., 1994). Ward, Wackman, and Wartella (1977) found that although lower income children receive more spending money, children's actual long-term savings increases with social class. Newson and Newson (1976) also found that more working-class than middle-class children spend all their allowance within the week and do not save it.

Table 12.5.

	Age	Source
M: "for things that they want, they are supposed to save their allowance"	Preschool	Sears, Maccoby, & Levin (1957, p. 321)
M is asked to hypothetically deal with C who brought flowers from neighbor's garden M: "I'd tell him that if he wanted to bring me a present he could save up all his pennies and buy one"	Preschool	Cook-Gumperz (1973, p. 242)
C: "Would you buy me one . . . I wanna get one" M: "Save up your allowance"	Preschool	Hall (CHILDES)
M: "I tell him he needs to save his money so he can purchase (what) he wants"	School	Isler, Popper, & Ward (1987, p. 165)
Talking of action figures C: "I got it with my own money . . . from my allowance" F: "That's right. How much allowance do you get? C: "Fifty cents a week" F asks the cost of the toy F: "So how many weeks' allowance is that? Can you figure that out?" C: "7 weeks"	5;9 years	MacWhinney (CHILDES)

& Teixeira, 2006). In the other strategy, putting money in the bank serves to make one forget that the money is there, "cos you can forget what's there," allowing one to pursue long-term savings goals. In keeping with this view, a 9-year-old explains, "I'd try and save up and keep it in my money box and forget about it and once mum gives me some more money, put it in my moneybox and forget about it again" (Sonuga-Barke & Webley, 1993, p. 56).[5]

In line with this, Ainslie identifies four strategies that individuals can use to commit themselves to their preferred delayed choices. First, they can make it physically impossible for themselves to choose a future alternative that is different from the one chosen now by "tying oneself to the mast." For instance, if one puts a timed lock on the refrigerator when one is not hungry, this obviates the possibility of opening the fridge when one is hungry.[6] Putting money into a closed bond in which one is penalized for taking the money out parallels this when it comes to money. Second, one can manipulate one's attention so as to avoid facing those options that tempt him. Third, one can attempt to directly control one's impulses, for instance by guiding one's thoughts in directions that make the temptations less appealing. Finally, one can establish personal rules that turn individual choices into principles, making deviations from those rules "immoral." Of course, there are ways of avoiding temptation that combine many of these strategies. In this vein, the father of a 12-year-old recounts, "I told him he could work in the garage with me, we made a deal, that he could earn so much and then we'd go put the CD (player) on layaway so he wouldn't be tempted to spend the money" (Palan & Wilkes, 1997, p. 161). In this context, making a deal with one's parent may be equivalent to invoking a personal principle and putting the item on layaway may be like putting a lock on the refrigerator door. Although research has not examined the ramification of this conceptualization, the bottom line is that one can combine diverse means of self-regulation. How children learn to do so has not been empirically addressed.

AFFECTIVE REACTIONS TO COPING AND SELF-REGULATING

Recall that the distinction between coping and self-regulation drawn above centers on who imposes the delay, another person or oneself. In light of the distinction drawn here between coping and self-regulation, one important issue to address is whether these two contexts differ psychologically in other ways as well. Specifically, are the affective reactions associated with successful coping versus self-regulation equivalent? Lagatutta (2005) compared children's and adults' predictions regarding the affective reactions of children who abided with or transgressed rules that were dictated by an authority figure or were spontaneously recalled by self. Both children and adults predicted that rule abiders would feel good and transgressors would feel bad and the source of the rule (i.e., self or mother) did not impact the likelihood of attributing negative emotions to characters who engaged in rule transgression. Transgressors were generally expected to experience

[5] Notice that this strategy is quite similar to one espoused by children who suggest that delayed rewards should be covered up because "it would seem like there were no marshmallows in this room" (Mischel & Mischel, 1983, p. 613).

[6] Of course, one can do the same for another person when this other person needs to lose weight. In this vein, a parent can avoid buying candies to prevent their children from getting cavities, the difference being that children do not have such second-order preferences.

negative emotions. Importantly, both children and adults attributed more positive emotions to characters who abided by the rules after recalling the rules themselves than after hearing the rules voiced by their mother. But why should rule abiders be expected to feel better when they abide by rules they themselves recall? Again, as in the case of strong threats, the mother's statement of the rules constitutes a salient external justification for rule following and leads one to discount possible internal motivation to comply. When rule abidance follows self-reminded rule generation, internal motivation to abide by the rules constitutes a more compelling explanation for having done so. This pattern of findings underlines the fact that even preschoolers apply the *discounting principle* (cf., Karniol & Ross, 1976, 1977; Lepper, 1981), with salient external causes undermining attributions to internal motivational sources of behavior. This parallels children's actual pattern of affective reactions in complying; children express more positive affect when obeying rules of their own accord than when doing so in response to parental control attempts (e.g., Kochanska, 2002).

Following self-generated rules, though, is difficult. Ainslie (2001) contends that one means of self-regulating is by avoiding those contexts in which one would have to invoke rules to deter oneself from engaging in those behaviors that are the focus of the rules. For instance, in trying to control a bad habit one can impose a physical distance between oneself and the opportunity to engage in a bad habit. Drinkers can avoid the streets where their favorite bars are located. This strategy is evident in the words of a 9-year-old who explains how he keeps healthy, saying, "sometimes I go out with my brother shopping, and get some vegetable or something. And I don't go to Woolworth's to get some sweets" (Mayall, 2002, p. 43). He deliberately avoids going into the store that holds the prospect of being tempted, acknowledging that being faced with the "forbidden sweets" would strain his ability to use self-imposed rules to guide his behavior. Research has not addressed children's strategies in such contexts.

RECURRING SELF-REGULATION

In the contexts discussed above, individuals faced situations of a nonrecurring nature, with a single choice point and a singular choice. But many contexts in which individuals need to self-regulate have multiple choice points (e.g., a dieter may skip lunch and have a high caloric dinner or snack; an individual who wants to reduce his caffeine intake may skip the 10 AM coffee but not the 2 PM one) and multiple choices (e.g., dinner menus are replete with high caloric items, most menus have both decaffeinated and caffeinated coffees). Moreover, in the majority of cases, no single choice point eliminates the possibility of actually attaining the more distant preference. A single piece of cake and a one time bout of drunkenness are not predictive of whether or not one can attain one's long-term preference of being thin or remaining sober. Missing one or two lectures of a course may not be critical to one's eventual grade. It is by *repeatedly* choosing the same immediately available alternatives that the distant outcome becomes an unavoidable result of previous choices. This is the case when resistance to temptation contexts involves desserts and other high caloric items; it is also the case when addictions are involved. In other words, unless one gets off the road on which desserts are staples, one cannot avoid reaching the overweight destination. The important aspect of this is that although at some point, one enters a highway with only one exit, there are many choice points along the road. The question then is to what extent one can see the last exit station at earlier points along the road. The same type of problem arises in contexts in which omission rather than commission of a given behavior is involved. For instance, I've often fought with my children about not brushing their teeth when they are really tired. After all, just one night of not brushing one's teeth is not disastrous to one's dental hygiene. However, repeated nights of not brushing one's teeth ensure the long-term outcome of rotting teeth and gingivitis. The issue of recurrent self-regulation has not been empirically examined.

However, in some recurrent contexts, self-perceptions may be more critical than self-control skills. Specifically, there are many instances in which individuals engage in certain behaviors because their prior behaviors have engendered changes in the way they perceive themselves. How we behave on one occasion may have an impact on the way we see ourselves, and because we now see ourselves in these new terms, our subsequent behavior is aligned with these new ways of seeing ourselves. This type of change in self-perception underlies the phenomenon known as "foot in the door." The door to door salesman knows this trick well. He asks you to "to spare him 5 minutes of your time." Once you've agreed and he sets his foot inside your door, he knows he has you. Chances are you will agree to buy from him whatever he wants you to buy. How does he do this? Research (Freedman & Fraser, 1966) suggests that once you agree to let the salesman in, you change your perception of yourself to see yourself as "a cooperative and kind individual." Individuals then strive to maintain their new self-image (cf., Bénabou & Tirole, 2006). Being a kind and cooperative individual means that you should consider his suggestions seriously – more seriously than if you saw yourself as an uncooperative individual. The trick then is to get you to see yourself in a particular way that serves the salesman's needs. Analogous to the above technique is the technique known as "door in the face," which similarly builds on changes in one's self-perceptions and which was discussed in the chapter on Manipulating Others.

Economists Bénabou & Tirole (2004) have presented a similar model of the role of self-perceptions in guiding self-regulation. They suggest that there are *internal* commitment mechanisms, or *personal rules*, that individuals adopt that allow them to commit to diets, monthly savings, and to jogging twice a week. In the model, people use their lapses of self-control to draw inferences about themselves, for example, "If I cannot turn down this drink, I might as well admit that I am still a hopeless alcoholic." Their model builds on two processes: (1) *time inconsistent preferences* and (2) *imperfect recall*, suggesting that the motives that lead up to choices are no longer accessible with complete accuracy or reliability once the choices are made. Loewenstein and Schkade (1999) refer to this as the "hot–cold empathy gap," with people failing to recall their cravings at the point at which their cravings have been satisfied. Moreover, recollections tend to be *self-serving*: people tend to remember their successes more than their failures (Ross, 1989), and as Bandura (e.g., 1999) has shown in the realm of morality, they tend to reframe their actions so as to see themselves as more beneficent than they actually are. The fear of *creating future precedents*, then, serves as an incentive that helps counter the bias toward immediate gratification. In the Bénabou and Tirole model, the degree of self-control increases as confidence in one's own willpower increases. Self-control is greater when such contexts are recurring, and externally imposed controls and incentives reduce individuals' trust in themselves as to their ability to self-control, thus inhibiting the emergence of autonomous self-regulation. These processes are mediated by causal attributions as to why one did, or did not, engage in self-regulation in a given context. The fear of appearing to be unable to engage in self-regulation drives individuals to treat each decision point as a test of their willpower, with the possibility of both beneficially or harmfully, guiding self-regulation. If each decision is seen as a possible precedent for one's future decisions, lapses in self-regulation today raise the prospect of similar lapses in the future. Implicit in the model is the preference to engage in self-regulation, a second-order preference that evaluates ongoing behavior as aligned, or misaligned with that preference. In this view, individuals can develop strategies of record keeping that facilitate more accurate appraisals of one's self-control abilities and are self-reinforcing to the extent that they actually reflect the engagement of self-regulation. Bénabou and Tirole's model builds on other findings indicating that people impose self-controls on their spending, earmarke monies for specific uses, and are loathe to change such earmarking.

A similar view is espoused by Kanfer, Stifter, & Morris (1981). They contend that the psychological processes involved in self-regulation are similar to those in altruism, with the central difference being the beneficiary of the outcome, not the process. To elaborate, in self-regulation, the person gives up rewards or tolerates an aversive situation to attain long-term positive benefits for himself. In altruism, a person forfeits a reward or endures an aversive situation to benefit another person. To test this equivalence, Kanfer and colleagues conducted two studies, in the first of which children 3.5 to 6 years old had to "work" at a sorting task that earned rewards that could be exchanged for toys. Stopping in the middle of the task would result in their getting nothing. After earning their rewards, the children were given a choice of continuing to work to benefit an anonymous child, an experimenter-selected classmate, a friend, themselves, or both a friend and themselves. As a control, they were given the choice of continuing to work at the sorting task without any promise of rewards. The alternative activity they could engage in was to play and children could either work or play for up to 15 minutes. Children who were not offered continued rewards for working or those whose work would benefit an anonymous child or an experimenter-selected classmate did not generally choose to continue working on the sorting task. In contrast, those whose work would benefit a friend, themselves, or both self and the friend, tended to continue working and did so during much of the allotted 15-minute period. Hence, children were willing to work to benefit a friend and to give up their play time for this benefit. This study underlines the sacrificial nature of friendship as perceived by children, even at these young ages.

Kanfer and his colleagues further suggest that sacrifice is much easier when the temptation to opt out of the delay period is removed as opposed to when there are continued opportunities to reverse the original decision and one can decide to terminate the delay at a later point in time. To examine what happens when there are continued opportunities to change one's mind, Kanfer and colleagues conducted a study, which required children to turn a crank to earn tokens that again could be exchanged for toys. After doing so, children were given an ongoing choice of continuing to turn the crank to earn rewards for an anonymous child, a friend, or for themselves, with the option of stopping and playing with other toys. The twist in this study was that they were instructed to continually ask themselves, "Do I want to turn the handle for another child/friend/myself or do I want to stop and play with the toys?" They were also told that they could provide one of two possible answers to this question, "Yes, I want to turn the handle" or "I want to play with the fun toys" and that they could stop turning the crank at any point in time. Framing the response in terms of wanting to play, led children to work more for their own benefit than for the benefit of others. Interestingly, research with adults using a different research paradigm has demonstrated the same pattern, with a focus on self's thoughts and feelings reducing helping and a focus on the thoughts and feelings of the needy other person increasing helping (Thompson, Cowan, & Rosenhan, 1980).

Thompson, Barresi, and Moore (1997) similarly argue that self-regulation and altruism have the same underpinnings. They consider the critical process to be imagining a non-current state of affairs, with the first of these concerning one's own future and the second, another person's future. From this perspective, altruism (i.e., concern for others) and prudence (i.e., concern for oneself) are the two pillars of organized social behavior, with the former requiring consideration of others' future preferences and prudence requiring consideration of one's own future preferences. Thompson and colleagues suggest that it is by using one's imagination that one can consider states of affairs that are different from those currently experienced, be they one's own or another person's. In this light, Jencks (1990) also argues that the mechanisms that make us take account of our own future self are much the same as those that make us take account of others. He suggests that "we empathize with the person we will later become and anticipate how he or she will feel if we choose a given course of action" (p. 55); from this perspective, imagining ourselves being poor and old leads us to engage in behaviors that are similar to those we engage in when we think of others being poor and old – we save for ourselves and we donate to others.

The ability to imagine noncurrent mental states of self or other as distinct from current experience allows one to implement behavior designed to bring about or prevent those future circumstances. But moreover, the imagined state of affairs needs to motivationally override current preferences. Imagining other people's or one's own future self induces empathy and empathy guides altruistic behavior. To test this conceptualization, Thompson, Barresi, and Moore (1997) presented 3- to 5-year-olds with a series of choices for which the rewards were stickers. Two kinds of choices were used: (1) a self-concerned choice in which children could choose between one immediate or two delayed stickers, and (2) an other-concerned choice in which children could choose between stickers for themselves only or for themselves and a teen confederate. To impose a cost on other-concern, they were also given choices in which they would get fewer stickers when they shared stickers than when they did not (e.g., two for self versus one for self and one for the other). To assess the impact of time, children were given choices between immediate rewards and delayed ones so that behaving altruistically imposed a temporal cost on self. First, 3-year-olds opted for smaller immediate rewards and 5-year-olds opted to for larger delayed rewards when the choice was self-concerned. When other-concerned choices did not require a temporal delay, 3-year-olds were as likely as 5-year-olds to opt to share with others but this was not the case when delay was involved. In addition, children who tended to share stickers in the future also tended to delay their own gratification, opting for larger, delayed rewards. In yet another study (Moore, Barresi, and Thompson, 1998), theory of mind performance in 4-year-olds was significantly correlated with the tendency to share in delay situations. Children who did well on theory of mind tasks tended to choose to share stickers with another child, even if it meant not being able to have the sticker now. In a longitudinal study in which preschoolers were assessed for prudence, altruism, and Theory of Mind but were also given a test of general intelligence (the Peabody Picture Vocabulary Test – PPVT), the correlation between performance on the theory of mind tasks and delayed sharing was not significant among younger children when general intelligence score was controlled, but was independent of general intelligence in the older children. The pattern of these data suggests that one needs to distinguish the representational abilities that underlie one's ability to self-regulate and to engage in altruistic behavior from the motivational underpinnings of the tendency to do so.

EMOTIONAL SELF-REGULATION

Societies have implicit rules relating to how emotions are to be expressed. In this context, there are societal rules about how long one can allow a child to cry. Guided by these rules, mothers invoke strategies that attempt to calm down an upset child, often using distraction to do so. Watson-Gegeo and Gegeo (1986) document that among the Kwará'ae, "distracting routines," techniques that serve to refocus the child's attention on something of interest (a bird, airplane, a passerby, a missing parent or sibling) are widely used to stop infants from fussing and crying. Such strategies are viewed as facilitating the child's detachment from the emotions being experienced, focusing his attention outside of himself, preferably on something social. In Tzeltal society, infants are also generally distracted by socialization agents when they are upset, at times being moved to alternative locations (Brown, 2002). Western mothers seem to use analogous distraction strategies in emotional contexts. A mother who is trying to get her preschooler to stop crying says, "You wanna go outdoors? You can go outside an' swing" (Wilson, Cameron, & Whipple, 1997). But mothers themselves may provide distractions, often involving toys in doing so. When children are upset mothers of Western children tend to use toys and activities as distracters, for example, "We'd play a game and he'd soon forget" (Cook-Gumperz, 1973, p. 248).

Eating can also be used as a distraction in dealing with upset children. Shutting children up with food rewards is also prevalent, for example, "supposing I was waiting for a bus somewhere and he was screaming his head off and I had in my pocket a plain biscuit I would give it to him to shut him up" (Charles & Kerr, 1988, p. 103). After sand goes into child's eye, teacher asks, "were they sore? Are they still sore now? Oh, you poor old thing. Do you think if you had a piece of apple, it would make them feel better?" (Peak, 1991, p. 202). Karen, at 31;4, relates that a child hit her at day care. When she is asked who hit her, she names the child and adds, "And I cried and Tova made me a bag (of goodies)."[7] In these instances, the adult offered children food and sweets as a means of distracting them.

Societies also have emotion display rules (Hochschild, 1979) that are conveyed to children during socialization. Individuals also need to control their emotions, often because society does not tolerate their expression (e.g., anger) and at other times because they do not wish to express them publicly (e.g., fear, crying). For instance, discussing anger, a 12-year-old girl says,

[7] Hebrew: "Ve-anni tivki ve-Tova assta li sakit."

You have to control it. I'm pretty good at that sometimes . . . . I just do it because I don't want to lose my friends, so I just control it . . . . I'll be mad at somebody; I'll want to say something . . . but I don't. I hold it back" Brown, 1998, p. 67.

When she is asked what would happen if she didn't control her anger, she says, "They'd probably be very very mad, and I want to stay friends with them so I don't say it" (ibid). As another girl explains, "Like you want to be careful not to get too angry or show them that you're angry or you'll totally lose a friend" (ibid, p. 68).

Socialization teaches children that crying also needs to be regulated. A mother talks to her preschooler about crying, saying,

'You hurt yourself and you cried and that's good to cry when you hurt yourself but you only cried for a little while and then you climbed back on your bike,' further explaining that when he was a little boy he would have acted otherwise, 'You would have run back to Mummy, crying really loudly, shouting, and you didn't do that, you acted like a big boy.' (Cloran, 1989, p. 119)

In fact, children openly discuss their younger crying self as opposed to their more mature, noncrying self. This is expressed by a girl of 4;9 who explains, "That's a good thing I won't cry when someone left me alone . . . well, when I was little I always cried when someone left me alone" (Garvey, CHILDES). In a similar fashion, children discuss their nonfearful current self as opposed to their earlier fearful self. Thus, a 4-year-old boy says to a peer, "When I was a little smaller, about this small, I was up high and I was so scared but now I'm so big that I'm not scared anymore"; she answers him, "I'm not scared either . . . . We're not going to be scared anymore" (Gottman, 1986b, p. 165). Of course, one does not know what these children actually felt when they were younger, but as 3- and 4-year-olds reflecting on themselves in the past, these statements reflect their emotional past as it could have been from the point of the view of their current emotional self.

Seeing oneself as a mature child who does not cry or express fear may well be the outcome of social message that public displays of emotion need to be curtailed as one gets older. As the song announces, "big girls don't cry" – but then, neither do boys. Children should not cry in public, despite being in pain (e.g., "Once I fell off my bike and it hurt bad but I didn't cry," Saarni, 1985, p. 199). Even children who are in the hospital for medical procedures need to regulate their emotions. In line with this, a child discusses being in the emergency room to get stitches for a cut and says, "I almost cried, but I didn't" (Engel, 1995, p. 194).

How do parental socialization practices convey these messages to children? Reminiscence talk, especially mothers' use of emotion language, has been found to predict both preschoolers' emotion understanding and their affective competence (e.g., Brown & Dunn, 1996; Denham, Zoller, & Couchoud, 1994; Fivush, 1993). Welch-Ross (1997) found that mother–child reminiscence contributed to theory of mind understanding in children, most likely because in such conversations, mothers clarified the thoughts, feelings, and motives of others, including themselves. In such conversations with their children, mothers elaborate the causal role that emotions and cognitions have in guiding human action and inaction, both alone and with others, laying the groundwork for children's understanding of the social world. On the other hand, while it is clear that parental strategies of emotion socialization are important, the data are not conclusive as to how parental socialization practices impact children's ability to self-regulate their emotions (Eisenberg, Cumberland, & Spinrad, 1998). Moreover, parental emotional socialization strategies appear to be associated with different outcomes in different societies (e.g., Cole & Dennis, 1998), suggesting that they work within a larger constellation of parental and social practices that have not yet been determined.

Gross (1998) has presented a process model of emotion regulation that differentiates regulatory processes undertaken before an emotion is generated, *antecedent-focused*, from those regulatory processes that occur after an emotion is generated, *response-focused*. Antecedent-focused strategies include: *situation selection* (avoid certain situation), *situation modification* (change aspects of the situation when in it), *attention deployment* (focus attention on certain aspects of the situation rather than others), and *cognitive change* (alter the meanings associated with certain aspects of the situation). Even young children evidence some antecedent-focused, self-regulatory strategies, as shown in Table 12.6.

According to Gross, response-focused strategies include altering the expression, experience, or physiology of an emotional response after it is experienced. Younger children do not appear to spontaneously evidence response-focused strategies whereas older children do appear to do so. For instance, a 12-year-old says that when she is angry, "I just go for a bike ride because I love riding my bike. Or I just go to my room and listen to my radio" (Brown, 1998, p. 66). In this example, the child substitutes an activity that she knows to be associated with positive affect. In the same context, another child says, "I'm just kind of doing other things and thinking other things and it just kind of goes away" (Brown, 1998, p. 101). A 12-year-old girl says that when she's angry "usually I can blow if off by reading. Reading fiction helps a lot . . . . " (ibid). In explaining how he copes with his anger at a friend, a 14-year-old explains, "Sometimes you got to get away for a while. Calm down a bit so you won't be so angry" (Selman, 1980, p. 110).

Why don't younger children evidence such strategies? They may not recognize these as strategies when parents use them or they may only gradually learn that such strategies are helpful in coping with negative affective experiences. For instance, a girl of 12 who moved to England when she was 9 years old explained that when she was sad, her mother "used to find things for me to do when I was feeling like that. Sometimes she would make cakes and I would help. Sometimes we got the bus and

Table 12.6.

	Age	Source
C: "I scared of the shark. Close my eyes"	28 mos.	Bretherton, Fritz, Zahn-Waxler, & Ridgeway (1986)
C: "Crash . . . . no watch" M: "You don't have to watch it sweetheart especially not if it upsets you"	30 mos.	Cameron-Faulkner, Lieven, & Theakston (2007)
C is scared of listening to a monster record C: "I'm not listening to that anymore. Not till I'm six – no way"	Preschool	Segal & Adcock (1981, p. 100)
T is getting ready to read a new book C: "Is there a part I won't like?" C asks teacher not to read a potentially sad page C leaves the room before page is read	Preschool	Paley (1990, p. 109)
T is getting ready to read "Goldilocks and the Three Bears" C: (whining) "I don't want to listen"	Preschool	Paley (1990, p. 157)
C tells of being scared by a character on TV C: "I didn't watch it and then left the TV without turning it off since I got so much frightened"	4;11 years	Ervin-Tripp & Kuntay (1997)
C: tells of scary movie on TV C: "I deliberately went to bed so I didn't see that bit"	15 years	Buckingham (1996, p. 144)

went shopping" (Knowles & Sixsmith, 1996, p. 129). Such experiences may teach children that "taking one's mind off it" is a successful strategy and that this can be done by engaging in alternate activities. As an 8-year-old who has learned this lesson indicates, "When you're busy, you don't have to think" (Singer, 1993, p. 8).

To get at some of these processes, Band and Weisz (1988) asked 6-, 9-, and 12-year-olds to recall a variety of stressful episodes, for instance, separation from a friend caused by moving to a different class or school, going for a medical injection, and being accidentally hurt. Children were asked to describe the incident, report on their thoughts and feelings, and to specify what they did to cope and how it helped them. Strategies were classified as reflecting *primary* or *secondary* control.[8] Classified as primary control strategies were: (1) *direct problem solving* (e. g., studying to improve one's grades, telling others to stop teasing, putting a band-aid on a cut); (2) *instrumental crying* (i.e., crying to get others to help); (3) *instrumental aggression* (e. g., beating up an annoying peer); and (4) *context avoidance* (e. g., staying away from kids who fight or tease). Five strategies were classified as secondary control: (1) eliciting social/spiritual support (e.g., telling others as a means of venting, praying), (2) emotional crying, (3) cathartic aggression (e.g., kicking a wall); (4) cognitive avoidance (e.g., watching TV to help forget about it – what I call self-distraction; and (5) pure cognition (e.g., daydreaming, convincing oneself that it wasn't such a bad grade – what I call *mind play*).

[8] Although Band and Weisz (1988) also identified a category they called *relinquishing control*, the latter responses were not analyzed because they represented less than 5 percent of all responses.

The results showed that the younger children used primary control strategies more than the older ones; concomitantly, the younger children used fewer secondary control strategies, either alone or in combination with primary control. Additionally, focusing on those strategies that are directed inward, to change our inner world, cognitive avoidance – which reflects the use of self-distraction – was the most commonly used, accounting for 44 percent of the responses for the medical context, for instance. Children reported that they coped by thinking happy thoughts to distract themselves from the pain of "getting a shot," for instance. Finally, pure cognition – which reflects *mind play* – was rather infrequent and did not differ significantly by age, ranging from 0 to 15 percent across children and contexts.

Similarly, in a study on surgical pain, children all reported using self-distraction, with the most common means of self-distraction involving reading, watching TV, and playing games. For example, a 10-year-old boy explained,

> I have read Donald Duck comics. This helps me to forget the pain. I can also get my thoughts elsewhere by playing Nintendo games. When I concentrate on playing I don't have much time to think about anything else. (Pölkki, Pietilä, & Vehviläinen-Julkunen, 2003)

AFFECTIVE CONTROL VIA MINIMIZATION

Minimization is a strategy of making events and outcomes appear to be less serious than they are first deemed to be. Taylor (1991) suggests that when facing a negative stimulus, people typically first mobilize to deal with it and then

Table 12.7.

	Age	Source
Experienced Outcomes		
C is upset, can't find piece of puzzle M helps him look for it M: "Never mind, Jeremy, we can do it as it is." C: "Gone, gone" M: "It doesn't matter. Look, Jeremy"	1;9	Urwin (1984, p. 313)
C talks of being scared in the pool M: "It's really nothing to be scared about in the pool. Daddy was there, and you've got a big floater"	Preschool	Wang (2001, p. 700)
C is sad after book is read to her M: "Come on it's just a book"	4 years	Gottman et al. (1987, p. 52)
C is upset, peer annoyed him at school M: "But Jason it's not worth it to get up upset or pay attention to him.... just ignore him ok?"	12 years	Ochs & Capps (2001, p. 282)
Self-Produced Outcomes		
C: "Ah! I step on (something)" F: "Don't worry about that. That's okay"	27 mos.	Warren, CHILDES
C spills coke, appears worried F tells her to cheer up M: "That's ok we'll get you some more"	Preschool	Pontecorvo, Fasulo, & Sterponi (2001, p. 349)
C breaks notebook divider M: "nothing to worry about. Just put some tape.... All right. Let's go"	8 years	Xu & Corno (1998, p. 413)
C's team lost a game F: "I know you lost, but that's okay"	Unknown	Kremer-Sadlik & Kim (2007, p. 41)

minimize its captivation of their attention. Negative stimuli initially produce an increase in the gathering of diagnostic information, a systematic elaboration of material, and a decreased use of heuristics. Once negative stimuli recede, they are "minimized." They are recalled less than positive events and are interpreted in ways that reduce their importance for the person. Such minimization is adaptive because it may help to minimize negative events to make sense of experience.

Minimization can be used *proactively* to try to alter the affective impact of anticipated events (e.g., failed exams, medical treatments), but it can also be used *retroactively* in the attempt to devalue the importance or affective impact of an outcome. Parents appear to use minimization strategically, both proactively and retroactively. Proactively, parents may invoke minimization strategically to shape the child's anticipated reactions to emotionally charged events. For instance, when a child says "I'm only getting a C on my report card in math," the answer is, "Yeh, but that's a passing grade" (Pomerantz, 1984, p. 87). Similarly, explaining what a peer does when a teen gets a bad grade, the teen speaker says: "don't worry about it. And she goes, there are other tests that you can do . . . that's just one bad grade" (Rawlins, 1992, p. 97). The expected aversiveness of the outcome has been minimized to make the outcome much more positive, as part of a series of grades that are all passing grades. Similarly, Denham (1998) talks about parents "redefining" affective experiences for children in a preemptive fashion, such as telling children that an expected injection will only pinch, rather than hurt. In more mundane contexts, when an 18-month-old is interpreted as being afraid of a dog, her mother says, "He won't hurt you. Don't worry" (Carew, 1976, p. 95).

Using minimization retroactively, parents can attempt to alter the relative importance or affective impact of an outcome that the child has interpreted in negative terms. When an 18-month-old child complains, apparently about a stick breaking, her mother says, "That's okay; shall we find another stick? Come on, let's see if we can find another" (Carew, 1976, p. 95). Minimization is especially prevalent in the context of children's emotional reactions, both to outcomes they experienced and to outcomes of their own making, as shown in Table 12.7.

In the above cases, the event is transformed by the parent *after* it occurs, minimizing its affective consequences as a means of having the child cope better with it. In this context, mothers sometimes explicitly remark on their role as requiring them to "make light of it or to make less light of it at that period, to shape his feelings towards sadness or towards anything" (Gottman et al., 1997, p. 53).

Interestingly, parents and teachers also retroactively minimize children's reaction to pain. When a child of 4;11 runs into the house and cries, "I fallen over," her mother responds, "Never mind, it's only a scratch" (Fletcher, CHILDES). A mother tells her preschool son "You had a needle, didn't you? . . . It didn't hurt you, did it?"

Table 12.8.

	Age	Source
C1 is upset at drawing over the lines C2: "it doesn't matter if you do go over the lines"	4;9 years	McTear (1985, p. 198)
C1 is upset C2: "Don't worry about that; it'll come off. It was on before and it came off before. Just don't worry about it, 'cause I'm not worried"	Preschool	Gottman (1986, p. 97)
C1 missed ball at third base, C2: "Don't worry, everyone makes mistakes"	12 years	Fine (1987, p. 88)

(Cloran, 1989, p. 120), attempting to retroactively minimize the pain the child experienced. A preschool teacher does the same, saying, "Have you hurt yourself? Never mind – rub it – it only stings for a minute" (Gardner & Cass, 1965, p. 67). In fact, Gardner and Cass (1965) found that preschool teachers often reacted to children's falling with statements like "that's not very bad" and "don't worry."

Although they discuss this strategy as "comfort and encouragement in the face of frustration and difficulty," Gerson and Schnabl-Brandes (1990) found minimization in the behavior of metaplot in Israeli kibbutzim who said things like: "Never mind that you've spilled a bit of paint on the floor, it's easy to clean up" and "Don't be so upset – this kind of puzzle is hard to put together the first time" (p. 40). Such verbalizations accounted for 7.7 percent of the behavior of metaplot toward children in Israeli kibbutzim. Urban Israeli preschool teachers also use minimization retroactively, trying to calm down upset children (e.g., "Never mind, Uri, that your clay table fell apart. You will learn how to make it firmer next time" Krown, 1974, p. 44). Sports coaches do the same. After missing a ball during a baseball game, a child is told by his coach, "That's all right, that's all right" (Fine, 1987, p. 32). Similarly, a baseball coach tells a 9-year-old who struck out, "Don't throw your bat. Even Mickey Mantle strikes out" (Fine, 1987 p. 69), thereby minimizing the aversiveness of this outcome.

Children appear to use minimization as a supportive strategy in their interactions with peers, as shown in Table 12.8.

These children are minimizing the impact of the troubling event as a means of making the other child feel better in contexts in which the other child is assumed by them to be experiencing negative affect. Older children appear to use minimization as a means of attempting to mediate between parties in conflict, similarly evidencing sensitivity to the conflicted parties' being upset over the issues in question. For instance, when Israeli children were in a state of *brogez*, third parties attempted to mediate, saying, "It's all nonsense. Not worth fighting because of this" (p. 472), and "For such a reason it is worth to quarrel?"[9] (Katriel, 1985, p. 480), minimizing the importance of the conflict as a means of calming down their peers.

Do children evidence minimization themselves? Older children do appear to do so in an anticipatory fashion, especially to cope with pain and medical treatments (e.g., Powers, 1999). Children 8 to 10 years old who were undergoing dental treatment said things like "it isn't really something to get upset about" (Curry & Russ, 1985, p. 214). A child who has to have dental anaesthesia explains, "I thought that the shot was just squirting water and it wasn't going into my skin" (Curry & Russ, 1985, p. 64), minimizing the pain of the injection to make it more tolerable. Similarly, a 12-year-old recounted, "Then I have kept on thinking that I am not hurting, there is no pain, there is no pain" (Pölkki, Pietilä, & Vehviläinen-Julkunen, 2003). In yet another context, a 10-year-old who said she was sad she couldn't take her dog on vacation and heard a computer Sage tell a story about a friend whom he'll never see again, responded, "You didn't see your friend ever again, but I will see my dog when we come back from vacation. I guess that is not that bad" (Bers & Cassell, 2000, p. 77), minimizing the aversiveness of the anticipated experience.

Younger children appear to deploy minimization *retroactively* (e.g., "it wasn't really that serious," Curry & Russ, 1985, p. 214), but it is not clear just how prevalent its use is. Orren, at 36;24, uses retroactive minimization when I commented that something he was building came apart and he answered, "It's not awful – I can build it again."[10] A girl of 3;10 referred to a broken tape recorder, saying "look it is broken. Never mind. That's nothing" (Toivainen, 1980, p. 35). In talking of her mother working late, a 15-year-old says, "but it doesn't matter. I'm still up then anyway" (Lewis et al, 1996, p. 59). Although they label it *distancing*, Causey and Dubow (1992) include retroactive minimization in their coping scale for children, for example, "make believe nothing happened."

What is the impact of minimization and does it enhance children's ability to cope with aversive contexts? Lukenheimer, Shields, and Cortina (2007) refer to minimization as *emotion–dismissing verbalizations* and suggest

[9] Hebrew; "Oof, hakol shtuyot. Lo shave' lariv biglal ze" and "Bishvil siba kazot kedai lariv?"

[10] Hebrew: "Ze lo nora – ani yaxol livnot at ze mexadash."

that they undermine children's emotion regulation. My own research suggests that they may be right. In a recent study (Karniol, unpublished) with fourth graders, children completed a self-control questionnaire (Rosenbaum & Ronen, 1992) and then responded in writing to a questionnaire regarding six settings that could occasion socialization practices by mothers (Cook-Gumperz, 1973).[11] Each setting was described as "Let's say . . . (this happened) . . . what would your mother say or do?" with three of the settings being potentially emotionally charged. Responses were coded as reflecting *minimization* (i.e., making outcomes seem less serious, "it's o.k.," "nothing happened"), *augmentation* (i.e., making outcomes seem more serious, "that's really awful"), *anger* (i.e., shouting, talking of being angry), and *miscellaneous*. Minimization serves to dampen the child's likely affective response and augmenting and anger serve to strengthen the child's likely affective response. Whereas boys and girls did not differ in their reports of mothers' use of minimization, they did differ in their reports of mothers' use of augmenting. Girls anticipated their mothers to augment more than boys. Interestingly, whereas augmenting was not expected to be differentially used by mothers of children high and low in affective control strategies, minimization was anticipated to be used more by mothers of children who were *low* in cognitive control strategies, and especially those who were also *high* in affective control strategies. This suggests that use of minimization by mothers may prevent children from attempting to control their own affective reactions.

To examine this possibility, my students and I (Karniol, Bohar, & Biran, unpublished) conducted a study with high school students, half of whom were in an ongoing year-long premilitary training course that demanded their presence on at least 85 percent of the sessions, thus providing a naturalistic group high in self-control. Each participant named a classmate who was not in the premilitary training course as a control group lower in self-control. Participants again completed two questionnaires, a self-control questionnaire for adolescents (Rosenbaum & Ronen, 1992 and a socialization questionnaire (modelled after Cook-Gumperz, 1973) that described five contexts in which the participant was to imagine himself and his parents' reactions. Two of the contexts described events that happened "when you were small": spilling wine on a table cloth during a family celebration and an accident in which a missed ball breaks the mother's favorite vase. Three of the settings referred to events that could happen currently: having a car accident in one's parents' car while out with friends, losing a soccer game by one point, and not getting the leading role in a school play. Adolescents indicated what their parents would say in response to the events described. First, those in the premilitary training course were in fact higher in self-control than their peers who were not in the course. The difference was particularly marked in the self-control of their emotions rather than their cognitions. Parental use of minimization was associated with *enhanced* self-control in the group not enrolled in the premilitary training course but with *reduced* self-control in the group in the premilitary training course. It would seem, then, that for adolescents high in self-control, parental use of minimization undermines their own attempts at affective control. It may well be that minimization serves to help young children cope with negative affect but that as children become able to deploy minimization themselves, its further use by parents is detrimental, because it prevents children from using minimization themselves. In fact, when parental strategies were differentiated by whether they referred to current or past events, only minimization for past events was found to be relevant for adolescents' current self-control.

[11] "Empirical attempts to relate parenting behaviors directly to children's self-control outcomes are often methodologically flawed. To focus on one problem, parents are often asked to report on both their own and children's behavior, and obtained correlations may well reflect shared method variance (cf., Hay & Forrest, 2006).

AFFECTIVE CONTROL VIA THOUGHT SUPPRESSION AND SUBSTITUTION

Parents also attempt to engender in their children thought suppression, telling the child not to think about the specified thought, as illustrated in Table 12.9.

But parents may combine thought suppression with thought substitution, suggesting replacing a specific thought with alternative, and, perhaps, less-disturbing thoughts as a means of influencing the child's current actions or emotional reactions. The provision of alternative thoughts can take several different forms. First, it can explicitly offer other things for the child to think about as a means of cheering him up. To quote one mother, "I do try to make him forget about it, cheer him up" (Gottman et al., 1997, p. 56). In fact, children often say that their parents and friends are able to cheer them up by providing substitute thoughts, as the following teens explain in Table 12.10.

In trying to cheer children up, parents often provide children with their own childhood memories. For instance, a mother says,

> what I try to do is remember my own childhood and I'll try to share that with him, you know, 'I remember when I felt that way . . . and I'll relate the story which usually helps cheers him up.' (Gottman et al, 1997, p. 60)

Peers also appear to use this strategy, as reported by a 16-year-old who said that when he broke up with a girlfriend, his friend "started telling me about all the girls he's gone with . . . and it just, I didn't feel as bad anymore" (Rawlins, 1992, p. 90). A 10-year-old girl explains this explicitly, saying,

> When people communicate they take an experience they had or think of something that the other person might want to hear, a same sort of problem, something familiar or similar, and they just tell it. (Bers & Cassell, 2000, p. 77)

Table 12.9.

	Age	Source
C: "See-saw" M: "Never mind about the see-saw, you can't go on the see-saw because it's too muddy" C: "see-saw" M: "Never mind about the see-saw. Come on"	18 mos.	Paprotté (1985, p. 445)
M explains what she would say to crying C M: "She can't expect to be invited to every party. She should just put it out of her mind"	Preschool	Applegate et al. (1985)
T: "You're not going to be playing today, so don't even think about it"	Kindergarten	Mody (2005, p. 65)
C asks T about the demise of the sun T: "We're not going to worry about the sun right now... we won't worry about that"	Sixth grade	Walther (1978, cited in Lindfors, 1999, p. 201)

Second, substitute thoughts can serve as distractions per se. In this vein, a mother talks of convincing her 5-year-old child to go to school, saying, "I'd chat to him and tell how the teacher would miss him.... I'd talk to him like that as he went to school to take his mind off it" (Cook-Gumperz, 1973, p. 245). Parents can also engender thought substitution by shifting current topics of conversation. For instance, a mother who is asked how she deals with a child who doesn't want to go to preschool, says, "I give him something to talk about, to distract him on the way to school" (Cook-Gumperz, 1973, p. 58). Similarly, a father who wants to distract a child who expressed a desire to have a bath says, "Mummy told me you were a good girl on the bus when you went to dancing school" (Clancy, Akatsuka, & Strauss, 1997, p. 57). In this context, almost any topic of conversation can provide a distraction. A mother explains about her 3-year-old, saying,

> he doesn't want to be put on his back to have his diaper changed, unless you're telling him a real good story or... got him totally distracted, so that he's not thinking about what you're doing. (Harkness, Super, & Keefer, 1992, p. 166)

Interestingly, children do appear to spontaneously engage in thought suppression. A school child whose mother wants to talk of her teacher's wake is told by her daughter, "I don't want to talk about sad parts" (Ochs & Capps, 2001, p. 274). Newson and Newson (1976) cite a mother who talks of her 7-year-old, saying, "if anything upsets her or she doesn't want it, she'll shut it off – she has this attitude, "Oh well, never mind, Mum, don't let's talk about it" (p. 42). An adolescent cancer patient relates: "I deal by trying not to think about it" (Kameny & Bearison, 2002, p. 162). But as quoted in the beginning of this chapter, children indicate that it is difficult to suppress thoughts. In fact, in line with this, Wegner's (1994) research on ironic processes has shown that attempts to suppress unwanted thoughts tend to backfire, becoming more prevalent after attempts to suppress them. As Elster (1983) contends, instructions not to think about something forbidden are often self-defeating.

A more successful strategy is to engage in thought suppression along with thought substitution (e.g., Hertel & Calcaterra, 2005). Children appear to acquire the understanding that engaging in thought substitution with thought suppression can facilitate their coping. When a 12-year-old is asked what he does when he wants to resist temptation, says, "I would close my eyes and think of all different things" (Sonuga-Barke & Webley, 1993, p. 40). Children appear to use these jointly in dealing with pain.

Table 12.10.

	Age	Source
Referring to Parents		
C: "Like when I fail a test or did something wrong, and then when I feel sad and stuff... He would just cheer me up"	Teen	Jeffries (2004, p. 119)
Referring to Friends		
C: "(Friends) "give you some optimistic viewpoints to help yourself"	17 years	
C: "When you're down about something or you're having a problem, they help cheer you up"	15 years	Rawlins (1992, p. 84)

For instance, in a study on postoperative pain, a child reported thinking about getting home as a means of combating the pain (Pölkki, Pietilä, & Vehviläinen-Julkunen, 2003); another child who was undergoing dental treatment said, "I tried to only think good thoughts, like that I would get a prize" (Curry & Russ, 1985, p. 64). An adolescent explains: "I just tried to get my mind off of the pain and think about something else, like going to Disneyland" (Stevens, 1989, p. 166). Orren, at 13 years old, got dehydrated and needed an intravenous line to be placed in his arm. The paramedic told him "Do you like watermelon? Have you ever eaten watermelon with ice cream? Think about eating watermelon with ice cream on a summer day."

Thought substitution can also serve to demotivate. For instance, a third grader explained that he would get himself to do homework by thinking he would get punished if he didn't finish it (Xu & Corno, 1998, p. 426). Social contexts can also engender thought suppression and thought substitution, as evident when an 11-year-old who had been excluded with her peer from a game of softball, eventually tells her peer, "Let's go do something. Let's not let this bug us. Let's go play on the teeter totter" (Goodwin, 2007, p. 363). Whereas above, children found physical means of self-distraction to get their minds off disturbing contexts, children also learn to do so psychologically, engaging mind play, to which I now turn in Chapter 13.

13 Mind Play: Applying Transformational Thought

A first grader explains what happens when he hurts his sister: 'So like, if they say, 'Now go to your room and think about what you've done,' I just go to my room and I think about something else. I use *my* will power not to think about what they want me to think about. Then I just look real sad when I come out and they think I was in there thinking about my dumb sister.'

(Carlisle, 1994, p. 212)

Rubin's son, Elihu, $2^1/_2$ years old, is crying. An older preschooler tries to appease him. 'Want some pizza?' He replies, 'No, I don't want pizza.' She offers: 'Want to ride my bicycle?' but he rejects the offer: "No, I don't want to ride on a bicycle." She tries again: "Want to see a dragon?" he stops crying and eagerly says 'Yes.'

(Rubin, 1980, p. 120)

In Chapter 10, I discussed transformational thought as occurring on three planes: (1) the *temporal plane*, allowing us to transform the present into the past and the realistic future; (2) the *imaginal plane*, transporting us into the imaginal future and into fictional worlds; and (3) the *plane of the mental*, imbuing others with covert psychological processes. As indicated in Chapter 10, being able to transform the *here-and-now* on the temporal, the imaginal, and the mental planes allows for the possibility of deploying transformations *strategically*, changing how we and others think and feel. In this chapter, I will show how transformational thought is deployed to cope psychologically with aversive situations, to garner motivational forces when they appear to be ebbing, to manipulate others' construals for one's own benefit as well as for these others' benefit, and to help others cope with aversive contexts or to "pep" them up. In contrast to pretend play in which imaginative worlds are insulated and do not have an impact on the postpretend world, the transformations conducted in mind play may have long-term implications for how individuals both behave and react psychologically (cf., Gendler, 2006). This chapter deals with the phenomenon of mind play as manifest in children and as fostered and induced in children by others. I discuss the various ways in which parents try to induce mind play in children for children's benefit and how children use mind play themselves and the strategies they use to attempt to induce mind play in others. The kinds of mind play discussed include: playing with context, playing with time, playing with pretense, and playing with perspective. The commonality between these strategies is their dependence on cognitive transformations along the three planes of transformation discussed earlier.

SELF-INDUCED MIND PLAY

What happens when we need to resign ourselves to the fact that our preferences are unattainable? We need to have psychological means of living with this knowledge. *Self-induced* mind play is the exertion of attempts to control our own psychological processes, attempting to suppress or stimulate thoughts and feelings and to engender different construals of current representations. Such attempts are often precipitated by having second-order preferences about the kinds of thoughts and feelings we want to have or that we think *should* have (cf., Wegner & Pennebaker, 1993). We don't want to think of the unattainability of the prom queen or of our lost wallet for the rest of our lives. That is, when we prefer not to think a given thought or experience a given emotion, we can attempt to influence that thought or emotion in various ways, using mind play to cope with *intrapersonal* preferential conflict. It is used to psychologically "alter our environment to suit our desires" (Gentner & Loewenstein, 2002) but also, to alter our desires to suit our environment. To quote Elster (1983), "our minds play all sorts of tricks on us, and *we on them*" (p. 111, emphasis added). The tricks we play on our own minds involve cognitive transformations of representations that are already in place, representations that for whatever reason, we prefer not to have. So we adopt a wide variety of strategies that transform how we think or feel in order to think or feel differently.

STRATEGIC INDUCTION OF MIND PLAY

As captured in the quotes at the beginning of this chapter, others often try to strategically induce mind play in us. March (1978) calls strategies for the induction of mind play "the engineering of choice," representing attempts to induce in others a reinterpretation of experience and behavior that "will facilitate posterior elaboration of a new understanding of personal preferences" (p. 601). In other words, individuals use these strategies to engender cognitive transformations in those whose preferences they want to influence. Doing so builds on the understanding of others as having preferences and psychological reactions to the attainment and thwarting of their preferences. March's primary concern is with strategic attempts to induce mind play *egoistically*. When we know that others' preferences are different than our own and that this may lead them to impede the pursuit of our preferences, we can attempt to induce mind play in these others because we want them to facilitate or at least not impede the pursuit of our preferences.

But as evident in the second epigraph of this chapter, strategic attempts to induce mind play can reflect different goals. First, they can be *prosocial*, undertaken as supportive actions aimed at helping others cope with their own dispreferred thoughts and feelings. The individual who strategically attempts to induce supportive mind play uses his knowledge of others' preferences, knowing that these others do not want to have a given thought or feeling, and he uses his knowledge of the kind of mind play that can be deployed to attempt to induce cognitive transformations in others to make them think and feel differently. As Burleson and Goldsmith (1998) note, "all any helper can do is assist the distressed other in developing new appraisals"; this is done by providing the other with possible cognitive transformations that facilitate such alternative construals. In fact, Sluzki (1992) sees all therapies as inducing transformations in patients' narratives, primarily but not limited to, transformations along the dimensions of time, space, and causality.

Strategic attempts to induce mind play can also be undertaken when one wants others to adopt one's *external* preferences (e.g., wanting my child not to drink or smoke). In such cases, it is the inducing agent who wants or does not want target others to have a particular construal. In using mind play to get others to adopt one's external preferences, the inducing individual attempts to align target others' preferences with his own external preferences, doing so by making others' preferences seem negative, by making one's own preferences seem positive, or by changing the context in which the issue in question is conceptualized.

Cross-cutting parental attempts to channel, temporize, and restrict their children's preferences, then, are strategies aimed at inducing mind play in children, strategies by which parents intentionally attempt to influence how children construe objects and activities, doing so by attempting to transform these objects and activities into cognitively different ones. Interestingly, over the preschool years at least, parents do not seem to vary the use of such strategies according to their children's age (e.g., Stansbury & Sigman, 2000). Yet, as I discuss later in this chapter, children start to use mind play to change their own construals, but they also attempt to induce mind play in their interaction with others, attempting to influence how these others construe objects and contexts.

PLAYING ALONG WITH THE MIND PLAY GAME

In attempting to induce mind play in others, these others have to be willing to play along with "the mind play game." One cannot elicit mental states in another person by issuing a command (Elster, 1983). As those who attempt to induce hypnosis know, not everyone is hypnotizable. In fact, children are more hypnotizable than adults (Plotnick, Payne, & O'Grady, 1991), and children who are prone to involvement in fantasy, whether in play or in daydreaming, are more likely to be hypnotizable (LeBaron, Zeltzer, & Fanurik, 1988). The need to "play along" with the attempt to induce mind play is captured well in the words of the first grader who was also cited above, in explaining to his peers how his parents deal with his hitting his younger sister. He says,

> Like they punish. Like going to my room and thinking about it, which is weird because you can't make another person's mind think about something *unless they want to* (emphasis added).... You don't understand about will power. Because like, your mother can't give you *your* willpower. (Carlisle, 1994, p. 212, original emphasis)

He resists his parents' mind play induction because he interprets such attempts in terms of a conflict of wills, his will versus that of his parents. In the same vein, a girl who had been diagnosed as paranoid schizophrenic complains about her mother, "She's always trying to teach me how to use my mind. You can't tell a person how to use their mind against their will" (Laing & Esterson, 1990, p. 44).[1] Yet both parents and children do attempt to get others to engage in mind play, generally assuming that the targets of their mind play induction will interpret such attempts as benign and will play along with the game. The game involves the induction of transformations of thought along the temporal plane, the imaginal plane, and the plane of the mental, as elaborated below.

PLAYING WITH CONTEXT

In playing with context, sometimes referred to as *reframing*, individuals provide new meaning to contexts and try to get others to construe experiences and events differently than they would otherwise. Watzlawick, Weakland, and Fisch explain that one changes

> the conceptual and/or emotional setting or viewpoint in relation to which a situation is experienced and to place it in another frame which fits the 'facts' of the same concrete situation equally well or even better, and thereby changes

[1] Interestingly, research suggests that in schizophrenogenic families, parents tend to engage in attempts at mind play induction more often than in normal families (e.g., Doane et al., 1982, 1987).

its entire meaning. (Watzlawick, Weakland, & Fisch, 1974, p. 95)

When playing with context concerns the inducing agent's external preferences, parents attempt both to encourage and to discourage behavior. In both cases, though, the goal is to get children to adopt parental external preferences. As to playing with context to encourage behavior, a mother explains,

You've got to take some notice of their likes and dislikes – if he doesn't want to do something I can usually persuade him . . . *by making it sound a nice thing to do*, I don't just tell him . . . . (Newson & Newson, 1976, p. 497, emphasis added)

There are several points that are relevant here. First, the mother plays with context when her external preferences are in conflict with those of her child. Second, she sees herself as able to cognitively transform her child's construals in the attempt to align his preferences with those. Third, she does so in an *anticipatory* manner as a means of getting him to engage in the behavior, providing a different way of thinking about a relevant event or outcome toward which the child was not positively inclined. To give a more explicit example of this, a preschooler refuses to go shopping with his parents. His father says, "Okay, you stay home and Mama and I will go out and eat chocolate ice cream." The child quickly chimed in that he wants to go too and the father feigned surprise, asking, "You do? You've changed your mind?" (Segal & Adcock, 1981, p. 156). By playing with context and making the shopping trip into an outing to eat chocolate ice cream, the father was able to get the child to join them. In this vein, to get a depressed 12-year-old to interact more with his peers, the therapeutic intervention included telling the child that withdrawing to his room was a good way "to get in touch with his sad feelings." He appeared confused and started to spend all his free time with his peers (Jessee et al., 1982, p. 316). An 11-year-old, who failed to learn to read, started reading when the context of reading was presented as looking at a map or an encyclopedia to prove his therapist wrong (Haley, 1973).

One can play with context by putting analogies and metaphors to work in an anticipatory fashion. For instance, mothers who want their children to clean the tell-tales sign of drinking milk from their face tell their toddlers and preschoolers "You have a nice moustache" (Tulviste, 2003) and that their mouth looks like "Santa with mustache" (Kobayashi, 2001, p. 126). These mothers, then, are guided by the assumption that they can change the context in which the child views having a dirty face. To do so, they searched for a different context, one that would lead children to clean off their faces without being explicitly told to do so. Mothers used their assumptions about their children's preferences, assumptions as to their children not wanting to have a moustache; if the mothers' assumptions are valid and their children would prefer not to embody this resemblance, then the children should eventually wipe off the tell-tale signs of milk. In this vein as well, the mother of a 21-month-old suggests, "Shall we get the scissors and give the plant a haircut?" (Hart & Risley, 1999, p. 107), presenting the mundane task of trimming the plant as a joint enterprise and as a potentially exciting endeavor in which plants, like children, may be expected to fight against such an imposition.

Of course, playing with context in an anticipatory fashion can be used to do the opposite, to dissuade a child from engaging in an activity the mother prefers the child *not* engage in. For instance, when a preschooler tries to put on a coat that's too small for her, her mother says, "it's too small, you don't like it anyway . . . it's for a baby. You're a little baby in that" (Walkerdine & Lucey, 1989, p. 166). Suggesting the event be recontextualized as "putting on baby clothes" served to dissuade the child from engaging in the behavior. Even more explicit about this undertaking, a mother who anticipated that her child would not be accepted to an elite private school, says, "I talked her out of it. I did a real marketing job on it. I just kept telling her it's just not the right place for her" (Chin, 2000, p. 155).

One can also play with context retroactively. When a Japanese 2-year-old says he is afraid of the doctor, his mother replies, "He isn't scary. He was kind, wasn't he?" (Clancy, 1999, p. 1415); the doctor's behavior is recontextualized by the mother in terms of kindness in her attempt to reduce the child's fear. In this vein, a mother explains that "there"ll be a troll or something like that on children's TV. Then we try to say that there's nothing to be afraid of" (Aukrust, 2001b, p. 241). Here again, the mother recontextualized the child's experience retroactively to make the experience seem more benign than originally construed. Gottman et al. (1997) recorded a mother who in dealing with her preschool daughter's sadness indicated that she would

try to bring things into her mind that make her feel better . . . . Like when she had a nightmare . . . . I said, 'Well, change the nightmare around so it wouldn't be a bad nightmare or a sad thing. It would be something better.' So she had a nightmare that the cat that she's going to get ate the goldfish that she just got. And then she turned and she said, 'The goldfish ate the cat.' So that changed it so she wasn't sad anymore. (Gottman, Katz, & Hooven, 1997, p. 322)

By encouraging her daughter to recontextualize the nightmare, which the daughter did by making the victim into the victimizer, the valence of the nightmare changed from scary to funny. Importantly, though, the daughter was unable to recontextualize her nightmare spontaneously and needed her mother's help in doing so. Therapeutic settings often are used for retroactive recontextualization. For instance, diabetic children were asked by a therapist: "what are some of the good things about having diabetes?" Although at first the children were stymied by this question, they subsequently recontextualized and came up with responses like "we don't get as many cavities because we don't eat candy," "diabetic summer camp and the canoe rides they have," and "the special things my mother fixes me to eat" (Fosson & deQuan, 1984, p. 44).

Playing with context, then, can serve as an important motivational resource, altering children's preferences and perhaps even their preference structure, making them more, or less, willing to engage in the behavior in question. However, children may not always be willing to play with context as suggested by others. A 3-year-old, who refused to get off a slide, finally came off it when the teacher recontextualized getting off the slide as a jumping game, asking: "Can you jump all the way to where I am?" (Bergin & Bergin, 1999, p. 201). In contrast, when a mother tries to get her preschooler to leave the playground and the child repeatedly refuses, the mother recontextualized, saying "I'll race you," and started counting to three. The child refused, saying "I don't want to" and the mother was forced to abandon the attempt (Gordon, 2008, p. 333).

Above, playing with context was induced by others retroactively and served to recontextualize unpleasant past experiences. But if the past is not pleasant to contemplate, we may want to transform the past ourselves to be able to live with it better. We may not want to live with our failures, our social disgraces, and our wrong choices. In each case, we may want to change the way we construe these events to achieve two ends: (1) to maintain our view of ourselves as wise, sane, and beneficent and (2) to harness our past in the service of our future. Achieving these two ends simultaneously is often difficult and we end up paying a price, either in terms of our ability to maintain a positive self-image or in terms of our ability to use the lessons of the past to pave our way into the future. We recontextualize the past when an outcome or behavior we engaged in is inconsistent with our preference for how it should have been: we failed a test, didn't get a job we applied for, or hurt a friend. We can cope by changing our attributions for what happened. We can blame others for our failures and we can make unnecessary assumptions about the way others would have behaved in the same context, thereby making our behavior and outcomes seem more normative. Moreover, we can rewrite the past (Ross, 1989), changing our perceptions of prior events to make them more consistent with the present, usually to make ourselves seem more rational and more beneficent.

Although psychologists have generally studied attribution processes by asking *why* questions, individuals often make spontaneous attributions for outcomes and behaviors that were unexpected or surprising to them (Wong & Weiner, 1981). We don't need to account to ourselves why we ate a delicious meal but we do need to account for why we ate a bad meal. Children make attributions for their own unexpected behavior and outcomes at very early ages. Karen, at 34;24, explains why she didn't get to the potty on time, saying, "I was looking for the magnets and didn't go to the potty – that's why it escaped from me."[2] She felt the need to account for her "accident" because she and her parents expected her not to have them any more. Parents similarly make attributions in such cases. When his 5-year-old son has a toileting accident and fears being spanked, the father says, "No . . . that happens when it gets cold . . . . But that's alright. It's sometimes you have to rush fast" (Hall, CHILDES).

The power of self-attributions is given special emphasis in Bandura's (1990, 1999, 2002) model of how individuals free themselves from experiencing guilt after doing harm to others. Specifically, Bandura contends that in the exercise of moral agency, people refrain from behaving in ways that violate their own moral standards, attempting to avoid their own self-censure. To do so, individuals monitor their conduct and the conditions under which it occurs, judge their actions in relation to their moral standards, and regulate their actions, being guided by the consequences they anticipate applying to themselves when they transgress. But individuals have a variety of strategies available that they can use to selectively disengage their moral self from transgressive or harmful behavior. Bandura suggests that there are four psychological means by which individuals can selectively disengage their moral agency: changing their perceptions of (1) the locus of the behavior, (2) the agent of the action, (3) the consequences of their behavior, and finally, (4) the victim of their actions. Individuals can change their perceptions of the locus of the behavior by construing their harmful behavior into righteous conduct. They can do so by using moral or ideological justifications, by using euphemistic language that portrays their behavior as benign, and by engaging in palliative comparison that renders their behavior more benevolent than some worse alternatives. Next, individuals can change their perceptions of their agentic role in the behavior in question, doing so by displacing responsibility to their superiors, by diffusing responsibility among all those involved in the decision or the behavior in question, and by taking solace in their degree of anonymity when such anonymity is offered to them by virtue of their role (e.g., Kelman & Hamilton, 1989; Zimbardo, 1995). As for the consequences of their actions, individuals can change their perceptions of such consequences, either minimizing their harmful consequences or even magnifying their potential positive consequences. Finally, individuals can change their perceptions of their victims, blaming them for being victims and dehumanizing them, divesting them of their human qualities. As a consequence of disengagement, behavior that would otherwise be viewed as immoral may come to be seen as morally justified.

Because attributions can be invoked retroactively to recontextualize events and outcomes, they can become powerful tools in the hands of psychologists who use attributional retraining (e.g., Wilson & Linville, 1982; Dweck, 2006). The guiding assumption of such retraining is that patterns of causal explanations for past success and failure, for instance, can have deleterious effects on current functioning. *Attributional retraining* procedures attempt to

[2] Hebrew: "ani xipasti at hamagnetim velo halaxti lasir – ze lama ze barax li."

shift people's explanations of previous failures from stable, uncontrollable causes (e.g., "I am not good at math") to unstable, controllable causes (e.g., "I don't work hard enough at math") and thereby to alter their related emotions, goals, and subsequent behavior. New attributions that serve to recontextualize past outcomes can serve as motivational resources, both in enhancing and decreasing motivation.

Once a situation is recontextualized, the individual can not only think about it differently but can also feel and behave differently. To illustrate, Peak (1991) relates an experience she had as an observer in a Japanese preschool. When she was repeatedly hit and kicked by one of the children, getting welts and wondering why none of the teachers was taking any notice of his aggressive behavior, she finally decided to broach the subject with the head teacher. Before she managed to do so, the teacher delivered a sermon to her about how different children have different means of trying to make friends, recontextualizing his aggressive behavior as "invitations to play" and implying that she herself had been rude to ignore these invitations, an interpretation that later proved to be correct.

Sports coaches engage in similar types of recontextualization. In trying to motivate his team to play better, a baseball coach recontextualizes the outcome of a game, saying, "It's not the umpire's fault or because it's too low or too high or any of that. It's nobody else's fault. It's your own fault, because you're not trying" (Turman, 2005, p. 66). Of course, as discussed above, playing with context can be undertaken when the target of induction does not want to play along.

Playing with context often takes the form of self-talk in which individuals convince *themselves* of the virtue of engaging in specific behaviors. A father talks about fatherhood, explaining,

> you just change your perspective on fun. Fun now to me is taking him places, taking him to the store, and, you know, taking him to the park and swinging him on the swing, instead of me being on the golf course with my buddies.... So I'm still having fun, it's just now it's a different kind of fun. (Palkovitz, 2002, p. 81)

In this instance, the father recontextualizes his own preferences. A mother expresses this explicitly in referring to her children's board games, explaining, "I made myself enjoy it and now I really do enjoy it. Because I thought it's no good unless I enjoy it, so I forced myself to enjoy the games" (Ribbens, 1994, p. 62).

Playing with context can also be used to *dissuade* oneself from one's preferences. A 6-year-old explains that when he tries to take sweets without permission, he gets sent up to his bedroom and then, when his mother calls him, he says, "I say that I don't want it any more" (Sonuga-Barke & Webley, 1993, p. 39). The child recontextualizes to align his preferences with those of his mother, convincing himself that he no longer wants the forbidden sweets. Referring to how to cope with waiting for a delayed food reward, an 11-year-old explains, "I would say' I'm stuffed. Then I would not want the marshmallows" (Mischel & Mischel, 1983, p. 609).

Playing with context to dissuade oneself is evident when children try to cope with being rejected by peers. A 3-year-old asks to play with two other girls. When she is rejected, she says, "I don't want to play anyway" (Pitcher & Schultz, 1983, p. 67). When two 4-year-olds are trying to decide on their respective roles in playing house, after one announces that she is the mommy, the other one asks what her role will be, insisting that she be the daddy. When this role is denied her, she answers, "Don't play house. I don't want to play house" (Gottman, 1986a, p. 96). As well, a preschooler rejects an offer to play saying, "I don't want to. I don't like to play house" (Garvey, 1993, p. 256). These children are all exhibiting what has come to be known as the *sour grapes* phenomenon. In Oesop's fable, the fox maneuvers his way into a vineyard and eats grapes till he is bursting. But then when he wants to leave the vineyard, he cannot get through the fence because he has become too fat to get through it. He stays in the vineyard until he loses the weight, and once he gets through the fence, he says to himself that the grapes were sour anyway. Elster (1983) defines the sour grapes phenomenon as the "adaptation of one's preferences to what is seen as possible" (p. 22), and hence it is viewed by Elster as an adaptive means of preference management. A child of 13;9 years captures the essence of this process, saying,

> you brainwash yourself into not liking it.... You keep telling yourself, I don't want to play this... you could keep on saying that and it would just take over your brain... and you just wouldn't want to play anymore (Selman, 1980, p. 104)

Doing so may not be functional in the long run, though and therapeutic interventions in such cases focus on how the child could get others to let him play, or to get them to compromise, and so forth (e.g., Spivack & Shure, 1974; Shure & Spivack, 1978).

Children also play with context strategically in their interactions with other children. For instance, in doll play, a child who assigns the less-favorable tasks to other children, tells a peer "You get to put the chapstick on her" (Shuy & Griffin, 1981, p. 281); she makes it seem that the task her peer was assigned is a reward, a more desirable task than it actually is. Kyratzis and Guo (2001) call these "mollifying statements" or "frame shifts," which highlight what the other is getting rather than on the alternative tasks that are being withheld from the child.

More interesting from my perspective are occasions when children strategically recontextualize objects and contexts in ways that make their requests to others appear more legitimate, especially after their requests are refused. This is often done by offering others transformations that imbue the object of contention with qualities that it did not have previously. Some illustrative examples are shown in Table 13.1.

Table 13.1.

	Age	Source
C1 wants her sister's new fancy socks Sister refuses Request is repeated and rejected again C1: "I need them for the birthday party" C2 agrees and they enact a birthday party scene	30 mos.	Haight & Miller (1993)
C1 wants toy pickle C2 has C2 refuses C1: "You have to make a pickle salad. So I'll put it in the pot. . . . I really need to make a pickle salad"	Preschool	Sheldon (1990)
C1 wants bus C2 has C1: "Give me the wee bus – it's going in the car wash, in the bus wash"	4 years	McTear (1985, p. 196)

By imaginally transforming the object or context so that the other child would likewise construe it in these new terms, the above children were able to bypass the other child's reluctance to comply with their requests. But note that in doing so, these children have essentially reconstituted the preferential conflict between themselves and the other child as an issue of how objects should be *construed* – as party socks, salad pickles, and dirty buses – rather than as a conflict regarding the need to share objects of contention.

The reconstrual of a conflict about sharing into a conflict about how objects and contexts are to be construed is also evident when children recontextualize objects and contexts as being jointly owned or as involving a joint enterprise, as shown in Table 13.2.

In these cases, children recontextualized the situation to get other children to accede to their preferences; because their requests are legitimate in the context of a joint enterprise, they were heeded. The strategic nature of such recontextualization is evident when a child changes her statement in midstream, to make her action seem to subserve both her own preferences and those of her peer, for example, "That's where it, where *we* want it" (de Hart, 1996, emphasis added). Again, though, reality has not changed; it is children's construals of the objects and contexts in questions that have been imaginally transformed.

More sophisticated still is what I call *mediational* recontextualization in which objects and contexts are presented in ways that explicitly serve to imaginally integrate the preferences of the parties in conflict, as shown in Table 13.3.

The above all reflect attempts to induce imaginal transformations that can serve to recontextualize the issue. Children thereby eliminated preferential conflict that would have disrupted their joint play. Importantly, both they and their peers were willing to transcend the *here-and-now* to perform the imaginal transformations together, because both of their preferences were satisfied in the course of doing so.

Above, children engaged play with context to transform it to make their appeals to others more legitimate. But children can also play with context in ways that focus on the other child's self-construal rather than on construal of the object of conflict. In this vein, a preschooler who refused to put on a hat was told by her age-mate, "You'll be the prettiest at the ball" (Malloy & McMurray, 1996, p. 193). That is, the child attempted to circumvent her peer's refusal by changing how the other child construed herself when interacting with the object in question.

Attempts to change others' self-construals can be used for the opposite end, to get others to relinquish an object of conflict. A sophisticated 3-year-old who wanted another child's play wig, and whose request for the wig was denied, said to the refusing child, "You know, Karen, I almost didn't recognize you with that ugly wig on," at which point Karen promptly took off the wig (Hazen, Black, & Fleming-Johnson, 1984, p. 31). In the same vein, a child of 3;11 years who wants her peer's crown tells her, "I should have the crown. Because it matches my dress. It looks ugly on you!" (Dunn, 1996, p. 192). This ploy that worked in her favor and she got the crown. One should note, though, that these attempts at playing with context work because the child who is inducing them takes these peers' preferences into account; the above children used their own preferences as a starting point for playing with context but the recontextualization worked because the other child's preferences, both positive and negative ones, were incorporated in the mind play induction.

Deception is a variant on playing with context. Guided by their understanding of others' preferences, children use deception to foster changes in others' construals of current contexts to their advantage, at first doing so to avert possible disciplinary consequences. A child of 23;9 gives a candy wrapper to her mother. When her mother says "You've eaten it," the toddler looks at the recording researcher, smirks, and says, "Lady ate it" (Howe, 1981, p. 85). The child took her mother's statement to mean that she should not have eaten the candy and found a deceptive

Table 13.2.

	Age	Source
Objects as Jointly Owned		
C2 is on car C1: "Pretend this was my car" C2 refuses C1: "Pretend this was our car" C2 agrees C1: Can I drive our car?" C2 agrees, leaves car	Preschool	Garvey (1975)
C1 wants phone "to call police" C2 refuses C1: "L, let's say this is our telephone, okay? Okay, L.? This will be ours" C2: "*okay*" C1: "Let's say I call the police now on our phone, okay?"	Preschool	Trawick-Smith (1992, p. 105)
C1 asks C2 to help him build a boat C2 refuses C1 repeats request, request is denied C1: "Let's say this is our boat and we'll build it together, okay?"	Preschool	Trawick-Smith (1992, p. 104)
Activities as Joint Enterprise		
C1 wants car C2 is driving C1: "I'll let you drive the car if you'll drive me to Grandmother's"	Preschool	Garvey (1984, p. 145)
Two girls want to check doll's ear C2 claims doll only needs one shot C1: "Well, let's pretend it's another day that we have to look in her ears together"	Preschool	Sheldon (1997, p. 236)

Table 13.3.

	Age	Source
Girls are building houses C1: "let's make a bridge"	4;6 years	
C2: "No, I don't wanna make a bridge" C1 insists C2: "No, a bridge house . . . . how about a bridge house"	4;1 years	Sheldon (1992, p. 109)
C1 wants to build a farm C2: "No, this is a museum where paintings are" C1 repeats her request that it be a farm C2: "Let's say it's a museum where farm animals can go. They can go to the museum, okay?"	Preschool	Trawick-Smith (1992, p. 107)
Male C1 wants to play superman Female C2 wants to play house Mutual shouting C1: "pretend this was Superman's house"	4 years	Gottman et al. (1997)
C1 wants a cardboard box to be a cave C2 wants to use the box to roll down a hill C2 suggests the box be a rolling cave	7 years	Trawick-Smith (1998, p. 242)

means of averting what she presumed to be a negative outcome. Similarly, a child of 22;21 who peed on the floor put her doll on the puddle and said about herself, "Debbie no dood it" (Church, 1966, p. 83). In blaming her doll, she assumed that her mother prefers that she not have toileting accidents, that her mother would want to chastise someone who did have a toileting accident, and by trying to avert this outcome, that her mother could be made to think that her doll was the culprit!

Deception can also be used in the attempt to promote more positive outcomes. For instance, a 26-month-old child who wanted to have a bath and was faced with an intransigent mother falsely indicated that she had a bowel movement in the hope that the mother would change her diaper and agree to give her a bath (Dunn, 1988). She used her knowledge of how her mother behaved in the past to attempt to initiate the same sequence of actions, assuming that her mother would follow through with the sequence despite the absence of the initiating event. These children were aware that they could induce others to have a different construal of the context by saying things and doing things that would lead to one interpretation – the one favored by the child. But to do so, these children had to imaginally recreate the sequence of events that could forestall disciplinary action on the mother's part in the first case and that would initiate favorable outcomes in the second case.

Children engage in deception in their interactions with peers as well. A preschooler whose persistent request to get a bike from a peer was refused, was told by the teacher not to fight over the bike. He subsequently walked over to the peer who refused to give over the bike and said, "Mrs. Shaw wants to talk to you – you've to go inside" (Sylva, Roy, & Painter, 1986, p. 78), which the other child did, leaving the bike prior to doing so. The deceptive child imaginally created a set of circumstances that would lead the other child to leave the bike and undertook to make these circumstances happen. Similarly, in a study in which second- and fourth-grade children had to act as pretend animals who needed to persuade other animals, they told the targets of their persuasion attempts that there was a fire in another part of the forest or that their favorite food was in a different location (Bisanz, 1982). That is, they imagined contexts in which other animals would willingly leave the location where they were at and would move to another location. Although the types of deception employed were not specified, Bragg, Ostrowski, and Finley (1973) found that deception was one of the major strategies used by 10-year-olds to persuade others to eat a cracker. Braginsky (1970) also found that among fifth graders who were to be rewarded with money for persuading other children to eat quinine-flavored (i.e., bitter) crackers, deception was the most common strategy deployed.

A very interesting example of deception occurs in somewhat older children in what Kochman (1972) refers to as *shucking,*

> speech behavior designed to work on the mind and emotions of the authority figure for the purpose of getting him to feel a certain way or give up something that will be to the other's advantage. (Kochman, 1972, p. 221)

Shucking is a means of talking one's way out of trouble, avoiding getting punished, and giving oneself a winning edge in dealing with authority figures. It differs from lying because it is like impromptu story-telling, being attuned to the needs and preferences of the individual being addressed. To illustrate the way shucking works, Kochman asked seventh graders to "talk their way out of trouble," given the following situations: "You're cursing at this old man and your mother comes walking down the stairs. She hears you." A shucking response would be, "I'd tell her that I was studying a scene in a school for a play" (ibid, p. 220). This response demonstrates an awareness of the impropriety of the action, awareness of the mother's potential anger, and an ability to use the imaginal plane to find a context under which such behavior would be deemed reasonable.

In the second situation, the child is asked "What if you were in a store and were stealing something and the manager caught you?" Shucking responses would be

> I would tell him that I was used to putting things in my pocket and then going to pay for them and show the cashier; I'd tell him that some of my friends were outside and they wanted some candy so I was goin to put it in my pocket to see if it would fit before I bought it. (Kochman, 1972, p. 220)

The above responses indicate awareness of the needs of the person being addressed and awareness of contexts under which the behavior could be considered "right." But the child's central task is to imagine contexts into which the event in question would fit without invoking others' wrath and spinning the inappropriate behavior seamlessly into it. Kochman found that adolescents were remarkably creative in providing shucking responses in such contexts, demonstrating an awareness of the types of transformations that others might well "buy into."

PLAYING WITH TIME

Parents and others can induce mind play in children by playing with time, using their ability to conduct thought transformations on the temporal plane to attempt to change the temporal framework in which events and outcomes are considered by children, as shown in Table 13.4.

When they play with time this way, adults reconstrue children's perceptions of negative events to reflect that events that happen in the here-and-now may be inconsequential in the larger, temporal frame of events in their life, orienting them toward the future rather than having them dwell on the past. Freud (1927) underlined the importance of doing so, saying, "(people) have to put themselves at a distance from it – the present, that is to say, must have become the past – before it can yield points of vantage

Table 13.4.

	Age	Source
C is upset, forgot book at friend's house M: "If we go and get it next time, things will be all right"	Preschool	Clancy, Akatsuka, & Strauss (1997, p. 56)
C is upset F: "Everything will be OK, when it's all over with. Later you'll be OK"	Preschool	Gottman, Katz, & Hooven (1997, p. 58)
In preschool, C got wet T: "Cheer up, Peter, we'll soon have you dry and comfortable again"	Preschool	Gardner & Cass (1965, p. 68)

from which to judge the future" (p. 5). A mother summarizes this attitude well, explaining what she says when her child is upset: "It's all going to be better. It's all past, you know, it's a big thing now but tomorrow it won't be a big thing" (Gottman et al., 1997, p. 58).[3]

Of course, parents can do the opposite, playing with time to make it seem as if the event or behavior in question is of greater importance than it actually is. For instance, a child could be told that losing a tennis game, getting an F on a report card, or failing to help an old lady across the street are behaviors that loom devastatingly in one's life. Sports coaches are notorious in playing with time this way, for instance, telling a high school team: "If you don't bust your butt on every single play tonight you will take it to your grave. You will regret it for the rest of your life and don't you forget that" (Turman, 2005, p. 131).

One can also play with time by changing the perceived relative balance of good and bad outcomes in one's life. This can be engendered by suggesting that "life is not a bowl of cherries," it has ups and downs and both must be coped with. Examples are provided in Table 13.5.

In this context, Bettelheim (1962) urged parents to tell their children that bad things can happen – that's how life is and that children need to face reality even when it is unpleasant. Interestingly, children do not apparently play with time themselves nor am I aware of their doing so as a supportive strategy with other children. However, Hermann et al. (2007) include statements that reflect playing with time (e.g., "Say to myself things will be OK"; "telling myself don't worry, everything will be OK") in their positive self-statements subscale of children's coping. Similarly, Ayers and his colleagues (1996) include items like "You told yourself that in the long run things would work out for the best" in the optimism subscale of children's coping. Consequently, playing with time this way is considered by theoreticians working in the field as an important strategy for children to deploy themselves in coping.

[3] Although I do not know of research in which children themselves have been found to play with time this way, assessments of children's coping styles often include items that index similar processes. For instance, Ayers and colleagues (1996) include the following item in their Optimism scale: "You told yourself that in the long run, things would work out for the best."

Another means of playing with time is the evocation of counterfactuals. Counterfactual thinking refers to the generation of imaginal alternatives to the reality that happened in the past or is ongoing in the present. Generating counterfactuals is a central aspect of human thinking. Hofstadter (1979) discusses subjective thought, finding the fact that humans constantly construct mental variants on the situations they face to be one of the most intriguing aspects of human cognition. He notes: "Think how immeasurably poorer our mental lives would be if we didn't have this creative capacity for slipping out of the midst of reality into soft 'what ifs!" (ibid, p. 643). To elaborate, conditional sentences set up antecedent–consequence pairings in which the antecedents can be either real or imaginal; counterfactual sentences are conditional sentences in which the antecedents are imaginal, they could have happened but they didn't. Generating counterfactuals, then, involves both the temporal and the imaginal plane of transformation. Although counterfactuals are similar in grammatical structure to conditionals (e.g., Orren, at 31;23, tells me about a shirt I was planning to put on, "If you will put it on you would look like a clown"[4]), they differ from them in that they are irreal – they deal with alternatives to reality, they describe the world as it could be or as it might have been, what Reilly (1986) calls *imaginative conditionals*. Freud (1899) talks of his unrequited love, saying that he was "building castles in the air," so as to improve the past (p. 313). Harley (2004) points out that *wanting* generally entails counterfactuality because one does not have what one wants. This aspect of *wanting* may well account for the fact that the ability to entertain counterfactual possibilities emerges in toddlerhood (e.g., German & Nichols, 2003).

When used strategically, counterfactuals can make others feel either better or worse. This is because thinking of how events could have turned out worse can make one feel better, and thinking of how events could have turned out better, makes one feel worse (Roese, 1997). Sports coaches use counterfactuals both to make their team players feel better (e.g., "Nobody need to look back and say if I just would have, I could have," Turman, 2005, p. 131) and to make them feel worse (e.g., "We could have had a better

[4] Hebrew: "At tassim at ze po at kmo tire' leiçan."

Table 13.5.

	Age	Source
C complains that peer runs faster M: "Well you know honey there's gonna be people who are gonna go faster than you through you life and there's gonna be people that go slower than you through your whole life. . . ."	5 years	Herot (2002, p. 169)
Responding to how they deal with C's negative affect M1: "when different things have happened, you know, we both try to explain that. That's kind of the way life is at times" M2: (teach C) "to roll with the punches and get on with his life"	Preschool	Gottman, Katz, & Hooven (1987, pp. 55, 65)
C tells T of a dog being run over by a car T: "That's very sad. That makes me feel very bad. But life's like that. We can't pretend it isn't can we?" C: "No" T: "'Cause things like that do happen. Sorry"	First grade	Michaels (1986, p. 98)
M: "You got to study hard and learn. It's gonna be some rough times, and it's gonna be some good times, but you got to keep going"	School	FitzSimmons (1999, p. 183)

half of football if we wouldn't have had some penalties and turnovers" (Turman, 2005, p. 127). In this vein, a baseball coach tells a child, "If you hadn't loafed on the way to first, you would have made it" (Fine, 1987, p. 63).

Adults generate counterfactuals *strategically* in their interactions with others, often by invoking counterfactual roles. Fillmore (1987) gives the example of the sentence: "If I were your father, I would spank you." This sentence can be construed in two different hypothetical worlds: one world in which this statement is said by someone who would like to be in the role of the child's father's so he could effect a punishment that the child's real father is apparently unwilling to administer. The second hypothetical world is one in which the person who says this is setting up a contrast between his own lenient means of discipline and the child's father's presumed harsher ones. The importance of such counterfactuals is that they are used to get others to contrast the world *as is* with the world as it could have been otherwise and to either enjoy or suffer from this hypothetical contrast.

Also in this genre, Lakoff (1996) differentiates the sentences *If I were you, I'd hate me* versus *If I were you, I'd hate myself*. Lakoff suggests that each of these sentences sets up two worlds, the real world and a hypothetical world, and that the speaker's locus of subjectivity in the real world replaces the hearer's subjectivity in the hypothetical world. This is done by creating a hypothetical person who is in the hearer's situation. In the first case, this hypothetical person is infused with the subjectivity of the speaker who must have done something awful to the real person being spoken to, who in turn, has not denounced the speaker. In the second case, the hypothetical person is also infused with the subjectivity of the speaker but the speaker indicates that the hearer should have denounced *his own* actions. This implies that the first sentence should be read as: *If I were you and the recipient of my own immoral actions, I would denounce me*, whereas the second sentence should read as: *If I were you and the agent who performed those immoral actions, I would denounce my own actions*. Here, again, the counterfactual is used to indicate to others alternative paths that could have been taken in a given context. Parents may well deploy counterfactuals as a means of engendering changes in their children's affective reactions to past experiences, but there is no research that I know of which has addressed this possibility.

When do children generate their own counterfactuals? They do so in contexts in which reality counters their preferences, as evident in Table 13.6.

Notice that in all these instances, children are expressing a preference for the current state of affairs to be otherwise and are specifying what the preferred state of affairs actually is. As these examples illustrate, then, children use counterfactuals to transform a current context into another context that is better aligned with their preferences. The fact that they understand counterfactuals as invoking alternatives to reality is evident when a child of 42 months says, "It would be good if Zorro existed because one could call him, he would protect me"[5] (Champaud, CHILDES).

Whereas young children appear to generate counterfactuals quite easily, they do not apparently want to entertain counterfactuals that other people suggest to them. Table 13.7 shows examples provided by Reilly (1986).

[5] French: "Ça serait bien si Zorro existait parc(e) qu'on pourrait l'appeler, it me protegerait."

Table 13.6.

	Age	Source
Lightbulb is out C: "If I had a ladder, I would climb up it and change that light bulb"	3;2 years	Shatz (1994, p. 180)
C doesn't want cheese sauce C: "I would like the cheese sauce if it were made with chocolate milk"	Preschool	Fiese, Foley, & Spagnola (2006 p. 74)
C looks at doll in research lab C: "I wish I had that doll at home"	Preschool	Radke-Yarrow, Belmont, Nottelmann, & Bottomly (1990, p. 357)
C1 pretends to go so sleep, addressing C2 C: "I wish I had my cozy blanket here, don't you?"	Preschool	Gottman (1986b, p. 167)
C: "If only I was like Barbie (i.e., the doll) I could get stuff at the mall, too"	8 years	Wason-Ellam (1997, p. 435)

Reilly (1986) contrasts this with children's willingness to adopt the pretend framework, saying, that children are unable "to integrate and encode this conceptual ability of hypothesizing imaginary situations into the conditional structure at the initial states of their conditional careers" (p. 326).

I rather doubt Reilly's account and suspect that the generation of counterfactuals is related to children's preferences. That is, children generate counterfactuals when their preferences are jarred; being offered counterfactuals that do not relate to their preferences leads to their rejection by young children. In fact, adults tend to use counterfactuals as a means of coping with negative events, "undoing" them mentally, contrasting *what is* with "what might have been" and how these aversive outcomes could have been avoided. Children as well have been found to undo negative events but not positive ones (German, 1999). This is well illustrated in the following. A father is trying to get his third grader to do math homework and says, "Let's say Kevin has sixteen dollars." His daughter responds, "Wow, I wish I was Kevin" (Xu & Corno, 1998, p. 427). In other words, children generate counterfactuals to cope with contexts that are aversive to them, imagining an alternative world in which their preferences are better aligned with reality. In keeping with this, finding a car ride uncomfortable with too many people in it, a girl of 4;1 years refers to their station wagon when she says, "We shoulda taked the grey car 'cuz it has a way-back" (Reilly, 1986, p. 322). If children are asked what could have made an aversive experience better, then, they can offer counterfactuals. But the counterfactuals are generated to alter their own actual aversive experiences. Because counterfactuals are generated in reaction to aversive outcomes, they can also be used to alter thoughts and emotions, specifying the irreal conditions that could alter them.

Above, counterfactuals were generated when the world *as is* countered the world *as preferred*. Counterfactuals can also concern one's own past behavior, "undoing" actions that led to unfavorable outcomes (e.g., "if only I studied more" as a reaction to failing a test, "if only I hadn't driven so fast," after having a car accident). Presumably such counterfactuals are functional in altering one's future behavior so that these aversive outcomes do not recur. Yet some individuals do not appear to be able to generate functional counterfactuals. In a recent series of studies (Karniol, Rotman, & Gershfeld, unpublished), my students and I examined the use of counterfactuals in aggressive adolescents. In the first study, male adolescents in a boarding school for youngsters with behavioral problems read a scenario in which they were provoked into an aggressive altercation in which an innocent bystander was ultimately hurt. They were then asked to generate counterfactuals focusing on self ("if only I . . ."), focusing on the provoking other ("if only he . . ."), or without being given a focus ("if only . . ."). Those provided with a self-focus generated primarily functional counterfactuals in which their own aggressive behavior was "undone"

Table 13.7.

	Age	Page
A: "What if your car broke on the way?" C: "Well, but when we drove here, our car didn't broke. . . . It doesn't break. I told you"	34 mos.	321
A asks what if the dog bites her C: "Her doesn't bite me"	34 mos.	324
A: "What if you eat three ice cream cones" C: "You don't have three hands"	3;9 years	324

(e.g., "if only I hadn't hit him back"). Those provided with a provoking-other focus "undid" the provocation (e.g., "if only he hadn't butted into line that night"). But when no focus was provided, these aggressive youngsters generated primarily dysfunctional counterfactuals in which they "undid" the behavior of the provoking-other, avoided being where the altercation occurred (e.g., "if only I hadn't gone to see a movie that night"), or invoked *greater* rather than less aggressive behavior on their part (e.g., "If only I had pounded him and knocked him down"). They did not "undo" their own aggressive behavior.

In a second study, high school students completed a self-reported aggression questionnaire and described an aggressive incident in which they had participated. Ten days later, they read a scenario similar to the one in the first study and generated counterfactuals when given a self-focus, a provoking-other focus, or no focus. Surprisingly, those children who scored higher in aggression did not differ from their less aggressive peers in generating dysfunctional counterfactuals when no focus was provided. But those children who scored higher in aggression evidenced two patterns that were not evident in the less aggressive youngsters. They were more likely to generate counterfactuals in which they changed their behavior to be *more* aggressive and ones in which they avoided being where the altercation occurred (e.g., "If only I hadn't gone out that night"). That is, they did not "undo" their own aggressive behavior and generated counterfactuals that are not instructive for how they should behave in the future. It seems that aggressive adolescents do generate counterfactuals, but ones that either render irrelevant the role of their own aggressive behavior in producing the negative outcome or ones in which their aggressive behavior is more "successful" in preventing the negative outcome from occurring.

Importantly, the "undoing" of behaviors that lead to aversive outcomes is associated with feelings of regret. As an eighth grader states, "after I do something bad I realize that it was wrong and I wish that I could rewind what I did and not do that bad thing" (Schultz & Selman, 1989, p. 149). If aggressive individuals do not anticipate experiencing regret, they may engage in behavior that nonaggressive individuals avoid because of anticipated regret (cf., Karniol, 1981), thus feeding into the cycle of aggression (cf., Barriga et al., 2001).

PLAYING WITH PRETEND FRAMEWORKS

Previously, parents were discussed as fostering adoption of the *pretend* framework for the purpose of play, transforming time and reality to create pretend worlds with their children. Once children understand that such transformations are possible, they can be swept into pretend worlds for other purposes as well. The *pretend* framework can be used to transform time and context strategically to manipulate children's preferences, to channel, temporize, and restrict their preferences (cf., Gordon, 2008).

In the food domain, when children are unwilling to eat, mothers channel children's preferences by playing the airplane game (e.g., Newson & Newson, 1968; Widdowson, 1981), bringing the airplane (i.e., the spoon) to land in the airport (i.e., children's mouths); a father attempts to distract his child from a fight with a sibling, asking, "Do you wanna half of a muffin? Here it comes" and after making loud airplane noises and saying "Flyin'," lands the muffin on the child's plate (Gough, 1984, cited in Hatch, 1992, p. 34). Some children were fed while taken on pretend rides to their aunts or grandmothers. Parents are quite innovative in using pretense to get their children to eat dispreferred foods. For instance, mothers fed their children "cabbage that makes your hair curl" or foods that "makes ears waggle" (Newson and Newson, 1968). A preschooler who explains the difference between eating at home and eating at preschool explains that at preschool, "You don't get to be a dragon" (Wesslén, Sepp, & Fjellström, 2002, p. 267). The father of a child of 4;2 years who doesn't like his dinner says to him: "Why don't you pretend that your food's uh green eggs and ham and let's eat" (Gleason, CHILDES). In this vein, a student reported an incident with her 5-year-old nephew who wanted chicken fingers, was told there weren't any, and was asked to pretend that the rice was chicken fingers. At first he balked, but then he started to play along, eating the rice and commenting what tasty chicken fingers he was eating. In this vein, Kurt Lewin (1935) remarked,

> a child that does not like a certain food eats it without ado if the goblin on the end of the spoon is to be buried, or if the spoon, as train, is to enter the station of the mouth . . . imbedding a separate task in another mental sphere . . . may radically change the valence of the activity. (Lewin, 1935, p. 168)

Teachers also invoke pretense strategically to channel behavior. After children refuse to come into the classroom, the teacher says, "let's use those sticks to pretend we're a band and we can march around the room" (Elgas, Klein, Kantor, & Fernie, 1988, p. 147).

Pretend can also be induced to help children cope with aversive situations. This is evident when a child is asked to transform a marshmallow into a "little cloud floating in the sky" in the context of coping with delay of gratification (e.g., Mischel & Baker, 1975). In a similar fashion, a preschool teacher calms down a child who is upset about a clay puppet that has lost an ear, saying "Oh, pretend he has had a fight with another cat" (Gardner & Cass, 1965, p. 67). Gardner, Sonuga-Barke, and Sayal (1999) found that in attempting to get their children to comply on a toy clean-up task, less than 10 percent of the mothers used what they called "imaginative strategies" (e.g., "Raccoon will help you to tidy. He wants to see how fast you can pick everything up"), concluding that this is an important individual difference in mothers. Although there is no research regarding this point, it may be easier for parents to take advantage of pretend frameworks that have been already adopted rather than to initiate new pretend frameworks in an instrumental fashion. A mother who is playing fairies with her preschooler, tells her "Fairy godmother, I think you better sit down and eat your yogurt because it's almost nap time" (Gordon, 2008, p. 321). There may also be cultural differences in the invocation of pretend by parents. Specifically, Haight and colleagues (1999) found that whereas American parents initiated pretend play primarily in order to involve children in fantasy, Chinese parents were more likely to use pretense to teach children about proper conduct. Thus, they saw the benefits of the *pretend* framework in terms of its socialization function rather than its intellectual function.

There is a variety of therapeutic practices (e.g., Freeman, Epston, & Lobovits, 1997; Lazarus & Abramovitz, 1962) that capitalize on pretense to achieve therapeutic goals. In all these techniques, children are given instructions as to the kinds of imaginal transformations that they should attempt to perform. This step necessarily builds on young children's ability to perform imaginal transformations, with even 2-year-olds being able to pretend to dry a surface made "wet" by a physical transformation that "spills" the pretend liquid (e.g., Harris & Kavanaugh, 1993) and 3- to 5-year-olds being able to make an imaginary balloon stretch by thinking about it (Estes, Wellman, & Woolley, 1989). That is, children can imagine a context, imagine a transformation of that context, and adjust their behavior to suit the imagined transformed consequence. Given the above, one can instruct children as to what they should pretend. In this vein, an 8-year-old who suffered nightmares was induced to make a monster run around in red underwear, sing opera, and turn around in circles. She was subsequently able to imaginally fence off the entrance to a cave out of which a threatening crocodile was emerging (Freeman et al., 1997). In line with this, Hall, Kaduson and Schaefer (2002) include among their play therapy techniques a game called "Party Hats on Monsters," in which the child is urged to draw a feared object like a monster and then draw a party hat on it, being told that by changing the drawing, he can also change the picture in his head. A monster with a party hat can't be all that scary.

Some therapeutic uses of pretense involve imaginally transforming the context. A child who suffered from encopresis (i.e., the inability to regulate defecation) had the problem transformed into "outwitting Sneaky Poo." This transformed context allowed him to overcome his problem, explaining that he managed to overcome it "because he was always bossing me around and I decided to boss him around" (Freeman, Epston, & Lobovits, 1997, p. 101). By imagining a battle between his willpower and that of Sneaky Poo, an anthropomorphized version of the problem, the child went into battle to gain control over his soiling. Again transforming the context, a 10-year-old who was scared of the dark was asked to imagine that Superman has asked him to wait in a nearly dark room for instructions regarding his impending mission (Lazarus & Abramovitz, 1962). With the help of this pretense, the child was able to stay in the dark room by himself. Importantly, neither the child nor the parents were apparently able to imaginally transform the context themselves in a way that would enable the child to overcome it. The help of an outsider, in this case, a therapist, was needed to do so.

Imaginal transformations can also involve transforming oneself. If they can pretend to be someone with magic powers, children can then imagine having these powers themselves and can behave in line with these imaginary powers. In this vein, a therapist who wants to get a maladjusted boy who is often bullied to stop his victimization suggests to him that he is "King Kong, just a big hunk of muscle, all powerful, and no one could stand up to you" (Corsini, 1966, p. 22); by adopting this pretense, the boy was able to fight back and the victimization stopped. Similarly, a child who experienced temper tantrums became a Temper Tamer, with a pouch containing a spyglass, a whistle, and a tiny notebook, to be used for spying on Temper, blowing the whistle when it was detected, and keeping score of successful taming (Freeman et al., 1997). Nelson (2007) enlists the help of a technique called "What would Superman do?" in which children harness the power of the superhero, being asked to imagine how he (or alternative heroes of their own making) would deal with the situation and are urged to adopt similar strategies to deal with problems (cf., Rubin & Livesay, 2006). Some children do, however, require the relevant superhero props (e.g., the red cape) to imaginatively conduct this transformation and to enact the skills in question.

Note that above, children were asked to pretend that they were someone else with specific powers that the child himself presumably does not have. Pretending to be that other person leads to the incorporation of those qualities that are lacking in oneself and this can facilitate change in one's behavior, to manifest those missing qualities. Paley (e.g., 1990, 2004), who documented her magical career experiences as a preschool teacher, suggested to an overly bossy child who interfered with others' block play that he pretend to be a Good Player who always lets people build their own way. The child willingly plays along; he knows how to pretend to be a Good Player and says to another child, "Hey, Teddy, put those blocks anyhow you want! I'll help you" (p. 100). From that point on, when the child was being unruly, Paley would say to him, "Hey, Franklin, you're pretending the wrong boy, remember?" (2004, p. 100). In another instance, a preschool child who knocked over a girl's dishes while being an Angry Wolf was told, "then be somebody else . . . you're spoiling everyone's play . . . could you pretend to be a wolf that doesn't knock over things?" (Paley, 1990, p. 89, 91).

Of course, fostering pretense in this manner or therapeutically cannot succeed unless there is a willingness on the child's part to "play along" with the attempt to engage in pretense to transform the way he thinks about the problem domain. The importance of this is underlined in a series of studies in which my students and I (Karniol, Galili, Shtilerman, Bar, & Naim, unpublished)

Table 13.8.

	Age	Source
C is upset T: "Let's make believe that it's tomorrow. Let's pretend it's tomorrow and.... Will you cry again?"	Kindergarten	Blaise (2005)
T wants children to run faster T: "Pretend you are bicycles flying down the street"	Preschool	Tobin, Wu, & Davidson (1989, p. 81)
T wants to leave classroom T: "I want you to curl up on the floor and go to sleep like little dormice"	Preschool	King (1978, p. 52)
T: "All the animals crouch down and all the flowers stand up tall; those children with wings *fly* to the other side..." (emphasis added).	Preschool	Sylva, Roy, & Painter (1986, pp. 113, 114)
Teacher tries to help C plan a tripod T: "Can you imagine for a minute that you're taking a photograph. How high would be comfortable?" C: "This is what I done – trying to find that out.... just pretend that I was looking through and...."	7 years	Wells (1981b, p. 269)

asked preschoolers to delay gratification while wearing a cape. In the first study, instructions as to the qualities that Superman embodies resulted in greater delay gratification than simple provision of the cape without such instructions. In the second study, when the cape was introduced as the cape of Dash (from the children's film *The Incredibles*), a superhero who is impulsive and incapable of delaying gratification, the majority of children refused to put on the cape but those who did, were unable to delay gratification as compared to a group to whom the same cape was introduced as Superman's cape. That is, children can refuse to adopt certain imaginal transformations. It is important to note, though, that the same cape led to different behavioral outcomes because of how it was construed by children.

This is further underlined in the work of Durrant (1995). He uses *pretend* as a therapeutic tool, suggesting to patients that they act "as if" a miracle solution has been found for their problem. If one pretends that the problem has been resolved, one can engage in behaviors that are consistent with the miracle; one doesn't try to be different but merely pretends to be different. The pretense allows the patient to practice more acceptable behavior, engendering positive social reactions that can then serve to reinforce the acceptable behavior. In this vein, in teaching social skills to children, therapists ask children to pretend that aversive outcomes have happened and to offer alternative means of dealing with the situation (Cartledge & Milburn, 1980). In what Morgan and Skovholt (1977) call "guided fantasy," individuals are told to let their imagination take them 10 years into the future as an aid in career counseling.

The *pretend* framework can also be invoked to foster better communication, often in classroom contexts. When a teacher asks a child to explain how to makes candles, she says, "Tell the kids how you do it from the very start. Pretend we don't know a thing about candles" (Michaels, 1986, p. 105). That is, she asks the child to assume children's and her own state of knowledge to be other than it is and to imaginally work out the implications of this assumption in providing the explanation. Similarly, Simons and Murphy (1986) cite an instance of a preschooler who starts explaining a game during circle time and is interrupted by the teacher who says, "Pretend I can't see it" (p. 204). If the child pretends, he will presumably explain better, taking into account his audience's state of ignorance. The request to pretend need not be explicitly stated. When a teacher is encouraging a fifth grader to understand visual perspective, she asks, "if someone watching that video who wasn't here the first day wanted to know if you were in the class, would they be able to tell?" (Putney et al., 2000, p. 98). Here, then, the teacher is creating pretend others who are not privy to the context and asking as to how they could be informed in their state of ignorance. But the opposite pretense may also be invoked. In a study on talk-aloud protocols during problem solving in adults, the instructions included, "Pretend there is no one here but yourself" (Krutetskii, 1976, as cited in Ericsson & Simon, 1984, p. 81).

The *pretend* framework can be used to engender more creative and different ways of doing things and of thinking about things, as illustrated in Table 13.8.

In a study (Heffner, Greco, & Etfert, 2003) that gave children either literal or metaphoric instructions (e.g., "pretend you are a turtle going into its shell"), children were found to prefer the metaphoric instructions. In fact, the "turtle technique" (Schneider, 1974) teaches children anger control by suggesting they pretend to be a turtle, withdrawing into its shell, thinking calming thoughts, and coming out of their shell when they are calm. The technique has been found to be effective in both educational and therapeutic settings (e.g., Robin, Schneider, &

Table 13.9.

	Age	Source
C1 tells C2 she's tired C2 offers her a plastic building block C2: "They make you better. Do you want one? They make you better."	33 mos.	Garvey (1984, p. 158)
C1 hit C2 C1: "Do you like apples?" C2: "No" C1: "Do you like bananas?" C2: "Yes" C1 picks offers C2 a plastic block C1: "Here's a banana" C2 laughs, both play grocery store	Preschool	Spivack & Shure (1974, p. 64)
C1 claims he cannot participate in cleanup C1: "I can't get out. I'm all locked up." C2: "Here, Jason. Here's the key. I found it. There, I unlocked you"	Preschool	Paley (1990, p. 43)

Dolnick, 1976). Similarly, Bedford (1986) uses a technique he calls "Instant Replay" in which children are to pretend that they can access a television replay button and they "could do it all over again," thus essentially engaging counterfactual thought to improve their problem solving strategies.

Unsurprisingly, pretend can be invoked to facilitate more creative writing. In this vein, a primary school teacher suggests to students that to write a story, they should "imagine you had some special way of becoming invisible so that no-one knew you were there . . . ," "imagine some of the things people would say when you surprised or shocked them," or "pretend you were at home and went round moving things and frightening your Mum . . . or what about pretending you are invisible and playing football?" (Pollard, 1985, pp. 174–175). The imaginal nature of pretend in writing is evident in the description provided by a 9-year-old boy as to how he could write a story if he were Wonder Boy. He explains: "he could stop and imagine he was in the story, then stop and write that down. Then he would go back into imagining himself into the story . . . ." (Freeman, Epston, & Lobovits, 1997).

The *pretend* framework can also be used to foster learning. Lepper and Malone (1987) conducted a study to examine the impact of embedding educational material in a "fantasy context" of instructional computer games. In a two-part study, students first ranked four games in order of preference and then chose one of the games to work on. The majority of the games chosen were ones that contained fantasy context. Next, children "played" and each game contained a varied number of fantasy constructs. Students with games that contained more fantasy constructs played longer and remembered more of the content material. Malone and Lepper concluded that embedding fantasy in educational material has a positive effect on both motivation and learning. In fact, logical reasoning tasks that are embedded in fantasy story contexts are solved more easily by children (e.g., Dias, Roazzi, O'Brien, & Harris, 2005 Seier, 1994). Moreover, presenting the same computer game as a male adventure (i.e., Pirates) versus a female adventure (i.e., Honeybears) had an impact on the way boys and girls played, with boys performing equally well on both versions and girls being significantly more successful on the female version than on the male version (Light & Littleton, 1999).

Children can use *pretend* strategically to transform others' construals in ways that further their own preferences. For instance, a 9-year-old, who wanted to get some clothes to the laundry room in the basement but didn't feel like doing so herself, asked her 4-year-old sibling, "Do you want to be Santa Claus?" When the younger child happily assented, the older one handed her the laundry and said, "Here's your toys. Now take them to the children in the basement," embedding the request in the context of a pretend game (Ervin-Tripp & Mitchell-Kernan, 1977, p. 9). That is, by imagining a context that would get her younger sister to willingly take things to the basement, the older child was able to successfully invoke such a context, based on her understanding of the younger sibling's preferences and of her willingness to adopt the pretend framework. Similarly, when two 7-year-olds want to get a child of 2;8 into a car during play, they ask her to get in, and when she dawdles, one yells, "There's a wolf. There's a wolf out there!" and the other nearly screams, "Get in! Get in!" (Ervin-Tripp, Guo, & Lampert, 1990, p. 317). Here again, the first child imagined a context that could be used to get the younger child into the car and the peer recognized the framework and embellished it to further their manipulative attempt.

Children can also invoke the pretend framework *proactively* to help other children cope with negative affect and other difficulties, as shown in Table 13.9.

Across these examples, children imaginally created contexts that could potentially resolve the other child's problem and invoked the pretend framework as a means of helping the other child cope with aversive contexts.

The pretend framework can also reflect proactive consideration. When a Batman-caped preschooler is upset because he can't cram his tricycle into a full station wagon, his sister offers, "Batman, you don't need a bike. You can *fly* over everyone faster than their bikes" (Ervin-Tripp & Gordon, 1986, p. 89), a suggestion the child gratefully accepted. Similarly, a second grader explains that when her little brother is too tired to walk, they "tell him pretend you're a puppy and we're taking you for a walk. Then he's happy" (Paley, 2004, p. 106). In essence, then, these children are using imaginal worlds to find solutions for other children's problems in the real world.

Notice, though, that in order to use pretend strategically whether to manipulate others for their own benefit or to help others cope better, children need to adopt a working framework that relates others' psychological processes to their behavior. In this framework, people's psychological states determine their behavior and if one alters these underlying psychological states, one can induce changes in behavior (cf., Vinden, 2000). As Vinden concludes, children become both *mind readers*, individuals who attempt to draw inferences about both their own and others' psychological processes (cf., Karniol, 1990b), and *mind actors*, individuals who use their own psychological processes in guiding their behavior. As discussed earlier, both of these abilities emerge out of the way adults talk to children, of children's, their own, and others people's covert psychological processes. This is why children's use of mental state terms is so strongly predicted by their parents' use of such terms (e.g., Meins & Fernyhough, 1999).

Children can also invoke imaginal worlds to cope with their own aversive real world problems, doing so either in a retroactive, or a proactive, manner. Doing so in a retroactive manner, a child can "undo" unpleasant experiences by engaging the pretend framework. For instance, when reenacting a trip to Disney World when the family car ran out of gas and an unpleasant wait on the turnpike had to be endured, a toddler says, "We go to Disney World. I start motor, we need gas, we don't run out of gas," and pretends to drive into a gas station (Segal & Adcock, 1981, p. 64). A 3-year-old who got burned by hot water plays with a toy figure and says, "Better turn the cold water on, he got to turn off the hot," and turns off the water in imaginary gestures (Wolf, 1990, p. 203). Similarly, pretending to go to Disney World, a preschooler says, "We're going to see Small World.... We're not going to Haunted Mansion. It's too scary. Those ghosts scare me" (Segal & Adcock, 1981, p. 65). Presumably, having been scared in the past, the child avoids the scary experience in the pretend scene that he creates in the present. When a 12-year-old complains to his mother about a boy who annoyed him at school and his mother suggests ignoring him, the son asks, "I just pretend that Jeremy Murray wasn't there?" and the mother responds, "uh hmm. That's a smart way" (Ochs & Capps, 2001, p. 282).

Pretense can also be used by children to cope proactively, "online," with their own aversive experiences. In this context, children "summoned" pretend friends when having to deal with the dark, with feared showers, and with machine monsters (Segal & Adcock, 1981). One child used his invisible friend's magic power to turn ghosts in the Haunted House at Disney World into the child's friendly ones. Children who were required to delay gratification and were given no instructions as to what to do, reported that they had passed the time by "playing a rocket game" or "I made believe I was flying an airplane and bad guys were after me" (Singer, 1973, p. 71). In a similar delay context, a child explained "I'd pretend I was a fish and was swimming" (Yates, Yates, & Beasley, 1987). A 9-year-old who is discussing adopting a Wonder Boy perspective offers, "Try to turn dishwashing from work to fun. Pretend the dishtowel is a mine in a mine field. But instead of the mine blowing up, it blows the dishes dry" (Freeman, Epston, & Lobovits, 1997, p. 41).

In her research with chronically ill school children, Clark (2003) found that they often use what she calls *imaginal coping*, the use of imagination to transform and reframe aversive situations.[6] For instance, a child explained,

> Sometimes I play games when I do my breathing machine. I pretend I have a friend who is a dragon, and the dragon breathes smoke. You know the steam coming from the machine? That's dragon smoke. Another game is, I have a toy airplane. I fly my airplane through the steam. I pretend to fly away, to a place away from this. (Clark, 2003, p. 60)

In general terms, then, children can use the *pretend* framework, drawing on their understanding of imaginal worlds to cope with the world when it is unpleasant or aversive. As Ervin-Tripp and her colleagues (1990) note, perhaps the most interesting development in school age children is the growth of "rich and inventive strategies for reframing the situation, typically through pretense" (p. 317).

From my perspective, the ability to deploy imaginal transformations undergrids the correlation between preschool delay ability and Quantitative SAT scores (Mischel, Shoda, & Rodriguez, 1989), a correlation that was discussed in Chapter 12. Quantitative SAT scores assess mathematical ability and mathematics is predicated on transformational thought (Piaget, Henriques, & Ascher, 1992); reasoning transformationally is critical to children's mathematical thinking (Harel & Sowder, 2005) as well as to successful performance in other academic subjects (Jensen, 1998). Importantly, though, as discussed in

[6] Clark actually only discussed imaginal coping in the context of children who need to deal with the hardships of illness. I have taken the liberty of generalizing her definition.

Chapter 10, transformational thought is the basis for pretend play, and engaging in play fosters the development of math skills in kindergarten children (Ainlie, 1990; Jarrell, 1998), most likely because fundamental concepts in early childhood math involve making comparisons and transformations, abilities that are inherent in pretend play and which, for Piaget, represent the essence of intelligence. In turn, the ability to engage in transformational thought for the purpose of coping with aversive contexts emerges out of the pretend play, which engages transformational thought and solidifies its use for strategic purposes.

Moreover, the ability to conduct imaginal transformations is critical to adult creativity (Root-Bernstein & Root-Bernstein, 2006). As a MacArthur Fellow[7] explains, "in a real sense, to do theory is to explore imaginary worlds because all models are simplified versions of reality" (p. 416). Yet another MacArthur Fellow elaborates, "a lot of original ideas in science come from some kind of mind play that stays within the bounds of reality, but still asks about something that you have never seen or known to happen" (p. 421). Playing with the irreal in childhood, both in pretend play and in coping, involves transformational thought on the temporal and imaginal planes and serves to prepare children for using transformational thought in their everyday adult lives as well.

The interplay between the ability to deploy imaginal transformations in pretense and performance on various social and cognitive tasks is evident in young children. To illustrate, Saltz, Dixon, and Johnson (1977) found that children who were instructed to engage in thematic fantasy play were better able to resist touching a forbidden toy, especially if instructed to think about their favorite story or look at a picture book while waiting. In a short-term longitudinal study, preschool children's sociodramatic play was predictive of their clean-up behavior about 5 months later, with concurrent clean-up behavior, age, and vocabulary partialled out[8] (Elias & Berk, 2002). Finally in this context, pretend play and coping ability are also related. Children whose quality of play was judged to be more imaginative in first and second grade evidenced more varied and more efficacious coping on a hypothetical coping task in fifth and sixth grades (Russ, Robins, & Christiano, 1999). As well, children's play predicted cognitive coping with an invasive dental procedure (Christano & Russ, 1996), emphasizing the critical role of mind play involving transformations on the imaginal plane in children's development.

[7] The MacArthur award, sometimes known as the Genius Award, is a $500,000 prize awarded with no strings attached to a limited number of unique individuals who have been recognized for their exceptional promise and creativity across domains of endeavor. Vivian Paley, whose work was mentioned above, was awarded a MacArthur Award in 1989.

[8] Vaughn, Kopp, and Krakow (1994) have shown the important role that emergent language abilities play in the self-control of children 24–30 months of age.

PLAYING WITH PERSPECTIVE

Whereas other types of mind play were deployed to transform contexts to make them better aligned with one's preferences, *perspective setting* (Graumann, 2002) is a means of mind play used to get children to adopt different perspectives, generally to "get a handle" on other people's preferences and likely affective reactions. But how does one set perspectives for others?

There are various ways of doing so. First, in the context of chastising children, parents imaginally transform their children from perpetrators into victims. To illustrate, a mother who is trying to discourage grabbing of objects from others, says to her toddler, "How would you like it if somebody took something which belonged to you?" (Cook-Gumperz, 1973, p. 67). That is, the mother implicitly invokes the imaginal plane because the child is being asked to think of self as victim whereas in fact, in the real world, he is the perpetrator. At the same time, though, she induces a temporal transformation since the child's hypothetical future preferences rather than his actual real-world preferences are invoked. Yet despite the fact that the question is posed in the conditional, children may rely on their past experiences of being victimized in attempting to reply with their hypothetical preferences in such contexts.

This is also the case when such perspective setting is implemented in a declarative fashion. That is, rather than asking the child as to his hypothetical preferences, the parent focuses on what the child's preferences would be in the relevant context. To illustrate, the mother of a preschooler who is tormenting her baby sister says, "C'mon, you wouldn't like someone shouting at you if you were sad, now stop it!" (Walkerdine & Lucey, 1989, p. 25). Here again, both the temporal domain and the imaginal domain are invoked since the child is being asked to imaginally become the person being shouted at and to access his hypothetical preferences in that transformed context. Notice that in doing so, the child's own preferences in the current context are rendered irrelevant; it is no longer of any concern why the child as agent engaged in the behavior in question. The transformation has made him the future recipient of the victimizing action and the focus is on his own preference structure in this new temporal context.

Whereas above, mothers were referring to the child's preference structure as the recipient of their own actions (i.e., "you don't/wouldn't like it if..."), their victim was left out of the new perspective, being alluded to in generic terms as *someone* or *somebody* who would victimize them. One can also conduct a double transformation of roles, in which the perpetrator becomes victim, but also, the victim becomes the victimizer. For instance, a child who grabbed a toy from a friend was chastised and told, "You can't go around grabbing things. Would you like it if he did that to you?" (Shure, 1985, p. 201). Similarly, a mother who is attempting to get a younger sibling to stop bothering an older one asks, "How do you think you would

Table 13.10.

	Age	Source
T: "How do you think Lori felt when you said that?"	Preschool	Kontos (1999, p. 369)
T. "How do you think Robert felt when you pushed him?"	Preschool	Shure (1982, p. 143)
C grabs racing car from peer M: "How do you think your friend feels when you grab toys?"	4 years	Shure (1985, p. 201)
M: "How do you think Andrea will feel if you don't let her read her book now?"	Preschool	Shure & Spivack (1978, p. 116)

feel if Andrea bothered you when you were busy?" (Shure & Spivack, 1978, p. 116). In these examples, mothers are engaged in two processes. First, they conduct a double transformation in querying about the child's hypothetical preferences as victim rather than as perpetrator, while at the same time making the victim into the perpetrator. In doing so, though, children's own preferences as perpetrators are rendered irrelevant. Only their preferences as hypothetical victims are being queried about. Second, they conduct a transformation on the temporal plane, getting the child to respond to questions regarding his own hypothetical future preferences. Of course, again, to answer the question, the child may draw on his past experiences in similar contexts in which he was victimized, whether by the actual victim or by someone else. In fact, mothers can make children into victims without querying as to their hypothetical preferences. Rather, they can refer to victims' generic experiences of being victimized. For instance, in intervening in preschoolers' sibling conflicts, mothers reacted with comments like, "You don't like it when he does that to you" (Perlman & Ross, 2005), and "It doesn't feel good when he takes your toys, does it?" (Ross et al., 1994). Here as well mothers are conducting double transformations but instead of asking the child, they are telling the child what the affective implications of such double transformations are.

Notice that in the above instances, children maintained their own identity and only their roles were reversed. Transformations that require role reversals are relatively easy because one maintains one's own preference structure. One does not need to become somebody else. This makes it easy for children to use when the person in the role is an adult rather than a child because one does not need to adopt the adult's preference structure, only his role. For instance, a mother who is explaining what she would do if her child stopped talking to his father because of a broken promise says, "I'd say how would he like it if no one talked to him that would make him sad wouldn't it" (Cook-Gumperz, 1973, p. 243). Similarly, when a mother indicates she can't read a book to her child because she is making dinner and the child persists, the mother asks "How would you feel if you came home from a day's work tired and hungry and dinner wasn't ready?" (Shure & Spivack, 1978, p. 140). The child is asked to keep his own preference structure but to feed it with events that are likely to be experienced by an adult – namely his father. Nevertheless, if the adults' and the children's understanding of these events differ, then age may well be relevant in the conclusion one draws as a result of such transformations (e.g., "fathers are not sad, so he wouldn't care").

Perspective setting can also attempt to induce transformations only on the mental plane, focusing on the psychological impact of one's behavior on others. Specifically, such practices do not engage the child's own preference structure but attempt to guide him to access the preference structure of others. For instance, when a child tells his mother that he broke a toy, she asks, "How do you think I feel when I pay good money to buy you toys and you just break them like that" (Shure & Spivack, 1978, p. 136). The mother's question requires the child to draw an inference as to how *she* feels and relies on the child's understanding of her, or generic mothers', preference structure. Answering her question does not require him to abandon his own preference structure, only to access hers. Additional examples of such questioning practices are shown in Table 13.10.

Irrespective of whether the questions are posed regarding the past, the timeless present, or the future, the child needs to use the plane of mental transformations to respond. Across the board, the child can draw on his understanding of generic others' psychological processes in doing so. Anyone in the same context would be expected to have the same reactions as the child about whom one is being questioned. Consequently, one can use generics, substituting generic terms for the specific other about whom one is being questioned. To illustrate, in a discussion group with school children, the counselor asks, "How do people feel when someone says something like that about them?" (Selman, Levin, & Brion-Meisels, 1982, p. 88); using the term "people" clarifies that anyone is that context would be expected to have similar reactions.

This becomes even more blatant when children are simply told, rather than asked, how the other person feels. For instance, when a preschooler is fighting with a boy over a book, the teacher says, "Well, it's Gabriel's and he doesn't want you to read it right now. So why make him unhappy . . . " (Hall, CHILDES). Similarly, when a preschool teacher says, "When you said that to Mary, she probably felt upset" (Kontos, 1999, p. 369), here again there is a contingency between what one says or

Table 13.11.

	Age	Source
Dolls and Stuffed Animals		
C tries to tie ribbons on doll's hat M: "We mustn't pull too hard or we'll hurt the baby, Honey"	21 mos.	Bloom (1970, p. 46)
C is brushing a toy dog M: "You might hurt the doggie if you brush his hair"	24 mos.	Bernstein (CHILDES)
Japanese C plays with doll's earring M: "if you pull it (the earring) off, it will hurt her"[9]	24 mos.	Clancy (1986)
Inanimate Objects		
Japanese C is dropping apples on floor M: "If you do that kind of thing, Mr. Apple says 'Ouch'"[10]	23 mos.	Clancy (1986)
Japanese C is banging toy airplane M: "I feel sorry for the airplane"	25 mos.	Clancy (1986)

does and others' psychological reactions as victims of one's actions, with the implicit message being that others' affective reactions are to be used as input in guiding our behavior toward them. Importantly, though, neither of these children represents a unique individual – anyone else in the same context would experience the same reactions.

The fact that perspective setting can be conducted either in a generic or a specific fashion is important because children need to learn that their behavior generally impacts others the same way; the individual whose psychological experiences the child is asked to consider is not a unique entity but rather, an exemplar of generic others. This issue is very interesting in light of the fact that parents use the same type of perspective setting in attempting to deter children from hurting their pets and their dolls. For instance, "John don't do that to the kitten! Why? Because it might hurt him . . . . Would you like me to push your neck down like that? No . . . . Well the kitty doesn't like it either" (Herot, 2002, p. 173). A 5-year-old is playing with the dog and his mother says,

> You stop bloody tormenting that dog! You horrible thing, you are." After she threatens to hit him with a stick and he cries, she holds him and says, "How would you like me to do that to you? You wouldn't like it, would you? Would you? Well, neither does the dog. (Wells, 1986, p. 75)

The children in these contexts are being asked to lay aside the differences between humans and animals, to view the pet as having preferences and psychological reactions, just like humans do. In these instances, though, because the pet cannot be made into the perpetrator, the mothers conduct the transformation by making the child the victim and making themselves, rather than the dog, the perpetrator. Of course, the same thing can be done with respect to human victims as well (e.g., "Would you like me to bite your foot?" Halle & Shatz, 1994, p. 92).

In this context, it is important that children may also be warned by mothers not to hurt their dolls, stuffed animals, and other inanimate objects, as shown in Table 13.11. Note that Japanese mothers have been found to be very likely to use such warnings (e.g., Clancy, 1986).

Parental use of such messages may have two functions. One function is to teach the child about the potential hazards of hurting others, with dolls, toy dogs, and other objects being anthropomorphized, serving as placeholders for the potential impact of the child's behavior on real people. The other less interesting function from the current perspective may well be to avoid potential damage to the toy itself. In this vein, we also get "My rug doesn't like (children's snacks)" (Mody, 2005, p. 58).

The important aspect of this, though, is that first, children apparently learn to refer to inanimate objects as having human-like experiences. A sophisticated 2-year-old sees her father chopping an onion and says, "Chuck, chuck, chuck. That's what the knife said to the onion" (Scollon & Scollon, 1981, p. 91), creating a world in which knives and onions engage in human-like conversations. When his bottle gets plugged, Orren, at 36;5 explains, "the bottle doesn't want me to drink milk."[11] Similarly, a child of 3;8 years who does not want to eat, explains, "the hunger has gone shopping, it's gone to work"[12] (Elbers & van Loon-Vervoorn, 1998b, p. 366). If fathers can go to work and disappear for hours at a time, why can't hunger? Consequently, children can also anthropomorphize and invoke the psychological reactions of objects in their interactions with other children, saying things like: "Why do you do that to the poor little table?" (Piaget, 1926, p. 191).

Children also start to set perspectives in their interactions with other children, using this strategy primarily in

[9] Japanese: "tottara itai yo, oneesan itai yo."
[10] Japanese: "Sonna koto susu n dattara ringoan itai itteru wa yo."
[11] Hebrew: "habakbuk lo roçe she-ani yishte xalav."
[12] Dutch: "De honger is boodschappen doen, die is naar het werk."

chiding others as to how to behave. In this vein, a 5-year-old tells her 3-year-old younger sister,

Don't ever bite on Barbie's feet. How would you like it if somebody came up and bited on your feet? Tropical Skipper doesn't like it. How would you like it if she came up and ate, bited on your foot? (Haight & Miller, 1993, p. 10)

Similarly, after a bout of name calling, a fifth grader asks a peer, "How would you like it if someone called you..." (Goodwin, 2006, p. 164).

Perspective setting can also be conducted in ways that require one to engage in transformations that invoke all three planes of transformation, by explicitly asking one to imaginally become the other person and generating one's own likely preference structure as that other person. This can take the form of, "if you were him," "Imagine if that were you" or "How would you feel if you were him?" attempts to get one to put oneself in a specific other's place, often to get perpetrators to imagine themselves being victims. The common thread running through such strategies of perspective setting is that they build on both pretense and counterfactuals; one can never be someone else but one can entertain being someone else on the plane of the irreal, whether it be a doctor, Superman, or one's victimized sibling. Having experience with being other people in pretend play presumably makes this self-into-other imaginal transformation easy. But putting oneself imaginally into *specific* other people's shoes as a victim is quite a problem. Specifically, one needs to draw inferences about how that specific other differs from generic others in whose shoes one could also step. How does my sister's preference structure differ from those of other children, or for that matter, from my own preferences? And why should strategies that center on getting the child to metaphorically put himself in a specific other person's shoes promote positive behavior and discourage negative behavior?

In fact, the instruction to metaphorically put oneself in someone else's shoes is not generally geared to differentiating that other person from generic others. Rather, it is a means of concretizing others and setting up both reversibility (i.e., if you can hit him, he can hit you) as well as setting up an equivalence between the preference structure of the person being instructed to take this transformed perspective and the individual whose perspective is to be adopted. That is, the request to imagine self in a specific other person's shoes, making oneself a victim rather than a perpetrator, is made so as to engender better understanding of the preference structure that is relevant when one is the beneficiary or the victim of the action (e.g., "if you were him..."). Importantly, there is an implicit assumption that once the victimized other's preference structure is exposed via the adoption of this transformed perspective, it will become a relevant criterion in determining future action that violates such preferences.

Notice, though, that the additional step of specifying that one should not engage in behavior that counters other people's preferences is seldom specified. Although perspective setting reflects an *if–then* contingency, with the antecedent being the likely affective consequences to others of the child's engaging in a given behavior, and the consequent being the lesson being taught – "then don't do it to others," this logical step is often unstated and the underlying assumption – that other people's preferences are relevant to guiding one's own behavior – is not spelled out. Mothers engage in perspective setting to get the child to see that his behavior conflicts with the preferences of the target of his behavior and they assume that once the child has "seen the light," this light will serve to guide his behavior in the future. That is, perspective setting attempts to bring to the fore other people's preferences and to make these preferences more important in guiding one's behavior than one's own preferences. When parts of this complex tale are omitted, the expectation is that the child will "fill in the blanks," to understand that if he would have a negative reaction to such an outcome, so would the person in whose shoes he is supposed to be in this exercise. Whether the child actually does fill in the blanks where necessary is unclear.

The concomitant assumption in guiding perspective setting is that if children understand that their own affective experiences were negative or would be negative in a given context, they will translate such understanding into behavioral guidelines in interacting with others. That is, if I don't like it, others won't like it. And I should be sufficiently concerned with other people's likes and dislikes to guide my future behavior in this light, so as to avoid inducing such negative experiences in others. This issue is succinctly summarized in the sage Hillel's view of the Bible's teachings:

That which is hateful to you, do not do to your fellow man. That is the whole Torah. The rest is commentary; go and learn it. (Babylonian Talmud, Tractate Shabbat 31a)

Hillel's summary crystallizes three issues. First, other people's preferences are to be taken seriously in guiding our own actions. Second, one can "crack" into other people's preference structure by using our own preferences as the guidelines for our behavior toward them. But notice that it is one's fellow man who is the focus of these guidelines, a generic individual whose specific interests cannot be identified, because he is a figment of our imagination. This contrasts with similar dictums, such as the Golden Rule, which refer to one's victim or one's neighbor who are both identifiable and self-concerned, just as we are (e.g., Paley, 1990, trained her preschool teachers with the rule: "I must not do to a child that which I would not have done to me," p. 91). Third, if I can put myself in someone else's shoes to discover what I should not do to him, presumably he can also put himself into my shoes to discover what he should not do to me. That is, perspectives should be reversible and this is what makes perspective taking and perspective setting such a powerful tool in social life. After a girl pushed her sibling off a scooter, the mother asks, "Is that

Table 13.12.

	Age	Source
C2 tattled on C1 C1: "If it was you, how would you feel? I feel sad. If it was me, I wouldn't tell"	Kindergarten	Mody (2005, p. 111)
C: "I know that if it were my turn to get snacks and you didn't let me, I would be angry"	School	Selman, Levin, & Brion-Meisels (1982, p. 84)
C: "I don't like people who talk about other people behind their backs because it's – they wouldn't like it if they were talked about, and I don't think it's right"	Adolescent	Secord & Peevers (1974, p. 138)
C explaining why her teachers don't like her C: "If I was in their place, I wouldn't like me 'cos the way I act"	Teen	Furlong (1976, p. 42)

the way you like to be treated?" When the daughter shakes her head *no*, the mother continues, "Then don't do it to other people" (Grieshaber, 2004, p. 184). The lesson being taught is a generic one rather than one that is restricted to one's sibling. This is emphasized in the words of a sophisticated 15-year-old who explains, "you gotta really feel that you'd be happy the way things went if you were in your friend's shoes" (Selman, 1980, p. 111).

In the above, the logic of the argument is that other children's aversive reactions to the behavior or speech that is directed at them should serve as implicit reasons to avoid engaging in the same behavior in the future. Yet the child is not explicitly told that one should avoid making others unhappy or upset. Moreover, there is no analogy drawn between self and other; what is emphasized is the psychological impact of one's actions on others. This is problematic for two reasons. First, one can attempt to infer what someone else feels but draw the wrong inference. For instance, after a child grabs a toy from another child, he's asked as to the other's likely affective reaction and responds, "He feels good. He don't like that old toy anyway" (Shure & Spivack, 1978, p. 126). Second, one can draw the correct inference but be unconcerned with others' affective reaction. In this vein, after a mother questions how one's friend feels when others grab toys from him, a preschooler responds, "Mad, but I don't care, it's mine" (Shure & Spivack, 1978, p. 36). When a child tells her mother that her friend might hit her, she adds, "I don't care 'cause I can beat her" (ibid, p. 127). As well, when a mother intervenes after a fight and asks a child "Don't you want your friend to be happy?" the child answers vehemently "NO!" (Shure & Spivack, 1978, p. 126). Thus, the major gap here is between knowing how another person feels and caring about that outcome, an issue I will return to in Chapter 14. But notice that here too the implicit assumption is that if the child understands the negative affective experiences of the other, this understanding will serve to engender more positive future behavior. The child is supposed to use his inferences as to others' likely negative reactions as reasons for refraining from such behavior. There is an implicit assumption that if the hypothetical experience counters one's own preferences, then that behavior is to be refrained from so that others' preferences are not jarred in the real world. For instance, a 10-year-old explains, "Like say you're about to step on an ant, and you get in the ant's shoes and you wouldn't want to be killed or something; so I wouldn't really step on the ant" (Selman & Damon 1975, p. 71). Importantly, children do create such hypothetical worlds in which they invoke other people's preferences. Matthews (1984) documents the father of a 3-year-old who is eating a banana and asks the child, "You don't like bananas, do you, Steve?"; his son answers, "No, if you were me, you wouldn't like bananas either. Then, who would be the daddy?" (p. 113). The child was creating a hypothetical world in which his father was him, with the same preferences that he had,[13] but he recognized that by setting up this hypothetical world, he was removing his father from the Daddy role and that this role would no longer be occupied.

Often, children invoke perspective setting to change how others behave toward them, as shown in Table 13.12.

The contrast between the hypothetical and the real world created in such conditionals is crystallized in the following. A 12-year-old who told his therapist he was not scared when looking over the ledge of a skyscraper was told by the therapist that he himself would have been scared. The child replied,

> Well . . . if I were a therapist and I was trying to get a kid to see that it was all right to admit that he feels frightened about some things, I might say that I would be afraid to show him that it was okay to show that you were scared . . . But I'm not a therapist and I'm also not afraid of anything. (Selman, 1980, p. 266)

[13] An important aspect of such sentences is that they only make sense when the hypothetical world is set up so that the hypothetical people that are projected have normal reactions to events and such normalcy can be used to make sense of the wills, judgments, and affective reactions that are expressed in the sentence. This is precisely the same normalcy assumption that guided the formulation of my S-A-D model for understanding other people's covert psychological processes, as discussed in Chapter 4.

Viewed in this light, perspective setting involves attempts to get children to use different information than they would ordinarily use to guide their behavior toward others. It can also be used to garner different information about how one should behave in contexts that do not involve victims. For instance, in one attempt to solve conflicts between peers, the question is termed as "What would you have to do in John's place to get Peter to play with you?" (Montangero, Pons, & Cattin, 2000). In turn, perspective taking reflects attempts to adduce different information into the current context. In particular, when children play with perspective, they draw on their store of knowledge of the world and the people in it. For instance, a 4-year-old says, "I wouldn't eat dishes if I were him. If my name was Cookie Monster I would eat a whole bunch of sweets... they're not good for you though" (Hart & Risley, 1995, p. 90). That is, playing with perspective allows children to solidify their knowledge and expand their understanding of the social world and the behavior of others in that world. Importantly, when individuals play with perspective, they cannot adduce information that is not within their own representational systems. This means that play with perspective should be viewed as the application of new interpretational structures that engender different construal of the context in question.

To elaborate, research indicates that the adoption of different perspectives on the same context or representation can lead to variations recall and in the inferences drawn. For instance, Anderson and Pichert (1978) gave participants a passage to read, with half being asked to read it from the perspective of prospective home buyer and half from the perspective of a burglar. First, the perspective adopted influenced the content of recall, with each perspective leading to more recall of perspective-relevant items. Then, when participants were subsequently given the alternative perspective, they recalled more items, especially ones that were more aligned with the new perspective adopted. Similarly, Santioso, Kunda, and Fong (1990) led some participants to think that being introverted was desirable while others were led to think that being extraverted was desirable. They were then asked to recall memories of past behaviors related to being introverted or extraverted. Those participants who were led think introversion was desirable were more likely to recount introverted memories first and to produce more introverted memories than those participants who were led to think extraversion was desirable. This pattern affirms that adopting different perspectives and different motives alters the way memory search is conducted.

This is also the case with the adoption of physical perspectives. Nigro and Neisser (1983) found that they could induce participants to recall different images when viewed from a field perspective (i.e., looking out from one's own eyes) than from an observer perspective (i.e., looking at oneself from an outside perspective). Such manipulations of perspective have also been found to alter participants' subjective feelings (Kross, Ayduk, & Mischel, 2005) and the number of affective experiences recalled (McIsaac & Eich, 2002). Hence, adopting different perspectives implies searching one's memory in a way that is more consistent with these alternative perspectives, suggesting that one can guide one's own memory search in the direction implied by the perspective to be adopted. This is why Piaget accorded such importance to the child's ability to take different perspectives. As Piaget and Inhelder (1968/1973) summarize,

> throughout our life, we reorganize our memories and ideas of the past, conserving more or less the same material, but adding other elements capable of changing its significance, and above all, of changing our viewpoint. (Piaget & Inhelder, 1968, p. 381)

Piaget further elaborates the importance of perspective, saying that formal reasoning demands

> a sort of detachment from one's own point of view or from the point of view of the moment, enabling one to place oneself at that of others... deduction must detach itself from reality and take up its stand upon the plane of the purely possible.... It is only from the moment that a child can detach himself from his personal beliefs and enter into any foreign point of view that he really will know what is meant by a hypothesis. (Piaget 1979, pp. 71–72)

But adopting alternative viewpoints builds on the inherent reversibility of the individuals whose viewpoints are being taken. This is critical for two reasons. First, reversibility implies an intrinsic similarity between people. By denying similarity between self and other, one legitimizes dehumanizing him, allowing one to mistreat him. In Bandura's (2002) model, dehumanization works by denying the "like me" aspect of others, serving to suppress possible empathy for one's victim.

The adoption of different perspectives is a critical aspect of both Rawls's (1971) Theory of Justice and Kant's Categorical Imperative. To elaborate, Rawls's *original position* is a hypothetical situation in which rational individuals, assumed to be acting on behalf of and representing the interests of concrete individuals, are portrayed as choosing those principles of behavior that would best serve the interests of those they represent. The unique nature of this representation is that Rawls equips these rational individuals with a veil of ignorance, which serves to hide the particular characteristics, preferences, and interests of the parties they represent. The *veil* renders all concrete individuals the same – generic individuals – whose preferences can be assumed to be the same and can further be assumed to be best served by equal distribution of all goods and services. But the guiding principle that governs choices is still the self-interest of the individuals being represented by the chooser. The critical issue here is that each hypothetical agent cannot gain special benefits for those he represents because the veil hides their particular preferences; his task, then, becomes that of ensuring that no one's preferences are compromised. Harsanyi (1976) discusses this in terms of impersonal choice, contexts in which the individual either does not know how his choice would affect his personal interests or disregards them at the moment of choice. This is precisely the opposite of the Kantian, and Kohlbergian (e.g., Kohlberg, 1976), view of the ideal observer. Kant's ideal observer arrives at impartiality by *integrating* information about all relevant parties and giving the preferences of each individual the same weight in arriving at a just solution. The burden on the ideal spectator, then, is to include the perspectives of everyone, to universalize. Thus, Kant's categorical imperative focuses on all humans and how one would prefer people to act toward all human beings, rather than simply toward oneself. Piaget (1969) summarizes this aptly saying that formal thought demands "the possibility of placing oneself at every point of view and of abandoning one's own"; but furthermore, one needs to establish "a purely possible world" wherein one performs one's deductive work (pp. 71–72). Yet irrespective of which philosophical position one adopts, playing with perspective is the means of confronting other people's preferences. This leads us to Chapter 14 in which the focus is how individuals mind, or do not mind, others' preferences.

14 Minding One's Own Versus Others' Preferences: Altruism, Aggression, and Morality

5-year-old John objects to Adam taking blocks from him, saying, 'Hey, don't take wood from my property.' Adam answers, 'Well, we're sharing wood.' When John denies this, Adam returns the blocks. Later, John requests, 'Hey, I need some of your wood, please?' and Adam replies, 'Here friend.' (Pitcher & Schultz, 1983, p. 67)

Knowing other people's preferences is a necessary but not sufficient prerequisite to becoming a social being. Sociality is determined by whether, and how, knowing other people's preferences has an impact on the pursuit of our own preferences. The way one's own behavior relates to other people's actual or presumed preferences guides the labeling and evaluation of behavior, both by those whose preferences are affected and by others who are privy to its impact. In this chapter, I discuss the interplay between our preferences and the preferences of others as this interplay is manifest in altruism, aggression, and morality.

HOW PREFERENCES RELATE TO ALTRUISM, AGGRESSION, AND MORALITY

Individuals can pursue their own preferences with, or without, regard to other people's preferences, yielding the following continuum, as illustrated in Table 14.1 and elaborated below.

A. Self-Regarding Behavior

As discussed by economists (e.g., Camerer & Fehr, 2006), behavior is self-regarding when it is undertaken in the pursuit of our own preferences without regard for other people's preferences. The *inconsiderate* or *egoistic* person does not evidence concern with the preferences, outcomes, or behavior of others, as long as they do not have an impact on the pursuit of his own preferences. Jencks (1990) defines egoistic behavior in terms of three criteria: (1) the subjective definition of one's own welfare does not relate to the welfare of others; (2) one's behavior indicates a lack of concern with the welfare of others; and (3) one's concern with the welfare of others is viewed as an instrumental means of promoting one's own selfish ends; "Let me do my thing and to hell with you" is the egoist's motto.

In contrast, the *aggressive* individual acts to further his own preferences, despite knowing that such preferences may conflict with those of others. He may also actively prevent others from fulfilling their preferences and physically attempt to impose his own preferences on them. For the aggressive individual, it's "Either get out of my way, or else . . . . " More extreme, the spiteful person is viewed (e.g., Fehr & Fischbacher, 2002) as willing to *decrease* others' outcomes, even at a personal cost to himself, for example, "I'll show you . . . . "

B. Other-Regarding Behavior

On the more positive side, behavior undertaken in light of other people's preferences is discussed as *other-regarding*. When individuals behave in ways that are mindful of others' preferences, they exemplify being *considerate*. One can be considerate of others by *commission* (e.g., turn off the radio when someone is sleeping) or by *omission*, (e.g., not turn on the radio when someone is sleeping). I refer to these, respectively, as proactive and preemptive consideration.

Behavior that furthers others' preferences and does not further our own preferences, or possibly even sets them back, is *altruistic*. The defining characteristic of altruistic behavior is that it does not benefit the acting individual. Economists (e.g., Andreoni, 1990) differentiate *pure altruism* from *warm-glow altruism*. In the former, the individual wants to improve the actual outcomes of the other person, and in the latter, he derives positive affect out of doing "the right thing" but evidences little concern with others' welfare (e.g., donate money to a beggar to make oneself feel good but remain unconcerned with the beggar's plight). This implies that many "altruistic" behaviors are impure, involving both pure altruism and warm glow altruism. Yet psychologists (cf. Batson, 1991) generally accept the warm glow as an *incidental* outcome of pure altruism, with Batson claiming that altruistic individuals are motivated to improve the target's well-being and that feeling good about oneself is a possible consequence but not the goal of the altruistic act.

Table 14.1.

Self-Regarding Behavior	Other-Regarding Behavior	Group-Regarding Behavior
Egoistic	Considerate	Moral
Inconsiderate	Helpful	Just
Aggressive/spiteful	Altruistic	

C. Group-Regarding Behavior

At the end of this continuum, in *moral* or *just* behavior, the preferences of generalized others – not one's own preferences or those of specific others – guide one's behavior. Sen (1977) discusses moral behavior as *group-interested*, being concerned with the preferences of the general public or the general good rather than the preferences of any particular person. Since the general public is an abstract notion, morality reflects concern with the preferences of generic others "who populate our imagination" (Jencks, 1990, p. 59), fictions we use to guide our behavior.

In this light, social life pivots on the way we choose to mind, align, or misalign, our preferences with those of specific and generic others. Social life affords us many occasions that are conducive to minding and aligning our preferences with those of others, but it also affords us occasions when preferences are misaligned and can foster preferential conflict. Yet even in contexts in which one *could* remain unconcerned with others' preferences, people often take others' preferences into account (e.g., Bowles & Gintis, 2006), furthering such preferences even at a cost to themselves.

This implies that we act as decision makers, determining whether to relinquish our own preferences and give priority to others' preferences or whether to get others to delay or relinquish their preferences, giving priority to our own preferences or even imposing our preferences on them. Letting someone into the cafeteria line, accommodating a coworker by agreeing to delaying one's lunch break, lending someone our class notes, or refusing to accommodate others in these contexts, all reflect the prominence of others' preferences in our lives. The mark of social intelligence is our knowing how to navigate the social world in the pursuit of our preferences, avoiding or negotiating conflict with others who are likewise pursuing their preferences. The seeds of such social intelligence are planted in contexts in which young children need to resolve conflicts between their own preferences and those of others, as discussed in the next section

RESOLVING PREFERENTIAL CONFLICTS OVER OBJECTS AND SPACE

Each person involved in preferential conflict wants his preferences to hold sway so that he can enjoy the objects or space in question without intervention until he decides otherwise. Yet there is no a priori reason why one's preferences should hold sway over the preferences of others. Cultures develop norms of fairness that can be alluded to in resolving preferential conflicts over objects and space. Cultures also socialize consideration of others' preferences, teaching children that others' preferences need to be taken into account in interacting with them.

Turning to norms first, cultures provide definitions of fairness that govern how preferential conflicts are to be resolved and children learn which ones confer them rights over objects and space. For instance, ownership confers rights over objects, entitling one to refuse to share (Ross, 1996), as acknowledged by a preschool teacher who rejects a child's request for a book, saying, "Well, it's Gabriel's and he doesn't want you to read it right now"(Hall, CHILDES). Saying "mine!" and "my . . . ," what Painter (1984) calls *claim staking*, is young children's common means of dealing with conflict with both peers and siblings and increases dramatically after 24 months of age (Hay, 2006), as shown in Table 14.2. Notwithstanding the above object-centered conflicts between peers and siblings, the above children do implicitly accept the claim that ownership confers rights over objects. Violating the principle of ownership, then, requires justification of its violation. Thus, when a preschooler challenges a peer, saying, "My pencil! You have my pencil! Give me my pencil!" the attacked child responds, "Oh Jeez sorry I didn't know it was yours" (Kyratzis & Guo, 1996, p. 562).

Because they undermine the possibility of claim staking, such conflicts may be more frequent in families that promulgate common object ownership. When a child of 7;6 refuses to share, saying, "I bought that with my money and nobody's help," his father answers, "Well we share everything in this family, and that's all!" (MacWhinney, CHILDES). Educational settings are ones in which claim staking is often undermined because such settings provide objects and materials that are commonly shared. This is evident when a child of 6;5 denies that a pencil is his friend's, saying, "it belongs to everybody, to all the children . . . it belongs to Mlle L. because she bought it, and it belongs to all the children as well" (Piaget, 1926, p. 71).

When ownership cannot be invoked, parents and teachers may be faced with the onerous tasks of determining alternative criteria of fairness as well as ensuring understanding of these criteria and monitoring their implementation. Of these tasks, the first seems easiest. Parents seem to have an intuitive understanding of the criteria of fairness they find relevant and they allude to them, either implicitly or explicitly, in trying to resolve preferential conflicts. Ensuring understanding and monitoring adherence seem to be underplayed in their socialization attempts, as I discuss later. Moreover, criteria of fairness are generally invoked retroactively rather than proactively, with preferential conflicts being used as contexts for socializing criteria of fairness and to teach sharing (e.g., Beck & Wood, 1993).

Table 14.2.

	Age	Source
Conflicts with Peers		
To a 2-year-old:		
"Get out of my space. This is *my* space"	4 years	Ervin-Tripp & Gordon (1986, p. 83)
Yelling at peer		
C: "Hands off the car, it's mine!"		
C: "Don't touch my stuff, I won't let you"	Preschool	Tulviste & Koor (2005)
Arguing about a board:		
C: "That was mine. You go get your own. That was mine so go get your own"	Preschool	Corsaro & Rizzo (1990, p. 32)
Conflicts with Siblings		
C: "No, no, Sam – Benjy's ball, quit it"	22;11	Church (1966, p. 154)
Snatching object		
C: "That's my, that's Hal"	Toddler	Painter (1984, p. 216)
M questions C1 for grabbing doll from older sib		
C: "But it's mine!"	4 years	
C2: "She took it first"	6 years	Shure & Spivack (1978, p. 31)
Arguing with older sibling		
C: "It's mine too"		
C2: "No, I just share it with you"		
C: "Yes, and when you share it, it's mine with yours. Both together, it's ours"		
C2: "... yes, but I'm in charge here 'cause it was mine"	Preschool	Phinney (1986, p. 55)

A second normative criterion is "finders' keepers" – whoever is first to access an object has rights to it. Friedman and Neary (2008) found that children 2 to 4 years old apparently use what they call "a first possession heuristic" so that whoever is considered to have had access to an object first is deemed to be its rightful owner. This may well account for the fact that preschool children often invoke having first access to objects as justifications for their right to them. For instance, a preschooler demands a block taken from near where she was sitting, saying, "I had it first... but I had it first.... I had that first" (Corsaro & Rizzo, 1990, p. 32). Similarly, preschool boys are playing and one asks the other for some crackers being used as pretend bullets. The child being approached says, "I found it and I don't have to – give – any – to you unless you – . . . " (Corsaro, 1985, p. 115). A preschool teacher uses the same argument, saying, "Anthony, go away, please. Stephen was there first" (Gardner & Cass, 1965, p. 83).

An additional norm has to do with taking turns, specifying that everyone is entitled to a turn, whether objects or space is involved. When objects are involved, socialization agents tend to refer to the need to share whereas when space is involved, they tend to refer to the need to turn take. In both cases, though, the critical processes are engendering perceptions of shareability or of turn taking as feasible and explicating how sharing or turn taking are to be implemented. Socialization agents often erroneously appear to construe instructions to share and turn take as self-explanatory. Some examples, at home and in school, are shown in Table 14.3.

But how are children to share in the above contexts? In many cases, sharing actually means turn taking, or relinquishing one's turn with the object of contention, as shown in Table 14.4. In turn taking, one individual needs to wait while the other benefits from the object of conflict. This in itself is difficult both because of the aversiveness of the delay, and because of the frustration of seeing others enjoy the object of contention. Socialization agents, then, need to foster perceptions of turn taking as feasible, establish temporal criteria for turns, and verify the occurrence of turn taking. This may be why some preschool settings regulate sharing by specifying when children need to exchange items or leave certain play areas. For instance, when a child rejects a green marker, saying "I don't want a green one," the teacher answers, "Well the next time we change, I'll give you the color you want" (Eder, 1982, p. 254). In a preschool where an hourglass was used to regulate children's activities, a 4-year-old explains to a peer, "when it goes all the way through there it's your turn, all right?," advising her when all the sand has passed and her turn has come (Rubin, 1980, p. 57).

Yet often, socialization agents fail to establish criteria for turn taking, varying widely in the socialization practices they adopt when turn taking issues arise. Howes, Unger, and Matheson (1992) interviewed mothers of toddlers regarding a vignette concerning sharing of toys. Some mothers thought sharing was important and that children need externally imposed rules to regulate turn taking, even using timers and physically modeling trading of toys. In their view, parents need to intervene when

Table 14.3.

	Age	Source
At Home		
K refuses to share toy with peer M: "You have to learn to share" K: "I don't know how to share"	33;28	Karniol (Diary, Karen)
Siblings in conflict over doll M: "You must learn to share your toys"	Preschool	Shure & Spivack (1978, p. 31)
Peers in conflict M: "Both of you want to play with the clay. How can both of you play with it?" C: "share it" M: "Good"	Preschool	Shure & Spivack (1978, p. 126)
At School		
Children quarrel over a spade T points to another spade T: "there's one, all right," C: "I don't want that one" T: "You have to share"	Preschool	Tizard & Hughes (1984, p. 228)
T: "Kyle, you need to share your marker with Derrick"	Preschool	Kontos (1999, p. 369)
Fighting over a rocking horse T: "We've got to share. We've only got one horse and we've got two kids who want it"	Preschool	Hall (CHILDES)

a problem arises, with their primary strategies being distracting the child from the object of contention or removing the toy. Other mothers indicated they would only intervene in a crisis, explaining that children need to learn to cope with preferential conflict (e.g., "as a rule I let them play and fight out the battles"; Sears, Maccoby, & Levin, 1957, p. 243). Finally, some mothers maintained that children have a right not to share, saying, "they have the right to continue playing with it and not just because another child wants to play with it give it up. If they choose to (i.e., share), that is wonderful" (ibid, p. 86). In fact, in home observations, parents were found to intervene in less than half the conflicts between their preschool children (Perlman & Ross, 2005; Perozynski & Kramer, 1999), doing so primarily when asked to intervene or when conflict escalates dangerously, with intervention occurring primarily in conflict about sharing and physical aggression (Ross et al., 1994). But parental interventions often refer to the norms discussed above.

In this context, it is sometimes unclear which norm takes precedence over another. Intervening in an argument over a spade, the teacher says, "I think Kevin was using it first, Donna." When the child insists that she had it first, the teacher says, "You have it back in a minute, all

Table 14.4.

	Age	Source
C grabs toy M: "You should either play together or take turns . . . Children must learn to share"	Preschool	Shure (1985, p. 201)
T gives C hammer T: "You must share them. When you've finished hammering for a while, put it down and then someone else can use it"	Preschool	Gardner & Cass (1965, p. 81)
Two Cs fighting over doll T: "Billy, Jennifer would like to have a turn with it now. When she's through, you may have another turn"	Preschool	Genishi & Di Paolo (1982, p. 64)
T: "Let's let David have his turn now, and then somebody else can do it"	Preschool	Eder (1982, p. 228)

Table 14.5.

	Age	Source
Focusing on Politeness		
C wants toy bear C2 is holding		
M: "OK, well ask Judy nicely for him. You can take turns, I know"	33 mos.	Garvey (1984, p. 109)
C complains about a peer		
T: "Perhaps you haven't asked him nicely. It's very important how you ask. Go and ask Bobby nicely"	Preschool	Gardner & Cass (1965, p. 87)
C wants C2 to relinquish toy		
T: "Well, ask him nicely to leave your boat alone"	Preschool	Gardner & Cass (1965, p. 81)
Focusing on Turn Duration		
T commends C for turn taking, adding		
T: "You had a turn and then it was his turn, but you didn't give him many minutes to play with it did you. Do you understand? We must take turns because we've only got one"	Preschool	Gardner & Cass (1965, p. 68)
T: "How long have you had this drum, old chap? A long time? Let someone else have a turn"	Preschool	Gardner & Cass (1965, p. 81)

right?" and tells the boy to give it back to her when he's finished (Tizard & Hughes, 1984, p. 228). The implication is that the first possession norm is less important than the norm than everyone should have a turn. The importance of the turn-taking norm may be conveyed explicitly. When a 4-year-old complains that her older siblings won't give her a turn at hopscotch, the mother questions whether they've had a turn, commands them to give her a turn, and when they resist, she repeats, "Well, you give her a turn" (Whiting & Edwards, 1988).

Importantly, though, as Bruner (1978b) argues, when a 26-month-old child says, "I first" in the context of peer play, this constitutes "a claim," reflecting her understanding of turn-taking norms and her assumption that "her interlocutors know of the same rule and that they will accept her claim, unless they have reason to challenge it" (p. 108). This is why children acknowledge the legitimacy of other's rights to turn take, both as turn takers and as turn awaiters, with turn takers saying things like "This is my last turn. Here you can have it" (Alloway, 1999, p. 161). In keeping with this, a girl of 5;1 delays complying with her friend's request, saying "I'm nearly finished. Just one more to do. That's the last one" (McTear, 1981, p. 122). Recipients of such temporizing attempts apparently accept such temporization, with turn awaiters expressing similar acknowledgements: "Can I have a turn, please," "Can I do that, please, now?" (Garvey, 1984, p. 113). Garvey (1984) found that when sharing or turn taking were proposed, 77 percent of all conflicts were terminated. In fact, Garvey (1984) found that the majority of turn-taking requests occurred when the child interacting with the object appeared to have some claim to it. For instance, when a preschooler grabs an eraser and another child wants it back, he's told "I'm using it" and the reply is, "I know, I'm waiting for you" (Corsaro & Maynard, 1996, p. 168). When others don't abide by turn-taking rules for play, children may opt out of playing with them, for example, when an older sibling asks a 4-year-old child to play hopscotch, he refuses, saying, "you don't let it be my turn" (Sealey, 2000, p. 156).

When a given context is viewed as subject to turn taking, parents and teachers may focus on the politeness of rejected requests to turn take as well as the duration of the turn-taking interval, as shown in Table 14.5. In the first set of examples, the bottleneck is viewed as inhering in the politeness of the request (e.g., a British teacher explains "If you are nicely mannered people are always pleased to help you," King, 1978, p. 55) rather than abuse of turn duration, whereas in the second set, abuse of the duration of the turn was viewed as the problem.

Whereas adult intervention of this type teaches children the criteria that guide turn taking, adult intervention can be a mixed blessing. It may solve the immediate conflict. But the prime purpose of intervention should be to redefine contexts as involving shareables or as subject to turn taking and to set up criteria that govern sharing and turn taking. In fact, both parents and teachers tend to intervene without achieving these goals, thereby potentiating the recurrence of conflict, as shown in Table 14.6. The children above were not advised how to negotiate turn taking, and continued to quibble so that the threat was eventually carried out. Children do learn the structure of such threats, though, for example, a preschooler who saw boys fighting over a toy she brought to school, yelled, "Share! Share! . . . If you don't share, I'll have to put it back in my cubby" (Meyer, 2003, p. 95).

SHARING AND FOSTERING SHARING

The way sharing is socialized varies by culture. For instance, Japanese mothers apparently encourage their

Table 14.6.

	Age	Source
At Home		
F: "ask Jennifer if she wants to draw with the chalk.... Which one do you want give Jennifer?" C: "Nothing" F: "Nomi, that's not one of the choices.... I'll take both pieces of chalk away if you don't give Jennifer one"	3;4 years	Sachs (CHILDES)
M insists children share dolls M: "I'll have to take them away"	Preschool	Shure & Spivack (1978, p. 32)
M wants siblings to share	24 mos.	
M: "I'll take it away, I don't want no fighting"	4 years	Ross (1996, p. 93)
At School		
C refuses to share toy brought from home T: "Share, Brent. If you can't share then the car goes back in your cubby"	Preschool	Meyer (2003, p. 94)
fighting over book C screams: "she won't share" T: "If we do not share I will put it up"; conflict continues T takes the book, puts it up on a shelf	Preschool	Kovarsky, Stephan, & Braswell (1994, p. 175)

children to share primarily by indicating that they themselves want some of the relevant item, saying, "Gee, I want to drink too" or "As for me, coffee is good. Please give me coffee" (Clancy, 1986, p. 229).[1] In this vein, during toy play, a mother asks her child, "Will you bake a fish for me? I'd sure like to have a fish baked" (p. 230). These mothers did not explicitly ask the child to share but rather made an indirect request alluding to their preferences. In contrast, American mothers tell their children explicitly to share and instruct them to make offers of consumables. When a toddler offers her mother candy, her mother suggests she offer some to the other adults present, saying, "Go ask Peggy and Terry if she wants some candy. If they want some candy." The child then asks "want some?" (Miller, 1982, p. 102). As the mother of a 2-year-old explains, she expects mothers to chastise their children for not sharing, to say, "that's not nice. Give 'em all some" (Miller, 1992, p. 58). Needing to share toys is also emphasized, especially during playdates, with children being told, "you let your guests play with your toys . . . and not "snatch it away from them, 'it's mine'" (Newson & Newson, 1968, p. 113). The implication of what needs to be done in such contexts is clear. Others have preferences that are to be taken into account and they too are entitled to enjoy the object of conflict.

Interestingly, children may be advised to share not with specific others but with all those present, as shown in Table 14.7. But contrast the above generic statements with the following, in which a preschool child at sandplay is told by the teacher, "Come on, David, you can't use all the sand . . . let Alan have some too" (Tough, 1973, p. 52)

Children do, in fact, appear to learn to share things that come in quantities, and especially food items, with both family and peers, as shown in Table 14.8.

The willingness to share in such contexts may well emerge out of children's perception that there is an abundant supply of the object in question and after they ensure that they got their fair share. According to *Just World Theory* (Lerner, 1980), we only worry about whether others have received their just desserts after ensuring that our own just claims have been adequately met. In line with this, when they are offered goodies, children frequently ask regarding their absent sibling's share. To illustrate, at 18;28, when Matthew's mother gives him a cracker, he reaches toward the box saying his version of his sister's name. When he gets the second cracker, he goes and offers it to her (Dunn, 1988). Similarly, after being given a goody Orren, at 31;21, admonishes me in both languages,[2] saying, "Karen too when Karen come home give Karen Bamba," an Israeli corn-based snack. While out shopping with her mother, a child is allowed to have a bag of candy. She then turns to her mother and, referring to her sibling, asks, "Should we bring a bag of candy for John too?" (Pettersson, Olsson, & Fjellström, 2004, p. 322). This pattern needs to be contrasted with contexts in which children fight with their siblings over the need to share objects and sweets.

[1] Kaye and Charney (1980) document a similar pattern with a mother who asks a child to give her a knife (e.g., "Well what about me? Give me a knife, I have to have one too," p. 220).

[2] Hebrew: "Karen tavo habaita at titen la bamba gum."

Table 14.7.

	Age	Source
At dinner, C takes too many peaches M: "Adam, there are other people at this table," asks C to put some back	Preschool	Ochs, Pontecorvo, & Fasulo (1996, p. 37)
C hogs flour at playtime T: "Oh, Lucy – not all the flour dear – leave some for the next people"	Preschool	Tough (1973, p. 52)

SHARING AND FRIENDSHIP

Children do not generally share with everyone. Sharing and turn taking are associated with friendship and liking. By definition, friends are supposed to engage in sharing and turn taking. Doing so indicates mutual liking; refusing to do so is a mark of disliking or friendship breakdown. Concomitantly, one likes one's friends because they share and sharing serves as an index of liking and friendship. On getting a bowl from a peer, a 5-year-old says, "Thank you. You're my best friend" (Pitcher & Schultz, 1968, p. 68). A 3-year-old attempts to capitalize on past sharing, asking, "Do you like me? Remember when I gave you a gumball?" (Pitcher & Schultz, 1983, p. 67). Being friends justifies complying with requests to share. When a child of 6;8 asks whether he can play, his playmate of 7;6 answers, "It's my game, you can play, you're my friend" (Sluckin, 1981, p. 45).

In fact, refusals to share are often met with reminders regarding the friendship status between the supplicant and the refuser. A 5-year-old child approaches a peer who is eating some crisps, puts out his hand and says, "I'm your friend, let me have some" – and his request is granted (Sluckin, 1981, p. 61). Given the norm of sharing, individuals who share are labeled "nice" and those who do not share are negatively evaluated. Preschool teachers commend sharing, saying: "I like the way you shared your toy with Trent" (Kontos, 1999), "you gave that teapot to Jimmy. That was nice of you" (Edwards, 1987, p. 143), and "Mazal, you shared the doll's clothes today with Sarah in such a grown-up way" (Krown, 1974, p. 44). Both teachers and parents also label not sharing in negative terms. A Japanese mother chides her child for not sharing, saying "If we don't say "Help yourself" to them, it's no good" (Clancy, Akatsuka, & Strauss, 1997, p. 53). When a child refers to cookies that her mother baked, saying "I'm gonna eat all of them," the mother says, "Oh, you're being selfish are ya" (Walkerdine, 1988, p. 132). Similarly, when Simone, at 22 months, won't share a blanket while pretending to sleep, her father laments, "Oh Mone! Don't be so mean to me. I'd like to sleep a little too. OK?"[3] (Miller, 1979). He uses the adjective *mean* to negatively label not sharing. Though children may not know how to share, such incidents teach them that sharing is valued and not sharing is frowned on.

Friendship also leads to *ritualized sharing* (Katriel, 1987), which dictates within-group allocations. For instance, Katriel surveys ritualized sharing in Israeli children's peer groups, in which giving friends a bite of whatever one has bought or brought is a social imperative, "something you must do even though you would prefer not to" (p. 314). When an American child on a baseball team buys gum, the other children congregate, making it seem "like feeding time at the aquarium, with Dino tossing out gum to a sea of outstretched hands" (Fine, 1987, p. 45). Children themselves acknowledge the force of ritualized sharing. In discussing their friendship group, girls explain that "if we've got biscuits we share them all around," and that when a girl brings an apple she gives everybody a bite (Meyenn, 1980, p. 122). The *ought* aspect of such sharing is emphasized when the above girls further explain that "You have to lend things to each other . . . giving each other crisps" (p. 126). Not sharing in such contexts is viewed as justifying aggressive responses toward the "mean" individual.

Concomitantly, children learn that behavior is evaluated in terms of its relation to other people's preferences (e.g., "If you're mean, no one will come play with you," Mody, 2005, p. 110) and they start to label both themselves and others in terms of their patterns of sharing and lack of it. After her mother asks her to share a book with her and she refuses, a child, at 25;7, talks to herself saying, "Mommy some. Me some. There. Share," and again, "give Mummy book. Be kind" (Oldenburg, 1990, p. 33). A 4-year-old asks his friend, "Are you mad?" and the friend answers, "Yeah. You know that wasn't very nice to take that away from me" (Gottman, 1986b, p. 172). A peer tells a 3-year-old, "You're selfish Margaret . . . you won't give me your scissors." When the girl who had been labeled "selfish" hands over something else later, the recipient tells the teacher, "Teacher, I told Margaret she's not selfish" (Paley, 1986, p. 95). In a poignant example, a girl prays, "Jesus help me not to be like my brother Adam and take other people's turn in the front of the car. Thank you that I'm not mean like him" (Ochs & Capps, 2001, p. 234).

Given the norm of sharing with one's friends, refusing to share with friends needs to be justified. When a girl is reminded of their friendship status when she

[3] German: "Ach Mone! Nun sei doch nicht so grausam zu mir. Ich will doch auch'n bisschen heia machen. Hm?"

Table 14.8.

	Age	Source
Addressing Family Members		
Eating cake, breaks off piece, brings to M's mouth C: "Some Mummy?"	22 mos.	Painter (1984, p. 198)
C: "Want some too?," "Wanna bite?"	23 mos.	Tomasello (1992)
Child gets ice cream, addresses grandmother: C: "You want some ice cream too?"	29 mos.	Shatz (1994, p. 128)
Addressing Peers		
During tea party with real food, to girl of 32 mos. C: "Would you like a chocolate-covered nut, too?" After girl accepts and eats, offers again, C: "Here's a nut. Want it?"	33 mos.	Garvey (1984, p. 98)
C has a frozen lollipop, pushes it in peer's mouth C: "Go on, have a bit"	Preschool	Sylva, Roy, & Painter (1986, p. 84)

refuses to share, she retorts, "I forgot. We can still share roller skates" (Pitcher & Schultz, 1983, p. 67). Similarly, a kindergarten child explains, "Remember yesterday you hit me with that plant?... because I wouldn't give you none of my fruit snack 'cause I forgot. I forgot!" (Dyson, 1993, p. 72). When no justifications are offered for refusing to share, then, children may perceive it as legitimate to threaten or aggress against those who do not share, as shown in Table 14.9.

Children do in fact carry out such threats as evident when a toddler explains, "I hit him because he did not give me the toy" (Golinkoff & Hirsh-Pasek, 1999, p. 184). Similarly, on being asked why he was bitten at day care, Orren, at 31;11, answers "Because I take to Avishay the penguin," elaborating that the other child refused to share the toy. In fact, Troop-Gordon and Asher (2005) found that when others represented obstacles to preference fulfillment in hypothetical vignettes, many 9- to 12-year-old children indicated a desire to revenge or retaliate, changing their strategies to be more aggressive.

There are, however, contexts in which refusing to share is viewed as legitimate. One is not expected to share with others who are mean, unkind, or aggressive. A 5-year-old tells her friend, "You hit me, so you're not going to have my candy" (Pitcher & Schultz, 1983, p. 47). Katriel (1985) found that when children were *brogez*, the Hebrew term for being in a state of conflict with another child, this provided justifications for refusing to play with him, not sharing, and not helping him when in need. In this vein, a preschooler tells her peers, "Don't talk to Alison! One day she was being mean and not giving me my book" (Kyratzis & Green, 1997, p. 25).

AGGRESSION

When is aggression justified? Children often get mixed messages regarding aggression, ones that may make it difficult to abstract when and why they should refrain from aggressive behavior. First, they may be warned against aggressing despite being physically punished themselves. Second, children may be physically punished for their aggressive behavior. For instance, a child who pulls the ears of a toy rabbit is warned: "If I catch you pulling Mike's ears I'm going to give you a good spanking" (Clancy, Akatsuka, & Strauss, 1997, p. 30). Older children state explicitly that their involvement in physical altercations may lead to being physically punished: "they'll beat me up," explaining "Slap on my back, or on my face" (Mayall, 2002, p. 124). In fact, children's uncertainty as to adult reactions to aggression results in reduced aggression

Table 14.9.

	Age	Source
C (to peer): "Give me a sweet or I'll hit you"	3 years	Tough (1977, p. 66)
C (to peer) "If you don't let me I'll bust your head"	5 years	Pitcher & Schultz (1983, p. 51)
C1 asks C2 for ruler Request is ignored, C1 repeats it twice C2: "Huh?" C1: "Will you please gimme the ruler before I knock you down"	12 years	Mitchell-Kernan & Kernan (1977, p. 205)

Table 14.10.

	Age	Source
C says she spits at boys who try to kiss her M: "Oh that's not nice you just... you just tell them you don't want them to do that or you won't play with them"	Preschool	Herot (2002, p. 172)
C complains about his friends M: "You just tell them, just tell them you don't want them to do that or you won't play with them"	4 years	Beals (1993, p. 506)
M: "The next time she comes when she starts scratching you have to tell her okay? Next time you tell her.... Tell her "stop doing that. I don't like that. That's not nice"	5 years	Herot (2002, p. 165)

when an authority figure is present (Karniol & Heiman, 1987) and lower retaliation rate to hurts inflicted by adults (Lambert, 1974). Children and mothers acknowledge this, saying, "I would get angry but I would not show it" (Wilson, 1974, p. 170), and "he knows not to show his anger to us" (Rothbaum, Morelli, Pott, & Liu-Constant, 2000, p. 342).

On the other hand, children are often encouraged to retaliate, with some mothers even elaborating how children should retaliate, suggesting to a 7-year-old, "well go and hit them back then; if you can't hit them, kick them back" (Newson & Newson, 1976, p. 202). Such instructions were also given to girls: "I'll give you a shilling.... If you can't hit him, kick him as hard as you can and he won't do it again" (Newson & Newson, 1976, p. 52). The legitimacy of retaliating may also be conveyed to children by other children, as when a first-grade girl says to a kindergarten boy, "don't let them (the other boys) pick on you, OK? If somebody hit you, you better hit them back. See, if you just take a stick..." (Dyson, 1993, p. 63).

The dilemma children face in this domain may be compounded by the fact that some parents warn their children of being physically punished for *failing* to retaliate. The mother of a 4-year-old reported that she told her daughter, "Go and hit Susan back, else Mummy'll smack you" (Newson & Newson, 1968, p. 127). In fact, Newson and Newson (1968, 1976) found that the mothers of many 4- and 7-year-old children warned them that they would be physically punished *unless* they retaliate physically when attacked.

But the message conveyed to children often centers on the need to stand up for one's rights by hitting back, for example, "I don't want her to come running. I'm like, defend yourself and fight it out" (Kasserow, 1999, p. 218). In this vein, a mother tells a preschooler, "Everytime he hits you, hit him back. I don't want you to be so timid.... If you don't learn to defend yourself, kids will keep on hitting you" (Shure & Spivack, 1978, p. 118). When a 2-year-old and her 5-year-old cousin are fighting over a doll, the mother intervenes, telling the toddler to say "keep off"; the toddler then swats the older child, saying, "keep off, my baby" (Miller, 1982, p. 102). The mother does not respond, thereby legitimizing aggression as a means of defending possessions. When a middle-school girl tells of a fight with a friend, she indicates that her mother "said to keep at it until she cries," adding, "I couldn't.... I can't do things like that" (Meyenn, 1980, p. 132). It is the child, and not the mother, who indicates reluctance to aggress.

Parents may also sanction sibling retaliation in teaching children to stand up for their rights. When a child complained that her older sister squeezed her, the mother said, "well, thump her one," complaining, "now they thump each other and then come crying afterwards" (Backett, 1982, p. 149). When a child takes her sister's straw, she is told, "Give her back her straw before she hits you" (Tizard & Hughes, 1984, p. 147), with the mother implicitly legitimizing aggression in the service of getting back one's possessions. Similarly, a father relates, "his brother used to push him around when he was little.... I'm glad to see he does it every once in a while" (Gottman Katz, & Hooven 1997, p. 78). Aggression can also be legitimized by statements that imply that aggression was a justified retaliation for a prior act of aggression, for example, "Listen to this. How come you scratched Ivan today?.... How come? What had Ivan been doing to you?"[4] (Ochs & Shohet, 2006, p. 46).

Rather than urging children to stand up for themselves, parents may promote the strategy of retaliating verbally to physical acts of aggression by others, as shown in Table 14.10.

Although parents who urge verbal rather than physical retaliation may differ in other ways as well, research has not addressed such possible differences.

Yet another approach parents may take is that aggression is legitimate toward some people, but not others, often focusing on others' sex or friendship status. In this vein, a mother explains that she taught her son "You beat up little boys but you don't beat up little girls" (Sears, Maccoby, & Levin, 1957, p. 399). In fact, a child who talked of hitting

[4] Italian: "Ascolta una cosa. Come mai oggi hai graffiato a Ivan tu?... Come mai? Che t'aveva fato Ivan?"

both boys and girls was asked, "You don't punch girls, do you?" (Cloran, 1989, p. 121). Girls themselves echo the view that boys are not allowed to hit girls, for example, "You're not supposed to slap girls, 'cause – girls are not that strong, like boys" (Dyson, 1994, p. 219), implying that boys are fair game. As for others' friendship status, when a child of 2;6 tells her mother, "I hit Janna's nose." Her mother answers, "Janna's your friend. You shouldn't hit your friend in the nose" (Warren, CHILDES). A Japanese preschool teacher tells a child, "this isn't your big brother, so don't punch or wallop your friends" (Peak, 1991, p. 161), thereby implying that hitting one's siblings is legitimate. The messages conveyed above are that some targets are legitimate as victims of aggression while certain targets, like one's friends, are not legitimate victims, and one should refrain from aggressing against them.

Such messages may also convey that refraining from aggression can serve as an index of one's friendship status. Karen, at 29;29, gives voice to this connection when she says, "Ashley doesn't know how to be a friend . . . she was in the restaurant and she pushed Karen," relating a 3-week-old episode. A preschooler relates why she doesn't like a peer, explaining, "When I was about four she pulled my hair" (Kyratzis & Green, 1997, p. 25). This linkage is also evident when a child of 3;7 asks, "Will you come and play with me if I don't hit you?" (Shields, 1978). Consequently, being reminded of one's friendship status can be used to deter aggression. When a boy of 6;9 wants to beat up an age-mate, a third child intervenes, saying, "He's your friend really, isn't he, isn't he?" (Sluckin, 1981, p. 630). Being friends precludes aggressing against those defined as one's friends and reminders of one's friendship status should deter aggression.

Interestingly, in some cultures, aggressive behavior and fighting are viewed as legitimate, natural responses and as important for children's emergent ability to deal with conflicts with peers. The view in Japan, for instance, is that fights

> are an important experience in acquiring proper social attitudes and behavior . . . . Through fighting, children communicate their own needs and desires to others, come to accept others' needs and desires, and learn the rules of child society . . . through fighting, children come to understand others' viewpoints and learn tolerance, self-restraint, and self assertiveness. (Peak, 1991, pp. 159–160)

In this view, children should not be "deprived of natural opportunities" to develop these skills. Guided by this approach, a Japanese teacher says,

> We don't encourage children to fight, but children need to fight when they are young if they are to develop into complete human beings . . . it is by fighting and experiencing what it feels like to hit someone and hurt them and to be hit and be hurt that they learn to control this urge to fight. (Tobin, Wu, & Davison, 1989, p. 33)

Moreover, an assistant principal even said that as the preschool year progresses, they put fewer toys out "to give children additional opportunities to learn to share and to deal with the conflicts which arise" (ibid).[5] From this perspective, then, a child who provokes fights serves a valuable social function, giving others a chance to learn and rehearse strategies for resolving conflict and to serve as mediators in others' conflicts. Yet from the perspective of Dodge's (1986; Crick & Dodge, 1994) social cognitive model of aggression, the aggressive child is prone to misinterpret and misconstrue cues in the social environment. Nonintervention by adults in such contexts does not serve to disabuse the aggressive child of his biased perceptions.

Even if fighting is viewed as a natural and necessary part of socialization, parents may draw the line at the use of either real or makeshift weapons. The mother of a 4-year-old explains that children can't do a great deal of harm with their hands, indicating that she intervenes when they use spades (Newson & Newson, 1968). Questioned as to what he thinks when another child hits him, a child tells his mother, "That I will shoot him . . . . I got a gun, I'm gonna shoot him." The mother does not indicate that this is unacceptable and merely asks, "You're gonna shoot Johnny?" (Fivush, 1994, p. 150). She makes such retaliation an acceptable response.

Yet guns are not unique in terms of their harmful potential. Children resort to using all kinds of objects as weapons. A 35-month-old says to his younger sister, "I hit you next time. So stop acting bad. You talking back? . . . One more time, I'm whipping your butt," and he hits her with a stick (Hart & Risley, 1999, p. 163). In the narratives they collected from children, Peterson and McCabe (1983) found children who indicated either wanting to hit, hitting, or being hit with milk bottles, brooms, and rakes. Yet in some sense, restrictions against the use of weapons are futile because any object can serve as a weapon and children can pretend that any object is a real weapon. A preschool teacher explains that disallowing war toys or toy guns is a hard rule to enforce "since children can pick up a block or a banana and go "bang bang" (Tobin, 1989, p. 142). Engel (2005) describes a situation in which a preschooler wants to pretend Lego pieces are guns, saying, " 'member that shooting killing game. Let's play that," and his peer replies "No we can't play that. Laurie said shooting is not okay" but a few minutes later, joins in saying, "I shoot it at you and you die" (p. 520). Paley (1984) notes that in her kindergarten, fingers and sticks served equally well as pretend weapons and were accompanied by loud "bang, bang" noises.

AVOIDING HARM TO OTHERS

Children need to understand why aggression is negatively evaluated; such understanding is not intuitive. A child may

[5] The impact of toy scarcity is unclear. Hayes (2005) found that having too few dolls in a preschool led to children's attempts to resolve the scarcity by negotiating. But providing more play materials has been found to increase positive interactions and reduce aggression (Prescott, 1987; Smith & Connolly, 1977).

Table 14.11.

	Age	Source
Sitting on mother's knee, C kicks her M: "Don't kick because that hurts"	24 mos.	Dunn (1988, p. 27)
C kicks mother M: "Now don't kick Mommy. That hurts. Now that isn't nice." C does it again M: "No kicking. That hurts now. That's not nice." C says she is playing M: "Well, you can play but not hurt. You're kicking and that hurts"	4 years	Whiting & Edwards (1988, p. 114)
C1 tosses blocks to C2 C2: "Don't throw it, it hurts me, it's not funny"	Preschool	Pitcher & Schultz (1983, p. 7)
C to peer who hurt him C: "stop it. You hurt my head"	Preschool	Garvey (1975)

understand that he is in pain after being the victim of aggression but may not infer that pain is also experienced by the targets of his aggression. Adults' role in this context is to foster such understanding, to clarify that others experience pain when they are the victims of aggression. Adults' most prevalent reaction, though, is to demand cessation of the hurtful behavior, often without elaborating why. To illustrate, when a toddler repeatedly hits his mother's face with a pom-pom, she admonishes him, saying, "Don't ever do that again, Tony!" (Wells, 1986, p. 11) – not explicating that it hurts her, that one shouldn't hurt others, and so forth. Parents may also provide evaluative labels, indicating that hitting is *bad*, or *not nice*, without explaining why. Children may, then, learn to apply evaluative labels without adequate understanding of why these labels are being used. Parents may also provide *inappropriate* evaluative labels. For instance, a mother admonishes a child for grabbing a toy, saying, "Grabbing is not nice" (Shure, 1985, p. 201) and a child pretending to be a Blue Fairy who attempted to grab her mother's yogurt was asked, "Didn't they teach you manners at fairy school?" (Gordon, 2008, p. 339). In these instances, grabbing was evaluated as not nice and rude rather than as aggressive. Consequently, children may learn to apply inappropriate evaluative labels for their own behavior.

Often, when the negative consequences of aggression are referred to, it is their impact on the person admonishing the child, whether it is a parent or a peer, that is addressed, as shown in Table 14.11.

Messages as to why aggressive behavior should be refrained from are perhaps more convincing when they allude to their potential impact on third parties. Such messages can be proactive or retroactive. A preschool teacher proactively warns a child, "Don't sit on his legs, darling, I'm sure you'll hurt him" (Gardner & Cass, 1965, p. 86). Generally, though, such messages tend to be issued retroactively, after someone has been hurt, for example, a mother tells her 4-year-old, "Well, when you go on a swing, you've gotta watch that its not anywhere near Richard before you start moving" (Wootton, 1986, p. 151), clarifying this *after* the younger brother had been hit in the head by the older child's swing. In fact, children start to allude to the potential impact of their behavior on specific others, as when a 7-year-old child explains, "When I hit my little brother, he's allowed to hit me back but I must never hit him because he's smaller and I could hurt him badly" (Robinson & Rackstraw, 1972b, p. 318).

The problem with such admonitions, though, is that they do not make it clear that the younger sibling or the peer victim is not unique in this context and that anyone in the path of the swing would be similarly hurt. Note the contrast with admonitions that warn of the impact of the child's behavior on generic others, both at home and at preschool, as shown (with emphasis added) in Table 14.12. These admonishments make it explicit that one's behavior victimizes others, not necessarily those others whom one has hurt in the past or the specific others whom one has victimized. This is also well illustrated in the words of an English mother whose 3-year-old says, "I want to kick you!"; she responds, "You mustn't kick people" (Dunn & Brown, 1991, p. 162), turning the issue into a generic one, referring to anyone else that the child may want to kick. Even clearer about the generic implications of physical victimization, a mother explains,

> If she kicked me or if she slapped me, I'd slap her back. I just told her that it doesn't feel good to get slapped. If she didn't want to get slapped herself, not to slap other people. The reaction would be the same in anyone that got slapped – they wouldn't like it. (Sears, Maccoby, & Levin, 1957, p. 249)

It may well be, though, that statements about specific others are more likely to be made by victims and statements about generic others are made by observers. For instance, after being the victim of aggression in

Table 14.12.

	Age	Source
At Home		
C hits playmate		
M: "Did you hit Susan? Why would you hit Susan? You don't want to hurt *people*.... No, Todd. You mustn't hit *people*"	22 mos.	Zahn-Waxler, Radke-Yarrow, & King (1979)
M: "Yes, but I did ask you to use the end swing, the rope one, in case that one bashes into *someone*"	Preschool	Tizard & Hughes (1984, p. 141)
C hit sister with a ball		
M: "So next time you don't throw your ball at *people*, okay?"	Preschool	Fung & Chen (2001, p. 426)
At School		
Two C's fighting		
T: "It's wrong to pinch *people*.... It hurts when you pinch and *people* don't like it"	Preschool	Meyer (2003, p. 82)
C grabs object		
T: "Listen, I think if you hit *people* like that you do have to go away. Better not do that anymore y'know. *People* really don't like it"	Preschool	Newman (1978, p. 248)
C's mistreat other C		
T: "We expect thoughtfulness, to be thinking of other *people* – not hurting *people*"	Preschool	Reid (1999, p. 182)
C1 pushes C2		
T: "Dan, you cannot push *people* in school"	Preschool	Malloy & McMurray (1996, p. 201)
C hit a peer		
T: "Hey, Hey, you shouldn't hit *people* like that"	Preschool	Peak (1991, p. 160)

retaliation for not having something shared, the victim says, "James, you couldn't just slap me with that plant"; and another boy responds, "Lamar, 'cause you can't hit nobody" (Dyson, 1993, p. 72). Whereas the child who was hit is making a statement about not hitting one's friends, the nonvictimized child makes a more general statement about hitting people. To the best of my knowledge, research has not addressed the possible socialization differences of using specific versus generic others as possible victims. Yet this may be an important variable given that Zahn-Waxler, Radke-Yarrow, & King (1979) found that children whose mothers frequently verbalized absolute principles regarding the need to refrain from hurting others evidenced more reparation at a later time period.

Even with the best of intentions, though, hurting others cannot be avoided entirely. Children are taught that when they do hurt others, apologies need to be expressed, as shown in Table 14.13.

Children thereby learn that hurting others, even accidentally, cannot be justified and they learn to apologize for accidentally inflicting hurt on others, as shown in Table 14.14.

Of course, saying *sorry* spontaneously also reflects one's recognition of self as having the potential of being a harm-doer.

SYMPATHY FOR AND CONSIDERATION OF OTHERS

In addition to learning to refrain from hurting others, children need to learn consideration for others. In this context, I differentiated earlier between *proactive consideration* in which one does something to benefit the other directly versus *preemptive consideration* in which one avoids doing something that could potentially disturb others. In addition, one needs to differentiate between concern with others' physical states and concern for their psychological states. Young children evidence surprising sensitivity to others' aversive states. For instance, Wolf (1982) reports an instance when she fell and hurt her nose, subsequently sitting and rubbing her nose in pain. The 14-month-old child that she was observing hugged her and offered her his security blanket. His remarkable behavior reflects the understanding that being hugged and holding one's security blanket are helpful – at least to him. Older children seem to focus on the target's needs and evidence context-appropriate consideration. When I was sitting on the beach and indicated being cold, Karen, at 22 months, says, "Have to bring Mummy a shirt; Otherwise it's cold." She had taken my statement of being cold as reflecting a need to be covered. Evidencing similar concern, Orren, at 34;26, says, "Mommy take an umbrella 'cause I don't want that the rain will drop on your coat and you

Table 14.13.

	Age	Source
M: "Look what you did – you got her all wet. You better tell her that you are sorry!"	24 mos.	Budwig, Strage, & Bamberg (1986, p. 90)
C grabs toy from peer M verifies that he wouldn't like it M: "Tell him you're sorry"	Preschool	Shure (1985, p. 201)
T: "Do you have something to say to Steven, What do you have to say to him?"	Preschool	Kovarsky, Stephan, & Braswell (1994, pp. 176–177)
C steps on teachers' toe T: "Oh Jim what should you say?" C: "Sorry, Miss Y" T: "There, you know what to say"	Preschool	Gardner & Cass (1965, p. 108)
Two children are fighting T: "I want you to figure out a way to play together. Why don't you both say you're sorry?"	Preschool	Tobin et al. (1989, p. 132)
C1 is crying after being hit by C2 T: "Your friend is crying. Now we're going to say that we're sorry"	Preschool	Peak (1991, p. 160)

will get sick."[6] When Karen, at 31;5, wants her father to come to the playground with her she tells him, "You also need a hat – there's wind."[7] Similarly, Karen, at 2;8;29, tells her toy bear, "if you're cold Tati I will put a jacket (on you) and then you won't be cold."[8] Such concern is also evident when a girl of 4;3 who is learning English explains that she is dressing the dolls warmly, saying, "I playing it's cold day" (Keller-Cohen & Gracey, 1979, p. 206). Above, others' physical state is of concern for the child and the solution offered reflects an understanding of what can be done to resolve the problem. When one is cold, one needs to put on warmer clothes; when one doesn't want to get rained on, one needs to take an umbrella. This is what mothers do for children themselves (e.g., when a preschooler complains of being cold while waiting for the bus, his mother answers, "Poor thing! If you're so cold, put on my shawl," Akatsuka, 1986, p. 341). But children's actions above evidence understanding that the same solutions can be used to solve other people's problems.

Proactive consideration is also evident when children warn others of potential danger, as shown in Table 14.15.

Importantly, the type of proactive concern evidenced above appears to have the other child's welfare in mind and does not carry any apparent benefit to the children issuing these warnings. In fact, older children define friendship by alluding to this type of concern over the welfare of others. Selman (1979, cites a 13-year-old who explains that "if he gets sick, you kind of start worrying about him . . . a close friend you worry about more than yourself, Well, maybe not more, but about the same." In this vein, a middle school girl explains regarding a friend that "Sometimes when I know Stacey doesn't have lunch, I go, 'Stacey go do you want this? Stacey, you can have this" (Kaplan, 2000, p. 500). As Sullivan (1953) noted, friendship entails "a new sensitivity to what matters to another person," a concern with the other's happiness rather than "what should I do to get what I want."

On the psychological plane, proactive consideration can take many forms. First, it can be manifest in expressions of sympathy, for example, as Orren, at 33;6, says to Karen, "I'm very sad that your stomach hurts."[9] Second, it can include offering means of distraction. The child perceives a psychological problem and attempts to solve it, by distracting the other child from the problem, for instance. When he sees Karen crying, Orren, at 33;6, says to her, "Karen don't cry I love you very much. Can you come to the show?"[10] (i.e., come to put on a show with me). The distraction is often in the form of offers of toys and other objects, as shown in Table 14.16.

In all these cases, these very young children are not only evidencing remarkable sensitivity to others' states, but they are also quite sophisticated in terms of what they do. This is also evident in children's play, when they offer to "help" dolls that are upset. For instance, Orren, at 35;11, says, "All day I give him kisses" and when he is asked why, he says, "I want him to calm down."[11] A Japanese preschool teacher embraces the same strategy, explaining that "Children aren't good at changing their own mood,

[6] Hebrew: "Ima tikax mitria she-ani lo roça she-hageshem yetaftef lax al ha-me'il ve-at tiheyi xola."

[7] Hebrew: "gum atta çrixa kova – yesh ruax."

[8] Hebrew: "Im kar lecha Tati ani assim lexa jacket veaz lo yiheye lexa kar."

[9] Hebrew: "Açuv li meod shekoev lax habeten."

[10] Hebrew: "Karen al tivki ani meod ohev otax. At yexola lavo lahaçaga?"

[11] Hebrew: "Ani kol hayom noten lo neshikot." Lama? "Ani roçé she-hu yiraga."

Table 14.14.

	Age	Source
C climbs on mother to examine a light switch M: "You're hurting me!" C: "Sorry. Sorry. Sorry. I don't mean to"	26 mos.	Dunn (1988, p. 32)
C hits cat C: "I'm sorry ditty"	24 mos.	Nelson & Bonvillian (1982)
C bumps into toddler sibling C: "Oh, I'm sorry, Fred. I'm sorry. I wasn't watching"	Toddler	Howe (1991, p. 1506)
C runs her tricycle through a boy's sand castle C2: "You shouldn't wreck it" C1: "I'm sorry, John," helps rebuild the sandcastle	Preschool	Denham (1998, p. 171)
C is chastised for hitting a playmate Picks up flower petal, smiles, gives it to her C: "Here"	Preschool	Zahn-Waxler, Radke-Yarrow, & King (1979)

Table 14.15.

	Age	Source
Younger child touches electric socket C: "Why do you mess with the socket, because it'll shock you"	3;3 years	Slama-Cazacu (1977, p. 109)
Pretend mother to two boys C: "Get off the porch! It's dangerous. Get off that porch. Get off it. It's dangerous. You'll fall off it"	Preschool	Corsaro & Rizzo (1990, p. 29)
Boy of 4 climbs barrow, female peer warns G: "Don't Mick, you might hurt yourself. Mick, it's not funny and you might hurt yourself and you might cry"	5;3 years	Campbell & Smith (2001, p. 94)
Warning younger sib about touching the medicine cabinet C: "You'll go to the hospital, and you'll stay in the hospital for a long, long time; and you won't see Mommy and Daddy And you won't have no toys to play with – just lay in bed all the time and get needles"	Kindergarten	Sears, Maccoby, & Levin (1957, p. 377)
Two girls playing outside with a boy C: "Don't" C2: "Mark, you're breakin the ice" C: "And you're going to fall in" C2: "You'll get wet"	9 years	Sealey (2000, p. 155)

Table 14.16.

	Age	Source
Offers of Toys		
Peer crying, C pats him, picks up toy, gives toy to crying child	16 mos.	Rubin (1980)
Peer crying, C rubs peer's arm, hands him toys C: "Nice Jerry"	22 mos.	Zahn-Waxler, Radke-Yarrow, & King (1979)
Sibling crying, C shows toy car C: "There's this man in here. What's this, Len? What's this, Len?"	30 mos.	Dunn (1988, p. 94)
Other Objects		
Peer upset C: "Tulio, I made you something. Look this is for you. Now do you feel better?"	3 years	Paley (1986, p. 95)
Peer crying C: "You can wear one of my scarfs. Don't cry"	Preschool	Pitcher & Schultz (1983, p. 66)
Peer crying C: "You wanna hold my pound puppy?"	Preschool	Paley (1990, p. 99)

Table 14.17.

	Age	Source
K: "Don't want Daddy to wake up Mummy. Mummy is sleeping. Have to be quiet"	22 mos.	Karniol (Diary, Karen)
Baby sister is sleeping, adult enters C: "Don't ring the bell either. Jenny will wake up"	Toddler	Bloom (1970)
O: "You need to be quiet." M: Why? O: "'Cause grandma is resting and if no no be quiet grandma can't rest"	3;3 years	Karniol (Diary, Karen)

so you have to help them feel happy again" (Peak, 1991, p. 180), with her solution being to "bring them toys or something like that." Older children offer different sort of distraction. When a boy of 9;1 cries after a fight, an age-mate asks him, "Do you want to play with us," and they walk off together (Sluckin, 1981, p. 58).

Children also evidence consideration in various preemptive contexts, including keeping quiet when parents are on the phone and when others are sleeping. For instance, Karen, at 22;15, indicates understanding of the potential impact of her own actions for others when she says, "Have to be a good girl, then Mommy can talk on the phone." Similarly, at 20;0, she says, "Daddy sleeping – listen to music not now." In other words, she recognized that her own desire to listen to music must be delayed because it would disturb her father's nap. In the same vein, Orren, at 33;24, asks to be read a story and says, "I agree that afterwards you will rest and I won't disturb you."[12] A Polish child of 5;7 asks her mother, "Will I not disturb you, if I am drawing here?" and her mother replies that she will not disturb her, allowing her to draw (Przetacznik-Gierowska & Ligeza, 1990, p. 85). These children have recognized the need for their preferences to be coordinated temporally with those of family members who have their own needs and preferences.

Children also evidence consideration when they tell others that they too need to behave in ways that reflect their concern with other people's preferences, as evident in Table 14.17. Such instructions reflect children's concern with the well-being of both family members and others. Przetacznik-Gierowska (1995) found that sentences like "Be quiet – somebody is sleeping" were frequent in toddlers in a Polish day care, generally referring to other sleeping children.

Pretend play is also replete with statements focused on the need to consider the welfare of dolls and pretend others. A 28-month-old child tells a peer, "Quiet Jacus, the doll is asleep, you will wake up the doll" (Przetacznik-Gierowska, 1995). Such concern is also reflected in the words of a girl of 3;9 who tells a peer, "Pretend I whisper 'cause you're sleeping" (Chafel, 1987, p. 36). Playing house, a child of 4;2 tells the pretend father, "let's pretend when you came home I that I was, I was, that I told you to be quiet because the baby was sleeping" (Katz, Kramer, & Gottman, 1992, p. 140).

Children also evidence joint proactive and preemptive consideration, expressing concern for others and telling third parties to do the same. A mother talks of her older child, saying, "very perceptive, very tuned into other people's feelings, and if I'm not well she will sense it immediately and she will help" (Ribbens, 1994, p. 52). A 15-year-old explains that when they suspected that their mother was sad, they would ask "are you feeling sad . . . don't you feel well?' and tell younger siblings, "to be quiet and do our bedrooms or something. My sister sits on her knee and hugs her around the neck . . . and we try to be really good and not bother her . . . like not tell her things that might worry her" (Knowles & Sixsmith, 1996, p. 126). A 12-year-old relates that "whenever my mom is like down or something, I make her this nice little meal, she gets all happy" (Kaplan, 2000, p. 489), similarly evidencing concern with their mother's psychological state.

Adults, both at home and at school, attempt to foster consideration for others, often using the impact of the behavior on generic others as reasons for doing so, as shown in Table 14.18. The teachers above phrased their requests in generic terms that are applicable beyond the preschool. That is, they implied that no one would like to suffer the relevant fate. Contrast these last generic examples with "Richard, please sit down so Emily can see" (Dickinson & Smith, 1994, p. 121), or "Can you move over so that Katy can sit down, Owen?" (Wood, McMahon, & Cranstoun, 1980, p. 41) in which the consequences to a specific other person are delineated. In using generics, then, children are not warned to desist behaving toward the target of their actions but toward either all the children in their class or to children as a generic category. This is also reflected in a teacher's comment that "Good citizens don't bother other children who are trying to learn, do they?" (Kounin, 1970, p. 102). In this vein, Clancy (1986) documents the way Japanese children are socialized to care about others, often using appeals to the imagined reactions of *hito*, generic other people, who are fictionalized embodiments of a Superego that

[12] Hebrew: "Ani maskim she axar kax tanooxi weani lo afria lax."

Table 14.18.

	Age	Source
At Home		
M: "You can choose where you want to play so the water won't be in *anybody*'s way"	Toddler	Shure & Spivack (1978, p. 151)
C has left toys on stairs M: "Get your toys off these steps. *Someone* might trip over them and get hurt"	Preschool	Shure & Spivack (1978, p. 142)
C wants to put feet on chair M: "When you put your feet on the chair, *somebody* can sit down and get all dirty.... *People* don't like to get their clothes dirty"	Preschool	Shure & Spivack (1978, p. 150)
At School		
C dumped Lego blocks T: "I want you to go over there and clean up... before *someone* steps on them and gets hurt"	Preschool	Tobin, Wu, & Davidson (1989, p. 133)
T: "Jane, please keep your feet off the seat, *people* will get their clothes dirty from your muddy shoes"	Preschool	Gardner & Cass (1965, p. 57)
T: "Mathilde, could you sit on your bottom so the *people* behind you can see"	Preschool	Teale, Martinez, & Glass (1989, p. 168)
T: "Sabrina & Carolyn, sit down, uh, on the floor so *everyone* can, so you can see"	Preschool	King (1978, p. 41)

monitors and evaluates children's behavior in an ongoing fashion.

Children need not only consider the potential physical damage they inflict on others; they also need to be concerned with potential psychological damage. Socialization agents can induce such understanding by discussing the association between emotional reactions and negative outcomes. In fact, parents often discuss emotions with children, focusing primarily on negative events (Reese, Haden, & Fivush, 1996), and preschool children may well refer to the impact of their actions on others's feelings (e.g., "I'm hurting your feelings, 'cause I was mean to you," Bretherton, 1991, p. 65). In this context, though, the critical issue is who the experiencer of the negative emotion is. Is the victim of one's actions the sole experiencer of negative emotions or do one's actions carry implications for generic others as well? Dunn (1988) found that mothers of children 18 to 36 months old were equally likely to cite their own and others' feelings in attempting to resolve conflicts between themselves and their child or between an older sibling and their child. But the emphasis is generally on the specific individuals involved as victims. For instance, a preschool teacher chastises a child, saying, "You can't go pushing and stomping like that, William. Look, you made Marni cry and you knocked over all her dishes" (Paley, 1990, p. 89). Another time this same child was told, "you've really upset Tim. Look at him crying" (ibid, p. 91). After a preschool child was sat on by several other children, the teacher explains, "Now Con has been hurt and his feelings have been hurt, haven't they Con?" (Reid, 1999, p. 182).

The generic implications of one's actions may be emphasized as well. In this light, a preschool teacher explains that "We're not gonna call them other names because it might hurt their feelings," and "somebody might be upset if their basket gets broken" (Kovarksy, Stephan, & Braswell, 1994, pp. 176–177). A preschool teacher tells a child who grabbed a box from a peer, "Children don't like it when you take their things away by force" (Krown, 1974, p. 48), again focusing on the generic implications of the child's actions rather than their impact on the specific child who was victimized. Interestingly, a mother chastises her child who had called a neighbor "ugly," saying to the child, "that's not nice to do that. You make people sad when you do that. You don't say it to people. You don't hurt their feelings. They might get mad at you" (Becker, 1990, p. 17). There are multiple reasons provided by the mother in this context, then: a moral evaluation of the act as not nice; the possibility of hurting others and making them sad; and the prospect of their getting angry at the child. This is also the message conveyed by a mother who plays cards with her preschooler who does not want to accept a random distribution. The mother says, "Well, lovey, that's sort of cheating, isn't it? ... You don't play if you're cheating ... people won't want to play with you if you cheat" (Tizard & Hughes, 1984, p. 56). This last point is also underlined in the words of a preschool teacher who says, "You made (child's name) mad. Screaming at people makes them mad at you" (Applegate, 1980, p. 86). Again, then, much of such socialization is undertaken in generic terms, referring to *someone* and *people*, rather than to the specific child who was the victim of the act.

The use of generics in such contexts teaches children that everyone is alike in terms of their reactions to physical and psychological pain. Children too start to allude to generic others' feelings as reasons for avoiding specific ways of behaving and talking. When a preschooler admonishes another child for saying *shut up*, she says, "Well, you're not 'posed to say that, you're not s'posed to say dirty words to people 'cause it could hurt the other person's feelings" (Rizzo, 1989, p. 66). The child then asks her whether it hurt her feelings and she answers in the affirmative. Notice, though, that the child doing the chastising does not say directly that her feelings were hurt; rather, just like adults, she uses the generic *people* to indicate the nature of her claim.

HELPING AND ALTRUISM

Helping and altruism require one to delay or forego one's own preferences for the benefit of others' preferences. Emergent altruism is evident when a 3-year-old child at play is approached by a peer who asks him to tie her shoes. He stops playing, saying to his playmate, "Okay. Wait a minute, Erik. I have to tie Mollie's shoe" (Paley, 1986, p. 78). Tying his friend's shoe is viewed as an imperative and as such, it takes precedence over other activities that one may be engaged in.

In what contexts do children encounter the need to help or be altruistic? Turning to helping first, children are often asked to provide help to mothers when mothers (1) are busy doing something else, (2) don't feel like doing it, (3) can't do something on their own. At around 24 months, parents start asking children to help them, for instance, "Can you bring me my purse," "Can you put that in the trash" (Hart & Risley, 1999, p. 61), and "Kate, you know where my tweezers are, please, bring them . . . " (Varenne, 1990, p. 275). When Hal is 25;12, his mother asks, "Will you shut the door for me darling?"; he answers *yes* and shuts the door (Painter, 1984, p. 257). In cross-cultural research, children of these ages were asked to help perform simple tasks like feed chickens, gather fruit, and bring things from a local shop. As they get older, the types of help requested of children become more complex. The mother of a 5-year-old asks, "Allison, put that in the bin for me please. . . . Allison can you put this in the fridge for me please?" (Grieshaber, 2004, p. 126). When Penny's mother asks her "Will you do me a favor? . . . Go upstairs and take the sheets off Paul's bed," preschooler Penny answers her "All right" and as she goes up, she asks, "And bring them down"? (Wells, 1985, p. 76). Preadolescents and adolescents are expected to help in more varied ways, explaining: "When she wants me to cook the dinner, I try to cook the dinner . . . (Mayall, 2002, p. 107), "I do the washing up sometimes" (ibid, p. 93) and "I do housework, I clean dishes, do the Hoovering" (ibid, p. 95).

Mothers use their young children as supplements rather than supplants; they could do all of the above activities themselves. Their request that the child help them is a time-saving device. What the child does, the mother does not need to do. But mothers often address requests to children as a teaching device, wanting them to learn how to engage in the behavior in question. Children under 2 years old were found to help mothers mop, dust, and polish, with children being encouraged to do so in parallel to their mothers (Dunn & Wooding, 1977). In addition, though, mothers want to foster feelings of being helpful in the child. A mother lets her 4-year-old dry spoons, saying, "it's kind of a game we play, Oh, I'm helping Mummy" (Newson & Newson, 1968, p. 70). When Allison, at 20;21, wipes the chair with a napkin, her mother says, "You're a big help. You're pretty good to have around" (Bloom, 1973, p. 223). A child of 4;9 who asks for directions in grating a lemon for a cake is finally told, "Thank you. That was a help" (Wells, 1986, p. 54).

Grusec and Redler (1980) found that children whose helpfulness was attributed to being a helpful and kind person were more likely to help in the future. In this context, then, the use of evaluative labels is viewed as necessary to induce children to make a self-attribution, for example, "I'm just that kind of person – who helps people, and is considerate." Parents then need to engage in evaluative labeling, for example, a parent tells a preschooler, "That was nice of you to help" (Piotrowski, 1997). A preschool teacher remarks to boys who brought in a toad for "show-and-tell," "Thank you very much, boys. It was very kind of you to bring the toad for us to see" (Gardner & Cass, 1965, p. 85). Another teacher similarly says, "I want Paul to sit by me because he has been so *nice* and *helpful*" (King, 1978, p. 54). A preschool child who refused to clean up but after repeated requests agreed to do so was finally told, "You're a good helper George" (Bergin & Bergin, 1999, p. 201). Even more telling, a preschool teacher says to a child who is rocking a doll, "This reminds me of that book I read yesterday, Corduroy, remember? You're as kind to that baby as Lisa in the book is to the toy bear" (Paley, 1990, p. 91). These adults are aware of the importance of labeling behavior in dispositional terms. Contrast this with the situational attribution of a teacher who tells a child, "last time he was really crying and you helped him handle his disappointment," and the child responds, "Yeah, I handled it" (Blaise, 2005, p. 139).

Children do in fact start to refer to themselves as being kind, helpful, and considerate. A 4-year-old says to his nursery school teacher, "Remember that day when I gave Colin a truck he needed? That was a very nice thing to do, don't you think, Miss Beyer" (Beyer, 1956, p. 347). Karen, at 26;8, says, "Karen is helping Mummy to fix this bed for Mummy and Daddy to sleep." A 5-year-old girl is asked what kind of girl she is and says, "Nice . . . Because . . . help mummy, help tidy up . . . help mummy find slugs in the garden . . . help mummy Hoover" (Moore & Beazley, 1996, p. 72). A 13-year-old girl says, "I don't want people to think of me as being mean, only thinking of myself. . . . I want them to think that I care about other people" (Brown, 1998, p. 58). An adolescent explains that her mother is suffering from postpartum depression and says, "I sometimes look after my sister for an hour like, if she (the mother) has to go to the doctor," also relating that

> like if the baby's crying, instead of saying, Mum, the baby's crying, just go and pick her up. Or if there's loads of dishes in the sink, don't say, Mum, shall I wash the dishes, just go and wash a few dishes. Just to help her. (Mayall, 2002, pp. 92–93)

Children are also urged to help others in preschool, at times because these others need help but at times, to stop the child's ongoing behavior. As an instance of real helping, a preschool teacher says, "Stephen, this is rather too heavy to carry on your own, help him, John" (ibid, p. 87). Similarly, a preschool teacher gives a child some blue paper to make the sky and asks, "Who'd like to help David to make this picture?" As for stopping ongoing behavior, when a preschooler is teasing another child, the teacher urges, "John, help Ernie and leave Chris alone" (Gardner & Cass, 1965, p. 83). All these diverse behaviors have been homogenized under the umbrella term of *helping*.

There are many instances in which children offer unsolicited help to others, often younger peers, using situational cues to infer that their help is needed. A 4-year-old approaches a 2.5-year-old who is having trouble putting on his jacket and says, "It's okay. When I was little I couldn't do that. I'll help you. I'll take care of you today" (Rand, 1976). A boy who sees a peer having trouble with the lid of a can of Play-Doh says, "I'll do it, Gao. I'm here to help you" (Kyratzis & Guo, 2001, p. 62). Pitcher and Schultz (1983) found that preschool girls spend much time pretending to take care of babies and of sick people; but older ones and boys do so as well. For instance, Orren, at 30;12, is playing with his stuffed bears and asks, "Why are you sad? Your Daddy went to work? I'll take care of you."[13] Pretending to find a lost girl, a 3.5-year-old says, "She's all alone. We have to take care of her." A peer adds, "Sit down, lost girl. Are you hungry?" (Paley, 1986, p. 134). The same helpfulness is evident when a girl of 10;4 tells a younger girl, "We were the first to find you and we have to look after you" (Sluckin, 1981, p. 64).

Berman (1986) found that 5- to 6-year-olds confronted with a 3- to 4-year-old with whom they could share cookies or crayons or whom they could help by picking up spilled items evidenced more of these behaviors when they were older and male than when they were younger and female. At the same time, though, girls showed more interest and interacted more with a 13-month-old toddler, and this difference increased with age. On the other hand, Dunn (1988) found the same rate of solicited and unsolicited sharing in children of 18, 24, and 36 months and their older siblings.[14]

Chapman and colleagues (1987) found that preschool to sixth-grade children who were exposed to situations in which they could potentially provide help to a kitten (i.e., by undoing the latch of its cage and finding the can opener needed to open its cat food), express sympathy or provide physical help to an adult in pain, help the mother of a crying infant by finding the infant's bottle, or express a desire to help a crying infant, were more likely to help when older. As well, the best predictor of their helping was their inference that a fictional story character experienced guilt for causing another person distress, with guilt coded when the story character was described as feeling remorse, personal blame, or expressing responsibility for the victim's state of well-being (e.g., "She's sorry she pushed him down"). Inferences about story characters' desire to provide victims with comfort or help (e.g., "She's trying to cheer her up") and empathic reactions were also predictive of children's likelihood of helping in the above contexts. Whereas above, taking responsibility for one's actions was examined in a projective context, in a study with kindergarten and first grade children who were left along in a room and heard sounds of another child falling, children were more likely to help if they were told that they were in charge and needed to take care of things (Staub, 1970).

Children also offer to help others when they hear them utter declaratives that indicate their current state and these are interpreted as expressions of a need for help. For instance, when a first grader says, "Stuck on another word," a boy says to a peer, "Well, you help her, Al" (p. 230) and when later she sighs, he suggests, "Ask Mary this time" (Wilkinson et al, 1981, p. 231). Hence, her statement was interpreted by him as a request for help and her behavior affirmed that this interpretation was correct. Similarly, when a first grader complains that she can't draw frogs properly and people laugh at her frog, another girl says, "I'll draw you a frog, Eugenie" (Dyson, 1993, p. 97).

However, children may be leery of offering unsolicited help because they may be uncertain whether their help will be accepted. Adults often reject offers of help when such offers are experienced as threatening their self-esteem, making them feel dependent and inferior (e.g., Nadler & Fisher, 1986). Refusals of offers of help are more prevalent when the offer is made by a similar other and when the other is not defined as a friend (Clark, 1983). In line with this, when an agemate offers to help a first grader draw a frog, the offer is refused with "No. . . . Not nobody mess up my picture" (Dyson, 1993, p. 97). Similarly, when she is offered help, a girl of 5;1 refuses the offer, saying, "no don't I can do all that" (McTear, 1985, p. 110).

ACTS OF ALTRUISM

Altruism differs distinctly from helping. The most clear-cut acts of altruism are ones in which a person takes a

[13] Hebrew: "Lama ata açuv? Aba shelxa halax la-avoda? Ani atapel bexa."

[14] Eisenberg and Neal (1979) found that whereas somewhat older children's moral reasoning on a hypothetical dilemma was uncorrelated with their unsolicited helping, their sociability was correlated with it, underlining that unsolicited helping at these ages is a function of children's relationships with others, as I contend here.

risk with his own life to save that of another person. In this context, it is important to note that children are never asked to save others, except in the context of pretend play. However, they are exposed to acts of altruism in the media and this may teach them the kinds of behavior required in such contexts. As a pretend lifeguard, Clark's son Damon, at 31;18, says, "I'm going to dive in and get people from getting into trouble" (Clark & Carpenter, 1989, p. 351). Preschoolers who were enacting a fire script called for people to move out of the way, got the fire engine to the location of the fire, took off the ladder, and talked about "rescuing the burning people" (Sylva et al., 1986, p. 260). Similarly, a 3-year-old says, "the building's all on fire . . . a man at the top . . . can't get down . . . put it up . . . the fire's burning . . . . get the man down . . . down" (Tough, 1977, p. 59). A 4-year-old who pretended that his fort with all his animals is on fire, said, "I have to get everything out," and threw all the animals out to save them (Segal & Adcock, 1981, p. 121).

Children also know that medical interventions may be needed in such contexts. A pretend mother at preschool says, "My baby's on fire. I need to get him to the doctor" (Pitcher & Schultz, 1983, p. 160). In playing trains, when a child pretends that a train has crashed, he yells "get an ambulance!" (Sylva et al. 1986, p. 56). Playing with his father, a 4-year-old pretends there's a fire and when his father asks whether they should rescue the people, the boy answers that he's crawling in the fire and says, "Put them in the ambulance. I'm taking them to the hospital . . . . Well, we have to get the dog out and the mommy and the daddy" (Segal & Adcock, 1981, p. 102).

Children may also learn how to intervene in emergencies from pretend play "accidents," which parents use as opportunities for socializing concern for others. A British mother is playing trains with her son who is 2;10. When the train stops due to "engine trouble," the mother asks what should be done and the child says "nothing." The mother replies, "you can't just leave the people there, had you better get an ambulance or a fire engine out: or a relief train? . . . . You can't just leave people stuck in the middle of nowhere, can you?" (Manchester corpus, CHILDES). Similarly, when a child pretend plays that there's a fire, his mother asks "If there's a fire, what should you do?" phrasing the need to help in terms of *should* (Clancy, Akatskua, & Strauss, 1997, p. 56).

Real accidents that happen at home or preschool are also occasions to teach children what one does when others are hurt or in trouble. Meyer (2003) recorded a preschool teacher saying, "Tracy, when someone falls you see if they're all right. Tracy, if someone falls, check if they're OK" (p. 39). Notice again that the references are to generic others who need to be helped. Socialization agents refer to *someone*, *everyone*, and *people* as the targets of one's help attempts and the impersonal *you* is used to underline who is supposed to engage in such activities. In line with this, in preschool, Corsaro (1985) found that when a child was distressed or injured in their vicinity, other children would stop their own activities, often comforting the hurt child until an adult arrived to take of the child. After a 4-year-old preschooler falls, a peer rushes over and asks, "Are you OK Mick? Do you want a hand?" (Campbell & Smith, 2001, p. 94). Anyone who is hurt needs help and it behooves everyone who witnesses his state of need to offer help. A 12-year-old explains that he helps his mother, saying, "And if she's not well, call the doctor . . . like in January . . . . So I called the hospital and they came and . . . " (Mayall, 2002, p. 107).

Children are also socialized to behave altruistically by hearing stories of altruism, often at dinnertime. For instance, after the mother of three children tells of a car accident she had that day, the father recounts an incident the previous day, the story of the runaway watermelon:

> So I stopped the car quickly and ran, and managed to catch the watermelon that was rolling in the bag, and it came to no harm, I returned it safe and sound into the arms of the little girl." The mother asks, "You braked, got off the car and saved the watermelon?" The father answers, "I gave her a watermelon and saved the life of the family there . . . I mean the woman's problem was either the watermelon or the child . . . she decided child, but the child decided watermelon. (Blum-Kulka, 1997, p. 133)

The message transmitted by the father is that even as an uninvolved bystander, one must help others in situations that are potentially dangerous and one does not do it for any potential gain. Dinnertime conversation is also used to narrate stories of moral behavior. A mother tells of having received too much change at a store, and after he hears the story, the father says, "You're not supposed to consider . . . whether it's the ethic – right thing to do is to say, "Hey lady – you – you gave me too much money" (Abu-Akel, 2002). We don't know how hearing such stories impacts on children, and we don't know how children transition into being altruistic adults.

MORALITY

Morality involves foregoing our own immediate preferences and pursuing the preferences of the general public, the common good (Dawes, 1980). Kagan (1990) gives the example of an individual who goes for a walk and picks up a piece of glass so that others would not step on it. Doing so involves costs to self (i.e., loss of time and possibly getting a cut) and does not offer any immediate benefits to oneself. The potential benefit of this moral act requires an understanding of the concept of generic others, individuals who are anonymous to self and whose preferences can only be conceptualized in abstract terms. It may well be this abstractness makes moral behavior so difficult. Public appeals to help children in Third World countries often focus on one specific child as a means of fostering concern over the plight of the numerous others that the depicted child represents. Nevertheless, moral behavior requires us to understand generic others' preferences and to mind such preferences in our behavior.

Yet moral behavior is rendered difficult because individuals often misperceive what the general public wants or prefers. Such misperceptions can be of two kinds. First, the individual can misperceive others' preferences as matching his own. This phenomenon is known as *false consensus*, perceiving one's own characteristics, opinions, traits, and preferences as relatively common (e.g., Ross, Greene, & House, 1977; Krueger & Clement, 1997). The other type of misperception is *false uniqueness*, misperceiving that others' preferences mismatch one's own, viewing oneself as falsely unique or uncommon in one's preferences (e.g., Mullen, Dovidio, Johnson, & Copper, 1992). False uniqueness occurs when an individual who engages in a given behavior estimates that the general public is less likely to engage in that behavior than is estimated by a person who engages in an alternative behavior. In the moral domain, both false consensus and false uniqueness are important, because if few people behave immorally, it probably takes a very immoral person to engage in such behavior. On the other hand, if everyone behaves immorally, then immoral behavior cannot be used to draw inferences about the person's moral stature. Hence, individuals should be more willing to engage in immoral behaviors when they assume behaviors are consensual than when they perceive such behaviors as deviant. In fact, knowing how others behave in a given context has an impact on one's own likelihood of behaving the same way. Frey and Meier (2004) found that individuals who were informed that the rate of contribution for their own university was relatively high contributed significantly more than those who were informed that the rate of contribution was low. But this effect was primarily due to the influence of knowledge about others' behavior on those who were inconsistent in their own past choices. Those who were consistent in their donation behavior, either contributing regularly in the past or refraining from contributing in the past, were not affected by knowledge of others' contributions.

Why would this be the case? This is because there are two pathways to morality.[15] Yet each of these pathways reflects the imaginary presence of generic others. In the first of these paths, the imaginary presence of generic others has an impact on moral choice and behavior by way of perceptions of the preferences of generic others and the adoption of their presumed preferences in guiding one's own behavior. In line with this, Bicchieri (1993) defines norms as behavioral regularities that arise because (1) almost everyone prefers to conform to the norm on the condition that almost everyone else conforms to and (2) almost everyone believes that almost every one else conforms to the norm. Norms, then, emerge out of the interplay between one's own preferences, one's external preferences about the behavior of others, one's beliefs about the preferences of generic others, and one's attempts to systematically align these beliefs and preferences.

The second pathway invokes generic others via the moral judgments that accompany the contemplation of immoral behavior prior to its being undertaken and that arise subsequent to its performance. That is, moral judgments have both a deterrent and a punitive function. One reacts to one's contemplated choices by invoking self-admonishments and one self-administers postbehavioral rewards and punishments that reflect possible mismatches between one's actions and one's second-order preferences. That is, moral judgments serve to relate one's own behavior to one's second-order preferences, with such second-order preferences relating to the kind of person one wants to be. They are removed from current contexts and are represented in the form of ideals that one wants to attain or maintain. As discussed earlier, though, second-order preferences also reflect societal ideals. This view of how moral judgments work is evident in approaches that emphasize the relevance of moral behavior to one's self-concept (e.g., Bénabou & Tirole, 2006; Blasi, 1987; Gibbs, 1991), approaches that underline the "ought" self as distinct from one's actual or "ideal" self (e.g., Higgins, 1987), and approaches that focus on the cognitive transformations individuals deploy to maintain images of themselves as moral beings (e.g., Bandura, 1999; Barriga, Morrison, Liau, & Gibbs, 2001). This is why most people do not take advantage of opportunities to steal or cheat, do not damage public property wantonly, do stop to help when they see someone who is hurt, and do return lost wallets to their owners. On the other hand, the above also accounts for why delinquents and psychopaths differ from most individuals in the relevance of morality to their self, in their tendency to deploy self-serving cognitive transformations to justify their immoral behavior as discussed in Chapter 13, and in their moral judgments, to which I now turn.

MORAL JUDGMENT

Once children learn that sharing, helping, and acts of altruism are an integral part of social life, they start to evaluate and pass judgments on others' behavior. For instance, Orren, at 33;12, complains, "Daddy, you promised me that you would come afterwards to check me so why aren't you checking me?"[16] The child invokes his understanding of promises as something that one must keep, essentially telling his father that he's not behaving appropriately. When a child complains to her mother about a friend, saying, "she didn't even say sorry about what she said yesterday," she similarly passes moral judgment on her friend, reflecting her understanding that when one hurts another person, apologies are needed (Thomas-Lepore, Bohanek, Fivush, & Duke, 2004).

Children also use this understanding in resolving moral dilemmas relating to being moral, helpful, or aggressive.

[15] Although there are debates about the role of affect in moral judgments (e.g., Haidt, 2001), affect appears to be involved in reactions to others' violations of moral and social rules but not to the resolution of moral dilemmas (cf., Monin, Pizarro, & Beer, 2007), which is my focus.

[16] Hebrew: "Abba atta hivtaxta li she-atta axar-kax tivdok otti. Az lama atta lo bodek otti?"

What are moral dilemmas? They are contexts in which an individual needs to decide between alternative actions, usually when one of the choices represents a moral issue (e.g., helping another person, saving a life) and the other represents either a self-serving behavior (e.g., getting to work or to a party) or a socially mandated one (e.g., contravening a law). Piaget (1932/1965), who first studied children's moral judgments, found that at young ages, the children are concerned with the negative outcomes of behavior to the acting individual, view rules as emanating from authority (whether parental, social, or divine), and are concerned with the likely punishments associated with rule violation. Piaget's tenet was that as children are exposed to peers and their perceptions of parental authority are undermined, they start to view rules as social instruments that are alterable by mutual consent and they become concerned with issues of justice.

Kohlberg (1969) suggested that Piaget's analysis was deficient on two grounds. The first of these is that Piaget failed to capture the role of self-interest in guiding young children's judgments; they allow their own preferences and the preferences they attribute to others to dominate their judgments as to what should be done. A young child would argue that the instrumentality of an action in fulfilling one's own preferences should be the guidepost to deciding on a line of action. Second, Kohlberg argued that Piaget did not differentiate moral decisions based on the need to uphold law and order from those based on principled thought. Based on a Kantian perspective, Kohlberg argued that acting morally entails adopting moral principles and using these principles as the basis for deciding and judging. The adoption of moral principles depends on the ability to suspend one's own interested perspective on the issue in question and to assume a transcendent, generalized perspective. By doing so, one becomes concerned with issues of justice and fairness, which Kohlberg sees as the ultimate basis of morality. He traced this development as occurring in six stages, with individuals passing through them as a function of their intelligence, their social role taking experiences, and their ability to adopt perspectives other than their own, culminating in adulthood.

Gilligan (1982) took issue with Kohlberg's analysis, arguing that there are multiple paths to being moral and that women adopt a different perspective. Rather than adopting a transcendental, generalized perspective, women adopt a relation-based perspective in which caring, concern, and responsibility for specific others is the foundation of morality. From her theoretical stance, men tend to think in abstract terms, emphasizing justice concerns and individual rights that are beyond the rights of any specific individual. Their concern is with righting the system rather than with directly ameliorating the welfare of those who suffer within the system. Gilligan argued that women's morality is a direct outcome of the caretaking role that women have played in social systems throughout history. This role has led women to be more concerned with the maintenance of social relations, to experience a sense of responsibility, and to extend help to those in need. Adopting this role promotes an ethic of care rather than an ethic of justice, with gender being the prime determinant of the ethic one adopts (cf., Karniol, Grosz, & Schorr, 2003; Karniol, Ekbali, & Vashdi, 2007).

The debate between Kohlberg and Gilligan revolves around what moral stance *should* be taken – whether a principled, abstract one is morally more advanced than a particularistic, relationship-maintaining one, or whether both should be viewed on an equal footing. This is not a debate that can be resolved by psychological argument but rather reflects a philosophical debate as to how morality should be conceptualized. Psychology can account for how morality is experienced and enacted, and how people use their value systems to resolve moral dilemmas. As Blasi (1987) argues, philosophical theory need not concern itself with the behaviors and feelings that are relevant to the psychologist's questions.

Turiel and his colleagues (e.g., 1978, 1983; Smetana, 1993) took issue with Kohlberg on different grounds, contending that children develop differentiated conceptions of social rules and that these conceptions arise due to the diverse social experiences that are associated with different rules. That is, societies and socialization agents do not respond to behavior in all domains the same way, responding differently to aggressive behavior than to impolite behavior or to pranks. The primary distinction is between responses to behavior classified as moral and as social-conventional. This distinction is important, because behavior in the moral domain has intrinsic consequences; it generally violates the rights and welfare of other people. These intrinsic consequences are both experienced by the child and focused on by socialization agents who underline the sanctity of other people's rights and welfare. Because of these intrinsic consequences, moral rules – as best exemplified in the Ten Commandments – are viewed as obligatory, nonalterable, and as having cross-situational validity. Behavior in the social-conventional domain does not generally have intrinsic consequences but rather, reflects the norms that govern social interaction. Such norms generally relate to what societies and families deem polite or acceptable behavior. They are arbitrary in that different norms could be adopted by mutual consent. Norms serve to guide one's behavior based on the expectation that others will adopt the same norm in guiding their behavior. On the other hand, once a social-conventional norm has been established, its violation may have intrinsic consequences. For instance, a teacher in North America would be greatly offended at being addressed by a first name because this contravenes the social-conventional norm of being addressed as *Mr.* or *Mrs.* plus one's last name. Yet in other societies, the opposite is the case; in Israel for instance, teachers are addressed either by their first names or as "teacher."

Finally, Turiel identifies the prudential domain that is concerned with one's safety and health; for instance, rules about wearing helmets when bike riding may be legally enforced, but they are prudential in that they are aimed at saving the lives of bike riders. The primary difference between moral rules and prudential rules then is that the former legislate interpersonal interaction and the latter govern personal action. In an extensive research program, Turiel and his students have skillfully demonstrated that children differentiate these domains (e.g., Turiel, Killen, & Helwig, 1987), citing fairness and others' welfare in justifying judgments of transgressions in the moral domain, norms and expectations in justifying judgments of transgressions in the social-conventional domain, and safety and health concerns in justifying transgressions in the prudential or personal domain.

Children as early as preschool were already found to evidence this differentiation, with social-conventional acts being evaluated with reference to the existence or nonexistence of a relevant rule. Smetana (2006) suggests that "from their experiences as victims and observers of transgressions, children develop prescriptive judgments of right and wrong" (p. 123). Specifically, she argues that social interactions in the three domains differ in terms of who responds to transgressions as well as the type of response that occurs. In the case of moral issues, children are urged to take the victim's perspective and to evaluate rights (e.g., "give it back, it's hers, how would you feel if she took yours?"). They themselves experience pain and emotional upset when their own rights are violated. The primary burden in establishing the differentiation between these three domains, then, is on socialization agents who need to respond in a domain-appropriate manner so that the differentiation can be made by children. Yet the evidence for domain-differentiated responsiveness by socialization agents is far from clear-cut.

How then do children as early as preschool develop this differentiated view of the domains? From my perspective, the moral domain, the social-conventional domain, and the prudential domain differ in the nature of preferential conflict inherent in them (cf., Skitka, Bauman, & Mullen, 2008). Preferential conflict emanates from different sources in each of these domains. In the moral domain, preferential conflict arises between our preferences and those of others, where enacting one's preferences conflicts or impedes others' first-order preferences; it "produces" victims, whose physical being, possessions, or rights are violated by such enactment. Becoming a victim means that one's preferences were not consulted, were ignored, or were setback in undertaking the relevant action in contexts in which such preferences were to have been considered. Moral rules reflect universal concerns that are equally relevant in one's home, at one's preschool, and in all social settings in which one interacts with others and in which one is expected to take their preferences into account (e.g., "You don't hurt other people"). Their breach makes one insensitive, aggressive, or delinquent. This is verifiable by engaging in role transformations, mentally switching places with the victim, thereby discovering that he is hurt. As a 16-year-old explains, one should help a bullied child because "you shouldn't really want that child to get hurt because you might get hurt if the situation was switched" (Eisenberg, 1992, p. 28).

In the social-conventional domain, preferential conflict arises between one's own preferences and the *external* preferences of either specific or generalized others. That is, social-conventional rules and norms can be translated from their generic phrasing (e.g., "we don't eat with our fingers") to reflect their external nature (i.e., "I/we/society don't want *you* to eat with your fingers"). They do not pertain to the first-order preferences of others. One could not say "your eating with your fingers prevents me from fulfilling my preferences" whereas one could say, "your taking my toy/hitting me prevents me from fulfilling my preferences."[17] Social-conventional rules tend to be context-bound (e.g., in school, you raise your hand before you speak, at preschool, you sit on a rug at story time) or time-bound (e.g., "in this house, we have a set bedtime – 7 o'clock, that's bedtime," Cook-Gumperz, 1973, p. 240) and may be object specific (e.g., "we don't jump on beds," "we don't eat out of glass cups" (cf., Shweder, Turiel & Much, 1981). Their breach makes one defiant, rude (e.g., not engaging in turn taking, talking with one's mouth full) or unruly.

In the prudential domain, the conflict is an *intra*personal one, between what one prefers in the short term versus the possible negative consequences of enacting such preferences (e.g., "don't touch the stove – you could get burned"). They are expressed by socialization agents whose roles require them to look out for those that are dependent on them. The breach of prudential rules may lead to being labeled careless or reckless. Here again, it makes little sense to tell someone to be careful with the stove because of the way such behavior has an impact on others' fulfillment of their preferences. My concern, then, is with the preference structure underlying moral judgments and the way the inferred preferences of specific and generic others are manifest in the judgment process, as discussed in the next section.

RECONCEPTUALIZING MORAL JUDGMENT

If one adopts the view that morality refers to contexts in which preferential conflict is resolved by relinquishing one's own preferences and helping others attain their preferences, then moral judgments necessarily refer to (1) whose preferences are relevant in resolving the dilemma, (2) whether immediate or long-term preferences are viewed as more important, and (3) whether the decision is based on others' current need states or their anticipated states as a consequence of the decision made. This yields a classification scheme that varies on three dimensions: (1) temporality of preferences, (2) whose

[17] Parents do say that their children's noncompliance with social-conventional rules makes them unhappy, though, but the force of the argument is still in the external nature of the preference being expressed by the parent.

Table 14.19.

		Temporality of Preferences		
		Present	Future Decision-Guiding	Future Decision-Reactive
	Self	I'd want to get to the party	I'd want others to help me If I was in that situation I would want somebody to help me	I'd be *un*happy that I *didn't help* him I'd feel guilty if I didn't help
Whose Preferences	Other	He needs help Her right was being violated	If I help him he can be saved He wants him to get him to the hospital	He'd be happy that I helped him They'd like her if she helped
	Third Parties	Teacher told me I had to	If I share, teacher will give me a good grade	She will be very happy because she knows the family will be happy[18]
	Generic Others	You have to help people who need help	Helping others can save lives If everyone helps we'd all be better off	They'd be happy if they had food I like to share to give others satisfaction

preferences are cited as justifications, and (3) whether future justifications are decision-guiding or decision-reactive, where the former invoke reasons for acting in a specific way, and the latter invoke the probable outcomes of acting in a specific way. This is shown in Table 14.19, with justifications taken primarily from Eisenberg (1992).

The advantage of conceptualizing moral judgment this way is that it places moral judgments in the context of preferences – one's own preferences versus other people's preferences – and in the context of time – past, present, or future time. It allows us to relate moral judgment more directly to social behavior and yields explicit hypotheses as to how these should relate to each other. This analysis can easily account for the pattern of justifications that children offer for actually engaging in helpful acts and in sharing with their peers in preschool. Responses like "she wanted some" and "he's hungry" (Eisenberg, 1992, p. 20) reflect concern with specific others' current needs. Responses such as "he'll save it (a seat) for me next time" and "he'll like me" (ibid) reflect concern with one's own future and are decision-guiding. A response like "If I share, the teacher will let me make popcorn later" (ibid), reflects a concern with the preferences of third parties as well as one's own future outcomes. But children's responses also evidence concern with generic others and their preferences, both in the present and in the future (e.g., "Candy should be shared to make the other children happy"; "I like to share to give others' satisfaction" (ibid, p. 25). Children may even express more explicit concern with generic others, saying, "I feel I have a responsibility to help other people in need" (Mussen & Eisenberg-Berg, 1977, p. 123). Contrast this with a child who says that "I would feel bad if I didn't help because I'd know that I didn't live up to my values" (ibid), clearly using his own future reactions as guides to what he should do in the present.

From this perspective, individuals can be placed on a continuum of self-concern versus other-concern that reflects the likelihood of their consideration of their own versus specific and generic other' preferences in their judgments. This framework allows us to understand justifications for not cheating, not helping, and sharing using the same conceptual tools. The child's own future preferences are provided as justifications for why a child should not help a child being bullied (e.g., "he'll get pushed over"); the child's own preferences or the victim's preferences serve as justifications for why a child should help the victim (e.g., "help him . . . (he might) not want the other kid to get hurt"; "help him . . . So the bully won't hurt him"). Older children refer explicitly to generic others, saying "People shouldn't just pick on each other . . . this is just the way humans should act toward each other." Generic others also feature in children's moral judgments as to why one should not cheat, for example, a 10-year-old who explains, "If everyone did that, no one will play anymore" (Piaget, 1965, p. 307). In the same vein, a teenager says, "Do unto others as you would have them do unto you,' an' if you do good deeds (and) you help other people, someone will help you" (FitzSimmons, 1999, p. 72).[19]

Although they do not apply these criteria systematically, Colby and Kohlberg's (1987) also accord importance to the individual whose preferences are cited, to generic others,

[18] A response provided in Rothbaum, Morelli, Pott, and Liu-Constant (2000, p. 341).

[19] One needs to differentiate the content of moral judgments from the means of arriving at moral judgments (cf., Turiel, 1978). Eisenberg (1977) confounds these, labeling the *means* by which individuals can know what others' needs/preferences are (e.g., "I know how he feels," Mussen & Eisenberg-Berg, 1977, p. 123) as types of justifications, but these do not constitute justifications for undertaking one versus another action to resolve the moral dilemma.

and to the temporal dimension in the resolution of moral dilemmas (e.g., whether someone should steal a potentially life-saving drug for his sick wife). Citing one's own future decision-guiding preferences (e.g., contending that one should not steal on behalf of a stranger because "the person may not even return you a favor," p. 71, coded Stage 2) is generally accorded a lower stage score than citing one's own future decision-reactive preferences (e.g., "It would be on my mind the rest of my life if I knew I could have helped . . . ," p. 31, coded Stage 5). Citing one's own present preferences is generally accorded a preconventional stage score (e.g., "Heinz wanted to keep her alive; "he wanted his wife to get well," p. 109) and citing the preferences of those who are helped or hurt is generally coded as conventional (e.g., "If he has any concerns over how Joe feels, he will . . . ," coded as Stage 3, p. 207; "he did it out of mercy for the suffering patient," coded as Stage 3, p. 410). Importantly, Colby and Kohlberg (1987) generally classify as Stage 5 justifications that refer to the preferences of generic others, for example, "the right to live is a universal thing, to be applied to all people whose lives can be saved" (p. 55) and people should act "for the good of society" (p. 444). In fact, they claim that "only by respecting claims universally can a person generate the solution that can be shared universally" (ibid, p. 232, Stage 5).

Justifications of the morality of gene therapy and cloning are similarly amenable to this preference-based coding scheme. For instance, Sadler (2004) found individuals who justified gene therapy in terms of "I don't like to see people suffer" (p. 348); others did so by stating that gene therapy "can help people live longer" (p. 348). Cloning was similarly justified by statements such as "you put yourself in that situation and you want to have a baby" (ibid, p. 349). Here too, the justifications referred to the preferences of self, specific others, and generic others.

Since moral dilemmas embody preferential conflict, it is the means by which individuals resolve preferential conflict that justifies their moral judgments as reflecting maturity or autonomy. In fact, as philosophers (e.g., Mongin, 2001) contend, ethical observers have representations of others' preferences and they use these representations in guiding their own decision making. Echoing Tyler's (2006) conclusion, our motivation to cooperate with others is rooted in social relationships and in moral judgments that give weight not only to our preferences but also to those of others, both specific and generic. This is what makes for social and moral human beings.

15 Tying Up

Throughout this book, I have presented preferences and preference management as the unifying theme of social development, suggesting that conveying our preferences to others, having them convey their preferences and their external preferences to us, and deciding how to implement this knowledge in guiding our behavior and pursuing our preferences is at the heart of human sociality. When infants are born, they are unable to pursue their preferences without others' help. As discussed in Chapters 1–4, mothers convey to infants the need to communicate their preferences so they can initiate preference alignment on their behalf, and infants' emergent capacities are used by them to communicate their preferences to others, and, gradually, to learn of others' preferences. We saw in Chapters 1 and 2 how gestures, and then language, are put to work to this end, as infants and children inform and tell others what they want and are told by others what they want for and from them. As part and parcel of doing so, as discussed in Chapters 3 and 4, children learn to think of themselves and of others as agents with preferences, with the perceived stability of preferences accounting for how both self and others are viewed. Concomitantly, as elaborated in Chapters 5–9, mothers' socialization practices and their responsiveness to children's expressed preferences implicitly expose children to parental preferences but they also reveal the self – other preference gap, both because children often recognize their own preferences to be different than the ones parents attempt to socialize and because repeated experiences with parents who are unwilling to accommodate to their preferences force children to confront this gap. This gap is evident to children when parents channel their preferences, temporize their preferences, restrict their preferences, and discipline them. Chapters 10–14 showed how becoming socialized involves developing means of bridging the self – other preference gap, attempting to change others' behavior and their construals to accommodate one's preferences. At the same time, socialization teaches children to resolve intrapersonal preferential conflict, to bind the time until the state of the world is aligned with their preferences and to change their own behavior and construals when such alignment is not possible. These abilities in turn emerge out of the understanding of preferences as both stable and unstable entities in oneself and in others, an understanding that can also guide the resolution of both interpersonal and intrapersonal preferential conflict. The resolution of such conflict calls transformational thought into play, requiring children to cope imaginatively with the intransigence of the physical and social world and deploying it in their own attempts to thwart or facilitate others' pursuit of their preferences. Transformational thought is acquired conversationally, with parental language that transports children to different temporal, imaginal, and mental worlds, licensing children to do likewise, as first evident in their pretend play and as manifest in mind play when they are older. It is children's means of adaptation to others' preferences that determines the stance they adopt on the continuum from self-regarding behavior, to other-regarding behavior, to group-regarding behavior. To the extent that generic others feature in their psychological world, children are more likely to adopt altruistic and moral behaviors that reflect their concern with other people's preferences.

This chapter summarizes some of the critical issues that my approach to preference management raises and places it in the context of alternative views of social development. I address the role of language, the intertwining of social and cognitive development, and the importance of both transformational thought and of the concept of generic others to preference management and to social development in general.

THE ROLE OF LANGUAGE

In this book, I traced the language infants and children use to express their preferences, to manage their own preferences, and to get others to satisfy their preferences, as well as the language socialization agents use to manage children's preferences. As evident in the tables throughout the book, children of all ages devote much of their talk to their own and other people's preferences. Note, though, that the divergent cultural practices characteristic of different parts of the world do not alter the need for children to pursue their preferences or to heed other people's preferences, or for parents to channel, temporize, restrict, and discipline their children. Language and everyday discourse universally serve as the primary medium through which cultural knowledge is "communicated and instantiated, negotiated and contested, reproduced and transformed" (Garrett & Baquedano-López, 2002); language in all societies gives voice to cultural values and both personal and societal preferences. As infants and children interact with others, they acquire linguistic and social skills but they also learn how to think, how to behave, and how to manage their preferences and their psychological reactions to the attainment and nonattainment of their preferences. Language is the universal means used to socialize children but language itself is socialized and concomitantly, language is the vehicle used for thinking, decision making, and self-regulating.

Importantly, from the current perspective, language is acquired to serve instrumental functions, and it is in this respect that Piaget fails to capture its critical role in social development. Specifically, Piaget's (1968) account does not adequately articulate the instrumental functions of language. Piaget contrasts his position regarding the functions of language with that of Bruner, claiming "a child's language is subordinated to his operational level, and does not constitute the formative mechanism of the operations" (p. 33). As Bruner (1986a) sees it, on the other hand, language is both a medium of communication and a medium for representing the world about which one is communicating; there is a mutual impact of language on thought and vice versa. This is because children internalize language as a cognitive instrument and use it to "represent and systematically transform the regularities of experience" (Bruner, 1964, p. 4). In addition, I share Bruner's claim that children do not learn to talk grammatically as part of an intellectual exercise; rather, they do so instrumentally, "in the interest of getting things done in the world: requesting, indicating, affiliating, protesting, asserting, possessing, and the rest" (Bruner, 1986a, p. 114). These functions serve to express children's preferences about what they want and what they want from others. Dewey (1897) echoes this claim, saying that "it is true that language is a logical instrument, but it is fundamentally and primarily a social instrument. Language is a device for communication." As we saw throughout this book, much of this communication concerns preferences, being evident in the way young children express their preferences about what they want for themselves, and for and from others. Social life demands that people communicate their preferences to each other. Sfard (2008) underlines this, saying, "We communicate in order to coordinate our actions and ascertain the kind of mutuality that provides us with what we need and cannot attain single-handedly" (p. 81). Language and cognition are instrumental to the attainment of preferences and for the intricate negotiations with other social beings that the mutual pursuit of preferences requires.

Yet in the prevailing view, interaction with other children, and not with parents or other adults, is the formative force in social development. Tomasello expresses this view in saying,

> discourse with other persons, perhaps especially siblings, is a prime mover in a child's coming to think of them as beings with desires, thoughts, and beliefs similar to her own but still different from hers – even when the discourse has no specifically mental terms in it. (Tomasello, 1999, p. 177)

Like Tomasello, Piaget (1959) accorded children's interaction and conflict with peers rather than with parents the critical role; Piaget did not endow parental language or socialization practices with any functional contribution to children's learning to adapt and adopt perspectives. This represents a major lacuna in Piaget's theory from my perspective. As the parent–child conversations in this book show, children negotiate with their parents in attempting to pursue their own preferences, in temporizing and rejecting parental preferences, and they converse with parents, as well as with other children and siblings, when they coordinate their activities and their play, a coordination of minds that facilitates the coordination of behavior. Denying parents' role in this process is tantamount to throwing out the baby with the bathwater. As I have traced in this book, it is *parental language* that sweeps children into linguistic perspective taking and *parental socialization practices* that provide children with the cognitive tools for bridging self–other preference gaps, when parents talk of people's preferences, discuss the need to take other people's preference into account, and demand behavior that reflects consideration of such preferences. Much of this occurs in the sphere of language, allowing for the conversational construction of meaning (Loos & Epstein, 1989) by the child. By way of this parent–child interactive process, infants and children learn that others are communicative and intentional beings who have preferences and that their preferences constitute relevant considerations in interacting with them. Children's language gradually indexes this knowledge, as they both question others as to their preferences and engage in linguistic practices that reflect their understanding that such preferences exist. Interaction with other children certainly facilitates and hastens this process but is not the critical variable. If it were, children in orphanages would be able to develop the necessary skills for these processes to develop by interacting with their orphan peers – but tragically they do not (Smyke et al., 2007).

THE INTERTWINING OF COGNITIVE AND SOCIAL DEVELOPMENT

Although child development is often portrayed as constituting two *separate* systems of thought (cf., El'konin, 1971) that unfold in two parallel lines – the line of development in the social domain and the line of development of intellectual or cognitive processes – both Freud and

Piaget recognized their indissociablity. Turning to Freud first, in discussing the tripartite division of personality, Freud (1933/1965) endowed the Id with the pleasure principle, the striving to obtain satisfaction. But being removed from reality, from time, and from negation, the Id was not accorded any means of interacting with the outside world. For this reason, the Ego develops. The Ego obtains its orders from the Id, but its primary function is to interpose "a postponement in the form of activity or thought" (p. 67), to delay acting according to the demands of the pleasure principle and adopt the reality principle. The reality principle both connects the child to the *here-and-now* and allows the child to respond as if the *here-and-now* were abstract. Thought transforms direct experience, allowing what Freud called "the mnemonic residues of experience" (p. 68) to guide the Ego to make decisions about the best means of fulfilling Id preferences. Freud (1924/1971) saw the transition from the pleasure principle to the reality principle by way of thought transformations as one of the most important advances in the development of the child.

But the Ego cannot deploy its cognitive processes and pursue reality without adequate consideration of *social reality*. Social reality, as conveyed by parental demands and restrictions, is independent of physical reality. Physical reality may determine whether we use windows or doors to exit from buildings, but it is social reality that determines how and where we eat, empty our bowels, and interact with others. Freud represented social reality in the Superego. The Superego is the site in which others' preferences are represented and it is the task of the Superego to "become increasingly aware of the presence and claims of others and of the necessity of restraining our own satisfactions where they conflict with those of others" (Flugel, 1961, p. 242). As Freud discussed it, then, the Ego serves two masters, the Id, representing one's own preferences, which need to be curtailed in light of physical reality, and the Superego, representing parental and societal preferences, which need to be taken into account by the Ego in its choice of actions. Although Freud saw this perpetual conflict as the inherent aspect of personality, the critical aspect of Freud's theory from the current perspective is that it makes language and cognition *instrumental* means to preference satisfaction. Even in describing the emergence of the Ego out of the Id, Freud kept the reins of personality in the hands of the Id, according it the source of psychic energy and endowing it with the ability to restrain the Ego by withdrawing such energy when preference satisfaction is thwarted.

For Piaget as well, cognitive development and social development are inextricably intertwined. In his words,

> Logical progress goes hand in hand with progress in socialization ... The social and the logical constitute the two indissociable aspects of a single and identical reality, that is at once social and individual. (Piaget, 1995, p. 145)

But how are the social and the intellectual related? For Piaget, intelligence and personality both require understanding of the relativity of one's own perspective. It is by interacting with others that we acquire the ability to reflect on the operations of our own mind. In this view,

> We reflect the operations of our mind by comparing them .... (man) rather than simply comparing his own operations among themselves, and thus remaining prisoner to a systematic illusion, he now confronts them with those of others and becomes able to "reflect" them ... by comparing his experiences with those of others. (Piaget, 1995, pp. 235–236)

It is by giving voice to one's own view of the world and hearing the voices of others' in expressing their possibly divergent views of the same world that one verifies and legitimizes one's perspective and builds an intelligent framework for interacting with the physical world and the social world. Personality, then, evolves by way of recognition of the limits of one's own perspective. As Piaget further notes,

> Personality involves consciously realizing the relativity of one's individual perspective and then relating it to the set of all other possible perspectives; so personality implies a coordination of the individual with the universal. (Piaget 1995, p. 219)

Why does Piaget accord social interaction and the meeting with other minds such importance? It is because one's behavior "necessarily has repercussions on other individuals; it is useful, harmful, or indifferent to them" (ibid, p. 100). That is, our behavior has the potential of furthering or thwarting other people's pursuit of their preferences. The fact that one's actions have implications for others means that to resolve potential preferential conflict, the child must necessarily learn to treat others as agents with preferences that may not match his own and cooperate with them in the attainment of their respective preferences. As a consequence, the child "no longer thinks only in terms of himself but also in terms of real or possible coordination of different points of view" (ibid, p. 144). Such coordination is considered by Piaget "an operatory transformation" (ibid, p. 309) involving both the differentiation of distinct perspectives and the integration of these perspectives to allow for social interaction and cooperation to take place. Piaget's view of the intertwining of the social and the cognitive in children's psychological lives is well-expressed in his claim that "the internal operations of the individual and the interpersonal coordination of points of view constitute a single and same reality, at once intellectual and social" (ibid, p. 307). The social and the cognitive, then, do not form parallel lines but intersecting lines that cross-fertilize and enrich each other in children's development, underlining the need to view the development of affect and intellect as a dynamic unity (cf., Vygotsky, 1966, 1981). It is this unity that undergrids the need to "throw some bridges across the river joining the intellectual and affective banks" (Odier, 1948/1965, p. 32). Yet the empirical bridges that have been constructed between the cognitive and affective banks, as discussed in previous chapters, need the support of the theoretical pillars provided by transformational thought, to which I now turn.

TRANSFORMATIONAL THOUGHT

Transformational thought is the basic conceptual tool that man has at his disposal. It allows us to revise knowledge and reconfigure it in new ways and use it flexibly for guiding our future behavior. To do so, we import the external world and represent it internally by transforming it, using those knowledge structures that we have available to do so (cf., Berlyne, 1965; Lawrence & Valsiner, 1993). But we also play with those representations that we already have, transforming them to deal with the world when it cannot be changed to support the pursuit of our preferences and attempting to impose transformations on others, both to manipulate them for our own purposes and to facilitate their coping with the world *as is* when it conflicts with the world *as preferred*. In particular, I delineated three planes of transformational thought that are critical for the preference management process.[1] The first plane of transformational thought involves transforming the *here-and-now* into the *neither-here-nor-now* on the temporal plane. The second plane of transformational thought is the imaginal plane, which allows us to create pretend worlds that may or may not have any basis in reality. The third plane of transformational thought involves mentalizing, that is, transforming the *here-and-now* into imaginary lines of thought and affective experiences in the minds of other people. The capacity for engaging in all three types of transformational thought emerges out of socialization and the conversational exchanges that typify such practices. As traced in several chapters, parents encourage children to leave the *here-and-now*, to transform reality *as is* into reality as *it was*, as it *will be*, as it *could be*, and to attempt to capture other people's reality as well.

A. Temporally and Imaginally Transforming Reality

Transformational thought, in which we detach ourselves from the current context, manipulate and change mental representations on the temporal or imaginal plane, allows us to recognize similarities between new problems and previously solved ones and to use analogical reasoning and our memories of previous solutions to guide our attempts to deal with current problems. As Chiappe and MacDonald (2005) have argued, general intelligence facilitates the solution of novel problems by decontextualization and abstraction. Decontextualization allows us to bypass the working of implicit and automatic processes in making inferences, judgments, and decisions (Stanovich & West, 2000). Transformational thought allows us to transport ourselves into past and future worlds as well as fictional worlds that we create in our own minds. This is why we can easily complete analogies like "unicorn is to horse as phoenix is to . . . " despite the fact that the former are mythical entities. In fact, transformational thought is implicated in several models of analogical reasoning (e.g., Hahn, Chater, & Richardson, 2003; Leech, Mareschal, & Cooper, 2007, 2008), providing a parsimonious account of the emergence of spontaneous analogies in young children (e.g., Tunteler & Resing, 2002), consistent with what we saw in earlier chapters. Rumelhart (1989) suggests that humans are uniquely capable of reasoning formally, but in addition they are able to reason by similarity and by mental simulation. The former uses the past as input for dealing with current contexts, and the latter enlists the imagination to create possible actions and possible consequences, and these serve to guide future behavior.

The seeds of transformational thought on the temporal and imaginal plane are planted early, being manifest in young children's use of deictic and generic pronouns, in children's ability to talk of the past, to allude to the future, to engage in analogical thinking, and to create pretend worlds in their play. Mothers scaffold children's use of decontextualization and recontextualization in the way they talk of the past and the future as well as in encouraging pretend play, thereby fostering children's own use of transformational and analogical thought (Morelock, Brown, & Morrissey, 2003). These transformational abilities are then brought to bear in contexts that require children to cope with situations in which others have temporized or blocked preference attainment, being evident in what children say to themselves in their own efforts to deal with such contexts and in other people's attempts to facilitate children's efforts to do so.

As we saw, transformational thought allows individuals to cope and to engage in mind play to cognitively transform contexts that are inherently aversive. As Schunk (1999) cogently claimed, it is by a transformation of social-to-self that self-control over one's own behavior is achieved and that the self-to-social transformation becomes possible as individuals both alter and adjust their social environments to suit their preferences and needs. But it bears recognition that self-control and social control processes share the same underpinnings (cf., Karpov & Haywood, 1998), with transformational thought being deployed both in self-control and in social control. As illustrated in Chapter 13 on Mind Play, children use transformational thought in contexts that require them to cope and also in contexts that require others to cope, offering them possible transformations to facilitate their coping. Doing so is both a cognitive achievement and a social achievement, underlining that these processes are intertwined in a way that disallows their disentanglement. But this intertwining

[1] Skirting the debate regarding the encapsulation or relative permeability of domains of knowledge (cf., Fodor, 1992; Mithen, 1996), while I see these planes as domain-specific, transformational thought as such is a process that knows no modular boundaries. The three planes can work independently as well as in concert with each other for both one's own and others' benefit as discussed in Chapter 13. This view accords well with Kutas's (2006) conclusion that there is no support for information encapsulation in the brain.

stems from the fact that transformational thought is critical for both. Transformational thought not only allows children to delay gratification of their own preferences but also to use this knowledge in getting others to delay gratification of their preferences for the benefit of mutual interaction and for coping with the world when it does not accommodate to their preferences.

This is why there is such an intricate weave in the fabric of children's social development. Cognitive abilities mesh with social ones and vice versa, with transformational thought providing the basic building blocks on which both are constructed. But transformational though is also critical for cognitive achievements, such as the conservation of mass and liquid (DeVries, 1997), and successful performance on false belief tasks (Bogdan, 2005), both of which require the coordination of past and present states and their mental transformation across time. We saw the ubiquitous nature of transformational thought in the link between children's delay behavior during the preschool years, their social skills, and their SAT scores 15 years later (Mischel, Shoda, & Rodriguez, 1989), in the relationship between children's play and their emergent math skills in kindergarten (Ainlie, 1990; Jarrell, 1998) and in the relationship between preschool mathematical abilities and performance on analogical reasoning tasks (e.g., White, Alexander, & Daugherty, 1998). Parents foster such processes when they encourage children to leave the current context and travel to alternative planes of possible existence.

B. Mentalizing

Transformational thought is also critical for thinking about other people's psychological experiences, *mentalizing*. Mentalizing is the elaboration of contexts into psychological fields of human thought, affect, and memory, depicting the paths into which others' psychological processes are likely to be channeled, allowing us to make inferences and predictions about them and their preferences and to take action in light of such anticipated psychological processes (Karniol, 1986, 1990a, 2003a).

Parents sow the seeds of such abilities in the manner in which they talk to their children. In fact, Fonagy and Target contend that

> the caregiver facilitates the creation of mentalizing models through complex linguistic and quasi-linguistic processes, primarily by behaving toward the child in such a way that the child is eventually led to postulate that his own behavior can be best understood if he assumes that he has ideas and beliefs, feelings and wishes, that determine his actions, and the reactions of others to him can then be generalized to other similar beings. (Fonagy & Target, 2006, p. 53)

As reviewed in earlier chapters, parental modes of thought and language are reflected in their children. For instance, patterns of maternal verbalization that allude to psychological processes predict infants' attachment security (Koren-Karie et al., 2002; Meins et al, 2001; Oppenheim & Koren-Karie, 2002), children's understanding of affective experiences (e.g., Dunn & Brown, 2001), their performance on Theory of Mind tasks (e.g., Hughes & Dunn, 2002), and children's own mentalizing at 45 and 48 months (Meins et al., 2002). As Bruner argues, language use is possible because we assume that others use the same rules of syntax for forming and comprehending speech, which means that others must use their mind the same way that we do. This assumption is critical for speech, but it is also critical for children to crack into the preference management process, when they express their preferences to others and attempt to negotiate their own preferences with others.

These intricate relations most likely account for the devastating impact of prolonged institutionalization and the inability to reverse its adverse effects when children are removed from such settings after age 2 (Smyke et al., 2007). Specifically, children in such settings lack caretaking others who attribute meaning to children' gestures and actions and children themselves do not have opportunities to triangulate and to attempt to alter foci, thus eliminating the need for language to be used instrumentally. But moreover, when others do not convey their intentions and do not infer children's intentions, children do not learn to mentalize and do not learn to treat others as psychological entities with preferences of their own.

As discussed earlier, the ability to conduct transformations on all three planes is a powerful tool that allows us to contemplate possible worlds and the possible psychological reactions of people in such possible worlds. This gives us the entry key to the world of fiction, as well as to the psychological world of real others, allowing us to bridge the self–other preference gap, to use transformational thought to manipulate others, to cope, and to traverse the bridge into altruistic and moral behavior. Moreover, it is our ability to conduct transformations simultaneously on all three planes that provides us with the ability to seamlessly comprehend stories that are internally coherent but violate what we know about the real world (e.g., understanding how a girl can comfort a depressed clock and why a peanut who is in love would be dancing with a smile on his face, Nieuwland & Van Berkum, 2006). As cited earlier, neuroscience evidence for the involvement of the same neural regions in episodic memory and recall, in prospection into the future, in making decisions about fictional others, in thinking of other people's psychological experiences, and in perspective taking, lends credence to the important role of the three planes of transformational thought that I identified in our social and intellectual lives.

C. Generic Others

Transformational thought allows for the creation of the concept of generic others, fictions that individuals use in guiding their own behavior and that potentiate the emergence of principled morality. This fiction is a product of what we know about others' preferences and how we perceive these preferences as relevant to our own preferences. Throughout this book, I have alluded to the importance of generic others as a fiction that is prevalent in parental socialization practices, in children's speech, and in guiding children's behavior. The assumption of generic others' normalcy governs all social interaction and importantly, behavior in the public domain, where normalcy coupled with rule-following create the semblance of social order amidst the chaos of interacting, idiosyncratic individuals.

Surprisingly, Freud did not incorporate the concept of generic others in the Superego. Although he claimed that social feelings rest on identification with other people, these others were parents, teachers, and other authority figures (e.g., Freud, 1923). The Freudian Superego remains tied to specific others and does not adopt the preferences of generic others as its moral guidepost (cf., Halton, 2004; Parsons, Bales, & Shils, 1955); thus Freud failed to equate the Superego with *principled* morality, according man the ability to engage in transformational thought but only in the service of protecting the Ego. He did not endow the Superego with similar transformational capacities.[2] In addressing this limitation in Freud's theory, Waelder (1960) suggests that the ability to step back and "assume an imaginary vantage point" from which to look at oneself critically is only implicit in the concept of Superego (p. 192). But as I discuss below, this imaginary vantage point, which allows for the emergence of the concept of generic others, is critical for social functioning and principled morality, as recognized by Piaget (1965) in his discussion of the importance of the "collective will" in autonomous moral thought in which personalities "are both conscious of themselves and able to submit their point of view to the laws of reciprocity and universality" (pp. 365, 368).

Generic others and the normalcy assumption have also been accorded important roles outside the field of psychology. Prince (1980), for instance, differentiates the virtual reader from the ideal reader, where the virtual reader is the reader imagined by the author as the eventual consumer of his work, "whom he bestows with certain qualities, faculties, and inclinations according to his opinion of men in general (or in particular)" (p. 9). Athens (1994) talks of *phantom communities* that populate the minds of criminals and support them in their antisocial behavior. In her remarkable book on perceptions of mass collectives, Mutz (1999) demonstrated that individuals have the ability to draw inferences about the attitudes and concerns of mass collectives, defined as groups with which individuals have no direct personal contact. This ability is of crucial importance in the American legal system because "the law presumes that people have the ability to assess the views of an average person, a reasonable person, and/or the consensus among large numbers of diffuse others with whom they may have no direct contact" and that in doing so they are not relying on their own personal judgments (Mutz, 1998, p. 193). Anderson (1983) has similarly talked of *imagined communities* of others whom one will never know but who populate our minds, underlining the importance of such imagined communities in the emergence and spread of nationalism. Generic others, then, serve an important role in our perceptions of the social world and the way we interact with others in it. As Boyer (2007) summarizes, "representations of agents *in absentia* are a constant feature of human thinking. Many, perhaps most, of our thoughts about other people are entertained when they are not around" (p. 246). Of course, some of these people are specific others, but as we saw above, generic others feature prominently in our thoughts.

This fiction was critical to both Cooley's discussion of *we* and to Mead's (1934) discussion of the *generalized other*. Cooley (1909) talked of *we* as a concept that operates exclusively in the world of our imagination. Mead also saw the generalized other as a fiction that emerges out of the child's participation in language practices, play, and games. In particular, in playing with other children, the child has to internalize not only the symbolic character of a specific other, but the roles of *all* others who are implicated with him in the same pretense. Moreover, as Nelson (1983) contends, in order to participate in social activities, children "must represent their own roles and the roles of others and be able to reciprocate the actions of others with appropriate actions of their own" (p. 135). Juggling these roles is fertile grounds for the development of both social and cognitive skills. Paley (1990) captures this in saying "the work of twenty-four children and their teachers as they analyze one another's clashing fantasies and conflicting desires provides training in the highest order of social responsibility and logical thought" (p. 98). For Mead, though, social play serves a further critical function because in play, the child must also comprehend the rules that govern different roles. This configuration of what Cronk (1973) calls "roles-organized-according-to-rules" brings the attitudes of all participants together to form a unity – this unity is what Mead calls the *generalized other*. The generalized other, then, is an organized and generalized attitude in reference to which the individual defines his own conduct. Importantly, though, the *I*, for Mead, becomes *Me* by transforming the present into the past, recalling memories of one's own prior actions and reflecting on them.

As well, though, Mead's formulation contains *a multiplicity of generalized others* (Cronk, 1973), which allows the individual to extend his conception of the generalized other by identifying himself with a "larger" community, the human race for instance. This provides

[2] In *Civilization and Its Discontents* (1930), Freud did stipulate that in many adults, guilt is changed to the extent that the role of parents is replaced by "the larger human community" (p. 125) but he did not specify how this transformation occurs. In his *New Introductory Lectures to Psychoanalysis* (1933/1965), on the other hand, Freud suggested that in addition to parents, other adult figures, teachers, and "people chosen as ideal models" (p. 64) become incorporated in the Superego, making the Superego more impersonal over time. Yet the power of the Superego comes from specific significant others who have been incorporated in it rather than from generic others.

people with a moral guidepost that allows them to oppose their own group by symbolizing and appealing to a "higher sort of community," questioning the morality of their own social group and providing the engine for moral and social change (cf., Kohlberg, 1976). Piaget (1965) elaborates this, saying, "common morality would thus be defined by the system of laws of perspective enabling one to pass from one point of view to the other, and allowing in consequence the making of a map or objective representation" (p. 351). Dewey (1897) also gives voice to this view, saying that through the demands of social situations, the child emerges "from his original narrowness of action and feeling," and conceives "of himself from the standpoint of the welfare of the group to which he belongs."

As Swanson (1988) contends, Freud, Piaget, and Mead are close on many fundamentals. They all assume that we become persons or selves because other people teach us that our desires and outlook may not be the same as theirs, because they require us to separate the two, and because they force us to take their preferences seriously. Autonomous morality emerges because individuals can "place themselves in reciprocal relationship with each other without letting the laws of perspective resultant upon this reciprocity to destroy their individual points of view" (Piaget, 1965, p. 397). We are social beings to the extent that we take into account our own preferences and the preferences of other people, both specific and generic, and guide our behavior accordingly. Through these processes, we thereby learn to behave in ways that "serve other people's interests, individual and collective, and not just our own" (Swanson, 1988, p. 8), playing a concert in which we each pull the strings of our own fiddle but must concomitantly listen attentively to the sounds emitted by other players and their instruments.

END NOTE

Kuran (1995) summarizes the three dominant conceptions of man in the social sciences: *homo economicus*, a utility-calculating, self-controlled man who takes little or no account of others or their preferences, whose nonselfish behavior derives from selfish preferences (Elster, 1983); *homo sociologicus*, a socially driven man who has no autonomous backbone and is primarily responsive to his knowledge of others' preferences; and *homo psychologicus*, best captured in Freud's portrait of the permanent struggle between the impulsive, pleasure-seeking Id and the internalized dictates of society as etched in the Superego. Skitka, Bauman, and Mullen (2008) have recently added yet another view of man as *homo moralis*, who is concerned with moral issues and not only driven by self-interest. These divergent conceptions all reflect an underlying core concern with our own and other people's preferences and the relative weights that such preferences are accorded in our social lives. But as this book has shown, there is yet another view that needs to be integrated into our conception of man: that of *homo transformatus*, who has internal conversations with himself and others, who responds to his own construction of the world, and who can both play with his own and others' representation of the world and adopt others' suggestions as to how the world should be mentally construed and reconstrued.

These divergent views of man must be integrated to account for human psychological functioning; preventing these independent streams from converging yields an erroneous picture of man and his social world. As illustrated in this book, in talking to others, children give voice to all these images, talking of their preferences, trying to get others to satisfy these preferences, and helping and hindering others in satisfying their preferences. In this process, they transform the real world, dealing with it in terms that are temporally, imaginally, and mentally removed from the physical world with which they interact, while at the same time they maintain both feet immersed in reality on the behavioral level. We should listen more often to these sometimes cacophonous voices, because they clearly ratify the simultaneous validity of all these conceptions and underline the need to draw a unified portrait in which our preferences – and our perceptions of others' preferences and our willingness to accommodate or thwart them – play a critical role. Tracing children's emergent language and demonstrating how they attempt to attain and negotiate their preferences with others provides us with a peephole for viewing this important process. To echo White,

> children's expressions have encouraged me to think past what I would have otherwise thought, to inquire about things that I would not otherwise have inquired about, and to question ideas and actions that I take for granted and that I would not otherwise have questioned. (White, 2000, p. 17)

I hope that in giving voice to infants', children's, and parents' language and allowing them to express and negotiate their respective preferences and cognitive transformations in this book, I have done the same and that the virtue of conceptualizing social development in terms of preference management will resonate in the scientific and larger community.

References

Abu-Akel, A. (2002). The psychological and social dynamics of topic performance in family dinner-time conversation. *Journal of Pragmatics, 34*, 1787–1806.

Acredolo, L. P., & Goodwyn, S. W. (1988). Symbolic gesturing in normal infants. *Child Development, 59*, 450–466.

Acredolo, L. P., & Goodwyn, S. W. (1998). *Baby Signs*. Chicago: Contemporary Books.

Addessi, E., Galloway, A. T., Visalberghi, E., & Birch, L. L. (2005). Specific social influences on the acceptance of novel foods in 2–5-year-old children. *Appetite, 45*, 264–271.

Adlam, D. S. (1977). *Code in Context*. London: Routledge & Kegan Paul.

Aijmer, K. (1996). *Conversational Routines in English: Convention and Creativity*. London: Longman.

Ainlie, J. (1990). Playing games and learning mathematics. In L. P. Steffe and T. Wood (Eds.), *Transforming Children's Mathematical Education: International Perspectives* (pp. 84–91). Hillsdale, NJ: Erlbaum.

Ainslie, G. (2001). *Breakdown of Will*. Cambridge, UK: Cambridge University Press.

Ainslie, G., & Haslam, N. (1992). Hyperbolic discounting. In G. F. Loewenstein & J. Elster (Eds.), *Choice over Time* (pp. 57–92). New York: Russell Sage Foundation.

Ainsworth, M. S. (1969). Maternal Sensitivity Scales, Scale 1 – Sensitivity versus Insensitivity to the Baby's Signals. Retrieved from http://www.psychology.sunysb.edu/attachment/pdf/mda_sens_coop.pdf

Ainsworth, M. S., Blehar, M. C., Waters, E., & Wall, S. (1978). *Patterns of Attachment: A Psychological Study of the Strange Situation*. Hillsdale, NJ: Erlbaum.

Akatsuka, N. (1986). Conditionals are discourse-bound. In E. C. Traugott, A. ter Meulen, J. S. Reilly, & C. A. Ferguson (Eds.), *On Conditionals* (pp. 333–351). Cambridge, UK: Cambridge University Press.

Allen, J. F. & Perrault, C. R. (1980). Analyzing intention in utterances. *Artificial Intelligence, 15*, 143–178.

Allen, R. (1995). "Don't go on my property!": A case study of transactions of user rights. *Language in Society, 24*, 349–372.

Alloway, N. (1999). Surveillance or personal empowerment? Macro- and micro-politics of gender and schooling. In B. Kamler (Ed.), *Constructing Gender and Difference: Critical Research Perspectives on Early Childhood* (pp. 153–166). Creskill, NJ: Hampton Press.

Altshuler, J. L., & Ruble, D. N. (1989). Developmental changes in children's awareness of strategies for coping with uncontrollable stress. *Child Development, 60*, 1337–1349.

Alwin, D. F. (1984). Trends in parental socialization values: Detroit, 1958–1983. *American Journal of Sociology, 90*, 359–382.

Alwin, D. F., & Jackson, D. J. (1982). Adult values for children: An application of factor analysis to ranked performance data. In R. M. Hauser, D. Mechanic, A. O. Haller, & T. S. Hauser (Eds.), *Social Structure and Behavior* (pp. 311–329). New York: Academic Press.

Andersen, E. S. (1986). The acquisition of register variation among Anglo-American children. In B. S. Schieffelin & E. Ochs, (Eds.), *Language Socialization across Cultures* (pp. 153–161). Cambridge, UK: Cambridge University Press.

Andersen, E. S. (1990). *Speaking with Style: The Sociolinguistic Skills of Children*. London: Routledge.

Anderson, B. (1983). *Imagined Communities: Reflections on the Origin and Spread of Nationalism*. London: Verso.

Anderson, R. C., & Pichert, J. W. (1978). Recall of previously unrecallable information following a shift in perspective. *Journal of Verbal Learning and Verbal Behavior, 17*, 1–12.

Andreoni, J. (1990). Impure altruism and donations to public goods: A theory of warm-glow giving. *Economic Journal, 100*, 464–477.

Antinucci, F., & Miller, R. (1976). How children talk about what happened. *Journal of Child Language, 3*, 167–189.

Applebee, A. N. (1978). *The Child's Concept of Story: Ages Two to Seventeen*. Chicago: University of Chicago Press.

Applegate, J. L. (1980). Person– and position–centered teacher communication in a day care center: A case study triangulating interview and naturalistic methods. *Studies in Symbolic Interaction, 3*, 59–96.

Applegate, J. L., Burleson, B. R., Burke, J. A., Delia, J. G., & Kline, S. L. (1985). Reflection-enhancing parental communication. In I. E. Sigel (Ed.), *Parental Belief Systems: The Psychological Consequences for Children* (pp. 107–142). Hillsdale, NJ: Erlbaum.

Ariel, S. (1984). Locutions and illocutions in make-believe play. *Journal of Pragmatics, 8*, 221–240.

Arlen, M. J. (1969). *Living-Room War*. New York: Viking Press.

Arminen, J. (2004). Second stories: The salience of interpersonal communications for mutual help in Alcoholics Anonymous. *Journal of Pragmatics, 36*, 319–347.

Aronsson, K., & Thorell, M. (2002). Voice and collusion in adult–child talk: Toward an architecture of intersubjectivity. In

S. Blum-Kulka & C. E. Snow (Eds.), *Talking To Adults: The Contribution of Multiparty Discourse to Language Acquisition* (pp. 277–293). Mahwah, NJ: Erlbaum.

Aschermann, E., Dannenberg, V., & Schulz, A. (1998). Photographs as retrieval cues for children. *Applied Cognitive Psychology, 12*, 55–66.

Astington, J. W. (2000). Language and metalanguage in children's understanding of mind. In J. W. Astington (Ed.), *Minds in the Making: Essays in Honor of David R. Olson* (pp. 267–284). Oxford: Basil Blackwell.

Atance, C. M., & O'Neill, D. K. (2005). Preschoolers talk about future situations. *First Language, 25*, 5–18.

Athens, L. (1994). The self as soliloquy. *Sociological Quarterly, 35*, 521–532.

Audet, L. R., & Ripich, D. N. (1994). Psychiatric disorders and discourse problems. In D. N. Ripich & N. A. Creaghead (Eds.), *School Discourse Problems*, 2nd ed. (pp. 191–227). San Diego, CA: Singular Publishing.

Aukrust, V. G. (2001a). Talk-focused talk in preschoolers – culturally formed socialization for talk? *First Language, 21*, 57–82.

Aukrust, V. G. (2001b). Agency and appropriation of voice – cultural differences in parental ideas about young children's talk. *Human Development, 44*, 235–249.

Aukrust, V. G. (2002). "What did you do in school today?" Speech genres and tellability in multiparty family mealtime conversations in two cultures. In S. Blum-Kulka & C. E. Snow (Eds.), *Talking to Adults: The Contribution of Multiparty Discourse to Language Acquisition* (pp. 55–83). Mahwah, NJ: Erlbaum.

Aukrust, V. G. (2004). Talk about talk with young children: Pragmatic socialization in two communities in Norway and the US. *Journal of Child Language, 31*, 177–201.

Aukrust, V. G., & Snow, C. E. (1998). Narratives and explanations during mealtime conversations in Norway and the U.S. *Language in Society, 27*, 221–246.

Autio, M. (2004). Finnish young people's narrative construction of consumer identity. *International Journal of Consumer Studies, 28*, 388–398.

Auwarter, M. (1986). Development of communicative skills: The construction of fictional reality in children's play. In J. Cook-Gumperz, W. A. Corsaro, & J. Streeck (Eds.), *Children's Worlds and Children's Language* (pp. 205–230). Berlin: Mouton de Gruyter.

Axia, G. (1996). How to persuade mum to buy a toy. *First Language, 16*, 301–317.

Ayers, T. S., Sandler, I. N., West, S. G., & Roosa, M. W. (1996). A dispositional and situational assessment of children's coping: Testing alternative models of coping. *Journal of Personality, 64*, 923–958.

Baars, B. J. (1988). *A Cognitive Theory of Consciousness*. New York: Cambridge University Press.

Backett, K. C. (1982). *Mothers and Fathers: A Study of the Development and Negotiation of Parental Behaviour*. London: Macmillan Press.

Band, E. B., & Weisz, J. R. (1988). How to feel better when it feels bad: Children's perspectives on coping with everyday stress. *Developmental Psychology, 24*, 247–253.

Bandura, A. (1965). Influence of model's reinforcement contingencies on the acquisition of imitative responses. *Journal of Personality and Social Psychology, 1*, 589–595.

Bandura, A. (1977). *Social Learning Theory*. Englewood Cliffs, NJ: Prentice-Hall.

Bandura, A. (1986). *Social Foundations of Thought and Action: A Social Cognitive Theory*. Englewood Cliffs, NJ: Prentice-Hall.

Bandura, A. (1990). Selective activation and disengagement of moral control. *Journal of Social Issues, 46*, 27–46.

Bandura, A. (1999). Moral disengagement in the perpetration of inhumanities. *Personality and Social Psychology Review, 3*, 193–209.

Bandura, A. (2002). Selective moral disengagement in the exercise of moral agency. *Journal of Moral Education, 31*, 101–119.

Bandura, A., Ross, D., & Ross, S. A. (1961). Transmission of aggression through imitation of aggressive models. *Journal of Abnormal and Social Psychology, 63*, 575–582.

Banks, S. M., Salovey, P., Greener, S., Rothman, A. J., Moyer, A., & Beauvais, J., & Epel, E. (1995). The effects of message framing on mammography utilization. *Health Psychology, 14*, 178–184.

Bannon, K., & Schwartz, M. B. (2006). Impact of nutrition messages on children's food choice: Pilot study. *Appetite, 46*, 124–129.

Barner-Barry, C. (1988). The structure of politically relevant behaviors in pre-school peer groups. In M. R. A. Chance (Ed.), *Social Fabrics of the Mind* (pp. 201–276). Hove, UK: Erlbaum.

Barnes, J. D. (2006). *Early Trilingualism: A Focus on Questions*. Clevedon, UK: Multilingual Matters.

Barnes, M. K., & Vangelisti, L. (1995). Speaking in a double-voice: Role making as influence in preschoolers fantasy play situations. *Research on Language and Social Interaction, 28*, 351–389.

Barnet-Verzat, C., & Wolff, F.-C. (2002). Motives for pocket money allowances and family incentives. *Journal of Economic Psychology, 23*, 339–366.

Barnett, M. A., King, L. M., & Howard, J. A. (1979). Inducing affect about self or other: Effects on generosity in children, *Developmental Psychology, 15*, 164–167.

Baron-Cohen, S. (1995). *Mindblindness: An Essay on Autism and Theory of Mind*. Cambridge, MA: MIT Press.

Barriga, A. Q., Morrison, E. M., Liau, A. K., & Gibbs, J. C. (2001). Moral cognition: Explaining the gender difference in antisocial behavior. *Merrill-Palmer Quarterly, 47*, 532–562.

Bartsch, K., & Wellman, H. M. (1995). *Children Talk about the Mind*. New York: Oxford University Press.

Bassano, D. (1996). Functional and formal constraints on the emergence of epistemic modality: A longitudinal study on French. *First Language, 16*, 77–114.

Bates, E. (1976). *Language and Context: The Development of Pragmatics*. New York: Academic Press.

Bates, E., Camaioni, L, & Volterra, V. (1979). The acquisition of performatives prior to speech. In E. Ochs & B. Schieffelin (Eds.), *Developmental Pragmatics* (pp. 111–129). New York: Academic Press.

Batson, C. D. (1991). *The Altruism Question*. Hillsdale, NJ: Erlbaum.

Batson, C. D., Early, S., & Salvarani, G. (1997). Perspective taking: Imagining how another feels vs. imagining how you would feel. *Personality and Social Psychology Bulletin, 23*, 751–758.

Baumrind, D. (1967). Child care practices anteceding three patterns of preschool behavior. *Genetic Psychology Monographs, 75*, 43–88.

Baumrind, D. (1971). Current patterns of parental authority. *Developmental Psychology Monographs, 4*, 1–103.

Baumrind, D. (1989). Rearing competent children. In W. Damon (Ed.), *Child Development Today and Tomorrow* (pp. 349–378). San Francisco: Jossey-Bass.

Baumwell, L., Tamis-LeMonda, C. S., & Bornstein, M. H. (1997). Maternal verbal sensitivity and child language comprehension. *Infant Behavior and Development*, *20*, 247–258.

Beach, B. A. (1988). Children at work: The home workplace. *Early Childhood Research Quarterly*, *3*, 209–221.

Beach, L. R. (1990). *Image Theory: Decision Making in Personal and Organizational Contexts*. New York: Wiley.

Beals, D. E. (1993). Explanations in low-income families' mealtime conversations. *Applied Psycholinguistics*, *14*, 489–513.

Bearison, D. J., & Cassel, T. Z. (1975). Cognitive decentration and social codes: Communicative effectiveness in young children from differing family contexts. *Developmental Psychology*, *11*, 29–36.

Beck, R. J., & Wood. D. (1993). The dialogic socialization of aggression in a family's court of reason and inquiry. *Discourse Processes*, *16*, 341–362.

Becker, J. A. (1988). "I can't talk, I'm dead": Preschoolers' spontaneous metapragmatic comments. *Discourse Processes*, *11*, 457–467.

Becker, J. A. (1990). Processes in the acquisition of pragmatic competence. In G. Conti-Ramsden & C. E. Snow (Eds.), *Children's Language*, Vol. 7 (pp. 7–24). Hillsdale, NJ: Erlbaum.

Becker, J. A. (1994). Pragmatic socialization: Parental input to preschoolers. *Discourse Processes*, *17*, 131–148.

Bedford, S. (1986). The "instant replay" game to improve rational problem solving. In C. E. Schaefer & S. E. Reid (Eds.), *Game Play: Therapeutic Use of Childhood Games*. New York: Wiley.

Bee-Gates, D. (2006). *I Want it Now: Navigating Childhood in a Materialistic World*. New York: Palgrave Macmillan.

Belk, R. W., Rice, C., & Harvey, R. (1985). Adolescents' reported saving, giving, and spending as a function of sources of income. *Advances in Consumer Research*, *12*, 42–46.

Bell, J. H., & Bromnick, R. D. (2003). The social reality of the imaginary audience: A grounded theory approach. *Adolescence*, *38*, 205–219.

Bellinger, D. C. (1979). Changes in the explicitness of mothers' directives as children age. *Journal of Child Language*, *6*, 443–458.

Bellinger, D. C., & Gleason, J. B. (1982). Sex differences in parental directives to young children. *Sex Roles*, *8*, 1123–1139.

Bénabou, R., & Tirole, J. (2004). Willpower and personal rules. *Journal of Political Economy*, *112*, 848–883.

Bénabou, R., & Tirole, J. (2006). Incentives and prosocial behavior. *American Economic Review*, *96*, 1652–1678.

Bennett, T., Emmison, M., & Frow, J. (1999). *Accounting for Tastes: Australian Everyday Cultures*. Cambridge, UK: Cambridge University Press.

Benson, J. B. (1997). The development of planning: Its about time. In S. Friedman & E. K. Scholnick (Eds.), *The Developmental Psychology of Planning: Why, How, and When do we Plan?* (pp. 43–75). Mahwah, NJ: Erlbaum.

Bentley, K. S., & Fox, R. A. (1991). Mothers and fathers of young children: Comparison of parenting styles. *Psychological Report*, *69*, 320–322.

Benveniste, E. (1971). *Problems in General Linguistics*. Coral Gables, FL: University of Miami Press.

Bergem, T. (1990). The teacher as moral agent. *Journal of Moral Education*, *19*, 88–100.

Bergin, C., & Bergin, D. A. (1999). Classroom discipline that promotes self-control. *Journal of Applied Developmental Psychology*, *20*, 189–206.

Beringer, G., & Garvey, C. (1983). Tag constructions: Structure and function in child discourse. *Journal of Child Language*, *9*, 151–168.

Berk, L. E. (1992). Children's private speech: An overview of theory and the status of research. In R. M. Diaz & L. E. Berk (Eds.), *Private Speech: From Social Interaction to Social Regulation* (pp. 17–53). Hillsdale, NJ: Erlbaum.

Berlyne, D. E. (1965). *Structure and Direction in Thinking*. New York: Wiley.

Berman, P. W. (1986). Young children's responses to babies: Do they foreshadow differences between maternal and paternal styles? In A. Fogel & G. F. Melson (Eds.), *Origins of Nurturance: Developmental, Biological and Cultural Perspectives on Caregiving* (pp. 25–51). Hillsdale, NJ: Erlbaum.

Bernstein, B. (1971). *Class, Codes, and Control (Vol. 1)*. London: Routledge & Kegan Paul.

Bernstein, B. (1974). *Class, Codes, and Control: Theoretical Studies toward a Sociology of Language (rev. ed.)*. New York: Schoken Books.

Berntsen, D. (1996). Involuntary autobiographical memories. *Applied Cognitive Psychology*, *10*, 435–454.

Bers, M. U., & Cassell, J. (2000). Children as designers of interactive storytellers "Let me tell you a story about myself . . . ." In K. Dautenhahn (Ed.), *Human Cognition and Social Agent Technology* (pp. 61–83). Amsterdam: John Benjamins Publishing.

Bettelheim, B. (1962). *Conversations with Mothers*. Oxford, UK: Free Press.

Beyer, E. (1956). Observing children in nursery school situations. In L. B. Murphy (Ed.), *Personality in Young Children (Vol. 1)* (pp. 337–377). New York: Basic Books.

Bicchieri, C. (1993). *Rationality and Coordination*. Cambridge, UK: Cambridge University Press.

Bickerton, D. (1995). *Language and Human Behavior*. Seattle, WA: University of Washington Press.

Bigelow, B. J., Tesson, G., & Lewko, J. H. (1996). *Learning the Rules: The Anatomy of Children's Relationships*. New York: Guilford Press.

Bin, Z. (1996) The little emperors' small screen: Parental control and children's television viewing in China. *Media, Culture and Society*, 18, 639–658.

Birch, L. L. (1980). Effects of peer models' food choices and eating behaviors on preschoolers' food preferences. *Child Development*, *51*, 489–496.

Birch, L. L., & Marlin, D. W. (1982). I don't like it, I never tried it: Effects of exposure on two-year-old children's food preferences. *Appetite*, *3*, 353–360.

Birch, L. L., Marlin, D. W., & Rotter, J. (1984). Eating as the "means" activity in a contingency: Effects on young children's food preferences. *Child Development*, *55*, 432–439.

Birch, L. L., McPhee, L. S., Bryant, J. L., & Johnson, S. L. (1993). Children's lunch intake: Effects of midmorning snacks varying in energy density and fat content. *Appetite*, *20*, 83–94.

Bisanz, G. L. (1982). Knowledge of persuasion and story completion: Developmental changes in expectations. *Discourse Processes*, *5*, 245–277.

Bischof-Kohler, D., & Bischof, N. (2007). Is mental time travel a frame of reference issue? *Behavioral and Brain Sciences*, *30*, 316–317.

Black, B. (1992). Negotiating social pretend play: Communication differences related to social status and sex. *Merrill-Palmer Quarterly*, *38*, 212–232.

Blaise, M. (2005). *Playing it Straight: Uncovering Gender Discourses in the Early Childhood Classroom*. New York: Routledge.

Blake, I. K. (1993). The social-emotional orientation of mother–child communication in African-American families. *International Journal of Behavioral Development*, *16*, 443–463.

Blasi, A. (1987). Comment: The psychological definitions of morality. In J. Kagan & S. Lamb (Eds.), *The Emergence of Morality in Young Children* (pp. 83–90). Chicago: University of Chicago Press.

Bloom, L. (1970). *Language Development: Form and Function in Emerging Grammars*. Cambridge, MA: MIT Press.

Bloom, L. (1973) *One Word at a Time: The Use of Single-Word Utterances before Syntax*. The Hague: Mouton.

Bloom, L. (1991). *Language Development from Two to Three*. Cambridge, MA: Harvard University Press.

Bloom, L., & Capatides, J. B. (1987). Sources of meaning in the acquisition of complex syntax: The sample case of causality. *Journal of Experimental Child Psychology*, *43*, 112–128.

Bloom, L., Lahey, M., Hood, L., Lifter, K., & Fliess, K. (1980). Complex sentences: Acquisition of syntactic connectives and the semantic relations they encode. *Journal of Child Language*, *7*, 235–261.

Bloom, L, Lightbown, P., & Hood, L. (1975). Structure and variation in child language. *Monographs of the Society for Research in Child Development*, *40* (Serial #160).

Bloom, L., Tackeff, J., & Lahey, M. (1984). Learning to in complement construction. *Journal of Child Language*, *11*, 391–406.

Blum-Kulka, S. (1997). *Dinner Talk: Cultural Patterns of Sociability and Socialization in Family Discourse*. Mahwah, NJ: Erlbaum.

Blum-Kulka, S. (2002). "Do you believe that Lot's wife is blocking the road (to Jericho)?": Co-constructing theories about the world with adults. In S. Blum-Kulka & C. E. Snow (Eds.), *Talking to Adults: The Contribution of Multiparty Discourse to Language Acquisition* (pp. 85–115). Mahwah, NJ: Erlbaum.

Blum-Kulka, S., House, J., & Kasper, G. (1989). Appendix: The CCSARP Coding Manual. In S. Blum-Kulka, J. House, & G. Kasper (Eds.), *Cross-Cultural Pragmatics: Requests and Apologies* (pp. 273–294). Norwood, NJ: Ablex.

Blum-Kulka, S., Huck-Taglicht, D., & Avni, H. (2004). The social and discourse spectrum of peer talk. *Discourse Studies*, *6*, 307–328.

Bogdan, R. J. (2005). Why self-ascriptions are difficult and develop late. In B. F. Malle & S. D. Hodges (Eds.), *Other Minds: How Humans Bridge the Divide between Self and Others* (pp. 190–213). New York: Guilford Press.

Bok, S. (1978). *Lying: Moral Choice in Public and Private Life*. New York: Vintage.

Bokus, B., & Shugar, G. W. (1979). What will a three-year-old say? An experimental study of situational variation. In O. K. Garnica & M. L. King (Eds.), *Language, Children and Society* (pp. 65–80). Oxford: Pergamon Press.

Bond, C. F. Jr., & Brockett, D. R. (1987). A social context-personality index theory of memory for acquaintances. *Journal of Personality and Social Psychology*, *52*, 1110–1121.

Bond, C. F. Jr., & Sedikides, C. (1988). The recapituation hypothesis in person retrieval. *Journal of Experimental Social Psychology*, *24*, 195–221.

Bonica, L. (1993). Negotiations among children and pretend play. In M. Stambak & H. Sinclair (Eds.), *Pretend Play among 3-Year-Olds* (pp. 55–77). Hillsdale, NJ: Erlbaum.

Borbely, C. J., Graber, J. A., Nichols, T., Brooks-Gunn, J., & Botvin, G. J. (2005). Sixth graders' conflict resolution in role plays with a peer, parent, and teacher. *Journal of Youth and Adolescence*, *34*, 279–291.

Bornstein, M. H., & Tamis-LeMonda, C. S. (1989). Maternal responsiveness and cognitive development in children. In M. H. Bornstein (Ed.), *Maternal Responsiveness: Characteristics and Consequences* (pp. 49–61). San Francisco: Jossey-Bass.

Bornstein, M. H., & Tamis-LeMonda, C. S. (1997). Maternal responsiveness and infant verbal abilities: Specific predictive relations. *Infant Behavior and Development*, *20*, 283–296.

Botzung, A., Denkova, E., & Manning, L. (2008). Experiencing past and future personal events: Functional neuroimaging evidence of the neural bases of mental time travel. *Brain and Cognition*, *66*, 202–212.

Bove, R. B., Valeggia, C. R., & Ellison, P. T. (2002). Girl helpers and time allocation in nursing women among the Toba of Argentina. *Human Nature*, *13*, 457–472.

Boucai, L., & Karniol, R. (2008) Suppressing and priming the motivation for motherhood, *Sex Roles*, *59*, 851–870.

Bowerman, M. (1985). Beyond communicative adequacy: From piecemeal knowledge to an integrated system in the child's acquisition of language. In K. E. Nelson (Ed.), *Children's Language*, Vol. 5 (pp. 369–398). Hillsdale, NJ: Erlbaum.

Bowerman, M. (1986). First steps in acquiring conditionals. In E. C. Traugott, A. ter Meulen, J. S. Reilly, & C. A. Ferguson (Eds.), *On Conditionals* (pp. 285–307). Cambridge, UK: Cambridge University Press.

Bowerman, M. (1973). *Learning to Talk: A Crosslinguistic Study of Early Syntactic Development, with Special Reference to Finnish*. Cambridge, UK: Cambridge University Press.

Bowles, S., & Gintis, H. (2006). Social preferences, homo economicus and zoon politikon. In C. Tilly & R. Goodin (Ed.), *Oxford Handbook of Contextual Political Analysis* (pp. 172–186). Oxford, UK: Oxford University Press.

Boyer, P. (2007). Specialized inference engines as precursors of creative imagination. In I. Roth (Ed.), *Imaginative Minds* (pp. 239–258). Oxford, UK: Oxford University Press.

Braungart, J. M., & Stifter, C. A. (1991) Regulation of negative reactivity during the strange situation: Temperament and attachment in 12-month-old infants. *Infant Behavior and Development*, *14*, 349–364.

Braunwald, S. R. (1985). The development of connectives. *Journal of Pragmatics*, *9*, 513–525.

Braunwald, S. R. (1995). Differences in the acquisition of early verbs: Evidence from diary data from sisters. In M. Tomasello & W. E. Merriman (Eds.), *Beyond Names for Things: Young Children's Acquisition of Verbs* (pp. 81–111). Hillsdale, NJ; Erlbaum.

Braunwald, S. R., & Brislin, R. W. (1979). The diary method updated. In E. Ochs & B. S. Schieffelin (Eds.), *Developmental Pragmatics* (pp. 21–42). New York: Academic Press.

Bragg, B. E. W., Ostrowski, M. V., & Finley, G. E. (1973). The effect of birth order and age of target on use of persuasive techniques. *Child Development*, *44*, 351–354.

Braginsky, D. (1970). Machiavellianism and manipulative interpersonal behavior in children. *Journal of Experimental Social Psychology*, *6*, 77–99.

Bredel, U. (2002). "You can say you to yourself": Establishing perspectives with personal pronouns. In C. F. Graumann & W. Kallmeyer (Eds.), *Perspective and Perspectivation in Discourse* (pp. 168–180). Amsterdam: John Benjamins.

Brehm, J. (1966). *A Theory of Psychological Reactance*. New York: Academic Press.

Brehm, S. S. (1981). Oppositional behavior in children: A reactance theory approach. In S. Brehm, S. M. Kassin, & F. X. Gibbons (Eds.), *Developmental Social Psychology* (pp. 96–121). New York: Oxford University Press.

Bretherton, I. (1984). Representing the social world in symbolc play: Reality and fantasy. In I. Bretherton (Ed.), *Symbolic Play: The Development of Social Understanding* (pp. 1–41). Orlando, FL: Academic Press.

Bretherton, I. (1991). Intentional communication and the development of an understanding of mind. In D. Frye & C. Moore (Eds.), *Children's Theories of Mind: Mental States and Social Understanding* (pp. 49–75). Hillsdale, NJ: Erlbaum.

Bretherton, I., & Beeghly, M. (1982). Talking about internal states: The acquisition of an implicit theory of mind. *Developmental Psychology*, *18*, 906–921.

Bretherton, I., Fritz, J., Zahn-Waxler, C., & Ridgeway, D. (1986). Learning to talk about emotions: A functionalist perspective. *Child Development*, *57*, 529–548.

Bridges, A., Sinha, C., & Walkerdine, V. (1981). The development of comprehension. In G. Wells (Ed.), *Learning through Interaction: The Study of Language Development* (pp. 116–156). Cambridge, UK: Cambridge University Press.

Bridges, L. J., & Grolnick, W. S. (1995). The development of emotional self regulation in infancy and early childhood. In N. Eisenberg (Ed.), *Review of Personality and Social Psychology*, Vol. 15, (pp. 185–211). New York: Sage.

Bridges, L. J., Grolnick, W. S., & Connell, J. P. (1997). Infant emotion regulation with mothers and fathers. *Infant Behavior and Development*, *20*, 47–57.

Brigaudiot, M., Morgenstern, A., & Nicolas, C. (1996). "Guillaume I va pas gagner, c'est d'abord Maman," Genesis of the first-person pronoun. In C. E. Johnson & J. H. V. Gilbert (Eds.), *Children's Language*, Vol. 9 (pp. 105–116). Mahwah, NJ: Erlbaum.

Broen, P. A. (1972). *The Verbal Environment of the Language-Learning Child*. Washington, DC: American Speech and Hearing Association.

Broeder, P. (1991). *Talking about People: A Multiple Case Study of Adult Language Acquisition*. Amsterdam: Swets & Zeitlinger.

Bronowski, J. (1977). *A Sense of the Future: Essays in Natural Philosophy*. Cambridge, MA: MIT Press.

Brown, J. R., & Dunn, J. (1991). "You can cry, Mum": The social and developmental implications of talk about internal states. *British Journal of Developmental Psychology*, *9*, 237–256.

Brown, J. R., & Dunn, J. (1996). Continuities in emotional understanding from 3 to 6. *Child Development*, *67*, 789–902.

Brown, L. M. (1998). *Raising their Voices: The Politics of Girls' Anger*. Cambridge, MA: Harvard University Press.

Brown, P. (2002). Everyone has to lie in Tzeltal. In S. Blum-Kulka & C. E. Snow (Eds.), *Talking to Adults: The Contribution of Multiparty Discourse to Language Acquisition* (pp. 241–275). Mahwah, NJ: Erlbaum.

Brown, R. (1958). *Words and Things: An Introduction to Language*. New York: Free Press.

Brown, R. (1973) *A First Language: The Early Stages*. Cambridge, MA: Harvard University Press.

Brown, R., Cazden, C., & Bellugi, U. (1968) The child's grammar from I to III. In J. P. Hill (Ed.), *Minnesota Symposium on Child Psychology* (pp. 28–73). Minneapolis: University of Minnesota Press.

Brown, R. (1980). The maintenance of conversation. In D. R. Olson (Ed.), *The Social Foundations of Language and Thought: Essays in Honor of Jerome S. Bruner* (pp. 187–210). New York: W. W. Norton.

Bruner, J. S. (1964). The course of cognitive growth. *American Psychologist*, *19*, 1–15.

Bruner, J. S., Jolly, A., & Sylva, K. (1976). *Play: It's Role in Development and Evolution*. New York: Basic Books.

Bruner, J. S. (1977). Early social interaction and language acquisition. In H. R. Schaffer (Ed.), *Studies in Mother–Infant Interaction* (pp. 271–289). London: Academic Press.

Bruner, J. (1978a). On prelinguistic prerequisites of speech. In R. N. Campbell & P. T. Smith (Eds.), *Recent Advances in the Psychology of Language: Language Development and Mother–Child Interaction* (pp. 199–214). New York: Plenum.

Bruner, J. S. (1978b). From communication to language: A psychological perspective. In I. Marková, (Ed.), *The Social Context of Language* (pp. 17–48). Chichester, UK: Wiley.

Bruner, J. (1983). *Child's Talk: Learning to Use Language*. New York: Norton.

Bruner, J. (1986a). *Actual Minds, Possible Worlds*. Cambridge, MA: Harvard University Press.

Bruner, J. (1986b). Play, thought, and language. *Prospects: Quarterly Review of Education*, *16*, 77–83.

Bruner, J., Roy, C., & Ratner, N. (1982). The beginnings of request. In K. E. Nelson (Ed.), *Children's Language*, Vol. 3 (pp. 91–138). Hillsdale, NJ: Erlbaum.

Brusdal, R. (2007). If it's good for the child's development then I say yes almost every time: How parents relate to their children's consumption. *International Journal of Consumer Studies*, *31*, 391–396.

Buckner, R. L., & Carroll, D. C. (2007). Self-projection and the brain. *Trends in Cognitive Sciences*, *11*, 49–57.

Buckingham, D. (1996). *Moving Images: Understanding Children's Emotional Responses to Television*. Manchester, UK: Manchester University Press.

Budwig, N. (1990). A functional approach to the acquisition of personal pronouns. In G. Conti-Ramsden & C. Snow (eds.), *Children's Language*, Vol. 7, (pp. 121–145). Hillsdale, NJ: Erlbaum.

Budwig, N. (1995). *A Developmental-Functionalist Approach to Child Language*. Hillsdale, NJ: Erlbaum.

Budwig, N. (1996). What influences children's patterning of forms and functions in early child language. In D. I. Slobin, J. Gerhardt, A. Kyratzis, & J. Guo (Eds.), *Social Interaction, Social Context, and Language: Essays in Honor of Susan Ervin-Tripp* (pp. 143–156). Mahwah, NJ: Erlbaum.

Budwig, N. (2002). A developmental-functionalist approach to mental state talk. In E. Amsel & J. P. Byrnes (Eds). *Language, Literacy, and Cognitive Development: The Development and Consequences of Symbolic Communication* (pp. 59–86). Mahwah, NJ: Erlbaum.

Budwig, N., Strage, A., & Bamberg, M. (1986). The construction of joint activities with an age-mate: The transition from caregiver–child to peer play. In J. Cook-Gumperz, W. A. Corsaro, & J. Streeck (Eds.), *Children's Worlds and Children's Language* (pp. 83–108). Berlin: Mouton de Gruyter.

Burns, S. M., & Brainerd, C. J. (1979). Effects of constructive and dramatic play on perspective taking in very young children. *Developmental Psychology*, *15*, 512–521.

Burleson, B. R., & Goldsmith, D. J. (1998). How the comforting process works: Alleviating emotional distress through conversationally induced reappraisals. In P. A. Andersen & L. K. Guerrero (Eds.), *Handbook of Communication and Emotion* (pp. 245–280). San Diego: Academic Press.

Bussey, K., & Bandura, A. (1992). Self regulatory mechanisms governing gender development. *Child Development, 63*, 1236–1250.

Butterworth, G. (1990). Self-perception in infancy. In D. Cicchetti & M. Beeghly (Eds.), *The Self In Transition: Infancy to Childhood* (pp. 99–119). Chicago: University of Chicago Press.

Butterworth, G. (2003). Pointing is the royal road to language for babies. In S. Kita (Ed.), *Pointing: Where Language, Culture and Cognition Meet* (pp. 9–33). Mahwah, NJ: Erlbaum.

Byrne, W. (1998). The distribution of generic objects: Lexicon, semantics, and pragmatics. In J.-P. Koenig (Ed.), *Discourse and Cognition: Bridging the Gap* (pp. 353–364). Stanford, CA: Center for the Study of Language and Information.

Callanan, M. A., & Oakes, L. M. (1992). Preschoolers' questions and parents explanations: Causal thinking in everyday activity. *Cognitive Development, 7*, 213–233.

Callanan, M. A., & Sabbagh, M. A. (2004). Multiple labels for objects in conversations with young children: Parents' language and children's developing expectations about word meanings. *Developmental Psychology, 40*, 746–763.

Calkins, S. D., & Johnson, M. C. (1998). Toddler regulation of distress to frustrating events: Temperamental and maternal correlates. *Infant Behavior and Development, 21*, 379–395.

Camaioni, L. (1979). Child–adult and child–child conversations: An intentional approach. In E. Ochs & B. S. Schieffelin (Eds.), *Developmental Pragmatics* (pp. 325–337). New York: Academic Press.

Camaioni, L. (1993). The development of intentional communication: A re-analysis. In J. Nadel & L. Camaioni (Eds.), *New Perspectives in Early Communication Development* (pp. 82–96). London: Routledge.

Camerer, C. F., & Fehr, E. (2006). When does "economic man" dominate social behavior? *Science, 311*, 47–52.

Cameron, C. A., Hunt, K., & Linton, M. J. (1996). Written expression as recontextualization: Children write in social time. *Educational Psychology Review, 8*, 125–150.

Campbell, S., & Smith, K. (2001). Equity observation and images of fairness in childhood. In S. Grieshaber & G. S. Cannella (Eds.), *Embracing Identity in Early Childhood Education: Diversity and Possibilities* (pp. 89–102). New York: Teachers College Press.

Cameron-Faulkner, T., Lieven, E., & Theakston, A. (2007). What part of no do children not understand?: A usage–based account of multiword negation. *Journal of Child Language, 33*, 251–282.

Cameron-Faulkner, T., Lieven, E., & Tomasello, M. (2003). A construction based analysis of child directed speech. *Cognitive Science, 27*, 843–873.

Cantor, N., Markus, H. R., Niedenthal, P. & Nurius, P. (1986). On motivation and the self concept. In R. M. Sorrentino & E. T. Higgins (Eds.), *Handbook of Motivation and Cognition* (pp. 96–121). New York: Wiley.

Cantor, N., Mischel, W., & Schwartz, J. C. (1982). A prototypic analysis of psychological situations. *Cognitive Psychology, 19*, 45–77.

Capps, L., & Ochs, E. (2002). Cultivating prayer. In C. E. Ford, B. A. Fox, & S. A. Thompson (Eds.), *The Language of Turn and Sequence* (pp. 39–55). Oxford: Oxford University Press.

Carew, J. V. (1976). *Observing Intelligence in Young Children: Eight Case Studies*. Englewood Cliffs, NJ: Prentice-Hall.

Carey, S., & Bartlett, E. (1978). Acquiring a single new word. *Papers and Reports on Child Language Development, 15*, 17–29.

Carlisle, L. (1994). Children's group discussions of literature: Fertile ground for informal oral language assessment. In K. Holland, D. Bloome, & J. Solsken (Eds.), *Alternative Perspectives in Assessing Chldren's Language and Literacy* (pp. 204–217). Norwood, NJ: Ablex.

Carlson, E. A. Sroufe, L. A. Egeland, B. (2004). The construction of experience: A longitudinal study of representation and behavior. *Child Development, 75*, 66–83.

Carpenter, M., Nagell, K., & Tomasello, M. (1988). Social cognition, joint attention, and communicative competence from 9 to 15 months of age. *Monographs of the Society for Research in Child Development, 63 (Serial #255)*.

Carrigan, M., Szmigin, I., Leek, S. (2006). Managing routine food choices in UK families: The role of convenience consumption. *Appetite, 47*, 372–383.

Carter, A. L. (1979a). Prespeech meaning relations: An outline of one infant's sensorimotor morpheme development. In P. Fletcher & M. Garman (Eds.), *Language Acquisition: Studies in First Language Development* (pp. 71–92). Cambridge, UK: Cambridge University Press.

Carter, A. L. (1979b). The disappearance schema: Case study of a second-year communicative behavior. In E. Ochs & B. S. Schieffelin (Eds.), *Developmental Pragmatics* (pp. 131–156). New York: Academic Press.

Cartledge, G., & Milburn, J. F. (1980). *Teaching Social Skills to Children*. New York: Pergamon Press.

Causey, D. L., & Dubow, E. F. (1992). Development of a self report coping measure for elementary school children. *Journal of Clinical Child Psychology, 21*, 47–59.

Chafel, J. A. (1987). Achieving knowledge about self and others through physical object and social fantasy play. *Early Childhood Research Quarterly, 2*, 27–43.

Chaillé, C. (1978). The child's conception of play, pretending, and toys: Sequences and structural parallels. *Human Development, 21*, 201–210.

Chandler, M. (1994). Self continuity in suicidal and nonsuicidal adolescents. *New Directions for Child Development, 64*, 55–70.

Chandler, M., Lalonde, C. E., Sokol, B. W., & Hallett, D. (2003). Personal persistence, identity development, and suicide: A study of native and non native North American adolescents. *Monographs of the Society for Research in Child Development, 68* (Serial #273).

Chang, C.-J. (2003). Talking about the past: How do Chinese mothers elicit narratives from their young children across time. *Narrative Inquiry, 13*, 99–126.

Chao, R. K. (1994). Beyond parental control and authoritarian parenting style: Understanding Chinese parenting through the cultural notion of training. *Child Development, 65*, 1111–1119.

Chapman, M., & Zahn-Waxler, C. (1982). Young children's compliance and noncompliance to parental discipline in a natural setting. *International Journal of Behavioral Development, 5*, 81–94.

Chapman, M., Zahn-Waxler, C., Cooperman, G., & Iannotti, R. (1987). Empathy and responsibility in the motivation of children's helping. *Developmental Psychology, 23*, 140–145.

Charles, N., & Kerr, M. (1987). Just the way it is: Gender and age differences in family food consumption. In J. Branner & G. Wilson (Eds.), *Give and Take in Families: Studies in Resource Distribution* (pp. 155–174). London: Allen & Unwin.

Charles, N., & Kerr, M. (1988). *Women, Food and Families*. Manchester, UK: Manchester University Press.

Charlesworth, W. R., & Kreutzer, M. A. (1973). Facial expressions of infants and children. In P. Ekman (Ed.), *Darwin and Facial Expression: A Century of Research in Review* (pp. 91–167). New York: Academic Press.

Charman, T., Ruffman, T., & Clemens, W. (2002). Is there a gender difference in false belief development? *Social Development*, *11*, 1–10.

Chiappe, D., & MacDonald, K. (2005). The evolution of domain-general mechanisms in intelligence and learning. *Journal of General Psychology*, *132*, 5–40.

Chiat, S. (2000). *Understanding Children with Language Problems*. Cambridge, UK: Cambridge University Press.

Chin, T. (2000). "Sixth grade madness": Parental emotion work in the private high school application process. *Journal of Contemporary Ethnography*, *29*, 124–163.

Chittenden, E., Salinger, T., & Bussis, A. M. (2001). *Inquiry into Meaning: An Investigation of Learning to Read*. New York: Teachers' College Press.

Christano, B. A., & Russ, S. W. (1996). Play as a predictor of coping and distress during an invasive dental procedure. *Journal of Clinical Child Psychology*, *25*, 130–138.

Christensen, P., & James, A. (2001). What are schools for? The temporal experience of children's learning in Northern England. In L. Alanen & B. Mayall (Eds.), *Conceptualizing Child-Adult Relations* (pp. 70–85). London: Routledge Falmer.

Chiu, C., Hong, Y., & Dweck, C. S. (1997). Lay dispositionism and implicit theories of personality. *Journal of Personality and Social Psychology*, *73*, 19–30.

Chu, J. Y. (2004). A relational perspective on adolescent boys' identity development. In N. Way & J. Y. Chu (Eds.), *Adolescent Boys: Exploring Diverse Cultures of Boyhood* (pp. 78–104). New York: New York University Press.

Church, J. (1966). *Three Babies: Biographies of Cognitive Development*. New York: Random House.

Cialdini, R. B., Vincent, J. E., Lewis, S. K., Catalan, J., Wheeler, D., & Darby, B. L. (1975). Reciprocal concessions procedure for inducing compliance: The door-in-the-face technique. *Journal of Personality and Social Psychology*, *31*, 206–215.

Cicourel, A. V. (1978) Interpretation and summarization: Issues in the child's acquisition of social structure. In J. Glick and A. Clarke-Stewart (Eds.), *Studies in Social and Cognitive Development* (pp. 251–281). New York: Gardner Press.

Clancy, P. M. (1986). The acquisition of communicative style in Japanese. In B. S. Schieffelin & E. Ochs, (Eds.), *Language Socialization across Cultures* (pp. 213–250). Cambridge, UK: Cambridge University Press.

Clancy, P. M., Akatsuka, N., Strauss, S. (1997). Deontic modality and conditionality in discourse: A cross-linguistic study of adult speech to young children. In A. Kamio (Ed.), *Directions in Functional Linguistics* (pp. 19–57). Amsterdam: John Benjamins.

Clancy, P. M. (1999). The socialization of affect in Japanese mother-child conversation. *Journal of Pragmatics*, *31*, 1397–1421.

Clark, C. D. (2003). *In Sickness and in Play: Children Coping with Chronic Illness*. New Brunswick, NJ: Rutgers University Press.

Clark, E. V. (1992). Conventionality and contrast: Pragmatic principles with lexical consequences. In A. Lehrer & E. F. Kittay (Eds.), *Frames, Fields and Contrasts* (pp. 171–208). Hillsdale, NJ: Erlbaum.

Clark, E. V. (1996). Early verbs, event types, and inflections. In C. E. Johnson & J. H. V. Gilbert (Eds.), *Children's Language*, Vol. 9 (pp. 61–73). Mahwah, NJ: Erlbaum.

Clark, E. V., & Carpenter, K. L. (1989). On children's uses of from, by, and with in oblique noun phrases. *Journal of Child Language*, *16*, 349–364.

Clark, H. H. (1992). *Arenas of Language Use*. Chicago: University of Chicago Press.

Clark, H. H. (1996). *Using Language*. Cambridge, UK: Cambridge University Press.

Clark, M. S. (1983). Reactions to aid in communal and exchange relationships. In J. D. Fisher, A. Nadler, & B. DePaulo (Eds.), *New Directions in Helping, Vol. 1. Recipient Reactions to Aid* (pp. 281–304). New York: Academic Press.

Clark, R. A., & Delia, J. G. (1976). The development of functional persuasive skills in childhood and early adolescence. *Child Development*, *47*, 1008–1014.

Clifford, E. (1959). Discipline in the home: A controlled observational study of parental practices. *Journal of Genetic Psychology*, *95*, 45–82.

Cloran, C. (1989). Learning through language: The social construction of gender. In R. Hasan & J. R. Martin (Eds.), *Language Development: Learning Language, Learning Culture* (pp. 111–151). Norwood, NJ: Ablex.

Cocking, R. R., & Copple, C. E. (1987). Social influences on representational awareness: Plans for representing and plans as representation. In S. L. Friedman, E. K. Scholnick, R. R. Cocking (Eds.), *Blueprints for Thinking: The Role of Planning in Cognitive Development* (pp. 428–465). Cambridge, UK: Cambridge University Press.

Cohler, B. J., & Grunebaum, H. J. (1981). *Mothers, Grandmothers, and Daughters*. New York: Wiley.

Colby, A., & Kohlberg, L. (1987). *The Measurement of Moral Judgment, Vol. II: Standard Issue Scoring Manual*. Cambridge, UK: Cambridge University Press.

Cole, P. A., & Dennis, T. A. (1998). Variations on a theme: Culture and the meaning of socialization practices and child competence. *Psychological Inquiry*, *9*, 276–278.

Cole, P. A., Bruschi, C. J., & Tamang, B. L. (2002). Cultural differences in children's emotional reactions to difficult situations. *Child Development*, *73*, 983–996.

Conway, M. A., & Bekerian, D. A. (1987). The role of situations in knowledge of emotions. *Cognition and Emotion*, *1*, 145–181.

Cook-Gumperz, J. (1973). *Social Control and Socialization: A Study of Class Differences in the Language of Maternal Control*. London: Routledge & Kegan Paul.

Cook-Gumperz, J. (1975). The child as practical reasoner. In. M. Sanches & B. G. Blount (Eds.), *Sociocultural Dimensions of Language Use* (pp. 137–162). New York: Academic Press.

Cook-Gumperz, J. (1981). Persuasive talk – The social organization of children's talk. In J. L. Wallat & C. Green (Eds.), *Ethnography and Language in Educational Settings* (pp. 25–50). Norwood, NJ: Ablex.

Cook-Gumperz, J. (1986). Language socialization and language acquisition. In J. Cook-Gumperz, W. A. Corsaro, & J. Streeck (Eds.), *Children's Worlds and Children's Language* (pp. 37–64). Berlin: Mouton de Gruyter.

Cook-Gumperz, J. (1995). Reproducing the discourse of mothering: How gendered talk makes gendered lives. In K. Hall & M. Bucholtz (Eds.), *Gender Articulated* (pp. 401–419). New York: Routledge.

Cooley, C. H. (1909). *Social Organization: A Study of the Larger Mind*. New York: Charles Scribner's & Son.

Cooper, C. R., Marquis, A., & Ayers-Lopez, S. (1982). Peer learning in the classroom: Tracing developmental patterns and consequences of children's spontaneous interactions. In L. C. Wilkinson (Ed.), *Communicating in the Classroom* (pp. 69–84). New York: Academic Press.

Corballis, M. (2007). The uniqueness of human recursive thinking. *American Scientist*, *95*, 240–248.

Corno, L. (1989). What it means to be literate about classrooms. In D. Bloome (Ed.), *Classrooms and Literacy* (pp. 29–52). Norwood, NJ: Ablex.

Corsaro, W. A. (1979a). Sociolinguistic patterns in adult-child interaction. In E. Ochs & B. S. Schieffelin (Eds.), *Developmental Pragmatics* (pp. 373–389). New York: Academic Press.

Corsaro, W. A. (1979b). "We're friends, right?" Children's use of access rituals in a nursery school. *Language in Society*, *8*, 315–336.

Corsaro, W. A. (1985). *Friendship and Peer Culture in the Early Years*. Norwood, NJ: Ablex.

Corsaro, W. A., & Maynard, D. W. (1996). Format tying in discussion and argumentation among Italian and American children. D. I. Slobin, J. Gerhardt, A. Kyratzis, & J. Guo (Eds.), *Social Interaction, Social Context, and Language: Essays in Honor of Susan Ervin-Tripp* (pp. 157–174). Mahwah, NJ: Erlbaum.

Corsaro, W. A., & Rizzo, T. A. (1990). Disputes in the peer culture of American and Italian nursery scool children. In A. D. Grimshaw (Ed.), *Conflict Talk: Sociolinguistic Investigations of Arguments in Conversations* (pp. 21–66). Cambridge, UK: Cambridge University Press.

Corsini, R. J. (1966). *Roleplaying in Psychotherapy: A Manual*. Chicago: Aldine.

Cotte, J., Ratneshiwar, S., & Mick, D. G. (2004). The times of their lives: Phenomenological and metaphysical characteristics of consumer timestyles. *Journal of Consumer Research*, *31*, 333–345.

Couch, C. J. (1984). *Constructing Civilizations*. Greenwich, CT: JAI Press.

Cournoyer, M., & Trudel, M. (1991). Behavioral correlates of self-control at 33 mos. *Infant Behavior and Development*, *14*, 497–503.

Crick, N. R., & Dodge, K. A. (1994). A review and reformulation of social-information processing mechanisms in children's social adjustment. *Psychological Bulletin*, *115*, 74–101.

Crockenberg, S., & Litman, C. (1990). Autonomy as competence in 2-year-olds: Maternal correlates of child defiance, compliance, and self-assertion. *Developmental Psychology*, *26*, 961–971.

Cronk, G. (1973). Symbolic interactionism: A "left-Meadian" interpretation. *Social Theory and Practice*, *2*, 313–333.

Csikszentmihalyi, M., & Schneider, B. (2000). *Becoming Adult: How Teenagers Prepare for the World of Work*. New York: Basic Books.

Cuff, E. C., & Hustler, D. (1981). Stories and story time in an infant classroom. In P. French & M. MacLure (Eds.), *Adult-Child Conversation* (pp. 111–141): London: Croom Helm.

Curran, J. M. (1999). Constraints on pretend play: Explicit and implicit rules. *Journal of Research in Childhood Education*, *14*, 47–55.

Currie, G. & Ravenscroft. I. (2003). *Recreative Minds: Imagination in Philosophy and Psychology*. New York: Oxford University Press.

Curry, S. L., & Russ, S. W. (1985). Identifying coping strategies in children. *Journal of Clinical Child Psychology*, *14*, 61–69.

Daly, K. J. (1996). *Families & Time: Keeping Pace in a Hurried Culture*. Thousand Oaks, CA: Sage Publications.

Daly, K. J. (2001). Controlling time in families: Patterns that sustain gendered work in the home. In K. J. Daly (Ed.), *Minding the Time in Family Experience: Emerging Perspectives and Issues* (pp. 227–250). Amsterdam: JAI Press.

Damon, W., (1977). *The Social World of the Child*. San Francisco: Jossey-Bass.

Damon, W., & Hart, D. (1988). *Self-Understanding in Childhood and Adolescence*. Cambridge, UK: Cambridge University Press.

Danby, S. (1998). The serious and playful work of gender: Talk and social order in a preschool classroom. In N. Yelland (Ed.), *Gender in Early Childhood* (pp. 175–205). London: Routledge.

Davidson, J. I. F. (1998). Language and play. In D. P. Fromberg & D. Bergen (Eds.), *Play from Birth to Twelve And Beyond: Contexts, Perspectives, and Meanings* (pp. 175–183). New York: Garland Publishing.

Davidson, R. G., & Snow, C. E. (1996). Five year olds' interactions with fathers versus mothers. *First Language*, *16*, 223–242.

Dawes, R. (1980). Social dilemmas. *Annual Review of Psychology*, *31*, 169–193.

Day, J. D., Borkowski, J. G., Punzo, D. & Howsepian, B. (1994). Enhancing possible selves in Mexican-American students. *Motivation and Emotion*, *18*, 79–103.

Deater-Deckerd, K. (1996). Within family variability in parental negativity and control. *Journal of Applied Developmental Psychology*, *17*, 407–422.

DeCharms, R. (1968). *Personal Causation*. New York: Academic Press.

De Geer, B. (2004). "Don't say it's disgusting!" Comments on socio-moral behavior in Swedish families. *Journal of Pragmatics*, *36*, 1705–1725.

De Geer, B., Tulviste, T., Mizera, L., & Tryggvason, M.-T. (2002). Socialization in communication: Pragmatic socialization during dinnertime in Estonian, Finnish, and Swedish families. *Journal of Pragmatics*, *34*, 1757–1786.

Degotardi, S., Torr, J., & Cross, T. (2008). "He's got a mind of his own": The development of a framework for determining mothers' beliefs about their infants' minds. *Early Childhood Research Quarterly*, *23*, 259–271.

De Hart, G. B. (1996). Gender and mitigation in 4-year-olds' pretend play talk with siblings. *Research on Language and Social Interaction*, *29*, 81–96.

De Houwer, A. (1990). *The Acquisition of Two Languages from Birth: A Case Study*. Cambridge, UK: Cambridge University Press.

Delamont, S. (1976). Beyond Flanders' fields: The relationship of subject matter and individuality to classroom style. In M. Stubbs & S. Delamont (Eds.), *Explorations in Classroom Observation* (pp. 101–131). Chichester, UK: Wiley.

Delamont, S. (1980). *Sex Roles and the School: Contemporary Sociology of the School*. London: Methuen.

DeLoache, J. S. (2002). The symbol-mindedness of young children. In W. W. Hartup & R. A. Weinberg (Eds.), *The Minnesota Symposia on Child Psychology*, Vol. 32, (pp. 73–101). Mahwah, NJ: Erlbaum.

DeLoache, J. S., & Burns, N. M. (1993). Symbolic development in young children: Understanding models and pictures. In C. Pratt & A. F. Garton (Eds.), *Systems of Representation in Young Children* (pp. 91–112). Chichester, UK: Wiley.

DeLoache, J. S., Miller, K. F., & Rosengren, K. S. (1997). The credible shrinking room: Very young children's performance with symbolic and nonsymbolic relations. *Psychological Science*, *8*, 308–313.

DeLoache, J. S., Uttal, D. H., & Rosengren, K. S. (2004). Scale errors offer evidence for a perception-action dissociation early in life. *Science*, *304*, 1027–1029.

Delgado-Gaitan, C. (1988). The value of conformity: Learning to stay in school. *Anthropology and Education Quarterly*, *19*, 354–381.

De Moura, S. L. (2007). Determinants of food rejection amongst school children. *Appetite*, *49*, 716–719.

Demuth, K. (1986). Prompting routines in the language socialization of Basotho children. In B. S. Schieffelin & E. Ochs (Eds.), *Language Socialization across Cultures* (pp. 51–79). Cambridge, UK: Cambridge University Press.

Denham, S. A. (1998). *Emotional Development in Young Children*. New York: Guilford.

Denham, S. A., Cook, M., & Zoller, D. (1992). "Baby looks very sad": Implications of conversations about feelings between mother and preschooler. *British Journal of Developmental Psychology*, *10*, 301–315.

Denham, S. A., Zoller, D., & Couchoud, E. A. (1994). Socialization of preschoolers' emotion understanding. *Developmental Psychology*, *30*, 928–936.

Deprez, V., & Pierce, A. (1993). Negation and functional projections in early grammar. *Linguistic Inquiry*, *24*, 47–85.

Derber, C. (1979). *The Pursuit of Attention: Power and Individualism in Everyday Life*. Oxford: Oxford University Press.

Desalles, J.-L. (2007). Storing events to retell them. *Behavioral and Brain Sciences*, *30*, 321–322.

DeTemple, J. M., & Beals, D. E. (1991). Family talk: Sources of support for the development of decontextualized language skills. *Journal of Research in Childhood Education*, *6*, 11–19.

Deuchar, M., & Quay, S. (2000). *Bilingual Acquisition: Theoretical Implications of a Case Study*. Oxford, UK: Oxford University Press.

DeVault, M. L. (1991). *Feeding the Family: The Social Organization of Caring as Gendered Work*. Chicago: University of Chicago Press.

DeVilliers, J. G. (1984). Form and force interactions: The development of negatives and questions. In R. L. Schiefelbusch & J. Pickar (Eds.), *The Acquisition of Communicative Competence* (pp. 194–236). Baltimore, MD: University Park Press.

DeVilliers, J., & DeVilliers, P. (2000). Linguistic determinism and the understanding of false belief. In P. Mitchell & K. Riggs (Eds.), *Children's Reasoning and the Mind* (pp. 191–228). Hove, UK: Psychology Press.

DeVilliers, J. G., & Pyers, J. E. (2002). Compliments to cognition: A longitudinal study of the relationship between complex syntax and false belief understanding. *Cognitive Development*, *17*, 1037–1060.

DeVilliers, P., & DeVilliers, J. G. (1979). Form and function in the development of sentence negation. *Papers and Reports on Child Language Development*, *17*, 57–64.

DeVries, R. (1997). Piaget's social theory. *Educational Researcher*, *26*, 4–17.

Dewey, J. (1897). My pedagogic creed. *School Journal*, *54*, 77–80.

Dias, M. G. B. B., Roazzi, A., O'Brien, D. P., & Harris, P. L. (2005). Logical reasoning and fantasy contexts: Eliminating differences between children with and without experience in school. *Interamerican Journal of Psychology*, *39*, 13–22.

Diaz, R. M. (1992). Methodological concerns in the study of private speech. In R. M. Diaz & L. E. Berk (Eds.), *Private Speech: From Social Interaction to Social Regulation* (pp. 56–81). Hillsdale, NJ: Erlbaum.

Dickinson, D. K. (1991). Teacher agenda and setting: Constraints on conversation in preschools. In A. McCabe & C. Peterson (Eds.), *Developing Narrative Structure* (pp. 255–301). Hillsdale, NJ: Erlbaum.

Dickinson, D. K., & Smith, M. W. (1994). Long-term effects of preschool teachers' book reading on low-income children's vocabulary and story comprehension. *Reading Research Quarterly*, *29*, 105–122.

Dienstbier, R. A., Hillman, D., Lehnhoff, J., Hillman, J., & Valkenaar, M. C. (1975). An emotion – attribution approach to moral behavior: Interfacing cognitive and avoidance theories of moral development. *Psychological Review*, *82*, 299–315.

Diessel, H. (2004). *The Acquisition of Complex Sentences*. Cambridge, UK: Cambridge University Press.

DiLalla, E. F., & Watson, M. L. (1988). Differentiation of fantasy and reality: Preschoolers' reactions to interruptions in their play. *Developmental Psychology*, *24*, 286–291.

Dimitracopoulou, I. (1990). *Conversational Competence and Social Development*. Cambridge, UK: Cambridge University Press.

Dix, T. (1991). The affective organization of parenting: Adaptive and maladaptive processes. *Psychological Bulletin*, *110*, 3–25.

Dix, T. (1992). Parenting on behalf of the child: Empathic goals in the regulation of responsive parenting. In I. Sigel, A. V. McGillicuddy-Delisi, & J. J. Goodnow (Eds.), *Parental Belief Systems: The Psychological Consequences for Children*, 2nd ed. (pp. 319–346). Hillsdale, NJ: Erlbaum.

Dix, T. (2000). What motivates sensitive parenting? *Psychological Inquiry*, *11*, 94–97.

Dix, T., Gershoff, E. T., Meunier, L. N., & Miller, P. C. (2004). The affective structure of supportive parenting: Depressive symptoms, immediate emotions, and child-oriented motivation. *Developmental Psychology*, *40*, 1212–1227.

Doane, J. A., et al. (1981). Parental communication deviance and affective style: Predictors of subsequent schizophrenia spectrum disorders in vulnerable adolescents. *Archives of General Psychiatry*, *38*, 679–685.

Doane, J. A., et al. (1982). Parental communication deviance as a predictor of competence in children at risk for adult psychiatric disorder. *Family Process*, *21*, 211–223.

Doane, J. A., et al. (1987). Communication deviance in adolescence and adulthood: A longitudinal study. *Psychiatry – Journal for the Study of Interpersonal Processes*, *50*, 5–13.

Dodge, K. A. (1986). A social information processing model of social competence in children. *Minnesota Symposia on Child Psychology*, *18*, 77–125.

Donaldson, M., & Wales, R. (1970). On the acquisition of some relational terms. In J. R. Hayes (Ed.), *Cognition and the Development of Language* (pp. 235–268). New York: Wiley.

Donkin, A. J., Neale, R. J., & Tilston, C. (1993). Children's food purchase requests. *Appetite*, *21*, 291–294.

Dore, J. (1978a). Preschool children's conversational performances. In K. Nelson (Ed.), *Children's Language*, Vol. 1 (pp. 397–444). New York: Gardner Press.

Dore, J. (1978b). Conditions for the acquisition of speech acts. In I. Marková (Ed.), *The Social Context of Language* (pp. 87–112). Chichester, UK: Wiley.

Dore, J. (1989). Monologue as reenvoicement of dialogue. In K. Nelson (Ed.), *Narratives from the Crib* (pp. 231–260). Cambridge, MA: Harvard University Press.

Dore, J., & Dorval, B. (1990). The politics of intimacy: A dialogical analysis of "being intimate" in a psychology experiment. *Advances in Discourse Processes*, Vol. 38 (pp. 78–100). Norwood, NJ: Ablex.

Dore, J., Gearhart, M., & Newman, D. (1978). The structure of nursery school conversation. In. K. Nelson (Ed.), *Children's Language*, Vol. 1 (pp. 337–395). New York: Gardner Press.

Dorval, B. (1990). Appendix. *Advances in Discourse Processes*, Vol. 38 (pp. 276–352). Norwood, NJ: Ablex.

Downey, T. W. (1987). Notes on play and guilt in child analysis. *Psychoanalytic Study of the Child*, *42*, 105–126.

Doyle, J. (2004). Prospects for preferences. *Computational Intelligence*, *20*, 111–136.

Dr. Seuss (1960). *Green Eggs and Ham*. New York: Random House.

Dubost, M. (1999). Le developpment des explications: Emergence et signification de 'parce que' dans l'interaction adulte-enfant. In E. Veneziano (Ed.), *La Conversation: Instrument, Objet et Source de Connaissance* (pp. 65–80). Paris: L'Harmattan.

Dunn, J. (1984). Pretend play in the family. In A. W. Gottfried & C. C. Brown (Eds.), *Play Interactions* (pp. 31–50). Lexington, MA: Heath.

Dunn, J. (1988). *The Beginnings of Social Understanding*. Cambridge, MA: Harvard University Press.

Dunn, J. (1996). Arguing with siblings, friends, and mothers: Developments in relationships and understanding. In D. I. Slobin, J. Gerhardt, A. Kyratzis, & J. Guo (Eds.), *Social Interaction, Social Context,and Language: Essays in Honor of Susan Ervin-Tripp* (pp. 191–204). Mahwah, NJ: Erlbaum.

Dunn, J. (2003). Emotional development in early childhood: A social relationship perspective. In R. J. Davidson, K. R. Scherer, & H. H. Goldsmith (Eds.), *Handbook of Affective Sciences* (pp. 332–346). Oxford: Oxford University Press.

Dunn, J., & Brown, J. (1991). Becoming American or English? Talking about the social world in England and the United States. In M. H. Bornstein (Ed.), *Cultural Approaches to Parenting* (pp. 155–172). Hillsdale, NJ: Erlbaum.

Dunn, J., & Brown, J. (2001). Relationships, talk about feelings, and the development of affect regulation in early childhood. In J. Garber & K. Dodge (Eds.), *Affect Regulation and Dysregulation in Childhood* (pp. 89–108). Cambridge, UK: Cambridge University Press.

Dunn, J., Brown, J., & Maguire, M. (1995). The development of children's moral sensibility: Individual differences and emotional understanding. *Developmental Psychology*, *31*, 649–659.

Dunn, J., & Dale, N. (1984). I a Daddy: 2-year-olds collaboration in joint pretend with sibling and with mother. In I. Bretherton (Ed.), *Symbolic Play: The Development of Social Understanding* (pp. 131–158). Orlando, FL: Academic Press.

Dunn, J. F., & Kendrick, C. (1982). *Siblings: Love, Envy and Understanding*. Cambridge, MA: Harvard University Press.

Dunn, J., & Munn, P. (1987). Development of justification in disputes with mother and sibling. *Developmental Psychology*, *23*, 791–798.

Dunn, J., & Wooding, C. (1977). Play in the home and its implications for learning. In B. Tizard & D. Harvey (Eds.), *Biology of Play* (pp. 45–58). London: Heinemann Medical Books.

Durrant, M. (1995) *Creative Strategies for School Problems: Solutions for Psychologists and Teachers*. New York: Norton.

Duranti, A., & Ochs, E. (1997). Syncretic literacy in a Samoan American family. In L. B. Resnick, R. Saljo, C. Pontecorvo, & B. Burge (Eds.), *Discourse, Tools, and Reasoning: Essays on Situated Cognition* (pp. 169–202). Berlin: Springer.

Dweck, C. S. (2006). *Mindset: The New Psychology of Success*. New York: Random House.

Dweck, C. S., Chiu, C., & Hong, Y. (1995). Implicit theories: Elaboration and extension of the model. *Psychological Inquiry*, *6*, 322–333.

Dworkin, R. (1978). *Taking Rights Seriously*. Cambridge, MA: Harvard University Press.

Dworkin, R. (1988). *The Theory and Practice of Autonomy*. New York: Cambridge University Press.

Dyson, A. H. (1993). *Social Worlds of Children Learning to Write in an Urban Primary School*. New York: Teachers' College Press.

Dyson, A. H. (1994). The ninjas, the X-Men, and the ladies: Playing with power and identity in an urban primary school. *Teachers College Record*, *96*, 219–239.

Eder, D. (1982). Differences in communicative styles across ability groups. In L. C. Wilkinson (Ed.), *Communicating in the Classroom* (pp. 245–264). New York: Academic Press.

Eder, R. A. (1989). The emergent personologist: The structure and content of $3\frac{1}{2}$-, $5\frac{1}{2}$-, and $7\frac{1}{2}$-year-olds' concepts of themselves and others. *Child Development*, *60*, 1218–1228.

Edwards, C. P. (1987). Culture and the construction of moral values: A comparative ethnography of moral encounters in two cultural settings. In J. Kagan & S. Lamb (Eds.), *The Emergence of Morality in Young Children* (pp. 123–154). Chicago: University of Chicago Press.

Eisenberg, A. (1992). Conflicts between mothers and their young children. *Merrill-Palmer Quarterly*, *38*, 21–43.

Eisenberg, A., & Garvey, C. (1981). Children's use of verbal strategies in resolving conflict. *Discourse Processes*, *4*, 149–170.

Eisenberg, A. R. (1985). Learning to describe past experiences in conversation. *Discourse Processes*, *8*, 177–204.

Eisenberg-Berg, N. (1979) The development of children's prosocial moral judgment. *Developmental Psychology*, *15*, 128–137.

Eisenberg-Berg, N., & Neal, C. (1979) Children's reasoning about their own spontaneous prosocial behavior. *Developmental Psychology*, *15*, 229.

Eisenberg, N. (1992). *The Caring Child*. Cambridge, MA; Harvard University Press.

Eisenberg, N., & Miller, P. A. (1992). The development of prosocial moral reasoning in childhood and mid-adolescence. In J. M. A. M. Janssens & J. R. M. Gerris (Eds.), *Child Rearing: Influence on Prosocial and Moral Development* (pp. 31–56). Amsterdam: Swets & Zeitlinger.

Eisenberg, N., Cumberland, A., & Spinrad, T. L. (1998). Parental socialization of emotions. *Psychological Inquiry*, *9*, 241–273.

Eisenberg, N., Wolchik, S. A., Hernandez, R., & Pasternack, J. F. (1985). Parental socialization of young children's play: A short-term, longitudinal study. *Child Development*, *56*, 1506–1513.

Ekman, P., Sorenson, E. R., Friesen, W. V. (1969). Pan-cultural elements in the facial displays of emotion. *Science*, *164*, 86–88.

Elbers, L., & van Loon-Verwoorn, A. (1998a). Contrast use in adult/child interaction: Effects on lexical development. In E. Veneziano (Ed.), *La Conversation: Instrument, Objet et Source De Connaissance* (pp. 229–264). Paris: L'Harmattan.

Elbers, L., & van Loon-Vervoorn, A. (1998b). Acquiring the lexicon: Evidence from Dutch research. In S. Gillis & A. De Houwer (Eds.), *The Acquisition of Dutch* (pp. 301–377). Amsterdam: John Benjamins.

Elgas, P. M., Klein, E., Kantor, R., & Fernie, D. E. (1988). Play and the peer culture: Play styles and object use. *Journal of Research in Childhood Education*, *3*, 142–153.

Elias, C., & Berk, L. E. (2002). Self-regulation in young children: Is there a role for sociodramatic play? *Early Childhood Research Quarterly*, *17*, 216–238.

Elkind, D. (1967). Egocentrism in adolescence. *Child Development*, *38*, 1025–1033.

El'konin, D. B. (1971). Toward the problem of stages in the mental development of children. *Soviet Psychology*, *4*, 6–20.

Elster, J. (1983). *Sour Grapes: Studies in the Subversion of Rationality*. Cambridge, UK: Cambridge University Press.

Ely, R., Gleason, J. B. (2006). I'm sorry I said that: Apologies in young children's discourse. *Journal of Child Language*, *33*, 599–620.

Ely, R., Gleason, J. B., Narasinhan, B., & McCabe, A. (1995). Family talk about talk: Mothers lead the way. *Discourse Processes*, *9*, 201–218.

Engel, S. (1995). *The Stories Children Tell*. New York: Freeman.

Engel, S. (2005). The narrative worlds of what is and what if. *Cognitive Development*, *20*, 514–525.

Engel, S., & Li, A. (2004). Narratives, gossip, and shared experience: How and what young children know about the lives of others. In J. M. Lucariello, J. A. Hudson, R. Fivush, & P. J. Bauer (Eds.), *The Development of the Mediated Mind: Sociocultural Context and Cognitive Development* (pp. 151–174). Mahwah, NJ: Erlbaum.

Ericsson, K. E., & Simon, H. A. (1984). *Protocol Analysis: Verbal Reports as Data*. Cambridge, MA: MIT Press.

Erickson, F. (1981). Timing and context in everyday discourse: Implications for the study of referential and social meaning. In W. P. Dickson (Ed.), *Children's Oral Communication Skills* (pp. 241–269). New York: Academic Press.

Erickson, F. (1990). The social construction of discourse coherence in a family dinner table conversation. *Advances in Discourse Processes*, Vol. 38 (pp. 207–239). Norwood, NJ: Ablex.

Eriksson, M., & Berglund, E. (1999). Swedish early communicative development inventories: Words and gestures. *First Language*, *19*, 55–90.

Ervin-Tripp, S. (1977). Wait for me, roller-skate! In S. Ervin-Tripp & C. Mitchell-Kernan (Eds.), *Child Discourse* (pp. 165–188). New York: Academic Press.

Ervin-Tripp, S., & Gordon, D. (1986). The development of requests. In R. L. Schiefelbusch (Ed.), *Language Competence: Assessment and Intervention* (pp. 61–96). San Diego, CA: College-Hill Press.

Ervin-Tripp, S., Guo, J., & Lampert, M. (1990). Politeness and persuasion in children's control acts. *Journal of Pragmatics*, *14*, 307–331.

Ervin-Tripp, S., & Kuntay, A. (1997). The occasioning and structure of conversational stories. In T. Givón (Ed.), *Conversation: Cognitive, Communicative, and Social Perspectives* (pp. 133–166), *Typological Studies in Language*, Vol. 34. Amsterdam: Benjamins.

Ervin-Tripp, S., & Mitchell-Kernan, C. (1977). *Introduction*. In S. Ervin-Tripp & C. Mitchell-Kernan (Eds.), *Child Discourse* (pp. 1–26). New York: Academic Press.

Ervin-Tripp, S., O'Connor, M. C., & Rosenberg, J. (1984). Language and power in the family. In M. Schulz & C. Kramerae (Eds.), *Language and Power* (pp. 116–135). Belmont, CA: Sage.

Estes, D., Wellman, H. M., & Woolley, J. D. (1989). Children's understanding of mental phenomena. *Advances in Child Development and Behavior*, *22*, 41–86.

Exline, V. M. (1947). *Play Therapy: The Inner Dynamics of Childhood*. Cambridge, MA: Houghton Mifflin.

Fader, A. (2006). Learning faith: Language socialization in a community of Hasidic Jews. *Language in Society*, *35*, 205–229.

Fagan, M. K. (2008). Toddlers' persistence when communication fails: Response motivation and goal subsititution. *First Language*, *28*, 55–69.

Fasulo, A., Liberati, V., & Pontecorvo, C. (2002). Language games in the strict sense of the term: Children's poetics and conversations. In S. Blum-Kulka & C. E. Snow (Eds.), *Talking to Adults: The Contribution of Multiparty Discourse to Language Acquisition* (pp. 209–237). Mahwah, NJ: Erlbaum.

Fehr, E., & Fischbacher, U. (2002). Why social preferences matter – the impact of non-selfish motives on competition, cooperation and incentives. *Economic Journal*, *112*, C1–C33.

Feigenbaum, P. (1992). Development of the syntactic and discourse structures of private speech. In R. M. Diaz & L. E. Berk (Eds.), *Private Speech: From Social Interaction to Social Regulation* (pp. 181–198). Hillsdale, NJ: Erlbaum.

Fein, G. G. (1984). The self-building potential of pretend play or 'I got a fish, all by myself'. In T. D. Yawkey & A. D. Pellegrini (Eds.), *Child's Play: Developmental and Applied* (pp. 125–142). Hillsdale, NJ: Erlbaum.

Fein, G. G. (1987). Pretend play: Creativity and consciousness. In D. Gorlitz & J. F. Wohlwill (Eds.), *Curiosity, Imagination, and Play: On the Development of Spontaneous Cognitive and Motivational Processes* (pp. 281–304). Hillsdale, NJ: Lawrence Erlbaum.

Feinman, S. (1992). *Social Referencing and the Social Construction of Reality*. New York: Plenum.

Feldman, C. F. (1989). Monologues as problem solving narrative. In K. Nelson (Ed.), *Narratives from the Crib* (pp. 98–119). Cambridge, MA: Harvard University Press.

Feldman, R. S., Jenkins, L., & Popoola, O. (1979). Detection of deception in adults and children via facial expressions. *Child Development*, *50*, 350–355.

Fenson, L. (1984). Developmental trends for action and speech in pretend play. In I. Bretherton (Ed.), *Symbolic Play: The Development of Social Understanding* (pp. 249–270). Orlando, FL: Academic Press.

Festinger, L. (1957). *A Theory of Cognitive Dissonance*. Stanford, CA: Stanford University Press.

Fiates, G. M. R., Amboni, R. D. de M. C., & Teixeira, E. (2006). Consumer behavior of Brazilian primary school students: Findings from focus group interviews. *International Journal of Consumer Studies*, *32*, 157–162.

Fiedler, F. F. (1967). *A Theory of Leadership Effectiveness*. New York: McGraw-Hill.

Fiese, B. H., Foley, K. P., & Spagnola, M. (2006). Routine and ritual elements in family mealtimes: Contexts for child well-being and family identity. *New Directions for Child and Adolescent Development*, *111*, 67–89.

Figueira, R. A. 1984) On the development of the expression of causativity: A syntactic hypothesis. *Journal of Child Language*, *11*, 109–127.

Fillenbaum, S. (1975). Inducements: On the phrasing and logic of conditional promises, threats, and warnings. *Psychological Research*, *38*, 231–250.

Fillmore, C. E. (1987). Varieties of conditional sentences. *Proceedings of the 3rd Eastern States Conference on Linguistics*, 163–182.

Fine, G. A. (1987). *With the Boys: Little League Baseball and Preadolescent Culture*. Chicago: University of Chicago Press.

Finley, G. E., & Humphreys, C. A. (1974). Naïve psychology and the development of persuasive appeals in girls. *Canadian Journal of Behavioral Science*, *6*, 75–80.

First, E. (1994). The leaving game, or I'll play you and you play me: The emergence of dramatic role play in 2-year-olds. In A. Slade & D. P. Wolf (Eds.), *Children at Play* (pp. 111–132). New York: Oxford University Press.

Fisher, L. O., & Birch, L. L. (1999). Restricting access to foods and children's eating. *Appetite*, *32*, 415–419.

FitzSimmons, E. (1999). *Teach Me: An Ethnography of Adolescent Learning*. Lanham, MD: International Scholars Publications.

Fivush, R. (1993). Emotional content of parent-child conversations about the past. In C. A. Nelson (Ed.), *Memory and Affect in Development: Minnesota Symposia on Child Psychology*, Vol. 23 (pp. 39–77). Hillsdale, NJ: Erlbaum.

Fivush, R. (1994). Constructing narrative, emotion, and self in parent–child conversation about the past. In U. Neisser & R. Fivush (Eds.), *The Remembering Self: Construction and Accuracy in the Self-Narrative* (pp. 136–157). Cambridge, UK: Cambridge University Press.

Fivush, R. (1998a). Methodological challenges in the study of emotional socialization. *Psychological Inquiry*, *8*, 281–283.

Fivush, R. (1998b). Gendered narratives: Elaboration, structure, and emotion in parent-child reminiscing across the preschool years. In C. P. Thompson, D. J. Herrmann, D. Bruce, J. D. Read, D. G. Payne, & M. P. Toglia (Eds.), *Autobiographical Memory: Theoretical and Applied Perspectives* (pp. 79–103). Mahwah, NJ: Erlbaum.

Fivush, R. (2004). Voice and silence: A feminist model of autobiographical memory. In J. M. Lucariello, J. A. Hudson, R. Fivush, & P. J. Bauer (Eds.), *The Development of the Mediated Mind: Sociocultural Context and Cognitive Development* (pp. 79–99). Mahwah, NJ: Erlbaum.

Fivush, R., Bohanek, J., Robertson, R., & Duke, M. (2004). Family narratives and the development of children's emotional wellbeing. In M. Pratt & B. H. Fiese (Eds.), *Family Stories and the Life Course: Across Time and Generations* (pp. 55–76). Mahwah, NJ: Erlbaum.

Fivush, R., & Fromhoff, F. A. (1988). Style and structure in mother-child conversations about the past. *Discourse Processes*, *11*, 337–355.

Fivush, R., Gray, J. T., & Fromhoff, F. A. (1987). Two-year-olds talk about the past. *Cognitive Development*, *2*, 393–409.

Fivush, R., & Slackman, E. (1986). The acquisition and development of scripts. In K. Nelson (Ed.), *Event Knowledge: Structure and Function in Development* (pp. 71–96). Hillsdale, NJ: Erlbaum.

Flavell, J. H. (1974) The development of inferences about others. In T. Mischel (Ed.), *Understanding Other Persons* (pp. 66–116). Oxford: Blackwell, Basil & Mott.

Fletcher, P. (1979). The development of the verb phrase. In P. Fletcher & M. Garman (Eds.), *Language Acquisition: Studies in First Language Development* (pp. 261–284). Cambridge, UK: Cambridge University Press.

Fletcher, P. (1985). *A Child's Learning of English*. Oxford: Basil Blackwell.

Flugel, J. C. (1961). *Man, Morals, and Society: A Psycho-Analytical Study*. New York: Viking Press.

Fodor, J. (1995) *The Elm and the Expert: Mentalese and its Semantics*. Cambridge, MA: MIT Press.

Folkman, S., & Lazarus, R. S. (1985). "If it changes it must be a process": Study of emotion and coping during three stages of a college examination. *Journal of Personality and Social Psychology*, *48*, 150–170.

Fonagy, P., Gergely, G., Jurist, E. L., & Target, M. (2002). *Affect Regulation, Mentalization, and the Development of the Self*. New York: Other Press.

Fonagy, P., & Target, M. (2006). The mentalization-focused approach to self pathology. *Journal of Personality Disorders*, *20*, 544–576.

Forbus, K. D., Gentner, D., & Law, K. (1995). MAC/FAC: A model of similarity-based retrieval. *Cognitive Science*, *19*, 141–205.

Forman, D. R., Aksan, N., & Kochanska, G. (2004). Toddlers' responsive imitation predicts preschool-age conscience. *Psychological Science*, *15*, 699–704.

Forrester, M. A. (2001). The embedding of the self in early interaction. *Infant and Child Development*, *10*, 189–202.

Forrester, M. A., & Reason, D. (2006). Competency and participation in acquiring mastery of language: A reconsideration of the idea of membership. *Sociological Review*, *54*, 446–460.

Förster, J., Friedman, R. S., & Liberman, N. (2004). Temporal construal effects on abstract and concrete thinking: Consequences for insight and creative cognition. *Journal of Personality and Social Psychology*, *87*, 177–189.

Forys, S. K. S., & McCune-Nicolich, L. (1984). Shared pretend: Sociodramatic play at 3 years of age. In I. Bretheron (Ed.), *Symbolic Play: The Development of Social Understanding* (pp. 159–191). Orlando, FL: Academic Press.

Fosson, A., & de Quan, M. M. (1984). Reassuring and talking with hospitalized children. *Child Health Care*, *13*, 37–44.

Foster, S. H. (1986). Learning discourse topic management in the preschool years. *Journal of Child Language*, *13*, 233–250.

Foster, S. H. (1990). *The Communicative Competence of Young Children: A Modular Approach*. London: Longman.

Fox, K. J. (1999). Reproducing criminal types: Cognitive training for violent offenders in prison. *Sociological Quarterly*, *40*, 435–453.

Fraisse, P. (1981). Cognition of time in human activity. In G. d'Yderwalle & W. Lens (Eds.), *Cognition in Human Motivation and Learning* (pp. 397–410). Hillsdale, NJ: Erlbaum.

Frankfurt, H. G. (1971). Freedom of the will and the concept of a person. *Journal of Philosophy*, *68*, 5–20.

Frankfurt, H. G. (1988). *The Importance of What We Care About*. Cambridge, UK: Cambridge University Press.

Frederick, S., Loewenstein, G., and O'Donoghue, T. (2002). Time discounting and time preference: a critical review. *Journal of Economic Literature*, *40*, 351–401.

Freedman, J. L., & Fraser, S. C. (1966). Compliance without pressure: The foot-in-the-door technique. *Journal of Personality and Social Psychology*, *4*, 195–202.

Freeman, J., Epston, D., & Lobovits, D. (1997). *Playful Approaches to Serious Problems: Narrative Therapy with Children and Their Families*. New York: Norton.

French, L. A. (1986). The language of events. In K. Nelson (Ed.), *Event Knowledge: Structure and Function in Development* (pp. 119–136). Hillsdale, NJ: Erlbaum.

French, L. A., & Nelson, K. (1985). *Young Children's Knowledge of Relational Terms: Some Ifs, Ors, and Buts*. New York: Springer-Verlag.

French, L., & Pak, M. K. (1995). Young children's play dialogues with mothers and peers. In K. E. Nelson & Z. Reger (Eds.), *Children's Language*, Vol. 8 (pp. 65–101). Hillsdale, NJ: Erlbaum.

French, P., & Woll, B. (1981). Context, meaning and strategy in parent-child conversation. In G. Wells (Ed.), *Learning through Interaction: The Study of Language Development* (pp. 157–182). Cambridge, UK: Cambridge University Press.

Freud, S. (1899). Screen memories. *The Standard Edition of the Complete Psychological Works of Sigmund Freud, Volume III (1893–1899): Early Psycho-Analytic Publications* (pp. 299–322). London: Hogarth Press.

Freud, S. (1901). On dreams. *The Standard Edition of the Complete Psychological Works of Sigmund Freud, 1900–1901: The Interpretation of Dreams (2nd Part) and On Dreams* (pp. 629–686). London: Hogarth Press.

Freud. S. (1908). Creative Writers and Day-Dreaming. *The Standard Edition of the Complete Psychological Works of Sigmund Freud, Volume IX (1906–1908): Jensen's 'Gradiva' and Other Works* (pp. 141–154). London: Hogarth Press.

Freud, S. (1911). Formulations on the two principles of mental functioning. *The Standard Edition of the Complete Psychological Works of Sigmund Freud, Volume XII (1911–1913): The Case of Schreber, Papers on Technique, and Other Works* (pp. 213–226). London: Hogarth Press.

Freud, S. (1913) Totem and Taboo. *The Standard Edition of the Complete Psychological Works of Sigmund Freud, Volume XIII (1913–1914): Totem and Taboo and Other Works* (xii–162). London: Hogarth Press.

Freud, S. (1917/1973). *Introductory Lectures on Psychoanalysis*. PFL Penguin Freud Library, Vol. 1. London: Penguin Books.

Freud, S. (1918/1946). *Totem and Taboo: Resemblances Between the Psychic Lives of Savages and Neurotics*. New York: Vintage Books.

Freud, S. (1923). The Ego and the Id. *The Standard Edition of the Complete Psychological Works of Sigmund Freud, Vol. XIV (1923–1925): The Ego and the Id and Other Works* (pp. 1–66). London: Hogarth Press.

Freud, S. (1924/1971). *A General Introduction to Psychoanalysis*. New York: Pocket Books.

Freud, S. (1927). The Future of an Illusion. *The Standard Edition of the Complete Psychological Works of Sigmund Freud, Vol. XXI (1927–1931): The Future of an Illusion, Civilization and Its Discontents, and Other Works* (pp. 1–56). London: Hogarth Press.

Freud, S. (1930). Civilization and Its Discontents. *The Standard Edition of the Complete Psychological Works of Sigmund Freud, Vol. XXI (1927–1931): The Future of an Illusion, Civilization and Its Discontents, and Other Works* (pp. 57–146). London: Hogarth Press.

Freud, S. (1933/1965). *New Introductory Lectures on Psychoanalysis*. New York: Norton.

Frey, B. S., & Meier, S. (2004). Social comparisons and pro-social behavior: Testing "Conditional Cooperation" in a field experiment. *American Economic Review*, *94*, 1717–1722.

Friedman, O., & Neary, K. R. (2008). Determining who owns what: Do children infer ownership from first possession? *Cognition*, *107*, 829–849.

Friedman, S. L., & Sherman, T. L. (1985). Mothers as mediators of their 2- to 4-year-olds' cognitive development. Paper presented at a symposium of the Society for Research in Child Development, Toronto, April.

Friedman, W. J. (2003). The development of a differentiated sense of the past and the future. In R. V. Kail (Ed.), *Advances in Child Development and Behavior*, Vol. 31 (pp. 232–269). San Diego, CA: Academic Press.

Frydenberg, E. (1997). *Adolescent Coping: Theoretical and Research Perspectives*. London: Routledge.

Fujita, K., Henderson, M. D., Eng, J., Trope, Y., & Liberman, N. (2006). Spatial distance and mental construal of social events. *Psychological Science*, *17*, 278–282.

Fujita, K., Trope, Y., Liberman, N., & Levin-Sagi, M. (2006). Construal level and self control. *Journal of Personality and Social Psychology*, *90*, 351–367.

Fung, H. (1999). Becoming a moral child: The socialization of shame among young Chinese children. *Ethos*, *27*, 180–209.

Fung, H., & Chen, E. C.-H. (2001). Across time and beyond skin: Self and transgression in the everyday socialization of shame among Taiwanese preschool children. *Social Development*, *10*, 420–437.

Fung, H., Miller, P. J., & Lin, L.-C. (2004). Listening is active: Lessons from the narrative practices of Taiwanese families. In M. Pratt & B. H. Fiese (Eds.), *Family Stories and the Life Course: Across Time and Generations* (pp. 303–323). Mahwah, NJ: Erlbaum.

Furlong, V. (1976). Interaction sets in the classroom: Towards a study of pupil knowledge. In M. Stubbs & S. Delamont (Eds.), *Explorations in Classroom Observation* (pp. 23–44). Chichester, UK: Wiley.

Furnham, A. (1999). Economic socialization: A study of adults' perceptions and uses of allowances (pocket money) to educate children. *British Journal of Developmental Psychology*, *17*, 585–604.

Furrow, D. (1992). Developmental trends in the differentiation of social and private speech. In R. M. Diaz & L. E. Berk (Eds.), *Private Speech: From Social Interaction to Social Regulation* (pp. 143–158). Hillsdale, NJ: Erlbaum.

Galda, L., & Pellegrini, A. D. (1988). Play talk, school talk, and emergent literacy. In S. Hynds & D. L. Rubin (Eds.), *Perspectives on Talk and Learning*. Urbana, IL: National Council of Teachers of English.

Galda, L., & Pellegrini, A. D. (1991). Longitudinal relations among preschoolers' symbolic play, metalinguistic verbs, and emergent literacy. In J. F. Christie (Ed.), *Play and Early Literacy Development* (pp. 47–67). Albany, NY: SUNY Press.

Gallagher, T. M., & Craig, H. K. (1987). An investigation of pragmatic connectors within preschool peer interaction. *Journal of Pragmatics*, *11*, 27–37.

Galloway, A. T., Fiorito, L. M., Francis, L. A., & Birch, L. L. (2006). "Finish your soup": Counter-productive effects of pressuring children to eat on intake and affect. *Appetite*, *46*, 318–323.

Gärdenfors, P. (2005) The detachment of thought. In C. E. Erneling & D. M. Johnson (Eds.), *The Mind as a Scientific Object: Between Brain and Culture* (pp. 323–366). Oxford, UK: Oxford University Press.

Gardner, D. E. M., & Cass, J. E. (1965). *The Role of the Teacher in the Infant and Nursery School*. Oxford, UK: Pergamon Press.

Gardner, F. E. M., Sonuga-Barke, E. J. S., & Sayal, K. (1999). Parents anticipating misbehaviour: An observational study of strategies parents use to prevent conflict with behaviour problem children. *Journal of Child Psychology and Psychiatry*, *40*, 1185–1196.

Gardner, J. M., & Turkewitz, G. (1982). The effect of arousal level on visual preferences in preterm infants. *Infant Behavior and Development*, *5*, 369–385.

Garnica, O. K. (1981). Social dominance and conversational interaction – the Omega child in the classroom. In J. L. Wallat & C. Green (Eds.), *Ethnography and Language in Educational Settings* (pp. 229–252). Norwood, NJ: Ablex.

Garrett, P. B., & Baquedano-López, P. (2002). Language socialization: Reproduction and continuity, transformation and change. *Annual Review of Anthropology*, *31*, 339–361.

Garvey, C. (1975). Requests and responses in children's speech. *Journal of Child Language*, *2*, 41–59.

Garvey, C. (1977). *Play*. Cambridge, MA: Harvard University Press.

Garvey, C. (1977b). Play with language. In B. Tizard & D. Harvey (Eds.), *Biology of Play* (pp. 74–99). London: Heinemann Medical Publications.

Garvey, C. (1984). *Children's Talk*. Cambridge, MA: Harvard University Press.

Garvey, C. (1993). Diversity in conversational repertoire: The case of conflicts and social pretending. *Cognition and Instruction*, *11*, 251–264.

Garvey, C., Berndt, R. (1977). Organization of pretend play. *JSAS Catalogue of Selected Documents in Psychology*, *7*, Manuscript #1589.

Garvey, C., & Kramer, T. L. (1989). The language of social pretend play. *Developmental Review*, *9*, 364–382.

Gauthier, I. (1999). Etude pragmatique des justifications et des simulations expressives du sein de la requête. In E. Veneziano (Ed.), *La Conversation: Instrument, Objet et Source de Connaissance* (pp. 45–63). Paris: L'Harmattan.

Gearhart, M., & Newman, D. (1980). Learning to draw a picture: The social context of an individual activity. *Discourse Processes*, *3*, 169–184.

Gehring, T. M., Wentzel, K. R., Feldman, S. S., & Munson, J. (1990). Conflict in families of adolescents: The impact of cohesion and power structures. *Journal of Family Psychology*, *3*, 290–309.

Gelman, R., & Shatz, M. (1977). Appropriate speech adjustments: The operation of conversational constraints on talk to two-year-olds. In M. Lewis & L. A. Rosenblum (Eds.), *Interaction, Conversation and the Development of Language* (pp. 27–61). New York: Wiley.

Gelman, S. A., Star, J. R., & Flukes, J. E. (2002). Children's use of generics in inductive inferences. *Journal of Cognition and Development*, *3*, 179–199.

Gelman, S. A., Taylor, M. G., & Nguyen, S. P. (2004). Mother–child conversations about gender: Understanding the acquisition of essentialistic beliefs. *Monographs of the Society for Research in Child Development*, *69* (Serial #275).

Gendler, T. S. (2006). Imaginative contagion. *Metaphilosophy*, *37*, 183–203.

Genishi, C., & Di Paolo, M. (1982). Learning through argument in preschool. In L. C. Wilkinson (Ed.), *Communicating in the Classroom* (pp. 49–68). New York: Academic Press.

Gentner, D., & Loewenstein, J. (2002). Relational language and relational thought. In E. Amsel & J. P. Byrnes (Eds.), *Language, Literacy, and Cognitive Development: The Development and Consequences of Symbolic Communication* (pp. 87–120). Mahwah, NJ: Erlbaum.

Gentner, D., & Medina, J. (1998). Similarity and the development of rules. *Cognition*, *65*, 263–297.

George, D. (2001). *Preference Pollution: How Markets Create the Desires We Dislike*. Ann Arbor, MI: University of Michigan Press.

Georgalidou, M. (2008). The conceptual parameters of linguistic choice: Greek children's preferences for the formation of directive speech acts. *Journal of Pragmatics*, *40*, 72–94.

Gergely, G. (1994). From self-recognition to theory of mind. In S. T. Parker, R. W. Mitchell, & L. Boccia (Eds.), *Self Awareness in Animals and Humans: Developmental Perspectives* (pp. 51–80). Cambridge, UK: Cambridge University Press.

Gergely, G. (2004). The role of contingency detection in early affect-regulative interactions and in the development of different types of infant attachment: Comment. *Social Development*, *13*, 468–478.

Gerhardt, J. (1991). The meaning and use of the modals HAFTA, NEEDTA and WANNA in children's speech. *Journal of Pragmatics*, *16*, 531–590.

German, T. P. (1999). Children's causal reasoning: Counterfactual thinking occurs for "negative" outcomes only. *Developmental Science*, *2*, 442–447.

German, T. P., & Nichols, S. (2003). Children's counterfactual inferences about long and short causal chains. *Developmental Science*, *6*, 514–523.

Gershoff, E. T. (2002). Corporal punishment by parents and associated child behaviors and experiences: A meta-analytic and theoretical review. *Psychological Bulletin*, *128*, 539–579.

Gershoff, E. T. (2002). Corporal punishment, physical abuse, and the burden of proof: Reply to Baumrind, Larzelere, and Cowan (2002), Holden (2002), and Parke (2002). *Psychological Bulletin*, *128*, 602– 611.

Gershoff, E. T., Miller, P. C., & Holden, G. W. (1999). Parenting influences from the pulpit: Religious affiliation as a determinant of parental corporal punishment. *Journal of Family Psychology*, *13*, 307–320.

Gerson, M., & Schnabl-Brandes, A. (1990). The educational approach of the metapelet of young children in the Kibbutz. In Z. Lavi (Ed.), *Kibbutz Members Study Kibbutz Children* (pp. 40–49). New York: Greenwood Press.

Gibbons, J., Anderson, D. R., Smith, R. N., Field, D. E., & Fischer, C. (1986). Young children's recall and reconstruction of audio and audiovisual narratives. *Child Development*, *57*, 1014–1023.

Gibbs, J. C. (1991). Sociomoral developmental delay and cognitive distortion: Implications for the treatment of antisocial youth. In W. M. Kurtines & J. L. Gewirtz (Eds.), *Handbook of Moral Behavior and Development. Vol. 3. Application* (pp. 95–110). Hillsdale, NJ: Erlbaum.

Gibbs, J. J., Giever, D., & Martin, J. S. (1998). Parental management and self-control: An empirical test of Gottfredson and Hirschi's general theory. *Journal of Research in Crime and Delinquency*, *35*, 40–70.

Gibson-Cline, J. (1996). *Adolescence: From Crisis to Coping: A Thirteen Nation Study*. Oxford: Butterworth-Heinemann.

Giddens, A. (1968). Power in the recent writing of Talcott Parsons. *Sociology*, *2*, 257–272.

Giffin, H. (1984). The coordination of meaning in the creation of shared make-believe reality. In I. Bretherton (Ed.), *Symbolic Play: The Development of Social Understanding* (pp. 73–100). Orlando, FL: Academic Press.

Gilbert, P., & Taylor, S. (1991). *Fashioning the Feminine: Girls, Popular Culture and Schooling*. North Sydney, Australia: Allen & Unwin.

Gilligan, C. (1982). *In a Different Voice: Psychological Theory and Women's Development*. Cambridge, MA: Harvard University Press.

Gilovich, T., & Savitsky, K. (1999). The spotlight effect and the illusion of transparency: Egocentric assessments of how we are seen by others. *Current Directions in Psychological Science, 8*, 165–167.

Ginott, H. (1965). *Between Parent and Child: New Solutions to Old Problems*. New York: Macmillan.

Gleason, J. B. (1987). Sex differences in parent–child interaction. In S. U. Phillips, S. Steele, & C. Tanz (Eds.), *Language, Gender, and Sex in Comparative Perspective* (pp. 189–199). Cambridge, UK: Cambridge University Press.

Gleason, J. B., & Ely, R. (1997). Input and the acquisition of vocabulary: Examining the parental lexicon. In C. Mandell & A. McCabe (Eds.), *The Problem of Meaning: Behavioral and Cognitive Perspectives* (pp. 221–260). Amsterdam: Elsevier.

Gleason, J. B., & Greif, E. B. (1983). Men's speech to young children. In B. Thorne, C. Kamarae, & N. Henley (Eds.), *Language, Gender, and Society* (pp. 140–150). Rowley, MA: Newbury House.

Gleason, J. B., Hay, D., & Cain, L. (1989). Social and affective determinants of language acquisition. In M. Rice & R. L. Schiefelbusch (Eds.), *The Teachability of Language* (pp. 171–186). London: Erlbaum.

Gleason, J. B., Perlmann, R. Y., & Greif, E. B. (1984). What's the magic word: Learning language through politeness routines. *Discourse Processes, 7*, 493–502.

Gleason, J. B., & Weintraub, S. (1978). Input language and the acquisition of communicative competence. In K. E. Nelson (Ed.), *Children's Language*, Vol. 1 (pp. 171–221). New York: Gardner Press.

Glucksberg, S., & Krauss, R. M. (1967). What do people say after they have learned to talk? Studies of the development of referential communication. *Merrill-Palmer Quarterly*, 13, 309–316.

Gnepp, J., & Chilamkurti, C. (1988). Children's use of personality attributions to predict other people's emotional and behavioral reactions. *Child Development, 59*, 743–754.

Gnepp, J., McKee, E., & Domanic, J. A. (1987). Children's use of situational cues to infer emotion: Understanding emotionally equivocal situations. *Developmental Psychology, 23*, 114–123.

Goldberg, S. (1982) Some biological aspects of early parent-infant interaction. In S. G. Moore and C. R. Cooper (Eds.), *The Young Child: Reviews of Research* (pp. 35–56). Washington, DC: National Association for the Education of Young Children.

Goldie, P. (2000). *The Emotions: A Philosophical Exploration*. Oxford: Clarendon Press.

Goldin-Meadow, S., & Butcher, C. (2003). Pointing toward two-word speech in young children. In S. Kita (Ed.), *Pointing: Where Language, Culture and Cognition Meet* (pp. 85–108). Mahwah, NJ: Erlbaum.

Goldman, A. I. (1992). In defense of the simulation theory. *Mind and Language, 7*, 104–119.

Goldman, S. R. (1982). Knowledge systems for realistic goals. *Discourse Processes, 5*, 279–303.

Golinkoff, R. M. (1983). The preverbal negotiation of failed messages: Insights into the transition period. In R. M. Golinkoff (Ed.), *The Transition from Prelinguistic to Linguistic Communication* (pp. 57–78). Hillsdale, NJ: Erlbaum.

Golinkoff, R. M. (1986). "I beg your pardon?": The preverbal negotiation of failed messages. *Journal of Child Language, 13*, 455–476.

Golinkoff, R. M., & Hirsh-Pasek, K. (1999). *How Babies Talk: The Magic and Mystery of Language in the first Three Years of Life*. New York: Penguin Books.

Golomb, C. (1979). Pretense play: A cognitive perspective. In N. R. Smith & M. B. Franklin (Eds.), *Symbolic Functioning in Childhood* (pp. 101–116). Hillsdale, NJ: Erlbaum.

Gomez, J. C. (1994). Mutual awareness in primate communication: A Gricean approach. In S. T. Parker, R. W. Mitchell, & L. Boccia (Eds.), *Self Awareness in Animals and Humans: Developmental Perspectives* (pp. 61–80). Cambridge, UK: Cambridge University Press.

Göncü, A., & Kessel, F. (1988). Preschoolers' collaborative construction in planning and maintaining imaginative play. *International Journal of Behavioral Development, 11*, 327–344.

Gopnik, A. (1993). How we know our minds: The illusion of first-person knowledge of intentionality. *Behavioral and Brain Sciences, 16*, 1–15.

Gopnik, A., & Astington, J. W. (1988). Children's understanding of representational change and its relation to the understanding of false belief and the appearance–reality distinction. *Child Development, 59*, 26–37.

Gopnik, A., & Wellman, H. M. (1994). The theory theory. In L. A. Hirschfeld & S. A. Gelman (Eds.), *Mapping the Mind: Domain Specificity in Cognition and Culture* (pp. 257–293). Cambridge, UK: Cambridge University Press.

Gopnik, A., & Meltzoff, A. N. (1994). Minds, bodies, and persons: Young children's understanding of the self and others as reflected in imitation and theory of mind research. In S. T. Parker, R. W. Mitchell, & L. Boccia (Eds.), *Self Awareness in Animals and Humans: Developmental Perspectives* (pp. 166–186). Cambridge, UK: Cambridge University Press.

Goodwin, M. H. (1990). *He-Said-She-Said: Talk as Social Organization Among Black Children*. Bloomington: Indiana University Press.

Goodwin, M. H. (2006). *The Hidden Life of Girls: Games of Stance, Status, and Exclusion*. Malden, MA: Blackwell.

Goodwin, M. H. (2007). Participation and embodied action in preadolescent girls' assessment activity. *Research on Language and Social Interaction, 40*, 353–375.

Gordon, C. (2002). "I'm Mommy and you're Natalie": Role reversal and embedded frames in mother–child discourse. *Language in Society, 21*, 679–720.

Gordon, C. (2008). A(P) Parent play: Blending frames and reframing in family talk. *Language in Society, 37*, 319–349.

Gordon, D., & Ervin-Tripp, S. (1984). The structure of children's requests. In R. L. Schiefelbusch & J. Pickar (Eds.), *The Acquisition of Communicative Competence*. (pp. 296–321). Baltimore, MD: University Park Press.

Gordon, R. (1986). Folk psychology as simulation. *Mind and Language, 1*, 158–171.

Gordon R. (1995). Simulation without introspection or inference from me to you. In M. Davies & T. Stone (Eds.), *Mental Simulation* (pp. 53–67). Oxford: Blackwell.

Gordon, T. (1976). *P. E. T. in Action*. Toronto: Bantam Books.

Gorn, G. J., & Goldberg, M. E. (1982). Behavioral evidence of the effects of televised food messages on children. *Journal of Consumer Research, 9*, 200–205.

Gottfredson, M., & Hirschi, T. (1990). *A General Theory of Crime*. Stanford, CA: Stanford University Press.

Gottman, J. (1986a). The observation of social process. In J. M. Gottman & J. G. Parker (Eds.), *Conversations of Friends:*

Speculations on Affective Development (pp. 51–100). Cambridge, UK: Cambridge University Press.

Gottman, J. (1986b). The world of coordinated play: Same- and cross-sex friendship in young children. In J. M. Gottman & J. G. Parker (Eds.), *Conversations of Friends: Speculations on Affective Development* (pp. 139–191). Cambridge, UK: Cambridge University Press.

Gottman, J. M., Katz, L. F., & Hooven, C. (1997). *Meta-emotion: How Families Communicate Emotionally*. Mahwah, NJ: Erlbaum.

Gough, J. (1984) *Play: A Case Study of Language and Pretense Play Within a Family Setting.* Unpublished Ph.D. Dissertation, Department of Applied Linguistics, UCLA.

Gough, B., & Reavey, P. (1997). Parental accounts regarding their physical punishment of children: Discourses of dis/empowerment. *Child Abuse and Neglect*, *21*, 417–430.

Gralinski, J. H., & Kopp, C. B. (1993). Everyday rules for behavior: Mothers' requests to young children. *Developmental Psychology*, *29*, 573–584.

Graue, M. E., & Walsh, D. J. (1998). *Studying Children in Context: Theories, Methods, and Ethics*. Thousand Oaks, CA: Sage.

Graumann, C. F. (2002). Explicit and implicit perspectivity. In C. F. Graumann & W. Kallmeyer (Eds.), *Perspective and Perspectivation in Discourse* (pp. 25–39). Amsterdam: John Benjamins.

Green, J., & Wallat, C. (1979). What is an instructional context? An exploratory analysis of conversational shifts across time. In O. Garnica & M. King (Eds.), *Language, Children, and Society: The Effects of Social Factors on Children Learning to Communicate* (pp. 159–188). Elmsford, NY: Pergamon Press.

Greenberg, S., & Formanek, R. (1974). Social class differences in spontaneous verbal interactions. *Child Study Journal*, *4*, 148–153.

Greenfield, P. M. (1980). Toward an operational and logical analysis of intentionality: The use of discourse in early child language. In D. R. Olson (Ed.), *The Social Foundations of Language and Thought: Essays in Honor of Jerome S. Bruner* (pp. 254–279). New York: Norton.

Greenfield, P. M., & Smith, J. H. (1976). *The Structure of Communication in Early Language Development*. New York: Academic Press.

Greenhalgh, L., & Chapman, D. I. (1995). Joint decision making. In R. M. Kramer & D. M. Messick (Eds.), *Negotiation as a Social Process* (pp. 166–185). Thousand Oaks, CA: Sage.

Grieshaber, S. (2004). *Rethinking Parent and Child Conflict*. New York: Routledge Falmer.

Grolnick, W. S., Bridges, L. J., & Connell, J. P. (1996). Emotion regulation in two-year olds: Strategies and emotional expression in four contexts. *Child Development*, *67*, 928–941.

Grolnick, W. S., Kurowsli, C. O., McMenamy, J. M., Rivkin, I., & Bridges, L. J. (1998). Mothers' strategies for regulating their toddlers' distress. *Infant Behavior and Development*, *21*, 437–450.

Gross, F. (1985). *Ideologies, Goals, and Values*. Westport, CT: Greenwood Press.

Gross, J. J. (1998). The emerging field of emotion regulation: An integrative review. *Review of General Psychology*, *2*, 271–299.

Grusec, J., & Dix, T. (1986). Socialization of prosocial behavior. In C. Zahn-Waxler, R. Iannotti, & M. Cummings (Eds.), *Altruism and Aggression* (pp. 218–237). New York: Cambridge University Press.

Grusec, J. E., & Goodnow, J. J. (1994) Impact of parental discipline methods on the child's internalization of values: A reconceptualization of current points of view. *Developmental Psychology*, *30*, 4–19.

Grusec, J. E., & Redler, E. (1980). Attribution, reinforcement, and altruism: A developmental analysis. *Developmental Psychology*, *16*, 525–534.

Guasti, M. T. (1993). Verb syntax in Italian child grammar: Finite and infinite verbs. *Language Acquisition*, *3*, 1–40.

Gumperz, J. J. (1982). *Discourse Strategies*. Cambridge, UK: Cambridge University Press.

Haden, C. A., & Fivush, R. (1996). Contextual variation in maternal conversational styles. *Merrill-Palmer Quarterly*, *42*, 200–227.

Hahn, U., Chater, N., & Richardson, L. B. (2003). Similarity as transformation. *Cognition*, *87*, 1–32.

Haidt, J. (2001). The emotional dog and its rational tail: A social intuitionist approach to moral judgment. *Psychological Review*, *108*, 814–834.

Haight, W. (1998). Adult direct and indirect influences on play. In D. P. Fromberg & D. Bergen (Eds.), *Play from Birth to Twelve and Beyond: Contexts, Perspectives, and Meanings* (pp. 259–265). New York: Garland Publishing.

Haight, W. L., & Miller, P. J. (1993). *Pretending at Home: Early Development in Sociocultural Context*. Albany, NY: SUNY Press.

Haight, W. L., Masiello, T., Dickson, K. L., Huckeby, E., & Black, J. E. (1994). The everyday contexts and social functions of spontaneous mother–child pretend play in the home. *Merrill-Palmer Quarterly*, *40*, 509–522.

Haight, W. L., Wang, X.-L., Fung, H. H. -T., Williams, K., & Mintz, J. (1999). Universal, developmental and variable aspects of young children's play: A cross-cultural comparison of pretending at home. *Child Development*, *70*, 1477–1488.

Haines, G. H. (1974). Process models of consumer decision making. In G. D. Hughes and M. L. Rays (Eds.), *Buyer/Consumer Information Processing* (pp. 89–107). Chapel Hill, NC: University of North Carolina Press.

Haley, J. (1973). *Uncommon Therapy: The Psychiatric Techniques of Milton H. Erickson*. New York: Norton.

Halford, J. G., Gillespie, J., Brown, V., Pontin, E. E., & Dovey, T. M. (2004). Effect of television advertisements for food on food consumption in children. *Appetite*, *42*, 221–225.

Hall, T. M., Kaduson, H. G., & Schaefer, C. E. (2002). Fifteen effective play therapy techniques. *Professional Psychology: Research and Practice*, *33*, 515–522.

Hall, W. S., & Cole, M. (1978). On participant's shaping of discourse through their understanding of the task. In K. Nelson (Ed.), *Children's Language*, Vol. 1 (pp. 445–465). New York: Gardner Press.

Halle, T., & Shatz, M. (1992). Mothers' social regulatory language to young children in family settings. *First Language*, *14*, 83–104.

Halliday, M. A. K. (1975). *Learning How to Mean*. London: Edwin Arnold.

Halliday, M. A. K. (1979). Development of texture in child language. In T. Myers (Ed.), *The Development of Conversation and Discourse* (pp. 72–87). Edinburgh: Edinburgh University Press.

Halliday, M. A. K. (1984). Language as code and language as behaviour: A systemic-functional interpretation of the nature and ontogenesis of dialogue. In R. P. Fawcett, M. A. K. Halliday, S. M. Lamb, & A. Makkai (Eds.), *The Semiotics of Culture and Language*, Vol. 1 (pp. 3–36). London: Frances Pinter Publishers.

Halton, E. (2004). The living gesture and the signifying moment. *Symbolic Interaction*, *27*, 89–113.

Hamann, C. (1996). Null-arguments in German child language. *Language Acquisition*, *5*, 155–208.

Hammock, T., & Brehm, J. W. (1966). The attractiveness of choice alternatives when freedom to choose is eliminated by a social agent. *Journal of Personality*, *34*, 546–554.

Hammond, K. J. (1989). *Case-Based Planning: Viewing Planning as a Memory Task*. San Diego, CA: Academic.

Hansson, S. O., & Grüne-Yanoff, T. (2006). Preferences. In E. N. Zalta (Ed.), *The Stanford Encyclopedia of Philosophy* (Winter 2006 Edition). http://plato.stanford.edu/archives/win2006/entrees/preferences/.

Harackiewicz, J. M. (1979). The effects of reward contingency and performance feedback on intrinsic motivation. *Journal of Personality and Social Psychology*, *37*, 1352–1363.

Harel, G., & Sowder, L. (2005). Advanced mathematical-thinking at any age: Its nature and development. *Mathematical Thinking and Learning*, *7*, 27–50.

Hargreaves, D. H., Hester, S. K., & Mellor, F. J. (1975). *Deviance in Classrooms*. London: Routledge & Kegan Paul.

Harkness, S., Super, C. M., & Keefer, C. H. (1992). Learning to be an American parent: How cultural models gain directive force. In R. D'Andrade & C. Strauss (Eds.), *Human Motives and Cultural Models* (pp. 163–178). Cambridge, UK: Cambridge University Press.

Harley, H. (2004). Wanting, having, and getting: A note on Fodor and Lepore 1998. *Linguistic Inquiry*, *35*, 255–267.

Harner, L. (1976). Children's understanding of linguistic reference to past and future. *Journal of Psycholinguistic Research*, *5*, 65–84.

Harner, L. (1980). Comprehension of past and future reference revisited. *Journal of Experimental Child Psychology*, *29*, 170–182.

Harper, L., & Sanders, K. (1975). The effect of adult's eating on young children's acceptance of unfamiliar foods. *Journal of Experimental Child Psychology*, *20*, 206–214.

Harrington, M. (2001) Gendered time: Leisure in family life. In K. J. Daly (Ed.), *Minding the Time in Family Experience: Emerging Prspectives and Issues* (pp. 343–382). Amsterdam: JAI Press.

Harris, M. (1992). *Language Experience and Early Language Development: From Input To Intake*. Hove, UK: Erlbaum.

Harris, P. L. (2000). *The Work of the Imagination*. Oxford: Blackwell.

Harris, P. L. (1993). Thinking by children and scientists: False analogies and neglected similarities. In L. A. Hirschfeld & S. A. Gelman (Eds.), *Mapping the Mind: Domain Specificity in Cognition and Culture* (pp. 294–315). Cambridge, UK: Cambridge University Press.

Harris, P. L., & Kavanaugh, R. D. (1993). Young children's understanding of pretense. *Society for Research in Child Development Monographs*, *58* (Serial #231).

Harris, P. L., & Núñez, M. (1996). Understanding of permission rules by preschool children. *Child Development*, *67*, 1572–1591.

Harsanyi, J. C. (1976) *Essays on Ethics, Social Behavior and Scientific Explanation*. Dordrecht, Holland: Reidel.

Harsanyi, J. C. (1988). Assessing other people's utilities. In B. R. Munier (Ed.), *Risk, Decision and Rationality* (pp. 127–138). Dordrecht, Holland: D. Reidel.

Hart, B., & Risley, T. R. (1995). *Meaningful Differences in the Everyday Experiences of Young American Children*. Baltimore, MD: Brookes Publishing,

Hart, B., & Risley, T. R. (1999). *The Social World of Children Learning to Talk*. Baltimore, MD: Brookes Publishing.

Hasan, R., & Cloran, C. (1990). A sociolinguistic interpretation of everyday talk between mothers and children. In M. A. K. Halliday, J. Gibbons, & H. Nicholas (Eds.), *Learning, Keeping and Using Language*, Vol. I (pp. 67–99). Amsterdam: John Benjamins.

Hassabis, D., & Maguire, E. A. (2007). Deconstructing episodic memory with construction. *Trends in Cognitive Sciences*, *11*, 299–306.

Hastings, P. D., & Grusec, J. E. (1998). Parenting goals as organizers of responses to parent-child disagreement. *Developmental Psychology*, *34*, 465–479.

Haswell, K., Hoch, E., & Wenar, C. (1982). Techniques for dealing with oppositional behavior in preschool children. *Young Children*, *3*, 13–19.

Hatch, E. (1992). *Discourse and Language Education*. Cambridge, UK: Cambridge University Press.

Hatch, E., Peck, S., & Wagner-Gough, J. (1979). A look at process in child second-language acquisition. In E. Ochs & B. S. Schieffelin (Eds.), *Developmental Pragmatics* (pp. 269–278). New York: Academic Press.

Haverkate, H. (1984). *Speech Acts, Speakers, and Hearers*. Amsterdam: John Benjamins.

Hay, C. (2001). Parenting, self-control, and delinquency: A test of self-control theory. *Criminology*, *39*,707–736.

Hay, C., & Forrest, W. (2006). The development of self-control: Examining self-control theory's stability thesis. *Criminology*, *44*, 739–774.

Hay, D. F. (2006). Yours and mine: Toddlers' talk about possessions with familiar peers. *British Journal of Developmental Psychology*, *24*, 39–52.

Hayakawa, S. I. (1972). *Language in Thought and Action*. New York: Harcourt Brace Jovanovich.

Hayes, R. (2005). Conversation, negotiation, and the word as deed: Linguistic interaction in a dual language program. *Linguistics in Education*, *16*, 93–112.

Haytko, D. L., & Baker, J. (2004). It's all at the mall: Exploring adolescent girls' experiences. *Journal of Retailing*, *80*, 67–83.

Hazen, N., Black, B., & Fleming-Johnson, F. (1984). Social acceptance: Strategies children use and how teachers can help children learn them. *Young Children*, *39*, 26–36.

Hazlitt, W. (1969). *An Essay on the Principles of Human Action and Some Remarks on the Systems of Hartley and Helvetius*. Gainesville, FL: Scholars' Facsimiles and Reprints (Originally published 1805).

Heal, J. (2003). *Mind, Reason and Imagination: Selected Essays in Philosophy of Mind and Language*. Cambridge, UK: Cambridge University Press.

Heath, S. B. (1986). What no bedtime story means: Narrative skills at home and school. In B. S. Schieffelin & E. Ochs (Eds.), *Language Socialization across Cultures* (pp. 97–124). Cambridge, UK: Cambridge University Press.

Heffner, M., Greco, L. A., & Etfert, G. H. (2003). Pretend you are a turtle: Children's responses to metaphorical versus literal relaxation instructions. *Child and Family Behavior Therapy*, *25*, 19–33.

Hegel, G. W. F. (1821/1996). *Philosophy of Right*. Amherst, NY: Prometheus Books.

Heider, F. (1958). *The Psychology of Interpersonal Relations*. New York: Wiley.

Hendy, H. M. (1999). Comparison of five teacher actions to encourage children's new food acceptance. *Annals of Behavioral Medicine*, *21*, 20–26.

Hendy, H. M., Williams, K. E., Camise, T. S., Eckman, N., & Hedemann, A. (2009). The parent mealtime action scale (PMAS). Development and association with children's development and weight. *Appetite, 52*, 328–339.

Herot, C. (2002). Socialization of affect during mealtime interactions. In S. Blum-Kulka & C. E. Snow (Eds.), *Talking to adults: The Contribution of Multiparty Discourse to Language Acquisition* (pp. 155–179). Mahwah, NJ: Erlbaum.

Heine, S. J., & Lehman, D. R. (1997). Culture, dissonance, and self affirmation. *Personality and Social Psychology Bulletin, 23*, 389–400.

Heilman, M. E., & Garner, K. A. (1975). Counteracting the boomerang: The effects of choice on compliance to threats and promises. *Journal of Personality and Social Psychology, 31*, 911–917.

Henwood, K., & Coughlan, G. (1993). The construction of "closeness" in mother–daughter relationships across the lifespan. In N. Coupland & J. F. Nussbaum (Eds.), *Discourse and Lifespan Identity* (pp. 191–214). Newbury Park, CA: Sage.

Hermann, C., Hohmeister, J., Zohsel, K., Ebinger, F., & Flor, H. (2007). The assessment of pain coping and pain–related cognitions in children and adolescents: Current methods and further development. *Journal of Pain, 8*, 802–813.

Herr, P. M., & Page, C. M. (2004). Asymmetrical association of liking and disliking judgments: So what's not to like? *Journal of Consumer Research, 30*, 588–601.

Hertel, P. T., & Calcaterra, G. (2005). Intentional forgetting benefits from thought substitution. *Psychonomic Bulletin and Review, 12*, 484–489.

Hess, R. D., & Handel, G. (1959). *Family Worlds: A Psychosocial Approach to Family Life*. Chicago: University of Chicago Press.

Higgins, E. T. (1981) Role taking and social judgment: Alternative developmental perspectives and processes. In J. H. Flavell & L. Ross (Eds.), *Social Cognitive Development* (pp. 119–153). New York: Cambridge University Press.

Higgins, E. T. (1987). Self-discrepancy: A theory relating self and affect. *Psychological Review, 94*, 319–340.

Higgins, E. T. (1998). Promotion and prevention: Regulatory focus as a motivational principle. In M. P. Zanna (Ed.), *Advances in Experimental Social Psychology*, Vol. 30 (pp. 1–46). San Diego, CA: Academic Press.

Higgins, E. T., & Bargh, J. A. (1987) Social cognition and social perception. *Annual Review of Psychology, 38*, 369–425.

Hochschild, A. (1979). Emotion work, feeling rules, and social structure. *American Journal of Sociology, 85*, 551–575.

Hodgson, J., Dienhart, A., & Daly, K. (2001). Time juggling: Single mothers' experience of time-press following divorce. *Journal of Divorce and Remarriage, 35*, 1–28.

Hoffman, M. L. (1976). Empathy, role taking, guilt, and the development of altruistic motives. In T. Lickona (Ed.), *Moral Development and Moral Behavior: Theory, Research, and Social Issues* (pp. 124–143). New York: Holt, Rinehart & Winston.

Hoffman, M. L., & Saltzstein, H. D. (1967). Parent discipline and the child's moral development. *Journal of Personality and Social Psychology, 5*, 45–57.

Hofstadter, D. (1979). *Gödel, Escher, Bach: An Eternal Golden Braid*. New York: Basic Books.

Hofstadter, D. & The Fluid Analogies Research Group (1995). *Fluid Concepts and Creative Analogies*. New York: Basic Books.

Holden, G. (1983). Avoiding conflict: Mothers as tacticians in the supermarket. *Child Development, 54*, 233–240.

Holden, G. W. (2002). Perspectives on the effects of corporal punishment: Comment on Gershoff (2002). *Psychological Bulletin, 128*, 590–595.

Holden, G. W., Coleman, S., & Schmidt, K. L. (1995). Why 3-year-old children get spanked: Parent and child determinants in a sample of college-educated mothers. *Merrill-Palmer Quarterly, 41*, 431–452.

Holden, G. W., Thompson, E. E., Zambarano, R. J., & Marshall, L. A. (1997). Child effects as a source of change in maternal attidues toward corporal punishment. *Journal of Social and Personal Relationships, 14*, 481–490.

Holden, G. W., & West, M. J. (1989). Proximate regulation by mothers: A demonstration of how differing styles affect young children's behavior. *Child Development, 60*, 64–69.

Holzman, M. (1972). The use of interrogative forms in the verbal interactions of three mothers and their children. *Journal of Psycholinguistic Research, 1*, 311–336.

Hood, L., & Bloom, L. (1979). What, when, and how about why: A longitudinal study of early expressions of causality. *Monographs of the Society for Research in Child Development*, 44 (Serial No. 181).

House, J. & Kasper, G. (1981). Politeness markers in English and German. In F. Coulmas Ed.), *Conversational Routine: Explorations in Standardized Communication Situations and Prepatterned Speech* (pp. 157–185). The Hague: Mouton.

Howe, C. (1981). *Acquiring Language in a Conversational Context*. London: Academic Press.

Howe, N. (1991). Sibling-directed internal state language, perspective taking, and affective behavior. *Child Development, 62*, 1503–1512.

Howe, N., & Rinaldi, C. M. (2004). 'You be the big sister': Maternal–preschooler internal state discourse, perspective-taking, and sibling caretaking. *Infant and Child Development, 13*, 217–234.

Howes, C., & Clements, D. (1994). Adult socialization of children's play in child care. In H. Goelman & E. V. Jacobs (Eds.), *Children's Play in Child Care Settings* (pp. 20–36). Albany, NY: SUNY Press.

Howes, C., Unger, O., & Matheson, C. C. (1992). *The Collaborative Construction of Pretend: Social Pretend Play Functions*. Albany, NY: SUNY Press.

Hsee, C. K. (1998). Less is better: When low-value options are valued more highly than high-value options. *Journal of Behavioral Decision Making, 11*, 107–121.

Hudson, J. A. (1986). Memories are made of this: General event knowledge and development of autobiographic memory. In K. Nelson (Ed.), *Event Knowledge: Structure and Function in Development* (pp. 97–118). Hillsdale, NJ: Erlbaum.

Hudson, J. A. (1990). The emergence of autobiographical memory in mother–child conversation. In R. Fivush and J. A. Hudson (Eds.), *Knowing and Remembering in Young Children* (pp. 166–196). Cambridge, UK: Cambridge University Press.

Hudson, J. A. (2002). "Do you know what we're going to do this summer?" Mothers' talk to preschool children about future events. *Journal of Cognition and Development, 3*, 49–71.

Hudson, J. A. (2004). The development of future thinking: Constructing future events in mother–child conversation. In J. M. Lucariello, J. A. Hudson, R. Fivush, & P. J. Bauer (Eds.), *The Development of the Mediated Mind: Sociocultural Context and Cognitive Development* (pp. 79–99). Mahwah, NJ: Erlbaum.

Hudson, J. A., & Nelson, K. (1986). Repeated encounters of a similar kind: Effects of familiarity on children's autobiographical memory. *Cognitive Development*, *1*, 253–271.

Hudson, J. A., & Shapiro, L. R. (1991). From knowing to telling: Children's scripts, stories, and personal narratives. In A. McCabe & C. Peterson (Eds.), *Developing Narrative Structure* (pp. 89–136). Hillsdale, NJ: Erlbaum.

Hudson, J. A., Shapiro, L. R., & Sosa, B. B. (1995). Planning in the real world: Preschool children's scripts and plans for familiar contexts. *Child Development*, *66*, 984–998.

Hudson, J. A., Sosa, B. B., & Shapiro, L. R. (1997). Scripts and plans: The development of preschool children's event knowledge and event planning. In S. L. Friedman & E. K. Scholnick (Eds.), *The Developmental Psychology of Planning: Why, How, and When Do We Plan?* (pp. 77–102). Mahwah, NJ: Erlbaum.

Hughes, C., & Dunn, J. (2002). "Why I say a naughty word": A longitudinal study of young children's account of anger and sadness in themselves and close others. *British Journal of Developmental Psychology*, *20*, 515–535.

Huston, A., Watkins, B., & Kunkel, D. (1989). Public policy and children's television. *American Psychologist*, *44*, 424–433.

Hutchby, I. (2005). "Active listening": Formulations and the elicitation of feelings-talk in child counseling. *Research on Language and Social Interaction*, *38*, 303–329.

Huttenlocher, J., Vasilyeva, M., Cymerman, E., & Levine, S. (2002). Language input and child syntax. *Cognitive Psychology*, *45*, 337–374.

Hutto, D. D. (1999). *The Presence of Mind*. Amsterdam: John Benjamins.

Hymes, D. (1972). On communicative competence. In J. B. Price & J. Holmes (Eds.), *Sociolinguistics: Selected Readings*. Baltimore, MD: Penguin.

Iannotti, R. J. (1985). Naturalistic and structured assessments of prosocial behavior in preschool children: The influences of empathy and perspective taking. *Developmental Psychology*, *21*, 46–55.

Igoa, C. (1995). *The Inner World of the Immigrant Child*. Mahwah, NJ: Erlbaum.

Imbens-Bailey, A. L., & Snow, C. E. (1997). Making meaning in parent-child interaction: A pragmatic approach. In C. Mandell & A. McCabe (Eds.), *The Problem of Meaning: Behavioral and Cognitive Perspectives* (pp. 261–295). Amsterdam: Elsevier.

Ingham, R. (1998). Tense without agreement in early clause structure. *Language Acquisition*, *7*, 51–81.

Insko, C., & Schopler, J. (1972). *Experimental Social Psychology*. New York: Academic Press.

Isler, L., Popper, E. T., & Ward, S. (1987). Children's purchase requests and parental responses: Results from a diary study. *Journal of Advertising Research*, *27*(5), 28–30.

Iverson, J. M., & Thal, D. J. (1998). Communicative transitions: There's more to the hand than meets the eye. In A. M. Wetherby, S. F. Warren, & J. Reichle (Eds.), *Transitions in Prelinguistic Communication*, Vol. 7 (pp. 59–86). Baltimore, MD: Brookes Publishing.

Iwamura, S. (1980). *The Verbal Games of Pre-School Children*. London: Croom Helm.

Iyengar, S. S., & Lepper, M. R. (1999). Rethinking the value of choice: A cultural perspective on intrinsic motivation. *Journal of Personality and Social Psychology*, *76*, 349–366.

Iyengar, S. S., & Lepper, M. R. (2000). When choice is demotivating: Can one desire too much of a good thing? *Journal of Personality and Social Psychology*, *76*, 995–1006.

Iyengar, S. S., & Lepper, M. R. (2002). Choice and its consequences: On the costs and benefits of self-determination. In A. Tesser, D. A. Stapel, & J. W. Wood (Eds.), *Self and Motivation: Emerging Psychological Perspectives* (pp. 71–96). Washington, DC: APA.

Jarrell, R. H. (1998). Play and its influence on the development of young children's mathematical thinking. In D. P. Fromberg & D. Bergen (Eds.), *Play from Birth to Twelve and Beyond: Contexts, Perspectives, and Meanings* (pp. 56–76). New York: Garland Publishing.

Jefferson, G. (1984). On stepwise transition from talk about trouble to inappropriate next-positioned matters. In J. M. Atkinson & J. Heritage (Eds.), *Structures of Social Action: Studies in Conversation Analysis* (pp. 191–222). Cambridge, UK: Cambridge University Press.

Jeffries, E. D. (2004). Experiences of trust with parents: A qualitative investigation of African American, Latino, and Asian American boys from low-income families. In N. Way & J. Y. Chu (Eds.), *Adolescent Boys: Exploring Diverse Cultures of Boyhood* (pp. 107–128). New York: New York University Press.

Jencks, C. (1990). Varieties of altruism. In J. J. Mansbridge (Ed.), *Beyond Self Interest* (pp. 54–67). Chicago: University of Chicago Press.

Jensen, A. (1998). *The g Factor: The Science of Mental Ability*. Westport, CT: Praeger.

Jones, E. E., & Davis, K. E. (1965). From acts to dispositions: The attribution process in person perception. In L. Berkowitz (Ed.), *Advances in Experimental Social Psychology*, Vol. 2 (pp. 219–266). New York: Academic Press.

Jones, E. E., & Nisbett, R. E. (1972). The actor and the observer: Divergent perceptions of the causes of behavior. In E. E. Jones, D. E. Kanouse, H. H. Kelley, R. E. Nisbett, S. Valins, & B. Weiner (Eds.), *Attribution: Perceiving the Causes of Behavior* (pp. 79–94). Morristown, NJ: General Learning Press.

Jessee, E. H., Jurkovic, G. J., Wilkie, J., & Chiglinsky, M. (1982). Positive reframing with children: Conceptual and clinical considerations. *American Journal of Orthopsychiatry*, *52*, 314–322.

Johnston, M. (1989). Moral reasoning and teachers' understanding of individuated instruction. *Journal of Moral Education*, *18*, 45–59.

Jones, J. M. (1988). Cultural differences in temporal perspectives: Instrumental and expressive behaviors in time. In J. E. McGrath (Ed.), *The Social Psychology of Time* (pp. 21–38). Newbury Park, CA: Sage.

Jordan, E., & Cowan, A. (1995). Warrior narratives in the kindergarten classroom: Renegotiating the social contract. *Gender and Society*, *9*, 727–743.

Junefelt, K., & Tulviste, T. (1998). American, Estonian, and Swedish mothers' regulation of their children's discourse construction. In M. C. D. P. Lyra & J. Valsiner (Eds.), *Construction of Psychological Processes in Interpersonal communication* (pp. 137–154). Stamford, CT: Ablex.

Kagan, C., & Lewis, S. (1996). Familes with parents who have multiple commitments. In M. Moore, J. Sixsmith, & K. Knowles (Eds.), *Children's Reflections on Family Life* (pp. 29–51). London: Falmer Press.

Kagan, J. (1990). The concepts of self: A dialogue of questions without answers. In D. Cicchetti & M. Beeghly (Eds.), *The Self in Transition: Infancy to Childhood* (pp. 363–383). Chicago: University of Chicago Press.

Kahneman, D., & Tversky, A. (1979). Prospect theory: An analysis of decisions under risk. *Econometrica, 47*, 263–291.

Kahneman, D., & Tversky, A. (1982). The psychology of preferences. *Scientific American, 246*, 160–170.

Kaiser, A. P., & Warren, S. F. (1988). Pragmatics and generalization. In R. L. Schiefelbusch & L. L. Lloyd (Eds.), *Language Perspectives: Acquisition, Retardation, and Intervention* (pp. 393–442). Austin, TX: Pro-Ed.

Kaiser, G. A. (1994). More about INFL-ection and agreement. In J. M. Meisel (Ed.), *Bilingual First Language Acquisition: French and German Grammatical Development* (pp. 131–160). Amsterdam: John Benjamins.

Kameny, R. R., & Bearison, D. J. (2002). Cancer narratives of adolescents and young adults: A quantitative and qualitative analysis. *Children's Health Care, 31*, 143–173.

Kamio, A. (2001). English generic *we, you* and *they*: An analysis in terms of territory of information. *Journal of Pragmatics, 33*, 1111–1124.

Kamler, B. (1999). This lovely doll who's come to school: Morning talk as gendered language practice. In B. Kamler (Ed.), *Constructing Gender and Difference: Critical Research Perspectives on Early Childhood* (pp. 191–213). Cresskill, NJ: Hampton Press.

Kanfer, F. H. (1979). Personal control, social control, and altruism, or can society survive the age of individualism. *American Psychologist, 34*, 231–239.

Kanfer, F. H., Stifter, E., & Morris, S. J. (1981). Self control and altruism: Delay of gratification for another. *Child Development, 52*, 674–692.

Kantor, R., Elgas, P. M., & Fernie, D. E. (1989). First the look and then the sound: Creating conversations at circle time. *Early Childhood Research Quarterly, 4*, 433–448.

Kaplan, E. B. (2000). Using food as a metaphor for care: Middle-school kids talk about family, school, and class relations. *Journal of Contemporary Ethnography, 29*, 474–509.

Karniol, R. (1980). A conceptual analysis of immanent justice responses in children. *Child Development, 51*, 118–130.

Karniol, R. (1982). Behavioral and cognitive correlates of various immanent justice responses in children: Deterrent versus punitive moral systems. *Journal of Personality and Social Psychology, 43*, 811–820.

Karniol, R. (1986). What will they think of next? Transformation rules used to predict other people's thoughts and feelings. *Journal of Personality and Social Psychology, 51*, 932–944.

Karniol, R. (1982b). Settings, scripts and self schemata: A cognitive analysis of the development of prosocial behavior. In N. Eisenberg (Ed.), *The Development of Prosocial Behavior* (pp. 251–278). New York: Academic Press.

Karniol, R. (1989). The role of manual manipulative stages in the infant's acquisition of perceived control over objects. *Developmental Review, 9*, 205–233.

Karniol, R. (1990a). Second language acquisition via immersion in daycare. *Journal of Child Language, 17*, 147–170.

Karniol, R. (1990b). Reading people's minds: A transformation rule model for predicting others' thoughts and feelings. *Advances in Experimental Social Psychology, 23*, 211–247.

Karniol, R. (1992). Stuttering out of bilingualism. *First Language, 12*, 255–283.

Karniol, R. (2003a). Egocentrism versus protocentrism: The status of self in social prediction. *Psychological Review, 110*, 564–580.

Karniol, R. (2003b). Protocentrism will prevail: A reply to Kruger (2003), Mussweiler (2003), and Sedikides (2003). *Psychological Review, 110*, 595–600.

Karniol, R., Ekbali, G. B., & Vashdi, D. R. (2007). The impact of parental status and gender role orientation on caring and postconventional reasoning in young marrieds. *Sex Roles, 56*, 341–350.

Karniol, R., Eylon, T., & Rish, S. (1997). Predicting you own and others' thoughts and feelings: More like a stranger than a friend. *European Journal of Social Psychology, 27*, 301–312.

Karniol, R., Grosz, E., & Schorr, I. (2003). Caring, gender role orientation, and volunteering. *Sex Roles, 49*, 11–19.

Karniol, R., & Heiman, T. (1987). Situational antecedents of children's anger experiences and subsequent responses to peer versus adult provokers. *Aggressive Behavior, 13*, 109–118.

Karniol, R., & Koren, L. (1987). How would you feel? Children's inferences regarding their own and others' affective reactions. *Cognitive Development, 2*, 271–278.

Karniol, R., & Miller, D. T. (1981). The development of self control in children. In S. Brehm, S. M. Kassin, & F. X. Gibbons (Eds.), *Developmental Social Psychology* (pp. 32–50). New York: Oxford University Press.

Karniol, R., & Miller, D. T. (1983). Why not wait? A cognitive analysis of self imposed delay termination. *Journal of Personality and Social Psychology, 45*, 935–942.

Karniol, R., & Ross, M. (1979). Children's use of causal attribution schema and the inference of manipulative intentions. *Child Development, 50*, 463–469.

Karniol, R., & Ross, M. (1996). The motivational impact of temporal focus: Thinking about the future and the past. *Annual Review of Psychology, 47*, 593–620.

Karniol, R., & Shomroni, D. (1999). What being empathic means: Applying the transformation rule approach to individual differences in predicting the thoughts and feelings of prototypic and nonprototypic others. *European Journal of Social Psychology, 29*, 45–59.

Karpov, Y. V., & Haywood, H. C. (1998). Two ways to elaborate Vygotsky's concept of mediation. *American Psychologist, 53*, 27–36.

Kasserow, A. S. (1999). De-homogenizing American individualism: Socializing hard and soft individualism in Manhattan and Queens. *Ethos, 27*, 210–234.

Katriel, T. (1985). *Brogez*: Ritual and strategy in Israeli children's conflicts. *Language in Society, 14*, 467–490.

Katriel, T. (1987). "Bexibudim!" Ritualized sharing among Israeli children. *Language in Society, 16*, 305–320.

Katz, L. F., Kramer, L., & Gottman, J. M. (1992). Conflict and emotions in marital, sibling, and peer relationships. In C. U. Shantz & W. W. Hartup (Eds.), *Conflict in Child and Adolescent Development* (pp. 122–149). Cambridge, UK: Cambridge University Press.

Kavanaugh, R. D., Whittington, S., & Cerbone, M. J. (1983). Mothers' use of fantasy in speech to young children. *Journal of Child Language, 10*, 45–55.

Kavanaugh, R. D. (2002). Caregiver-child social pretend play: What transpires? In R. W. Mitchell (Ed.), *Pretending and Imagination in Animals and Children* (pp. 91–101). Cambridge, UK: Cambridge University Press.

Kavanaugh, R. D., & McCall, R. B. (1983). Social influencing among two-year-olds: The role of affiliative and antagonistic behaviors. *Infant Behavior and Development, 6*, 39–52.

Kaye, K., & Charney, R. (1980). How mothers maintain "dialogue" with two-year-olds. In D. R. Olson (Ed.), *The Social Foundations of Language and Thought: Essays in Honor of Jerome S. Bruner* (pp. 211–230). New York: Norton.

Keenan, E. O., Schieffelin, B. B., & Platt, M. (1983). Questions of immediate concern. In E. Ochs & B. B. Schieffelin (Eds.), *Acquiring Conversational Competence* (pp. 114–126). London: Routledge & Kegan Paul.

Keller-Cohen, D., & Gracey, C. A. (1979). Learning to say *No*: Functional negation in discourse. In O. Garnica & M. King (Eds.), *Language, Children, and Society: The Effects of Social Factors on Children Learning to Communicate* (pp. 197–212). Elmsford, NY: Pergamon Press.

Kellermann, K., & Cole, T. (1994). Classifying compliance gaining messages: Taxonomic disorder and strategic confusion. *Communication Theory*, *4*, 3–60.

Kelley, H. H. (1971). *Attribution in Social Interaction*. Morristown, NJ: General Learning Press.

Kelly, V. E. (2001). Peer culture and interaction: How Japanese children express their internalization of the cultural norms of group life (Shudan Seikatsu). In H. Shimizu & R. A. LeVine (Eds.), *Japanese Frames of Mind: Cultural Perspective on Human Development* (pp. 170–201). Cambridge, UK: Cambridge University Press.

Kelman, H. C. (1974). Further thoughts on the processes of compliance, identification, and internalization. In J. Tedeschi (Ed.), *Perspectives on Social Power* (pp. 125–171). Chicago: Aldine.

Kelman, H. C., & Hamilton, V. L. (1989). *Crimes of Obedience: Toward a Social Psychology of Authority and Responsibility*. New Haven, CT: Yale University Press.

Kiebzak-Mandera, D. (2006). Speaker and hearer reference in Russian speaking children. In N. Gagarina & I. Gulzow (Eds.), *The Acquisition of Verbs and their Grammar: The Effect of Particular Languages* (pp. 319–344). Dordrecht, The Netherlands: Springer.

King, R. (1978). *All Things Bright and Beautiful? A Sociological Study of Infants' Classrooms*. Chichester, UK: Wiley.

Klein, G. A. (1993). A recognition-primed decision (RPD) model of rapid decision making. In G. Klein, J. Orasanu, R. Calderwood, & C. Zsambok (Eds.), *Decision Making in Action: Models and Methods* (pp. 138–147). Norwood, NJ: Ablex.

Kluckhohn, C. (1951). Values and value orientations in the theory of action. In T. Parsons & A. Shils (Eds.), *Toward a General Theory of Action* (pp. 388–433). Cambridge, MA: Harvard University Press.

Kluckhohn, F. K., & Strodbeck, F. L. (1961). *Variations in Value Orientations*. Evanston, IL: Row, Peterson & Co.

Knowles, K., & Sixsmith, J. (1996). Children's experiences in transnational families. In M. Moore, J. Sixsmith, & K. Knowles (Eds.), *Children's Reflections on Family Life* (pp. 115–134). London: Falmer Press.

Kobayashi, S. (2001). Japanese mother-child relationships: Skill acquisition before the preschool years. In H. Shimizu & R. A. LeVine (Eds.), *Japanese Frames of Mind: Cultural Perspective on Human Development* (pp. 111–140). Cambridge, UK: Cambridge University Press.

Kochanska, G. (1995). Children's temperament, mothers' discipline, and security of attachment: Multiple pathways to emerging internalization. *Child Development*, *66*, 597–615.

Kochanska, G. (2002) Commited compliance, moral self, and internalization: A mediational model. *Developmental Psychology*, *38*, 339–351.

Kochanska, G., Coy, K. C., & Murray, K. T. (2001). The development of self-regulation in the first four years of life. *Child Development*, *72*, 1091–1111.

Kochman, T. (1972). Black American speech events and a language program for the classroom. In C. B. Cazden, V. P. John, & D. Hymes (Eds.), *Functions of Language in the Classroom* (pp. 211–266). New York: Teachers' College Press.

Kockelman, P. (2004). Stance and subjectivity. *Journal of Linguisic Anthropology*, *14*, 127–150.

Kohlberg, L. (1966) A cognitive-developmental analysis of children sex role concepts and attitudes. In E. Maccoby (Ed.) *The Development of Sex Differences* (pp. 82–173). Stanford, CA: Stanford University Press.

Kohlberg, L. (1969). Stage and sequence: The cognitive-developmental approach to socialization. In D. A. Goslin (Ed.), *Handbook of Socialization Theory and Research* (pp. 347–480). Chicago: Rand McNally.

Kohlberg, L. (1976) Moral stages and moralization: The cognitive-developmental approach. In T. Lickona (Ed.), *Moral Development and Beahvior: Theory, Research, and Social Issues* (pp. 31–53). New York: Holt, Rinehart & Winston.

Kohn, M. L. (1959). Social class and parental values. *American Journal of Sociology*, *64*, 337–351.

Kohn, M. L. (1969). *Class and Conformity: A Study in Values*. Homewood, IL: Dorsey Press.

Kohn, M. L., & K. M. Slomczynski (1990). *Social Structure and Self-Direction: A Comparative Analysis of the United States and Poland*. Oxford: Basil Blackwell.

Kolodner, J. L. (1984). *Retrieval and Organization Strategies in Conceptual Memory: A Computer Model*. Hillsdale, NJ: Erlbaum.

Kontos, S. (1999). Preschool teachers' talk, roles, and activity settings during free play. *Early Childhood Research Quarterly*, *14*, 363–382.

Koos, O., & Gergely, G. (2001). A contingency-based approach to the etiology of "disorganized attachment": The "flickering switch" hypothesis. *Bulletin-of-the Menninger-Clinic*, *65*, 397–410.

Kopp, C. B. (1982). Antecedents of self regulation: A developmental perspective. *Developmental Psychology*, *18*, 199–214.

Koren-Karie, N., Oppenheim, D., Dolev, S., Sher, S., & Etzion-Carasso, A. (2002). Mother's insightfulness regarding their infants' internal experience: Relations with maternal sensitivity and infant attachment. *Developmental Psychology*, *38*, 534–542.

Kounin, J. S. (1970). *Discipline and Group Management in Classrooms*. Malabar, FL: R. E. Krieger Publishing.

Kovarksy, D., Stephan, T., & Braswell, M. (1994). Conflict talk in an Appalachian day care center. In D. N. Ripich & N. A. Creaghead (Eds.), *School Discourse Problems*, 2nd ed. (pp. 171–185). San Diego, CA: Singular Publishing.

Krafft, K. C., & Berk, L. E. (1998). Private speech in two preschools: Significance of open-ended activities and make-believe play for verbal self-regulation. *Early Childhood Research Quarterly*, *13*, 637–658.

Kremer-Sedlik, T., & Kim, J. L. (2007). Lessons from sports: Children's socialization to values through family interaction during sports activities. *Discourse and Society*, *18*, 35–52.

Kross, E., Ayduk, O., & Mischel, W. (2005). When asking "why" does not hurt. *Psychological Science*, *16*, 709–715.

Krown, S. (1974). *Threes and Fours go to School*. Englewood Cliffs, NJ: Prentice-Hall.

Krueger, J. (1998). On the perception of social consensus. In M. P. Zanna (Ed.), *Advances in Experimental Social Psychology*, Vol. 30 (pp. 163–240). New York: Academic Press.

Krueger, J., & Clement, R. W. (1997). Estimates of social consensus by majorities and minorities: The case for social projection. *Personality and Social Psychology Review*, *1*, 299–313.

Kuhn, D. (1999). Metacognitive development. In L. Balter & C. S. Tamis-LeMonda (Eds.), *Child Psychology: A Handbook of Contemporary Issues* (pp. 259–286). Philadelphia: Psychology Press.

Kuran, T. (1995). *Private Truths, Public Lies: The Social Consequences of Preference Falsification*. Cambridge, MA: Harvard University Press.

Kutas, M. (2006). One lesson learned: Frame language processing – literal and figurative – as a human brain function. *Metaphor and Symbol*, *21*, 285–325.

Kwan-Terry, A. (1990). The role of transfer in simultaneous language acquisition. In M. A. K. Halliday, J. Gibbons, & H. Nicholas (Eds.), *Learning, Keeping and Using Language*, Vol. I (pp. 55–66). Amsterdam: John Benjamins.

Kyratzis, A., & Ervin-Tripp, S. (1999). The development of discourse markers in peer interaction. *Journal of Pragmatics*, *31*, 1321–1338.

Kyratzis, A., & Green, J. (1997). Jointly constructing narratives in classrooms: Co-construction of friendship and community through language. *Teaching and Teacher Education*, *13*, 17–37.

Kyratzis, A., & Guo, J. (1996). "Separate worlds for girls and boys"? Views from U.S. and Chinese mixed-sex friendship groups. In D. I. Slobin, J. Gerhardt, A. Kyratzis & J. Guo (Eds.), *Social Interaction, Social Context, and Language: Essays in Honor of Susan Ervin-Tripp* (pp. 555–575). Mahwah, NJ: Erlbaum.

Kyratzis, A., & Guo, J. (2001). Preschool girls' and boys' verbal conflict strategies in the United States and China. *Research on Language and Social Interaction*, *34*, 45–74.

Kyratzis, A., Marx, T., & Wade, E. R. (2001). Preschoolers' communicative competence: Register shift is the marking of power in different contexts of friendship group talk. *First Language*, *21*, 387–431.

Ladd, G. W., Profilet, S. M., & Hart, C. H. (1992). Parents' management of children's peer relations: Facilitating and supervising children's activities in the peer culture. In R. D. Parke & G. W. Ladd (Eds.), *Family–Peer Relationships: Modes of Linkage* (pp. 215–253). Hillsdale, NJ: Erlbaum.

Lagattuta, K. H. (2005). When you shouldn't do what you want to do: Young children's understanding of desires, rules, and emotions. *Child Development*, *76*, 713–733.

Lagattuta, K. H., Wellman, H. M., & Flavell, J. H. (1997). Preschoolers' understanding of the link between thinking and feeling: Cognitive cuing and emotional change. *Child Development*, *68*, 1081–1104.

Laing, R. D., & Esterson, A. (1990). *Sanity, Madness and the Family*. London: Penguin Books.

Lakoff, G. (1987). *Women, Fire and Dangerous Things: What Categories Reveal About the Mind*. Chicago: University of Chicago Press.

Lakoff, G. (1996). Sorry, I'm not myself today: The metaphor system for conceptualizing the self. In G. Fauconnier & E. Sweetser (Eds.), *Spaces, Worlds, and Grammar* (pp. 91–123). Chicago: University of Chicago Press.

Lambert, W. (1974). Promise and problems of cross-cultural explanations of children's aggressive strategies. In J. De Wit and W. W. Hartup (Eds.), *Determinants and Origins of Aggressive Behavior* (pp. 437–457). The Hague: Mouton.

Lancy, D. F. (2007). Accounting for variability in mother–child play. *American Anthropologist*, *109*, 27–284.

Landesman, S. Jaccard, J., & Gunderson,V. (1991). The family environment: The combined influence of family behavior, goals, strategies, resources, and individual experiences. In M. Lewis & S. Feinman (Eds.), *Social Influences and Socialization in Infancy* (pp. 63–96). New York: Plenum Press.

Langacker, R. W. (2005). Dynamicity, fictivity, and scanning: The imaginative basis of logic and linguistic meaning. In D. Pecher & R. A. Zwaan (Eds.), *Grounding Cognition: The Role of Perception and Action in Memory, Language, and Thinking* (pp. 164–197). New York: Cambridge University Press.

Langer, E. J. (1989). *Mindfulness*. Reading, MA: Addison-Wesley.

Langer, E. J., Chanowitz, B., & Blank, A. (1978). The mindlessness of ostensibly thoughtful action. *Journal of Personality and Social Psychology*, *36*, 635–642.

Langford, D. (1981). The clarification request sequence in conversation between mothers and their children. In P. French & M. MacLure (Eds.), *Adult–Child Conversation* (pp. 159–184). London: Croom Helm.

Lanza, E. (1997). *Language Mixing in Infant Bilingualism: A Sociolinguistic Perspective*. Oxford, UK: Clarendon Press.

Larrick, R. P., & Blount, S. (1995). Social context in tacit bargaining games: Consequences for perceptions of affinity and cooperative behavior. In R. M. Kramer & D. M. Messick (Eds.), *Negotiation as a Social Process* (pp. 268–284). Thousand Oaks, CA: Sage.

Larzelere, R. E. (2000). Child outcomes of non-abusive and customary physical punishment by parents: An updated literature review. *Clinical Child and Family Psychology Review*, *3*, 199–221.

Laursen, B., & Koplas, A. L. (1995). What's important about important conflicts? Adolescents' perceptions of daily disagreements. *Merrill-Palmer Quarterly*, *41*, 536–553.

Lavelli, M., & Poli, M. (1998). Early mother-infant interaction during breast- and bottle- feeding. *Infant Behavior and Development*, *21*, 667–684.

Lawrence, J. A., & Valsiner, J. (1993). Conceptual roots of internalization: From transmission to transformation. *Human Development*, *36*, 150–167.

Lazarus, A. A., & Abramovitz, A. (1962). The use of "emotive imagery" in the treatment of children's phobias. *Journal of Mental Science*, *108*, 191–195.

LeBaron, S., Zeltzer, L. K., & Fanurik, D. (1988). Imaginative involvement and hypnotizability in childhood. *International Journal of Clinical and Experimental Hypnosis*, *36*, 284–205.

Lecuyer, E., & Houck, G. M. (2006). Maternal limit-setting in toddlerhood: Socialization strategies for the development of self regulation. *Infant Mental Health Journal*, *27*, 344–370.

Lederer, S. H. (2002). Collaborative pretend play: From theory to therapy. *Child Language Teaching and Therapy*, *18*, 233–255.

Leech, R., Mareschal, D., & Cooper, R. P. (2007). Relations as transformations: Implications for analogical reasoning. *Quarterly Journal of Experimental Psychology*, *60*, 897–908.

Leech, R., Mareschal, D. & Cooper, R. P. (2008). Analogy as relational priming: A developmental and computational perspective on the origins of a complex cognitive skill. *Behavioral and Brain Sciences*, *31*, 357–378.

Legerstee, M., & Barillas, Y. (2003). Sharing attention and pointing to objects at 12 months: Is the intentional stance implied? *Cognitive Development*, *18*, 91–110.

Lehr, S. (1990). Literature and the construction of meaning: The preschool child's developing sense of theme. *Journal of Research in Childhood Education*, *5*, 37–46.

Leifer, J., & Lewis, M. (1983). Maternal speech to normal and handicapped children: A look at question-asking behavior. *Infant Behavior and Development*, *6*, 175–187.

Lepper, M. R. (1973). Dissonance, self-perception, and honesty in children. *Journal of Personality and Social Psychology*. *25*, 65–74.

Lepper, M. R. (1981). Intrinsic and extrinsic motivation in children: Detrimental effects of superfluous social controls. *Minnesota Symposium on Child Development*, Vol. 14, 155–213.

Lepper, M. R. (1983). Social control processes and the internalization of social values: An attributional perspective. In E. T. Higgins, D. N. Ruble, & W. W. Hartup (Eds.), *Social Cognition and Social Development* (pp. 294–330). New York: Cambridge University Press.

Lepper, M. R., Greene, D., & Nisbett, R. E. (1973). Undermining children's intrinsic interest with extrinsic reward: A test of the "overjustification" hypothesis. *Journal of Personality and Social Psychology*, *28*, 129–137.

Lepper, M. R., & Malone, T. W. (1987). Intrinsic motivation and instructional effectiveness in computer-based education. In R. E. Snow & M. J. Farr (Eds.), *Aptitude, Learning, and Instruction: Vol. 3. Conative and Affective Process Analyses* (pp. 255–286). Hillsdale, NJ: Erlbaum.

Lepper, M., Sagotsky, G., Dafoe, J., & Greene, D. (1982). Consequences of superfluous social constraints on young children's social inferences and subsequent intrinsic interest. *Journal of Personality and Social Psychology*, *42*, 51–64.

Lerner, M. J. (1980). *The Belief in a Just World: A Fundamental Delusion*. New York: Plenum.

Leslie, A. M. (1987) Pretense and representations: The origins of "theory of mind". *Psychological Review*, *94*, 412–426.

Leslie, A. M. (1988) Some implications of pretense for the mechanisms underlying the child's theory of mind. In J. W. Astington, P. L. Harris, & D. R. Olson (Eds.), *Developing Theories of Mind* (pp. 19–46). New York: Cambridge University Press.

Levin, E. A. & Rubin, K. H. (1983). Getting others to do what you want them to do: The development of children's requestive strategies. In K. E. Nelson (Ed.), *Children's Language*, Vol. 4 (pp. 157–186). Hillsdale, NJ: Erlbaum.

LeVine, R. A. (1974). Parental goals: A cross-cultural view. *Teachers College Record*, *76*, 226–239.

LeVine, R. A. (1977). Child rearing as cultural adaptation. In P. H. Leiderman, S. R. Tulkin, and A. Rosenfeld (Eds.), *Culture and Infancy: Variations in the Human Experience* (pp. 15–27). New York: Academic Press.

Levinson, S. C. (1997). From outer to inner space: Linguistic categories and non-linguistic thinking. In J. Nuyts & E. Pederson (Eds.), *Language and Conceptualization* (pp. 13–45). Cambridge, UK: Cambridge University Press.

Levy, E. (1989). Monologue as development of the text-forming function of language. In K. Nelson (Ed.), *Narratives from the Crib* (pp. 123–170). Cambridge, MA: Harvard University Press.

Lewin, K. (1935). *A Dynamic Theory of Personality*. New York: McGraw-Hill.

Lewin, K. (1951). *Field Theory in Social Science*. New York: Harper.

Lewis, M., & Cherry, L. (1977). Social behavior and language acquisition. In M. Lewis & L. A. Rosenblum (Eds.), *Interaction, Conversation and the Development of Language*. (pp. 227–245). New York: Wiley.

Lewis, M. (1994). Myself and me. In S. T. Parker, R. W. Mitchell, & L. Boccia (Eds.), *Self Awareness in Animals and Humans: Developmental Perspectives* (pp. 20–34). Cambridge, UK: Cambridge University Press.

Lewis, S., Sixsmith, J., & Kagan, C. (1996). Dual career families. In N. M. Moore, J. Sixsmith, & K. Knowles (Eds.), *Children's Reflections on Family Life* (pp. 52–65). London: Falmer Press.

Liberman, N., Sagristano, M., & Trope, Y. (2002). The effect of temporal distance on level of mental construal. *Journal of Experimental Social Psychology*, *38*, 523–534.

Liberman, N., & Trope, Y. (1998). The role of feasibility and desirability considerations in near and distant future decisions: A test of temporal construal theory. *Journal of Personality and Social Psychology*, *75*, 5–18.

Liberman, N., Trope, Y., & Stephan, E. (2007). Psychological distance. In E. T. Higgins & A. W. Kruglanski (Eds.), *Social Psychology: Handbook of Basic Principles*, Vol. 2 (pp. 353–381). New York: Guilford Press.

Lieven, E. V. M. (1978). Turn-taking and pragmatics: Two issues in early child language. In R. N. Campbell & P. T. Smith (Eds.), *Recent Advances in the Psychology of Language: Language Development and Mother–Child Interaction* (pp. 215–236). New York: Plenum.

Light, P., Girotto, V., & Legrenzi, P. (1990). Children's reasoning on conditional promises and permissions. *Cognitive Development*, *5*, 369–383.

Light, P., & Littleton, K. (1999). *Social Processes in Children's Learning*. Cambridge, UK: Cambridge University Press.

Limber, J. (1973). The genesis of complex sentences. In T. Moore (Ed.), *Cognitive Development and the Acquisition of Language* (pp. 169–186). New York: Academic Press.

Lindfors, J. W. (1999). *Children's Inquiry: Using Language to Make Sense of the World*. New York: Teachers' College Press.

Livesley, W. J., & Bromley, B. D. (1973). *Person Perception in Childhood and Adolescence*. London: Wiley.

Lock, A. (1980). *The Guided Reinvention of Language*. London: Academic Press.

Loos, V., & Epstein, E. (1989). Conversational construction of meaning in family therapy: Some evolving thoughts on Kelly's sociality corollary. *International Journal of Personal Construct Psychology*, *2*, 149–167.

Loewenstein, G., & Schkade, D. (1999). Wouldn't it be nice? Predicting future feelings. In D. Kahneman, E. Diener, & N. Schwarz (Eds.), *Well-Being: The Foundations of Hedonic Psychology* (pp. 85–105). New York: Russell Sage Foundation.

Lowrey, T. M., Otnes, C. C., & Ruth, J. A. (2004). Social influences on dyadic giving over time: A taxonomy from the giver's perspective. *Journal of Consumer Research*, *30*, 547–558.

Lucariello, J., Kyratzis, A., & Engel, S. (1986). Event representations, context, and language. In K. Nelson (Ed.), *Event Knowledge: Structure and Function in Development* (pp. 137–160). Hillsdale, NJ: Erlbaum.

Lunkenheimer, E., Shields, A. M., & Cortina, K. S. (2007). Parental emotion coaching and dismissing in family interaction. *Social Development*, *16*, 232–248.

Luria, A. R. (1982). *Language and Cognition* (J. V. Wertsch, Ed.). New York: Wiley.

MacLure, M., & French, P. (1981). A comparison of talk at home and at school. In G. Wells (Ed.), *Learning Through Interaction: The Study of Language Development* (pp. 205–239). Cambridge, UK: Cambridge University Press.

Maccoby, E. E. (1980). *Social Development: Psychological Growth and the Parent-Child Relationship*. New York: Harcourt Brace Jovanovich.

Maccoby, E. E. (1998). *The Two Sexes: Growing Up Apart, Coming Together*. Cambridge, MA: Harvard University Press.

MacWhinney, B. (2000). *The CHILDES Project: Tools for Analyzing Talk*, 3rd ed. Mahwah, NJ: Erlbaum.

MacWhinney, B. (2005a). The emergence of linguistic form in time. *Connection Science*, *17*, 191–211.

MacWhinney, B. (2005b). The emergence of grammar from perspective. In D. Pecher & R. A. Zwaan (Eds.), *Grounding Cognition: The Role of Perception and Action in Memory, Language, and Thinking* (pp. 198–223). New York: Cambridge University Press.

Malloy, H. L., & McMurray, P. (1996). Conflict strategies and resolutions: Peer conflict in an integrated classroom. *Early Childhood Research Quarterly*, *11*, 185–206.

Maniacci, M. P., & Maniacci, S. V. (1989). Parental values as parameters for limit setting in a democratic atmosphere. *Individual Psychology*, *45*, 509–512.

Maratsos, M. (1973). Non-egocentric communication abilities in preschool children. *Child Development*, *44*, 697–700.

March, J. G. (1978). Bounded rationality, ambiguity, and the engineering of choice. *Bell Journal of Economics*, *9*, 587–608.

Marcos, H. (1991). Reformulating requests at 18 months: Gestures, vocalizations, and words. *First Language*, *11*, 361–375.

Marfo, K. (1992). Correlates of maternal directiveness with children who are developmentally delayed. *American Journal of Orthopsychiatry*, *62*, 219–233.

Markus, H. (1977). Self-schemata and processing information about the self. *Journal of Personality and Social Psychology*, *35*, 63–78.

Markus, H. R, & Smith, J. (1981). The influence of self schemata on the perception of others. In N. Cantor & J. F. Kihlstrom (Eds.), *Personality, Cognition, and Social Interaction* (pp. 233–262). Hillsdale, NJ: Erlbaum.

Markus, H. & Nurius, P. (1986). Possible selves. *American Psychologist*, *41*, 954–969.

Markus, H. & Ruvolo, A. (1989). Possible selves and personalized representations of goals. In L. A. Pervin (Ed.), *Goal Concepts in Personality and Social Psychology* (pp. 211–241). Hillsdale, NJ: Erlbaum.

Marquis, M., & Claveau, D. (2005). Repertoire of strategies used by French Canadian mothers living in Montreal to pressure their 10-year-old children to eat. *International Journal of Consumer Studies*, *29*, 254–260.

Marshall, L. J., & Levy, V. M., Jr. (1998). The development of children's perceptions of obstacles in compliance-gaining interactions. *Communication Studies*, *49*, 342–357.

Masataka, N. (2003). From index-finger extension to index-finger pointing: Ontogenesis of pointing in preverbal infants. In S. Kita (Ed.), *Pointing: Where Language, Culture and Cognition Meet* (pp. 69–84). Mahwah, NJ: Erlbaum.

Mason, J., & Falloon, J. (2001). Some Sydney children define abuse: Implications for agency in childhood. In L. Alanen & B. Mayall (Eds.), *Conceptualizing Child–Adult Relations* (pp. 99–113). London: Routledge Falmer.

Matta, J., Scheibehenne, B., & Todd, P. B. (2008). Predicting children's meal preferences: How much do parents know? *Appetite*, *50*, 367–375.

Matthews, G. B. (1984). *Dialogues with Children*. Cambridge, MA: Harvard University Press.

Mayall, B. (2000). Conversations with children: Working with generational issues. In P. Christensen & A. James (Eds.), *Research with Children: Perspectives and Practices* (pp. 120–135). London: Falmer Press.

Mayall, B. (2002). *Towards a Sociology of Childhood: Thinking from Children's Lives*. Buckingham, UK: Open University.

Maynard, A. (2002). Cultural teaching: The development of teaching skills in Maya sibling interactions. *Child Development*, *73*, 969–982.

Maynard, D. M. (1985). How children start arguments. *Language in Society*, *14*, 1–30.

McCabe, A. (1997). Narrative threads of metaphor. In C. Mandell & A. McCabe (Eds.), *The Problem of Meaning: Behavioral and Cognitive Perspectives* (pp. 347–375). Amsterdam: Elsevier.

McCabe, A., & Peterson, C. (1991). Getting the story: A longitudinal study of parental styles in eliciting narratives and developing narrative skill. In A. McCabe & C. Peterson (Eds.), *Developing Narrative Structure* (pp. 217–254). Hillsdale, NJ: Erlbaum.

McCune, L. (1993). The development of play as the development of consciousness. In M. H. Bornstein & A. W. O'Reilly (Eds.), *New Directions for Child Development*, *59*, 67–78.

McCune-Nicolich, L., & Fenson, L. (1984). Methodological issues in studying early pretend play. In T. D. Yawkey & A. D. Pellegrini (Eds.), *Child's Play: Developmental and Applied* (pp. 81–104). Hillsdale, NJ: Erlbaum.

McGillicuddy-De Lisi, A. V. (1985). The relationship between parental beliefs and children's cognitive level. In I. E. Sigel (Ed.), *Parental Belief Systems: The Psychological Consequences for Children* (pp. 7–24). Hillsdale, NJ: Erlbaum.

McGlaughlin, A., Morrissey, M., Empson, J. M., & Sever, J. (1981). Language performance of disadvantaged children at 30 months: Interpersonal and other environmental influences. In W. P. Robinson (Ed.), *Communication in Development* (pp. 109–128). London: Academic Press.

McGuire, W. J., & McGuire, C. V. (1986). Differences in conceptualizing self versus conceptualizing other people as manifested in contrasting verb types used in natural speech. *Journal of Personality and Social Psychology*, *51*, 1135–1143.

McGuire, W. J., & McGuire, C. V. (1988). Content and process in the experience of self. In L. Berkowitz (Ed.), *Advances in Experimental Social Psychology*, Vol. 21 (pp. 97–144). New York: Academic Press.

McIsaac, H. K., & Eich, E. (2002). Vantage point in episodic memory. *Psychonomic Bulletin and Review*, *9*, 146–159.

McNeill, D., & McNeill, N. (1968). What does a child mean when he says "no"? In E. Zale (Ed.), *Proceedings of the Conference on Language and Language Behavior* (pp. 51–62). New York: Appleton-Century-Crofts.

McShane, J. (1980). *Learning to Talk*. Cambridge, UK: Cambridge University Press.

McTear, M. F. (1981). Towards a model for analysing conversations involving children. In P. French & M. MacLure (Eds.), *Adult–Child Conversation* (pp. 187–209). London: Croom Helm.

McTear, M. F. (1985). *Children's Conversations*. Oxford, UK: Basil Blackwell.

Mead, G. H. (1934). *Mind, Self and Society*. Chicago: University of Chicago Press.

Mehan, H. (1979). *Learning Lessons: Social Organization in the Classroom*. Cambridge, MA: Harvard University Press.

Meins, E., & Fernyhough, C. (1999). Linguistic acquisitional style and mentalising development: The role of maternal mind-mindedness. *Cognitive Development*, *14*, 363–380.

Meins, E., Fernyhough, C., Fradley, E., & Tuckey, M. (2001). Rethinking maternal sensitivity: Mothers' comments on infants' mental processes predict security of attachment at 12 months. *Journal of Child Psychology and Psychiatry*, *42*, 637–648.

Meins, E., Fernyhough, C., Wainwright, R., Das Gupta, M., Fradley, E., & Tuckey, M. (2002). Maternal mind – mindedness and attachment security as predictors of theory of mind understanding. *Child Development*, *73*, 1715–1726.

Melara, R. D., & Nairne, J. S. (1991). On the nature of interactions between the past and the present. *Journal of Experimental Psychology: Learning, Memory, and Cognition*, *17*, 1124–1135.

Melges, F. T. (1982). *Time and the Inner Future: A Temporal Approach to Psychiatric Disorders*. New York: Wiley.

Meltzoff, A. N. (2007a). The "like me" framework for recognizing and becoming an intentional agent. *Acta Psychologica*, *124*, 26–43.

Meltzoff, A. N. (2007b). "Like Me": A foundation for social cognition. *Developmental Science*, *10*, 126–134.

Mennella, J. A., & Beauchamp, G. K. (1996). The human infants' response to vanilla flavors in mother's milk and formula. *Infant Behavior and Development*, *19*, 13–19.

Mennella, J. A., & Beauchamp, G. K. (2002). Flavor experiences during formula feeding are related to preferences during childhood. *Early Human Development*, *68*, 71–82.

Menyuk, P., Liebergott, J. W., & Schultz, M. W. (1995). *Early Language Development in Full-term and Premature Infants*. Hillsdale, NJ: Erlbaum.

Merker, B. (2007). Memory, imagination, and the asymmetry between past and future. *Behavioral and Brain Sciences*, *30*, 325–326.

Merritt, M. (1982). Distributing and directing attention in primary classrooms. In L. C. Wilkinson (Eds.), *Communicating in the Classroom* (pp. 223–244). New York: Academic Press.

Merritt, M. (1998). Of ritual matters to master: Structure and improvisation in language development at primary school. In S. M. Hoyle & C. T. Adger (Eds.), *Kids Talk: Strategic Language Use in Later Childhood* (pp. 134–150). New York: Oxford University Press.

Meskin, A., & Weinberg, J. M. (2003). Emotions, fiction, and cognitive architecture. *British Journal of Aesthetics*, *43*, 18–34.

Messer, D. G. (1981). Non-linguistic information which could assist the young child's interpretation of adults' speech. In W. P. Robinson (Ed.), *Communication in Development* (pp. 39–62). London: Academic Press.

Meyenn, R. J. (1980). School girls' peer groups. In P. Woods (Ed.), *Pupil Strategies: The Sociology of the School* (pp. 108–142). London: Croom Helm.

Meyer, J. (2003). *Kids Talking: Learning Relationships and Culture with Children*. Lanham, MA: Rowman & Littlefield.

Mezhevich, I. (2008). A time-relations approach to tense and mood. *Proceedings of the 27th West Coast Conference on Formal Linguistics* (pp. 326–327). Somerville, MA: Cascadilla Proceedings Project.

Michaels, S. (1986). Narrative presentations: An oral preparation for literacy with first graders. In J. Cook-Gumperz (Ed.), *The Social Construction of Literacy* (pp. 94–116). Cambridge, UK: Cambridge University Press.

Michaels, S. (1991) The dismantling of narrative. In A. McCabe & C. Peterson (Eds.), *Developing Narrative Structure* (pp. 303–352). Hillsdale, NJ: Erlbaum.

Mikeš, M., Dezső, L., & Vlahović, P. (1972). Sentence-programming span in child language. In K. Ohnesort (Ed.), *Colloquium Paedolingisticum, Proceedings of the First International Symposium of Paedolinguistics* (pp. 166–178). The Hague: Mouton.

Milburn, T. W., & Watman, K. H. (1981). *On the Nature of Threat*. New York: Praeger.

Miller, D. T. (1975). Ego involvement and attributions for success and failure. *Journal of Personality and Social Psychology*, *34*, 901–906.

Miller, D. T., & Karniol, R. (1976). The role of rewards in externally and self imposed delay of gratification. *Journal of Personality and Social Psychology*, *33*, 594–600.

Miller, D. T., & Karniol, R. (1976). Coping strategies and attentional mechanisms in self-imposed and externally-imposed delay situations. *Journal of Personality and Social Psychology*, *34*, 310–316.

Miller, D. T., Weinstein, S., & Karniol, R. (1978). Effects of age and verbalization on children's ability to delay gratification. *Developmental Psychology*, *14*, 569–570.

Miller, M. H. (1979). *The Logic of Language Development in Early Childhood*. Berlin: Springer-Verlag.

Miller, P., Danaher, D., & Forbes, D. (1986). Sex-related strategies for coping with interpersonal conflict in children aged five to seven. *Developmental Psychology*, *22*, 543–548.

Miller, P. J. (1982). *Amy, Wendy, and Beth: Learning Language in South Baltimore*. Austin, TX: University of Texas Press.

Miller, P. J., & Garvey, C. (1984). Mother-baby role play: Its origins in social support. In I. Bretherton (Ed.), *Symbolic Play: The Development of Social Understanding* (pp. 101–130). Orlando, FL: Academic Press.

Miller, P. J., Fung, H., & Mintz, J. (1996). Self-construction through narrative practices: A Chinese and American comparison of early socialization. *Ethos*, *24*, 237–280.

Miller, P. J., Sandel, T. L., Liang, C.-H., & Fung, H. (2001). Narrating transgressions in Longwood: The discourses, meanings, and paradoxes of an American socializing practice. *Ethos*, *29*, 159–186.

Miller, S. A., Davis, T. L., Wilde, C. A., & Brown, J. (1993). Parents' knowledge of their children's preferences. *International Journal of Behavioral Development*, *16*, 35–60.

Minami, M. (1997). Cultural constructions of meaning: Cross-cultural comparisons of mother–child conversations about the past. In C. Mandell & A. McCabe (Eds.), *The Problem of Meaning: Behavioral and Cognitive Perspectives* (pp. 297–345). Amsterdam: Elsevier.

Minami, M. (2002). *Culture-Specific Language Styles: The Development of Oral Narrative and Literacy*. Clevedon, UK: Multilingual Matters.

Minsky, M. (1986). *The Society of Mind*. New York: Simon & Schuster.

Minton, C., Kagan, J., & Levine, J. A. (1971). Maternal control and obedience in the two-year-old. *Child Development*, *42*, 1873–1894.

Mischel, H. (1984). From intention to action: The role of rule knowledge in the development of self regulation. *Human Development*, *27*, 124–128.

Mischel, H. N., & Mischel, W. (1983). The development of children's knowledge of self-control strategies. *Child Development*, *54*, 603–619.

Mischel, W., & Baker, N. (1975). Cognitive appraisals and transformations in delay behavior. *Journal of Personality and Social Psychology*, *31*, 254–260.

Mischel, W., & Moore, B. (1973). Effects of attention to symbolically presented rewards on self-control. *Journal of Personality and Social Psychology*, *28*, 172–179.

Mischel, W., & Ebbesen, E. B. (1970). Attention in delay of gratification. *Journal of Personality and Social Psychology*, *16*, 329–337.

Mischel, W., Cantor, N., & Feldman, S. (1996). Principles of self regulation: The nature of willpower and self-control. In E. T. Higgins & A. W. Kruglanski (Eds.), *Social Psychology: Handbook of Basic Principles* (pp. 329–360). New York: Guilford.

Mischel, W., & Mischel, H. N. (1976). A cognitive social-learning approach to morality and self-regulation. In T. Lickona (Ed.), *Moral Development and Behavior* (pp. 84–107). New York: Holt, Rinehart & Winston.

Mischel, W., Shoda, Y., & Rodriguez, M. L. (1989). Delay of gratification in children. *Science*, *244*, 933–938.

Mishler, E. (1979). "Wou' you trade cookies with the popcorn?" The talk of trades among six year olds. In O. Garnica & M. King (Eds.), *Language, Children, and Society: The Effects of Social Factors on Children Learning to Communicate* (pp. 221–236). Elmsford, NY: Pergamon Press.

Mishler, E. G. (1972). Implications of teacher strategies for language and cognition: Observations in first grade classrooms. In C. B. Cazden, V. P. John, & D. Hymes, (Eds.), *Functions of Language in the Classroom* (pp. 267–298). New York: Teachers' College Press.

Mitchell, L. (1982). Language styles of 10 nursery school children. *First Language*, *3*, 3–28.

Mitchell-Kernan, C., & Kernan, K. T. (1977). Pragmatics of directive choice among children. In S. Ervin-Tripp & C. Mitchell-Kernan (Eds.), *Child Discourse* (pp. 189–208). New York: Academic Press.

Mithen, S. (1996). *The Prehistory of the Mind: The Cognitive Origins of Art and Science*: London: Thames & Hudson.

Mithen, S. (2007). Seven steps in the evolution of human imagination. In I. Roth (Ed.), *Imaginative Minds* (pp. 3–30). Oxford, UK: Oxford University Press.

Mody, S. L. (2005). *Cultural Identity in Kindergarten: A Study of Asian Indian Children in New Jersey*. New York: Routledge.

Moerk, E. L. (1975). Verbal interactions between children and their mothers during the preschool years. *Developmental Psychology*, *11*, 788–794.

Moerk, E. L. (1983). *The Mother of Eve – as a First Language Teacher*. Norwood, NJ: Ablex.

Moltmann, F. (2006). Generic One, arbitrary PRO, and the first person. *Natural Language Semantics*, *14*, 257–281.

Mongin, P. (2001). The impartial observer theory of social justice. *Economics and Philosophy*, *17*, 147–179.

Monin, B., Pizarro, D. A., & Beer, J. S. (2007). Deciding vs. reacting: Conceptions of moral judgment and the reason-affect debate. *Review of General Psychology*, *11*, 814–834.

Montangero, J., Pons, F., & Cattin, J.-P. (2000). The diachronic approach and solutions to interpersonal conflicts. *British Journal of Developmental Psychology*, *18*, 415–429.

Montgomery, H. (1983). Decision rules and the search for a dominance structure: Towards a process model of decision making. In P. C. Humphreys, O. Svenson, & A. Vari (Eds.), *Analyzing and Aiding Decision Processes* (pp. 343–369). Amsterdam: North-Holland.

Montgomery, H. (1994). Towards a perspective theory of decision making and judgment. *Acta Psychologica*, *87*, 155–178.

Moore, B., Mischel, W., & Zeiss, A. (1976). Comparative effects of the reward stimulus and its cognitive representation on voluntary delay. *Journal of Personality and Social Psychology*, *34*, 419–424.

Moore, C., Barresi, J., and Thompson, C. (1998). The cognitive basis of prosocial behavior. *Social Development*, *7*, 198–218.

Moore, C., Jarrold, C., Russell, J., Lumb, A., Sapp, F., & MacCallum, F. (1995). Conflicting desire and the child's theory of mind. *Cognitive Development*, *10*, 467–482.

Moore, M., & Beazley, S. (1996). Split family life. In M. Moore, J. Sixsmith, & K. Knowles (Eds.), *Children's Reflections on Family Life* (pp. 66–80). London: Falmer Press.

Morelli, G. A., Rogoff, B., & Angelillo, C. (2003). Cultural variation in young children's access to work or involvement in specialized child-focused activities. *International Journal of Behavioral Development*, *27*, 264–274.

Morelli, G. A., & Tronick, E. Z. (1991). Parenting and child development in the Efe foragers and Lese farmers of Zaire. In M. H. Bornstein (Ed.), *Cultural Approaches to Parenting* (pp. 91–114). Hillsdale, NJ: Erlbaum.

Morelock,M. J., Brown, P. M., & Morrissey, A-M. (2003) Pretend play and maternal scaffolding: Comparisons of toddlers with advanced development, typical development, and hearing impairment. *Roeper Review: A Journal on Gifted Education*, *26*, 41–51.

Morgan, J. I., & Skovholt, T. M. (1977). Using inner experience: Fantasy and daydreaming in career counseling. *Journal of Counseling Psychology*, *24*, 391–397.

Morrow, L. M., & Rand, M. (1991). Preparing the classroom environment to promote literacy during play. In J. F. Christie (Ed.), *Play and Early Literacy Development* (pp. 141–165). Albany, NY: SUNY Press.

Mortimer, J. T., Dennehy, K., Lee, C., & Finch, M. D. (2004). Economic socialization in the American family: The prevalence, distribution, and consequences of allowance arrangements. *Family Relations*, *43*, 23–29.

Morton, A. (2003). *The Importance of Being Understood: Folk Psychology as Ethics*. New York: Routledge.

Muhlhausler, P., & Harré, R. (1990). *Pronouns and People: The Linguistic Construction of Social and Personal Identity*. Oxford, UK: Basil Blackwell.

Mullen, B., Dovidio, J. F., Johnson, C., & Copper, C. (1992). Ingroup-outgroup differences in social projection. *Journal of Experimental Social Psychology*, *28*, 422–440.

Müller, N. (1994). Parameters cannot be reset: Evidence from the development of COMP. In J. M. Meisel (Ed.), *Bilingual First Language Acquisition: French and German Grammatical Development* (pp. 235–269). Amsterdam: John Benjamins.

Müller, V., Sokol, B., & Overton, W. (1998). Reframing a constructivist model of the development of mental representation: The role of higher-order operations. *Developmental Review*, *18*, 155–201.

Murnighan, J. K., & Pillutla, M. M. (1995). Fairness versus self-interest: Asymmetric moral imperatives in ultimatum bargaining. In R. M. Kramer & D. M. Messick (Eds.), *Negotiation as a Social Process* (pp. 240–267). Thousand Oaks, CA: Sage.

Musatti, T., & Mayer, S. (1993). Pretend play in the schoolyard: Propagation of play themes among a group of young children.

In M. Stambak & H. Sinclair (Eds.), *Pretend Play Among 3-Year-Olds* (pp. 31–54). Hillsdale, NJ: Erlbaum.

Mussen, P., & Eisenberg-Berg, N. (1977). *Roots of Caring, Sharing, and Helping: The Development of Prosocial Behavior in Children*. San Francisco: Freeman.

Mutz, D. C. (1999). *Impersonal Influence: How Perceptions of Mass Collectives affect Political Attitudes*. Cambridge, MA: Cambridge University Press.

Nadler, A., & Fisher, J. D. (1986). The role of threat to self esteem and perceived control in recipient reactions to help: Theory development and empirical validation. In L. Berkowitz (Ed.), *Advances in Experimental Social Psychology*, Vol. 19 (pp. 81–122). New York: Academic Press.

Nagin, D. S., & Pogarsky, G. (2004). Time and punishment: Delayed consequences and criminal behavior. *Journal of Quantitative Criminology*, *20*, 291–317.

National Coalition to Abolish Corporal Punishment in the Schools. (2001). *Facts about corporal punishment*. Retrieved April 10, 2002, from www.stophitting.com/NCACPS/index.html.

Nelson, C. A. (2007). What would Superman do? In L. C. Rubin (Ed.), *Using Superheroes in Counseling and Play Therapy* (pp. 49–67). New York: Springer.

Nelson, K. (1983). The derivation of concepts and categories form event representations. In E. K. Scholnick (Ed.), *New Trends in Conceptual Representation: Challenges to Piaget's Theory?* (pp. 129–150). Hillsdale, NJ: Erlbaum.

Nelson, K. (1986). *Event Knowledge: Structure and Function in Development*. Hillsdale, NJ: Erlbaum.

Nelson, K. (1989). *Narratives from the Crib*. Cambridge, MA: Harvard University Press.

Nelson, K. (1996). *Language in Cognitive Development: Emergence of the Mediated Mind*. New York: Cambridge University Press.

Nelson, K. (1999). Levels and modes of representation: Issues for the theory of conceptual change and development. In E. K. Scholnick, K. Nelson, S. A. Gelman, & P. H. Miller (Eds.), *Conceptual Development: Piaget's Legacy* (pp. 269–291). Mahwah, NJ: Erlbaum.

Nelson, K. (2001). Language and the self: From the "Experiencing I" to the "Continuing Me." In C. Moore & K. Lemmon (Eds.), *The Self in Time: Developmental Perspectives* (pp. 15–34). Mahwah, NJ: Erlbaum.

Nelson, K., Engel, S., & Kyratzis, A. (1985). The evolution of meaning in context. *Journal of Pragmatics*, *9*, 453–474.

Nelson, K., & Gruendel, J. (1979). At morning it's lunchtime: A script view of children's dialogues. *Discourse Processes*, *2*, 73–94.

Nelson, K., & Hudson, J. A. (1988). Scripts and memory: Functional relationships in development. In F. E. Weinert & M. Perlmutter (Eds.), *Memory Development: Universal Changes and Individual Differences* (pp. 147–167). Hillsdale, NJ: Erlbaum.

Nelson, K., & Shaw, L. K. (2002). Developing a socially shared symbolic system. In E. Amsel & J. P. Byrnes (Eds.). *Language, Literacy, and Cognitive Development: The Development and Consequences of Symbolic Communication* (pp. 27–57). Mahwah, NJ: Erlbaum.

Nelson, K., & Seidman, S. (1984). Playing with scripts. In I. Bretherton (Ed.), *Symbolic Play: The Development of Social Understanding* (pp. 45–71). Orlando, FL: Academic Press.

Nelson, K. E. (1982). Early language development: Conceptual growth and related processes between 2 and $4^1/_2$ years of age. In K. E. Nelson (Ed.), *Children's Language*, Vol. 1 (pp. 467–556). New York: Gardner Press.

Nelson, K. E., & Bonvillian, J. D. (1978). Early semantic development: Conceptual growth and related processes between 2 and $4^1/_2$ years of age. In K. E. Nelson (Ed.), *Children's Language*, Vol. 1 (pp. 467–556). New York: Gardner Press.

Neuman, S. B., & Roskos, K. (1991). The influence of literacy-enriched play centers on preschoolers' conceptions of the functions of print. In J. F. Christie (Ed.), *Play and Early Literacy Development* (pp. 167–187). Albany, NY: SUNY Press.

Nevat-Gal, R. (2002). Cognitive expressions and humorous phrases in family discourse as reflectors and cultivators of cognition. In S. Blum-Kulka & C. E. Snow (Eds.), *Talking to Adults: The Contribution of Multiparty Discourse to Language Acquisition* (pp. 181–208). Mahwah, NJ: Erlbaum.

Newman, D. (1978). Ownership and permission among nursery school children. In J. Glick and K. A. Clarke-Stewart (Eds.), *The Development of Social Understanding* (pp. 213–249). New York: Gardner Press.

Newman, J., & Taylor, A. (1992). Effect of a means-end contingency on young children's food preferences. *Journal of Experimental Child Psychology*, *55*, 200–216.

Newson, J. (1979). The growth of shared understandings between infant and caregiver. In M. Bullowa (Ed.), *Before Speech: The Beginnings of Interpersonal Communication* (pp. 207–222). London: Cambridge University Press.

Newson, J., & Newson, E. (1968). *Four Years Old in an Urban Community*. London: Allen & Unwin.

Newson, J., & Newson, E. (1976). *Seven Years Old in the Home Environment*. New York: Wiley.

Nichols, S., & Stich, S. (2000). A cognitive theory of pretence. *Cognition*, *74*, 115–147.

Nichols, S., & Stich, S. (2004). Reading one's mind: Self awareness and developmental psychology. *Canadian Journal of Philosophy*, *Supp. 30*, 294–339.

Nicklaus, S., Boggio, J., Chabanet, C., & Issanchou, S. (2005). A prospective study of food variety seeking in childhood, adolescence, and early adult life. *Appetite*, *44*, 289–297.

Nieuwland, M. S., & Van Berkum, J. J. A. (2006). When peanuts fall in love: N400 evidence for the power of discourse. *Journal of Cognitive Neuroscience*, *18*, 1098–1111.

Nigro, G., & Neisser, U. (1983). Point of view in personal memories. *Cognitive Psychology*, *15*, 467–482.

Ninio, A., & Snow, C. E. (1996). *Pragmatic Development*. Boulder, CO: Westview Press.

Nisbett, R. E., & Wilson, T. D. (1977). Telling more than we can know: Verbal reports on mental processes. *Psychological Review*, *84*, 231–259.

Noelle-Neumann, E. (1984). *The Spiral of Silence – Our Social Skin*. Chicago: University of Chicago Press.

Nofziger, S. (2008). The "cause" of low self-control: The influence of maternal self-control. *Journal of Research in Crime and Delinquency*, *45*, 191–224.

Norton, D. G. (1993). Diversity, early socialization, and temporal development: The dual perspective revisited. *Social Work*, *25*, 82–90.

Nourot, P. M. (1998). Sociodramatic play: Pretending together. In D. P. Fromberg & D. Bergen (Eds.), *Play from Birth to Twelve and Beyond: Contexts, Perspectives, and Meanings* (pp. 378–391). New York: Garland Publishing.

Nucci, L. (2004). Social interaction and the construction of moral and social knowledge. In J. I. M. Carpendale & U. Müller (Eds.), *Social Interaction and the Development of Knowledge* (pp. 195–213). Mahwah, NJ: Erlbaum.

Nucci, L., & Smetana, J. G. (1996). Mothers' concepts of young children's areas of personal freedom. *Child Development, 67*, 1870–1886.

Oburu, P. O., & Palmérus, K. (2003). Parenting stress and self-reported discipline strategies of Kenyan caregiving grandmothers. *International Journal of Behavioral Development, 27*, 505–512.

Ochs, E. (1979). Introduction: What child language can contribute to pragmatics. In E. Ochs & B. S. Schieffelin (Eds.), *Developmental Pragmatics* (pp. 1–20). New York: Academic Press.

Ochs, E. (1986). From feelings to grammar: A Samoan case study. In B. S. Schieffelin & E. Ochs (Eds.), *Language Socialization across Cultures* (pp. 251–272). Cambridge, UK: Cambridge University Press.

Ochs, E. (1988). *Culture and Language Development*. New York: Cambridge University Press.

Ochs, E. (1992). Indexing gender. In A. Duranti & C. Goodwin (Eds.), *Rethinking Context: Language as an Interactive Phenomenon* (pp.335–358). Cambridge, UK: Cambridge University Press.

Ochs, E. (2004). Narrative lessons. In A. Duranti (Ed.), *A Companion to Linguistic Anthropology* (pp. 269–289). Oxford, UK: Blackwell.

Ochs, E., & Capps, L. (2001). *Living Narrative: Creating Lives in Everyday Storytelling*. Harvard University Press.

Ochs, E., Pontecorvo, C., & Fasulo, A. (1996). Socializing taste. *Ethnos, 61*, 7–46.

Ochs, E., & Schieffelin, B. (2001). Language acquisition and socialization: Three developmental stories and their implications. In A. Duranti (Ed.), *Linguistic Anthropology: A Reader* (pp. 263–301). Malden, MA: Blackwell.

Ochs, E., & Shohet, M. (2006). The cultural structuring of mealtime socialization. *New Directions for Child and Adolescent Development, 111*, 35–49.

Odier, C. (1948/1965). *Anxiety and Magic Thinking*. New York: International Universities Press.

O'Hanlon, W. H., & Weiner-Davis, M. (1989). *In Search of Solutions: A New Direction in Psychotherapy*. New York: Norton.

O'Kane, C. (2000). The development of participatory techniques: Facilitating children's views about decisions that affect them. In P. Christensen & A. James (Eds.), *Research with Children: Perspectives and Practices* (pp. 136–159). London: Falmer Press.

O'Keefe, B. J., & Benoit, P. J. (1982). Children's arguments. In J. R. Cox and C. A. Willard (Eds.), *Advances in Argumentation Theory and Research* (pp. 154–183). Carbondale, IL: Southern Illinois University Press.

Oldenburg, J. (1990). Learning the language and learning through language in early childhood. In M. A. K. Halliday, J. Gibbons, & H. Nicholas (Eds.), *Learning, Keeping and Using Language*, Vol. I (pp. 27–38). Amsterdam: John Benjamins.

Oldershaw, L., Walters, G. C., & Hall, D. K. (1986). Control strategies and noncompliance in abusive mother–child dyads: An observational study. *Child Development, 57*, 722–732.

Olson, D. R. (1980). Some social aspects of meaning in oral and written language. In D. R. Olson (Ed.), *The Social Foundations of Language and Thought: Essays in Honor of Jerome S. Bruner* (pp. 90–108). New York: Norton.

Olson, D. R. (1988). On the origins of beliefs and other intentional states in children. In J. W. Astington, P. L. Harris, & D. R. Olson (Eds.), *Developing Theories of Mind* (pp. 414–426). New York: Cambridge University Press.

Olson, D. R. & Hildyard, A. (1981). The role of nonverbal behavior in children's communication. In W. P. Dickson (Ed.), *Children's Oral Communication Skills* (pp. 313–335). New York: Academic Press.

Olson, D. R. & Campbell, R. (1993). Constructing representations. In C. Pratt & A. F. Garton (Eds.), *Systems of Representation in Children* (pp. 11–26). Chichester, UK: Wiley.

Olson-Fulero, L. (1982). Style and stability in mother conversational behavior: A study of individual differences. *Journal of Child Language, 9*, 543–564.

O'Neill, D. K. (1996). Two-year-old children's sensitivity to a parent's knowledge state when making requests. *Child Development, 67*, 659–677.

O'Neill, D. K., & Atance, C. M. (2000). "Maybe my daddy give me a big piano": The development of children's use of modals to express uncertainty. *First Language, 20*, 29–52.

Oppenheim, D., & Koren-Karie, N. (2002). Mothers' insightfulness regarding their children's internal worlds: The capacity underlying secure child-mother relationships. *Infant Mental Health Journal, 23*, 593–605.

Orellana, M. F. (1994). Appropriating the voice of the superheroes: Three preschoolers' bilingual language uses in play. *Early Childhood Research Quarterly, 9*, 171–193.

Orrel-Valente, J. K., Hill, L. G., Brechwald, W. A., Dodge, K. A., Pettit, G. S., & Bates, J. E. (2007). "Just three more bites": An observational analysis of parental socialization of children's eating at mealtime. *Appetite, 48*, 37–45.

Oster, H., & Ekman, P. (1978). Facial behavior in child development. *Minnesota Symposium on Child Psychology, 11*, 231–276.

Painter, C. (1984). *Into the Mother Tongue: A Case Study in Early Language Development*. London: Frances Pinter.

Painter, C. (1989). Language: A functional view of language development. In R. Hasan & J. R. Martin (Eds.), *Language Development: Learning Language, Learning Culture* (pp. 18–65). Norwood, NJ: Ablex.

Palan, M. K., & Wilkes, R. E. (1997). Adolescent-parent interaction in family decision making. *Journal of Consumer Research, 24*, 159–169.

Paley, V. G. (1984). *Boys and Girls: Superheroes in the Doll Corner*. Chicago: University of Chicago Press.

Paley, V. G. (1986). *Mollie is Three: Growing Up in School*. Chicago: University of Chicago Press.

Paley, V. G. (1990). *The Boy Who Would be a Helicopter*. Cambridge, MA: Harvard University Press.

Paley, V. G. (1999). *The Kindness of Children*. Cambridge, MA: Harvard University Press.

Paley, V. G. (2004). *A Child's Work: The Importance of Fantasy Play*. Chicago: University of Chicago Press.

Palkovitz, R. (2002). *Involved Fathering and Men's Adult Development: Provisional Balances*. Mahwah, NJ: Erlbaum.

Palmérus, K., & Jutengren, G. (2004). Swedish parents' self-reported use of discipline in response to continued misconduct by their preschool children. *Infant and Child Development, 13*, 79–90.

Paprotté, W. (1985). Metaphor and the first words. In W. Papprotté and R. Dirven (Eds.), *The Ubiquity of Metaphor: Metaphor in Language and Thought* (pp. 425–480). Amsterdam: John Benjamins.

Parker, J. (1986). Becoming friends: Conversational skills for friendship formation in young children. In J. M. Gottman & J. G. Parker (Eds.), *Conversations of Friends: Speculations on*

Affective Development (pp. 103–138). Cambridge, UK: Cambridge University Press.

Parkhurst, J., & Gottman, J. M. (1986). How young children get what they want. In J. M. Gottman & J. G. Parker (Eds.), *Conversations of Friends: Speculations on Affective Development* (pp. 315–345). New York: Cambridge University Press.

Parsons, T., Bales, R. F., & Shils, E. A. (1955). *Working Papers in the Theory of Action*. New York: The Free Press.

Patterson, C. J., & Carter, D. B. (1979). Attentional determinants of children's self-control in waiting and working situations. *Child Development*, *50*, 272–275.

Paxson, C., & Schady, N. (2005). *Cognitive development among young children in Ecuador: The roles of wealth, health and parenting*. The World Bank, Policy Research Working Paper no. 3605.

Payne, J. W. (1976). Task complexity and contingent processing in decision making: An information search and protocol analysis. *Organizational Behavior and Human Performance*, *16*, 366–387.

Pea, R. D. (1980). The development of negation in early child language. In D. R. Olson (Ed.), *The Social Foundations of Language and Thought: Essays in Honor of Jerome S. Bruner* (pp. 156–186). New York: Norton.

Peak, L. (1991). *Learning to Go to School in Japan: The Transition from Home to Preschool Life*. Berkeley: University of California Press.

Peak. L. (2001). Learning to become part of the group: The Japanese child's transition to preschool life. In H. Shimizu & R. A. LeVine (Eds.), *Japanese Frames of Mind: Cultural Perspectives on Human Development* (pp. 143–169). Cambridge, UK: Cambridge University Press.

Peake, P. P., Hebl, M., & Mischel, W. (2002). Strategic attention deployment for delay of gratification in working and waiting situations. *Developmental Psychology*, *38*, 313–326.

Pearlin, L. I. (1971). *Class Context and Family Relations: A Cross-National Study*. Boston: Little, Brown & Co.

Peirce, C. S. (1932). *Collected Papers of Charles Sanders Peirce* (Vols. 1–8). Cambridge, MA: Harvard University Press.

Perlman, M., & Ross, H. S. (2005). If–then contingencies in children's sibling conflicts. *Merrill-Palmer Quarterly*, *51*, 42–66.

Perlmutter, J. C., & Pellegrini, A. D. (1987). Children's verbal fantasy play with parents and peers. *Educational Psychology*, *7*, 269–281.

Perner, J. (1991). *Understanding the Representational Mind*. Cambridge, MA: MIT Press.

Perner, J., Leekam, S. R., & Wimmer, H. (1987). Three-year-olds' difficulty with false belief: The case for a conceptual deficit. *British Journal of Developmental Psychology*, *5*, 125–137.

Perozynski, L., & Kramer, L. (1999). Parental beliefs about managing sibling conflict. *Developmental Psychology*, *35*, 489–499.

Peters, A. M. (2000). From prosody to grammar in English: The differentiation of catenatives, modals, and auxiliaries from a single protomorpheme. In J. Weisshenborn & B. Hohle (Eds.), *Approaches to Bootstrapping: Phonological, Lexical, Syntactic and Neurophysiological Aspects of Early Language Acquisition*, Vol. 2 (pp. 121–156). Amsterdam: John Benjamins.

Peterson, C., & McCabe, A. (1983). *Developmental Psycholinguistics: Three Ways of Looking at a Child's Narrative*. New York: Plenum Press.

Pettersson, A., Olsson, U., & Fjellström, C. (2004). Family life in grocery stores – a study of interaction between adults and children. *International Journal of Consumer Studies*, *28*, 317–328.

Phinney, J. S. (1986). The structure of 5-year-olds' verbal quarrels with peers and siblings. *Journal of Genetic Psychology*, *147*, 47–60.

Piaget, J. (1926/1959). *The Language and Thought of the Child*. London: Routledge & Kegan Paul.

Piaget, J. (1928/1969). *Judgment and Reasoning in the Child*. Totowa, NJ: Littlefield, Adams.

Piaget, J. (1929/1975). *The Child's Conception of the World*. Totowa, NJ: Littlefield, Adams.

Piaget, J. (1932/1965). *The Moral Judgment of the Child*. New York: The Free Press.

Piaget, J. (1936/1952). *The Origins of Intelligence in Children*. New York: International Universities Press.

Piaget, J. (1946/1951). *Play, Dreams and Imitation in Childhood*. New York: Norton.

Piaget, J. (1964/1967). *Six Psychological Studies*. New York: Vintage Books.

Piaget, J. (1968). *On the Development of Memory and Identity*. Worcester, MA: Clark University Press.

Piaget, J. (1970). *Genetic Epistemology*. New York: Columbia University Press.

Piaget, J. (1995). *Sociological Studies*. London: Routledge.

Piaget, J., Henriques, G., & Ascher, E. (1992). *Morphisms and Categories: Comparing and Transforming*. Hillsdale, NJ: Erlbaum.

Piaget, J., & Inhelder, B. (1968/1973). *Memory and Inelligence*. London: Routledge & Kegan Paul.

Pine, K. J., & Nash, A. (2002). Dear Santa: The effects of television advertising on young children. *International Journal of Behavioral Development*, *26*, 529–539.

Piotrowski, C. (1997). Rules of everyday family life: The development of social rules in mother–child and sibling relations. *International Journal of Behavioral Development*, *21*, 571–580.

Pitcher, E. G. & Schultz, L. H. (1983). *Boys and Girls at Play: The Development of Sex Roles*. Santa Barbara, CA: ABC-CLIO, LLC.

Plotnick, A. B., Payne, P. A., & O'Grady, D. J. (1991). Correlates of hypnotizability in children: Absorption, vividness or imagery, fantasy play, and social desirability. *American Journal of Clinical Hypnosis*, *34*, 51–58.

Polakowski, M. (1994). Linking self- and social control with deviance: Illuminating the structure underlying a general theory of crime and its relation to deviant activity. *Journal of Quantitative Criminology*, *10*, 41–78.

Pölkki, T. P., Pietilä, A.-M., & Vehviläinen-Julkunen, K. (2003). Hospitalized children's descriptions of their experiences with postsurgical pain relieving methods. *International Journal of Nursing Studies*, *40*, 33–44.

Pollard, A. (1985). *The Social World of the Primary School*. London: Holt, Rinehart & Winston

Pomerantz, A. (1984). Agreeing and disagreeing with assessments: Some features of preferred/dispreferred turn shapes. In J. M. Atkinson & J. Heritage (Eds.), *Structures of Social Action: Studies in Conversation Analysis* (pp. 57–101). Cambridge, UK: Cambridge University Press.

Pontecorvo, C., & Fasulo, A. (1997). Learning to argue in family shared discourse: The reconstruction of past events. In L. B. Resnick, R. Saljo, C. Pontecorvo, & B. Burge (Eds.), *Discourse, Tools, and Reasoning: Essays on Situated Cognition* (pp. 406–439). Berlin: Springer.

Pontecorvo, C., Fasulo, A., & Sterponi, L. (2001). Mutual apprentices: The making of parenthood and childhood in family dinner conversations. *Human Development*, *44*, 340–361.

Pool, D. L., Shweder, R. A., & Much, N. C. (1983). Culture as a cognitive system: Differentiated rule understanding in children and other savages. In E. T. Higgins, D. N. Ruble, & W. W. Hartup (Eds.), *Social Cognition and Social Development: A Sociocultural Perspective* (pp. 193–213). New York: Cambridge University Press.

Posada, G., Carbonell, O. A., Alzate, C., & Plata, S. J. (2004). Through Colombian lenses: Ethnographic and conventional analyses of maternal care and their association with secure base behavior. *Developmental Psychology, 40*, 508–518.

Powers, S. W. (1999). Empirically-supported treatments in pediatric psychology: Procedure-related pain. *Journal of Pediatric Psychology, 24*, 131–145.

Prasada, S. (2000). Acquiring generic knowledge. *Trends in Cognitive Sciences, 4*, 66–72.

Pratt, C. (1978). *The Socialization of Crying*. Unpublished doctoral dissertation, Oxford University.

Pratt, T. C., Turner, M. G., & Piquero, A. R. (2004). Parental socialization and community context: A longitudinal analysis of the structural sources of low self control. *Journal of Research in Crime and Delinquency, 41*, 219–243.

Prescott, E. (1987). The environment as organizer of intent in child-care settings. In C. S. Weinstein & T. G. David (Eds.), *Spaces for Children: The Built Environment and Child Development* (pp. 73–88). New York: Plenum.

Prince, G. (1980). Introduction to the study of the narratee. In J. P. Tompkins (Ed.), *Reader-Response Criticism: From Formalism to Post-Structuralism* (pp. 7–25). Baltimore, MD: Johns Hopkins University Press.

Prinstein, M. J., La Greca, A. M., Vernberg, E. M., & Silverman, W. K. (1996). Children's coping assistance: How parents, teachers, and friends help children cope after a natural disaster. *Journal of Clinical Child Psychology, 25*, 463–475.

Pronin, E., & Ross, L. (2006). Temporal differences in trait self-ascription: When the self is seen as an other. *Journal of Personality and Social Psychology, 90*, 197–209.

Prusank, D. T. (1993). Contextualizing social control: An ethnomethodological analysis of parental accounts of discipline interactions. In N. Coupland & J. F. Nussbaum (Eds.), *Discourse and Lifespan Identity* (pp. 132–153). Newbury Park, CA: Sage.

Puhl, R. M., & Schwartz, M. B. (2003). If you are good you can have a cookie: How memories of childhood food rules link to adult eating behaviors. *Eating Behaviors, 4*, 283–293.

Putney, L. G., Green, J., Dixon, C., Duran, R., & Yeager, B. (2000). Consequential progressions: Exploring collective–individual development in a bilingual classroom. In C. D. Lee & P. Smagorinsky (Eds.), *Vygotskian Perspectives on Literacy Research: Constructing Meaning Through Collaborative Inquiry* (pp. 86–126). Cambridge, UK: Cambridge University Press.

Przetacznik-Gierowska, M., & Ligeza, M. (1990). Cognitive and interpersonal functions of children's questions. In G. Conti-Ramsden & C. E. Snow (Eds.), *Children's Language*, Vol. 7 (pp. 69–101). Hillsdale, NJ: Erlbaum.

Przetacznik-Gierowska, M. (1995). Functions of resultative coordinate constructions in early language and logical development: Insights form children's acquisition of Polish. In K. E. Nelson & Z. Reger (Eds.), *Children's Language*, Vol. 8 (pp. 203–223). Hillsdale, NJ: Erlbaum.

Pylyshyn, Z. (1984). *Computation and Cognition: Towards a Foundation for Cognitive Science*. Cambridge, MA: MIT Press.

Quay, S. (2008). Dinner conversations with a trilingual two-year-old: Language socialization in a multilingual context. *First Language, 28*, 5–33.

Radford, A. (1990). *Syntactic Theory and the Acquisition of English Syntax: The Nature of Early Child Grammars of English*. Oxford, UK: Blackwell.

Radke-Yarrow, M., Belmont, B., Nottelmann, E., & Bottomly, L. (1990). Young children's self conceptions: Origins in the natural discourse of depressed and normal mothers and their children. In D. Chicchetti & M. Beeghly (Eds.), *The Self in Transition: Infancy to Childhood* (pp. 345–361). Chicago: University of Chicago Press.

Raeff, C. (2003). Patterns of culturally meaningful activity: Linking parents' ideas and parent–child interaction. In C. Raeff & J. B. Benson (Eds.), *Social and Cognitive Development in the Context of Individual, Social, and Cultural Processes* (pp. 35–53). London: Routledge.

Rakoczy, H., Warneken, F., & Tomasello, M. (2008). The sources of normativity: Young children's awareness of the normative structure of games. *Developmental Psychology, 44*, 875–881.

Rand, H. Y. (1976). Multi-age groups: Let them reason together. *Day Care and Early Education, 3/4*, 24–27.

Rastall, P. (2003). What do we mean by we? *English Today, 19*, 50–53.

Rawlins, W. K. (1992). *Friendship Matters: Communication, Dialectics, and the Life Course*. New York: Aldine de Gruyter.

Rawls, J. (1971). *A Theory of Justice*. Cambridge, MA: Harvard University Press.

Read, B. K., & Cherry, L. J. (1978). Preschool children's production of directive forms. *Discourse Processes, 1*, 233–245.

Reeder, K. (1980). The emergence of illocutionary skills. *Journal of Child Language, 7*, 13–28.

Reeder, K. (1985). Classification of children's speech acts: A consumer's guide. *Journal of Pragmatics, 7*, 679–694.

Reeder, K. (1996). Children's attributions of speakers' pragmatic intentions. In M. Aldridge (Ed.), *Child Language* (pp. 149–164). Clevedon, UK: Multilingual Matters.

Reese, E., Haden, C. A., & Fivush, R. (1993). Mother-child conversations about the past: Relationships of style and memory over time. *Cognitive Development, 8*, 403–430.

Reese, E., Haden, C. A., & Fivush, R. (1996). Mothers, fathers, daughters, sons: Gender differences in autobiographical reminiscing. *Research on Language and Social Interaction, 29*, 27–56.

Reichman, R. (1990). Communication and mutual engagement. *Advances in Discourse Processes*, Vol. 38 (pp. 23–48). Norwood, NJ: Ablex.

Reid, J.-A. (1999). Little women/little men: Gender, violence and emobodiment in an early childhood classroom. In B. Kamler (Ed.), *Constructing Gender and Difference: Critical Research Perspectives on Early Childhood* (pp. 167–190). Cresskill, NJ: Hampton Press.

Reid, J. B. (1986). Social interactional patterns in families of abused and nonabused children. In C. Zahn-Waxler, R. Iannotti, & M. Cummings (Eds.), *Altruism and Aggression: Biological and Social Origins* (pp. 238–257). New York: Cambridge University Press.

Reilly, J. S. (1986). The acquisition of temporals and conditionals. In E. C. Traugott, A. ter Meulen, J. S. Reilly, & C. A. Ferguson (Eds.), *On Conditionals* (pp. 309–331). Cambridge, UK: Cambridge University Press.

Repacholi, B. M., & Gopnik, A. (1997). Early reasoning about desires: Evidence from 14- and 18- month-olds. *Developmental Psychology*, *33*, 12–21.

Reynolds, P. C. (1976). Squares and oblongs. In J. S. Bruner, A. Jolly, & K. Sylva (Eds.), *Play: Its Role in Development and Evolution* (pp. 621–635). New York: Basic Books.

Rheingold, H., & Cook, K. (1975). The contents of boys' and girls' rooms as an index of parents' behavior. *Child Development*, *46*, 459–463.

Ribbens, J. (1994). *Mothers and their Children: A Feminist Sociology of Childrearing*. London: Sage.

Riksen-Walraven, J. M., Meij, H. Th., van Roozendaal, J., & Koks, J., (1996). Mastery motivation in toddlers as related to quality of attachment. In D. J. Messer (Ed.), *Mastery Motivation in Early Childhood: Development, Measurement and Social Processes* (pp. 189–204). Routledge: New York.

Ritchie, K. L. (1999). Maternal behaviors and cognitions during discipline episodes: A comparison of power bouts and single acts of noncompliance. *Developmental Psychology*, *35*, 580–589.

Rizzo, T. A. (1989). *Friendship Development Among Children in School*. Norwood, NJ: Ablex.

Robin, A., Schneider, M., & Dolnick, M. (1976). The turtle technique: An extended case study of self-control in the classroom *Psychology in the Schools*, *13*, 449–453.

Robinson, W. P., & Rackstraw, S. J. (1972a). *A Question of Answers. Vol. I*. London: Routledge & Kegan Paul.

Robinson, W. P. & Rackstraw, S. J. (1972b). *A Question of Answers. Vol. II*. London: Routledge & Kegan Paul.

Roese, N. J. (1997). Counterfactual thinking. *Psychological Bulletin*, *121*, 133–148.

Rook, D. W. (1987). The buying impulse. *Journal of Consumer Research*, *14*, 189–199.

Root-Bernstein, M., & Root-Bernstein, R. (2006). Imaginary world play in childhood and maturity and its impact on adult creativity. *Creativity Research Journal*, *18*, 405–425.

Rosenbaum, M., & Ronen, T. (1992, January). *How did Israeli children and their parents cope with the threat of daily attack by Scud missiles during the Gulf War?* Paper presented at the Ministry of Education Conference on stress reaction of children in the Gulf War, Ramat Gan, Israel.

Ross, H. S. (1996). Negotiating principles of entitlement in sibling property disputes. *Developmental Psychology*, *32*, 90–101.

Ross, H. S., Filyor, R. E., Lollis, S. P., Perlman, M., & Marin, J. L. (1994). Administering justice in the family. *Journal of Family Psychology*, *8*, 254–237.

Ross, L. (1977). The intuitive psychologist and his shortcomings: Distortions in the attribution process. In L. Berkowitz (Ed.), *Advances in Experimental Social Psychology*, Vol. 10 (pp. 174–221). New York: Academic Press.

Ross, L., Greene, D., & House, P. (1977). The false consensus phenomenon: An attributional bias in self-perception and social-perception processes. *Journal of Experimental Social Psychology*, *13*, 279–301.

Ross, M. (1989). Relation of implicit theories to the construction of personal histories. *Psychological Review*, *96*, 341–357.

Rothbaum, F., Morelli, G., Pott, M., & Liu-Constant, Y. (2000). Immigrant-Chinese and Euro-American parents' physical closeness with young children: Themes of family relationships. *Journal of Family Psychology*, *14*, 334–348.

Rothbaum, F., Weisz, J. R., & Snyder, S. S. (1982). Changing the world and changing the self: A two-process model of perceived control. *Journal of Personality and Social Psychology*, *42*, 5–37.

Rothman, A. J., Salovey, P., Antone, C., Keough, K., & Martin, C. (1993). The influence of message framing on intentions to perform health behaviors. *Journal of Experimental Social Psychology*, *29*, 408–433.

Rout, U., Sixsmith, J., & Moore, M. (1996). Asian family life. In M. Moore, J. Sixsmith, & K. Knowles (Eds.), *Children's Reflections on Family Life* (pp. 100–114). London: Falmer Press.

Rozin, P., Riklis, J., & Margolis, L. (2004). Mutual exposure or close peer relationships do not seem to foster increased similarity in food, music or television program preferences. *Appetite*, *42*, 41–48.

Rubin, J. Z., & Brown, B. R. (1975). *The Social Psychology of Bargaining and Negotiation*. New York: Academic Press.

Rubin, J. Z., & Lewicki, R. J. (1973). A three factor experimental analysis of promises and threats. *Journal of Applied Social Psychology*, *3*, 240–257.

Rubin, L. C. (2007). Introduction: Look, up in the sky! An introduction to the use of superheroes in psychotherapy. In L. C. Rubin (Ed.), *Using Superheroes in Counseling and Play Therapy* (pp. 3–21). New York: Springer.

Rubin, L. C., & Livesay, H. (2006). Look, up in the sky! Using superheroes in play therapy. *International Journal of Play Therapy*, *15*, 117–133.

Rubin, Z. (1980). *Children's Friendships*. Cambridge, MA: Harvard University Press.

Ruby, P. & Decety, J. (2001). Effect of subjective perspective taking during simulation of action: A PET investigation of agency. *Nature Neuroscience*, *4*, 546–550.

Ruby, P., & Decety, J. (2003). What do you believe versus what you think they believe: A neuroimaging study of conceptual perspective-taking. *European Journal of Neursoscience*, *17*, 2475–2480.

Ruby, P., & Decety, J. (2004). How would *you* feel versus how do you think *she* would feel? A neuroimaging study of perspective-taking with social emotions. *Journal of Cognitive Neuroscience*, *16*, 988–999.

Ruble, D. N., & Frey, K. S. (1991). Changing patterns of comparative behavior as skills are acquired: A functional model of self evaluation. In J. Suls & T. Ashby (Eds.), *Social Comparison: Contemporary Theory and Research* (pp. 79–113). Hillsdale, NJ: Erlbaum.

Rumbaugh, D. M., & Gill, T. V. (1977). Language and language-type communication: Studies with a chimpanzee. In M. Lewis & L. A. Rosenblum (Eds.), *Interaction, Conversation and the Development of Language* (pp. 115–132). New York: Wiley.

Rumelhart, D. E. (1989). Toward a microstructural account of human reasoning. In S. Vosniadou & A. Ortony (Eds.), *Similarity and Analogical Reasoning* (pp. 298–312). New York: Cambridge University Press.

Russ, S. W, Robins, A. L., & Christiano, B. A. (1999). Pretend play: Longitudinal prediction of creativity and affect in fantasy in children. *Creativity Research Journal*, *12*, 129–141.

Saarni, C. (1985). Indirect processes in affect socialization. In M. Lewis & C. Saarni (Eds.), *The Socialization of Emotions* (pp. 187–209). New York: Plenum Press.

Sachs, J. (1983). Talking about the there and then: The emergence of displaced reference in parent–child discourse. In K. E. Nelson (Ed.), *Children's Language*, Vol. 4 (pp. 1–28). Hillsdale, NJ: Erlbaum.

Sachs, J. (1984). Children's play and communicative development. In R. L. Schiefelbusch & J. Pickar (Eds.), *The Acquisition of Communicative Competence* (pp. 110–140). Baltimore, MD: University Park Press.

Sachs, J. (1987). Preschool boys' and girls' language use in pretend play. In S. Philips, S. Steele, & C. Tanz (Eds.), *Language, Gender and Sex in Comparative Perspective* (pp. 178–188). Cambridge, UK: Cambridge University Press.

Sadler, T. D. (2004). Moral sensitivity and its contribution to the resolution of socio-scientific issues. *Journal of Moral Education*, *33*, 339–358.

Salo, I., & Svenson, O. (2001). Constructive psychological processes before and after a real-life decision. In C. M. Allwood & M. Selart (Eds.), *Decision Making: Social and Creative Dimensions* (pp. 137–151). Dordrecht, The Netherlands: Kluwer Academic.

Saltz, E., Dixon, D., & Johnson, J. (1977). Training disadvantaged preschoolers on various fantasy activities: Effects on cognitive functioning and impulse control. *Child Development*, *48*, 367–380.

Santioso, R., Kunda, Z. and Fong, G. (1990). Motivated recruitment of autobiographical memories. *Journal of Personality and Social Psychology*, *57*, 229–241.

Saudino, K. J., Wertz, A. E., Gagne, J. R., & Chawla, S. (2004). Night and day: Are siblings as different in temperament as parents say they are. *Journal of Personality and Social Psychology*, *87*, 698–706.

Saussure, F. de (1916/1983) *Course in General Linguistics* (Translated by Roy Harris). London: Duckworth.

Savić, S. (1980). *How Twins Learn to Talk: A Study of the Speech Development of Twins from 1–3*. London: Academic Press.

Schachter, F. F. (1979). *Everyday Mother Talk to Toddlers: Early Interventions*. New York: Academic Press.

Schaffer, H. R. (1991). The mutuality of parental control in early childhood. In M. Lewis & S. Feinman (Eds.), *Social Influences and Socialization in Infancy* (pp.165–184). New York: Plenum Press.

Schank, R. (1982). *Dynamic Memory: A Theory of Learning in Computers and People*. London: Cambridge University Press.

Schank, R. (1999). *Dynamic Memory Revisited*. Cambridge, UK: Cambridge University Press.

Schank, R., & Abelson, R. P. (1977). *Scripts, Plans, Goals and Understanding*. Hillsdale, NJ: Erlbaum.

Schank, R., & Wilensky, R. (1978) A goal-directed production system for story understanding. In D. A. Waterman & F. Hayes-Roth (Eds.), *Pattern-Directed Inference Systems* (pp. 415–430). Orlando, FL: Academic Press.

Scheff, T. (1967). Toward a sociological model of consensus. *American Sociological Review*, 32, 32–46.

Schelling, T. C. (1984). Self-command in practice, in policy, and in a theory of rational choice. *American Economic Review*, *74*, 1–11.

Schieffelin, B. B. (1979). Getting it together: An ethnographic approach to the study of the development of communicative competence. In E. Ochs & B. S. Schieffelin (Eds.), *Developmental Pragmatics* (pp. 1–20). New York: Academic Press.

Schieffelin, B. B. (1981). A developmental study of pragmatic appropriateness of word order and case marking in Kaluli. In W. Deutsch (Ed.), *The Child's construction of Language* (pp. 105–120). New York: Academic Press.

Schieffelin, B. B. (1983). Looking and talking: The functions of gaze direction in the conversations of a young child and the mother. In E. Ochs & B. B. Schieffelin (Eds.), *Acquiring Conversational Competence* (pp. 50–65). London: Routledge & Kegan Paul.

Schieffelin B. B., & Eisenberg, A. R. (1984). Cultural variation in children's conversations. R. L. Schiefelbusch & J. Pickar (Eds.), *The Acquisition of Communicative Competence* (pp. 378–420). Baltimore, MD: University Park Press.

Schieffelin, B. B. (1990). *The Give and Take of Everyday Life: Language Socialization of Kaluli Children*. New York: Cambridge University Press.

Schlyter, S. (2003). Development of verb morphology and finiteness in children and adults acquiring French. In C. Dimroth & M. Starren (Eds.), *Information Structure and the Dynamics of Language Acquisition* (pp. 15–44). Amsterdam: John Benjamins.

Schlyter, S. (2005). Adverbs and functional categories in L1 and L2 acquisition of French. In J.-M. Dewaele (Ed.), *Focus on French as a Foreign Language: Multidisciplinary Approaches* (pp. 36–62). Toronto: Multilingual Matters.

Schneider, M. R. (1974). Turtle technique in the classroom. *Teaching Exceptional Children*, *7*, 21–24.

Schneider, T. R., Salovey, P., Apanovitch, A. M., Pizarro, J., McCarthy, D., Zullo, J., et al. (2001). The effects of message framing and ethnic targeting on mammography use among low-income women. *Health Psychology*, *20*, 256–266.

Scholnick, E. K. (2002). Language, literacy, and thought: Forming a partnership. In E. Amsel & J. P. Byrnes (Eds.), *Language, Literacy, and Cognitive Development: The Development and Consequences of Symbolic Communication* (pp. 3–23). Mahwah, NJ: Erlbaum.

Scholnick, E. K., & Friedman, S. L. (1987). The planning construct in the psychological literature. In S. L. Friedman, E. K. Scholnick, & R. R. Cocking (Eds.), *Blueprints for Thinking: The Role of Planning in Cognitive Development* (pp. 3–38). Cambridge, UK: Cambridge University Press.

Scholnick, E. K., & Wing, C. S. (1992). Speaking deductively: Using conversation to trace the origins of conditional thought in children. *Merrill-Palmer Quarterly*, *38*, 1–20.

Schönenberger, M. (2001). *Embedding V-to-C in Child Grammar: The Acquisition of Verb Placement in Swiss German*. Dordrecht, Holland: Kluwer Academic.

Schrader, C. T. (1991). Symbolic play: A source of meaningful engagements with writing and reading. In J. F. Christie (Ed.), *Play and Early Literacy Development* (pp. 190–213). Albany, NY: SUNY Press.

Schunk, D. (1999). Social–self interaction and achievement behavior. *Educational Psychologist*, *34*, 219–227.

Schultz, J. (1979) It's not whether you win or lose: It's how you play the game. In In O. K. Garnica & M. L. King (Eds.), *Language, Children and Society* (pp. 271–292). Oxford: Pergamon Press.

Schultz, L. H., & Selman, R. L. (1989). Bridging the gap between interpersonal thought and action in early adolescence: The role of psychodynamic processes. *Development and Psychopathology*, *1*, 133–152.

Schutze, Y, Kreppner, K., & Paulsen, S. (1986). The social construction of the sibling relationship. In J. Cook-Gumperz, W. A. Corsaro, & J. Streeck (Eds.), *Children's Worlds and Children's Language* (pp. 129–145). Berlin: Mouton de Gruyter.

Schwartz, B. (2004). *The Paradox of Choice: Why More is Less*. New York: HarperCollins.

Schwartz, U. V. (1991). *Young Children's Dyadic Pretend Play: A Communication Analysis of Plot Structure and Plot Generative Strategies*. Amsterdam: John Benjamins.

Schwartzman, H. B. (1978). *Transformations: The Anthropology of Children's Play*. New York: Plenum.

Scollon, R. (1979). A real early stage: An unzippered condensation of a dissertation on child language. In E. Ochs & B. S. Schieffelin (Eds.), *Developmental Pragmatics* (pp. 215–227). New York: Academic Press.

Scollon, R., & Scollon, S. B. K. (1981). *Narrative, Literacy and Face in Interethnic Communication*. Norwood, NJ: Ablex.

Scorce, J. F., Emde, R. N., Campos, J., & Klinnert, M. (1985). Maternal emotional signaling: Its effect on the Visual Cliff Behavior of 1-Year-Olds. *Developmental Psychology*, *21*, 195–200.

Sealey, A. (1997). "Who do you think you are?" Four children's sociolinguistic strategies in the regulation of self. In L. Thompson (Ed.), *Children Talking: The Development of Pragmatic Competence* (pp. 22–35). Clevedon, UK: Multilingual Matters.

Sealey, A. (2000). *Childly Language: Children, Language and the Social World*. Harlow, UK: Pearson Education.

Searle, J. R. (1975) A taxonomy of illocutionary acts. In K. Gunderson (Ed.), *Language, Mind, and Knowledge* (pp. 344–369). Minneapolis: University of Minnesota Press.

Sears, R. R., Maccoby, E. E., & Levin, H. (1957). *Patterns of Child Rearing*. Stanford, CA: Stanford University Press.

Sears, R. R., Rau, L. & Alpert, R. (1965). *Identification and Child Rearing*. Stanford, CA: Stanford University Press.

Secord, Paul F., & Peevers, B. H. (1974). The development and attribution of person concepts.In T. Mischel (Ed.), *Understanding other persons* (pp. 117–142). Oxford, U.K.: Blackwell.

Segal, M., & Adcock, D. (1981). *Just Pretending: Ways to Help Children Grow through Imaginative Play*. Englewood Cliffs, NJ: Prentice-Hall.

Seier, W. L. (1994). The effects of a fantasy context, an obligation schema, and a rationale on children's conditional reasoning. *British Journal of Developmental Psychology*, *12*, 507–522.

Selman, R. D. (1979). *Assessing Interpersonal Understanding: An Interview and Scoring Manual in Five Parts Constructed by the Harvard–Judge Baker Social Reasoning Project*. Judge Baker Social Reasoning Project, Harvard University.

Selman, R. L. (1980). *The Growth of Interpersonal Understanding: Developmental and Clinical Analysis*. New York: Academic Press.

Selman, R. L. (1985). The use of interpersonal negotiation strategies and communicative competencies: A clinical–developmental exploration in a pair of troubled early adolescents. In R. A. Hinde, A.-N. Perret-Clemont, & J. Stevenson-Hinde (Eds.), *Social Relationships and Cognitive Development* (pp. 208–232). Oxford, UK: Clarendon Press.

Selman, R. L., & Damon, W. (1975). The necessity (but insufficiency) of social perspective taking for conceptions of justice at three early levels. In D. J. DePalma & J. M. Foley (Eds.), *Moral Development: Current Theory and Research* (pp. 57–74). Hillsdale, NJ: Erlbaum.

Selman, R. L., Levin, D. R., & Brion-Meisels, S. (1982). Troubled children's use of self-reflection. In F. C. Serafica (Ed.), *Social-Cognitive Development in Context* (pp. 62–99). New York: Guilford Press.

Semans, M. P., & Fish, L. S. (2000). Dissecting life with a Jewish scalpel: A qualitative analysis of Jewish-centered family life. *Family Process*, *39*, 121–139.

Sen, A. K. (1977). Rational fools: A critique of the behavioral functions of economic theory. *Journal of Philosophy and Public Affairs*, *6*, 317–344.

Sfard, A. (2008). *Thinking as Communicating: Human Development, the Growth of Discourses, and Mathematizing*. New York: Cambridge University Press.

Shafrir, U. (1999). Representational competence. In I. E. Sigel (Ed.), *Development of Mental Representations: Theories and Applications* (pp. 371–389). Mahwah, NJ: Erlbaum.

Shatz, M. (1974). The comprehension of indirect directives: Can two-year-olds shut the door? Paper delivered at the Linguistic Society of America, summer meeting.

Shatz, M. (1994). *A Toddler's Life: Becoming a Person*. New York: Oxford University Press.

Shatz, M., & Gelman, R. (1973). The development of communication skills: Modifications in the speech of young children as a function of listener. *Monographs of the Society for Research In Child Development*, *38* (Serial #152).

Shatz. M., Wellman, H., & Silber, S. (1983) The acquisition of mental verbs: A systematic investigation of the first reference to mental state. *Cognition*, *14*, 301–321.

Sheldon, A. (1990). Pickle fights: Gendered talk in preschool disputes. *Discourse Processes*, *13*, 5–13.

Sheldon, A. (1992). Conflict talk: Sociolinguistic challenges to self-assertion and how young girls meet them. *Merrill-Palmer Quarterly*, *38*, 95–117.

Sheldon, A. (1997). Talking power: Girls, gender enculturation and discourse. In R. Wodak (Ed.), *Gender and Discourse* (pp. 225–244). London: Sage.

Shennum, W. A., & Bugental, D. B. (1982). The development of control over affective expression in nonverbal behavior. In R. S. Feldman (Ed.), *Development of Nonverbal Behavior in Children* (pp. 101–121). New York: Springer-Verlag.

Sherman, A. (1997). Five-year-olds' perceptions of why we go to school. *Children and Society*, *11*, 117–127.

Sherman S. J., Skov, R. B., Hervitz, E. F., & Stock, C. B. (1981). The effects of explaining hypothetical future events: From possibility to probability to actuality and beyond. *Journal of Experimental Social Psychology*, *17*, 142–158.

Shields, M. M. (1978). Some communicational skills of young children – a study of dialogue in the nursery school. In R. N. Campbell & P. T. Smith (Eds.), *Recent Advances in the Psychology of Language: Language Development and Mother–Child Interaction* (pp. 313–335). New York: Plenum.

Shields, M. M. (1978). The child as psychologist: Construing the social world. In A. Lock (Ed.), *Action, Gesture and Symbol: The Emergence of Language* (pp. 529–552). London: Academic Press.

Shields, M. M. (1979). Dialogue, monologue and egocentric speech by children in nursery schools. In O. K. Garnica & M. L. King (Eds.), *Language, Children and Society* (pp. 249–270). Oxford, UK: Pergamon Press.

Shields, M. M., & Duveen, G. M. (1986). The young child's image of the person and the social world: Some aspects of the child's representation of persons. In J. Cook-Gumperz, W. A. Corsaro, & J. Streeck (Eds.), *Children's Worlds and Children's Language* (pp. 173–203). Berlin: Mouton de Gruyter.

Shimanoff, S. B. (1980). *Communication Rules: Theory and Research*. Beverly Hill, CA: Sage.

Shimizu, H. (2001). Beyond individualism and sociocentrism: An ontological analysis of the opposing elements in personal experiences of Japanese adolescents. In H. Shimizu & R. A. LeVine (Eds.), *Japanese Frames of Mind: Cultural Perspectives on Human Development* (pp. 205–227). Cambridge, UK: Cambridge University Press.

Shure, M. B. (1982). Interpersonal problem solving: A cog in the wheel. In F. C. Serafica (Ed.), *Social-Cognitive Development in Context* (pp. 133–166). New York: Guilford Press.

Shure, M. B. (1985). Interpersonal problem-solving: A cognitive approach to behaviour. In R. A. Hinde, A.-N. Perret-Clemont, & J. Stevenson-Hinde (Eds.), *Social Relationships and Cognitive Development* (pp. 191–207). Oxford, UK: Clarendon Press.

Shure, M. B., & Spivack, G. (1978). *Problem-solving Techniques in Child Rearing*. San Francisco: Jossey-Bass.

Shuy, R. W., & Griffin, P. (1981). Rules and roles: The "communication game" and speaker–listener processes. In W. P. Dickson (Ed.), *Children's Oral Communication Skills* (pp. 271–286). New York: Academic Press.

Shweder, R. A. (1982). Beyond self-constructed knowledge: The study of culture and morality. *Merrill-Palmer Quarterly*, *28*, 41–69.

Shweder, R. A., & Much, N. C. (1987) Determinations of meaning: Discourse and moral socialization. In W. M. Kurtines & J. L. Gewirtz (Eds.), *Moral Development Through Social Interaction* (pp. 197–244). Hillsdale, NJ: Erlbaum.

Shweder, R. A., Turiel, E., & Much, N. C. (1981). The moral intuitions of the child. In J. H. Flavell & L. Ross (Eds.), *Social Cognitive Development: Frontiers and Possible Futures* (pp. 288–305). Cambridge, UK: Cambridge University Press.

Sigel, I. E. (1970). The distancing hypothesis: A causal hypothesis for the acquisition of representational thought. In M. R. Jones (Ed.), *Miami Symposium on the Prediction of Behavior, 1968: Effects of Early Experience* (pp. 99–118). Coral Gables, FL: University of Miami Press.

Sigel, I. E. (1992). The belief–behavior connection: A resolvable dilemma? In I. E. Sigel, A. V. McGillicuddy-DeLisi, & J. J. Goodnow (Eds.), *Parental Belief Systems: The Psychological Consequences for Children* (pp. 433–456). Hillsdale, NJ: Erlbaum.

Sigel, E. I., & Cocking, R. R. (1977). Cognition and communication: A dialectic paradigm for development. In M. Lewis & L. A. Rosenblum (Eds.), *Interaction, Conversation and the Development of Language* (pp. 207–226). New York: Wiley.

Sigel, I. E., Stinson, E. T., & Flaugher, J. (1991). Socialization of representational competence in the family: The distancing paradigm. In L. Okagaki & R. J. Sternberg (Eds.), *Directors of Developmental Influences on the Development of Children's Thinking* (pp. 121–141). Hillsdale, NJ: Erlbaum.

Sigel, I. E., Stinson, E. T., Kim, M.-I. (1993). Socialization of cognition: The distancing model. In R. H. Wozniak & K. W. Fischer (Eds.), *Development in Context: Acting and Thinking in Specific Environments* (pp. 211–224). Hillsdale, NJ: Erlbaum.

Silverman, I. W. (2003). Gender differences in delay of gratification: A meta-analysis. *Sex Roles*, *45*, 451–464.

Silverstein, M. (1976). Shifters, linguistic categories, and cultural description. In K. H. Basso & H. A. Selby (Eds.), *Meaning in Anthropology* (pp. 11–56). Albuquerque, NM: University of New Mexico Press.

Simons, H. D., & Murphy, S. (1986). Spoken language strategies and reading acquisition. In J. Cook-Gumperz (Ed.), *The Social Construction of Literacy* (pp. 185–206). Cambridge, UK: Cambridge University Press.

Sinclair, J. McH., & Coulthard, R. M. (1975). *Towards an Analysis of Discourse: The English Used by Teachers and Pupils*. London: Oxford University Press.

Singer, D. (1993). *Playing for Their Lives: Helping Troubled Children through Play Therapy*. New York: The Free Press.

Singer, J. L. (1973). *The Child's World of Make-Believe*. New York: Academic Press.

Sixsmith, J., & Knowles, J. (1996). Home life in the "traditional family." In M. Moore, J. Sixsmith, & K. Knowles (Eds.), *Children's Reflections on Family Life* (pp. 12–28). London: Falmer Press.

Skinner, E. A., Edge, K., Alman, J., & Sherwood, H. (2003). Searching for the structure of coping: A review and critique of category systems for classifying ways of coping. *Psychological Bulletin*, *129*, 216–269.

Skitka, L. J., Bauman, C. W., & Mullen, E. (2008). Morality and justice: An expanded theoretical perspective and review. In K. A. Hedgvedt & J. Clay-Warner (Eds.), *Advances in Group Processes*, Vol. 25 (pp. 1–27). Bingley, UK: Emerald Group Publishing.

Slade, A. (1987). A longitudinal study of maternal involvement and symbolic play during the toddler period. *Child Development*, *58*, 367–375.

Slama-Cazacu, T. (1977). *Dialogue in Children*. The Hague: Mouton.

Slep, A. M. S., & O'Leary, S. G. (1998). The effects of maternal attributions on parenting: An experimental analysis. *Journal of Family Psychology*, *12*, 234–243.

Sluckin, A. (1981). *Growing Up in the Playground: The Social Development of Children*. London: Routledge & Kegan Paul.

Sluzki, C. E. (1992). A blueprint for narrative changes in therapy. *Family Process*, *31*, 217–230.

Smetana, J. (1993). Understanding of social rules. In M. Bennett (Ed.), *The Development of Social Cognition: The Child as Psychologist* (pp. 111–141). New York: Guilford.

Smetana, J., Kochanska, G., & Chuang, S. (2000). Mothers' conceptions of everyday rules for young toddlers: A longitudinal investigation. *Merrill-Palmer Quarterly*, *46*, 391–416.

Smetana, J. G. (2006). Social-cognitive domain theory: consistencies and variations in children's moral and social judgments. In M. Killen & J. G. Smetana (Eds.), *Handbook of Moral Development* (pp. 119–153). Mahwah, NJ: Erlbaum.

Smith, D. E., & Mosby, G. (2003). Jamaican child-rearing practices: The role of corporal punishment. *Adolescence*, *38*, 369–381.

Smith, J. (1999). Anticipating future life goals and managing personal development. In J. Brandstädter & R. M. Lerner (Eds.), *Action and Self Development: Theory and Research through the Life Span* (pp. 223–255). Thousand Oaks, CA: Sage.

Smith, L. B. (1987). From global similarities to kinds of similarities: The construction of dimensions in development. In S. Vosniadou & A. Ortony (Eds.), *Similarity and Analogical Reasoning* (pp. 146–178). Cambridge, UK: Cambridge University Press.

Smith, P. K. (1977). Social and fantasy play in young children. In B. Tizard & D. Harvey (Eds.), *Biology of Play* (pp. 123–145). London: Heinemann Medical Publications.

Smith, P. K. & Connolly, K. J. (1977). Social and aggressive behavior in preschool children as a factor of crowding, *Social Science Information*, *16*, 601–620.

Smyke, A. T., Koga, S. F., Johnson, E. E., Fox, N. A., Marshall, P. J., Nelson, C. A., & Zeanah, C. H. (2007). The caregiving context in institution-reared and family-reared infants and toddlers in Romania. *Journal of Child Psychology and Psychiatry*, *48*, 210–218.

Snow, C. E. (1972). Mothers' speech to children learning language. *Child Development*, *43*, 549–565.

Snow, C. E. (1977). Development of conversation between mothers and babies. *Journal of Child Language*, *4*, 1–22.

Snow, C. E. (1983). Saying it again: the role of expanded and deferred imitations in language acquisition. In K. E. Nelson (Ed.), *Children's Language*, Vol. 4 (pp. 29–58). Hillsdale, NJ: Erlbaum.

Snow, C. E. (1984). Parent–child interaction and the development of communicative ability. In R. L. Schiefelbusch & J. Pickar (Eds.), *The Acquisition of Communicative Competence* (pp. 72–107). Baltimore, MD: University Park Press.

Snow, C. E. (1990). Building memories: The ontogeny of autobiography. In D. Chicchetti & M. Beeghly (Eds.), *The Self in Transition: Infancy to Childhood* (pp. 213–242). Chicago: University of Chicago Press.

Snow, C. E., de Blauw, A., & van Roosmalen, G. (1978). Talking and playing with babies: The role of ideologies of child rearing. In M. Bullowa (Ed.), *Before Speech: The Beginning of Interpersonal Communication* (pp. 269–288). London: Cambridge University Press.

Snow, C. E., Perlmann, R. Y., Gleason, J. B., & Hooshyar, N. (1990). Developmental perspectives on politeness: Sources of children's knowledge. *Journal of Pragmatics*, *14*, 289–305.

Snyder, M. (1974). The self-monitoring of expressive behavior. *Journal of Personality and Social Psychology*, *30*, 52–537.

Snyder, M., & Gangestad, S. (1986). On the nature of self-monitoring: Matters of assessment, matters of validity. *Journal of Personality and Social Psychology*, *51*, 125–139.

Snyder, M. L., Stephan, W. G., & Rosenfield, D. (1976). Egotism and attribution. *Journal of Personality and Social Psychology*, *33*, 435–441.

Sonuga-Barke, E. J. S. & Webley, P. (1993). *Children's Saving: A Study in the Development of Economic Behavior*. Hove, UK: Erlbaum.

Speier, M. (1972). Some conversational problems for interactional analysis. In D. Sudnow (Ed.), *Studies in Social Interaction* (pp. 397–427). New York: The Free Press.

Sperry, L. L., & Sperry, D. E. (2000). Verbal and nonverbal contributions to early representation: Evidence from African American toddlers. In N. Budwig, I. C. Uzgiris, & J. V. Wertsch (Eds.), *Communication: An Arena of Development* (pp. 143–165). Stamford, CT: Ablex.

Spivack, G., & Shure, M. B. (1974). *Social Adjustment in Young Children: A Cognitive Approach to Solving Real-Life Problems*. San Francisco: Jossey-Bass.

Spock, B. (1968). *Baby and Child Care*. New York: Hawthorn Books.

Sproles, G., & Kendall, E. L. (1986). A methodology for profiling consumers' decision-making styles. *Journal of Consumer Affairs*, *20*, 267–279.

Stanovich, K. E., & West, R. F. (2000). Individual differences in reasoning: Implications for the rationality debate. *Behavioral and Brain Sciences*, *23*, 645–665.

Stansbury, K., & Sigman, M. (2000). Responses of preschoolers in two frustrating episodes: Emergence of complex strategies of emotion regulation. *Journal of Genetic Psychology*, *161*, 182–202.

Staton, A. Q. (1993). Transitions through the student career. In N. Coupland & J. F. Nussbaum (Eds.), *Discourse and Lifespan Identity* (pp. 154–172). Newbury Park, CA: Sage.

Staub, E. (1970). A child in distress: The effect of focusing responsibility on children on their attempts to help. *Developmental Psychology*, *2*, 152–153.

Steiner, J. E. (1973). The gustofacial response: Observation on normal and anencephalic newborn infants. In J. F. Bosma (Ed.), *Fourth Symposium an Oral Sensation and Perception*. Bethesda, MD: U.S. Department of Health, Education and Welfare.

Stella-Prorok, E. M. (1983), Mother-child language in the natural environment. In K. E. Nelson (Ed.), *Children's Language*, Vol. 4 (pp. 187–230). Hillsdale, NJ: Erlbaum.

Stenzel, A. (1994). Case assignment and functional categories of bilingual children: Routes of development and implications for linguistic theory. In J. M. Meisel (Ed.), *Bilingual First Language Acquisition: French and German Grammatical Development* (pp. 161–208). Amsterdam: John Benjamins.

Stern, C., & Stern, W. (1928). Die Kindersprache: Eine psychologische und sprachtheoretische Untersuchung [The language of children: A psychological and linguistic-theoretical investigation], 4th ed. Leipzig, Germany: Barth.

Stevens, M. (1989), Coping strategies of hospitalized adolescents. *Child Health Care*, *18*, 163–169.

Stevenson, O. (1954), The first treasured possession. *Psychoanalytic Study of the Child*, *9*, 199–217.

Stewart, B. R. (1958). Developmental differences in the stability of object preferences and conflict behavior. *Child Development*, *29*, 9–18.

Straus, M. A. (1994). *Beating the Devil out of Them*. New York: Lexington Books.

Straus, M. A., & Mouradian, V. E. (1998). Impulsive corporal punishment by mothers and antisocial behavior and impulsiveness of children. *Behavioral Sciences and the Law*, *16*, 353–374.

Straus, M. A., & Stewart, J. H. (1999). Corporal punishment by American parents: National data on prevalence, chronicity, severity, and duration in relation to child and family characteristics. *Clinical Child and Family Review*, *2*, 55–70.

Striano, T., Tomasello, M., & Rochat, P. (2001). Social and object support for early symbolic play. *Developmental Science*, *4*, 442–455.

Stubbs, M. (1976). Keeping in touch: Some functions of teacher talk. In M. Stubbs & S. Delamont (Eds.), *Explorations in Classroom Observation* (pp. 151–172). London: Wiley.

Suddendorf, T., & Corballis, M. C. (1997). Mental time travel and the evolution of the human mind. *Genetic, Social and General Psychology Monographs*, *123*, 133–167.

Suizzo, M.-A. (2004). Mother–child relationships in France: Balancing autonomy and affiliation in everyday interactions. *Ethos*, *32*, 293–323.

Sullivan, H. S. (1953). *The Interpersonal Theory of Psychiatry*. New York: W. W. Norton.

Sullivan, S. A., & Birch, L. L. (1990). "Pass the sugar, pass the salt": Experience dictates preference. *Developmental Psychology*, *26*, 546–551.

Sun, R. (1995). Robust reasoning: Integrating rule-based and similarity-based reasoning. *Artificial Intelligence*, *75*, 241–296.

Sun, R. (2007). The motivational and cognitive control in CLARION. In W. Gray (Ed.), *Modeling Integrated Cognitive Systems*. New York: Oxford University Press.

Svenson, O. (1992). Differntiation and consolidation theory of human decision making: A frame of reference for the study of pre- and post-decision processes. *Acta Psychologica*, *80*, 143–168.

Swan, M. (1995). *Practical English Usage*. Oxford, UK: Oxford University Press.

Swanson, G. E. (1988). *Ego Defenses and the Legitimation of Behavior*. Cambridge, UK: Cambridge University Press.

Sylva, K., Roy, C., & Painter, M. (1986). *Childwatching at Playgroup and Nursery School.* Oxford, UK: Basil Blackwell.

Sylvester-Bradley, B., & Trevarthen, C. (1978). Baby talk as an adaptation to the infant's communication. In N. Waterson & C. E. Snow (Eds.), *The Development of Communication* (pp. 75–92). London: Wiley.

Taeschner, T. (1983). *The Sun is Feminine: A Study on Language Acquisition in Bilingual Children*. Berlin: Springer–Verlag.

Tamis-LeMonda, C. S., & Bornstein, M. H. (1989). Habituation and maternal encouragement of attention in infancy as predictors of toddler language, play, and representational competence. *Child Development*, *60*, 738–751.

Tannen, D. (1990). Gender differences in conversational coherence: Physical alignment and topical cohesion. *Advances in Discourse Processes*, Vol. 38 (pp. 167–206). Norwood, NJ: Ablex.

Taylor, S. E. (1991). Asymmetrical effects of positive and negative events: The mobilization-minimization hypothesis. *Psychological Bulletin*, *110*, 67–85.

Teale, W. H., Martinez, M. G., & Glass, W. L. (1989). Describing classroom storybook reading. In D. Bloome (Ed.), *Classrooms and Literacy* (pp. 158–188). Norwood, NJ: Ablex.

Teale, W. H., & Sulzby, E. (1987). Literacy acquisition in early childhood: The roles of access and mediation in storybook reading. In D. Wagner (Ed.), *The Future of Literacy in a Changing World* (pp. 111–130). New York: Pergamon Press.

Terwogt, M. M., & Rieffe, C. (2003). Stereotyped beliefs about desirability: Implications for characterizing the child's theory of mind. *New Ideas in Psychology*, *21*, 69–84.

Thomas-Lepore, C. E., Bohanek, J., Fivush, R., & Duke, M. (2004). *"Today I . . . ": Ritual and Spontaneous Narratives During Family Dinners*. Working Paper no. 31, Emory Center for Myth And Ritual in American Life.

Thompson, C., Barresi, J., & Moore, C. (1997). The development of future-oriented prudence and altruism in preschoolers. *Cognitive Development*, *12*, 199–212.

Thompson, R. A., Laible, D. J., & Ontai, L. L. (2003). Early understanding of emotion, morality, and self: Developing a working model. In R. V. Kail (Ed.), *Advances in Child Development and Behavior*, Vol. 31 (pp. 139–171). Amsterdam: Academic Press.

Thompson, W. C., Cowan, C. L., & Rosenhan, D. L. (1980). Focus of attention mediates the impact of negative affect on altruism. *Journal of Personality and Social Psychology*, *38*, 291–300.

Thornton, R. (2002). Let's change the subject: Focus movement in early grammar. *Language Acquisition*, *10*, 229–271.

Timotijevic, L., & Breakwell, G. M. (2000). Migration and threat to identity. *Journal of Community and Applied Social Psychology*, *10*, 335–372.

Tizard, B., & Hughes, M. (1984). *Young Children Learning: Talking and Thinking in Home and At School*. London: Fontana.

Tobin, J. J., Wu, D. Y. H., & Davidson, D. H. (1989). *Preschool in Three Cultures: Japan, China, and the United States*. New Haven, CT: Yale University Press.

Todd, P. (1982). Tagging after red herrings: Evidence against the processing capacity explanation in child language. *Journal of Child Language*, *9*, 99–114.

Tomasello, M. (1992). *First Verbs*. New York: Cambridge University Press.

Tomasello, M. (1995). Pragmatic contexts for early verb learning. In M. Tomasello & W. E. Merriman (Eds.), *Beyond Names for Things: Young Children's Acquisition of Verbs* (pp. 115–146). Hillsdale, NJ; Erlbaum.

Tomasello, M. (1999). *The Cultural Origins of Human Cognition*. Cambridge, MA: Harvard University Press.

Torr, J. (2000). Thinking and saying in the classroom: An exploration of the use of projection by teachers and children. *Linguistics and Education*, *11*, 141–159.

Torrance, N., & Olson, D. R. (1985). Oral and literate competencies in the early school years. In D. R. Olson, N. Torrance & A. Hildyard (Eds.), *Literacy, Language, and Learning: The Nature and Consequences of Reading and Writing* (pp. 256–284). Cambridge, UK: Cambridge University Press.

Tough, J. (1973). *Focus on Meaning: Talking to Some Purpose with Young Children*. London: George Unwin.

Tough, J. (1976). *Listening to Children Talking: A Guide to the Appraisal of Children's Use of Language*. London: Ward Lock Educational.

Tough, J. (1977). *The Development of Meaning: A Study of Children's Language Use*. New York: Wiley.

Toivainen, J. (1980). *Inflectional Affixes Used by Finnish-Speaking Children Aged 1–3 Years*. Helsinki: Seura.

Torode, B. (1976). Teachers' talk and classroom discipline. In M. Stubbs & S. Delamont (Eds.), *Explorations in Classroom Observation* (pp. 173–192). Chichester, UK: Wiley.

Trawick-Smith, J. (1990). The effects of realistic versus nonrealistic play materials on young children's symbolic transformation of objects. *Journal of Research in Childhood Education*, *5*, 27–36.

Trawick-Smith, J. W. (1992). A descriptive study of persuasive preschool children: How they get others to do what they want. *Early Childhood Research Quarterly*, *7*, 95–114.

Trawick-Smith, J. (1998). A qualitative analysis of metaplay in the preschool years. *Early Childhood Research Quarterly*, *13*, 433–452.

Trawick-Smith, J. (1998). School-based play and social interactions: Opportunities and limitations. In D. P. Fromberg & D. Bergen (Eds.), *Play from Birth to Twelve and Beyond: Contexts, Perspectives, and Meanings* (pp. 241–247). New York: Garland Publishing.

Trawick-Smith, J. (2001). The play frame and the "fictional dream": The bidirectional relationship between metaplay and story writing. *Advances in Early Education and Day Care*, *11*, 339–355.

Trevarthen, C. (1977). Descriptive analyses of infant communicative behavior. In H. R. Schaffer (Ed.), *Studies in Mother-Infant Interaction*. (pp. 227–270). London: Academic Press.

Trommsdorff, G., & Lamm, H. (1975). An analysis of future orientation and some of its social determinants. In J. T. Fraser & N. Lawrence (Eds.), *The Study of Time, II*. Berlin: Springer-Verlag.

Troop-Gordon, W., & Asher, S. L. (2005). Modifications in children's goals when encountering obstacles to conflict resolution. *Child Development*, *76*, 568–582.

Trope, Y., & Liberman, N. (2003). Temporal construal. *Psychological Review*, *110*, 403–421.

Tsimpli, I.-M. (1996). *The Prefunctional Stage of First Language Acquisition*. New York: Garland Publishing.

Tulviste, T. (2003). Contextual variation in interactions between mothers and 2-year-olds. *First Language*, *23*, 311–325.

Tulviste, T., & Koor, M. (2005). "Hands off the car, it's mine" and "The teacher will be angry if we don't play nicely": Gender related preferences in the use moral rules and social conventions in preschoolers' dyadic play. *Sex Roles*, *53*, 57–66.

Tunteler E., & Resing W. C. (2002). Spontaneous analogical transfer in 4-year-olds: A microgenetic study. *Journal of Experimental Child Psychology*, *83*, 149–166.

Turiel, E. (1979). Distinct conceptual and developmental domains: Social convention and morality. In C. B. Keasey (Ed.), *Nebraska Symposium on Motivation* (pp. 77–116). Lincoln, NB: University of Nebraska Press.

Turiel, E. (1983). *The Development of Social Knowledge: Morality and Convention*. Cambridge, UK: Cambridge University Press.

Turiel, E., Killen, M., & Helwig, C. (1987). Morality: Its structure, functions, and vagaries. In J. Kagan & S. Lamb (Eds.), *Emergence of Morality in Young Children* (pp. 155–243). Chicago: University of Chicago Press.

Turman, P. D. (2005). Coaches' use of anticipatory and counterfactual regret messages during competition. *Journal of Applied Communication Research, 33*, 116–138.

Tversky, A., & Kahneman, D. (1986). Rational choice and the framing of decisions. In R. M. Hogarth & M. W. Reder (Eds.), *Rational Choice: The Contrast between Economics and Psychology* (pp. 67–94). Chicago: University of Chicago Press.

Tyler, T. R. (2006). *Why People Obey the Law*. Princeton, NJ: Princeton University Press.

Uccelli, P., Hemphill, L., Pan, B. A., & Snow, C. (1999). Telling two kinds of stories: Sources of narrative skills. In L. Balter & C. S. Tamis-LeMonda (Eds.), *Child Psychology: A Handbook of Contemporary Issues* (pp. 215–233). Philadelphia: Psychology Press.

United Nations (2007) *Study on Violence against Children*, A/61/299. Retrieved 9/8/09 from http://www.unicef.org/violencestudy/reports/SG_violencestudy_en.pdf

Unnever, J. D., Cullen, F. T., & Pratt, T. C. (2003). Parental management, ADHD, and delinquent involvement: Reassessing Gottfredson and Hirschi's General Theory. *Justice Quarterly, 20*, 471–500.

Urwin, C. (1984). Power relations and the mergence of language. In J. Henriques, W. Hollway, C. Urwin, C. Venn, & V. Walkerdine (Eds.), *Changing the Subject: Psychology, Social Regulation and Subjectivity* (pp. 264–322). Methuen: London.

Valsiner, J. (1987). *Culture and the Development of Children's Action*. Chichester, UK: Wiley.

Varela, J. A. (1971). *Psychological Solutions to Social Problems*. New York: Academic Press.

Varenne, H. (1990). Parents and their children at talk. *Advances in Discourse Processes*, Vol. 38 (pp. 239–265). Norwood, NJ: Ablex.

Varenne, H. (1992). *Ambiguous Harmony: Family Talk in America*. Norwood, NJ: Ablex.

Vaughn, B., Kopp, C. B., & Krakow, J. B. (1994). The emergence and consolidation of self-control from eighteen to thirty months of age: Normative trends and individual differences. *Child Development, 55*, 990–1004.

Veneziano, E. (2001). Displacement and information in child-directed talk. *First Language, 21*, 323–356.

Veneziano, E. (2002). Language in pretense during the second year: What it can tell us about "pretending" in pretense and the "know-how" about the mind. In R. W. Mitchell (Ed.), *Pretending and Imagination in Animals and Children* (pp. 59–72). Cambridge, UK: Cambridge University Press.

Vinden, P. G. (2000). Making up my mind: Learning the culture of Olson and OISE. In J. W. Astington (Ed.), *Minds in the Making: Essays in Honor of David R. Olson* (pp. 29–42). Oxford, UK: Basil Blackwell.

Volterra, V., & Antinucci, F. (1979). Negation in child study: A pragmatic study. In E. Ochs & B. S. Schieffelin (Eds.), *Developmental Pragmatics* (pp. 281–303). New York: Academic Press.

Volterra, V., Bates, E., Benigny, L., Bretherton, I., & Camaioni, L. (1979) First words in language and action: A qualitative look. In E. Bates (Ed.) *The Emergence of Symbols: Cognition and Communication in Infancy* (pp. 141–222). New York: Academic Press.

Vuchinich, S. (1990). The sequential organization of closing in verbal family conflict. In A. D. Grimshaw (Ed.), *Conflict Talk: Sociolinguistic Investigations of Arguments in Conversations* (pp. 118–138). Cambridge, UK: Cambridge University Press.

Vygotsky, L. S. (1934/1962) *Thought and Language*. Cambridge, MA: MIT Press.

Vygotsky, L. (1966). Play and its role in the mental development of the child. *Soviet Psychology, 12*, 6–18.

Vygotsky, L. (1981). The genesis of higher mental functions. In J. V. Wertsch (Ed.), *The Concept of Activity in Soviet Psychology* (pp. 144–188). Armonk, NY: Sharpe.

Vygotsky, L., & Luria A. (1994). Tool and symbol in child development. In R. van der Veer & J. Valsiner (Eds.), *The Vygotsky Reader* (pp. 99–174). Oxford, UK: Blackwell.

Waelder, R. (1960). *Basic Theory of Psychoanalysis*. New York: International Universities Press.

Wagner-Gough, J. (1975). Comparative studies in second language learning. *CAL-ERIC/CLL Series on Languages and Linguistics, No. 26*. Washington, DC: Center for Applied Linguistics.

Walker, B. M. (2004). Frames of self: Capturing working-class British boys' identities through photographs. In N. Way & J. Y. Chu (Eds.), *Adolescent Boys: Exploring Diverse Cultures of Boyhood* (pp. 31–58). New York: New York University Press.

Walkerdine, V. (1988). *The Mastery of Reason: Cognitive Development and the Production of Rationality*. London: Routledge.

Walkerdine, V., & Lucey, H. (1989). *Democracy in the Kitchen: Regulating Mothers and Socialising Daughters*. London: Virago.

Walkerdine, V., & Sinha, C. (1981). Developing linguistic strategies in young school children. In G. Wells (Ed.), *Learning Through Interaction: The Study of Language Development* (pp. 183–204). Cambridge: Cambridge University Press.

Wang, Q. (2001). "Did you have fun?" American and Chinese mother–child conversations about shared emotional experiences. *Cognitive Development, 16*, 693–715.

Wang, Q. (2004). The cultural context of parent–child reminiscing: A functional analysis. In M. Pratt & B. H. Fiese (Eds.), *Family Stories and the Life Course: Across Time and Generations* (pp. 279–301). Mahwah, NJ: Erlbaum.

Wang, Q., & Spillane, E. L. (2003). Developing autobiographical memory in the cultural contexts of parent–child reminiscing. In S. P. Shohov (Ed.), *Topics in Cognitive Psychology* (pp. 101–116). New York: Nova Science Publishers.

Wang, X., Bernas, R., & Eberhard, P. (2002). Variations of maternal support to children's early literacy development in Chinese and American Indian families: Implications for early childhood educators. *International Journal of Early Childhood, 34*, 9–23.

Ward, S., Wackman, D. B., & Wartella, E. (1977). *How Children Learn to Buy: The Development of Consumer Information-Processing Skills*. Beverly Hills, CA: Sage.

Wardle, J., Cooke, L. J., Gibson, L., Sapochnik, M., Sheiham, A., & Lawson, M. (2003). Increasing children's acceptance of vegetables: A randomized trial of parent-led exposure. *Appetite, 40*, 155–162.

Wason-Ellam, L. (1997). "If only I was like Barbie." *Language Arts, 74*, 430–437.

Watson, J. S. (2001). Contingency perception and misperception in infancy: Some potential implications for attachment. *Bulletin-of-the-Menninger-Clinic*, *65*, 296–320.

Watson, R. (1989). Monologue, dialogue, and regulation. In K. Nelson (Ed.), *Narratives from the Crib* (pp. 263–283). Cambridge, MA: Harvard University Press.

Watson-Gegeo, K. A., & Gegeo, D. W. (1986). The social world of Kwara'ae children: Acquisition of language and values. In J. Cook-Gumperz, W. A. Corsaro, & J. Streeck (Eds.), *Children's Worlds and Children's Language* (pp. 109–127). Berlin: Mouton de Gruyter.

Watson-Gegeo, K. A. (2001). Fantasy and reality: The dialectic of work and play in Kwara'ae children's lives. *Ethos*, *29*, 138–158.

Watzlawick, P., Weakland, J., & Frisch, R. (1974). *Change: Principles of Problem Formation and Problem Resolution*. New York: W.W. Norton.

Weatherby, A. M., Alexander, D. G., & Prizant, B. M. (1998). The ontogeny and role of repair strategies. In A. M. Wetherby, S. F. Warren & J. Reichle (Eds.), *Transitions in Prelinguistic Communication*, Vol. 7 (pp. 135–159). Baltimore, MD: Brookes Publishing.

Webley, P. (2005). Children's understanding of economics. In M. Barrett & E. Buchanan-Barrow (Eds.), *Children's Understanding of Society* (pp. 43–67). Hove, UK: Psychology Press.

Wegner, D. M. (1994). Ironic processes of mental control. *Psychological Review*, *101*, 34–52.

Wegner, D. M., & Pennebaker, J (Eds.). (1993). *Handbook of Mental Control*. Upper Saddle River, NJ: Prentice-Hall.

Weininger, O. (1988). "What if" and "as if": Imagination and pretend play in early childhood. In K. Egan & D. Nadaner, (Eds.), *Imagination and Education* (pp. 141–149). New York: Teacher's College Press.

Weir, R. H. (1962). *Language in the Crib*. The Hague: Mouton.

Weisner, T. S., & Gallimore, R. (1977). My brother's keeper: Child and sibling caretaking. *Current Anthropology*, *18*, 169–190.

Weiss, D. M., & Sachs, J. (1991). Persuasive strategies used by preschool children. *Discourse Processes*, *14*, 55–72.

Weist, R. M. (1986). Tense and aspect: Temporal systems in child language. In P. Fletcher and M. Garman (Eds.), *Language Acquisition: Studies in First Language Development* (pp. 356–374). Cambridge, UK: Cambridge University Press.

Weisz, J. R., Rothbaum, F. M., & Blackburn, T. F. (1984a). Standing out and standing in: The psychology of control in America and Japan. *American Psychologist*, *39*, 955–969.

Weisz, J. R., Rothbaum, F. M., & Blackburn, T. F. (1984b). Swapping recipes for control. *American Psychologist*, *39*, 974–975.

Weizman, E. (1989). Requestive hints. In S. Blum-Kulka, J. House, & G. Kasper (Eds.), *Cross-Cultural Pragmatics: Requests and Apologies* (pp. 71–95). Norwood, NJ: Ablex.

Welch-Ross, M. K. (1997). Mother–child participation in conversations about the past: Relations to preschoolers' theory of mind. *Developmental Psychology*, *33*, 618–629.

Wellman, H. M. (1988). First steps in the child's theorizing about the mind. In J. W. Astington, P. L. Harris, & D. R. Olson (Eds.), *Developing Theories of Mind* (pp. 64–92). New York: Cambridge University Press.

Wellman, H. M., Cross, D., & Watson, J. (2001). Meta-analysis of theory-of-mind development: The truth about false belief. *Child Development*, *72*, 655–684.

Wellman, H. M., Harris, P. L., Banerjee, M., & Sinclair, A. (1995). Early understanding of emotion: Evidence from natural language. *Cognition and Emotion*, *9*, 117–149.

Wells, G. (1981). Language as interaction. In G. Wells (Ed.), *Learning Through Interaction: The Study of Language Development* (pp. 22–72). Cambridge, UK: Cambridge University Press.

Wells, G. (1981). Language, literacy, and education. In G. Wells (Ed.), *Learning Through Interaction: The Study of Language Development* (pp. 240–276). Cambridge, UK: Cambridge University Press.

Wells, G. (1985). *Language Development in the Pre-school Years*. London: Cambridge University Press.

Wells, G. (1986). *The Meaning Makers: Children Learning Language and Using Language to Learn*. Portsmouth, NH: Heinemann.

Werner, H., & Kaplan, B. (1963). *Symbol Formation: An Organismic-Developmental Approach to Language and the Expression of Thought*. New York: Wiley.

Wesslén, A., Sepp, H., & Fjellström, C. (2002). Swedish preschool children's experience of food. *International Journal of Consumer Studies*, *26*, 264–271.

White, A. R. (1990). *The Concept of Imagination*. Oxford, UK: Basil Blackwell.

White, C. S., Alexander, P. A., & Daugherty, M. (1998). The relationship between young children's analogical reasoning and mathematical learning. *Mathematical Cognition*, *4*, 103–123.

White, H. (1986). Damsels in distress: Dependency themes in fiction for children and adolescents. *Adolescence*, *21*, 251–256.

White, J. D. (1976). *Talking with a Child*. New York: Macmillan.

White, M. (2000). *Reflections on Narrative Practice: Essays and Interviews*. Adelaide, Australia: Dulwich Centre Publications.

Whitehurst, G., Kedesdy, J., & White, T. G. (1982). A functional analysis of meaning. In S. A. Kuczaj (Ed.), *Language Development, Syntax and Semantics*, Vol. 1 (pp. 397–427). Hillsdale, NJ: Erlbaum.

Whiting, J. W. M., & Child, I. (1953). *Child Training and Personality: A Cross-Cultural Study*. Cambridge, MA: Harvard University Press.

Whiting, B. B., & Edwards, C. P. (1988). *Children of Different Worlds*. Cambridge, MA: Harvard University Press.

Whorf, B. (1956) On the connection of ideas. In J. B. Carroll (Ed.), *Language, Thought, and Reality: Selected Writings of Benjamin Lee Whorf*. Cambridge, MA: MIT Press.

Widdowson, J. D. A. (1979). *If You Don't Be Good: Verbal Social Control in Newfoundland*. St. John's: NFLD, Memorial University of Newfoundland.

Widdowson, J. (1981). Food and traditional verbal modes in the social control of children. In A. Fenton & T. Owen (Eds.), *Food in Perspective* (pp. 377–389). Edinburgh: John Donald.

Wijnen, F., & Verrips, M. (1998). The acquisition of Dutch syntax. In S. Gillis & A. De Houwer (Eds.), *The Acquisition of Dutch* (pp. 223–299). Amsterdam: John Benjamins.

Wiley, A. (1997). Religious affiliation as a source of variation in childrearing values and parental regulation of young children. *Mind, Culture, and Activity*, *4*, 86–107.

Wilkinson, A. (1991). Talking sense: The assessment of talk. In D. Booth & C. Thornley-Hall (Eds.), *The Talk Curriculum* (pp. 124–144). Portsmouth, NH: Heinemann.

Wilkinson, A. M. (1971). *The Foundations of Language: Talking and Reading in Young Children*. London: Oxford University Press.

Wilkinson, L. C., & Calculator, S. (1982). Effective speakers: Students use of language to request and obtain information and action in the classroom. In L. C. Wilkinson (Ed.), *Communicating in the Classroom* (pp. 85–99). New York: Academic Press.

Wilkinson, L. C., Clevenger, M., & Dollaghan, C. (1981). Communication in small instructional groups: A sociolinguistic approach. In W. P. Dickson (Ed.), *Children's Oral Communication Skills* (pp. 207–240). New York: Academic Press.

Willes, M. J. (1983). *Children into Pupils: A Study of Language in Early Schooling*. London: Routledge & Kegan Paul.

Williamson, P. A., & Silvern, S. B. (1991). Thematic-fantasy play and story comprehension. In J. F. Christie (Ed.), *Play and Early Literacy Development* (pp. 69–90). Albany, NY: SUNY Press.

Wilson, G., & Wood, K. (2004). The influence of children on parental purchases during supermarket shopping. *International Journal of Consumer Studies*, *28*, 329–336.

Wilson, R. W. (1974). *The Moral State: A Study of the Political Socialization of Chinese and American Children*. New York: The Free Press.

Wilson, S. R., Cameron, K. A., & Whipple, E. E. (1997). Regulative communication strategies within mother–child interaction: The implications for the study of reflection-enhancing parental communication. *Research on Language and Social Interaction*, *30*, 73–92.

Wilson, T. D. & Linville, P. W. (1982). Improving the academic performance of college freshmen: Attribution therapy revisited. *Journal of Personality and Social Psychology*, 42, 367–376.

Wimmer, H., & Perner, J. (1983) Beliefs about beliefs: Representations and constraining function of wrong beliefs inyoung children's understanding of deception. *Cognition*, *13*, 103–128.

Wing, L. A. (1995). Play is not the work of the child: Young children's perceptions of work and play. *Early Childhood Research Quarterly*, *10*, 223–244.

Wolf, D. P. (1982). Understanding others: A longitudinal study of the concept of independent agency. In F. E. Forman (Ed.), *Action and Thought: From Sensorimotor Schemes to Symbolic Operations* (pp. 297–327). New York: Academic Press.

Wolf, D. P. (1990). Being of several minds: Voices and versions of the self in early childhood. In D. Cicchetti & M. Beeghly (Eds.), *The Self in Transition: Infancy to Childhood* (pp. 183–212). Chicago: University of Chicago Press.

Wolf, D., & Grollman, S. (1982). Ways of playing: Individual differences in imaginative play. In K. Rubin & D. Pepler (Eds.), *The Play of Children: Current Theory and Research* (pp. 46–63). New York: Karger.

Wolf, D. P., Rugh, J., Altshuler, J. (1984). Agency and experience: Actions and states in play narratives. In I. Bretherton (Ed.), *Symbolic Play: The Development of Social Understanding* (pp. 195–217). Orlando, FL: Academic Press.

Wolfenstein, M. (1950). Some varieties of moral training of children. *Psychoanalytic Study of the Child*, *5*, 310–328.

Wong, P. T., & Weiner, B. (1981). Why people ask "why" questions, and the heuristics of attributional search. *Journal of Personality and Social Psychology*, *40*, 650–663.

Wood, D., McMahon, L., & Cranstoun, Y. (1980). *Working with Under Fives*. London: Grant McIntyre.

Wood, D., & Beck, R. J. (1994). *Home Rules*. Baltimore, MD: Johns Hopkins University Press.

Wootton, A. J. (1974). Talk in the homes of young children. *Sociology*, *8*, 277–295.

Wootton, A. J. (1981). The management of grantings and rejections by parents in request sequences. *Semiotica*, *37*, 59–89.

Wootton, A. J. (1986). Rules in action: Orderly features of actions that formulate rules. In J. Cook-Gumperz, W. A. Corsaro, & J. Streeck (Eds.), *Children's Worlds and Children's Language* (pp. 147–168). Berlin: Mouton de Gruyter.

Wootton, A. J. (1997). *Interaction and the Development of Mind*. Cambridge, UK: Cambridge University Press.

Wootton, A. J. (2007). A puzzle about please: Repair, increments, and related matters in the speech of a young child. *Research on Language and Social Interaction*, *40*, 171–198.

Wright, P. (1993). Mothers' ideas about feeding in early infancy. In I. St. James-Roberts, G. Harris, & D. Messer (Eds.), *Infant Crying, Feeding and Sleeping: Development, Problems and Treatments* (pp. 99–117). New York: Harvester Wheatsheaf.

Wright, P. Fawcett, J. N., & Crow, R. A. (1980). The development of differences in the feeding behaviour of bottle and breast-fed human infants form birth to two months. *Behavioural Processes*, *5*, 1–20.

Wrong, D. (1979) *Power: Its Forms, Bases and Uses*. New York: Harper & Row.

Wyckoff, J., & Unell, B. C. (1984). *Discipline Without Spanking or Shouting: Practical Solutions To the Most Common Preschool Behaviour Problems*. New York: Meadowbrooks.

Xu, J., & Corno, L. (1998). Case studies of families doing third-grade homework. *Teachers College Record*, *100*, 402–436.

Yang, S., & Rettig, K. D. (2003). The value tensions in Korean-American mother–child relationships while facilitating academic success. *Personal Relationships*, *10*, 349–369.

Yates, G. C. R., Yates, S. M., & Beasley, C. J. (1987). Young children's knowledge of strategies in delay of gratification. *Merrill-Palmer Quarterly*, *33*, 159–169.

Yont, K. M., Snow, C. E., & Vernon-Feagans, L. (2003). The role of context in mother–child interactions: An analysis of communicative intentions expressed during toy play and book reading with 12-month-olds. *Journal of Pragmatics*, *35*, 435–454.

Young, R. A., Faseluikho, M. A., & Valach, L. (1997). The role of emotion in the construction of career in parent–adolescent conversations. *Journal of Counseling and Development*, *76*, 36–44.

Yuill, N. (1997). English children as personality theorists: Accounts of the modifiability, development, and origin of traits. *Genetic, Social, and General Psychology Monographs*, *123*, 7–26.

Zahn-Waxler, C., Radke-Yarrow, M., & King, R. (1979). Child rearing and children's prosocial initiations toward victims of distress. *Child Development*, *50*, 319–330.

Zahn-Waxler, C., Iannotti, R., & Cummings, M. (1988). *Altruism and Aggression*. New York: Cambridge University Press.

Zajonc, R. B. (1984). On the primacy of affect. *American Psychologist*, *39*, 117–123.

Zeedyk, M. S. (1991). Developmental accounts of intentionality: Toward integration. *Developmental Review*, *16*, 416–461.

Zimbardo, P. G. (1995). The psychology of evil: A situationist perspective on recruiting good people to engage in anti-social acts. *Research in Social Psychology*, *11*, 125–133.

Zuckerman, M., Porac, J., Lathin, D., Smith, R., & Deci, E. L. (1978). On the importance of self-determination for intrinsically motivated behavior. *Personality and Social Psychology Bulletin*, *4*, 443–446.

Zukow, P. G., Reilly, J., & Greenfield, P. M. (1982). Making the absent present: Facilitating the transition from sensorimotor to linguistic communication. In K. E. Nelson (Ed.), *Children's Language*, Vol. 3 (pp. 1–90). Hillsdale, NJ: Erlbaum.

Subject Index

Name Index*

*t refers to Table on the cited page.